MARKETING

Canadian Edition

**Marketing
Canadian Edition**

ISBN-13: 978-0-07-098492-9
ISBN-10: 0-07-098492-1

1 2 3 4 5 6 7 8 9 10 QPD 0 9 8 7

Printed and bound in the United States of America.

Care has been taken to trace ownership of copyright material contained in this text; however, the
publisher will welcome any information that enables them to rectify any reference or credit for
subsequent editions.

Vice-President and Editor-In-Chief: Joanna Cotton
Senior Sponsoring Editor: Leanna MacLean
Senior Marketing Manager: Joy Armitage Taylor
Senior Developmental Editor: Suzanne Simpson Millar
Developmental Editor: James Booty
Photo/Permissions Research: Shelley Wickabrod
Editorial Associate: Stephanie Hess
Supervising Editor: Elizabeth Priest
Copy Editor: Erin Moore
Senior Production Coordinator: Jennifer Hall
Cover & Interior Design: Michelle Losier, Fine Lines Design
Cover Image: © Chris Rogers/Corbis
Page Layout: Valid Design and Layout/Valerie Bateman
Printer: Quebecor Printing Dubuque

Library and Archives Canada Cataloguing in Publication

Marketing / Dhruv Grewal ... [et al.].—Canadian ed.
Includes bibliographical references and index.

ISBN 978-0-07-098492-9

1. Marketing—Textbooks. I. Grewal, Dhruv

HF5415.M369645 2008   658.8   C2008-903627-1

To those who had a strong positive influence
on the early years of our careers:

James Littlefield, Professor of Marketing, Virginia Tech
Kent B. Monroe, John M. Jones Professor of Marketing,
University of Illinois
A. Coskun Samli, Professor of Marketing,
University of North Florida
Dianna L. Stone, Professor of Management,
University of Central Florida
—*Dhruv Grewal*

James L. Ginter, Professor Emeritus, The Ohio State University
Roger A. Kerin, Harold C. Simmons Distinguished Professor
of Marketing, Southern Methodist University
Mike Harvey, Hearin Professor of Global Business,
The University of Mississippi
Bernard J. LaLonde, Professor Emeritus, The Ohio State University
Barton A. Weitz, JCPenney Eminent Scholar, The University of Florida
—*Michael Levy*

Ken Danns, Professor, University of Guyana
Leland Paul, Professor, University of Guyana
Vinod Kumar, Professor, Eric Sprott School of Business,
Carleton University
Uma Kumar, Professor, Eric Sprott School of Business,
Carleton University
—*Ajax Persaud*

Gordon McDougall, Professor Emeritus,
School of Business and Economics, Wilfrid Laurier University
Auleen Carson, Retired Professor,
School of Business and Economics, Wilfrid Laurier University
David Goodwin, Professor,
Digital Arts Communication, University of Waterloo
Brad Davis, Professor of Marketing,
School of Business and Economics, Wilfrid Laurier University
—*Shirley Lichti*

about the authors

Dhruv Grewal

Dhruv Grewal, PhD (Virginia Tech), is the Toyota Chair in Commerce and Electronic Business and a professor of marketing at Babson College. His research and teaching interests focus on marketing foundations, marketing research, retailing, pricing, and value-based strategies. He was awarded the 2005 Lifetime Achievement in Behavioral Pricing Award by Fordham University. He is a "Distinguished Fellow" of the Academy of Marketing Science. He has also coauthored *Marketing Research* (2004, 2007).

Professor Grewal has published over 70 articles in journals such as *Journal of Marketing, Journal of Consumer Research, Journal of Marketing Research, Journal of Retailing,* and *Journal of the Academy of Marketing Science.* He currently serves on numerous editorial review boards, including *Journal of Retailing, Journal of the Academy of Marketing Science, Journal of Interactive Marketing,* and *Journal of Public Policy & Marketing.* He served as co-editor of *Journal of Retailing* from 2001–2007.

Professor Grewal has won many awards for his teaching including, 2005 Sherwin-Williams Distinguished Teaching Award, SMA; 2003 AMA Award for Innovative Excellence in Marketing Education; 1999 AMS Great Teachers in Marketing Award; Executive MBA Teaching Excellence Award (1998); School of Business Teaching Excellence Awards (1993, 1999); and Virginia Tech Certificate of Recognition for Outstanding Teaching (1989). He co-chaired: 1993 AMS Conference, 1998 Winter AMA Conference, a 1998 Marketing Science Institute Conference, 2001 AMA doctoral consortium, and 2006 Summer AMA Conference.

Professor Grewal has taught executive seminars and courses and/or worked on research projects with numerous firms, such as IRI, TJX, Radio Shack, Monsanto, McKinsey, Motorola, and numerous law firms. He has taught seminars in the U.S., Europe, and Asia.

Michael Levy

Michael Levy, PhD, is the Charles Clarke Reynolds Professor of Marketing and Director of the Retail Supply Chain Institute at Babson College. He received his PhD in business administration from The Ohio State University and his undergraduate and MS degrees in business administration from the University of Colorado at Boulder. He taught at Southern Methodist University before joining the faculty as professor and chair of the marketing department at the University of Miami.

Professor Levy has developed a strong stream of research in retailing, business logistics, financial retailing strategy, pricing, and sales management. He has published over 50 articles in leading marketing and logistics journals, including the *Journal of Retailing, Journal of Marketing, Journal of the Academy of Marketing Science,* and *Journal of Marketing Research.* He currently serves on the editorial review board of the *Journal of Retailing, Journal of the Academy of Marketing Science, International Journal of Logistics Management, International Journal of Logistics and Materials Management, ECR Journal,* and *European Business Review.* He is coauthor of *Retailing Management,* 6e (2007), the best-selling college-level retailing text in the world. Professor Levy was co-editor of *Journal of Retailing* from 2001–2007.

Professor Levy has worked in retailing and related disciplines throughout his professional life. Prior to his academic career, he worked for several retailers and a housewares distributor in Colorado. He has performed research projects with many retailers and retail technology firms, including Accenture, Federated Department Stores, Khimetrics, Mervyn's, Neiman Marcus, ProfitLogic (Oracle), Zale Corporation, and numerous law firms. He co-chaired the 1993 Academy of Marketing Science conference and the 2006 Summer AMA conference.

Ajax Persaud, PhD, is an Associate Professor of Marketing and Director, MSc in Management, at the Telfer School of Management, University of Ottawa, with more than 15 years of post secondary teaching experience at colleges and universities in Canada and overseas. Professor Persaud has taught many undergraduate and graduate courses such as Marketing, Electronic Marketing, Digital Marketing Technologies, High-Tech Marketing, Marketing Strategy, New Product Development, Entrepreneurial Finance, R&D Management, Technology and Innovation Management, Economics, and Quantitative Methods. He has received several awards and nominations for teaching and research excellence. In 2005, he was awarded the University of Ottawa Excellence in Education Prize for excellence in teaching and research.

Professor Persaud has published material in journals, conference papers, and four books, including *E-Business Innovations: Cases and Readings* and *Managing Innovations through Corporate Global R&D.* His research has been published in leading journals such as *Journal of Product Innovation Management, IEEE Transactions on Engineering Management, Journal of Technology Transfer,* and the *Canadian Journal of Administrative Sciences.* He has also served as academic reviewer for many journals including *Journal of Product Innovation Management, IEEE Transactions on Engineering Management,* and *Journal of Asia Pacific Marketing.*

He has also delivered many executive seminars and workshops and has consulted for many small businesses in Guyana and Canada. He is an active community volunteer with both his time and money for many worthy causes and charities, focusing on education and disadvantaged children and youths.

Shirley Lichti, BA, MA, has taught in the School of Business and Economics at Wilfrid Laurier University since 1993 as a part-time and full-time instructor. She has taught a range of undergraduate and graduate courses, including Introductory Marketing; Building and Managing Products, Services and Brands; Integrated Marketing Communications; and Consumer Behaviour. Shirley has an extensive background in marketing, advertising, promotion, and training, developed during a 14-year career with IBM. She has worked in Canada, the Caribbean, and Japan.

A dedicated educator, Shirley was recognized with the 2002 SBE Outstanding Teacher Award. She was honoured to be included as one of Laurier's "Most Popular Professors" in the *MacLean's Guide to Canadian Universities* in 2003, 2004, 2005, and 2006. In 2007, Shirley was recognized by the Ontario Ministry of Training, Colleges and Universities with The LIFT Award for Teaching Excellence.

She also runs Marketing Magic, a Waterloo-based marketing communication consulting and training company. She has been a featured keynote speaker at conferences and has developed and delivered marketing seminars and workshops for many organizations. Her clients include small companies, ranging from the Stratford Festival to Fortune 500 companies such as Manulife Financial, Scotiabank, and Lexus Canada.

Shirley has written a regular marketing column for *The Record* for over 10 years. She has been an active board member and volunteer in many organizations including ViaSource, Communitech, the Business Success for Women Conference, K-W Business Women's Association, and the K-W Sexual Assault Support Centre.

brief contents

table of contents

3 Ethics and Socially Responsible Marketing 56

4   Analyzing the Marketing Environment   82

"I guess it is easy being green."

Presenting the 36 mpg Ford Escape Hybrid, the most fuel-efficient SUV on Earth.* How green is that?
www.fordvehicles.com

ESCAPE HYBRID   *Ford*

SECTION SIX   Value Delivery: Designing the Marketing Channel and Supply Chain   359

SECTION SEVEN   Value Communication   416

Marketing, First Canadian Edition— An integrated, practical approach

We are proud to say that our book integrates the Canadian Marketing Association's definition of marketing. It takes a value-based perspective and emphasizes the process of creating, communicating, and delivering value to customers, as well as managing relationships in ways that benefit both the organization and its stakeholders.

One of the challenges in teaching marketing is that textbooks tend to "chunk" learning by chapter content. While that approach helps students understand the theory related to marketing research, consumer behaviour, or global marketing, it doesn't always allow them to understand the big picture—how all aspects of marketing fit together. We want students to see marketing as an integrated process. To illustrate this, we follow two brands extensively throughout the book— BlackBerry and Dove—from research and product design to pricing and integrated marketing communications. To a lesser extent, we return to other Canadian examples such as Fairmont Hotels and WestJet to show their marketing efforts in a broader context.

A unique perspective that sets this book apart from others is its focus not just on what marketing is, but also on how and why it's done. Content is woven together to ensure that students develop a deep understanding of marketing principles and can apply them to solve marketing challenges, make sound decisions, and formulate strategies. Examples are carried throughout chapters. Inset boxes provide detailed illustrations of ethics, adding value, Internet marketing, as well as entrepreneurial and small business marketing. Student feedback that told our approach "helped to demonstrate the concepts in real scenarios in the business world." The pedagogy developed in the text is also carried through the Online Learning Centre, which provides Interactive Toolkit Exercises, Videos, Interactive Quizzes, and several other learning supplements.

Our book was tested in classrooms at Wilfrid Laurier University to gauge students' assessments of how well it helped them learn and apply marketing principles. Similarly, more than a dozen students from the University of Ottawa and Carleton University who had recently completed a marketing principles course compared our book to the book used in their course. Feedback from over 700 students told us the book was "very easy to read and understand." One student wrote, "This would have to be my favourite text I've read in university. I found all the examples and concepts to be so interesting and I truly looked forward to reading the text. I've learned a lot through reading this text and it has made me question whether a career in marketing would be beneficial to me rather than accounting." Others commented that they "enjoyed the cases and examples because they were current and applicable." Several students remarked that the smooth flow from theory to example made it extremely easy for them to digest the material without frustration.

Feedback from instructors who used the text was also very favourable. One professor wrote, "I really like the text. I like the writing style for a university student. I like the examples. I especially like the PowerPoint support. I think it is the first time I haven't had to really change much in my prep."

We're sure you too will find that *Marketing*, First Canadian Edition, truly uses an integrated, practical approach.

what is *marketing*?

The function of marketing is multi-faceted, but its fundamental purpose is to create value. Consider these examples:

Not too long ago water was simply one of the most basic natural elements. It came out of a faucet in your home and was consumed for the purposes of drinking, washing, etc. Taking a cue from European firms like Perrier in France and San Pellegrino in Italy, firms such as Aberfoyle Springs, Clearly Canadian, Canadian Springs, and Montclair have created new products that customers find valuable by bottling water in attractive and easy-to-carry packages. Today, bottled water is a $35-billion worldwide industry with global consumption topping 154 billion litres, up 57 percent from five years earlier.

Why do people buy roughed-up jeans for well over a hundred dollars when they could buy Wrangler jeans at Wal-Mart for under twenty? The answer lies in marketing brand value: Brands such as Diesel and Seven for All Mankind have created a cache for their brands with edgy advertising and innovative washes and styles. When trendsetters start to wear these brands, others follow.

Regardless of your age, your gender, or the city in which you live, you already know something about marketing. You have been an involved consumer in the marketing process since childhood when, for example, you accompanied your mother or father to the grocery store and asked to buy a particular brand of cereal because you saw a friend eating it or heard about it on television. The prize inside the box of cereal was of value to you as a child; the nutritional information offered on the box panel was of value to your mother or father. Once you begin to explore the many ways in which companies and brands create value for their customers through marketing, you will also begin to appreciate the complex set of decisions and activities that are necessary to provide you with the products and services you use every day.

preface

The prevalence and power of the Internet has created a marketplace of more informed and savvy customers than ever before. Those who teach the marketers of the future need to account for the consumer's ability to assess the marketplace at their fingertips and discern good value from poor value. *Marketing*, First Canadian Edition, is all about the core concepts and tools that help marketers create value for customers. Throughout this book you will find many examples that define how companies create value for customers through branding, packaging, pricing, retailing, service, and advertising. We introduce the concept of value in Chapter 1 and carry it through the entire text.

• **The first section** of the text contains four chapters and the central theme of the section is "Assessing the Marketplace." Following an introduction to marketing in Chapter 1, Chapter 2 then focuses on how a firm develops a marketing plan. A central theme of the chapter is how firms can effectively create, capture, deliver, and communicate value to their customers. Chapter 3 focuses attention on Marketing Ethics and Socially Responsible Marketing. An ethical decision framework is developed and presented, and the key ethical concepts are linked back to the marketing plan introduced in Chapter 2. Finally, Chapter 4 and presented in the Appendix at the end of the text. (Analyzing the Marketing Environment) focuses on how marketers can systematically uncover and evaluate opportunities. Key elements of scenario planning are introduced and presented to demonstrate how to analyze and capitalize on opportunities presented.

• **The second section** of the book deals with "Understanding the Marketplace" and is composed of three chapters. Chapter 5 on Marketing Research and Information Systems identifies the various tools and techniques that marketers use to uncover these needs and ensure that they create goods and services that provide value to their target markets. Chapter 6, Consumer Behaviour, focuses on all aspects of understanding why consumers purchase products and services. The consumer decision process is highlighted. Chapter 7, Business-to-Business Marketing, focuses on all aspects pertaining to why and how business-to-business buying takes place.

• **The third section** of the book deals with "Targeting the Marketplace." Chapter 8 focuses on Segmentation, Targeting, and Positioning. In this chapter, we focus on how firms segment the marketplace, pick a target market, and then position their good/service in line with their customers' needs and wants.

• *Marketing*, First Canadian Edition, devotes three chapters to Value Creation. The first two, Chapter 9, "Product, Branding, and Packaging Decisions," and Chapter 10, "Developing New Products" cover the development and management of products and brands. While many of the concepts involved in developing and managing services are similar to those of physical brands, Chapter 11, "Services: The Intangible Product" addresses the unique challenges of the marketing of services.

• Pricing is the activity within a firm responsible for Transacting Value by bringing in money and affecting revenues. Chapter 12 examines the importance of setting the right price, the relationship between price and quantity sold, break-even analysis, the impact of price wars, and how the Internet has changed the way people shop.

• One important reason why Wal-Mart has become the world's largest retailer is their Value Delivery system. They time the delivery of merchandise to get to stores just in time to meet customer demand. To achieve this, they have initiated many innovative programs with their vendors and developed sophisticated transportation and warehousing systems. *Marketing*, First Canadian Edition, devotes two chapters to value delivery. Chapter 13 takes a look at marketing channels, distribution strategy, and supply chain, while Chapter 14 concentrates on retailing.

• Today's methods of **Value Communication** are more complex because of new technologies that add e-mail, Blogs, Internet, and Podcasts to the advertising mix that once only utilized radio and television to relay messages to consumers. *Marketing*, First Canadian Edition, devotes two chapters to value communication. Chapter 15 introduces the breadth of integrated marketing communications. Chapter 16 is devoted to advertising, sales promotions, and personal selling.

• Most firms are involved in **Global Marketing** at some level. In less than 10 years, Lululemon has been transformed into a global company and a great Canadian success story in the athletic and sportswear industry. But even small entrepreneurial firms are also involved because they get their materials, products, or services from firms located in other countries. Chapter 17 is devoted exclusively to this topic.

Adding Value

The value theme is integrated throughout the text in the **Adding Value** boxes that occur in each chapter. These features illustrate how firms find ultimate success by adding value to their products and services.

Adding Value | 1.1 | Bottled Water: Commodity or Super Premium?

Creating value isn't always about offering low prices. Take bottled water for example. Is bottled water better than tap water in Canada? Some bottled water begins the same place as the water that comes from your tap and on its label you may see its origin listed as "public Source." Canadians are divided on the merits of tap water versus bottled water but it hasn't stopped us from consuming more bottled water than ever. Global consumption of bottled water tops 154 billion litres (41 billion gallons), up 57 percent from the 98 billion litres consumed five years earlier. In 2006, almost 3 out of 10 households drank predominantly bottled water whether they had a private or municipal water source. This boom in consumption has moved the product beyond niche markets and into the mainstream. Bottled water has become a basic staple to many Canadians.

Adding value to a commodity and charging consumers a premium for a product they can get for free from their taps requires an exceptional strategy—and that is precisely what Voss has done—successfully! VOSS Artesian Water, which competes in the super premium market, derives its product from underground aquifers shielded for centuries from pollutants by layers of rock and ice. With prices of over $15 for an 800-ml glass bottle, its value proposition is built on more than just a pristine product. VOSS founders, Ole Christian Sandberg and Christopher Harlem, knew that their packaging would also need to reflect the purity of the water source to define and differentiate their brand. They enlisted the help of Neil Kraft, a former Calvin Klein creative director, who noted that while premium bottled water was purchased to reflect one's style, taste, and sophistication, the bottles on the market were unsophisticated and lacked style. Taking inspiration from the fragrance industry, a unique cylindrical glass

bottle was chosen. The brand name, set in lowercase type, was silk-screened in grey directly on the bottle so as not to obscure the purity of its contents. Even the cap, in silver plastic, the same diameter as the bottle, was unique.

The last part of the company's value added strategy involved limiting distribution exclusively to upscale establishments: fine restaurants, hotels, clubs, and spas, first in Europe and eventually in North America. VOSS quickly gained popularity helped along by its trendy bottle being seen in the hands of worldwide celebrities. Apparently, Madonna took a liking to it. On the other hand, NAYA successfully targets ordinary consumers with its simple message of *source of well being.* Although VOSS and NAYA both sell water, they add value to different customer segments in different ways.

A differentiation strategy that revolves around stunning cylindrical glass bottles and exclusive distribution helped VOSS Artesian Water develop a trendy image and significant market share in the super premium market. Meanwhile, Naya targets mainstream consumers using a simple message based on health and well-being.

Features inside *Marketing,* First Canadian Edition

In addition to our emphasis on value in *Marketing,* First Canadian Edition, you will also find integrated and highlighted coverage of ethics, entrepreneurship, Internet marketing, services, and globalization within the framework of the marketing discipline:

• *Marketing,* First Canadian Edition, contains an entire chapter on **Marketing Ethics**. Placed early in the text (Chapter 3), it provides rich illustrations of corporate responsibility, and introduces an ethical decision-making framework that is useful for assessing potential ethically troubling situations that are posed throughout the rest of the book. It therefore sets the tone for ethical material in each subsequent chapter.

 In addition, Chapters 2 to 17 each contain an **Ethical Dilemma box** with a compelling ethical discussion and end of chapter discussion questions that force students to consider and evaluate each situation.

• **Entrepreneurship**. An entrepreneurial spirit pervades most marketing innovations and is necessary to keep firms growing and healthy. *Marketing,* First Canadian Edition, nurtures that entrepreneurial spirit by providing examples of young entrepreneurial firms and successful entrepreneurs such as Lululemon, Kicking Horse Coffee, Kettleman's Bagels, and more.

And each chapter contains an **Entrepreneurial Marketing box** that depicts recognizable and interesting young entrepreneurial firms.

• **Internet Marketing boxes** further explore the growing use of the Internet as a distribution channel as well as a marketing tool.

For example, Chapter 6 includes a discussion of Canada's Expedia.ca as an example of presenting alternatives for travel, by allowing for choices such as by price, interest, date, hotel, and packages, and is a major player on the competitive market today.

Reinforcing learning

Learning Objectives

Listed at the beginning of each chapter, **Learning Objectives** show students the main concepts discussed inside. These Learning Objectives are then presented in the margins throughout the chapter when they are introduced. At the end of each chapter, the Learning Objectives are then revisited and reviewed, reinforcing for students the key sections in the chapter, and allowing them to follow their own progress to know where they need help.

Opening Vignette

Each chapter begins with an Opening Vignette that helps to introduce and illustrate some of the main content that follows. These vignettes have been carefully selected to pique student interest and are designed to provide real world examples of how the theory has been applied by a variety of companies.

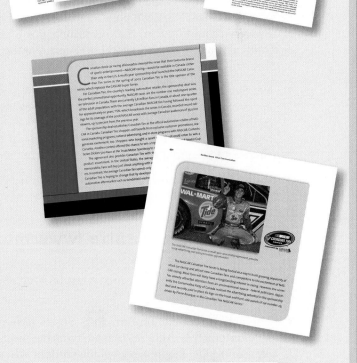

Chapter Roadmap

Each chapter consists of a Chapter Roadmap representing the main steps that describe a chapter. Then in the chapter, each step is explained in detail, allowing students to easily absorb/understand the information. The Chapter Roadmap serves as a useful study tool for students.

why will **students enjoy using this book?**

- **A Compelling Read.** *Marketing*, First Canadian Edition, was written with the student in mind. The examples are current and appealing, and feature a wide range of products and services that will be recognizable to a diverse group of readers. A draft version of the text was used at Wilfrid Laurier University in the fall of 2007 and received extremely favourable reviews from students.

- ## Unique End-of-Chapter Applications and Exercises

  - **Marketing Applications.** Student-tested at Wilfrid Laurier and University of Ottawa, these Marketing Application questions encourage students to become more critical in their thinking of how marketing theory relates to practice.

  - **Ethical Dilemma.** At least one of the Marketing Applications in each chapter poses an ethical dilemma based on material covered in the chapter. For instance, in Chapter 17 on global marketing, we pose the issue of offshore tax preparation work being done at a local accounting firm that communicates a personal commitment to each customer. Students can apply the ethical decision-making framework introduced in Chapter 3 to these marketing situations.

  - **Net Savvy.** Each chapter contains two exercises that drive students to the Internet to apply material covered in the text. For example, in Chapter 16 on advertising we direct students to the Concerned Children's Advertisers website, one of the major self-regulatory bodies for children's advertising at www.cca-kids.ca/. We ask students to choose a PSA and discuss how these ads are used to deliver CCA's message.

  - **End-of-Chapter Cases.** Each chapter ends with a two or three page case covering a current marketing idea, concept, or company.

- ## Online Learning Centre (www.mcgrawhill.ca/olc/grewal)

  The Online Learning Centre (OLC) will help students use *Marketing*, First Canadian Edition, effectively, and reinforce what they've learned in the text. Some of the features on the OLC include:

  - **Interactive Student Toolkit.** Sophisticated, fun, and instructive, the Tool Kit is a set of interactive exercises that are working models of the concepts presented in the text. An icon in the chapters shows the student where the Tool Kit content can be used and students can go to the OLC for these resources.

  - **Videos.** Compelling videos feature firms in the text book such as M&M Meat Shops, Holiday Inn Express, and Netflix. The bottled water industry is also covered in a long segment which integrates several key concepts discussed in the text.

  - **Supplemental textbook material**
    - Glossary
    - Chapter Summaries
    - Multiple-Choice questions with feedback

Marketer's Showdown is an online, interactive video case program that puts you in the middle of dynamic marketing strategy decision-making with real marketers. Nine cases take you through up-to-the-minute issues in the music industry, the automotive industry, and the soft drink industry.

You get to analyze the marketing problem, choose a proposed solution, and then watch your proposal debated by marketing professionals. After the debate, you can change your mind or stick to your guns. Then see what the outcome is. Just like real life, not every good decision leads to a good outcome! Are you ready to tackle a complex marketing problem? Find out, with Marketer's Showdown.

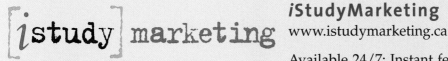

iInteract iLearn iSucceed

*i*StudyMarketing

www.istudymarketing.ca

Available 24/7: Instant feedback so you can study when you want, how you want, and where you want: www.istudymarketing.ca. This online *i*Study space was developed to help you master the concepts and achieve better grades with all of the learning tools you've come to expect (e.g., multiple-choice and true/false quizzes) plus learning objects, marketing plan resources, flashcards, videos, and added quizzes, including chapter-by-chapter diagnostic assessments that point you to the concepts you need to focus on to improve your grades. Pick and choose from all of these features to develop your own personalized study plan. *i*Study offers the best, most convenient way to interact, learn, and succeed.

*i*StudyMarketing can be purchased through the Online Learning Centre (www.mcgrawhill.ca/olc/grewal) or through the *i*StudyMarketing web-site.

Instructors: Please contact your *i*Learning Sales Specialist for more information on how to make *i*StudyMarketing part of your students' success.

We've created this book and support package to give you the best possible learning experience. We truly hope that you fully enjoy this book and the tools that accompany it.

why will **instructors** enjoy using this book?

- **Assessment.** The **Interactive Student Tool Kit** (see page xxvi) contains up to three gradable assignments on each of the following concepts:

- SWOT Analysis (Chapter 2)
- Compensatory versus Non-compensatory Consumer Decision Making (Chapter 6)
- Vendor Evaluation Analysis (Chapter 7)
- Market Positioning Map (Chapter 8)
- Service Quality (Chapter 11)
- Break-even Analysis (Chapter 12)
- Developing an Advertisement (Chapter 16)

- **Instructor Supplements.** A broad spectrum of high-quality supplements compliment this text, and are available on the Online Learning Centre (www.mcgrawhill.ca/olc/grewal):

- **PowerPoint presentations** for each chapter contain photos, screen captures, key terms, exhibits, and commentaries, to provide visuals in your lectures.

- **Instructor's Manual.** This manual includes lecture notes as well as end-of-chapter solutions, but you will also find additional assignments, examples, and in-class activities that you can use to enhance your lectures.

- **Videos** of more than 15 segments in a variety of lengths will provide flexibility for your class. Firms featured in the videos include M&M Meat Shops, Holiday Inn Express, and Netflix, as well as a long segment on the bottled water industry.

- **Test Bank.** One of the most important aspects of the teaching package is the test bank. *Marketing,* First Canadian Edition, addresses this important resource with a test bank which was designed by a focus group of instructors. It provides more than 100 questions per chapter, each keyed to chapter Learning Objectives and noted for level of difficulty. A mix of true/false, multiple-choice, short answer, and essay questions are included, and labelled as Conceptual, Applied, or Application driven.

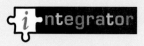

- **Integrator.** Keyed to the chapters and Learning Objectives, the Integrator ties together all the elements in your resource package, guiding you to where you'll find corresponding coverage in the supplemental material. Link to the Integrator from the Online Learning Centre, at www.mcgrawhill.ca/olc/grewal.

- ***i*Learning Services** McGraw-Hill Ryerson offers a unique *i*Services package designed for Canadian faculty. Our mission is to equip higher education providers with superior tools and resources required for excellence in teaching. For additional information, visit www.mcgrawhilll.ca/highereducation/iservices.

acknowledgments

We could not have completed this text without the help of others. In particular, we would like to thank Stacey Biggar who diligently worked with us throughout the project as an invaluable research assistant, writer, and proofreader. We could not have met our many deadlines without her. Our thanks go as well to the many Wilfrid Laurier University students and professors who took the time to provide us with feedback on the chapter content, cases, and exercises of first draft materials.

Additionally, we would like to thank Bernadette Franjieh and Neil Parker who made significant contributions as research assistants during the early writing stages and to our many student reviewers including Tracy Longchamps, Angie Kelly, Sushil Dahiya, Philip Plante-Ajah, Xu Xi Liu, Emilio Franco, Irfan Butt, Aaron Dobson, Sachit Harish, Danielle Sauve, Nadine Wasfi, Annie Nguyen, Shelina Jamal, Jenna Krishnan, Bernie Maclean, and Savita Kapoor.

A special thanks to the many talented staff members at McGraw-Hill Ryerson— Leanna MacLean, Emma Gain, Marcia Luke, Suzanne Simpson Millar, Erin Moore, Elizabeth Priest, James Booty, and Joy Armitage Taylor. You made our jobs so much easier. It was a pleasure working with you.

We gratefully acknowledge feedback and constructive criticism from marketing colleagues across Canada.

Cathy Ace	Simon Fraser University
Rick Appleby	Okanagan University College
Jim Beatty	George Brown College
Onur Bodur	Concordia University
Pat Browne	Kwantlen University College
Mark Cleveland	University of Western Ontario
Scott Colwell	University of Guelph
Brian Cronin	Seneca College
Paul Cubbon	University of British Columbia
Tanya Drollinger	University of Lethbridge
Lisa Giguere	Wilfrid Laurier University
Sarah Holding	Malaspina College
Geof Malleck	University of Waterloo
Gordon McFarlane	Langara College
Brent McKenzie	University of Western Ontario
R. Sachdev	University of Ontario Institute of Technology
Janice Shearer	Mohawk College
Simon Sigue	Athabasca University
Harvey Skolnick	Sheridan College
Peter Stasiuk	Durham College
Heather Stevens	George Brown College
Medhi Zahaf	Lakehead University

I would like to thank my wife, Vidya, and kids, Priya and Ryan, for their love, support, and humour that made writing this book enjoyable.　　　　—Ajax Persaud

For my husband, John and son, Stephen, who patiently supported and encouraged me throughout the process of research and writing.　　　　—Shirley Lichti

CHAPTER 1

LEARNING OBJECTIVES

After studying this chapter, you should be able to:

LO 1 Define marketing and explain its core concepts

LO 2 Discuss how marketers create value for a product or service

LO 3 Explain the four orientations of marketing

LO 4 Discuss the role of customer relationship management in creating value

LO 5 Discuss the importance of marketing both within and outside the firm

Overview of Marketing

The BlackBerry wireless solution, from Research In Motion (RIM), is one of Canada's most recent successful and innovative products.[1] The BlackBerry solution offers more than just a cool gadget; it is a truly innovative service that not only changed the way business executives, managers, professionals, and sales people globally communicate and work but also the speed and timeliness with which crucial business decisions are made and implemented. Executives and sales people from around the world talk about how using the BlackBerry solution enhances their ability to access key corporate information and connect with their coworkers in real time from anywhere, anytime. The resulting efficiency has resulted in sales deals being closed faster and key decisions being communicated to decision-makers, even when they are on the golf course. The BlackBerry smartphone has become the one device that many business people find hard to function without.

The BlackBerry solution, the brainchild of Mike Lazaridis, is based on a paper he wrote in three hours on his basement computer in 1997. That paper has changed the way users globally talk, work, and even move their thumbs—the BlackBerry solution is now available on over 300 networks in over 120 countries. Today, the BlackBerry smartphone is to business professionals as Google is to Internet searching—the world's leading and most preferred wireless, mobile communications device. It's sleek, elegant, fast, and highly valued by professionals who need a wireless solution to stay connected and be accessible no matter where they are. The BlackBerry smartphone is more than just a mobile e-mail device; it is business professionals' phone, organizer, instant messenger, GPS, Internet browser, and media player. It keeps mobile professionals connected to the people, data, and resources that drive their day—providing a world of information at their fingertips.

Mike Lazaridis and two friends, Doug Fregin and Mike Barnstijn, launched their entre-preneurial venture, Research In Motion Limited (RIM) in 1984, while they were still university students. Headquartered in Waterloo, Ontario, RIM has offices in North America, Europe, and Asia Pacific. RIM's portfolio of award-winning products, services, and embedded tech-nologies include the BlackBerry wireless platform, the wireless device product line, software development tools, radio-modems, and software/hardware licensing agreements. Extensive product lines have been developed, for example the BlackBerry smartphones, which include the BlackBerry 7100, 7200, 8700, and 8800 series as well as the BlackBerry Curve and Black-Berry Pearl series. These product lines are offered at price points that meet the needs and wants of both businesses and consumers around the world.

Despite fierce competition from some similarly priced devices and solutions from Palm, HP, Sony, Good Technology Inc., Microsoft, and a patent lawsuit from NTP, RIM has achieved phenomenal growth. RIM's sales grew from US$85 million in 2000 to US$3.04 billion in 2007. Over 35 percent of 2007 revenues were from global sales outside North America. Between 2001 and 2007, the company grew its workforce from about 1250 employees to more than 7000 employees. Currently, RIM has over 12 million users globally.

In addition to meeting its customer needs with an impressive portfolio of innovative products, RIM has made excellent customer care a top priority. It has increased the number of employees providing customer care, improved the number of service contracts to users, and developed training programs for corporate customers. This focus on the customer helps RIM ensure that BlackBerry is "always on, always connected" satisfying users who demand information in real time.

Describe the value RIM's BlackBerry provides users. What do you consider are the main reasons for RIM's phenomenal growth and success? (Visit http://rim. com/ to learn more.)

What is Marketing?

Unlike other subjects you may have studied, marketing is already very familiar to you. You start your day by agreeing to do the dishes in exchange for a freshly made cup of coffee. Then you fill up your car with gas. You attend a class that you have chosen and paid for. After class, you pick up lunch at the cafeteria, have your hair cut, buy a few songs from Apple's iTunes, and watch a movie. In each case, you have acted as the buyer and made a decision about whether you should part with your time and/or money to receive a particular service or merchandise. If, after you return home from the movie, you decide to auction a CD on eBay, you have become a seller. And in each of these transactions, you were engaged in marketing.

When you buy a song on iTunes, you are engaging in marketing.

This chapter will look at the definition of marketing and how it is used to create value in products or in services. We will see how the interrelated marketing mix—or 4Ps—create, transact, communicate, and deliver value. As well, we will look at where marketing happens and how it has evolved over the years into today's concept of value-based marketing. Lastly we will discuss why marketing is an important function for any successful firm. Refer to the chapter roadmap to guide you through the chapter contents.

The Canadian Marketing Association states that "**Marketing** is a set of business practices designed to plan for and present an organization's products or services in ways that build effective customer relationships."[2] What does this definition really mean? Good marketing is not a random activity; it requires thoughtful planning with an emphasis on the ethical implications of any of those decisions on consumers and society in general. Firms develop a **marketing plan** (Chapter 2) that specifies the marketing activities for a specific period of time. The marketing plan is also broken down into various components—how the product or service will be conceived or designed, how much it should cost, where and how it will be promoted, and how it

marketing
A set of business practices designed to plan for and present an organization's products or services in ways that build effective customer relationships.

marketing plan
A written document composed of an analysis of the current marketing situation, opportunities and threats for the firm, marketing objectives and strategy specified in terms of the four Ps, action programs, and projected or pro forma income (and other financial) statements.

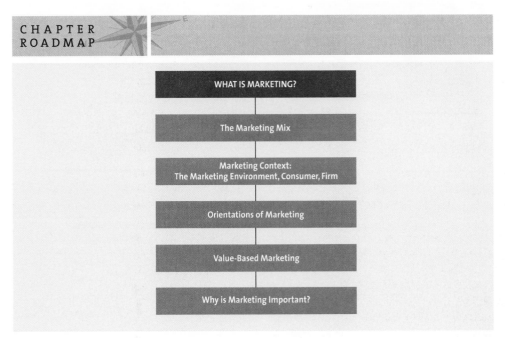

CHAPTER ROADMAP

- WHAT IS MARKETING?
- The Marketing Mix
- Marketing Context: The Marketing Environment, Consumer, Firm
- Orientations of Marketing
- Value-Based Marketing
- Why is Marketing Important?

will get to the consumer. In any exchange, the buyer and the seller should be satisfied with the value they obtained from a transaction. In our previous example, you should be satisfied or even delighted with the iTune you downloaded and Apple should be satisfied with the amount of money it received from you. The core aspects of marketing are shown in Exhibit 1.1. Let's see how they look in practice.

Marketing is about Satisfying Customer Needs and Wants

Understanding and satisfying consumer needs and wants is fundamental to marketing success. A **need** is when a person feels deprived of the basic necessities of life such as food, clothing, shelter, or safety. A **want** is the particular way in which the person chooses to fulfill his or her need, which is shaped by a person's knowledge, culture, and personality. For example, when we are hungry, we need something to eat. Some people may want a plate of spaghetti and meatballs to satisfy that hunger whereas others want a salad and soup instead. The topic of understanding customer needs is described in detail in Chapter 6, which deals with consumer behaviour.

In order to understand customer needs and wants, the company must first identify the customers or **market** for its product or service. Generally, the market for a firm's offerings consists of all consumers who need or want a company's products or services and have the ability and willingness to buy. Although marketers would prefer to sell their products and services to everyone, it is not practical to do so.

need
A person feeling physiologically deprived of basic necessities, such as food, clothing, shelter, and safety.

want
The particular way in which a person chooses to satisfy a need, which is shaped by a person's knowledge, culture, and personality.

market
Refers to the groups of people to whom an organization is interested in marketing its products, services, or ideas.

LO **1**

EXHIBIT | **1.1** | Core Aspects of Marketing

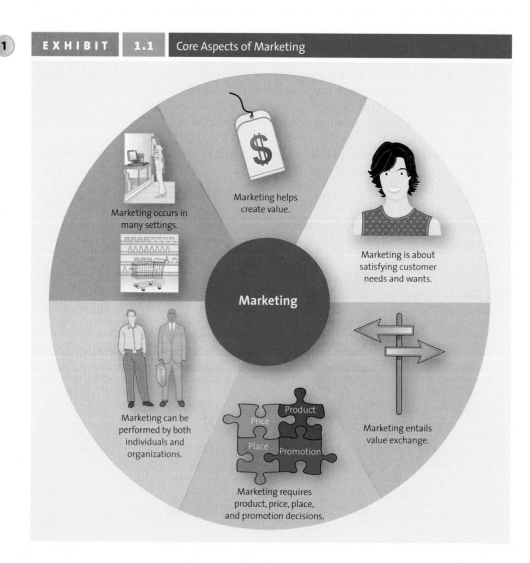

Marketing occurs in many settings.

Marketing helps create value.

Marketing is about satisfying customer needs and wants.

Marketing

Marketing can be performed by both individuals and organizations.

Price Product
Place Promotion

Marketing requires product, price, place, and promotion decisions.

Marketing entails value exchange.

Thus, marketers divide the market into sub-groups or segments of people to whom they are interested in marketing their products, services, or ideas. For example, even though the marketplace for toothpaste users may include most of the people in the world, the makers of Crest could divide them into adolescent, adult, and senior users or perhaps into smokers, coffee drinkers, and wine drinkers. If you manufacture toothpaste that removes tar and nicotine stains, you want to know for which market segments your product is most relevant and then make sure that you build a marketing strategy that meets the needs and wants of the target groups or **target market**. The process of how companies segment the market for their products and services and then choose which segment to target and how best to reach the segment is described in Chapter 8. The process of identifying customer segments the company wants to target with its products and services requires market research. The types of market research that help marketers make good decisions about various aspects of the marketing mix are discussed in Chapter 5.

target market
The customer segment or group to whom the firm is interested in selling its products and services; potential customers who have both an interest in the product or service and an ability to buy.

exchange
The trade of things of value between the buyer and the seller so that each is better off as a result.

Marketing Entails Value Exchange

Marketing is about an **exchange**—the trade of things of value between the buyer and the seller so that each is better off as a result. As depicted in Exhibit 1.2, sellers provide goods or services, then communicate and facilitate the delivery of their offering to consumers. Buyers complete the exchange by giving money and information to the seller. Suppose you learn about a new Nelly Furtado CD by reading your favourite entertainment magazine, which published a review of the CD and included an ad noting that the CD was available online at iTunes. You go online and purchase the CD. Along with gathering your necessary billing and shipping information, iTunes creates a record of your purchase: information that may be used in the coming months to inform you of the introduction of her next album or a concert near you. Thus, in addition to making money on this particular transaction, iTunes can use the information you provided to facilitate an exchange in the future and solidify a relationship with you—additional value for both you and iTunes.

When you purchase a new Nelly Furtado CD, you are engaging in a marketing exchange. You get the CD, and the exchange partners get money and information about you.

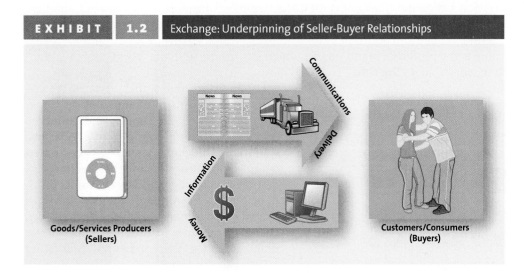

| **EXHIBIT** | **1.2** | Exchange: Underpinning of Seller-Buyer Relationships |

Communications
Delivery
Information
Money

**Goods/Services Producers
(Sellers)**

**Customers/Consumers
(Buyers)**

LO **2**

EXHIBIT **1.3** Marketing Mix Decisions

Product/Service
Brand
Size
Quality
Features
Packaging
Warranty

Creating value

Product

List Price
Discounts
Allowances
Costs
Payment Period
Credit Terms

Transacting value

Price

Target Market

Communicating value

Promotion

Advertising
Sales Promotion
Personal Selling
Public Relations
Direct Marketing
Electronic Media

Delivering value

Place

Marketing Channels
Distribution Intensity
Locations: retailers, online
Supply Chain
Logistics

Marketing Requires Product, Price, Place, and Promotion Decisions

marketing mix (four Ps)
Product, price, place, and promotion—the controllable set of activities that a firm uses to respond to the wants of its target markets.

goods
Items that can be physically touched.

Marketing traditionally has been divided into a set of four interrelated decisions known as the **marketing mix**, or **four Ps**: product, price, place, and promotion as shown in Exhibit 1.3.[3] Together, the four Ps comprise the marketing mix, which is the controllable set of activities that the firm uses to respond to the wants of its target markets. But what does each of them mean?

Product: Creating Value   One main purpose of marketing is to create value by developing a variety of offerings, including goods, services, and ideas, to satisfy customer needs. Take, for example, water. Not too long ago, consumers perceived this basic commodity as simply water. It came out of a faucet and was consumed for drinking and washing. But taking a cue from European firms like Perrier (France) and San Pellegrino (Italy), several Canadian-based firms such as Clearly Canadian, Canadian Springs, and Montclair have created a product with benefits that consumers find valuable. In addition to easy access to water, an essential part of this created value is the product's brand image, which lets users say to the world, "I'm healthy," "I'm smart," and "I'm chic."[4]

Clearly Canadian has created a product with benefits that consumers find valuable.

Goods are items that you can physically touch. Roots clothing, Molson Canadian beer, and Kraft Dinner, and countless other products are examples of goods. The example of ImaSight, a small Quebec-based company producing imaging technology, demonstrates how it adds value to its products by producing high quality, low-cost digital X-ray images which doctors can easily manipulate in order to make better diagnoses (See Entrepreneurial Marketing 1.1 later in this chapter.)

Unlike goods, **services** are intangible customer benefits that are produced by people or machines and cannot be separated from the producer. Air travel, banking, insurance, beauty treatments, and entertainment all are services. If you attend a hockey or football game, you are consuming a service. Getting money from your bank using an ATM or teller is another example of using a service. In this case, cash machines usually add value to your banking experience by being conveniently located, fast, and easy to use.

Many offerings represent a combination of goods and services. When you go to Hakim Optical, for example, you have your eyes examined (service) and purchase new contact lenses (good). If you enjoy Norah Jones's music, you can attend one of her concerts that can be provided only at a particular time and place. At the concert, you can purchase one of her CDs—the tangible good that has provided you with a combination of a good and a service.

Many offerings are a combination of goods and services. At a Norah Jones concert you can enjoy the concert (a service) and buy her CD (a good).

Ideas include thoughts, opinions, philosophies, and intellectual concepts that also can be marketed. Groups promoting bicycle safety go to schools, give talks, and sponsor bike helmet poster contests for the members of their primary target market—children. Then their secondary target market segment, parents and siblings, gets involved through their interactions with the young contest participants. The exchange of value occurs when the children listen to the sponsor's presentation and wear their helmets while bicycling, which means they have adopted, or become "purchasers," of the safety idea that the group marketed.

Price: Transacting Value Everything has a price, though it doesn't always have to be monetary. **Price**, therefore, is everything the buyer gives up—money, time, energy—in exchange for the product. Marketers must determine the price of a product carefully on the basis of the potential buyer's belief about its value. For example, Air Canada can take you from Toronto to Vancouver or New York. The price you pay depends on how far in advance you book the ticket, the time of year, whether you want to fly economy or business class, and more recently whether or not you have luggage to check in. Passengers now get a discount on their ticket if they do not have any check-in luggage. If you value the convenience of buying your ticket at the last minute for a ski trip between Christmas and New Year's Day and you want to fly business class, you can expect to pay four or five times as much as you would for the cheapest available ticket. That is, you have traded off a lower price for convenience. For marketers, the key to determining prices is figuring out how much customers are willing to pay so that they are satisfied with the purchase and the seller achieves a reasonable profit.

Place: Delivering Value The third P, place, describes all the activities necessary to get the product from the manufacturer or producer to the right customer. Place decisions are concerned with developing an efficient system for merchandise to be distributed in the right quantities, to the right locations, and at the right time in the most efficient way in order to minimize systemwide costs while satisfying the service levels required by their customers.[5] Many marketers initially overlook the importance of distribution management because a lot of the activities are behind the scenes. But

service
Intangible customer benefits that are produced by people or machines and cannot be separated from the producer.

ideas
Include thoughts, opinions, philosophies, and intellectual concepts.

price
The overall sacrifice a consumer is willing to make—money, time, energy—to acquire a specific product or service.

The Country Grocer is Canada's first independently owned grocery store to sell groceries online.

without a strong and efficient distribution system, merchandise isn't available when or where customers want it. They are disappointed, and sales and profits suffer. Place or distribution activities and decisions are discussed in detail in Chapter 13.

To illustrate how distribution delivers the value proposition, consider the experience of the Country Grocer, a small Ottawa-based independent grocery store. The Country Grocer was the first independently owned grocery store in Canada to offer online groceries. As an independent store, you might think that its customers would come from within a couple of kilometres of the store. The reality is that the Country Grocer, through its Internet site (www.thecountrygrocer.com), gets more than 30 percent of its online sales from the eastern Arctic (Iqaluit) and about 5 percent from customers in the United States. Customers place their orders through the website and the Country Grocer ensures that their purchases are delivered on time.[6]

Promotion: Communicating Value   Even the best products and services will go unsold if marketers cannot communicate their value to customers. Countless Internet companies sank in the late 1990s, at least partly because they did not communicate successfully with their customers. Some such firms had great products at very fair prices, but when customers could not find them on the Internet, the companies simply failed. Promotion is communication by a marketer that informs, persuades, and reminds potential buyers about a product or service to influence their opinions or elicit a response. Promotion generally can enhance a product or service's value, as

Parasuco is known for its provocative advertising that appears on billboards and the use of celebrities as a way to market their denim lines.

happened for Parasuco jeans. The company's provocative advertising has helped create an image that says more than "Use this product and you will look good." Rather, the promotion sells youth, style, and sex appeal.

Marketing is Shaped by Forces and Players External to the Firm

It is important to recognize that a company's marketing activities are not only influenced by factors within the company but also by forces, organizations, and individuals external to the company as shown in Exhibit 1.4. External forces such as social, technological, economic, competitive, and regulatory changes shape a company's marketing activities. For instance, two current social trends that are reshaping the marketing activities of most firms are concerns about the environment and obesity. In response to these concerns, marketers are beginning to use more environmentally friendly packaging for their products; some are even using alternative materials in their products. In response to the obesity trend, marketers try to distinguish their products by using labels such as non-fat, low-fat, fat-free, sugar-free, and cholesterol-free.

EXHIBIT 1.4 The Marketing Environment

(Concentric diagram. Outer ring: Competitors, Political/Regulatory, Demographics, Economic, Social/Cultural Trends, Technology. Middle ring: Marketing Mix Decisions — Product, Price, Promotion, Place. Centre: Target Market.)

As well, a firm's relations with suppliers, distributors, other intermediaries (e.g., financial institutions, advertising agencies, market research firms) and advocacy groups (e.g., Greenpeace, PETA) affect its marketing decisions. Suppliers can exert substantial influence on a company's marketing activities with devastating consequences. For example, Lululemon claimed that its VitaSea shirts were made from 24 percent seaweed, providing health benefits. Yet independent testing showed no difference between a regular cotton t-shirt and Lululemon's VitaSea shirt. The company said that it took the word of its suppliers who made the claim and that they did not do any testing to verify the supplier's claim. Regardless, Lululemon is facing lawsuits from angry customers who felt they were deliberately deceived by the company. Only time will tell the extent to which the negative publicity from its false claims have hurt the Lululemon brand.[7] Advocacy groups such as People for the Ethical Treatment of Animals (PETA), often target the marketing practices of specific firms (Kentucky Fried Chicken) or industries (meat industry) with hard-hitting ads such as the ones shown in the photo. PETA's ads and marketing messages have nevertheless turned many customers away from these products and have forced marketers to change some of their business practices. The influence of all of these forces is discussed in greater detail in Chapter 4.

PETA's ads target the meat and fur industries by encouraging customers to turn away from these products.

Marketing Can Be Performed by Both Individuals and Organizations

Imagine how complicated the world would be if you had to buy everything you consumed directly from producers or manufacturers. You would have to go from farm to farm buying your food and then from manufacturer to manufacturer to purchase the table, plates, and utensils you need to eat that food. Fortunately, marketing intermediaries, such as retailers, accumulate merchandise from producers in large amounts and then sell it to you in smaller amounts. The process in which businesses sell to consumers is known as **B2C (business-to-consumer) marketing**, whereas the process of selling merchandise or services from one business to another is called **B2B (business-to-business) marketing**. Some companies, like General Electric, are engaged in both B2B and B2C marketing at the same time. However, with the advent of various auction sites, such as eBay, consumers have started marketing their products and services to other consumers, which requires a third category in which consumers sell to other consumers: **C2C marketing**. These marketing transactions are illustrated in Exhibit 1.5. Individuals can also undertake activities to market themselves. When you apply for a job, for instance, the research you do about the firm, the résumé and cover letter you submit with your application, and the way you dress for an interview and conduct yourself during it are all forms of marketing activities. Accountants, lawyers, financial planners, physicians, and other professional service providers also market their services.

B2C (business-to-consumers) The process in which businesses sell to consumers.

B2B (business-to-business) The process of selling merchandise or services from one business to another.

C2C (consumer-to-consumer) The process in which consumers sell to other consumers.

Marketing Occurs in Many Settings

Most people think of marketing as a way for a firm to make profits, but marketing works equally well in the nonprofit sector. Think about what influenced your selection of your college or university, other than family, friends, and convenience. It's likely that your college has a sophisticated marketing program to attract and retain students. Hospitals, theatres, charities, museums, religious institutions, politicians, and even governments rely on marketing to communicate their message to their constituents.

In addition, marketing isn't useful only in countries with well-developed economies. It can also jump-start the economies of less developed countries by actually putting buyers and sellers together to create new markets. A Piece of Africa, for example, buys art from African artists and, through its website, makes that art available to customers all over the world; thereby creating a market that otherwise would not exist. Customers become exposed to an array of products from various countries that previously would have been available only through expensive galleries, and the tribal artists can spend their earnings locally, which stimulates the local economy.

EXHIBIT   1.5   Marketing Can Be Performed by Both Individuals and Organizations

| Firm (Makes Monitors) | Firm (Dell–Sells PCs & Monitors) | Consumer A | Consumer B |

B2B   B2C   C2C

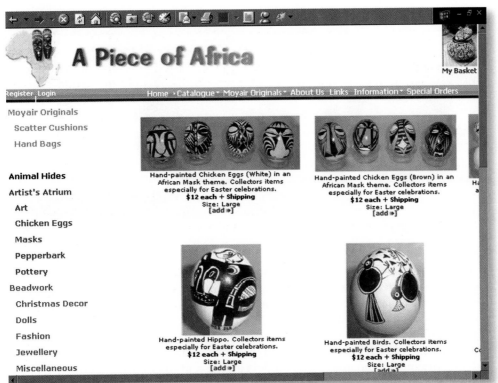

A Piece of Africa buys art from African artists and, through its website (www.bizinsa.com/apieceofafrica), makes that art available to customers all over the world, thereby creating a market that otherwise would not exist.

Finally, the firm donates 3 percent of the online sales to goodwill projects in Africa, which solidifies its socially responsible appeal.

Marketing is often designed to benefit an entire industry, which can help many firms simultaneously. The dairy industry has used a very successful, award-winning campaign with its slogan "Got Milk," aimed at different target segments. This campaign has not only created high levels of awareness about the benefits of drinking milk but also increased milk consumption in various target segments,[8] possibly through the use of celebrities such as Angelina Jolie and athletes such as boxer Oscar de la Hoya. Overall, this campaign benefits the entire dairy industry, not just one dairy farmer.

Now that we've examined what marketing is and how it creates value, let's consider how it fits into the world of commerce, as well as into society in general.

Marketing Helps Create Value

Marketing didn't get to its current prominence among individuals, corporations, and society at large overnight. To understand how marketing has evolved into its present-day, integral business function of creating value, let's look for a moment at the four different marketing orientations and some of the milestones in marketing's history (Exhibit 1.6).

The dairy industry's "Got Milk" ad campaign has created high levels of awareness about the benefits of drinking milk and has increased milk consumption by using celebrities like Hilary Duff in its ads.

LO **3**

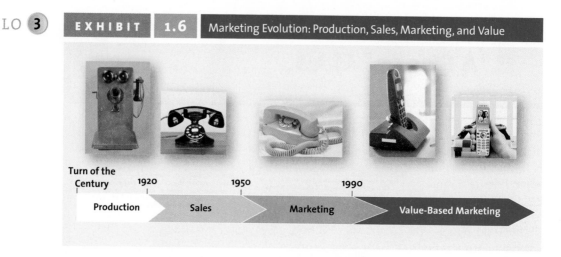

EXHIBIT | **1.6** | Marketing Evolution: Production, Sales, Marketing, and Value

Turn of the Century   1920   1950   1990

Production | Sales | Marketing | Value-Based Marketing

Production-Oriented Era   Around the turn of the 20th century, most firms were production oriented and believed that a good product would sell itself. Henry Ford, the founder of Ford Motor Co., once famously remarked, "Customers can have any colour they want so long as it's black." Manufacturers were concerned with product innovation, not with satisfying the needs of individual consumers, and retail stores typically were considered places to hold the merchandise until a consumer wanted it. Product-oriented companies focus on developing and distributing innovative products with little concern whether the products best satisfy customers' needs.

Sales-Oriented Era   Between 1920 and 1950, production and distribution techniques became more sophisticated, however, the Great Depression and World War II conditioned customers to consume less. As a result, manufacturers had the capacity to produce more than customers really wanted to buy. Firms found an answer to their overproduction in becoming sales oriented; they depended on heavy doses of personal selling and advertising. Marketing was essentially reduced to a selling function where companies try to sell as much as possible of the products they make rather than focus on making products consumers really want.

Market-Oriented Era   After World War II, soldiers returned home, got new jobs, and started families. At the same time, manufacturers turned from focusing on the war effort and toward consumer products. Suburban communities sprouted up around the country, and the new suburban fixture, the shopping centre, began to replace cities' central business districts as the hub of retail activity and a place to just hang out. Some products, once in limited supply because of World War II, became plentiful. Canada entered a buyer's market—the customer became king! When consumers again had choices, they were able to make purchasing decisions on the basis of factors such as quality, convenience, and price. Manufacturers and retailers thus began to focus on what consumers wanted and needed before they designed, made, or attempted to sell their products and services.

Value-Based Marketing Era   Most successful firms today are market oriented.[9] That means they have gone beyond a production or selling orientation and attempt to discover and satisfy their customers' needs and wants. Better marketing firms recognized that there was more to good marketing than simply discovering and providing what consumers wanted and needed; to compete successfully, they would have to give their customers greater value than their competitors.

value
Reflects the relationship of benefits to costs, or what the consumer *gets* for what he or she *gives*.

   Value reflects the relationship of benefits to costs, or what you *get* for what you *give*.[10] In a marketing context, customers seek a fair return in goods and/or services for their hard-earned money and scarce time. They want products or services that meet their specific needs or wants and that are offered at competitive prices. The challenge for firms is to find out what consumers are looking for and attempt to provide those goods and services but still make a profit.

Every value-based marketing firm must implement its strategy according to what its customers value. Depending on the specific product or service for sale, these valuable benefits could include speed, convenience, size, accuracy, price, cost-savings, or user-friendliness. Sometimes providing greater value means providing a lot of merchandise for relatively little money, such as a Whopper for 99¢ at Burger King or a diamond for 40 percent off the suggested retail price at Costco. But value is in the eye of the beholder and doesn't always come cheap. Satisfied Lexus buyers probably believe their car is a good value because they have received a lot of benefits for a reasonable price. Similarly, teenagers may be willing to pay a premium for Apple's iPod because of its extraordinary design and packaging, even though cheaper substitutes are available. This is the power of marketing in general and branding in particular. The bottled water story in Adding Value 1.1 shows how marketers add value for consumers to a rather ordinary product like water. The story of ImaSight's technology described in Entrepreneurial Marketing 1.1 on page 19 illustrates other aspects of value beyond just monetary cost and price.

Adding Value   1.1   Bottled Water: Commodity or Super Premium?[11]

Creating value isn't always about offering low prices. Take bottled water for example. Is bottled water better than tap water in Canada? Some bottled water begins the same place as the water that comes from your tap and on its label you may see its origin listed as "public source." Canadians are divided on the merits of tap water versus bottled water but it hasn't stopped us from consuming more bottled water than ever. Global consumption of bottled water tops 154 billion litres (41 billion gallons), up 57 percent from the 98 billion litres consumed five years earlier. In 2006, almost 3 out of 10 households drank predominantly bottled water whether they had a private or municipal water source. This boom in consumption has moved the product beyond niche markets and into the mainstream. Bottled water has become a basic staple to many Canadians.

Adding value to a commodity and charging consumers a premium for a product they can get for free from their taps requires an exceptional strategy—and that is precisely what Voss has done—successfully! VOSS Artesian Water, which competes in the super premium market, derives its product from underground aquifers shielded for centuries from pollutants by layers of rock and ice. With prices of over $15 for an 800-mL glass bottle, its value proposition is built on more than just a pristine product. VOSS founders, Ole Christian Sandberg and Christopher Harlem, knew that their packaging would also need to reflect the purity of the water source, to define and differentiate their brand. They enlisted the help of Neil Kraft, a former Calvin Klein creative director, who noted that while premium bottled water was purchased to reflect one's style, taste, and sophistication, the bottles on the market were unsophisticated and lacked style. Taking inspiration from the fragrance industry, a unique cylindrical glass bottle was chosen. The brand name, set in lowercase type, was silk-screened in grey directly on the bottle so as not to obscure the purity of its contents. Even the cap, in silver plastic, the same diameter as the bottle, was unique.

The last part of the company's value added strategy involved limiting distribution exclusively to upscale establishments: fine restaurants, hotels, clubs, and spas, first in Europe and eventually in North America. VOSS quickly gained popularity helped along by its trendy bottle being seen in the hands of worldwide celebrities. Apparently, Madonna took a liking to it. On the other hand, NAYA successfully targets ordinary consumers with its simple message of *source of well being*.[12] Although VOSS and NAYA both sell water, they add value to different customer segments in different ways.

A differentiation strategy that revolves around stunning cylindrical glass bottles and exclusive distribution helped VOSS Artesian Water develop a trendy image and significant market share in the super premium market. Meanwhile, Naya targets mainstream consumers using a simple message based on health and well-being.

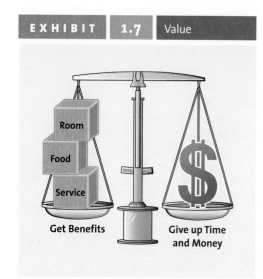

EXHIBIT 1.7 Value

Room

Food

Service

Get Benefits

$

Give up Time and Money

value-based marketing
Marketing that focuses on providing customers with benefits that far exceed the cost (money, time, effort) of acquiring and using a product or service while providing a reasonable return to the firm.

In the next section, we explore the notion of value-based marketing further. Specifically, we look at various options for attracting customers by providing them with better value than the competition does. Then we discuss how firms compete on the basis of value. Finally, we examine how firms transform the value concept into their value-driven activities.

What is Value-Based Marketing?

Consumers make explicit and/or implicit trade-offs between the perceived benefits of a product or service and their costs. Customers naturally seek options that provide the greatest benefits at the lowest costs. Marketing firms attempt to find the most desirable balance between providing benefits to customers and keeping their costs down, as illustrated in Exhibit 1.7.

To better understand value and to develop a **value-based marketing** orientation, a business must also understand what customers view as the key benefits of a given product or service and how to improve on them. For example, some benefits of staying at a Four Points Sheraton hotel might include the high level of service quality provided by the personnel, the convenience of booking the room via Sheraton's website, and the overall quality of the room and meals offered. In broader terms, some critical benefits may be service quality, convenience, and merchandise quality.

The other side of the value equation entails the firm's ability to provide either a better product/service mix at the same cost or the same level of quality and convenience for a lower cost. The customer's potential cost elements, in terms of value-based marketing strategies, for the Sheraton hotel in our example would include the price of the room and meals, the time it takes to book a room or check in at the hotel, and the risk of arriving at the hotel and finding it overbooked.

How Firms Compete on the Basis of Value

With such a simple formula, marketers should be able to deliver value consistently, right? Well, not exactly. In today's quickly changing world, consistently creating and delivering value is quite difficult. Consumer perceptions change quickly, competitors constantly enter markets, and global pressures continually reshape opportunities. Thus, marketers must keep a vigilant eye on the marketplace so they can adjust their offerings to meet customer needs and keep ahead of their competition.

Value-based marketing, however, isn't just about creating strong products and services; it should be at the core of every firm's functions. For example, Wal-Mart does not serve those customers who are looking to impress their friends with conspicuous consumption. Rather, it is for those who want convenient one-stop shopping and low prices—and on those values, it consistently delivers. But good value is not limited to just low prices. Although Wal-Mart carries low-priced pots, pans, and coffee pots, cooking enthusiasts may prefer the product selection, quality, and expert sales assistance at a Paderno outlet. The prices there aren't as low as at Wal-Mart, but Paderno customers believe they are receiving good value—because of the selection, quality, and service they receive—when they shop there. Even nonprofit organizations need to focus on creating value to ensure the services they provide to stakeholders are of high quality while also minimizing the total fundraising required.

How Do Firms Become Value Driven?

Firms become value driven by focusing on three activities. (See Exhibit 1.8.) First, they share information about their customers and competitors across their own organization and with other firms that might be involved in getting the product or service to the marketplace, such as manufacturers and transportation companies. Second, they strive to balance their customers' benefits and costs. Third, they concentrate on building relationships with customers.

Sharing Information In a value-based, marketing-oriented firm, marketers share information about customers and competitors that has been collected through customer relationship management, and integrate it across the firm's various departments. The fashion designers for Zara, the Spain-based fashion retailer, for instance, collect purchase information and research customer trends to determine what their customers will want to wear in the next few weeks; simultaneously, the logisticians—those persons in charge of getting the merchandise to the stores—use the same purchase history to forecast sales and allocate appropriate merchandise to individual stores. Sharing and coordinating such information represents a critical success factor for any firm. Imagine what might happen if Zara's advertising department were to plan a special promotion but not share its sales projections with those people in charge of creating the merchandise or getting it to stores.

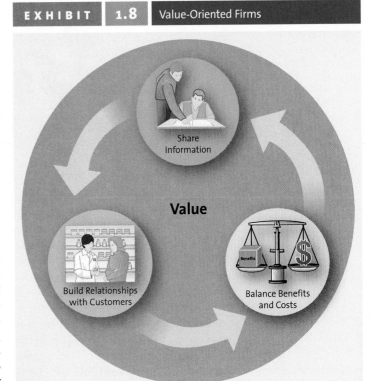

EXHIBIT **1.8** Value-Oriented Firms

Balancing Benefits with Costs Value-oriented marketers constantly measure the benefits that customers perceive against the cost of their offering. In this task, they use available customer data to find opportunities in which they can better satisfy their customers' needs and in turn develop long-term loyalties. Such a value-based orientation has helped Canadian Tire and Wal-Mart outperform other department stores, and WestJet and Southwest Airlines to outperform mainstream carriers. Also, as noted in the opening vignette, RIM not only offers its customers the innovative, feature-packed portfolio of BlackBerry products, it also offers high quality customer service at a competitive price. By establishing contracts with wireless carriers such as AT&T and Bell South, it gained a solid footing before competitors like Nokia entered the market. RIM's marketing savvy in making customer value the centrepiece of its strategy is one of the reasons why it has been able to beat the competition.

Until recently, it sometimes cost more to fly within Europe than to fly from the United States to Europe. But low-frills, low-cost carriers such as Ryanair and EasyJet,[13] modelled on Southwest Airlines and Jet Blue, now offer customers what they want: cheap intra-Europe airfares. Like their American counterparts, Ryanair and EasyJet offer no food service and generally fly to and from out-of-the-way airports like Stansted, about 34 miles northeast of London. But many customers find value despite such minor inconveniences. Consider,

Fashion designers for Zara, the Spain-based fashion retailer, collect purchase information and research customer trends to determine what their customers will want to wear in the next few weeks. They share this information with other departments to forecast sales and coordinate deliveries.

To provide a great value, U.K.-based EasyJet offers no food service and generally flies to and from out-of-the-way airports.

LO **4**

transactional orientation
Regards the buyer-seller relationship as a series of individual transactions, so anything that happened before or after the transaction is of little importance.

relational orientation
A method of building a relationship with customers based on the philosophy that buyers and sellers should develop a long-term relationship.

customer relationship management (CRM)
A business philosophy and set of strategies, programs, and systems that focus on identifying and building loyalty among the firm's most valued customers.

for example, the London to Salzburg, Austria route for $65 or London to Sweden for $70. Values such as these are also what have given low-cost carriers in the United States approximately 25 percent of the market share. They are so popular that conventional airlines have started their own low frills/low cost airlines: Singapore Airlines provides Tiger and Australia's Qantas offers Jetstar.

Building Relationships with Customers During the past decade or so, marketers have begun to realize that they need to think about their customer orientation in terms of relationships rather than transactions.[14] A **transactional orientation** regards the buyer–seller relationship as a series of individual transactions, so anything that happened before or after the transaction is of little importance. For example, used car sales typically are based on a transactional approach; the seller wants to get the highest price for the car, the buyer wants to get the lowest, and neither expects to do business with the other again.

A **relational orientation**, in contrast, is based on the philosophy that buyers and sellers should develop a long-term relationship. According to this idea, the lifetime profitability of the relationship matters, not how much money is made during each transaction. For example, UPS works with its shippers to develop efficient transportation solutions. Over time, UPS becomes part of the fabric of the shippers' organizations, and their operations become intertwined. In this scenario, they have developed a long-term relationship.

Firms that practise value-based marketing also use a process known as **customer relationship management (CRM)**, a business philosophy and set of strategies, programs, and systems that focus on identifying and building loyalty among the firm's most valued customers.[15] Firms that employ CRM systematically collect information about their customers' needs and then use that information to target their best customers with the products, services, and special promotions that appear most important to those customers.

Why Is Marketing Important? LO **5**

Marketing was once only an afterthought to production. Early marketing philosophy went something like this: "We've made it; now how do we get rid of it?" Today, marketing has evolved into a major business function that crosses all areas of a firm or organization, as illustrated in Exhibit 1.9. Marketing works with other departments such as R&D, engineering, and production to ensure that high-quality, innovative products that meet customers' needs are available in the right quantity, at the right price, and at the right place, that is, wherever they want to purchase it. It creates mutually valuable relationships between the company and its suppliers, distributors, and other external firms that are involved in the firm's marketing process. It identifies those elements that local customers value and makes it possible for the firm to expand globally.

EXHIBIT 1.9 Importance of Marketing

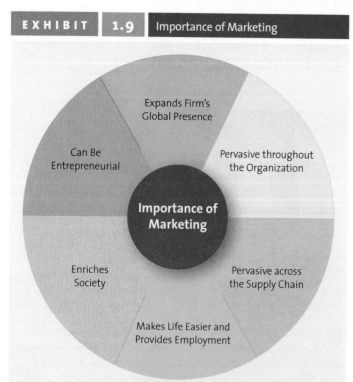

Importance of Marketing

- Expands Firm's Global Presence
- Pervasive throughout the Organization
- Pervasive across the Supply Chain
- Makes Life Easier and Provides Employment
- Enriches Society
- Can Be Entrepreneurial

Entrepreneurial Marketing

1.1 ImaSight—Get Clear[16]

ImaSight, a small Quebec-based company, is emerging as a key player in the digital radiography industry. What makes ImaSight radiography technologies innovative and special? Their technology uses a unique patent-pending charge couple device (CCD) imaging process, which has the potential to deliver very high quality images at very low costs. ImaSight sees a huge market opportunity in small medical clinics and hospitals that need a more efficient, less-expensive, and a better alternative to film X-ray technologies. This includes the veterinary market, chiropractors, human care clinics, and even developing countries. Let's examine more closely some of the value ImaSight is offering the marketplace.

Traditionally, X-rays are taken using films, which require a substantial amount of time to photograph, develop, and diagnose. Furthermore, if the image is not clear, the X-rays have to be retaken, and patients have to return to the laboratory. Once the X-rays are taken, the films must be physically delivered to the doctor, which often leads to long delays up to several days. Poor quality images can lead to improper diagnosis and doctors cannot easily share the X-rays with colleagues who are not physically present. Moreover, traditional film X-ray technologies require the use of harmful chemicals for processing and physical space to store the film.

The advent of digital imaging is changing all of this and ImaSight's technology is making a huge difference. Founded in 2001 by Jean Caseault, the leading-edge CCD technology ImaSight4600 digital sensor and imaging tool produces a high quality

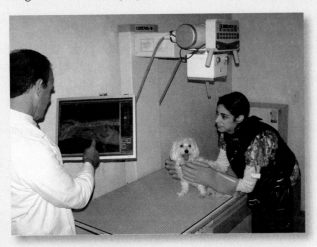

ImaSight4600 Vision tool is designed to help professionals make a better diagnosis without the hassle of learning complicated imaging software.

image on a computer display in seconds. All images are processed and stored automatically. Flexible image enhancements eliminate the need for retakes. This technology cuts the time needed to take a picture and get it to the doctor by 67 percent. Film processing and time constraints are no longer an issue! Fewer retakes leads to increased productivity and a substantial reduction in overall operating and maintenance costs. Like more expensive digital radiography machines, the ImaSight4600 provides an electronic picture that can be viewed on a large monitor, e-mailed to specialists, archived in a network server, or burned onto a CD and sent home with the patient—only at a lower cost. The device helps specialists perform better diagnostics by allowing them to zoom in and out, magnify an area, add diagnostic comments, print images, or share images via e-mail with other professionals. The flexibility, efficiency, and improved diagnostic quality made possible is extraordinary compared to traditional X-ray films.

This new technology can be used to retrofit medical clinics that have traditional film X-ray technology, for just a fraction of the cost. According to John Brooks, ImaSight's CEO, to achieve the digital image quality that you get with the ImaSight4600, you will need to pay at least $100,000 on the market today. A veterinary hospital could convert to the ImaSight sensor for less than $50,000. The ImaSight technology allows specialists to see more patients, better utilize the physical space in their hospitals and medical clinics, and eliminate the need for expensive and harmful chemicals.

Marketing has had a significant impact on consumers as well. Without marketing, it would be difficult for any of us to learn about new products and services. You may even decide to pursue a career in marketing after you graduate.

Marketing Expands Firms' Global Presence

A generation ago, Coca-Cola was available in many nations, but Levi's and most other American and Canadian brands were not. But today most jeans, including Levi Strauss & Co. and Parasuco, are made in places other than Canada and the United States and available nearly everywhere. Thanks to MTV and other global entertainment venues, cheap foreign travel, and the Internet, you share many of your consumption behaviours with college and university students in countries

These brands can be found in many countries.

all over the globe. The best fashions, music, and even food trends disseminate rapidly around the world.

Take a look at your next shopping bag. Whether it contains groceries or apparel, you will find goods from many countries—produce from Mexico, jeans from Italy, t-shirts from China. Global manufacturers and retailers continue to make inroads into the Canadian market. Companies such as Honda, Sony, and Heineken sell as well in Canada as they do in their home countries. Sweden's fashion retailer H&M operates in 22 countries, including Canada;[17] its upscale competitor, Spain's Zara, operates in 62, including Canada.[18] Starbucks even adjusted its menu to meet customer wants in the Japanese market more effectively. How does marketing contribute to a company's successful global expansion? Understanding customers is critical. Without the knowledge that can be gained by analyzing new customers' needs and wants on a segment-by-segment, region-by-region basis—one of marketing's main tasks—it would be difficult for a firm to expand globally.

Marketing is Pervasive across the Organization

In value-based marketing firms, the marketing department works seamlessly with other functional areas of the company to design, promote, price, and distribute products. Consider the Scion, a new car and brand designed by Toyota for the less affluent youth market, which sometimes has been referred to as "Generation Y."[19] Scion's marketing department worked closely with engineers to ensure that the new car exceeded customers' expectations in terms of design but remained affordable. The company also coordinated the product offering with an innovative communications strategy. Because Generation Y is famous for its resistance to conventional advertising, Scion introduced a virtual road race in which participants received mileage points for sending Scion e-cards. The more "places" they visited, the more mileage points they received. At the end of the competition, each driver's points were totalled and compared with other racers' scores. The driver with the most points won an onboard navigation system worth more than $2,000. In addition, because Scion is a new car, the marketing department must work closely with the distribution department to ensure that advertising and

Starbucks has adjusted its menu to meet customer wants in the Japanese market more effectively.

Toyota introduced a virtual road race in which participants received mileage points for sending Scion e-cards. At the end of the competition the driver with the most points won an onboard navigation system worth more than $2,000.

promotions reach all distributors' territories and that distribution exists where those promotions occur. Marketing thus is responsible for coordinating all these aspects of supply and demand.

Marketing is Pervasive across the Supply Chain

Firms typically do not work in isolation. Manufacturers buy raw materials and components from suppliers, which they sell to retailers or other businesses after they have turned the materials into their products (see Exhibit 1.10). Every time materials or products are bought or sold, they are transported to a different location, which sometimes requires that they be stored in a warehouse operated by yet another organization. The group of firms that make and deliver a given set of goods and services is known as a **supply chain**. Supply chain management is discussed in detail in Chapter 13 but for now let us consider the value of supply chain in marketing.

Often, some supply chain participants take a transactional orientation in which each link in the chain is out for its own best interest. Manufacturers, for example, want the highest price, whereas retailers want to buy the product at the lowest cost. Supply chain members do not enjoy any cooperation or coordination. But for the supply chain to provide significant value to the ultimate customer, the parties must establish long-term relationships with one another and cooperate to share data, make

supply chain
The group of firms that make and deliver a given set of goods and services.

EXHIBIT	1.10	Supply Chain

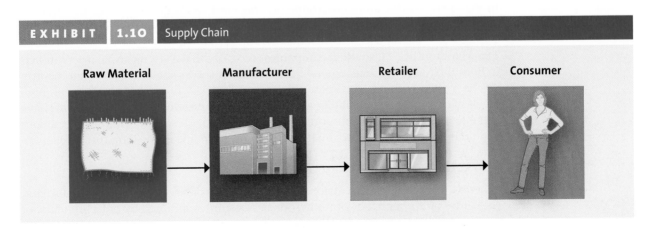

Raw Material   Manufacturer   Retailer   Consumer

joint forecasts, and coordinate shipments. Effectively managing supply chain relationships often has a huge impact on a firm's ability to satisfy the consumer, which results in increased profitability for all parties.

Consider Loblaw, Canada's largest food distributor, and its relationships with its manufacturers and trading partners. A couple of years ago, Loblaw's supply chain system suffered from several inefficiencies which drove up its costs substantially.[20] For example, inaccurate demand forecasts led trading partners to stock huge inventory in order to meet unpredictable demand. Inefficient use of customer data meant that stock replenishment was made by estimation rather than true customer data. Disconnected supply chain systems, limited collaboration, reduced information sharing, and supply variability led to poor quality information on which to base sales forecasts, production plans, and replenishment schemes. The company has since made many changes to improve the efficiency of its supply chain. Loblaw's participation in a radio frequency identification (RFID) pilot project for the grocery industry conducted by the Canadian RFID centre will help them understand and experience how RFID may drive business benefits.

Marketing Makes Life Easier and Provides Career Opportunities

Marketers provide you, as a consumer, with product and service choices, as well as information about those choices, to ensure that your needs are being met. They balance the product or service offering with a price that makes you comfortable with your purchase, and after the sale, they provide reasonable guarantees and return policies. Marketing's responsibility also includes offering pleasant and convenient places for you to shop. In essence, marketers make your life easier, and in that way, they add value.

Marketing also offers a host of career opportunities that require a variety of skills. On the creative side, positions such as artists, graphic designers, voice talent, animators, music composers, and writers represent just a few of the opportunities available to talented individuals. On the analytical side, marketing requires database analysts, market researchers, and inventory managers who can quickly digest information, cross-reference data, and spot trends that might make or break a company. On the business side, marketing requires strategists, project/product/brand managers, sales associates, and analysts who are capable of designing and implementing complex marketing strategies that increase the bottom line.

Marketing Enriches Society

Should marketing focus on factors other than financial profitability, like good corporate citizenry? Many of Canada's best known corporations seem to think so, because they encourage their employees to participate in activities that benefit their communities and invest heavily in socially responsible actions and charities. For example, Petro-Canada has invested heavily in a number of community partnership programs in the areas of education, environment, and local community groups. In addition, Petro-Canada is the exclusive oil and gas national partner of the Vancouver 2010 Winter Olympic Games and is a dedicated supporter of athletes and coaches in Canadian communities.[21] Canadian companies recognize that a strong social orientation is in both their and their customers' best interest. It shows the consumer that the firm can be trusted with their business. Also, investors view firms that operate with high levels of corporate responsibility and ethics as safe investments. Similarly, firms have come to realize that good corporate citizenship through socially responsible actions should be a priority because it will help their bottom line in the long run.[22]

Marketing Can Be Entrepreneurial

Whereas marketing plays a major role in the success of large corporations, it also is at the centre of the successes of numerous new ventures initiated by entrepreneurs, or people who organize, operate, and assume the risk of a business venture.[23] Key to the success of many such entrepreneurs is that they launch ventures that aim to satisfy unfilled needs. Some examples of successful ventures (and their founders) that understood their customers and added value include

- Research In Motion (Mike Lazaridis)
- *The Oprah Winfrey Show* and other ventures (Oprah Winfrey).

As noted in the opening vignette, Mike Lazaridis is best known for inventing the BlackBerry solution, a wireless, mobile communication device and software platform and for founding the highly successful company, Research In Motion. The company continues to grow and is recognized as the global leader for wireless, mobile communication particularly among business executives, managers, and professionals. In 2007, Mike Lazaridis was listed in *Forbes* magazine as among the world's richest people.[24]

Mike Lazaridis, co-CEO of Research In Motion, is best known for inventing the BlackBerry.

Another extraordinary entrepreneur and marketer is Oprah Winfrey. A self-made billionaire before she turned 50, Oprah went from being the youngest person and first African-American woman to anchor news station WTVF-TV in Nashville, Tennessee, to being only the third woman in history to head her own production studio. Under the Oprah Winfrey banner, you can find Harpo Productions, Inc.; *O, The Oprah Magazine; O at Home* magazine; Harpo Films; and the Oxygen television network. In addition, Oprah's philanthropic contributions are vast and varied. Through the Oprah Winfrey Foundation, women around the world enjoy a champion supporting their rights to education and empowerment. Her humanitarian efforts in Africa have helped thousands of children get a better start in life, and her efforts in the United States resulted in President Bill Clinton signing into law the national "Oprah Bill" to establish a national database of convicted child abusers.[25]

Both of these distinguished entrepreneurs had a vision about how certain combinations of products and services could satisfy unfilled needs. Each understood the marketing opportunity (i.e., the unfilled need), conducted a thorough examination of the marketplace, and developed and communicated the value of their product and services to potential consumers.

When you think of Oprah Winfrey, think big: Harpo Productions, Inc.; O, The Oprah Magazine; O at Home magazine; Harpo Films; the Oxygen television network, not to mention her philanthropic work with the Oprah Winfrey Foundation.

Learning Objectives Review

1) Define marketing and explain its core concepts

2) Discuss how marketers create value for a product or service

3) Explain the four orientations of marketing

4) Discuss the role of customer relationship management in creating value

5) Discuss the importance of marketing both within and outside the firm

1) In definition form, "Marketing is a set of business practices designed to plan for and present an organization's products or services in ways that build effective customer relationships." Marketing strives to *create value* in many ways. If marketers are to succeed, their customers must believe that the firm's products and services are valuable; that is, they are worth more to the customers than they cost.

Marketers also enhance the value of products and services through various forms of *communication*, such as advertising and personal selling. Through communications, marketers educate and inform customers about the benefits of their products and services and thereby increase their perceived value.

Marketers facilitate the *delivery of value* by making sure the right products and services are available when, where, and in the quantities their customers want. Better marketers are not concerned about just one transaction with their customers; they recognize the value of loyal customers and strive to develop *long-term relationships* with them.

2) Value represents the relationship of benefits to costs. Firms can improve their value by increasing benefits, reducing costs, or both. The best firms integrate a value orientation into everything they do. If a move doesn't increase benefits or reduce costs, it probably shouldn't occur. Marketers also have found that providing good value is one of the best ways to maintain a sustainable advantage over their competitors.

Firms become value driven by finding out as much as they can about their customers and those customers' needs and wants. They share this information with their partners, both up and down the supply chain, so the entire chain collectively can focus on the customer. The key to true value-based marketing is the ability to design products and services that achieve the right balance between benefits and costs—not too little, not too much.

Finally, value-based marketers aren't necessarily worried about how much money they will make on the next sale. Instead, they are concerned with developing a lasting relationship with their customers so those customers return again and again.

3) Firms that are *production-oriented* tend to believe that a good product will sell itself. Manufacturers are concerned with product innovation, not with satisfying the needs of individual consumers, and keep producing with the assumption that people will buy it. Marketing with this orientation is simply about informing the customer that a product exists, if used at all.

In the case of a *sales-orientation*, firms rely on a sales team in order to sell. Production is maximized and then heavy doses of personal selling and advertising help distribute and sell the product. The role of marketing is focused only on the sale of products.

If a firm is *market-oriented* it celebrates the customer. Here the customer can decide what is best for them, based on the attributes of a product or service. Rather than simply produce and sell, manufacturers with this orientation seek to learn customer needs and wants and design products to fit the customers. Marketing plays an important role to communicate the different attributes, or value, created by each product.

Most successful firms today have transcended other views and instead support a *value-based marketing orientation*. In addition to discovering needs and wants, it is critical to deliver more value to customers than competitors. Value reflects the relationship of benefits to costs, or what you get for what you give. Marketing here plays an integral role not only in creating and delivering that valuable product, but also in communicating the value especially in relation to other products available, and transacting the value through to customers.

4) Building strong relationships with customers is important to creating value and is the central concept of the relational orientation. Unlike the transactional orientation, here firms adopt a business strategy that identifies customers and focuses on building strong relationships with them. This is known as *customer relationship management* (CRM), and maximizes the long-term value of the buyer-seller relationship rather than trying to maximize the profit from each transaction. CRM often includes collecting customer information in order to target specific promotions or offers to customers who would benefit most.

5) The marketing function is important both within and outside the firm. Many brands and stores now appear in multiple countries, which complicates the challenge for marketers. Successful firms integrate marketing throughout their organizations so that marketing activities coordinate with other functional areas such as product design, production, logistics, and human resources.

Marketing also helps facilitate the smooth flow of goods through the supply chain, all the way from raw materials to the consumer. From a personal perspective, the marketing function facilitates your buying process, and knowledge of marketing will help you in virtually any career you may decide to pursue.

Marketing also can be important for society through its embrace of solid, ethical business practices. For instance, a firm clearly has "done the right thing" when it sponsors charitable events, but that effort also helps endear customers to the firm. Finally, marketing is a core cornerstone of entrepreneurialism. Not only have many great companies been founded by outstanding marketers, but an entrepreneurial spirit pervades the marketing decisions of firms of all sizes.

Key Terms

- B2C (business-to-consumers), 12
- B2B (business-to-business), 12
- C2C (consumer-to-consumer), 12
- customer relationship management (CRM), 18
- exchange, 7
- goods, 8
- ideas, 9

- market, 6
- marketing, 5
- marketing mix (four Ps), 8
- marketing plan, 5
- need, 6
- price, 9
- relational orientation, 18
- service, 9

- supply chain, 21
- target market, 7
- transactional orientation, 18
- value, 14
- value-based marketing, 16
- want, 6

Concept Review

1. What is marketing and why is it important?

2. Is the marketing mix (4Ps) enough to guarantee successful marketing? Explain.

3. Explain how a strike at one of the company's supplier firms or a new technology would influence the company's marketing efforts?

4. Discuss the main elements of value-based marketing. List four ways in which marketing helps to create value.

5. Explain the relationship between customer value and customer satisfaction.

6. Generally, all companies are in business to generate profits and increase shareholder value. Yet, the Canadian Marketing Association's definition of marketing given on page 5 does not explicitly mention profits or shareholder value. Why do you think these are not included in the definition? Should they be included?

7. Today, many marketers are not interested in selling their products and services to everyone who wants it, but only to selected target markets. What do you think the main reasons are for targeting specific market segments?

8. Give reasons why you think understanding customer needs and wants is fundamental to marketing success. How can marketers go about understanding customer needs and wants?

9. Which marketing orientation would most likely help a company build strong customer relationships that are profitable? Why?

10. Explain how customer value is created or increased when the company's marketing department works closely with other departments within the firm as well as with the firm's suppliers and customers.

Marketing Applications

1. When apparel manufacturers develop their marketing strategies, do they concentrate on satisfying their customers' needs or wants? What about a utility company? A cellular phone company?

2. Choose a product that you use every day. Describe its 4Ps.

3. Provide examples of three firms that are involved in both B2C and B2B marketing.

4. Pick a firm that you believe provides its customers with good value. Justify your answer by explaining how the firm competes on value.

5. Assume you have been hired by the marketing department of a major consumer products manufacturer such as Colgate-Palmolive. You are having lunch with some new colleagues in the finance, manufacturing, and logistics departments. They are arguing that the company could save millions of dollars if they just got rid of the marketing department. Develop an argument that would persuade them otherwise.

6. Why do marketers find it important to embrace societal needs and ethical business practices? Provide an example of a societal need or ethical business practice being addressed by a specific marketer.

7. Visit the website of Rogers Communications (http://rogers.com/) and compare the 4Ps marketing mix for its BlackBerry 8800 and BlackBerry Pearl. What factors might explain the differences you observe?

8. For many consumers the difference between Dasani water made by Coca-Cola (www.dasani.com/) and Aquafina made by Pepsi (www.aquafina.com/) is hardly noticeable. However, both companies and their loyal customers would argue that there are many differences between these two brands of water. What is your view? Explain how customer perceptions and emotions may influence the way they value a company's product.

9. As described in this chapter, customer relationship management is a very important aspect of value-based marketing. Pick any one of Canada's major retailers, e.g., The Bay (www.hbc.com/), Loblaws (www.loblaws.ca/), or Shoppers Drug Mart (www.shoppersdrugmart.ca/), and explain how they go about building strong customer relationships with their customers.

10. Apple's iPhone is seen by many industry analysts as a competitor to RIM's BlackBerry Pearl. Visit Apple's website (www.apple.com) and Rogers Communications website (http://rogers.com/) to learn more about these two products. What do you think the main value proposition is for each product? Which company do you think will come out as the winner and why?

Net Savvy

1. Happy Planet (www.happyplanet.com/), a Vancouver-based organic juice producer is an emerging player in the organic beverage market supplying all of Canada and some of the U.S. with organic juice. Visit its website and describe how it delivers value above and beyond that provided by traditional grocery retailers. Describe the ways in which the company communicates this value through its website.

2. Lands' End (www.landsend.com) has successfully built its market share by providing great value to consumers. Visit its website and describe the ways in which it creates value for consumers and how it differs from a traditional apparel store. Although it is common for Lands' End to underprice its competition, consumers can also accrue nonmonetary benefits. Identify some of these.

Chapter Case Study

EBAY: CREATING VALUE IN THE MARKETPLACE[26]

With 180.6 million registered users and net revenues of $4.55 billion, eBay has become the most popular shopping site for goods and services for a diverse community of consumers and businesses.[27] Founder Pierre Omidyar attributes much of its success to its trust among that community of users.

Originally introduced to create an efficient forum for people to trade with one another, eBay pioneered online trading by developing a Web-based community of browsers, buyers, and sellers. Initially, eBay capitalized on increases in consumer-to-consumer (C2C) transactions through traditional channels such as classified advertisements, collectibles shows, garage sales, flea markets, and auction houses. But the company has grown beyond individual consumers with individual sales to include merchants, small to medium-sized businesses, global corporations, and government agencies that sell office supplies, raw materials, and furniture in bulk. In addition to facilitating trading, eBay provides a place for socialization and discussion. Trading activities in individual categories often evolve into unique communities of buyers and sellers who maintain category-specific bulletin boards and chat rooms. To make trading easier, eBay also sponsors payment services, insurance, shipping, authentication, appraisal, vehicle inspection, and escrow services.

Online buyers typically enter the site through eBay's home page, which contains a listing of major product categories and featured items. (A sample page is presented in Exhibit C1.1.) Users can search for specific items by browsing within a category, and then they "click through" to a detailed description of a particular item. Users also can perform a keyword search for specific items, in response to which the site's search engine generates lists of relevant items with links to the detailed descriptions. Furthermore, users can search for a particular bidder or seller by name to review that person's listings and feedback history or for products by a specific region or other attributes.

A registered user who has found a desired item can enter a bid for the maximum amount he or she is willing to pay at that time. In the event of competitive bids, the eBay service automatically increases bidding in increments from the current high bid up to the bidder's maximum price. For those listings that offer the "Buy-It-Now" feature, the user may purchase the item by accepting the Buy-It-Now price established by the seller.

EXHIBIT	C1.1	eBay's Home Page

eBay views its market as comprised of both sellers and buyers and has developed services to satisfy both in a vibrant trading environment. Various dimensions distinguish the two; for example, sellers range from individuals selling a few personal items to large companies liquidating excess stock. However, both buyers and sellers can benefit from eBay's rating systems, which gather aggregated ratings from buyers after each transaction. The overall score then is available to browsers when they want to gather information about a seller.

To maintain a strong sense of community, trust, and safety, eBay has fostered an honest and open marketplace in which individual users are treated with respect. The site also commits to several trust and safety initiatives designed to bolster its reputation as a safe place to trade, such as user verification, a requirement that new sellers have a credit card on file, insurance, vehicle inspections, escrow, authentication, and appraisal, as well as a well-articulated privacy statement. As a founding member of the Online Privacy Association, it also has built a reputation for leading the way to protect consumer privacy on the Internet.

Questions

1. According to the breakdown presented in Exhibit 1.6, which of the four orientations best describes eBay? Justify your answer.

2. Does eBay create greater value for buyers of collectables, beyond that provided by traditional channels? For sellers? Explain your answers in terms of greater benefits, reduced costs, or a combination.

3. Visit the eBay website to explore some of its features. How well does eBay facilitate the exchanges of goods? Does it have the same potential for exchanges that involve services? Explain your answer.

CHAPTER 2

LEARNING OBJECTIVES

After studying this chapter you should be able to

LO **1** Describe how a firm develops and implements a marketing plan

LO **2** Conduct a SWOT analysis and explain its use in marketing planning

LO **3** Explain how a firm chooses what group(s) of people to pursue with its marketing efforts

LO **4** Describe how the marketing mix increases customer value

LO **5** Describe how firms grow their businesses

Developing Marketing Strategies

Managers at Disney noticed that attendance at their theme parks was declining.[1] Visitors cited long lines and high ticket prices as the major deterrents to visiting the theme park. Disney was challenged to adjust its strategy to create a better in-park experience and deliver more value for the $63-a-day ticket price.

Their answer: A strategy heavy on technology that makes the park experience more personal and relevant to each visitor. To reinvent the customer experience, influence visitor behaviour, and ease crowding throughout the parks, it combined global positioning satellites, smart sensors, wireless technology, and mobile devices.

Consider "Pal Mickey." The 26-cm doll, available for rent or purchase, is equipped with a central processing unit, an internal clock, small speakers, and an infrared sensor. As patrons move through the park, the sensor acquires wireless data uploads from beacons concealed in lampposts, rooftops, and bushes. When the doll receives information, it giggles and vibrates, which means "It's time to tell a secret" about shorter lines for rides in the area, the time of the upcoming parade, or trivia about the area in which the patron is walking. Pal Mickey also contains 700 prerecorded

Disney is investing in technologies like Pal Mickey to provide a better in-park experience and deliver more value to its customers.

messages to keep kids entertained with jokes and games while they wait in line. Pal Mickey speaks Spanish too!

The concept of working with data to create a more individual experience has migrated to other applications as well. For example, Disney plans to send text messages about dinner reservations, fireworks displays, and tee times via a visitor's cell phone or PDA. If a visitor spends a long time in the Dinosaur Exhibit at Animal Kingdom and purchases dinosaur merchandise, Disney figures that he or she might like to receive a special e-mail notification about an upcoming DVD release about dinosaurs. With Disney's digital-imaging services, park visitors can even view pictures taken throughout the day on their hotel television sets and purchase them with the touch of a button.

In the first part of this chapter, we examine the various levels of strategic planning and discuss each of the steps involved in the strategic marketing planning process. We then consider ways of analyzing a marketing situation, as well as identifying and evaluating marketing opportunities. We also examine some specific strategies marketers use to grow a business. Finally, we consider how the implementation of the marketing mix increases customer value. Refer to the chapter roadmap to guide you through the chapter contents.

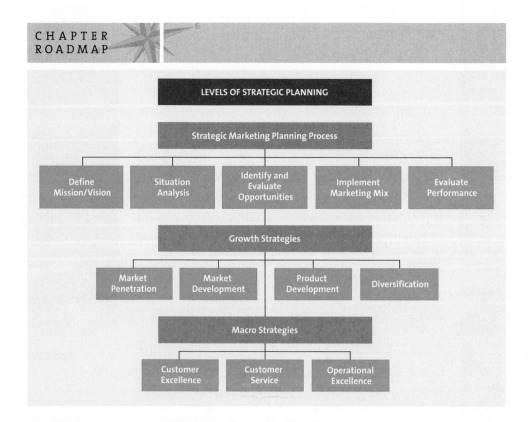

Levels of Strategic Planning in Corporations

Effective marketing doesn't just happen. Firms like Disney carefully plan their marketing strategies to react to changes in the environment, the competition, and their customers. Strategic planning in most organizations occurs on at least two levels, the corporate level and the functional level (see Exhibit 2.1). Corporate level planning is done by the company's top management and focuses on the overall direction of the entire company. Senior managers decide on the business of the company, define the company's mission or vision, and set objectives or goals for the company. Corporate level planning focuses on the long-term direction of the company, which is updated regularly in order to respond to changes in the business environment. Generally, large corporations have various business functions such as human resources, research and development, finance, manufacturing, and marketing. Each of these functions usually undertakes some form of planning. The marketing function develops marketing plans for the company's various products, brands, and markets. These plans could take the form of annual plans or three to five year plans.

In addition to corporate and functional level strategic planning, large companies that operate several business lines may see each of its strategic business units (SBUs) develop strategic plans for their products and markets they serve. An SBU is a division of the company that can be managed somewhat independently from other divisions since it markets a specific set of products to a clearly defined group of customers. For example, Disney has four business units—media networks, parks and resorts, studio entertainment, and consumer products—that focus on different customer segments with different products. Each of these units develops plans for the products and markets under their control. It is important to recognize that the marketing function may also be involved in both corporate level and SBU-level planning because of its focus on creating value for customers and the company. Marketing can advise top management where business opportunities exist as well as possible threats to their businesses. Similarly, marketing can advise SBUs of changing consumer trends or to develop customer service and loyalty programs for all business units. In the remainder of this chapter, we focus on the marketing planning process for a particular product, brand, or market.

EXHIBIT 2.1	Levels of Strategic Planning		
Levels of Planning	**Scope**	**Duration**	**Strategic Focus**
Corporate Planning	Entire firm	Long-term (5 years)	Define the company's mission, set company's goals, and establish the business portfolio
Strategic Business Unit (SBU)/Division Planning (applies only to large firms with more than one distinct line of businesses)	Single SBU within the firm	Medium to Long-term (3 to 5 years)	Set goals and establish portfolio of products and markets for the business unit
Functional Planning e.g., Marketing Planning	Product portfolio, single product, brand or market	Short-term to medium term (1 to 3 years)	Develop marketing plans for specific products, brands, or markets

LO ❶ # The Strategic Marketing Planning Process

strategic marketing planning process
A set of steps a marketer goes through to develop a strategic marketing plan.

planning phase
Where marketing executives and other top managers (1) define the mission or vision of the business, (2) evaluate the situation by assessing how various players, both in and outside the organization, affect the firm's potential for success, and (3) identify and evaluate different opportunities by engaging in segmentation, targeting, and positioning, and develop the marketing mix, 4Ps.

implementation phase
Where marketing managers implement the marketing mix, allocate resources, and develop the marketing organization.

control phase
The part of the strategic marketing planning process when managers evaluate the performance of the marketing strategy and take any necessary corrective actions.

The **strategic marketing planning process** (see Exhibit 2.2) represents a set of steps a marketer goes through to develop a strategic marketing plan.[2] A marketing plan is a written document composed of an analysis of the current marketing situation, opportunities and threats for the firm, marketing objectives and strategy specified in terms of the 4Ps, action programs, and projected or pro-forma income (and other financial) statements.[3] As shown in Exhibit 2.2, the three major phases of the strategic planning process are planning, implementation, and control.

In Step 1 of the **planning phase**, marketing executives, in conjunction with other top managers, define the mission and/or vision of the business. For the second step, they evaluate the situation by assessing how various players, both inside and outside of the organization, affect the firm's potential for success (Step 2). In the third step, marketing managers identify and evaluate different opportunities by engaging in a process known as segmentation, targeting, and positioning (STP). They are then responsible for developing the marketing mix using the 4Ps. In the **implementation phase**, Step 4, marketing managers are responsible for implementing the marketing mix strategy, which requires obtaining adequate resources through a budget, developing the marketing organization, and establishing schedules and timelines for the various marketing activities of the 4Ps. Finally, the **control phase** is for evaluating the performance of the marketing strategy and taking any necessary corrective actions (Step 5).

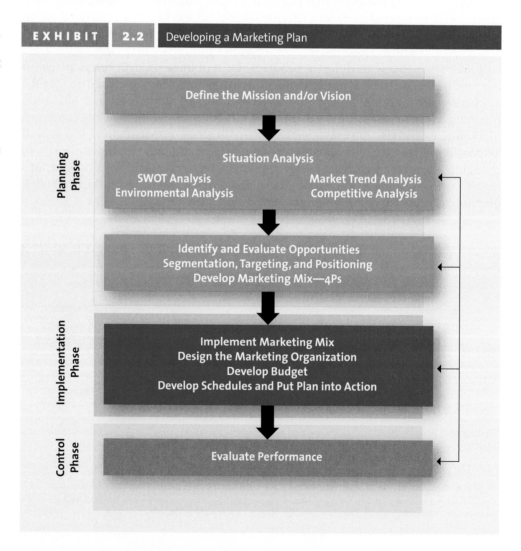

| **EXHIBIT** | **2.2** | Developing a Marketing Plan |

Planning Phase

Define the Mission and/or Vision

Situation Analysis
SWOT Analysis   Market Trend Analysis
Environmental Analysis   Competitive Analysis

Identify and Evaluate Opportunities
Segmentation, Targeting, and Positioning
Develop Marketing Mix—4Ps

Implementation Phase

Implement Marketing Mix
Design the Marketing Organization
Develop Budget
Develop Schedules and Put Plan into Action

Control Phase

Evaluate Performance

| EXHIBIT | 2.3 | Sample Outline of a Marketing Plan |

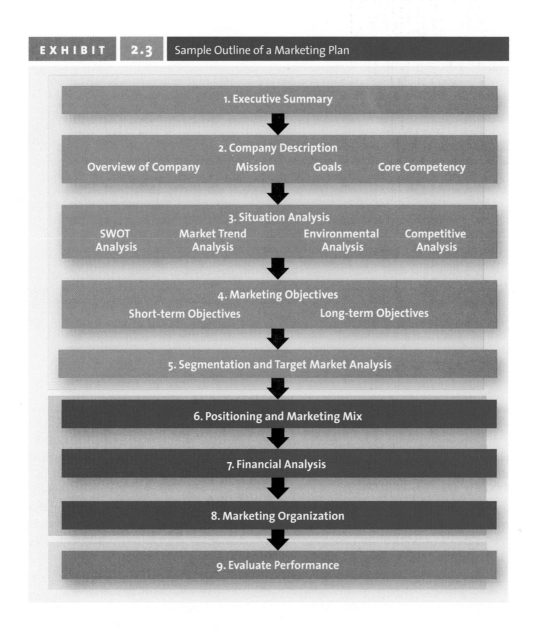

1. Executive Summary

2. Company Description
Overview of Company　　Mission　　Goals　　Core Competency

3. Situation Analysis
SWOT Analysis　　Market Trend Analysis　　Environmental Analysis　　Competitive Analysis

4. Marketing Objectives
Short-term Objectives　　Long-term Objectives

5. Segmentation and Target Market Analysis

6. Positioning and Marketing Mix

7. Financial Analysis

8. Marketing Organization

9. Evaluate Performance

As indicated in Exhibit 2.2, it is not always necessary to go through the entire process for every evaluation (Step 5). For instance, a firm could evaluate its performance in Step 5, then go directly to Step 2 to conduct a situation audit without redefining its overall mission.

Although there are substantial variations in the formats of marketing plans, most marketing plans consist of the elements listed in the sample outline as shown in Exhibit 2.3 above. A sample marketing plan utilizing this outline is provided in the Appendix to this book.

Step 1: Define the Business Mission

The **mission statement**, a broad description of a firm's objectives and the scope of activities it plans to undertake,[4] attempts to answer two main questions: What type of business are we? and What do we need to do to accomplish our goals and objectives? These fundamental business issues must be answered at the highest corporate levels before marketing executives can get involved. Most firms want to maximize stockholders' wealth by increasing the value of the firm's stock and paying dividends.[5] However, owners of small, privately held firms frequently have other objectives,

mission statement
A broad description of a firm's objectives and the scope of activities it plans to undertake; attempts to answer two main questions: What type of business is it? What does it need to do to accomplish its goals and objectives?

EXHIBIT	**2.4**	Mission Statements

The Heart and Stroke Foundation mission is to improve the health of Canadians by preventing and reducing disability and death from heart disease and stroke through research, health promotion, and advocacy.

Coca-Cola states its mission this way:
The Coca-Cola Company exists to benefit and refresh everyone it touches. The basic proposition of our business is simple, solid and timeless. When we bring refreshment, value, joy and fun to our stakeholders, then we successfully nurture and protect our brands, particularly Coca-Cola. That is the key to fulfilling our ultimate obligation to provide consistently attractive returns to the owners of our business. Thus, in its mission statement, Coca-Cola recognizes that it must bring value to all the parties with which it interacts—customers, suppliers, employees, and shareholders. Within this framework, marketing holds the primary responsibility of enhancing the value of the company's products for its customers.

Disney, with its many business units, broadly describes its mission as its commitment to producing creative entertainment experiences based on story telling.

Sources: "About Us" www.heartandstrokefoundation.ca; www2.coca-cola.com/ourcompany/ourpromise.html; and "Company Overview" www.corporate.disney.go.com.

such as achieving a specific level of income and avoiding risks. (See Exhibit 2.4 above for several mission statement examples.)

Nonprofit organizations, such as the Heart and Stroke Foundation have nonmonetary objectives like improving the health of Canadians through research, health promotion, and advocacy. Coca-Cola's mission statement recognizes that it must bring value to all the parties with which it interacts—customers, suppliers, employees, and shareholders.[6] Disney's mission statement is sufficiently broad to encompass the many different types of businesses it operates. For all three firms, marketing holds the primary responsibility of enhancing the value of the company's products for its customers and other constituents.

Another key goal or objective often embedded in a mission statement is building a **sustainable competitive advantage**, namely, something the firm can persistently do better than its competitors. Although any business activity a firm engages in can be the basis for a competitive advantage, some advantages are sustainable over a longer period of time, whereas others, like low prices, can be duplicated by competitors almost immediately.[7] For example, in the very competitive airline industry, discount carriers such as WestJet realize that it is unlikely to obtain long-term advantage by competing directly on price with larger air carriers such as Air Canada. Instead, WestJet focuses its marketing efforts on providing top quality and friendly service. Thus, it is not surprising that WestJet is widely recognized among Canadians for its friendly crew and excellent service.[8] The image that WestJet is a leader in Canada for low-cost, high-value friendly airline service is not easy for other airlines to copy and thus can provide it with a long-term (i.e., sustainable) competitive advantage.

A competitive advantage acts like a wall that the firm has built around its position in a market. This wall makes it hard for outside competitors to contact customers inside—otherwise known as the marketer's target market. Of course, if the marketer has built a wall around an attractive market, competitors will attempt to break down the wall. Over time, advantages will erode because of these competitive forces, but by building high, thick walls, marketers can sustain their advantage, minimize competitive pressure, and boost profits for a longer time. Thus, establishing a sustainable competitive advantage is key to long-term financial performance.

sustainable competitive advantage Something the firm can persistently do better than its competitors.

Step 2: Conduct a Situation Analysis Using SWOT

After developing its mission, a firm next must perform a **situation analysis**, using a SWOT analysis that assesses both the internal environment with regard to its **S**trengths and **W**eaknesses and the external environment in terms of its **O**pportunities and **T**hreats.

Let's look at how a corporation like The Walt Disney Company (Disney) might conduct the SWOT analysis pictured in Exhibit 2.5. The strengths (Exhibit 2.5, upper left) are positive and internal attributes of the firm. In addition to Disney being known as one of the world's best known brands, another strength is its many diverse businesses. They operate in four very distinct businesses: media networks, studio entertainment, parks and resorts, and consumer products. These diverse businesses provide opportunities for growth and reduce the firm's overall risk. Its cable stations appeal to a broad range of interests and age groups with channels such as ABC, Lifetime Television, A&E, Toon Disney, SoapNet, and ESPN. The penetration rates of its cable network channels in 2006 include: ESPN with 92 million subscribers, ABC Family with 91 million subscribers, Disney Channel with 89 million subscribers, and Toon Disney with 57 million subscribers.[9] Disney owns and operates Disneyland in California, Walt Disney World Resort, and Disney Cruise Line, both in Florida, while earning royalties from Tokyo Disneyland Resort. It also has a 41 percent equity stake in Euro Disney. Under the names of Walt Disney Pictures, Touchstone, Miramax, and Dimension, Disney produces and distributes movies worldwide. Its consumer products segment licenses the Walt Disney name and uses Disney Stores and catalogues in direct retail distribution.

The opportunities (Exhibit 2.5, lower left) are positive aspects of the external environment. Like Disney's strengths, it has many opportunities, not the least of which is its ability to build its current brand and businesses both in the U.S. and globally. For instance, release of some videos such as *Pirates of the Caribbean* and *Finding Nemo* are demonstrating consistently strong sales. The acquisition of Pixar Animation Studios is expected to restrengthen its position as the leader in animated films. Walt Disney World Resort is seeing record numbers of visitors during the holidays, and Disney Princess Cruise Lines is also posting record numbers. Disney launched its Disney Channel and Toon Disney channel in India and Disney's Asian television service is available in seven Asia-Pacific regions: Australia, Korea, Malaysia, South Korea, Singapore, Brunei, and the Philippines. The Disney name is a recognized brand globally, and when people see it on any of its products they know they will be entertained. For example, the Disney brand drives around US$10 billion of international retail consumer products sales annually.[10] The growth opportunities in these and other markets are enormous.

situation analysis Second step in a marketing plan; uses of a SWOT analysis that assesses both the internal environment with regard to its **S**trengths and **W**eaknesses and the external environment in terms of its **O**pportunities and **T**hreats.

EXHIBIT	2.5	SWOT Analysis for Disney	
Environment	**Evaluation**		
	Positive		**Negative**
Internal	**Strengths** • Diverse businesses—operates in four business lines: media networks, parks and resorts, studio entertainment, and consumer products • Well-known brand image		**Weaknesses** • Over-reliance on relationships • Seasonal fluctuations • Risky foreign operations • Weak performance of some business lines • Lacklustre performance of Hong Kong Disneyland Resort
External	**Opportunities** • Expand into international markets • Expand existing business in the U.S. • Expand cruise line business • Build new attractions for theme parks		**Threats** • Increasing competitive pressures • Piracy of its media assets • Regulatory risks

Home release of some Disney videos such as Pirates of the Caribbean *and* Finding Nemo *are demonstrating consistently strong sales.*

Every firm has its weaknesses, and Disney is no different. The weaknesses (Exhibit 2.5, upper right) are negative attributes of the firm. For instance, it relies heavily on its relationships with cable operators to expand its distribution. Without them, their continued growth would be in jeopardy. Also, the natural seasonal fluctuations inherent in the tourism industry affect its theme park and resort operations. The linked nature of Disney's businesses can have a domino effect. If a movie is not successful, then its merchandise will not sell either. For example, revenues from its studio entertainment and consumer products divisions fell sharply, more than 15 percent, between 2004 and 2006. Continued weak performance would substantially weaken the firm's revenues and profitability. Finally, foreign operations are fraught with risk. Euro Disney, for instance, was not successful when it first opened. Similarly, the Hong Kong Disneyland Resort has not yet lived up to expectations. A recent study showed that 70 percent of local residents had a negative opinion of the resort and there are ticketing problems and employee relations issues at the resort. This negative situation could tarnish Disney's image and future growth in Asia.[11]

Threats (Exhibit 2.5, lower right) are negative aspects of the external environment. For Disney, stiff competition in all markets can have a negative impact on their businesses. For example, the Disney's studio and broadcasting services face stiff competition from other television networks (such as CBS and Fox), satellite television, and cable television. This could affect Disney's ability to raise advertising revenues from its media properties. In addition, technology has made it easy for consumers to pirate Disney's digital content—movies, songs, DVDs, TV shows, etc.—that could adversely affect its revenues and profitability. Similarly, its parks and resort business face stiff competition for visitors from the likes of Paramount Parks and smaller local U.S. based amusement parks around the country. Finally, the media business is heavily regulated in both the U.S. and internationally and this could limit the ability of Disney to offer certain programs, for example, there are restrictions on commercial time during children's programming. Also, accidents at its theme parks could lead to tighter safety regulations of its theme park operations.[12]

LO ③ Step 3: Identify and Evaluate Opportunities Using STP (Segmentation, Targeting, and Positioning)

STP
The processes of segmentation, targeting, and positioning that firms use to identify and evaluate opportunities for increasing sales and profits.

After completing the situation audit, the next step is to identify and evaluate opportunities for increasing sales and profits using **STP** (segmentation, targeting, and positioning). With STP, the firm must first understand customer needs and wants through market research, then divide the market or customers into subgroups or segments, determine which of those segments it should pursue or target, and finally decide how it should position its products and services to best meet the needs of those chosen targets.

market segment
A group of consumers who respond similarly to a firm's marketing efforts.

market segmentation
The process of dividing the market into groups of customers with different needs, wants, or characteristics—who therefore might appreciate products or services geared especially for them.

Segmentation Many types of customers appear in any market, and most firms cannot satisfy everyone's needs. For instance, among Internet users, some do research online, some shop, some look for entertainment, and many may do all three. Each of these groups might be a **market segment** consisting of consumers who respond similarly to a firm's marketing efforts. The process of dividing the market into groups of customers with different needs, wants, or characteristics—who therefore might appreciate products or services geared especially for them—is called **market segmentation**. For example, Disney targets its Pleasure Island to singles and couples, Epcot to families with older children and adults, and the Magic Kingdom to families with younger children. Firms identify segments in various ways. For instance, Disney may use demographics like gender, age, and income to identify the young families it is pursuing for the Magic Kingdom; but use psychological or behavioural factors, like those who like to party or go dancing, to identify the singles and couples it is pursuing for Pleasure Island. Firms may also segment consumers based on socio-cultural factors as discussed in Chapter 8.

Frito Lay targets several markets with many different types of chips.

Targeting   After a firm has identified the various market segments it might pursue, it evaluates each segment's attractiveness and decides which to pursue using a process known as **target marketing** or **targeting**. From our previous example, Disney realizes that the Magic Kingdom's primary appeal is to young families, so the bulk of its marketing efforts for this business are directed toward that group. Similarly, potato chip manufacturers have divided the market into many submarkets or segments. Frito Lay Canada, for instance, makes its cheesy Doritos chips for the teen segment and its wasabi and curry Lay chips for Asian Canadians.[13] The criteria used to evaluate the attractiveness of a target segment are also described in Chapter 8.

target marketing/targeting
The process of evaluating the attractiveness of various segments and then deciding which to pursue as a market.

Positioning   Finally, when the firm decides which segments to pursue, it must determine how it wants to be positioned within those segments. **Market positioning** involves the process of defining the marketing mix variables so that target customers have a clear, distinctive, desirable understanding of what the product does or represents in comparison with competing products. Positioning is what consumers think and feel about a brand or product. All marketers would like consumers to think of their brand or product in the way the company wants to present it to them but few are able to so effectively. Disney, for instance, defines itself as an entertainer and most consumers perceive Disney as an entertainment provider. Its Florida Walt Disney World Resort owns and operates four theme parks, 17 hotels and resorts, as well as golf courses, water parks, a sports complex and a retail and dining complex.

market positioning
Involves the process of defining the marketing mix variables so that target customers have a clear, distinctive, desirable understanding of what the product does or represents in comparison with competing products.

After identifying its target segments, a firm must evaluate each of its strategic opportunities. Firms typically are most successful when they focus on those opportunities that build on their strengths relative to those of their competition. In Step 4 of the strategic marketing planning process, the firm implements its marketing mix and allocates resources to different products and services.

Set Marketing Objectives   Normally the marketing manager is responsible for setting the marketing specific objectives for the product or brand over the life of the plan. These objectives may include market share, revenues and profitability targets, unit sales volume, and brand awareness. Depending on the duration of the plan, these objectives usually cover one year to five years.

Develop Marketing Mix

LO **4**

When the firm has identified and evaluated different growth opportunities by performing an STP analysis, the real action begins. It has decided what to do, how to do it, and how many resources should be allocated to it. In this step of the planning process, marketers develop the marketing mix—product, price, promotion, and place—for each product and service on the basis of what they believe their target markets will value (Exhibit 2.6). Each element of the 4Ps must be fully integrated in order to achieve a coherent strategy.

Product and Value Creation   Products, which include services, constitute the first of the 4Ps. Because the key to the success of any marketing program is the creation of value, firms attempt to develop products and services that customers

| EXHIBIT | 2.6 | Developing the Marketing Mix |

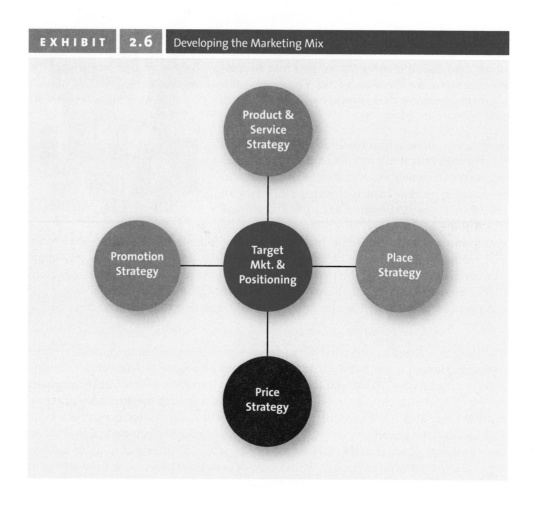

perceive as valuable enough to buy. Sirius Satellite, for instance, understood that the radio marketplace was full of opportunities. Sirius is one of two existing satellite radio companies. Satellite radio is a service that customers pay for through a subscription plan. Customers can choose the radio that suits their needs best. They can choose table top, car, or portable units. These radios display the singer and song title on the screen. Sirius also offers a *sportster* unit, which allows the user to choose the type of sport updates they would like to see scroll live across the screen.

Sirius created value for a product and market that didn't previously exist.

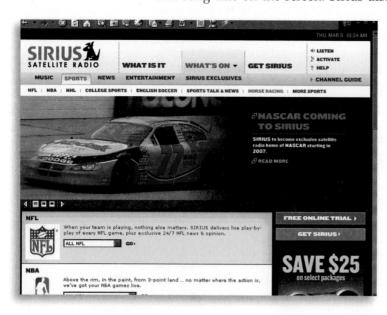

Sirius and satellite radio have over 120 stations of music and talk radio stations with an extensive music catalogue. Unlike terrestrial radio, Sirius, with its continental reach, can offer shows such as *The Bob Dylan Hour* that would normally have too small an audience to support it. Sirius radio has added value to generic radio services through a pay service, specialized receivers, and a broad range of stations that allow Sirius consumers to customize their own radio experience.

Price and Value for Money   Recall that the second element of the marketing mix is price. As part of the exchange process, a firm provides a product or a service, or some combination thereof, and in return it receives money. Value-based marketing requires that firms charge a price that customers perceive as giving them good value for the products and services they receive. Firms practise three types of pricing strategies. The first pricing strategy, **cost-based pricing**, is when a firm determines the costs of producing or providing its product and then adds a fixed amount above that total to arrive at the selling price. For example, most university bookstores purchase textbooks at the publisher's wholesale price and then mark them up by a certain percent, usually between 20 to 30 percent. The second type, the **competitor-based pricing** strategy, is when a firm prices below, at, or above its competitors' offerings. For example, Chapters bookstore might decide to take the top 10 books on *The Globe & Mail* bestseller list and price them $2 less than either Zellers or Wal-Mart.

Although relatively simple to implement, neither of these methods alone ensures that customers will perceive they are getting good value for the products or services. That perception requires the third approach, termed **value-based pricing**, in which the firm first determines the perceived value of the product from the customer's point of view and then prices accordingly. For example, the bookstore might determine from its prior experience that students have various attitudes toward textbooks and their prices: some students want a new book, whereas others accept a used one for a lesser price. Giving them a choice of both options provides value to both groups.

However, value-based pricing remains one of the least understood areas of business decision making, even though it is one of the few business activities with a direct impact on profits. Clearly, it is important for a firm to have a clear focus in terms of what products to sell, where to buy them, and what methods to use in selling them. But pricing is the only activity that actually brings in money by influencing revenues. If a price is set too high, it will not generate much volume. If a price is set too low, it may result in lower-than-necessary margins and profits. Therefore, price should be based on the value that the customer perceives. Pricing decisions and strategies are discussed in detail in Chapter 12.

Place and Value Delivery   For the third P, place, the firm must be able to, after it has created value through a product and/or service, make the product or service readily accessible when and where the customer wants it. Consider how Lee Valley Tools (described in Internet Marketing 2.1) has integrated its stores and catalogue operations with its Internet operations and used place to create value in its delivery process. Lee Valley, one of the world's leading mail-order and retail suppliers of woodworking and gardening tools, saw the Internet as another delivery channel that complements its existing operations and thus, established a fully operational e-commerce website. Through its website, leevalley.com, Lee Valley is able to reach a wider market segment more efficiently and cost-effectively. Also, through its website, customers are provided with more detailed information about the company's products, training seminars, and woodworking and gardening tips and advice. Thus, Lee Valley turned the integration of its different channels into a seamless customer experience, a key value driver for the company.[14]

Promotion and Value Communication   The fourth and last P of the marketing mix is promotion. Marketers communicate the value of their offering, or the value proposition, to their customers through a variety of media including television, radio, magazines, sales promotion, publicity, the sales force, and the Internet—the last boon for specialty retailers across the globe. It is now possible for firms in out-of-the-way locations to expand their market area to the whole world. For example, Canadians living in places such as Africa, Australia, and New Zealand can order their favourite authentic Canadian products they cannot find in these countries through the Ottawa-based Country Grocer website, www.thecountrygrocer.com.[15] Similarly, Kicking Horse Coffee, located in the heart of the Canadian Rockies—about 150 km from Banff and 877 km from Vancouver, BC—sells over

cost-based pricing
A pricing strategy that involves first determining the costs of producing or providing a product and then adding a fixed amount above that total to arrive at the selling price.

competitor-based pricing
A strategy that involves pricing below, at, or above competitors' offerings.

value-based pricing
A pricing strategy that involves first determining the perceived value of the product from the customer's point of view and then pricing accordingly.

Internet Marketing

2.1   Lee Valley Tools Ltd.—Delivering Value through Integrated Channels

Statistics Canada data show that 60 percent of Canadian companies still do not have a website. And, of the 40 percent that do, the overwhelming majority use it only to provide information about their company and products rather than for conducting e-commerce.[16] Lee Valley Tools is among the small minority of firms that use its website for e-commerce. Lee Valley Tools delivers strong value to its customers by seamlessly integrating its mail-order operations with its physical stores and online operations. By linking its bricks, clicks, and mail-order operations into an integrated business, Lee Valley Tools is able to get a better understanding of its customers' needs and preferences and thus is better able to serve their needs. It uses its website to communicate with its customers and build strong relationships, to teach customers about the proper use and care for the tools they buy, and to provide technical information and tips about woodworking and gardening. Customers have come to trust not only the company and its tools but also the additional information it provides on its website. Lee Valley Tools has used its website to take its business to a higher level, and in the process, deliver substantially more value to its customers at no additional costs! The website is a focal point for engaging customers in a dialogue and helps build strong, lasting, profitable relations with them—no surprise that the majority of its customers are repeat customers.

Lee Valley Tools Ltd. began 30 years ago as a catalogue mail-order supplier of woodworking and gardening tools by entrepreneur, Leonard Lee. Over the years, Lee has opened 11 stores across Canada and in 2000 launched a fully-functional e-commerce website. Based in Ottawa, Lee Valley Tools has grown to become one of the world's leading mail-order and retail suppliers of very innovative woodworking and gardening tools. The company that started out with just three employees now employs around a 1000 people. Its continued success

is credited to its three guiding principles established by Lee when he first started the company—customer satisfaction, integrity, and treating customers as friends. As part of its customer satisfaction guarantee, a customer can return "any product within 3 months at no cost to the customer; we return every penny you paid us, plus, for shipments within North America, we will refund your return parcel post costs."[17]

Apart from ordering tools through its website, Lee Valley uses its website to tell customers of upcoming training seminars that are held in its physical stores. These seminars teach customers about the use and care of the tools and to demonstrate new, innovative tools being developed. The website also contains a variety of technical articles on woodworking and gardening that help customers learn more and enjoy their favourite activity. The regular e-newsletter, which customers sign up for, provides technical information, trade show dates, company news, special event dates and other topics of interest to woodworkers and gardeners. Customers can even send letters about their experiences with specific tools, which are posted on the company's website for everyone to view. Lee Valley Tools is extending its customer base one customer at a time.

Customers purchase woodworking and gardening tools by catalogue, phone, website, or in-store.

20,000 kg per week of its more than 21-flavour organic Fair Trade Coffee to consumers and retail stores across Canada, United States, and Holland. Kicking Horse Coffee is now the national leader in grocery-store sales of super-premium coffee—ahead of even the mighty Starbucks.[18] These retailers and thousands like them have added value to their offerings through their efficient and effective communications strategies.

Marketers therefore must consider which are the most efficient and effective methods to communicate with their customers, which goes back to understanding customers, the value created, and the message being communicated. Recently, an increasing number of companies are using the Internet and their own websites to advertise and communicate with their customers and build closer relationships. For example, visitors to Sears Canada website, sears.ca, could win either a Kenmore Elite™ HE5t Laundry Team or one of three free trips to Jamaica, Cuba, or St. Lucia, without even making a purchase; they only had to sign up and answer a simple skill testing question![19] Research has shown that this type of campaign is much more effective than either mail or TV advertising. Nevertheless, marketers must balance the effectiveness of their value communication activities with their costs. For example, Google offers a service called AdWord Select that charges advertisers on the basis of the number of actual clicks on their advertisements, not when, where, or how often it was placed, which is a more common strategy among traditional media outlets.[20] In addition to the Internet, many Canadian companies spend a large portion of their marketing budgets on sales promotions because Canadian consumers are increasingly becoming more value-conscious. In fact, spending on sales promotion has exceeded spending on advertising in Canada.[21]

Companies need to ensure their promotional strategies are in line with their corporate vision. That's not always as easy as it sounds. Ethical Dilemma 2.1 examines a promotional tactic that caused concerns as Lululemon worked to expand its retail presence in Canada.

Step 4: Implement the Marketing Mix: Allocating Resources

After developing the marketing mix, marketing managers must allocate the resources needed to put the plan into action. This involves developing a budget, setting schedules for various tasks, and designing the marketing organization. At this stage, marketing managers must make important decisions about how they will allocate their scarce resources to their various products and services. Marketers have several tools to help them allocate resources. In portfolio analysis, for example, management evaluates the firm's various products and businesses—its "portfolio"—and allocates resources according to which products are expected to be the most profitable for the firm in the future. A popular tool for portfolio analysis—the BCG Matrix—was developed by the Boston Consulting Group and is described on the next page. Portfolio analysis is typically performed at the **strategic business unit (SBU)** or **product line** level of the firm, though managers can also use it to analyze brands or even individual items. An SBU is a division of the company that can be managed somewhat independently

strategic business unit (SBU)
A division of the firm itself that can be managed and operated somewhat independently from other divisions and may have a different mission or objectives.

product line
A group of products that consumers may use together or perceive as similar in some way.

Ethical Dilemma

2.1 Lululemon: Bare It All, Even If You Don't Want To!

Not long ago, Lululemon, Canada's newest fashion outlet for Yoga-inspired men's and women's athletic wear ran a promotion publicizing the opening of their new Kingston, Ontario store.[22] The first 30 customers to enter their store clad only in their underwear were offered a free top and bottom. Girls planned to enter the store in their underpants, hide their breasts with their hands and sprint to the nearest clothing rack. Some hoped to wear their bras as well. Only minutes before the opening, the girls were told that bras were a no-go and they could not cover their breasts with their hands, all the while the cameras rolled, even following the girls while they tried on the clothes. When the girls asked them to back away, camera opera-

tors backed away but still kept on taking pictures. A similar event like this was held in Vancouver earlier. According to a Lululemon spokesperson, "this was an event of choice and the people who participated chose to have some fun and went home with a free Lululemon outfit. Everyone was very happy with the results of the event." Interestingly, Lululemon's Yoga-inspired brand promises women a lifestyle of fun, health, balance, and even empowerment. Is this empowerment or objectification of women? Were the girls exploited because they were photographed naked? Because the girls were told in advance of the nature of the promotion (although it seems not to the full extent), does it make it ethically acceptable?

from other divisions since it markets a specific set of products to a clearly defined group of customers. For example, Loblaw Companies Limited consists of its general merchandise, drugstores, President's Choice® brand, and financial products and services operations.[23] Each of these is an SBU. A product line, in contrast, is a group of products that consumers may use together or perceive as similar in some way. There are several product lines within Loblaws' PC Financial® services SBU: PC banking, PC Mastercard, mortgages, and insurance.

relative market share
A measure of the product's strength in a particular market, defined as the sales of the focal product divided by the sales achieved by the largest firm in the industry.

market growth rate
The annual rate of growth of the specific market in which the product competes.

BOSTON CONSULTING GROUP'S PORTFOLIO ANALYSIS

One of the most popular portfolio analysis methods, developed by the Boston Consulting Group (BCG), requires that firms classify all their products into a two-by-two matrix, as depicted in Exhibit 2-7.[24] The circles represent brands, and their sizes are directly proportion to the brands' annual sales. The horizontal axis represents the relative market share, a measure of the product's strength in a particular market, which we define as the sales of the focal product divided by the sales achieved by the largest firm in the industry. The vertical axis is the market growth rate, or the annual rate of growth of the specific market in which the product competes. Market growth rate thus measures how attractive a particular market is. Each quadrant has been named on the basis of the amount of resources it generates for and requires from the firm.

Stars. Stars (upper left quadrant) occur in high growth markets and are high market share products. That is, stars often require a heavy resource investment in such things as promotions and new production facilities to fuel their rapid growth. As their market growth slows, stars will migrate from heavy users of resources to heavy generators of resources and become cash cows.

EXHIBIT	**2.7**	BCG Growth-Share Matrix

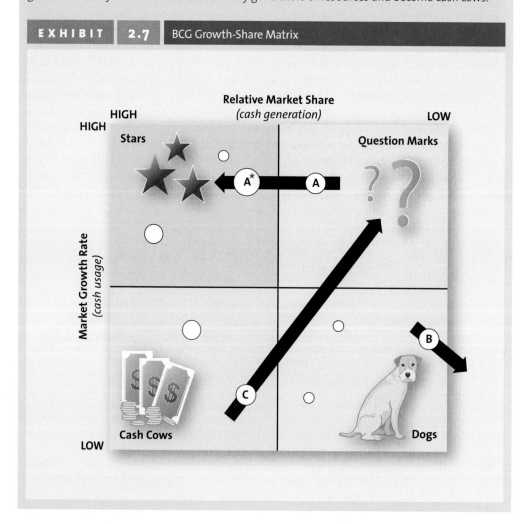

Cash cows. Cash cows (lower left quadrant) are in low growth markets but are high market share products. Because these products have already received heavy investments to develop their high market share, they have excess resources that can be spun off to those products that need it. For example, in Exhibit 2.7, Brand C uses its excess resources to fund products in the question mark quadrant.

Question marks. Question marks (upper right quadrant) appear in high growth markets but have relatively low market shares; thus, they are often the most managerially intensive products in that they require significant resources to maintain and potentially increase their market share. Managers must decide whether to infuse question marks with resources generated by the cash cows, so that they can become stars, or withdraw resources and eventually phase out the products. Brand A, for instance, is currently a question mark, but by infusing it with resources, the firm hopes to turn it into a star.

Dogs. Dogs (lower right quadrant) are in low growth markets and have relatively low market shares. Although they may generate enough resources to sustain themselves, dogs are not destined for stardom and should be phased out unless they are needed to complement or boost the sales of another product or for competitive purposes. In this case, the company has decided to stop making Brand B.

Although quite useful for conceptualizing the resource allocation task, the BCG approach, and others like it, are often difficult to implement in practice. In particular, it is difficult to measure both relative market share and industry growth. Furthermore, other measures easily could serve as substitutes to represent a product's competitive position and the market's relative attractiveness. Another issue for marketers is the potential self-fulfilling prophecy of placing a product into a quadrant. That is, suppose a product is classified as a dog though it has the potential of being a question mark. The firm might reduce support for the product and lose sales to the point that it abandons the product, which might have become profitable if provided with sufficient resources.

Because of these limitations, many firms have tempered their use of matrix approaches to achieve a more balanced approach to allocating their resources. Instead of assigning allocation decisions to the top levels of the organization, many firms start at lower management levels and employ checks and balances to force managers at each level of the organizational hierarchy to negotiate with those above and below them to reach their final decisions.

In addition to allocating resources, marketing managers must develop schedules—timelines for each activity and the personnel responsible for the respective activity to avoid bottlenecks and ensure smooth and timely implementation of the marketing mix activities. Also, marketers must design the organization that will be responsible for putting the plan into action. This organization is usually represented in the form of an organizational chart as shown in the sample marketing plan in the Appendix at the back of the textbook. In most established companies, the marketing organization already exists and it is just a matter of simply assigning responsibilities to various employees within the marketing department. The marketing organization is usually responsible for the day-to-day operational decisions involved in executing the plan.

These screen shots show some of the business lines of President's Choice, which is a company within the Loblaw Group of Companies .

Step 5: Evaluate Performance and Make Adjustments

The final step in the planning process includes evaluating the results of the strategy and implementation program. The firm must determine why it achieved or did not achieve its performance goals. Was the success or failure due to factors that were within the firm's control? For instance, did it spend too much to buy its parts or ingredients? Were the results due to economic or competitive factors such as a new product in the marketplace? Understanding the causes of the performance, regardless of whether that performance exceeded, met, or fell below the firm's goals, enables firms to make appropriate adjustments.

Typically, managers begin by reviewing the implementation programs, and their analysis may indicate that the strategy (or even the mission statement) needs to be reconsidered. Problems can arise both when firms successfully implement poor strategies and when they poorly implement good strategies.

To evaluate a brand, a manager could measure brand awareness (i.e., how aware customers are of the brand name), the number of people who bought the product, or what the repeat purchase rate is. To evaluate the performance of a specific item, the manager would consider sales, profitability, and turnover.[25]

As an illustration of how a firm evaluates its performance and makes appropriate adjustments, consider the case of Canada's Fairmont Hotel and Resort, the largest luxury hotel company in North America. Recently, the company developed a guest data warehouse in order to maintain guest profile information across all its properties; target guest segments with personalized communications, incentives, and discounts; better manage its loyalty program; and acquire new guests and build loyalty. This data warehouse is seamlessly integrated with Fairmont's website, the hotel's central reservation and property management systems, and can gather guest information from all touch points (media through which customers come into contact with Fairmont). As a result of this guest warehouse, Fairmont is able to maximize its revenues by focusing its marketing and brand-building efforts on higher-value guest segments. It can also, for the first time, measure the effectiveness of segmented marketing initiatives.[26]

Strategic Planning is Not Sequential

The planning process in Exhibit 2.2 suggests that managers follow a set sequence when they make strategic decisions. Namely, after they've defined the business mission, they perform the situation analysis, identify strategic opportunities, evaluate alternatives, set objectives, allocate resources, develop the implementation plan, and, finally, evaluate their performance and make adjustments. But actual planning processes can move back and forth among these steps. For example, a situation analysis may uncover a logical alternative, even though this alternative might not be included in the mission statement, which would mean that the mission statement would need to be revised. The development of the implementation plan also might reveal that insufficient resources have been allocated to a particular product for it to achieve its objective. In that case, the firm would need to either change the objective or increase the resources; alternatively, the marketer might consider not investing in the product at all.

Now that we have gone through the steps of the strategic marketing planning process, let's look at some strategies that have been responsible for making many marketing firms successful.

LO ⑤ Growth Strategies

Firms consider pursuing various market segments as part of their overall growth strategies, which may include the four major strategies shown in Exhibit 2.8.[27] The rows distinguish those opportunities a firm possesses in its current markets from

EXHIBIT	2.8	Market/Product and Services Strategies

Markets	Products and Services	
	Current	**New**
Current	Market Penetration	Product Development
New	Market Development	Diversification

those it has in new markets, whereas the columns distinguish between the firm's current marketing offering and that of a new opportunity. Let's consider each of them in detail.

Market Penetration

A **market penetration strategy** employs the existing marketing mix and focuses the firm's efforts on existing customers. Such a growth strategy might be achieved by attracting new consumers to the firm's current target market or encouraging current customers to patronize the firm more often or buy more merchandise on each visit. A market penetration strategy generally requires greater marketing efforts, such as increased advertising, additional sales and promotions, or intensified distribution efforts in geographic areas in which the product or service already is sold.

For example, Canada's Fairmont Hotel and Resorts offer customers numerous promotions and discount packages all year round for staying at Fairmont Hotels and Resorts. Its *Only One Way Summer Rates* discount package offers customers a discount on one night accommodation at the Fairmont during the summer months. With this promotion, customers who book for a minimum of two nights before a certain date and pay with any American Express® Card receive up to a $50 food and beverage credit per night for stays between May and September or can earn double airline miles from its participating airline partners.[28] Its President Club membership program offers its 800,000 members—half of them Canadians, many benefits such as allowing them to reserve Adidas apparel and footwear in their personal sizes, plus selected equipment, and have it waiting in their rooms as part of its Fairmont Fit Program.[29]

market penetration strategy
A growth strategy that employs the existing marketing mix and focuses the firm's efforts on existing customers.

Market Development

A **market development strategy** employs the existing marketing offering to reach new market segments, whether domestic or international. International expansion is generally riskier than domestic expansion because firms must deal with differences in government regulations, cultural traditions, supply chain considerations, and language. The Fairmont Hotel and Resorts formed a joint venture in 2007 with Jin Jiang International Group, the largest hotel group in China, to reopen The Peace Hotel, a Shanghai landmark for over a century. The joint venture company is called the Jin Jiang Fairmont Hotel and is scheduled to reopen in 2010. In the future, the company plans to open Fairmont Hotels and Resorts in Vancouver, Cairo, Abu Dhabi, South Africa, and other parts of Asia and the Middle East where it has very few properties.[30] Similarly, Forever 21, a Los Angeles-based pioneer of "cheap

market development strategy
A growth strategy that employs the existing marketing offering to reach new market segments, whether domestic or international.

Fairmont is practising a market development strategy by opening hotels and resorts in places like China, like this one in Shanghai.

chic" clothing that sells "ripped-from-the-runway" fashion aimed at teens and college and university students, has recently opened its flagship Canadian boutique across the street from Toronto's Eaton Centre. It plans to follow the footsteps of H&M of Sweden and Zara of Spain and open more stores across Canada.[31]

Product Development

product development strategy
A growth strategy that offers a new product or service to a firm's current target market.

The third growth strategy option, a **product development strategy**, offers a new product or service to a firm's current target market. Fairmont Hotels and Resorts wanted to migrate its existing customers to its website from existing channels, so it developed a website that simplifies the booking steps, shortens the timeframe required to complete the booking process, and can provide relevant, value-added packages and promotions during the booking process. To further enhance its e-business initiative, Fairmont now offers visitors secured wired and wireless connectivity throughout its properties. According to Fairmont's VP of Technology, "we have guests that actually host their own servers, and who actually work out of our hotels, out of meeting rooms, and out of guestrooms. Some even run mail servers." The idea is to make professional visitors as productive in their hotel rooms as they are in the corporate office.[32]

Diversification

diversification strategy
A growth strategy whereby a firm introduces a new product or service to a market segment that it does not currently serve.

A **diversification strategy**, the last of the growth strategies from Exhibit 2.8, introduces a new product or service to a market segment that is currently not served. Diversification opportunities may be either related or unrelated. In a related diversification opportunity, the current target market and/or marketing mix shares something in common with the new opportunity. In other words, the firm might be able to purchase from existing vendors, use the same distribution and/or management information system, or advertise in the same newspapers to target markets that are similar to their current consumers. In contrast, in an unrelated diversification, the new business lacks any common elements with the present business. As part of its related diversification strategy, Fairmont Hotels and Resorts acquired Delta Hotels, Canada's largest first-class hotel company that caters to a lower market segment than the Fairmont.[33] Additionally, the Fairmont Hotel and Resorts also owns a 35-percent investment stake in the Real Estate Investment Trust (REIT) Legacy.[34] Entrepreneurial Marketing 2.1 describes Kicking Horse Coffee's success–growth strategy.

Macro Strategies

Growth strategies are not the only way a firm might improve its business. For example, macro strategies, or overarching strategies, focus on elements of excellence to create and deliver value and to develop sustainable competitive advantages. As we depict in Exhibit 2.9, many marketing firms have turned to three such strategies—also called value disciplines—to give them a sustainable long-term advantage over their competition.[35]

customer excellence
Involves a focus on retaining loyal customers and excellent customer service.

operational excellence
Involves a firm's focus on efficient operations and excellent supply chain management.

product excellence
Involves a focus on achieving high-quality products; effective branding and positioning are key.

- **Customer excellence**, which focuses on retaining loyal customers and excellent customer service.
- **Operational excellence** through efficient operations and excellent supply chain management.
- **Product excellence**, or achieving high-quality products; effective branding and positioning are key.

Customer Excellence

Customer excellence is achieved when a firm develops value-based strategies for retaining loyal customers and provides outstanding customer service.

Entrepreneurial Marketing

2.1 | Kicking Horse Coffee—Kicking Ass![36]

Legend has it that the Kicking Horse Pass was one of the final hurdles in the development of the railway linking British Columbia to the rest of Canada. It is from this legendary pass that Kicking Horse Coffee derived its name. The company was started in 1996 by Elana Rosenfeld and Leo Johnson, two Torontonians who love the outdoors. It is their love for the outdoors that led them to the small but scenic town of Invermere, British Columbia, where Kicking Horse Coffee is located. Kicking Horse Coffee is nestled in the heart of the Canadian Rockies, some 150 km west from the world famous mountain town of Banff and 877 km east of Vancouver.

The couple's initial plan was to produce and distribute organic coffee. Kicking Horse Coffee offers a 21-flavour portfolio of the very best organic, Fair Trade coffee in Canada that is roasted and blended at 914 metres above sea level. Currently, the company sells over 20,000 kilos of coffee per week to grocery stores and restaurants in Canada, the U.S., and Holland, employs 15 people, owns a 20,000-square foot office and roasting facility, and projects annual revenues of close to $10 million. Kicking Horse Coffee even climbed to number 1 nationally in grocery-store sales of super-premium coffee—ahead of even the mighty Starbucks and Timothy's World Coffee. Did Elana Rosenfeld and Leo Johnson plan for this growth? Hardly! Flashback to 1996, when Elana wrote, "if we can sell 350 pounds per week, we are laughing". Their phenomenal sales were beyond their wildest imagination and they were unable to meet the unexpected strong demand for their coffee. Could they have been the victim of their own success by not being able to meet demand as a reliable supplier?

Elana Rosenfeld admitted that initially they did not adopt formal business planning but relied on an on-the-fly sort of approach. They only adopted formal

Kicking Horse Coffee offers 21 flavours of organic coffee.

business planning after realizing that they were unable to satisfy the skyrocketing demand for their coffee—demand surged by more than 229 percent within a three-year period! The couple was so engrossed with trying to fill increasing orders that they had no time to think about planning although they realized that they had to plan if they were going to scale their company to keep up with booming sales. It was time to get serious about planning. Luckily, in late 2005, the Business Development Bank of Canada awarded Kicking Horse $5,000 worth of consulting, which Rosenfeld says was "invaluable, absolutely necessary" advice on planning. They developed detailed sales forecasts and projected future capital needs using a more systematic approach to anticipate space, people, and equipment requirements. They hired two experienced managers to bring more structure to production and have become more disciplined in choosing which opportunities to pursue. They also found a balance that allows the company to grow fast, but not so fast that the co-founders must break their "never any overtime" pledge to themselves and their dozen staff. "In our tenth year in business," says Rosenfeld, "we're slowly coming out of our infancy." She noted that although clients such as Safeway, Loblaw, and Provigo still can't get as much Kick Ass Coffee as they could sell, production is ramping up and they are starting to close the gap between supply and demand.

Rosenfeld points to two key benefits from her planning mindset: it has made day-to-day operations smoother and freed up more time for the co-founders to set the overall direction. "Part of planning is articulating who you are and what you believe in so you can stay on the path," she says. This has helped them resist retailers who've urged them to sell bulk ground coffee, which would compromise quality because ground coffee quickly goes stale when exposed to the air.

Retaining Loyal Customers Customer loyalty means that customers are committed to buying from a particular firm. Sometimes, the methods a firm uses to maintain a sustainable competitive advantage help attract and maintain loyal customers. For instance, having a strong brand, unique merchandise, and superior customer service all help solidify a loyal customer base. But in addition, having loyal customers is, in and of itself, an important method of sustaining an advantage over competitors. Loyalty is more than simply preferring to purchase from one firm instead of another;[37] it means that customers are reluctant to patronize competitive firms. For example, loyal customers continue to buy Nike running shoes even if Reebok shoes are available at more convenient locations or provide a slightly superior assortment or slightly lower prices.

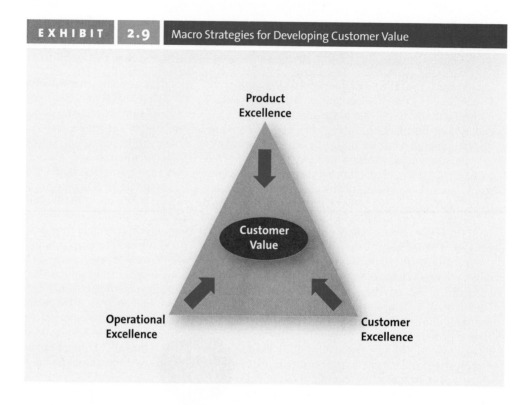

EXHIBIT 2.9 Macro Strategies for Developing Customer Value

More and more firms realize the value of achieving customer excellence through focusing their strategy on retaining their loyal customers. For instance, a good dry cleaner doesn't think in terms of washing and pressing a single shirt for $2. Instead, it is concerned with satisfying the customer who spends $25 per week, 50 weeks a year, for 10 years or more. This customer isn't a $2 customer; he's a $12,500 customer. Viewing customers with a life-time value perspective, rather than on a transaction-by-transaction basis, is key to modern customer retention programs.[38]

The world's largest independent credit card issuer, MBNA, recognizes the significant value of serving and retaining loyal customers.[39] According to the company's estimates, a 5-percent decrease in defection rates—that is, decreasing the number of customers who move to another bank—increases its average customer value by more than 125 percent. In turn, MBNA believes that by decreasing its defection rate by 10 percent, it could double the average amount of time customers remain with the company and increase its profits sixteenfold. In general, experts suggest that companies can boost profits by almost 100 percent if they can retain an additional 5 percent of their customers[40]

Marketers use several methods to build customer loyalty. One such way involves developing a clear and precise positioning strategy. For instance, loyal Bell Sympatico High Speed Internet consumers value its fast, efficient, and helpful customer service so much that they would not move to other service providers even though they might save a few dollars by switching. Another method of achieving customer loyalty creates an emotional attachment through loyalty programs.[41] Loyalty programs, which constitute part of an overall customer relationship management (CRM) program as we described in Chapter 1, prevail in many industries from airlines to hotels to movies theatres to retail stores. Three-quarters of Canadians and Americans belong to at least one loyalty program.[42] Although, the benefits to consumers of loyalty programs are limited since only a small percentage of customers save enough points to claim their rewards, loyalty programs are a boon to marketers. With such programs, companies can combine membership data with customer purchase data in order to develop a profile of the customer. Companies often use this data to tailor their offering to better meet the needs of their loyal customers. For instance, by analyzing their databases, financial institutions such as Bank of Montreal develop profiles of customers who have defected in the past and use that information to identify customers who may defect in the future. Once it identifies these customers, the firm can implement special retention programs to keep them.

Customer Service

Marketers may also build sustainable competitive advantage by offering excellent customer service,[43] though consistently offering excellent service can prove difficult. Customer service is provided by employees, and invariably, humans are less consistent than machines. Firms that offer good customer service must instill its importance in their employees over a long period of time so that it becomes part of the organizational culture.

Although it may take considerable time and effort to build a reputation for customer service, once a marketer has earned a good service reputation, it can sustain this advantage for a long time because a competitor is hard pressed to develop a comparable reputation. Adding Value 2.1 describes the entrepreneurial quest for superb customer service by Virgin Atlantic's founder Richard Branson.

Operational Excellence

Firms achieve operational excellence, the second macro success strategy, through their efficient operations and excellent supply chain management. All marketers strive for efficient operations to get their customers the merchandise they want, when they want it, in the required quantities, and at a lower delivered cost than that of their competitors. By so doing, they ensure good value to their customers, earn profitability for themselves, and satisfy their customers' needs. In addition, efficient operations enable firms to either provide their consumers with lower priced merchandise or, even if their prices are not lower than those of the competition, to use the additional margin they earn to attract customers away from competitors by offering even better service, merchandise assortments, or visual presentations.

Firms achieve these efficiencies by developing sophisticated distribution and information systems as well as strong relationships with vendors. Similar to customer relationships, vendor relations must be developed over the long term and generally cannot be easily offset by a competitor.[44] Telus Corporation, Canada's second largest telecommunications company, has over 4.5 million wireless subscribers, 4.7 million wireline network access lines and 1 million Internet subscribers. Customer service is a key differentiator in this industry because price competition is fierce. Assessing its customer service performance, Telus found that its current customer service management application was cumbersome and inefficient for its customer service representatives (CSRs) to use. For example, CSRs had to undergo extensive training and took a long time to learn the application before they became comfortable. Also, several screens would ask CSRs to enter the same information repeatedly and multiple applications were required to serve the same customer. Thus, the possibility for errors was substantial and CSRs spent considerable amounts of time trying to resolve customer enquiries—valuable time that could be spent up-selling and cross-selling to customers. To rectify the situation, Telus implemented its Smart Desktop, a much easier and efficient application, at more than 1000 customer service sites at a cost of $6.5 million. The results on operational efficiency are impressive: training time for existing staff and

Some firms develop a sustainable competitive advantage through operational excellence with efficient operations and excellent supply chain management.

Adding Value

2.1 Customer Service at Virgin Atlantic

Virgin Atlantic, the second largest long-haul international airline, operates services out of London's Heathrow and Gatwick airports to 22 destinations across the world—Shanghai, the Caribbean, and, of course, the United States.[45] Virgin's customer service orientation is heralded in its mission statement: "to grow a profitable airline that people love to fly and where people love to work."

In an age of dwindling airline services and disgruntled passengers, Virgin Atlantic set out to distinguish itself by providing the best possible service at the best possible price for all classes of tickets. Moreover, it set out to do so differently than anyone else. The result is a loyal group of travellers, agents, and employees who know the value of excellent customer service.

What does Virgin do that makes it so special? Consider the offerings in the box below. While economy service is good, there are lots of extras for premium economy. Upper service is just out of sight!

Virgin Atlantic retains loyal customers through great customer service.

Service Class	Distinctive Features
Upper	<ul><li>In-flight massages and manicures</li><li>Airport lounges with putting greens</li><li>Full-service spas and beauty salons</li><li>Onboard stand-up bars</li><li>Full reclining seats</li><li>Free limousine transfer</li><li>Drive-through check-in service standard with fare</li></ul>
Premium Economy	<ul><li>Dedicated check-in</li><li>Fast Track processing line</li><li>Priority baggage handling</li><li>20 cm more leg room than standard in the industry</li></ul>
Economy	<ul><li>Full in-flight meals</li><li>Free individual entertainment for each seat (28 channels with movies, television shows, and games)</li><li>Free drinks</li><li>Amenity kits with stylishly fun socks, eye shades, tooth brushes, combs, rejuvenating toiletries, and seat-back stickers with slogans like "Do Not Disturb," "Wake Me For Meals," and "Wake Me For Duty Free."</li></ul>

new hires was considerably reduced as well as the volume of call transfers—estimated savings were over $1.3 million. Additionally, CSRs up-selling and cross-selling activities increased by over 25 percent across all products and more than 125 percent in one of its products. Telus won the 2006 CIPA Silver Award of Excellence in Efficiency for its efficiency and operational improvements.[46]

Product Excellence

Product excellence, the third macro success strategy, occurs through branding and positioning. Some firms have difficulty developing a competitive advantage through their merchandise and service offerings, especially if competitors can deliver similar products or services easily. However, others have been able to maintain their sustainable competitive advantage by investing in their brand itself; positioning their product or service using a clear, distinctive brand image; and constantly reinforcing that image through their merchandise, service, and promotion. For instance, *The Globe and Mail* and *Interbrand's* top Canadian brands—RBC Financial Group, Shoppers Drug Mart, Bell, Tim Hortons, Molson, Rona, and Loblaw—are all leaders in their respective industries, at least in part because they have strong brands and a clear position in the marketplace.[47]

One of the world's top known brands, Lexus, was conceived in 1983 when Toyota Chairman Eiji Toyoda determined that the "time is right to create a luxury vehicle to challenge the best in the world." The Lexus 400 and ES250 were introduced in 1989; by 1990, the LS 400 was acclaimed by the trade press and industry experts as one of the best vehicles in the world.[48] Today, the Lexus brand is synonymous with luxury and quality. How did Toyota take the Lexus concept from obscurity to a tangible vehicle that rivals such long-standing brands as Mercedes, BMW, and Porsche? Lexus developed its brand by focusing on the most important variables that predict whether a person will purchase a new luxury car: income, current car ownership, age of current vehicle, and distance from a dealership.

Lexus achieves customer value by creating a luxurious, high quality automobile.

Armed with this information, the company created integrated marketing campaigns to cater to specific market profiles. For example, an early campaign sent a safety kit or picnic basket to those potential customers who test drove a Lexus. Although these promotional items were expensive, the company found that the offer was necessary to get the busy luxury car buyers to visit its dealerships.[49]

In most cases, however, a single strategy, such as low prices or excellent service, is not sufficient to build a sustainable competitive advantage.[50] Firms require multiple approaches to build a "wall" around their position that stands as high as possible. For example, WestJet Airlines has achieved success by providing customers with good value that meets their expectations, offering good customer service, maintaining good customer relations, and offering great prices. The company has consistently positioned itself as a carrier that provides good service at a good value—customers get to their destination on time for a reasonable price. At the same time, its customers don't have extraordinary expectations and don't expect food service, seat assignments, or flights out of certain airports.[51] By fulfilling all of these strategies, WestJet has developed a huge cadre of loyal customers and has built a very high wall around its position as the value player in the Canadian airline industry.

In this chapter we considered how a firm develops its marketing strategy by completing a marketing plan. In particular, we described how firms analyze their marketing situation, evaluate it, and then develop a segmentation, targeting, and positioning strategy in response. Then we studied how the marketing mix can be used to increase customer value. Finally, we detailed several generic strategies for growing a business and three overarching macro strategies that many firms have implemented successfully.

WestJet Airlines provides good service at a good price—a good value—and they have fun doing it!

Learning Objectives Review

1) Describe how a firm develops and implements a marketing plan

2) Conduct a SWOT analysis and explain its use in marketing planning

3) Explain how a firm chooses what group(s) of people to pursue with its marketing efforts

4) Describe how the marketing mix increases customer value

5) Describe how firms grow their businesses

1) A marketing plan is composed of an analysis of the current marketing situation, its objectives, the strategy for the 4Ps, and appropriate financial statements. A marketing plan represents the output of a three-phase process: planning, implementation, and control. The planning phase requires that managers first define the firm's mission and vision, which helps to answer the questions, "What business are we in now, and what do we intend to be in the future?" In the planning phase, managers conduct a situation analysis, identify and evaluate opportunities through segmentation, targeting, and positioning, and develop the marketing mix, 4Ps. In the second phase, implementation, the firm specifies, in more operational terms, how it plans to implement its mission and vision. Specifically, managers focus on implementing the marketing mix, allocate resources, design the marketing organization, and develop schedules and action plans. Finally, in the control phase, the firm must evaluate its performance to determine what worked, what didn't, and how performance can be improved in the future.

2) Recall that SWOT stands for strengths, weaknesses, opportunities, and threats. A SWOT analysis occurs during the second step in the strategic planning process, the situation analysis. By analyzing what the firm is good at (its strengths), where it could improve (its weaknesses), where in the marketplace it might excel (its opportunities), and what is happening in the marketplace that could harm the firm (its threats), managers can assess their firm's situation accurately and plan its strategy accordingly.

3) Once a firm identifies different marketing opportunities, it must determine which are the best to pursue. To accomplish this task, marketers go through a segmentation, targeting, and positioning (STP) process. Firms segment various markets by dividing the total market into those groups of customers with different needs, wants, or characteristics who therefore might appreciate products or services geared especially toward them. After identifying the different segments, the firm goes after, or targets, certain groups on the basis of the firm's perceived ability to satisfy the needs of those groups better and more profitably than competitors. To complete the STP process, firms position their products or services according to the marketing mix variables so that target customers have a clear, distinctive, and desirable understanding of what the product or service does or represents relative to competing products or services.

4) The marketing mix consists of the 4Ps—product, price, promotion, and place—and each P contributes to customer value. To provide value, the firm must offer a mix of products and services at prices their target markets will view as indicating good value. Thus, firms make trade-offs between the first two Ps, product and price, to give customers the best value. The third P, promotion, informs customers and helps them form a positive image about the firm and its products and services. The last P, place, adds value by getting the appropriate products and services to customers when they want them and in the quantities they need.

5) Firms use four basic growth strategies: market penetration, market development, product development, and diversification. A market penetration strategy directs the firm's efforts toward existing customers and uses the present marketing mix. In other words, it attempts to get current customers to buy more. In a market development strategy, the firm uses its current marketing mix to appeal to new market segments, as might occur in international expansion. A product development growth strategy involves offering a new product or service to the firm's current target market. Finally, a diversification strategy takes place when a firm introduces a new product or service to a new customer segment. Sometimes a diversification strategy relates to the firm's current business, such as when a women's clothing manufacturer starts making and selling men's clothes, but a more risky strategy is when a firm diversifies into a completely unrelated business. Great marketing firms also employ three macro strategies to achieve their sustainable competitive advantage: customer excellence through retaining loyal customers and providing excellent customer service, operational excellence through efficient supply chain management and operations, and product excellence through branding and positioning.

Key Terms

- competitor-based pricing, 39
- control phase, 32
- cost-based pricing, 39
- customer excellence, 46
- diversification strategy, 46
- implementation phase, 32
- market development strategy, 45
- market growth rate, 42
- market penetration strategy, 45
- market positioning, 37

- market segment, 36
- market segmentation, 36
- mission statement, 33
- operational excellence, 46
- planning phase, 32
- product development strategy, 46
- product excellence, 46
- product line, 41
- relative market share, 42
- situation analysis, 35

- STP, 36
- strategic business unit (SBU), 41
- strategic marketing planning process, 32
- sustainable competitive advantage, 34
- target marketing/targeting, 37
- value-based pricing, 39

Concept Review

1. Briefly describe the activities involved at each of the three phases of the marketing planning process: (1) planning, (2) implementation, and (3) control.

2. What is meant by a mission or vision statement? What purpose does a mission statement serve and how does it influence marketing planning?

3. What does SWOT mean? List two benefits of SWOT analyses. What do you think the differences are between a SWOT analysis for the entire firm and a SWOT analysis for a product?

4. What type of information is required to conduct a SWOT analysis and where do marketers typically look for this information?

5. Why are segmentation, targeting, and positioning (STP) crucial for identifying and evaluating market opportunities? How does STP influence the development of the marketing mix—4Ps?

6. Describe the four growth strategies that firms typically pursue. Use a fast food restaurant or a grocery chain in Canada (e.g., Loblaws, Safeway, or Food Basics) to illustrate each of the four growth strategies.

7. Of the four growth strategies described in the chapter, which is the most risky? Which is the easiest to implement? Why?

8. Identify and describe three macro strategies or value disciplines that firms could use to grow their business. What other strategies could companies use to compete in the market?

9. What are the four components of the BCG Matrix? When would "stars" be preferred over "cash cows"?

10. Explain why in the BCG Matrix all products start out as questions marks and either end up as stars, cash cows, or as dogs.

Marketing Applications

1. How has WestJet Airlines created a sustainable competitive advantage?

2. Perform a SWOT analysis for your faculty, college, or university.

3. Describe the primary target markets for the Toronto Blue Jays, Victoria's Secret, and Gatorade. How do these three firms position their products and services so that they appeal to their respective target markets?

4. Pick your favourite product, service provider, or retailer. How do they add value through the implementation of the 4Ps?

5. Choose three retailers. You believe the first builds customer value through product excellence, the second through operational excellence, and the third through customer excellence. Justify your answer.

6. Visit the website of your bank and try to identify how it uses STP to develop various types of bank accounts (products) and charge different fees (price) for different types of accounts.

7. Value-based pricing strategies require that firms first determine the perceived value of their product or service from the customer's point of view and then price them accordingly. Now, consider your cell phone service provider. In your opinion, what value do you get from your cell phone plan? Do you consider it good value for money? Why?

8. You and a few of your classmates are planning to open a new spa facility near the campus of your university. Explain how you would segment the market for your services, which segment would you target, and how would you position your spa to the chosen target market.

9. Describe the pricing strategies you will use to charge customers for your products and services. What are the advantages and disadvantages of your chosen pricing strategies?

10. Make a list of the promotion strategies you would use to promote your spa starting with the most important one to the least important one. Explain the pros and cons of your top two promotion strategies.

Toolkit

SWOT ANALYSIS

Assume you are a marketing analyst for a major company and are trying to conduct a situation analysis using SWOT analysis. Use the toolkit provided at www.mcgrawhill.ca/olc/grewal, and complete the SWOT grids for each company using the appropriate items.

Net Savvy

1. Petro-Canada is considered a progressive company in terms of its values and the mission statement that drives its business. Visit its website (www.petro-canada.ca) and review the portion that discusses the company, its mission, and its values. Discuss aspects of its mission and values that might be considered progressive. Do you believe its progressive attitude creates a special position in the market that contributes to a sustainable competitive advantage?

2. More and more firms seem to be entering the dating service industry. Visit LavaLife (www.lavalife.com) and tour its website to find the types of activities and methods such companies use to help match compatible couples. Now, analyze the environment that might affect Internet dating services using a SWOT analysis.

Chapter Case Study

TORONTO FOOTBALL CLUB: REBIRTH TO EXCITEMENT[52]

The sold-out crowd of 20,148 roared at the first home game of the Toronto Football Club.[53] On April 28, 2007, fans of all ages and backgrounds united to cheer on their team as they battled the Kansas City Wizards.[54] Many were dressed from head to toe in Toronto FC gear, waving scarves of red and white. The crowd went into hysterics when Toronto player Andy Welsh had a chance to score—but was denied. Despite the high-energy of the crowd, Kansas was too tough a challenge for Toronto FC and the final score was 1–0.[55]

This was the first re-appearance of professional soccer in Canada since 1984 when the Toronto Blizzards folded after their governing league was dismantled. Despite past challenges for the sport, the future looked promising. Excitement from the recent FIFA World Cup still lingered, and soccer had become the most televised sport in Canada. At any given time, fans have the opportunity to watch one of more than 500 soccer games on cable television—more than anywhere else in the world.[56] Even veteran English soccer fans were impressed with the excitement from Toronto fans.[57]

Bringing the Toronto FC to life required a venue where games could be played. The approval of the expansion team couldn't happen until a stadium was planned. Negotiations between municipal, provincial, and federal government as well as private enterprises and the Major League Soccer (MLS) organization required immense coordination and concrete business plans. In October 2006 a tentative deal was struck delivering the funds for a new $62.8 billion stadium with five key financiers. The open-air BMO Field was completed just in time for Toronto FC's first game with a total capacity of 20,000.[58]

The portfolio of teams managed by Maple Leaf Sports Entertainment lent great expertise to the new team. Some of Canada's leading sports franchises handled by the company include the Toronto Maple Leafs and the Toronto Raptors. While success on the field can often create new fans, the company knew it wasn't all about winning. For example, the Leafs haven't won a Stanley Cup since 1967, yet year after year the strong brand provides value and consistently sells out the Air Canada Centre.

For the Toronto FC, success would ultimately be measured by continued fan enrolment, making sure that new fans joined the franchise more quickly than any that left. Even before the team set foot on the new field, the company had to form a strategy for long-term business success, which included the following objectives:

1. Build a strong brand to establish the new team
2. Over-deliver value in all interactions with fans

The first step in building the brand was to ensure the team could be embraced not only by Toronto, but also as the soccer team for Canada. Team emblems and merchandise were created with red and white colours, and a generic name with the hope that fans would begin to develop nicknames organically.[59] Later, when games began, the matches were broadcast publicly on CBC so fans could watch at home. In the community, MLSE worked hard to give back to the less fortunate by fundraising for Right to Play, a humanitarian organization that engages children and youth in regular, organized sports activities.[60]

One critical decision in providing value was ticket pricing. With a certain supply of 20,000 seats and uncertain demand, MLSE needed to be strategic. Introductory prices were set low by league standards in hopes that corporations and hard-core fans would consume many of the season tickets. Ticket prices were initially set lower at launch in an aim to over-deliver value to fans. Season tickets were $285–$1820 per game, Single tickets were $525–$1840 per game, youth tickets were $304–$874 per game, and single game group pricing as low as $19 per ticket. Toronto FC were interested in attracting fans with a deep-rooted love for the game—the ones who used to sit at home and watch soccer on Italian and other European stations and had a favourite team or player in another country—the ones who really get fired up about soccer. This coupled with news of player acquisitions and potential game schedules created a surprisingly large demand for ticket sales, and 14,000 season's ticket packages quickly sold out. Most surprising though was the diversity of fan demographics, including much unexpected interest from young career professionals.[61] The remaining 6000 seats were reserved for half-season packages and single game sales, to keep accessibility for fans from all income brackets.

Other key decisions for providing value included bringing popular teams to Toronto. High-calibre international teams like SL Benfica and Aston Villa were expensive to host, but guaranteed that many fans would be interested in watching the matches. Even if the cost of these teams exceeded the revenues they brought in for Toronto, it ensured growth of those enrolled in the franchise. Another unique element that added value was the approachability of key Toronto FC decision makers. Before the team even played its first game, public announcements invited fans to join the players and head coach Mo Johnston to discuss soccer one-on-one. Popularity of these events resulted in the addition of more dates for soccer enthusiasts to discuss the game.[62]

The season opened with a slow start for Toronto. The opener on April 7, 2007 against Chivas USA in California ended in a loss of 1-0. One loss rolled into another and another. The Toronto FC players couldn't seem to score a goal or rack up a win for four games straight. The loss couldn't silence the Toronto fans, though. Their passion shone and continued to support the team, selling out every single home game. The players' hard work and the devoted followers were finally rewarded on May 11, 2007 when the club conquered the Chicago Fire with a 3-1 win.[63] The stadium erupted with cheers and praise.

With sold out season's tickets and the proverbial monkey off their backs, the focus for MLSE becomes future success. What can the Toronto FC do to secure the successful future of their young MLS team? What will keep the fans coming back?

Questions

1. What do you think the company's mission is? Comment on the appropriateness of its mission.
2. Conduct a situation analysis for Toronto FC using SWOT. To what extent are the company's objectives appropriate for long term success?
3. What do you perceive as Toronto FC's competitive advantage? To what extent is this competitive advantage sustainable over time?
4. Who do you think is Toronto FC's target market?
5. What can Toronto FC do to keep existing fans loyal to the franchise?

CHAPTER 3

Ethics and Socially Responsible Marketing

enu Foods,[1] based in Mississauga, Ontario, is the leading North American private-label/contract manufacturer of wet pet food products sold by 17 of the top 20 retailers in North America under store labels such as Master Choice, Compliments, and Select. The company also manufactures for several national brands including Procter & Gamble's *Iams* and Colgate-Palmolive's *Hill's Pet Nutrition*. Its products are marketed nationwide by retailers such as Safeway, Wal-Mart, PetSmart, and Pet Valu.

The pet food market in North America is estimated to be worth US$10 billion. Since its establishment in 1971, Menu Foods worked diligently to establish and maintain its reputation as a quality manufacturer of pet food. It had not experienced any food safety-related problems until March 16, 2007 when it issued a voluntary recall of its "cuts and gravy" style pet food. This unfortunate event was not caused by unclean facilities, poor manufacturing processes, lax inspection, or similar problems. Rather, the recall was caused by contaminated wheat gluten obtained from one of its suppliers, ChemNutra, a Chinese company. The chemical melamine found in the wheat gluten was identified by the U.S. Food and Drug Administration (FDA) as the cause for thousands of dogs and cats to become ill or die after consuming the food.

The fallout from the recall has been enormous for Menu Foods, its shareholders and customers. Over 60 million cans and pouches of cat and dog food labelled under almost 100 brands were recalled at an estimated cost of $40 million. The company lost more than half of its value within one week—the stock price dropped from $7.40 the day before the recall to $3.90 by March 20; a whopping 52 percent decline! The recall angered loyal customers, with many openly saying that they would not buy Menu Foods again. Class action law suits on behalf of pet owners were filed in Toronto, Montreal, Chicago, and elsewhere. Pebbles, shown in the photo, is the Los Angeles–area Yorkshire terrier who died on March 22 after eating pet food suspected of containing contaminated wheat gluten.

The huge financial cost and damage to Menu Foods' reputation aside, let's examine the company's reaction to the crisis. The chief spokesperson for Menu Foods throughout the crisis was its CEO, Paul Henderson, who distributed press releases and gave press conferences to explain the ongoing situation. He admitted that the first reports of illnesses and deaths due to kidney failure came in late February but that the company delayed its recall until weeks after complaints first surfaced to confirm suspicions that cats and dogs were dying from eating its food and not for other reasons.

The company then conducted tests for industry-recognized causes of renal failure. All tests revealed no problems. Only after the company conducted its own feeding studies was an alarm raised even though none of its tests revealed a link to pet deaths. The voluntary recall was made as a proactive step with the CEO explaining that the health and well-being of pets was paramount to Menu Foods.

After the recall was announced, Menu Foods immediately advised its customers and pet owners to stop feeding their pets the recalled brands and return them to retailers for a full refund. Customers were also advised to see a veterinarian immediately if their pet was showing any signs of illness after consuming any recalled pet food. Menu Foods offered to cover the vet bills. The company updated its website, enhanced its call centre capabilities to better respond to consumer requests for information, and contacted over 200,000 customers to deal with their concerns. At the same time, retailers were contacted by mail and telephone to ensure that all recalled pet products were taken off their shelves. Henderson announced that Menu Foods was working with the FDA and commercial laboratories to identify the cause of the deaths. Menu Foods also hired a marketing communications firm to help it deal with the crisis in order to minimize the impact on the future of the company.

About a week after the recall, the FDA announced it had identified the cause of the problem. Henderson noted that Menu Foods had stopped using the wheat gluten product from ChemNutra on March 6, when they suspected a "coincidental event"—production associated with the complaints coincided with the introduction of an ingredient from a new supplier. He reassured customers that

Pebbles has become the "poster pet" for canine and feline victims of Menu Foods.

increased testing of all raw materials and finished goods meant that its other products were safe to use and would soon be returning to store shelves. And he announced that the company was working with the U.S. Congress, FDA, the Pet Food Institute, and other interested parties to prevent similar occurrences in the future.

In spite of the actions taken by Menu Foods, some critics felt that the company waited too long—almost three weeks—before it made the recall. They argued that in these situations speed, directness, and transparency are important and that the company should have acted faster. On the other hand, others believed that Menu Foods did its best given the situation. Nevertheless, the impact of the recall was explosive. Its share price took three distinct hits in the first six months, falling to just over $2. In the end the company lost an estimated 80 percent of its contract business. The long-term impact still remains to be seen. Do you think Menu Foods handled this crisis in an ethical and socially responsible manner? Do a quick search on the Internet to get an update of this story.

Which is a more important corporate objective: making a profit, or obtaining and keeping customers?[2] Although firms cannot stay in business without earning a profit, using profit as the sole guiding light for corporate action can lead to short-term decisions that may in fact cause the firm to lose customers in the long run. As we saw in the opening vignette, Menu Foods tried to maintain a strong relationship with its customers by removing close to 100 brands of its pet food from the market, foregoing profit instead of looking toward a short-term, bottom-line result.

When customers believe that they can no longer trust a company or that the company is not acting responsibly, they will no longer support it by purchasing its products or services or investing in its stock. For marketers, the firm's ability to build and maintain consumer trust by conducting ethical transactions must be of paramount importance.

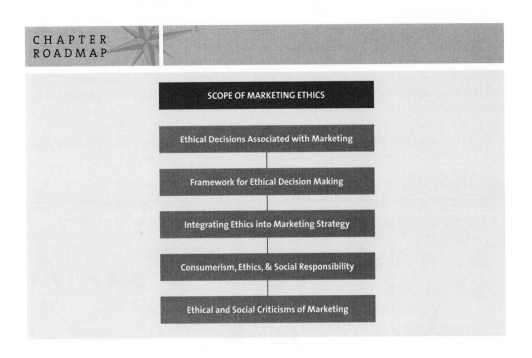

CHAPTER ROADMAP

SCOPE OF MARKETING ETHICS

Ethical Decisions Associated with Marketing

Framework for Ethical Decision Making

Integrating Ethics into Marketing Strategy

Consumerism, Ethics, & Social Responsibility

Ethical and Social Criticisms of Marketing

In this chapter, we start by examining what marketing ethics is and why behaving ethically is so important to successful marketing. We then discuss how firms can create an ethical climate among employees and how individual behaviour can affect the ability of the firm to act ethically. To help you make ethical marketing decisions, we also provide a framework for ethical decision making and then examine some ethical issues within the context of the strategic marketing planning process (from Chapter 2). Finally, we present some scenarios that highlight typical ethical challenges marketing managers often must face. Refer to the chapter roadmap to guide you through the chapter contents.

The Scope of Marketing Ethics

business ethics
Refers to a branch of ethical study that examines ethical rules and principles within a commercial context, the various moral or ethical problems that might arise in a business setting, and any special duties or obligations that apply to persons engaged in commerce.

marketing ethics
Refers to those ethical problems that are specific to the domain of marketing.

 LO **1**

Business ethics refers to a branch of ethical study that examines ethical rules and principles within a commercial context, the various moral or ethical problems that might arise in a business setting, and any special duties or obligations that apply to persons engaged in commerce.[3] The cartoon below illustrates the importance of making good ethical decisions. **Marketing ethics**, in contrast, examines those ethical problems that are specific to the domain of marketing. Because the marketing profession often is singled out among business disciplines as the root cause of a host of ethical concerns (for example, unethical advertising or the promotion of shoddy products), anyone involved in marketing activities must recognize the ethical implications of their actions. These can include societal issues, such as the sale of products or services that may damage the environment; global issues, such as the use of sweatshops; and individual consumer issues, such as deceptive advertising and the marketing of dangerous products.[4]

Ethical Issues Associated with Marketing Decisions

Unlike other business functions like accounting or finance, people in marketing interact directly with the public. Because they are so much in the public's eye, it should not be surprising that marketing and sales professionals sometimes rank poorly in ratings of the most trusted professions. In a recent Gallup survey, most professions were rated much higher than marketing—car salespeople came in last and advertising practitioners fared only slightly better but not as well as lawyers![5] (See Exhibit 3.1.) For marketers, who depend on the long-term trust of their customers, this low ranking is very disappointing.

Yet there is some good news. In a recent survey, it was found that more than two-thirds of Canadians pay attention to issues related to corporate ethics and social responsibility and that three-quarters of Canadian firms are actively engaged in key corporate social responsibility activites.[6] Many consumers remain highly skeptical of business, however, and especially of marketing. But because the marketing function interacts with so many entities outside the firm on a regular basis, it has a tremendous opportunity to build the public's trust. As many marketing executives correctly believe, creating an ethical climate that establishes the health and well-being of consumers as the firm's number one priority just makes good business sense.

Creating an Ethical Climate in the Workplace

The process of creating a strong **ethical climate** within a marketing firm (or in the marketing division of any firm) includes having a set of values that guides decision making and behaviour. Everyone within the firm must share the same understanding of these values and how they translate into the business activities of the firm, and they must share a consistent language to discuss them.

Once the values are understood, the firm must develop a set of explicit rules and implicit understandings that govern all the firm's transactions. Top management must commit to establishing an ethical climate, but employees throughout the firm also must be dedicated because the roots of ethical conflict often are the competing values of individuals. Each individual holds his or her own set of values, and sometimes those values result in conflicts between employees or even within them. For instance, a sales person may feel pressure to make a sale because her family depends on her for support, but at the same time she may feel that the product she is selling is not appropriate for a particular customer. Once the rules are in place, there must be a system of controls that rewards appropriate behaviour—that is, behaviour consistent with the firm's values—and punishes inappropriate behaviour.

Many professions, including marketing, have their own codes of ethics that firms and individuals in the profession agree to abide by. The generally accepted code in marketing, developed by the Canadian Marketing Association (see Exhibit 3.2), flows from general norms of conduct to specific values to which marketers should aspire. Each sub-area within marketing, such as marketing research, advertising, pricing, and so forth, has

ethical climate
The set of values within a marketing firm, or in the marketing division of any firm, that guides decision making and behaviour.

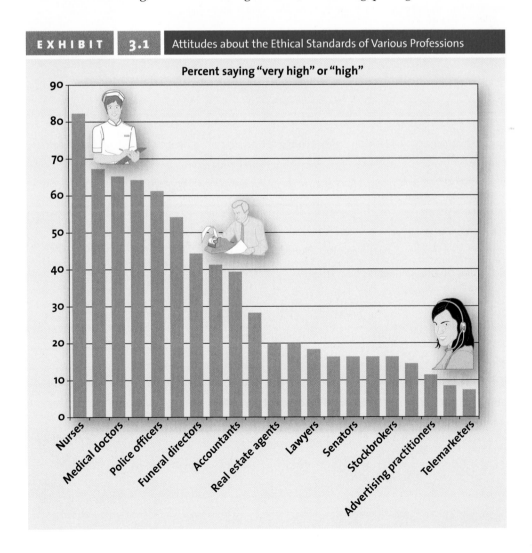

| EXHIBIT | 3.1 | Attitudes about the Ethical Standards of Various Professions |

Percent saying "very high" or "high"

EXHIBIT   3.2   Canadian Marketing Association's Code of Ethics

ETHICAL NORMS AND VALUES FOR MARKETERS

B. Purpose of CMA Code of Ethics and Standards of Practice

The CMA Code of Ethics and Standards of Practice (the "Code") is designed to establish and maintain standards for the conduct of marketing in Canada.

Marketers acknowledge that the establishment and maintenance of high standards of practice are a fundamental responsibility to the public, essential to winning and holding consumer confidence, and the foundation of a successful and independent marketing industry in Canada.

Members of the Canadian Marketing Association recognize an obligation—to the consumers and the businesses they serve, to the integrity of the discipline in which they operate and to each other—to practice to the highest standards of honesty, truth, accuracy, fairness and professionalism.

E. Responsibility for Marketing Communications

Marketers are responsible for the content of their marketing communications and the practices of their suppliers and advertising agencies when in the course of executing marketing communications on their behalf. This responsibility extends to suppliers which are not CMA members.

H. Overarching Ethical Principles

H2 Truthfulness: Marketing communications must be clear and truthful. Marketers must not knowingly make a representation to a consumer or business that is false or misleading.

Universal Marketing Practices

These practices apply regardless of industry sector, sub-discipline or marketing medium employed.

I1 Accuracy of Representation

I1.1 Marketers must not misrepresent a product, service or marketing program and must not mislead by statement or manner of demonstration or comparison.

I2 Clarity

Marketing communications must be executed in a manner that is simple and easy to understand

I5 Disguise

I5.1 Marketers must not engage in marketing communications in the guise of one purpose when the intent is a different purpose.

J. Protection of Personal Privacy

All consumer marketers must abide by the *Personal Information Protection and Electronics Documents Act* (PIPEDA), and/or applicable provincial privacy laws and the following ten Privacy Principles from the National Standard of Canada and five additional requirements as outlined in this section.

J5 Source of Personal Information

Marketers must provide consumers with the source of their personal information, upon request.

L. Special Considerations in Marketing to Teenagers

L2 Responsibility

Marketing to teenagers imposes special responsibilities on marketers. Marketers will use discretion and sensitivity in marketing to teenagers, to address the age, knowledge, sophistication and maturity of teenagers. Marketers should exercise caution that they do not take advantage of or exploit teenagers.

P. Protection of the Environment

Marketers recognize and acknowledge a continuing responsibility to manage their businesses to minimize environmental impact.

Q. Enforcement Procedures for the CMA Code of Ethics and Standards of Practice

Q1 Upon receipt of a consumer complaint regarding violation of this Code, whether regarding a member or a non-member, the Canadian Marketing Association will contact the organization and use the Association's internal mediation procedures to attempt to resolve the consumer complaint.

Source: www.the-cma.org.

its own code of ethics that deals with the specific issues that arise when conducting business in those areas.

Now we examine the role of the individuals within the firm and how they contribute to the firm's ethical climate.

The Influence of Personal Ethics

Every firm is made up of individuals, each with his or her own needs and desires. Let's look at why people may make unethical decisions and how firms can establish a process for decision making that ensures individuals choose ethical alternatives more often.

Why People Act Unethically Every individual is a product of his or her culture, upbringing, genes, and various other influences. In spite of these factors, however, people do continue to grow emotionally in their understanding of what is and is not ethical behaviour. For example, a six-year-old child might think nothing of bonking a brother on the head with a toy; but adults are expected to recognize that violence is an unethical means to interact with others. All of us vary in the way we view various situations, depending on our own level of understanding about ethical dilemmas.

It is not always clear why people act unethically and sometimes illegally, but when they do act in this manner, many people may be harmed. Here is Conrad Black facing the media during his trial.

Recent corporate scandals at companies such as Enron, WorldCom, Bre-X, Nortel Networks, and Hollinger Corp. have many people asking two simple questions: What makes people take actions that create so much harm? Are all the individuals who engaged in that behaviour just plain immoral or unethical? These questions have very complex answers.

In many cases, people must choose between conflicting outcomes. For example, a brand manager for a car company discovers, from conversations with a member of the development team, that a potentially dangerous design flaw resides in the hot new energy-efficient hybrid model that is set to go into full production shortly. The brand manager can: delay production and remedy the design flaw, which pushes production off schedule, delays revenue, and may result in layoffs and loss of a bonus, or stay on schedule, put the flawed design into production, and hope it does not result in injuries to consumers and loss of revenue for the firm. This type of dilemma with its competing outcomes occurs nearly every day in thousands of different business environments.

When asked in a survey whether they had seen any unethical behaviour among their colleagues, chief marketing officers responded that they had observed employees participating in high pressure, misleading, or deceptive sales tactics (45 percent); misrepresenting company earnings, sales, and/or revenues (35 percent); withholding or destroying information that could hurt company sales or image (32 percent); and conducting false or misleading advertising (31 percent).[7] Did all the marketers in these situations view their actions as unethical? In making marketing decisions, managers are often faced with the dilemma between doing what is beneficial for them and possibly the firm in the short run, and doing what is right and beneficial for the firm and society in the long run.

What is the "real" price? Did the manager bring the t-shirts in at an artificially high level and then immediately mark them down?

For instance, a manager might feel confident that earnings will increase in the next few months and therefore believe it benefits himself, his branch, and his employees to exaggerate current earnings just a little. Another manager might feel considerable pressure to increase sales in a retail store, so she brings in some new merchandise, marks it at an artificially high price, and then immediately puts it on sale. Consumers are deceived into thinking they are getting a good deal because they view the initial price as the "real" price. Each decision may have been justifiable at the time for the individual but also had potentially serious ethical and legal consequences for the company.

To avoid these ethical consequences, the long-term goals of the firm must be aligned with the short-term goals of each individual within the firm. In our hybrid car example, the brand manager's short-term drive to receive a bonus conflicted with the firm's long-term aim of providing consumers with safe, reliable cars. As discussed in the previous section, to align personal and corporate goals, firms need to have a strong ethical climate, explicit rules for governing a firm's transactions including a code of ethics, and a system for rewarding and punishing behaviour. In the next section, we discuss this link between ethics and social responsibility by businesses.

LO ❷

The Link between Ethics and Corporate Social Responsibility

corporate social responsibility
Refers to the voluntary actions taken by a company to address the ethical, social, and environmental impacts of its business operations and the concerns of its stakeholders.

Corporate social responsibility describes the voluntary actions taken by a company to address the ethical, social, and environmental impacts of its business operations and the concerns of its stakeholders.[8] For a company to act in a socially responsible manner, the employees within the company must also maintain high ethical standards and recognize how their individual decisions lead to the collective actions of the firm. Firms with strong ethical climates tend to be more socially responsible.

Ideally, firms should implement programs that are socially responsible, AND employees should act in an ethically responsible manner. (See Exhibit 3.3, upper left quadrant.) But being socially responsible is generally considered beyond the norms of corporate ethical behaviour. For example, a firm's employees may conduct their activities in an ethically acceptable manner but still not be considered socially responsible because their activities have little or no impact on anyone other than their closest stakeholders: their customers, employees, and stockholders (Exhibit 3.3, upper right quadrant). In this case, employees would not, for instance, be involved in volunteer activities to clean up a local park or coach the community's youth baseball league—socially responsible activities that improve the communities in which the company operates.

Likewise, some firms that are perceived as socially responsible can still take actions that are viewed as unethical (Exhibit 3.3, lower left quadrant). For instance, a firm might be considered socially responsible because it makes generous donations to charities but is simultaneously involved in questionable sales practices. For example, both Sears Canada and Suzy Shier, two very socially responsible companies were fined by the Competition Bureau for questionable business practices.[9] Suzy Shier advertised price tags on its garments indicating "regular" and "sale" prices, which did not meet the requirement for doing so because the garments had not been sold in any significant quantity nor for any reasonable period of time at the "regular" price. Ethically, how do we characterize a firm that obtains its profits through illicit actions but then donates a large percentage of those profits to charity? The worst situation, of course, is when firms behave both unethically AND in a socially unacceptable manner (Exhibit 3.3, lower right quadrant). For example, Premier Fitness Club was fined $30,000 in April 2007 for four violations of the

EXHIBIT 3.3	Ethics versus Social Responsibility	
	Socially Responsible	**Socially Irresponsible**
Ethical	Both ethical and socially responsible	Ethical firm not involved with the larger community
Unethical	Questionable firm practices, yet donates a lot to the community	Neither ethical nor socially responsible

Vision

RBC's vision for corporate responsibility is to sustain our company's long-term viability while contributing to the present and future well-being of our stakeholders. We strive to operate our business with integrity, have a positive economic impact, promote environmental sustainability, create a workplace of choice, and contribute to communities.

Principles	**Business practices**	**Economic impact**
	• Comply with laws and regulations • Manage under strong governance • Operate with ethical business practices • Provide products and access to banking services responsibly • Protect and educate consumers	• Provide strong returns to shareholders • Pay fair share of taxes • Support small business and community economic development • Foster innovation and entrepreneurship • Purchase goods and services responsibly
Workplace and employment	**Environment**	**Community**
• Respect diversity • Foster a culture of employee engagement • Provide competitive compensation and total rewards • Provide opportunities for training and development	• Lend responsibly • Leverage "green" business opportunities • Reduce operational footprint	• Provide donations with a lasting social impact • Sponsor key community initiatives • Enable employees to contribute

Employment Standards Act (ESA 2000) in connection with wages owed to former employees and in November 2007 paid a $200,000 settlement to the Competition Bureau for misleading advertising.[10] Both of these situations go against the norms of socially acceptable business practices.

Consumers and investors increasingly appear to want to purchase products and services from and invest in companies that act in socially responsible ways. According to the Conference Board of Canada, corporate social responsibility is the business issue of the 21st century. The importance of corporate social responsibility is underlined by the finding that a majority of Canadians have rewarded or punished companies for their corporate citizenship. About 55 percent said they consciously decided to buy a product or service from one company over another because they felt the company was a good corporate citizen. Fifty-two percent consciously refused to support companies they felt were not socially responsible.[11]

The Royal Bank of Canada (RBC) recognizes that it makes good business sense to adopt the principles of sustainable development, which could provide short- and long-term returns for its shareholders, clients, and employees while preserving the environment for future generations. RBC's beliefs led it to purchase 1000 megawatt hours of green power, mitigating 640 tonnes or 7 percent of greenhouse gas emissions annually. It also reduces its paper consumption by approximately 20 tonnes by providing clients the option of receiving electronic rather than paper statements.[12]

Companies earn both tangible and intangible benefits for acting in a socially desirable manner (see Adding Value 3.1); it just makes good business sense to take actions that benefit society.

Saturn's 300th playground—Cambridge Street Public School in Ottawa.

Consider, for example, companies such as Tim Hortons and Saturn Canada, which have established strong programs to support Canadian children. The Tim Hortons Children's Foundation was established in 1975 to honour Tim Horton's love for children and his desire to help those less fortunate. To support this initiative, Tim Hortons storeowners hold an annual Camp Day, donating coffee sales and collecting public donations. In 2007, the foundation raised over $8.3 million, enabling it to send 12,000 kids from economically disadvantaged homes to camp.[13]

Another program, Saturn Canada's Playground Program, is a part of the automotive company's community-comes-first philosophy of meeting the needs of its neighbours. Employees and customers are invited to help create safe, fun places for Canadian children to play. Over the years, more than 300 playgrounds have been built or restored as part of Saturn's playground program.[14] Corporations such as

Adding Value	3.1	**ALDO Fights AIDS Globally—Hear No Evil, See No Evil, and Speak No Evil** [15]

ALDO, the global fashion footwear and accessories brand, has been involved with the fight against AIDS since 1985. ALDO has teamed up with YouthAIDS (an HIV/AIDS education and prevention initiative) and 21 Hollywood celebrities to raise awareness and educate young people about HIV/AIDS. Through its well-known ALDO Fights AIDS campaign, ALDO raised over $3 million to support YouthAIDS' HIV/AIDS programs in over 60 countries. To date, the campaign has protected over 585,000 people from HIV/AIDS.

The ALDO Fights AIDS campaign targets youths because they are most at risk for contracting HIV. Each day there are 14,000 newly infected people and more than half of these are youth between the ages of 15 to 24, most of whom do not know they carry the deadly virus. ALDO and YouthAIDS are determined to reverse this trend. The campaign is a simple but powerful way of raising funds and communicating its message. The diverse group of celebrities donates their time, energy, and talent, YouthAIDS develops innovative and effective HIV/AIDS programs, and ALDO raises funds through the sale of its special edition, fashion-forward "Empowerment Tags" and "Celebrity Tote Bags." Using the theme "Hear No Evil, See No Evil, and Speak No Evil," the campaign seeks to break the silence about HIV/AIDS and educate and empower young people. The empowerment tags, which are strung on leather straps and engraved with "Hear," "See," or "Speak" on one side and the AIDS ribbon on the other, can be purchased at ALDO stores worldwide and on www.youthaids-aldo.org. The tags and tote bags retail for $5, with 100% of the net proceeds benefiting

ALDO's "Hear," "See," or "Speak" campaign raises millions of dollars for HIV/AIDS programs.

YouthAIDS. Another key piece of the campaign is a series of powerful black-and-white images of celebrities with strong messages about HIV/AIDS shot by world-renowned photographer Peter Lindbergh. The campaign is featured in over 22 countries and is seen by millions in major markets including New York, Los Angeles, San Francisco, Montreal, Toronto, London, Johannesburg, Sydney, and Singapore. By leveraging its corporate assets, ALDO has changed the lives of millions of people globally.

RBC, Tim Hortons, Saturn Canada, and many others, increasingly include socially responsible programs when planning and defining their strategic initiatives. But unfortunately, being a socially responsible corporation does not ensure that all members of the firm or all subunits within it will act ethically; rather, it means only that the firm is committing time and resources to projects in the community that may not directly relate to generating profit.

We cannot expect every member of a firm to always act ethically. However, a framework for ethical decision making can help move people to work toward common ethical goals.

A Framework for Ethical Decision Making

LO **3**

Exhibit 3.4 outlines a simple framework for ethical decision making. Let's consider each of the steps.

Step 1: Identify Issues

The first step is to identify the issue. For illustrative purposes, we'll investigate the use (or misuse) of data collected from consumers by a marketing research firm. One of the issues that might arise is the way the data are collected. For instance, are the respondents told about the real purpose of the study? Another issue questions whether the results are going to be used in a way that might mislead or even harm the public.

Step 2: Gather Information and Identify Stakeholders

In this step, the firm focuses on gathering facts that are important to the ethical issue, including all relevant legal information. To get a complete picture, the firm must also identify and discuss with the individuals and groups that have a stake in how the issue is resolved.

Stakeholders typically include the firm's current and retired employees, suppliers, the government, customer groups, stockholders, environmentalists, and members of the community in which the firm operates. Beyond these, many firms now also analyze the needs of the industry and the global community, as well as "one off" stakeholders, such as future generations.

Exhibit 3.5 illustrates a stakeholder analysis matrix for our example.[16] Notice that each stakeholder has responsibilities to the others; in this case, the marketing researcher has ethical responsibilities to the public, the research subjects, and the client company, while the client has ethical responsibilities to the researcher, the subjects, and the public. Acknowledging the interdependence of responsibilities ensures that everyone's perspective is considered in the firm's decision making.

EXHIBIT 3.4 Ethical Decision-Making Framework

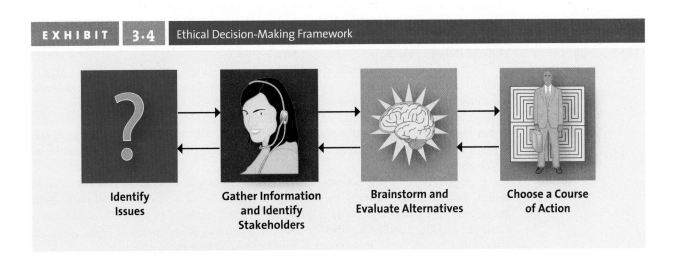

| Identify Issues | Gather Information and Identify Stakeholders | Brainstorm and Evaluate Alternatives | Choose a Course of Action |

EXHIBIT	3.5	Stakeholder Analysis Matrix for a Marketing Research Firm

Stakeholder	Stakeholders' Concerns	Result or Impact on the Stakeholder	Potential Strategies for Obtaining Support and Diminishing Impact
The Public	• Get inaccurate and biased results. • Publish false, misleading, or out of context results.	• Lose trust in marketing research professionals. • Lose trust in the marketing research process.	• Report accurate results. • Report study context and methodology. • Comply with Canadian Marketing Association's (CMA) Code of Ethics.
The Subjects/ Respondents	• Invade privacy. Privacy will be compromised if they answer the survey. • Use marketing research as a guise to sell consumers goods or services.	• Lose trust in the marketing research process. • Refuse to participate in future marketing research projects. • Provide incorrect information.	• Comply with Canadian Marketing Association's (CMA) Code of Ethics. • Protect respondent's confidential data. • Report aggregate, rather than individuals' results.
The Client	• Conduct research that was not needed. • Use an inadequate sample to generalize to their target market. • Disclose sensitive data to others.	• Reduce their spending and reliance on marketing research. • Make marketing decisions without doing research or doing inadequate research.	• Ensure that the marketing research vendor signs a confidentiality agreement. • Comply with Canadian Marketing Association's (CMA) Code of Ethics.

Step 3: Brainstorm and Evaluate Alternatives

After the marketing firm has identified the stakeholders and their issues and gathered the available data, all parties relevant to the decision should come together to brainstorm any alternative courses of action. In our example, these might include halting the market research project, making responses anonymous, instituting training on the CMA Code of Ethics for all researchers, and so forth. Management then reviews and refines these alternatives, leading to the final step.

Step 4: Choose a Course of Action

The objective of this last step is to weigh the various alternatives and choose a course of action that generates the best solution for the stakeholders using ethical practices. Management will rank the alternatives in order of preference, clearly establishing the advantages and disadvantages of each. It is also crucial to investigate any potential legal issues associated with each alternative. Of course, any illegal activity should immediately be rejected.

To choose the appropriate course of action, marketing managers will evaluate each alternative using a process something like the sample ethical decision-making evaluation questionnaire in Exhibit 3.6. The marketer's task here is to ensure that he or she has applied all relevant decision-making criteria and to assess his or her level of confidence that the decision being made meets those stated criteria. If the marketer isn't confident about the decision, he or she should reexamine the other alternatives.

By using this ethical framework, decision makers will include the relevant ethical issues, evaluate the alternatives, and choose a course of action that will help them avoid serious ethical lapses. The illustration of using traffic lights to identify and compare healthy foods described in Ethical Dilemma 3.1 on page 71 highlights the ethical challenges companies must address in marketing their products.

EXHIBIT 3.6	Ethical Decision-Making Evaluation Questionnaire					
				Confidence in Decision		
		Not Very Confident			Confident	
Criteria		**1**	**2**	**3**	**4**	**5**
1. Have I/we thought broadly about any ethical issues associated with the decision that must be made?						
2. Have I/we involved as many possible people who have a right to offer input into or have actual involvement in making this decision and action plan?						
3. Does this decision respect the rights and dignity of the stakeholders?						
4. Does this decision produce the most good and the least harm to the relevant stakeholders?						
5. Does this decision uphold relevant conventional moral rules?						
6. Can I/we live with this decision alternative?						

Source: Adapted from Kate McKone-Sweet, Danna Greenberg, and Lydia Moland, "Approaches to Ethical Decision Making," Babson College Case Development Center, 2003.

Integrating Ethics into Marketing Strategy

LO **4**

Ethical decision making is not a simple process, though it can get easier as decision makers within the firm become accustomed to thinking about the ethical implications of their actions from a strategic perspective. In this section, we examine how ethical decision making can be integrated into the strategic marketing planning process introduced in Chapter 2. Exhibit 3.7 summarizes the process, with an emphasis on identifying potential ethical pitfalls during each stage.

The questions vary at each stage of the strategic marketing planning process. For instance, in the planning stage the firm will decide what level of commitment to its ethical policies and standards it is willing to declare publicly. In the implementation stage, the tone of the questions switches from "can we?" serve the market with the firm's products or services in an ethically responsible manner to "should we?" be engaging in particular marketing practices. The key task in the control phase is to ensure that all potential ethical issues raised during the planning process have been addressed and that all employees of the firm have acted ethically. Let's take a closer look at how ethics can be integrated at each stage of the strategic marketing planning process.

Ben and Jerry's Ice Cream's mission statement is known for reflecting its strong ethical climate

Planning Phase

Marketers can introduce ethics at the beginning of the planning process simply by including ethical statements in the firm's mission or vision statements. Many Canadian firms such as RBC, Sleep Country, and others have a clearly articulated ethical and corporate social responsibility policies and programs, recognizing that profits and social responsibility go hand in hand. Some firms use mission statements that include ethical precepts for shaping the organization. The mission statements from organizations such as The Body Shop and Ben and Jerry's Ice Cream are known for reflecting strong ethical climates. Even large firms such as General Mills provide a statement of "values" that defines the priorities of the organization and its commitment to pro-

EXHIBIT 3.7 Ethical Issues and the Marketing Plan

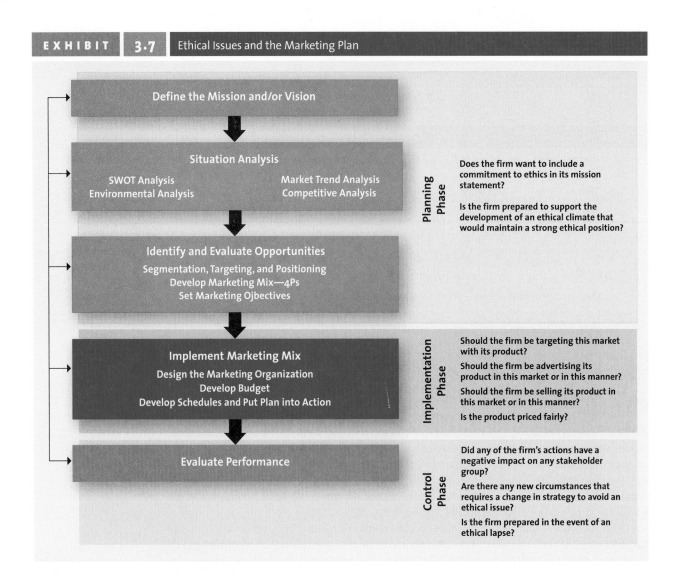

Define the Mission and/or Vision

Situation Analysis

SWOT Analysis
Environmental Analysis

Market Trend Analysis
Competitive Analysis

Planning Phase

Does the firm want to include a commitment to ethics in its mission statement?

Is the firm prepared to support the development of an ethical climate that would maintain a strong ethical position?

Identify and Evaluate Opportunities

Segmentation, Targeting, and Positioning
Develop Marketing Mix—4Ps
Set Marketing Ojbectives

Implement Marketing Mix

Design the Marketing Organization
Develop Budget
Develop Schedules and Put Plan into Action

Implementation Phase

Should the firm be targeting this market with its product?

Should the firm be advertising its product in this market or in this manner?

Should the firm be selling its product in this market or in this manner?

Is the product priced fairly?

Evaluate Performance

Control Phase

Did any of the firm's actions have a negative impact on any stakeholder group?

Are there any new circumstances that requires a change in strategy to avoid an ethical issue?

Is the firm prepared in the event of an ethical lapse?

moting those values in all that the firm does. Every year, General Mills issues a report discussing how the firm has performed against its own standards of ethical conduct.[17]

For example, General Mills recently announced it would be switching to whole grains in all its breakfast cereal lines—making it the first of the mass-marketed cereal manufacturers to do so. This switch has been applauded by nutritionists who claim it dramatically improves the dietary benefits of the cereals. General Mills made the switch not necessarily to increase consumer demand; rather, in keeping with its stated values, it improved its cereal products to improve the health of its consumers.[18]

During planning, ethical mission statements can take on another role as a means to guide a firm's SWOT analysis. Fetzer Vineyards (see Entrepreneurial Marketing 3.1 on page 72), for example, has what most of us would consider an ambitious mission statement.

General Mills is switching to whole grains in all of its breakfast cereal lines, which should improve the dietary benefits.

Implementation Phase

An important element of Fetzer's continued commitment to its mission statement is that the values stated

Obesity is fast becoming a pandemic in Canada. A study of almost 11,000 Canadians aged 20 to 56 over an eight-year period by Statistics Canada concluded that 1.1 million adult Canadians went from being overweight to obese. The data show that 63 percent of Canadians are either overweight or obese. The fight against obesity has led to a proliferation of diet plans, exercise routines, books on dieting and weight loss, and fitness gyms. This situation is not unique to Canada since both Britain and the United States are battling similar challenges. The latest salvo in this battle to buck the obesity trend is a plan by Britain's Food Standards Agency (FSA) to use traffic light labelling to identify and classify foods according to certain nutrients, for example, the amounts of fat, saturated fat, sugars, and salt they contain.

Kraft's traffic light labelling on packaging identifies fat, sugar, and salt content in its food products.

The concept is quite simple. A red light label on the food package means that the food is high in something that you should cut down on—eat occasionally or as a treat. Amber means that the food isn't high or low in the nutrient, so it's an OK choice. Green means the food is low in bad nutrients—the more green lights, the healthier the choices. According to the FSA, the traffic light labelling is intended to help consumers make informed choices that will help them get overall balance in their diet. Additionally, signpost labelling puts consumers in control and makes it easier for them to compare products, which will eventually lead them to make healthier choices. Traffic light labelling will not replace but complement the nutritional information normally found on food packages. The FSA even claims that its research over a 20-month period shows that consumers love this approach. Hence, the FSA has embarked on an aggressive advertising campaign to create awareness among consumers of traffic light labelling. The idea is that once consumers become aware of and understand it, they can ask their grocery stores to use this type of labelling. What does the food industry (grocery stores and food manufacturers) think of the idea? It's a bad idea which should be scrapped immediately and they will use whatever means necessary to kill it. One FSA official described the food industry opposition to the ideas as "the most ferocious we've ever experienced." Kellogg's director of communications said that "in principle we could never accept traffic light labelling."

The food industry prefers to use the Guideline Daily Amounts (GDAs) system developed by food manufacturers and retailers. A coalition of food companies such as Kellogg's, Tesco, Danone, Unilever, Nestlé, and Kraft are planning a major campaign to advertise their GDA system. The FSA insisted that it will recommend that the food industry put traffic light labels on their food package. Many consumer groups feel that having different labelling schemes would confuse consumers. In fact, Britain's National Heart Forum accuses the food industry of using GDA figures that are misleading so as to make their foods seem healthier than they are. For example, adult guidelines are used in products targeted to children, even though children's targets are different than those of adults. As well, GDAs for Tesco cola are calculated on the basis for 100 ml when a typical can is 330 ml.

The National Heart Forum stated that, "at a time when consumers want help to eat more healthy, some manufacturers and retailers are failing their customers by using labels that are misleading. Some even appear to be manipulating the labels to promote their products rather than inform." Shouldn't customer focused companies give consumers what they want—traffic light labelling? Is the response of the food industry ethical? Would traffic light labelling work in Canada? How might the decision-making questionnaire in Exhibit 3.6 help retailers and manufacturers in this situation?

in it remain consistent with the values of the company's primary target market. Sometimes, however, a firm's choice of target market for its products can lead to charges of unethical behaviour. In segmenting a market, the marketer determines what aspects of the product, service, and overall marketing effort are important to particular groups of consumers. Groups may be responsive to the firm's efforts and still not represent an appropriate target market; thus, the firm can serve this market but should not.

Entrepreneurial Marketing

3.1 Fetzer Vineyards' Mission Is Win–Win

The Fetzer Vineyards' mission statement begins like this:

> We Make Our Wines Responsibly. Please Drink Them Responsibly.

In 1958, Barney and Kathleen Fetzer purchased a run-down ranch in Mendocino, California, converted it into a vineyard, and created Fetzer Vineyards. Over time, the Fetzers have added other vineyards and are now the sixth-largest producer of premium wines in the United States. Fetzer Vineyards is unique in that its mission, in addition to providing the highest quality wine, is to protect the environment and benefit society.

The mission statement continues:

- We are an environmentally and socially conscious grower, producer, and marketer of wines of the highest quality and value.

- Working in harmony and with respect for the human spirit, we are committed to sharing information about the enjoyment of food and wine in a lifestyle of moderation and responsibility.

Fetzer Vineyards produces organic wines.

- We are dedicated to the continuous growth and development of our people and business.[20]

While seeking to live up to this ambitious mission statement, Fetzer has been able to identify opportunities that others without a similar focus probably would have missed. For example, Fetzer is committed to using only organic grapes in its Bonterra line, which means it contains no pesticides, no fungicides, and no fertilizers. This decision has actually translated into a cost savings for the firm because it no longer needs to purchase chemicals or supervise the level at which they are used on the grape fields.[21] Fetzer also has initiated innovative educational programs for its employees, including a very successful English as a Second Language program. Already consistent with the mission statement, these initiatives also provide win–win situations for the firm, its employees, and the community at large. Fetzer is a successful firm whose customers get healthier products, whose employees have greater access to education, and whose immediate community enjoys a healthier environment.

Procter & Gamble (P&G) teamed up with "tween" retailer Limited Too on a promotion featuring P&G's Secret Sparkle Body Spray. The promotion offered a contest open only to girls aged 7 to 14 years. But even as this group was being targeted, the Sparkle Body Spray product carried a warning label on its own packaging stating that it was to be kept out of children's reach. The spray also was being advertised in teen and tween magazines that attracted audiences under the age of 12 years.[22] Clearly, this promotion to young girls was inappropriate according to P&G's own labelling and was terminated when the Children's Advertising Review Unit of the Better Business Bureau stepped in and requested that P&G stop promoting the product to children. Had P&G considered all the potential ethical dilemmas at the implementation stage in its strategic marketing planning process, it might have avoided the issue of promoting spray to the same children it warned not to use the product. The Lesson: Even big companies with years of marketing experience and good ethical standards can make mistakes or bad decisions. Hence, marketers should always be vigilant.

The question of resource allocation in the implementation phase can also be an ethical minefield, and perhaps no business is more susceptible to charges of unethical resource allocation than the pharmaceutical industry. For example, AIDS activists claim that pharmaceutical companies are not doing enough to develop affordable drugs for underdeveloped countries to treat AIDS among their poor citizens. Some public health officials also have sounded alarm bells about the lack of research into the next generation of antibiotics, at a time when bacteria continues to become increasingly resistant to existing drugs. Critics of the pharmaceutical industry can also point to the increasing number of "lifestyle" drugs, such as those for erectile dysfunction, obesity, male-pattern baldness, nail fungus, and such, as possible causes for the lack of new treatments for serious diseases, even though the pharmaceutical companies vehemently deny that they have been transferring assets from research on treatments for life-threatening illnesses to fund lifestyle drugs.

Sourcing decisions are another problem area for some firms. Charges that they use sweatshop labour to produce their goods have been made against many well-known companies. Locating production in an underdeveloped country can make economic sense, because it allows the company to take advantage of the lower production costs offered in poorer nations, but it also opens a Pandora's Box of ethical issues, the most prominent of which deals with responsibility. Who is responsible for ensuring that the workers in the factories that produce the goods are treated fairly and paid a living wage? Recently, Coca-Cola has been facing strong opposition from students across university campuses in both Canada and the United States regarding its business practices in Columbia and elsewhere. Students from over a dozen of Canada's largest universities and colleges are pressuring their university's administration not to renew contracts with Coca-Cola.[23] Even the public faces of firms, such as Mary-Kate and Ashley Olsen and Kathy Lee Gifford, have been faulted for failing to take responsibility for the conditions in factories that produce products bearing their names. Environmental organizations have also joined the attack recently, noting that many overseas factories do not maintain the highest environmental standards.

Miriam Papps is part of the Students Against Sweatshops, a University of Waterloo group urging students to investigate companies' ethics before buying their products.

Once the strategy is implemented, controls must be in place to be certain that the firm has actually done what it has set out to do. These activities take place in the next phase of the strategic marketing planning process.

Control Phase

Like any activity in the control phase of the strategic marketing planning process, managers must be evaluated on their actions from an ethical perspective. Systems must be in place to check whether each potentially ethical issue raised in the planning process was actually successfully implemented. Systems used in the control phase must also react to change. The emergence of new technologies and new markets ensures that new ethical issues continually arise. Many firms have emergency response plans in place just in case they ever encounter a situation where their products are tampered with or there is an industrial accident at a manufacturing plant. These plans are designed to ensure the public, the employees, and all other stakeholders that the firm is aware of the potential for problems and equipped to deal with it appropriately. Firms that respond in the first few hours of a crisis with an organized plan and with compassion for those affected suffer fewer long-term negative effects on their reputation, credibility, and level of trust among consumers.[24]

Ethics thus remains a crucial component of the strategic marketing planning process and should be incorporated into all the firm's decision making. Internet Marketing 3.1 illustrates the case of Turnitin.com, a plagiarism service that has raised several important ethical questions regarding its service.

Understanding Ethics Using Scenarios

In this section, we present a series of ethical scenarios designed to assist you in developing your skills at identifying ethical issues. There is no one right answer to the dilemmas below, just as there will be no correct answers to many of the ethical situations you will face throughout your career. Instead, these scenarios can help you develop your sensitivity toward ethical issues, as well as your ethical reasoning skills.

Exhibit 3.8 provides simple tests to assist you in evaluating these scenarios. By asking yourself these simple questions, you can gauge your own ethical response.

Internet Marketing

3.1 Turnitin.com—Plagiarism Prevention or Copyright Infringement?[25]

Turnitin.com is the world's first Internet-based plagiarism detection service. It was started by a group of researchers at UC Berkeley to monitor the recycling of research papers in their large undergraduate classes. Today, it is the Internet's most widely used and trusted resource for preventing the spread of Internet plagiarism. Turnitin.com has attracted a lot of media attention in Canada and the United States for a variety of reasons. It seems that teachers and educators love it but students don't like it at all. The ease with which information can be copied and pasted or downloaded from the Internet make such a detection service appealing to educators since it helps them easily catch cheaters. According to Turnitin.com, its services are being used by thousands of institutions in over 90 countries to catch cheaters. The company claims that educators using its services notice a significant reduction in the incidence of plagiarism. These days Turnitin.com has evolved its services from just plagiarism to developing a full suite of solutions that is designed to help realize the Internet's full educational potential. The company claims that its suite of educational products help eliminate abuse of the Internet as a research tool and assists teachers and professors to become more efficient in teaching and grading students' works through features such as its peer review system, GradeBook, and GradeMark. Further, the Turnitin solution fully and easily integrates with WebCT, Blackboard, Moodle, ANGEL and other course management systems. Turnitin.com prides itself in its database of intellectual property—papers, articles, assignments, and other works—which it claims contains millions of previously submitted student papers.

Papers are also compared to databases of academic and professional content not available on the public Internet, including millions of articles and abstracts from over 10,000 journals and periodicals. Turnitin.com is a subscription based service where users can purchase a single campus licence, multiple campus licence, department licence, or individual licence, depending on their needs. The costs and benefits of each type of licence vary.

The question most critics ask is where and how does Turnitin get its database of student papers? Some students whose papers have been archived on Turnitin.com are suing the company, arguing that they own the copyright for their own work and Turnitin shouldn't have the right to use it and sell it without their explicit permission. Other critics of Turnitin argue that Canadian students should not be forced to file their work in an American database because that amounts to refusing to respect the legitimate personal security, privacy, and copyright concerns of their owners. One Canadian professor at Wilfrid Laurier University has developed a unique and successful approach to combating plagiarism that is based on educating university students in frosh week about plagiarism—what is it, how to detect it, and how to prevent it—by using fellow students to deliver the message. Initial results suggest that this program is making a difference. Should Canadian schools demand that students submit their works to Turnitin.com in order to monitor plagiarism or should they adopt approaches similar to Wilfrid Laurier University? Do you consider Turnitin.com services ethical even though students do not have the right to refuse to submit their works?

Scenario 1: Who is on the Line?

A California company, Star38, has invented a computer program that allows certain telephone users to avoid caller ID systems. For $19.99 per month and $.07 per minute, a caller can log on to the company's website, type in the number he or she wants to call, and the number he or she wants to appear on the caller ID screen of the receiving phone. For an additional fee, the caller can create a name to appear along with the phony phone number. Star38 intends to sell its service to collection agencies, private detectives, and law enforcement agencies.

Is this an ethical business plan? Would your answer be the same if Star38 sold its services to any individual who signed up?

Marvin Smith, who runs a collection agency in Winnipeg, Manitoba, is considering signing up for Star38. Should he?[26]

EXHIBIT | **3.8** | The Six Tests of Ethical Action

The Publicity Test
- Would I want to see this action that I'm about to take described on the front page of the local paper or in a national magazine?
- How would I feel about having done this if everyone were to find out all about it, including the people I love and care about the most?

The Moral Mentor Test
- What would the person I admire the most do in this situation?

The Admired Observer Test
- Would I want the person I admire most to see me doing this?
- Would I be proud of this action in the presence of a person whose life and character I really admire?
- What would make the person I admire most proud of me in this situation?

The Transparency Test
- Could I give a clear explanation for the action I'm contemplating, including an honest and transparent account of all my motives, that would satisfy a fair and dispassionate moral judge?

The Person in the Mirror Test
- Will I be able to look at myself in the mirror and respect the person I see there?

The Golden Rule Test
- Would I like to be on the receiving end of this action and all its potential consequences?
- Am I treating others the way I'd want to be treated?

Source: Tom Morris, *The Art of Achievement: Success in Business and in Life,* Fine Communications, 2003.

Scenario 2: Giving Credit Where Credit isn't Due

A catalogue retailer that carries home and children's items, such as children's furniture, clothing, and toys was seeking a way to reach a new audience and stop the declining sales and revenue trends it was suffering. A market research firm hired by the cataloguer identified a new but potentially risky market: lower-income single parents. The new market seems attractive because of the large number of single parents, but most of these homes are severely constrained in terms of their monetary resources.

The research firm proposed that the cataloguer offer a generous credit policy that would allow consumers to purchase up to $500 worth of merchandise on credit without a credit check, provided they sign up for direct payment of their credit account from a chequing account. Because these are high-risk consumers, the credit accounts would carry extremely high interest rates. The research firm believes that even with losses, enough accounts will be paid off to make the venture extremely profitable for the catalogue retailer.

Should the cataloguer pursue this new strategy?

Scenario 3: The Jeweller's Tarnished Image

Sparkle Gem Jewellers, a family-owned and operated costume jewellery manufacturing business, traditionally sold its products only to wholesalers. Recently however, Sparkle Gem was approached by the charismatic Barb Stephens, who convinced the owners to begin selling through a network of distributors she had organized. The distributors recruited individuals to host "jewellery parties" in their homes. Sparkle Gem's owners, the Billing family, has been thrilled with the revenue generated by these home parties and started making plans for the expansion of the distributor network.

However, Mrs. Billing just received a letter from a jewellery party customer, who expressed sympathy for her loss. Mrs. Billing was concerned and contacted the letter writer, who told her that Barb Stephens had come to the jewellery party at her church and told the story of Sparkle Gem. According to Barb's story, Mrs. Billing was a young widow struggling to keep her business together after her husband died on a missionary trip. The writer had purchased $200 worth of jewellery at the party and told Mrs. Billing that she hoped it helped. Mrs. Billing was stunned. She and her very much alive husband had just celebrated their 50th wedding anniversary.

What should Mrs. Billing do now?

Scenario 4: No Wonder It's So Good

Enjoy Cola is a new product produced by ABC Beverage and marketed with the slogan "Relax with Enjoy." Unlike other colas on the market, Enjoy does not contain caffeine and therefore is positioned as the perfect beverage to end the day or for a slow-paced weekend, and as a means to help consumers relax and unwind. The market response has been tremendous, and sales of Enjoy have been growing rapidly, especially among women.

ABC Beverage decided not to list on the ingredient label that Enjoy contains a small amount of alcohol because it is not required to do so by the government unless the alcohol content is more than 1 percent.

Mia Rodriquez, the marketing director for Enjoy, only recently learned that Enjoy contains small amounts of alcohol and is troubled about ABC's failure to disclose this information on the ingredients list. If the alcohol content is less than 1 percent, the beverage is not an alcoholic beverage. Currently there is not a requirement to list alcohol on the label if it is under that 1 percent. She worries about the impact of this omission on consumers who have alcohol sensitivities or those who shouldn't be consuming alcohol, such as pregnant women and recovering alcoholics.

What should Mia do? What would you do in Mia's place?

Scenario 5: Bright Baby's Bright Idea

Bartok Manufacturing produces a line of infant toys under the "Bright Baby" brand label. The Consumer Product Safety Commission (CPSC) recently issued a recall order for the Bright Baby car seat gym, a very popular product. According to the CPSC, the gym contains small parts that present a choking hazard. The CEO of Bartok Manufacturing, Bill Bartok, called an executive meeting to determine the firm's strategy in response to the recall.

Mike Henderson, Bartok's CFO, stated that the recall could cost as much as $1 million in lost revenue from the Bright Baby line. Noting that there had been no deaths or injuries from the product, just the *potential* for injury, Mike proposed that the remaining inventory of car seat gyms be sold in Mexico, where there are no rules such as the CPSC's. Sue Tyler, the marketing director for Bartok, recommended that the product be repackaged and sold in Mexico under a different brand name so that the Bright Baby name would not be associated with the product. Bill, though a bit leery of the plan, agreed to go along with it to avoid the monetary losses.

What would you have recommended to the CEO?

LO ⑤ # Consumerism, Ethics, and Social Responsibility

As shown throughout this chapter, companies that do not pay sufficient attention to ethical conduct and strong corporate responsibility are often targeted by consumer groups and other advocacy groups for negative publicity and even boycott of their products. *Consumer Reports* and *Lemon Aid* are two key publications that are dedicated to inform and protect consumers from harmful products and poor business practices by marketers. *Consumer Reports* states its mission as: *We test, inform, and protect.* **Consumerism**—a social movement aimed at protecting consumers from business practices that infringes upon their rights—and enhanced environmental awareness and activism are two key factors that have been driving the trend toward greater CSR in Canada. Today, more than 75 percent of Canadian companies have established corporate social responsibility (CSR) policies and projects that support their communities.[27]

consumerism
A social movement aimed at protecting consumers from business practices that infringe upon their rights.

Many companies have established CSR programs that enable consumers to safely dispose of the products they buy in order to minimize the harmful effects on the environment. For example, Mountain Equipment Co-op offers a recycling program where customers can bring their worn-out polyester garments back to a store to be recycled into new items[28] and Loblaw has introduced reusable shopping bags made from 100 percent recycled material.[29] Similarly, personal computer vendors such as Dell and Hewlett Packard have begun to collect used equipment for recycling. All HP laser cartridges come with instructions for returning the old cartridges. Cell phone manufacturers are also starting to promote recycling of old phones and batteries, encouraging consumers to drop them off at collection depots across the country. Even governments have gotten into the action. For example, the government of Prince Edward Island has established its Lead Acid Take Back Program[30] and imposed regulations that require retailers to charge $5 on new battery purchases unless an old battery is returned within 30 days. The program focuses on lead acid batteries; this includes all vehicle batteries (car, truck, snowmobile, motorcycle, off-road vehicle, ride-on lawnmower batteries). Similarly, the Ontario government introduced its wine and liquor bottle recycling program where consumers are given a refund when they take their empty bottles to the Beer Store for recycling rather than throwing them in their Blue Box or garbage bins.

President's Choice Greenest Shopping Bag

Consumers increasingly want to purchase products and services from companies that act in socially responsible ways. Most large companies understand this and actively promote their efforts. Guelph-based The Co-operators, a co-operatively owned insurance company, has built a reputation for caring about its member's needs and the quality of life in their communities. Safety-related events such as car-seat inspection clinics and bike safety rodeos, anti-drinking and driving initiatives, and sponsorship of the Block Parent Program of Canada are funded by its Community Economic Development program. Like many other companies with corporate social responsibility programs, The Co-operators has a focus on what's known as the triple bottom line, meaning the economic, social, and environmental sustainability of a company.[31]

A relevant question is: are consumers doing their part to promote and support various CSR programs aimed at protecting the environment? When you buy a new digital camera or cell phone, do you first consider what will happen to your old one? When you buy a popular Harry Potter book, do you care that British author J.K. Rowling, has expressed a desire for her books to be printed on forest friendly paper?[32] American consumers boycotted U.S. publishers and ordered *Harry Potter and the Half-Blood Prince* from Canadian Raincoast Books, which has been printing the books on recycled paper since 2003.[33] What do you think? Should marketers take more responsibility for educating consumers on the downside of consumption or is it up to consumers to take a proactive role?

Ethical and Social Criticisms of Marketing

The discussion so far suggests that marketers, whether fairly or unfairly, are often criticized for some of their marketing practices. This is particularly the case when marketers, whether deliberately or unintentionally, breach the trust of their customers or the general public by engaging in unethical or illegal marketing practices. For example, companies that promote their products and services to vulnerable groups such as young children, people who are addicted to alcohol, tobacco, and gambling, or seniors who are not capable of making an informed decision are often deemed unscrupulous and ethical. Although promoting products and services to these groups is not illegal, it does raise serious questions about the ethical conduct of companies. A Dolce & Gabbana ad was outlawed in several European countries on moral grounds since it reinforces stereotypes about rape and sexuality. Although there was nothing illegal about the ad, Dolce & Gabbana responded by pulling the ad. In other situations, marketers may engage in illegal practices such as bait-and-switch, deceptive advertising regarding the prices, sales, and features of their products. Although companies are often penalized when they are caught, this does little to boost customers' confidence and trust in marketers. Another criticism of marketing is the tendency to make grossly exaggerated claims about product benefits. This practice is very prevalent among marketers of beauty, anti-aging, and certain health products. Finally, marketers are criticized for making people feel that they are more valued for the products they use than for who they really are as individuals. For instance, young kids and teenagers often feel more popular or better than their friends if they wear high fashion brand name clothing, shoes, and accessories.

Learning Objectives Review

1) Explain why marketers should be concerned about ethics

2) Describe the characteristics of a socially responsible firm

3) Explain how a firm could make ethically responsible decisions

4) Discuss how ethics and social responsibility can be integrated into a firm's marketing strategy

5) Discuss how consumers foster ethical and socially responsible business practices.

1) The most important reason to worry about making ethically correct decisions is that it is simply the right thing to do! Being a part of an ethically responsible firm should be important to every employee, but it is particularly important to marketers because they interact most directly with customers and suppliers, which offers them a multitude of opportunities to address ethically challenged issues. It is often challenging to make ethically correct decisions because they can conflict with other personal or corporate objectives.

2) Individuals and firms can (and should) act ethically, but the outcome of their acts may not affect anyone other than the firm's immediate stakeholders, such as its employees, customers, and suppliers. To be socially responsible, a firm also must take actions that benefit the community in a larger sense, such as helping people who have been affected by a natural disaster like a hurricane. Socially responsible firms try to conduct their business operations in such a way as to eliminate or minimize the negative impacts on the natural environment and vulnerable groups of consumers such as children, the aged, and the disabled. They also inform consumers of potential harmful effects of their products, promote their products and services in a truthful and responsible way, and are quick to take corrective actions when deficiencies in their products and services are revealed.

3) First, firms can include ethics and social responsibility in their corporate mission. Second, they should institute policies and procedures to ensure that everyone working for the firm is acting in an ethically responsible manner. Third, firms can model their ethical policies after a well-

established code of ethics like the one provided by the Canadian Marketing Association. Fourth, when making ethically sensitive decisions, firms can utilize an ethical decision-making evaluation questionnaire, such as that described in Exhibit 3.6. Firms could also recognize and reward employees for making ethical decisions.

4) Firms can ensure that ethics and social responsibility issues are an integral part of their planning processes. These considerations even could be integrated into the firm's mission statement, as long as top management commits to supporting a strong ethical climate within the organization. When considering their marketing strategy, firms should ask not only "can we implement a certain policy?" but also "should we do it?" Firms should ensure that their marketing mix—4Ps—are held to the highest standard of social responsibility, that is, they must develop safe products, price their products fairly at all times, promote it truthfully, and distribute without undue discrimination. Finally, in the control phase, marketers must determine whether they truly have acted in an ethical and socially responsible manner. If not, they should quickly rectify the situation.

5) Consumerism—aimed at protecting consumers from business practices that infringe upon their rights—has been a major force driving the trend towards increased ethics and CSR. Unfortunately, many consumers are not making full use of the many CSR programs established by corporations and governments to foster greater environmental responsibility. Also, consumers have levelled many ethical and social criticisms of marketing, especially when marketers breach the trust of consumers with inappropriate business practices.

Key Terms

- business ethics, 60
- consumerism, 76
- corporate social responsibility, 64
- ethical climate, 61
- marketing ethics, 60

Concept Review

1. Explain the meaning of ethics and corporate social responsibility (CSR) in marketing. What are the main differences between ethics and social responsibility?

2. List four factors that determine whether an individual or firm will act ethically. List the different ways firms could demonstrate their commitment to corporate social responsibility.

3. Describe how firms can integrate ethics and corporate social responsibility into their marketing strategy.

4. Explain how the ALDO Fights AIDS campaign is adding value to the company's offering to consumers.

5. Is it possible for companies that have a code of ethics to behave unethically? Why and how might this happen?

6. What is consumerism? Name two organizations that you think are at the forefront of consumerism in Canada. How has consumerism helped foster ethical behaviour and good CSR in Canadian companies?

7. Is it ever possible to eliminate or reduce the social and ethical criticisms of marketing? What actions might help in this regard?

8. It seems that academic fraud is more prevalent because of the volume of information that is available on the Internet and the ease with which technologies can be used by students, almost undetected, to download and share various information with colleagues. Apart from using services such as Turnitin.com as described in Internet Marketing 3.1, what other measures can universities take to combat this situation?

9. Many commentators suggest that socially responsible marketing is not only a fad but can actually enhance the revenues and profitability of a firm. Explain how socially responsible marketing may contribute to improved revenues and profitability. Can you name one or two firms in Canada that explicitly make the claim that their CSR efforts have resulted in increased revenues and profitability?

10. Many marketers have developed programs to help consumers dispose of their products after use in safe and environmentally responsible ways, either through recycling or by taking the used product to a retailer or depot. Yet, tonnes of recyclable materials end up in landfills all across Canada. What factors do you think might explain the behaviours of consumers who do not dispose of their products in an environmentally friendly manner?

Marketing Applications

1. Why are marketers likely to be faced with more ethical dilemmas than members of other functional areas of the firm, like finance, accounting, or real estate?

2. Develop an argument for why a pharmaceutical firm should build and maintain an ethical climate.

3. An insurance company gives generously to charities and sponsors cancer awareness programs. It also makes it difficult for elderly consumers to make claims on policies that they have owned for years. Evaluate this company from an ethical and social responsibility perspective.

4. A Canadian clothing manufacturer is negotiating with a company in Brazil to make a new line of sweatshirt. The manufacturer wants a high quality sweatshirt at a reasonable cost but is concerned that the Brazilian workers will be underpaid and asked to work long hours in unpleasant conditions. Develop a stakeholder analysis matrix similar to that in Exhibit 3.5 to assess the impact of this decision on the relevant stakeholders.

5. Based on the clothing manufacturing scenario you developed for Question 4, provide responses to the ethical decision-making evaluation questionnaire from Exhibit 3.6. Provide a rationale for your confidence score for each question.

6. A company that makes granola and other "healthy" snacks has the following mission statement: "Our goal is to profitably sell good-tasting, healthy products and to better society." Although its products are organic, they also are relatively high in calories. The company gives a small portion of its profits to the United Way. Evaluate the mission statement.

7. The granola company described in the last question is thinking about starting an advertising campaign directed at children that would air on Saturday morning television. Explain why you think it should or should not do so.

8. A health inspector found some rodent droppings in one batch of granola made by this same company. What should the company do?

9. A women's clothing retailer has been found guilty of misleading pricing practices. In spite of significant fines, its pricing practices remain unchanged. Explain how consumerism could force the company to act more ethically in the future.

10. Consumers who were unhappy about the Canadian seal hunt expressed their displeasure by promoting an international boycott of Canadian seafood. While this action might prompt the sealing industry to change, it could also result in job losses in the fishing industry. Are consumers taking the most ethical approach?

Net Savvy

1. Perhaps no subdiscipline of marketing receives more scrutiny regarding ethical compliance than direct marketing, a form of nonstore retailing in which customers are exposed to and purchase merchandise or services through an impersonal medium such as telephone, mail, or the Internet.[34] Ethical issues in direct marketing cover a broad spectrum because this means of selling is conducted through all forms of communication. The Canadian Marketing Association (CMA) takes ethics very seriously and has several programs to ensure that its member organizations comply with its Code of Ethics. Go to the website for the Canadian Marketing Association (www.the-cma.org/) and type the word *ethics* in the search box. Discuss the results of your search. How many different ways did you find that the CMA was involved in assisting consumers and the industry to create a more ethical marketplace?

2. An increasing number of firms are stating their strong commitment to corporate social responsibility initiatives. The Corporate Social Responsibility Newswire Service keeps track of these various initiatives and posts stories on its website about what various corporations are doing. Go to www.csrwire.com/ and choose one story. Write a description of the corporation and the initiative.

Chapter Case Study

HOW BIG IS YOUR FOOTPRINT?[35]

People, communities, corporations and countries are growing more concerned about climate change. Since the Industrial Revolution alone, "concentrations of carbon dioxide have increased by 30 percent, methane by 145 percent, and nitrous oxide by 15 percent,"[36] all of which is caused by our increasingly sophisticated and mechanized lifestyle. We need the biggest, the fastest, and the strongest car, and often fail to consider the possible effects that this has caused our environment, in particular the burning of fossil fuels such as coal, oil, and natural gas to generate electricity in factories and cars. As individuals, we have cleared more land for human use in the past 100 years than in all of prior human history. This has resulted in the loss of forests and wetlands, which absorb and store greenhouse gases and naturally regulate the atmosphere. The bottom line is that climate change needs to be tackled on a global scale. Carbon dioxide lasts for hundreds of years in the atmosphere, and emissions mix easily, no matter where they're from. However, there is hope. With more global awareness of the harmful toxins we input in our environment, many people have taken the next step of making small changes that can add up in the effort to reduce the world's emissions of greenhouse gases.

In the United Kingdom, doing the right thing for the environment has become a new passion and an obsession for some. In a country famed for its fads, the latest is all about a personal question; how big is your carbon footprint? Carbon footprint is "a measure of the impact human activities have on the environment in terms of greenhouse gases produced, measured in units of carbon dioxide."[37] Things we do that pollute our environment form the measure of our individual footprint. On average, a British individual generates about six tonnes of carbon emissions each year. Britain's new national obsession has proved to be beneficial to the environment, as many people have stepped up to the challenge of reducing such staggering numbers. Whether you're in Aberdeen or Wales, carbon neutral cabs can be found just about anywhere, prepared to take you to carbon sensitive stores selling carbon friendly goods.[38] Many are seeking the help of carbon coaches who assess their home, and offer alternative suggestions to reduce their footprint.

Where less is more, the practice of offsetting has been ever growing. Carbon offsetting, which has been around for over a decade, has only recently been growing in popularity. It is another way individuals are attempting to counter damage done through the release of carbon emissions. Carbon offset schemes set prices on the amount it costs to mitigate the harm from emissions, and then invests that amount in something ecologically sound on your behalf. The basic argument for offsetting schemes is that while such tactics do not reverse the damage that has already been caused, it's one more thing we can do to improve our environment. Offsetting programs include such things as the planting of trees to absorb excess carbon, using solar power energy generation, switching to low-energy light bulbs and driving more fuel efficient cars. Saving the environment is no longer an individual concern. Many corporations too are taking up the challenge of saving the environment as part of their responsibilities to the society. Dell Computers, for instance, recently launched a *Plant a Tree for Me* program that is sending donations from computer buyers to the conservation fund. The cost is $6 for a desktop computer, figuring the trees planted for that amount will cover the pollution caused by making the computer within 70 years.[39] Airline agencies such as Travelocity have even set goals to get 10 percent of travellers to ante up.[40] Air Canada has also joined the bandwagon partnering with Zerofootprint, a tree planting offsetting organization, to give Air Canada's customers the option to purchase a carbon offset for their trip. A calculator is used to determine the amount of carbon dioxide their trip will generate and the cost to offset it. Customers are offered an easy way to pay the cost of offsetting their trip either with their ticket purchase or at another time. For example, based on the specifications of Air Canada's current aircraft, it will cost $19.20 for a customer to offset their share of carbon emissions on a return flight from Toronto to London and $12.80 for a return flight from Vancouver to Montreal.[41]

As one of the world's leading carbon offset and climate consulting business, The Carbon Neutral Company specializes in carbon offsetting programs, climate-consulting reduction strategies, and marketing services to clients. The Carbon Neutral Company sources and supplies carbon offsets from worldwide technology and forestry projects, and have purchased credits from over 170 projects covering five continents. Clients are provided with resources to help them understand their carbon risk along with a reduction, avoidance, and offset program to meet commercial objectives.[42]

In Canada, government agencies and corporations have taken environmental initiatives to reduce their carbon footprint. For example, the Ontario government is working with the Recycling Council of Canada and grocer and retail associations to reduce the use of plastic bags in Ontario by 50 percent by 2012. Ontarians will be given incentives to use reusable cloth or canvas bags for shopping. If successful, this scheme will reduce the daily use of plastic bags in Ontario from about 7 million to 3.5 million or four plastic bags per day per person. [43] The federal government environmental plan hopes to reduce the amount of emissions produced by the average consumer through tactics such as, setting fuel-efficiency standards that all cars and light trucks built after 2011 must meet. Plans of creating and improving emissions standards for items like dishwashers, dehumidifiers, hot tubs, and gas-fired furnaces are to be executed, as well, eradicating the use of incandescent light bulbs by 2012. Corporations such as Loblaw Companies Limited are creating environmentally friendly grocery bags—the President's Choice Greenest Shopping Bag—to reduce the number of plastic grocery bags that congest landfills.

With the increase in awareness about the harmful emissions we release into our environment, we should all play our roles in reducing such effects. Changes cannot be made overnight, but rather one day at a time. So next time you go to grab the car keys, think about how BIG your footprint is.

Questions

1. In your opinion, how effective are the practices of carbon offsetting in reducing the amount of emissions produced?

2. What role can consumers play in combating the amount of emissions produced? Provide three specific examples not listed in the case.

3. Suggest alternate ways (apart from offsetting schemes) that can be used to reduce our carbon footprints.

CHAPTER 4

LEARNING OBECTIVES

After studying this chapter, you should be able to:

LO **1** Explain how a firm's core competencies, customers, and partners influence its marketing strategy

LO **2** Identify and explain the factors in a firm's macroenvironment

LO **3** Understand how marketers use scenario planning to make marketing decisions and strategies

Analyzing the Marketing Environment

Although it's taken a while for consumers to accept responsibility for the planet, today it seems just about everyone has gone green. Loblaw, which first introduced environmentally friendly products 20 years ago, recently sensed consumers were ready to do more and launched reusable shopping bags made from 85 percent recycled material. At 99 cents a bag, stocks were sold out in only three weeks.[1]

Cloth and reusable bags aren't new. They've been available for decades. However, Al Gore's documentary, *An Inconvenient Truth*, had a tremendous impact on consumer attitudes, creating the perfect marketing environment to introduce a move away from plastic bags. Improved consumer awareness certainly helps, too.

Other countries had already initiated change with Ireland passing a bag tax in 2002 and South Africa banning plastic bags in 2003.[2] In 2007, San Francisco became the first city in North America to ban plastic grocery bags in grocery stores and pharmacies.[3] The small town of Leaf Rapids, in Northern Manitoba, followed this lead becoming the first municipality in Canada to ban plastic shopping bags.[4] In the spring of 2007, the Ontario government announced a partnership with the Recycling Council of Ontario to cut the number of plastic bags used in half within five years.[5] Loblaw furthered their green commit-

President's Choice Canada's Greenest Shopping Bag. Pay 99ᶜ for a bag and get 50 PC points each time you use it.

ment by opening Ontario's first bagless grocery store in Milton recently. Ontario residents are estimated to use 7 million plastic bags each day or about four per person.[6]

To encourage shoppers to use their own bags, some retailers offer incentives. Loblaw shoppers can earn 50 PC points for every reuseable bag they tote when paying with a PC Financial MasterCard or bank card. Mountain Equipment Co-op donates 5 cents to an environmental charity when customers use their own bags. And with such a shift in the marketing environment, many marketers are rethinking how they sell products and services.

A Marketing Environment Analysis Framework

As the opening vignette of this chapter suggests, marketers have become more aware of recent changes in what their customers want with regard to environmentally friendly programs and products and have adapted their product and service offerings accordingly to meet those needs. By paying close attention to customer needs and continuously monitoring the environment in which a firm operates, a good marketer can identify potential opportunities. Many marketers get their ideas for new products or services from monitoring and studying the marketing environment, as demonstrated in the case of Simply Audiobooks at the end of this chapter. Analyzing the marketing environment also helps marketers assess their continued strengths and value of their products and services or any weaknesses resulting from changes in the marketing environment.

Our chapter roadmap shows how companies analyze their marketing environment starting with the framework. At the heart of the analysis is, as always, the consumer. Consumers may be influenced directly by the immediate actions of the focal

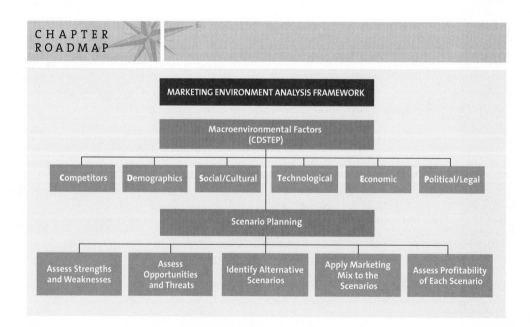

company, the company's competitors, and the corporate partners that work with the firm to make and supply products and services to consumers. The firm, and therefore consumers indirectly, is influenced by the macroenvironment, which includes influences such as competitors and demographics, as well as social and cultural, technological, economic, and political and legal factors. We'll discuss each of these components in detail in this chapter and suggest how they interrelate.

The consumer is the centre of all marketing efforts. One of the goals of value-based marketing is to provide greater value to consumers than competitors offer. This provision requires that the marketing firm looks at the entire business process from a consumer's point of view.[7] Consumers' needs and wants, as well as their ability to purchase, are affected by a host of factors that change and evolve over time. Firms use a variety of tools to keep track of their competitors' activities and communicate with their corporate partners. Furthermore, they monitor their macroenvironment to determine how such factors influence consumers and how they should respond to them. Sometimes, a firm can even anticipate trends.

For example, pharmaceutical companies have done an excellent job of monitoring consumers and responding to their needs and market trends. On the basis of observing and monitoring the aging baby boomer generation of consumers, they have made and marketed drugs to lower cholesterol, improve sexual performance, slow down aging, and stem hair loss. What's next on the list? Imagine the needs and wants of these consumers, and the answer—a new array of "lifestyle drugs, including those that improve intelligence, with the first step being memory enhancers"[8]—may appear obvious.

Successfully Leveraging Company Capabilities

LO **1**

In the firm's microenvironment, the first factor that affects the consumer is the firm itself. Successful marketing firms focus their efforts on satisfying customer needs that match their core competencies. The primary strength of Apple, for instance, rests in the design, manufacture, distribution, and promotion of Macintosh computers, but it has successfully leveraged its core competency in the digital audio player arena with its iPod after recognizing a trend among consumers for sleek but functional portable music players, which can become part of their personal accessory. Marketers can use an analysis of the external environment, like the SWOT analysis described in Chapter 2, to categorize an opportunity as either attractive or unattractive and, if it appears attractive, to assess it relative to the firm's existing competencies.

Building Relationships with Corporate Partners

The next factor that affects decision making is the firm's corporate partners. Few firms operate in isolation. For example, automobile manufacturers collaborate with suppliers of sheet metal, tire manufacturers, component part makers, unions, transport companies, and dealerships to produce and market their automobiles successfully. Even firms like Dell, which makes its own computers and sells them to customers, must purchase components, consulting services, advertising, and transportation from others. Those parties that work along with the focal firm can be viewed as its corporate partners.

Let's consider the role these partners play and how they work together with the firm to create one efficient manufacturing system. Companies such as Toyota, Dell, General Motors, and Ford have long realized the importance of their various corporate partners. Toyota, like many automobile companies, engages in a **just-in-time (JIT) inventory system** that keeps inventories of automobile components to a minimum because the company only orders them from suppliers to arrive just in time to be used. But even the best JIT systems face unforeseen situations, as Adding Value 4.1 illustrates.

just-in-time (JIT) inventory systems Inventory management systems designed to deliver less merchandise on a more frequent basis than traditional inventory systems; the firm gets the merchandise "just in time" for it to be used in the manufacture of another product; also known as *quick response (QR) systems* in retailing.

Adding Value | 4.1 | Toyota and a Little Help from Its Friends

Early one morning, a factory that supplied brake fluid proportioning valves to Toyota's 20 automobile plants in Japan was engulfed in flames.[9] Scheduled to produce 14,000 cars per day with JIT inventories that used a window of about four hours, Toyota faced a crippling dilemma that could have shut down its production for weeks. Acting quickly, Toyota acquired the blueprints for the valve, improvised tooling systems, and set up makeshift production lines within hours of the fire. The key to success was intense, rapid coordination across a diverse group of suppliers and other supply chain partners.

As a testament to Toyota's strong relationships with its suppliers and partners, four days later, 36 of Toyota's suppliers, aided by more than 150 other subcontractors, had created nearly 50 separate lines producing small batches of the brake valves. Thanks to their corporate partners, Toyota's production lines started up again and a disaster was averted.

At this Toyota plant in Georgetown, Kentucky, parts and materials arrive just in time for production.

LO ② Macroenvironmental Factors

macroenvironmental factors
Aspects of the external environment that affect a company's business, such as competitors, demographics, social/cultural trends, technological advancements, economic conditions, and political/regulatory factors (CDSTEP).

In addition to understanding their customers, the company itself, and their corporate partners, marketers must also understand the **macroenvironmental factors** that operate in the external environment, namely, the **c**ompetitors, **d**emographics, **s**ocial and cultural issues, **t**echnological advances, **e**conomic situation, and **p**olitical/regulatory environment, or CDSTEP, as shown in Exhibit 4.1. As discussed in Entrepreneurial Marketing 4.1, having a thorough understanding of these factors can be critical to a company's success.

| EXHIBIT | 4.1 | The Macroenvironment |

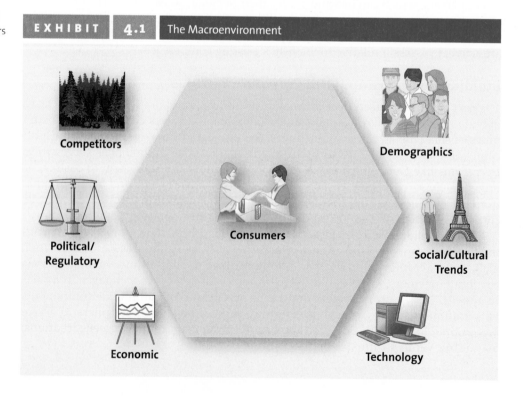

4.1 Dussault Custom Ink—Meshing Rock and Hip Hop![10]

Meet Jason Dussault of Vancouver, the owner and creative mind behind Dussault Custom Ink, a unique and forward thinking, high-end street wear clothing line. Dussault grew up listening to everything from hip hop to rock, spending late nights watching horror movies and sketching art. He always wanted to get into fashion in a unique way by bringing his artwork, love of rock music and fashion together in a way that people would really want to wear the clothes. But more than this, he wanted to "create a place where people could come in and say, "Wow! I really like that design but I wish I could tweak it a bit!" Now they can, at Dussault Custom Ink in Vancouver. As Jason puts it, "whatever you want, we will custom make it for you."

Since its launch in 2005, Dussault Ink has met with remarkable success. It is the top selling line at Leone's 12 Boutique, a Vancouver fashion institution that caters to those with only the most discerning tastes. Most clothing lines want (or pay) a celebrity to wear their clothing but celebrities seem to naturally gravitate towards the Dussault Custom Ink line of hoodies, jeans, and

Celebrities, such as legendary rockstar Gene Simmons, have gravitated toward Dussault Custom Ink clothing.

t-shirts. Why? According to Jason, it's because they have that authentic "rock star" look that lots of people want. According to one fashionista, the clothes are eclectic and gritty on the outside and velour-lined on the inside. They reflect a bad-boy street culture and are cross-stitched with playful contradiction. Some of his more notable customers include Pamela Anderson, Jessica Alba, Nicole and Lionel Richie, Kid Rock, Gene Simmons, and The Black Eyed Peas.

Dussault Custom Ink made its U.S. debut at the 2007 Magic Convention in Las Vegas, the place where you find the hottest and newest trends amidst the "who's who" of the fashion industry. In his first appearance at the convention, he walked away with the award for Most Innovative Booth Design. Since his success at Magic, Jason Dussault has become a celebrity in his own right and is much sought after by TV, radio stations, and online magazines for interviews, like Extra, CityTV, Much Music, e-talk Daily and All Hip Hop.com. He now has a store in Las Vegas and has teamed up with Gene Simmons to launch the MoneyBag line.

Critical understanding of the very competitive fashion market has helped Dussault succeed. A competitive analysis showed him a niche that other competitors weren't satisfying. After an analysis of the economic health and

demographic trends of the youth in the area, Dussault went to work. Attracting style-savvy consumers with disposable income is key. His secret for success is attention to detail and making each pair of Dussault jeans like a limited art edition. They are signed, dated, and numbered in sequence on the inside back pocket. For example, Dussault Edition One is limited to only 1500 pairs of unique jeans. With no two pairs the same you will hold onto your Dussault jeans forever. The reason Jason Dussault has included so few is because it forces him to stay on top of fashion and what is going on in pop culture and to set new trends. Edition One collection is still in demand although the 1500 pairs are sold out.

When you come to Dussault Ink you can pick your own embroidery thread for the Booty Pocket from the limitless colour combinations in the jean book. The Booty Pocket design is Dussault's signature. Dussault Jeans have a hidden secret—on every jean there is a piece of vintage fabric sewn into the inside belt line. Soft against the skin this piece complements the Booty Pocket embroidery colours. The only person who knows your hidden secret is you. Jason describes his Dussault Custom Ink Hoodie this way: "we use Chinese Silk to line the Hoodies and embroidered patches to embellish the back. We also love the smell of bleach, so we use it to affect the material and create a unique splash of texture. The handpainted sections gracefully age and crack, with the dignity of a silver screen star." He claims that Dussault jeans and hoodies can be worn anywhere, to every occasion, any day or night of the week. And Dussault line of fashion wear is made in Canada.

What is the source of his inspiration? It comes from the horror flicks he loved to watch like *The Outsiders, The Warriors*, and *House of a 1000 Corpses*. In addition, he is surrounded by a team of fashionistas, rockers, tattoo artists, rappers, and graphic designers. He has drawn inspiration from many different people to create the perfect blend of magic, nostalgia, and future all in one line.

This inspiration comes at a price. Hoodies for men retail for $630 and women's for $430. Custom designs could cost about $2500. Jeans retail for $270 and t-shirts for $84. Needless to say, an in-depth understanding of macroenvironmental factors such as competitors, economics, and demographics is essential to Dussault's success.

Competitors

It is critical that marketers understand their firm's competitors, including their strengths, weaknesses, and likely reactions to the marketing activities their own firm undertakes. Predicting new product launches and anticipating marketing campaigns helps firms remain competitive by allowing them to develop similar products or conversely, communicate with consumers in new and different ways than their rivals. It can also serve to highlight new market trends or reinforce ones already understood.

competitive intelligence (CI) Used by firms to collect and synthesize information about their position with respect to their rivals; enables companies to anticipate market developments rather than merely react to them.

Firms use **competitive intelligence (CI)** to collect and synthesize information about their position with respect to their rivals. In this way, CI, or business intelligence (BI) as it is often called, enables companies to anticipate market developments rather than merely react to them.[11] In Canada, an Ipsos Reid study conducted on behalf of the Marketing Research and Intelligence Association reports that while overall awareness of various business intelligence components ranges from medium to high among BI decision-makers and business executives, existing BI activities are fairly limited in practice, and require more resources and attention in the future. The study found that less than half of BI decision-makers say that their company is involved in various BI initiatives.[12]

The strategies to gather CI can range from simply sending a retail employee to a competitive store to check merchandise, prices, and foot traffic to more involved methods, such as:

- Reviewing public materials including websites, press releases, industry journals, annual reports, subscription databases, permit applications, patent applications, and tradeshows.
- Interviewing customers, suppliers, partners, or former employees.
- Analyzing a rival's marketing tactics, distribution practices, pricing, and hiring needs.

These more sophisticated CI strategies are implicitly obvious in the modern razor market. Although men and women have been shaving for thousands of years, it wasn't until 1901 that anyone tried to sell a disposable, thin piece of metal sharp enough to shave hair. In its first year of production, the Gillette Safety Razor Company, as it was known then, sold 50 razor sets. The following year it sold 12 million—obviously, the company anticipated a need well. Today, American men spend almost $2 billion annually on razors and blades. In 2003, Gillette, the Canadian market leader with a 76-percent market share, changed the landscape again by launching

Who copied whom? Gillette and Schick introduced similar razors almost simultaneously.

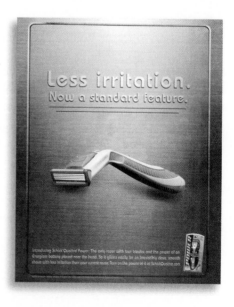

the enormously successful Mach3, a three-blade razor.[13] Not to be outdone, Energizer Holding, the owner of Schick, introduced the Quattro razor, the world's first four-blade razor in 2003. The resulting battle for the title of "best razor" and for market share has resulted in a costly promotional and pricing battle. Razors that normally retail for up to $10 are being given away for free, and coupons for the corresponding razor blades appear everywhere.[14] In situations such as this, it becomes critical for firms like Gillette and Schick to keep close tabs on each other's activities using CI techniques. If Schick hadn't paid attention to the release of the Mach3, it may never have introduced the Quattro.

Although CI is widely regarded as a necessary function in today's world, certain methods of obtaining information have come under ethical and legal scrutiny. Take for example Gillette's case against Schick. Within hours of the press release introducing the Quattro in August 2003, Gillette had filed a patent infringement lawsuit claiming that the Quattro violates its Mach3 system's technology patent.[15] To file the suit so quickly, Gillette must have known about the impending launch well before Schick announced it, but how the company found out forms the core of the ethical question. According to the court papers that Gillette filed two weeks later, "a company engineer shared the results of scientific tests conducted on 10 Quattro cartridges obtained by the company." Schick quickly questioned how Gillette obtained the cartridges prior to their commercial release in an ethically appropriate manner. But Schick's ethical argument apparently held little sway, as the U.S. Appeals Court ruled on April 29, 2005, that Gillette's patent could extend to four or even five blades and was not limited to the number of blades currently installed in the Mach3.[16] Armed with this ruling, Gillette and Schick continue to compete head-to-head. Gillette released the manual and battery operated Fusion, one-upping the Quattro with five blades. Schick, in anticipation of the Fusion, created three stylized versions of the Quattro, the Schick Quattro Chrome, Midnight, and Power to appeal to shavers on a more aesthetic level.[17]

Another misuse of competitive intelligence can be seen in Air Canada's case against WestJet. A lawsuit centred on allegations that WestJet management used the password of a former Air Canada employee to access a website maintained by Air Canada to download confidential information. WestJet countersued by alleging Air Canada used private investigators to search through recycling material at the home of a WestJet executive. WestJet later accepted full responsibility for such misconduct, which was unethical and unacceptable. Even worse, this practice was undertaken with the knowledge and discretion of the highest management levels of WestJet and was not halted until discovered by Air Canada. WestJet apologized to its competitor and Air Canada top executive Robert Milton. WestJet will also pay $5 million to Air Canada for its investigation and litigation costs, and make a $10-million donation to children's charities in the names of both airlines.[18]

Demographics

Demographics indicate the countable characteristics of human populations and segments, especially those used to identify consumer markets. Typical demographics such as age—which includes generational cohorts—gender, race, and income are readily available from market research firms like ACNielsen, Ipsos Reid, Leger Marketing, and Statistics Canada. For instance, ACNielsen collects information about television viewership and sells it to networks and potential advertisers. The networks then use this information to set their advertising fees, whereas advertisers use it to choose the best shows on which to advertise. For a show popular among the desirable 18- to 35-year-old viewing segment, a network can charge the highest fees. But advertisers also might want to know whether a show is more popular with women than men or with urban or rural viewers. Demographics thus provide an easily understood "snapshot" of the typical consumer in a specific target market.

demographics
Countable characteristics of human populations and segments, especially those used to identify consumer markets such as age, gender, income, and education.

Marketers position their products and services differently depending on which generational cohort they are targeting.

In the next few sections, we examine how firms use some such demographics to assess their customers' needs and therefore position themselves to deliver better value for those customers' desired merchandise and services.

generational cohort
A group of people of the same generation—typically have similar purchase behaviours because they have shared experiences and are in the same stage of life.

Generational Cohorts A group of people of the same generation, **generational cohorts** have similar purchase behaviours because they have shared experiences and are in the same stage of life. For instance, baby boomers (people born after World War II, 1946–1964) and generation Xers (people born between 1965 and 1976) both gravitate toward products and services that foster a casual lifestyle; however, they tend to do so for different reasons.[19] The aging baby boomers, who grew up with jeans and khakis and brought casual dressing into the business arena, are often trying to maintain their youth. Gen Xers, in contrast, typically wear jeans and khakis because they are less impressed with the symbols of conspicuous consumption that their parents seem to have embraced. Although there are many ways to cut the generational pie, we discuss five major groups, as listed in Exhibit 4.2.

seniors
North America's fastest-growing generational cohort; people aged 63 and older.

Seniors Seniors make up Canada's fastest-growing group.[20] Between 1981 and 2005, the number of **seniors** in Canada grew from 2.4 million to 4.2 million. Their share of the population increased from 9.6 percent to 13.1 percent. According to Statistics Canada, between 2006 and 2026 the number of seniors is projected to increase from 4.3 million to 8 million and will comprise 21.2 percent of the Canadian population. But just because they are a large segment, are they necessarily an important market segment for marketers to pursue? They're more likely to complain, need special attention, and take time browsing before making a purchase compared with younger groups. However, they generally have time to shop and money to spend.

In the past, seniors were very conservative with their savings because they wanted something to pass on to their children. But that attitude appears to be changing. Perhaps you have seen the bumper sticker: "I am spending my children's inheritance"?[21] Older people seem to be buying goods and services at the same pace as younger generations. What do they spend their money on? Travel, second homes, luxury cars, electronic equipment, investments, home furnishings, and clothing are frequent purchases. For example, computer use among seniors jumped seven-fold from 3.4 percent in 1997 to 23 percent in 2004. Internet use among seniors more than doubled within three years—from 11 percent in 2000 to 28 percent in 2003.[22]

EXHIBIT 4.2	Generational Cohorts				
Generational Cohort	Tweens	Gen Y	Gen X	Baby Boomers	Seniors
Range of Birth Years	1996-2000	1977-1995	1965-1976	1946-1964	Before 1946
Age in 2008	8-12	13-31	32-43	44-62	63 and older

Specifically, seniors tend to like "made in Canada" items and recognizable brand names (but generally not designer labels), value, quality, and classic styles. They're typically loyal and willing to spend but are extremely quality conscious and demand hassle-free shopping, particularly in terms of convenient locations. Because most mature customers don't need the basics, they would prefer to buy a few high-quality items rather than a larger number of low-quality items.[23]

Baby Boomers   After World War II, the birth rate in Canada rose sharply, resulting in a group known as the **baby boomers**, the 10 million Canadians born between 1946 and 1964. Although the baby boomer generation spans 20 years, experts agree that its members share several traits that set them apart from those born before World War II. First, they are individualistic. Second, leisure time represents a high priority for them. Third, they believe that they will always be able to take care of themselves, partly evinced by their feeling of economic security, even though they are a little careless about the way they spend their money. Fourth, they have an obsession with maintaining their youth. Fifth and finally, they will always love rock 'n roll.

baby boomers
Generational cohort of people born after World War II, between 1946 and 1964.

The baby boomers' quest for youth, in both attitude and appearance, provides a constantly growing market. For instance, boomers spend $30 billion per year on anti-aging products and therefore have reenergized businesses ranging from food and cosmetics to pharmaceuticals and biotechnology.[24] Salon services used to be a purely feminine domain, but with boomers turning 50 at the rate of seven per minute, providers are recognizing the potential of positioning themselves as being in the rejuvenation business. In ways that previous generations would have considered unthinkable, men have begun pampering themselves with salon services such as manicures, facials, and pedicures. Indeed, many boomers, including older baby boomers, are driving sports cars and going on adventure-based vacations.

Generation X   The next group, **generation X** (Xers), includes those born between 1965 and 1976 and represents some 5 million Canadians or about 14 percent of the Canadian population.[25] Vastly unlike their baby boomer parents, Xers are the first generation of latchkey children—those who grew up in homes in which both parents worked. These young adults, having grown up in times of economic recession are more likely than previous generations to be unemployed, carry higher debt loads, more likely to live

generation X
Generational cohort of people born between 1965 and 1976.

No matter how old they get, baby boomers will always love rock n' roll.

longer with their parents compared to baby boomers at their age who couldn't wait to get out, travel the world, and move far away from their parents.[26]

Gen Xers possess considerable spending power because they tend to wait to get married and buy houses later in life. They're much less interested in shopping than their parents but far more cynical, which tends to make them astute consumers. They demand convenience and tend to be less likely to believe advertising claims or what salespeople tell them. Marketing to Gen Xers is difficult, but word-of-mouth advertising from people they know and trust can give marketers the credibility needed to market to this cohort. Because of their experience as children of working parents who had little time to shop, Xers developed shopping savvy at an early age and knew how to make shopping decisions by the time they were teenagers. As a result, they grew more knowledgeable about products and more risk averse than other generational cohorts. Finally, Gen Xers are much less interested in status products than older generations, not because they can't afford luxury brands, but because they just don't see the point. Many companies such as Harley-Davidson and the Starwood Hotel chain have developed products targeted specifically to Gen Xers.

generation Y
Generational cohort of people born between 1977 and 1995; biggest cohort since the original postwar baby boom.

Multitasking is no big deal for Gen Y.

Generation Y   Born between 1977 and 1995, they represent about 7 million Canadians or about 20 percent of the population.[27] This group also varies the most in age, ranging from teenagers to young adults who have their own families.[28] **Generation Y**, also called the "echo boom" generation, grew up in a more media-intensive and brand-conscious era than their parents. Thus, they are more skeptical about what they hear in the media, which makes marketing to this group even more challenging. If a Gen Y member believes the sell is "too hard," (s)he won't buy. Regardless of where they live, they watch an hour less of television than an average household, accept the use of personal Internet time at work, and expect a healthy option at fast-food restaurants.[29] Gen Yers are Internet- and technology-savvy and love digital electronics such as cell phones, digital music players, digital cameras, and videogames. In the next 10 years or so, many Gen Yers will be starting new families and would be prime targets for homes and durable household products such as appliances, furniture, and gardening equipment and tools. Most experts believe the reason for the similarities among this

EXHIBIT **4.3**	Generational Cohort Comparisons	
Baby Boomers	**Generation X**	**Generation Y**
Diversity as a cause	Accept diversity	Celebrate diversity
Idealistic	Pragmatic/cynical	Optimistic/realistic
Mass movement	Self-reliant/individualistic	Self-inventive/individualistic
Conform to the rules	Reject rules	Rewrite the rules
Killer job	Killer life	Killer lifestyle
Became institutions	Mistrust institutions	Irrelevance of institutions
TV	PC	Internet
Have technology	Use technology	Assume technology
Task-technology	Multitask	Multitask fast
Ozzie and Harriet	Latch-key kids	Nurtured
Other boomers	Friend-not family	Friends-family

Source: "Gen Y and the future of mall retailing," *American Demographics*, December 2002 24. (11) p. J1.

broad group is, quite simply, the Internet. To appeal to the first generation tied together by a worldwide media Web, market-savvy firms can spot trends in one country and market them in others. Many firms such as Abercrombie and Fitch, Tommy Hilfiger, DKNY, American Eagle, and Hard Candy specifically target Gen Yers.

Exhibit 4.3 on the previous page provides some interesting comparisons between baby boomers and their children—generation X and generation Y.

Tweens   Tweens—not quite teenagers, but not young children either—sit in beTWEEN. The importance of **tweens** to marketers stems from their immense buying power, estimated at $2.9 billion annually in Canada and $260 billion annually in the United States.[30] In China, this trend appears even more significant; as a result of China's 1979 one-child policy for families, parents and grandparents are intensely focused on the needs of their only child and spend nearly 40 percent of their household income on their "little emperor or empress."[31] These kids may look and act like children, but they sometimes surprise their parents and marketers by consuming like teenagers. Like their big brothers and sisters in generation Y, much of their market power comes from tweens' strong influence on family purchases.

Watch out for tweens. They are fast, multitasking, technology-savvy, and easily bored.

tweens
Generational cohort of people born between 1996 and 2000; not quite teenagers, but not young children either: in beTWEEN.

In Canada, tweens spend their money mainly on food and drinks, electronics (gaming consoles and games, digital music players, cell phones, and computers) and clothing. They learn about new products mainly from TV shows and friends. Although they enjoy the attention they get from marketers, they are not an easy group to market to. Three in four Canadian tweens make shopping decisions jointly with their parents.[32] Tweens are also known as speeders, because they do everything at lightning speed.[33] The first generation born after the emergence of the Internet, technology has no novelty for them. They communicate with friends via instant messenger, talk on a cell phone, and watch television simultaneously. Marketers reach this group primarily through television and the Internet, but because many parents limit television viewing times, the Internet provides a huge media opportunity. Marketers must be careful with this cohort though; once they get bored, tweens are gone, off doing something else. So firms need to engage them quickly and with sincerity. Many companies such as McCain Foods with its frozen pizza and Sony with its PlayStation have developed innovative media campaigns to market to this group.

And what do tweens like? In the food industry, they lean toward products like Heinz's green ketchup and Yoplait's GoGURT. For toys and clothing, they have made Build-A-Bear Workshop, Claire's, and Limited Too immensely popular. However, because they have little of their own money, tweens tend to be value conscious, which makes them key targets for retailers such as The Gap, Wal-Mart, and Old Navy.

Income   The median income of Canadian families in 2006 was approximately $58,300.[34] Canadians may be classified into distinct groups based on their income and other factors like background, education, and occupation—upper class, middle class, working class (or low income earners), and under classs (at or below poverty). *Upper class* consumers are very affluent and their spending patterns are not influenced by economic conditions. They have high discretionary incomes and tend to purchase luxury items. Their family income is usually in excess of $70,000. They are more likely to be highly educated and work in managerial and executive roles. *Middle class* families earn between $30,000 to $70,000 with the majority tending towards the higher end of this scale. They can afford a good life most of the time. They tend to be care-

This water cannon electric boat from Hammacher Schlemmer is a rechargeable electric watercraft powerful enough for riders to navigate lakes and ponds for up to six hours per charge, and it has a built-in motorized water cannon that can continuously spray a stream of water up to 10 metres. It can be yours for only $1995.95.

ful about their spending and are often value-conscious. *Working class* or low income families earn between $20,000 and $30,000, barely sufficient income to cover their basic needs. *Under class* families earn less than $20,000 and often rely on assistance to cover their basic needs. According to the 2000 Census, the richest 30 percent of the households in Canada received 49.2 percent of all household income, whereas the bottom 30 percent accounted for merely 14.3 percent.[35] The increase in wealthy families may be due to the maturing of the general population, the increase in dual-income households, and the higher overall level of education. Family income distribution in Canada varies by province, education level, gender, and profession. This broad range in incomes creates marketing opportunities at both the high and low ends of the market.

Although some marketers choose to target only affluent population segments, others have had great success delivering value to middle- and low-income earners. Consider, for example, the toy water cannon electric boat presented by the specialty retailer Hammacher Schlemmer versus the mass appeal of Wal-Mart's everyday low prices (EDLP), which has made it the world's largest toy retailer. Toy buyers at Wal-Mart are looking for inexpensive products; those at Hammacher Schlemmer go to great lengths to find exclusive, one-of-a-kind products, like a radio-controlled paraglider.

Another aspect of the income demographic relates to the concept of value. Why are customers searching for this value more today than in recent decades? During the first three decades after World War II, most families experienced real income growth, but between 1980 and 2005, that growth began to idle. Between 1980 and 2005, median earnings among the top 20 percent of earners increased by 16.4 percent. In contrast, median earnings among those in the bottom 20 percent fell 20.6 percent. Median earnings among those in the middle 20 percent stagnated, increasing by only 0.1 percent.[36] In 2005, the richest families on average earned about 10 times more than the poorest families!

Education Studies show that higher levels of education lead to better jobs and higher incomes.[37] Moreover, average annual earnings are higher for those with degrees than for those without. For example, 60 percent of Canadians with just a high school education level earn less than $20,000 per year and 60 percent with university degrees earn more than $80,000. In 2000, Canadians with a university degree earned on average over $72,000, those with a college diploma earned on average less than $50,000, and those with less than a high school education earned on average about $36,000.[38]

For some products, marketers can combine education level with other data like occupation and income and obtain pretty accurate predictions of purchase behaviour. For instance, a full-time college or university student with a part-time job may have relatively little personal income but will spend his or her disposable dollars differently than would a high school graduate who works in a factory and earns a similar income. College and university students tend to be engaged in playing sports and going to clubs, whereas the high school graduate more likely watches sports and goes to bars. Marketers are therefore quite cognizant of the interaction among education, income, and occupation.

Since women are such an important segment of their customers, Rona, the giant home improvement chain, has designed their stores with women in mind.

Gender Years ago, gender roles appeared clear, but those male/female roles have been blurred. This shift in attitude and behaviour affects the way many firms design and promote their products and services. For example, more firms are careful about gender neutrality in positioning their products and, furthermore, attempt to transcend gender boundaries whenever they can.

From cars to copiers, sweaters to sweeteners, women make the majority of purchasing decisions and then influence most of the remainder. For instance, despite the traditional view that hardware stores appeal mostly to men, women shoppers are so important to Rona, the home improvement chain, that the stores have been designed with women in mind.[39] Furthermore, women now head more than 20 percent of Canadian households.[40] Clearly, the working women's segment is a large, complex, and lucrative market.

But that doesn't mean marketers have forgotten about men. The days of commercials that show Mom alone with the kids are over. To reflect changing family roles, commercials for most children's gear now include Dad interacting with the kids and being involved in purchase decisions. Although the gap is narrowing, men still earn more money than women—in 2005 women entering the workforce (aged 25 to 29) earned 15 percent less than men or 85 cents for each dollar earned by men.[41]

Women are no longer the only family member doing the grocery shopping.

Social and Cultural Trends

Various social and cultural trends shape consumer values in Canada, the United States, and around the world. Social concerns include greener consumers, privacy concerns, and time-poor society. Cultural influences include ethnicity, cultural differences, and subcultures, (See Exhibit 4.4.)

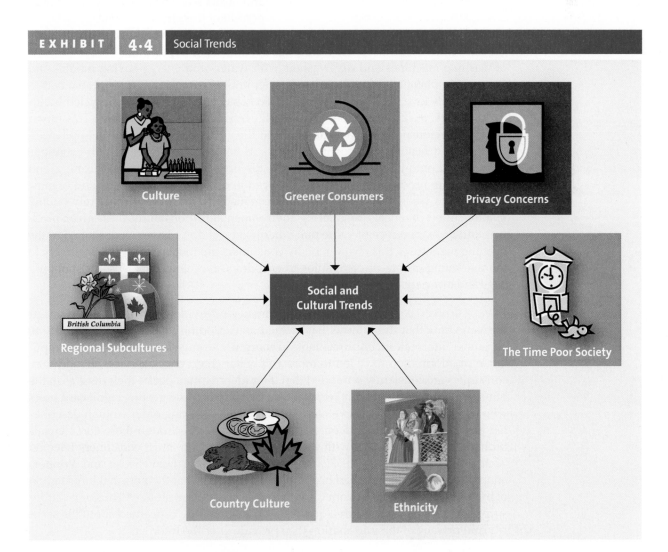

EXHIBIT 4.4   Social Trends

Culture

Greener Consumers

Privacy Concerns

Regional Subcultures

Social and Cultural Trends

The Time Poor Society

Country Culture

Ethnicity

green marketing
Involves a strategic effort by firms to supply customers with environmentally friendly merchandise.

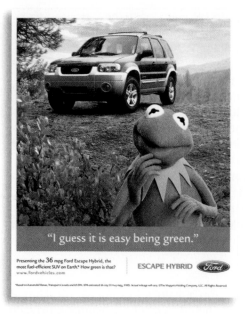

"I guess it is easy being green."

Presenting the 36 mpg Ford Escape Hybrid, the most fuel-efficient SUV on Earth.* How green is that? www.fordvehicles.com   ESCAPE HYBRID   *Ford*

Based on Automobile News, Transport Canada and US EPA. EPA estimated 36 city/31 hwy mpg, FWD. Actual mileage will vary. ©The Muppets Holding Company, LLC. All Rights Reserved.

Spawned by environmental concerns and rising gas prices, consumers are demanding more fuel-efficient hybrid cars.

Greener Consumers[42]   Green marketing involves a strategic effort by firms to supply customers with environmentally friendly merchandise. Although this "green" trend is not new, it is growing. Many consumers, concerned about everything from the purity of air and water to the safety of beef and salmon, believe that each person can make a difference in the environment. A study found that more than 90 percent of Canadians feel that individuals can take action to reduce air pollution. For example, more than half of Canadian households now recycle their soft drink bottles, cardboard boxes, and newspapers. In many cities across Canada, the use of pesticides on lawns is banned and many consumers are trying alternative, environmentally friendly lawn care treatment. Despite these positive efforts, much more needs to be done since, for example, Ontario residents and businesses combined recycled only 25 percent of their trash in 2006.[43]

The demand for green-oriented products has been a boon to the firms that supply them. For instance, marketers encourage consumers to replace their older versions of washing machines and dishwashers with water- and energy-saving models and to invest in phosphate-free laundry powder and mercury-free, rechargeable batteries. Canada's love affair with recycling also has created markets for recycled building products, packaging, paper goods, and even sweaters and sneakers. This raised energy consciousness similarly has spurred the growth of more efficient appliances, lighting, and heating and cooling systems in homes and offices. Health-conscious consumers continue to fuel the markets for organic foods, natural cleaning and personal care products, air- and water-filtration devices, bottled water, and organic fertilizers, as well as integrated pest management systems that do not rely on any manufactured chemicals. By offering environmental responsibility, these green products add an extra ounce of value that other products don't have. As described in the opening vignette of this chapter, many consumers are responding very positively to the marketing efforts of companies to encourage recycling and reuse of shopping bags and a variety of other products.

Privacy Concerns   More and more consumers worldwide sense a loss of privacy. At the same time that the Internet has created an exploding volcano of accessibility to consumer information, improvements in computer storage facilities and the manipulation of information have led to more and better credit check services. In addition, consumers are constantly reminded that their identity may not be their own, as in the humourous series of Citibank commercials that depict unsuspecting credit card users who have had their identities stolen. In one, a sweet-looking older woman describes her new pickup truck in a deep, masculine voiceover. Although these commercials promote a new credit card with identity theft protection, most consumers have no such protection. In early 2007, the parent company of HomeSense and Winners announced that its system had been compromised and that the personal information of millions of customers in both Canada and U.S. had been stolen.[44] Thus, it is hardly surprising that more than three-quarters of Canadians are concerned about the security and privacy of the information they provide over the Internet.[45]

The Time-Poor Society Reaching a target market has always been a major challenge, but it is made even more complicated by several trends that increase the difficulty of grabbing those markets' attention. First, in the majority of families, both parents work, and the kids are busier than ever. For example, on average, Canadians worked 8.9 hours during a typical workday in 2005 but 25 percent said they devote more than 10 hours a day to their work. Thus, Canadians have less time for leisure and to spend with family. In 2005 Canadian workers spent about 200 hours less with family than they did two decades earlier.[46]

Second, consumers have many more choices about the ways they might spend their dwindling leisure hours. When *Leave It to Beaver* ruled television, most viewers could choose from only three or four channels, plus a handful of AM radio stations. Today, they have hundreds of each. Competing with television and radio are DVDs, MP3 players, cell phones, pagers, personal computers, and the Internet. Third, many consumers attempt to cope with their lack of leisure time by multitasking—watching television or listening to music while talking on the telephone or doing homework. Their divided attention simply cannot focus as well on advertisements that appear in those media.

When Leave It To Beaver *was on TV in the 1950s, viewers had only three or four channels from which to choose.*

Marketers must respond to the challenge of getting consumers' attention by adjusting, such as by moving their advertising expenditures from traditional venues like print media to movie screens, fortune cookies, baggage claim conveyor belts, billboards, and ads in airports and on taxis, buses, and mass transport vehicles.[47] Retailers are doing their part by making their products available to customers whenever and wherever they want. For instance, retailers like Sears Canada and The Bay are becoming full-fledged multichannel retailers that offer stores, catalogues, and Internet shopping options. Others, like Loeb, Shopper's Drug Mart and Wal-Mart, have extended their hours of operation so that their customers can shop during hours that they aren't working. In addition, automated processes like self-checkout lanes and electronic kiosks speed the shopping process and provide customers with product and ordering information.

Self-checkout lanes speed the shopping process, but do they improve customer service?

Ethnicity Statistics Canada data show that the ethnic composition of Canada has been changing over the last two decades and will continue to change in the next decade. Current research shows that 1 out of every 5 Canadians was not born here, counting for nearly 70 percent of Canada's population growth. If this trend continues Canada's population growth will be attributed exclusively to immigration by 2030.[48] The two fastest-growing groups are the Chinese (from Hong Kong, mainland China, and Taiwan) and South Asians (from India, Pakistan, Sri Lanka, and Bangladesh). It is estimated that ethnic groups or visible minorities will make up about 8.5 million or 23 percent of Canada's population by 2017 because of immigration and increasing birth rates among various ethnic groups.[49] Many new immigrants choose to settle in Montreal, Toronto, or Vancouver, however areas like Calgary, Edmonton, Winnipeg, and London are growing in popularity. These groups of South Asians and Chinese are typically young, educated, and wealthy. Currently, more than a quarter of all visible minorities in Canada are under 14 years, thus, they are likely to have considerable influence over the economy in the future. South Asians are the largest ethnic group in Ontario.[50]

From a marketer's perspective, the growing number of ethnic groups or visible minorities represents both a challenge and huge marketing opportunity. The chal-

Canada is a mosaic, made up of people from every corner of the world.

lenge is for marketers to understand the culture, value, and spending patterns of the various groups and figure out the best way to communicate with them and serve them. A recent *Marketing Magazine* report describes the way Canada's big banks typically approach the burgeoning Chinese and South Asian markets as "everyone is doing the same thing." The creative director of Fat Free Communications, a Toronto ad agency, argues that most bank advertising employs "very superficial ways of acknowledging the community, which a lot of people in the community actually find irritating." Chris Bhang, a vice president at Allard Johnson Direct, admonishes marketers to "be colloquial, be creative but be relevant." In terms of the marketing opportunity, it is estimated that ethnic groups spend over $42 billion on retail goods and services and the average Chinese household spends $63,500 per year compared to the Canadian average of $58,500. In general, ethnic Canadians spend more than their white counterparts on big-ticket items such as cars, clothing, and home furnishings. Many also have an affinity for brand-name products because they equate them with quality.[51]

The Royal Bank of Canada (RBC) realizing that much of its future growth will come from ethnic markets has recently developed new products, several targeted to these customers. For example, a bank's standard credit scoring is based on residence history, work experience, and credit history, but obviously somebody new to Canada isn't going to bring that Canadian history with them. So, RBC developed its secured Visa option, which allows people to more easily build credit history. RBC also launched Internet-based account opening so newcomers can deposit their assets and establish a relationship with RBC before arriving in Canada. The "Welcome to Canada" site at www.rbc.com/canada is in English and Chinese. The company even ran TV ads that show an immigrant couple and their young daughter as they navigate their way through open houses, car lots, and job interviews. The family then meets with an RBC banker, who has the same ethnicity, and the ads sign off with "it's another way RBC is putting us first." Five ads were created using the same storyline, but with different talent and language in each, including English, Punjabi, Hindi, Mandarin, and Cantonese.[52]

Despite these efforts, RBC and some of the other big Canadian banks have some catching up to do. According to Solutions Research Group's *Diversity in Canada* study, TD Canada Trust has the largest share of the ethnic market. The bank scored highest among South Asians, with 43 percent naming it as their primary financial institution—higher than CIBC, RBC, and Scotiabank combined. TD Canada Trust was also number one with Chinese Canadians, with a 29 percent share.[53]

culture
The set of values, guiding beliefs, understandings, and ways of doing things shared by members of a society; exists on two levels: visible artifacts (e.g., behaviour, dress, symbols, physical settings, ceremonies) and underlying values (thought processes, beliefs, and assumptions).

country culture
Entails easy-to-spot visible nuances that are particular to a country, such as dress, symbols, ceremonies, language, colours, and food preferences, and more subtle aspects, which are trickier to identify.

Culture   We broadly define **culture** as the shared meanings, beliefs, morals, values, and customs of a group of people.[54] Transmitted by words, literature, and institutions, culture gets passed down from generation to generation and learned over time. You participate in many cultures: Your family has a cultural heritage; your school or workplace also shares its own common culture. In a broader sense, you also participate in the cultural aspects of the town and country in which you live. The challenge for marketers is to determine whether their culture can serve as a relevant identifier for a particular group of people who would be interested in purchasing the firm's products and services. Our various cultures influence what, why, how, where, and when we buy. Two dimensions of culture that marketers must take into account as they develop their marketing strategies are the culture of the country and that of a region within a country.

Country Culture   The visible nuances of a **country's culture**, such as artifacts, behaviour, dress, symbols, physical settings, ceremonies, language differences, colours and tastes, and food preferences, are easy to spot. But the subtle aspects of culture generally are trickier to identify and navigate. Volkswagen has successfully marketed its Turbo Diesel Injection in Canada to a young, environmentally friendly, slightly offbeat subsegment of the population by providing subtle cultural cues in its promotions with its "1000 kms per tank" campaigns.

Regional Subcultures   The region in which people live in a particular country affects the way they react to different cultural rituals, or even how they refer to a particular product category. As a resident of Quebec, you are 25 percent less likely to buy a hot prepared meal or reheatable meal than a resident of Ontario. This is attributed to Quebec women's desire to cook and be involved in their family's lives. As well, Quebec consumers are less price sensitive when grocery shopping than residents of Ontario. In Quebec the most popular stores are IGA and Metro, as compared with No Frills and Food Basics in Ontario.[55] These kinds of differences can be the insight that helps a marketer make a strong connection with a consumer, rather than communicating the same way to all Canadians.

Another example of a regional subcultural difference is how we refer to our beverages. For instance, 37 percent of Canadians refer to carbonated beverages as "soda," whereas another 40 percent call it "pop," and an additional 17 percent call any such beverage a "Coke," even when it is Pepsi. Eat lunch in British Columbia, and you'll have the best luck ordering a pop, but if you head to Quebec for dinner, you'd better order your "soft-drink." Imagine the difficulty these firms have in developing promotional materials that transcend these regional boundaries.[56]

To find and develop methods to make life easier for many diverse consumers in a time-poor society, marketers often rely on technology, another macroenvironmental factor and the topic of the next section.

Technological Advances

Technological advances have accelerated greatly during the past few decades, improving the value of both products and services. Since the birth of the first generation Y baby in 1977, the world has realized the commercial successes of cellular telephones, MP3 players, Internet access, personal digital assistants (PDAs), WiFi, and digital cameras. Flat-screen and high-definition televisions, as well as video on demand, have begun to change the way we view television, and their impact is only expected to increase in the next few years. Exhibit 4.5 showcases some of the recent major achievements in technology. On the retail side, firms are able to track an item from the moment it was manufactured, through the distribution system, to the retail store, and into the hands of the final consumer using radio frequency identification device (RFID) chips that are affixed to the merchandise. Because they are able to determine exactly how much of each product is at a point in the supply chain, retailers also can communicate with their suppliers—probably over the Internet—and collaboratively plan to meet their

technological advances Technological changes that have greatly contributed to the improvement of the value of both products and services in the past few decades.

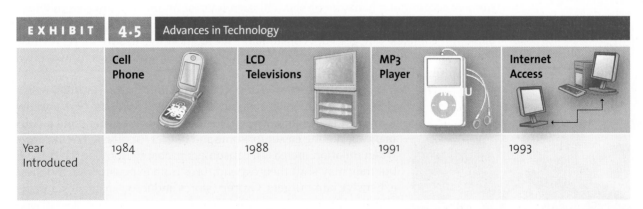

EXHIBIT 4.5	Advances in Technology			
	Cell Phone	**LCD Televisions**	**MP3 Player**	**Internet Access**
Year Introduced	1984	1988	1991	1993

Source: Dan Nystedt, "U.S. marks new cell phone record in 2005," *InfoWorld* April 07, 2006, www.infoworld.com (accessed August 25, 2006); "World Fact Book," www.cia.gov (accessed August 25, 2006); Ilse Jurrien, "Consumer electronic sales record in 2006," www.letsgodigital.org January 5, 2006 (accessed August 25, 2006).

inventory needs. In 2005, Canadians spent on average close to $900 per household on cell phones and other wireless devices, digital cameras, and Internet access—well over $3 billion in total.[57] See Internet Marketing 4.1.

Other areas of technical advance include how we bring media into our homes. Popular movies are now on blu-ray disc or high definition digital video disc (HD DVD) and the latest sportscasts are available via high definition television (HDTV). Gaming consoles have come a long way as well to include Sony's Playstation 3 and Microsoft's Xbox 360, with faster central processing units and stronger graphics, both capable of online networking and data and photo storage. The Nintendo Wii has also revolutionized home gaming with its hand-held remote that detects movement in three directions. Rather than sitting on the couch to play a game with friends you can now literally get into the action and swing to hit a homerun or jump up to volley a ball. All three consoles feature 3D perspectives that greatly increase the challenge of the games. Not only do all of these technological advances offer higher quality products, they also create buzz and a sense of novelty for their industries, and new opportunities to communicate with consumers. Different technology adoption levels also matter to marketers when communicating a new product or using a new media type.

Economic Situation

economic situation
Economic changes that affect the way consumers buy merchandise and spend money, both in a marketer's home country and abroad; see *inflation, foreign currency fluctuations*, and *interest rates*.

inflation
Refers to the persistent increase in the prices of goods and services.

foreign currency fluctuations
Changes in the value of a country's currency relative to the currency of another country; can influence consumer spending.

interest rates
These represent the cost of borrowing money.

Tourists from other countries flock to the U.S. to shop because the value of the dollar is low compared to their own currency.

Marketers monitor the general **economic situation**, both in their home country and abroad, because it affects the way consumers buy merchandise and spend money. Some major factors that influence the state of an economy include the rate of inflation, foreign currency exchange rates, and interest rates.

Inflation refers to the persistent increase in the prices of goods and services.[58] Increasing prices cause the purchasing power of the dollar to decline; in other words, the dollar buys less than it used to.

In a similar fashion, **foreign currency fluctuations** can influence consumer spending. For instance, on January 21, 2007 one Canadian dollar was worth $0.6179 U.S., the lowest exchange rate ever between these two currencies. By the beginning of May 2007, the value of the Canadian dollar relative to the U.S. dollar increased to $0.9071.[59] It hit parity in early September then rose as high as $1.10 before returning close to parity in the late fall. As the value of the Canadian dollar increases compared with the U.S. dollar, merchandise made in Canada and exported to the U.S. becomes more costly to Americans, whereas products made in the United States cost less for Canadian consumers.

Finally, **interest rates** represent the cost of borrowing money. For example, when customers borrow money from a bank, they agree to pay back the loan, plus the interest that accrues. The interest, in effect, is the cost to the customers or the fee the bank charges those customers for borrowing the money. Likewise, if a customer opens a savings account at a bank, he or she will earn interest on the amount saved, which means the interest becomes the fee the consumer gets for "loaning" the money to the bank. If the interest rate goes up, consumers have an incentive to save more, because they earn more for loaning the bank their money; when interest rates go down, however, consumers generally borrow more.

How do these three important economic factors—inflation, foreign currency fluctuations, and interest rates—affect a firm's ability to market goods and services? Shifts in the three economic factors make marketing easier for some and harder for others. For instance, when inflation increases, consumers probably don't buy less food, but they may shift their expenditures from expensive steaks to less expensive hamburgers. Grocery stores and inexpensive restaurants win, but expensive restaurants lose. Consumers also buy less discretionary merchandise. For instance, the sale of expensive jewellery, fancy cars, and extravagant vacations will decrease, but curiously,

| Internet Marketing | **4.1** | **Voice over Internet Protocol—A World of Possibilities?**[60] |

In the beginning, there was the landline telephone, which we have all used. Then came cell phones—most of us have one. Now there's Voice over Internet Protocol (VoIP) phones, which only a few of us have. Just about 10 percent of Canadian households have VoIP/cable phones, although the trend is increasing. Basically, VoIP is the family of technologies that allow the Internet to be used for voice applications, such as telephony, voice instant messaging, and teleconferencing. PC to Phone VoIP refers to using your Internet-connected computer to make calls to conventional phones around the world. So, what's the big deal about VoIP?

For starters, VoIP phone saves users money on calls, moves, and changes. Because your telephone number is associated with your IP phone rather than your physical location, you can take your phone with you when you move offices or homes and simply plug it into a VoIP-ready jack and you are ready to make calls—no delays! IP phones can access the company phone directory, allowing users to find the most up-to-date phone numbers right on their phones. Further, when you travel you can take your VoIP phone with you while keeping the same number and have no break in service. You can even take it on vacation with you! And, if you don't want to take your phone when you travel, you can use "soft phone" which is software that turns your laptop into a phone that can simulate your work phone. For example, when someone calls your work number, your laptop rings making it seem like you are sitting at your desk. You can even do call transfer or conference calls just as if you were in the office—all this from anywhere in the world! Not only can you be easily reached but there are no surprise charges for the people who call you since it is just like they are calling your office (or home) phone. But replacing the company's traditional switchboard with IP telephony just to cut cost is the most basic use of the VoIP—it can deliver much more.

VoIP not only creates significant functionality but could increase productivity and foster collaboration because it can converge voice, video, and data communication on to one single channel. The capability of VoIP phones to work seamlessly with the range of wireless devices including PDAs provides even more functionality. According to John Arnold, founder of J Arnold & Associates, a Toronto-based consultancy specializing in VoIP, the ultimate goal for VoIP will be advanced integration with back-end business systems. He uses the example of supply chain management, in which a back-end inventory system notices stocks have dropped below a certain threshold. The system could arrange a conference call between the supplier and the vendor, and dial them both after checking their availability status. They could even use their VoIP-enabled phones to share access to an image viewer to review product designs. Although such developments may be far into the future, they open a world of possibilities for new business opportunities. But how is it being used today in Canada?

British Columbia School District 67 has revolutionized the school communications network in Okanagan Skaha. The School District, which has just 5 IT staff and 19 buildings to manage, worked with the City of Penticton to run its own fibre optic cable along local telephone poles, escaping the high costs of leasing unused fibre from local telecommunications firms. Danny Francisco, IT manager for the district, said the project is now handling VoIP-based calls for both the district and the city. The school is also busy hooking the VoIP network up to the loudspeaker system so that someone can pick up an IP handset and page, or have it display text messages on your computer.

Legal firm Fraser Milner Casgrain, installed nearly 700 VoIP phones in its Toronto offices alone in order to deliver extra functionality to its lawyers. These units serve up a full intranet-based telephone directory on the handsets screen. The company also put IP phones into lawyers' homes, making it easy to re-route calls to them when they are not in the office. Voicemails arrive as e-mails, which makes it easier to keep up-to-date on client communication. The company has also been using its network for video conferencing. Future developments will include the ability to deliver client notes to IP phone using incoming caller ID information, so lawyers can access relevant client information when they pick up their phones.

The National Ballet School's Toronto location has a state-of-the-art network which supports IP telephony. The School envisions delivering student schedules and cafeteria menus to IP phone screens. The school also installed softphones on its laptops so staff travelling for auditions can stay on the school's telephone network.

the sale of low-cost luxuries, such as personal care products and home entertainment, tends to increase. It appears that, instead of rewarding themselves with a new Lexus or a health spa vacation, consumers buy a few cosmetics and rent a movie.

Another, perhaps unexpected, result of the strengthening of the Canadian dollar compared with the U.S. dollar is that it might allow Canadian manufacturers to win and U.S. makers to lose, i.e., imports of raw material from the U.S. are cheaper. During such inflationary times, "made in America" claims become more important in the U.S., which means that Canadian manufacturers and U.S. retailers that specialize in Canadian merchandise must decide whether they should attempt to maintain their profit margins or accept a lower price to keep their U.S. customer base. Finally, when interest rates go up, consumers tend to save more, which makes it easier for financial institutions to sell products like mutual funds. But at the same time, people have less incentive to buy discretionary products and services because they are enticed by the higher interest rates to save. Therefore, though a financial institution's investment division might benefit, its mortgage department might suffer because people don't buy houses when they feel they are not getting good value for the money they must spend and borrow.

Political/Regulatory Environment

political/regulatory environment
Comprises political parties, government organizations, and legislation and laws that promote or inhibit trade and marketing activities.

The **political/regulatory environment** comprises political parties, government organizations, and legislation and laws. Organizations must fully understand and comply with any legislation regarding fair competition, consumer protection, or industry-specific regulation. Since the turn of the century, the government has enacted laws that promote both fair trade and competition by prohibiting the formation of monopolies or alliances that would damage a competitive marketplace, fostering fair pricing practices for all suppliers and consumers, and promoting free trade agreements among foreign nations.

Legislation also has been enacted to protect consumers in a variety of ways. First, regulations require manufacturers to abstain from false or misleading advertising practices that might mislead consumers, such as claims that a medication can cure a disease when in fact it causes other health risks. Second, manufacturers are required to identify and remove any harmful or hazardous materials (e.g., asbestos) that might place a consumer at risk. Third, organizations must adhere to fair and reasonable business practices when they communicate with consumers. For example, they must employ reasonable debt collection methods and disclose any finance charges; as we note in Ethical Dilemma 4.1 with Payday loans on page 104.

Last but not least, the government enacts laws focused on specific industries. These laws may be geared toward increasing competition, such as the deregulation of the telephone and energy industries. Or they may be in response to current events, such as the laws passed following the terrorist attacks of September 11, 2001, when the U.S. government ushered through the Air Transportation Safety and System Stabilization Act to ensure that airlines could remain in business. A short list of some of the most significant legislation affecting marketing interests appears in Exhibits 4.6 and 4.7.

EXHIBIT 4.6 Major Federal Legislation to Protect Competition and Consumers	
Access to Information Act Bankruptcy Act	Standards Council of Canada Act
Bills of Exchange Broadcasting Act Canada Agricultural Product Standards Act Canada Corporations Act Canada Small Business Financing Act	Small Loans Act Textile Labelling Act Trade-Marks Act True Labelling Act Weight and Measures Act Winding-up Act
Canada Dairy Products Act Canada Human Rights Act **Competition Act** Consumer Packaging and Labelling Act Copyright Act Criminal Code Department of Consumer and Corporate Affairs Electricity and Gas Inspection Act	Food and Drugs Act Income Tax Act Interest Act Investment Canada Act Lobbyist Registration Act Patent Act Official Languages Act Personal Information Protection and Electronic Documents Act (PIPEDA) Privacy Act

EXHIBIT	4.7	Marketing Practices Covered by the Competition Act

Law	Description
Price	
Price fixing	Sellers conspire to set the price of a product, usually higher than it would be in a free market.
Price discrimination	Charging different prices to different (competing) buyers for goods of the same quality and of the same quantity
Predatory pricing	Pricing that is intended to drive competitors out of the market or keep competitors from entering the market—usually low prices
Resale price maintenance	Manufacturers or channel members try to influence the price at which the product is sold to subsequent purchasers
Bid Rigging	Sellers collude to set prices in response to bids or quotations for products
Promotion	
Misleading advertising	All types of advertising about a product or service that are false or misleading
Bait-and-switch	Sellers try to attract customers to their stores by offering a low price on a product (bait) but once in the store try to persuade customer to buy a higher-priced item (switch)
Referral selling	Incentives offered to consumers to provide the names of other potential consumers
Distribution (Place)	
Refusal to deal	A seller refuses to sell products or services to legitimate buyers
Exclusive dealing	A seller refuses to sell to other channel members unless that member agrees to buy exclusively from that particular seller
Pyramid selling	Schemes where salespersons are paid to recruit other salespeople. and each new salesperson pays for the right to recruit other salespeople, with some of that money going to earlier recruiters. Participants are often asked to buy specific quantity of goods or are knowingly sold unreasonable quantities of goods and are not allowed to return the goods on commercially reasonable terms.

Scenario Planning

LO **3**

Now that we have examined how the macroenvironment impacts a company, its competition, its corporate partners, and, most important, the way these entities market to customers, let's look at a process called **scenario planning** that integrates this information as a means to understand the potential outcomes of different applications of a firm's marketing mix.[61] By using the strategy elements that we discussed in Chapter 2, scenario planning enables a firm to predict, monitor, and adapt to the ever-changing future. All firms face strategic challenges in dealing with the opportunities and uncertainties of the marketplace due to the changes in cultural, demographic, social, technological, economic, and political forces. Thus, anticipating and interpreting change, and leveraging resources to address those changes, are key to developing winning value-based strategies.[62]

As an outcome, a scenario planning exercise like the one outlined in Exhibit 4.8 on page 105, develops a set of possible conclusions based on the plausible alternatives that a firm might pursue. By looking at alternative courses of action and imagining what might happen if they were taken, managers can better prepare for the future. To demonstrate how scenario planning works, we investigate a scenario plan for Loblaw to determine which strategic directions the giant grocer might pursue in coming years.

scenario planning
A process that integrates macroenvironmental information in an attempt to understand the potential outcomes of different applications of a firm's marketing mix; enables a firm to predict, monitor, and adapt to the ever-changing future.

Ethical Dilemma ✋

4.1   Payday Loans—Valuable Service or Predatory Lenders?[63]

Consumers with poor credit ratings or who need cash to get by until their next paycheque are prime targets for payday lenders. Payday lenders serve these riskier consumers with higher than market rate loans. For many consumers who have declared bankruptcy or have fallen on financial hard times, these lenders provide a needed service. Changing personal economic factors such as unemployment, unexpected expenses, or an upcoming celebration can also be reason to use such a service.

According to the Canadian Payday Loan Association, its 23 member companies service nearly 2 million Canadians a year through 500 retail financial services outlets across Canada with short-term loans in small amounts to help cover unanticipated expenses. Further, its members adhere to a strict Code of Best Business Practices and observance of this code is closely monitored and strictly enforced by an independent Ethics and Integrity Commissioner. Despite this claim, more than a dozen lawsuits have been filed across Canada against a variety of payday loan operators. The suits allege that the fees and interest charges levied for short-term loans—often for just a week or two—far exceed the maximum allowed interest rate, which is 60 percent maximum. Some estimates put the cost (interest plus fees) for some payday loans at an effective annual interest rate of more than 1000 percent! According to the Financial Consumer Agency of Canada, in addition to interest, borrowers may face various fees such as administration fee/processing fee/convenience charges/verification fee, broker's fee, collection fees, early repayment fee, initial or one-time set-up fee, loan repayment fee/first-party cheque-cashing fee, locate fee,

return fee/non-sufficient funds (NSF) fee, and roll-over fee/renewal fee/finance charge/additional charge/extension fee. Thus, a $300 payday loan, due in two weeks, may cost you between $30 and $105, depending on the fees that apply (visit www.fcac-acfc.gc.ca/ to learn more). In a recent court case in British Columbia, a Payday company asked the court to make a distinction between interest rates and the exorbitant fees and service charges that the industry routinely bills its customers. It also contended that the Criminal Code should only apply to loan sharks and not to payday loan operators. The judge rejected the company's arguments. During the trial, the court heard that the company charged a 21 percent interest rate plus a processing fee of $9.50 for every $50 borrowed. It also added a $75 fee for any cheques returned and, in cases where loan payments were delayed, charged a fee of $25 for every $100 deferred. Critics argue that often the people who take these loans are already vulnerable and unable to get out of debt—they have to keep borrowing these loans to make ends meet—or they lose any asset they place as security for the loans.

Payday lenders—are they creditors or sharks? You decide.

Despite these criticisms, Payday loan operators claim that they provide a legitimate and much-needed financial service to ease short-term financial needs. They also claim that their business is carried out in a friendly, professional, and open retail environment by thousands of small business people and their customers consistently express high levels of customer satisfaction. Finally, they provide employment for thousands of Canadians. Are Payday lenders providing much-needed service as they claim or are they predators as their critics deem them?

Step 1: Assess Strengths and Weaknesses

Step 1 includes the first half of a SWOT analysis: Assess the firm's strengths and weaknesses.

Strengths   Loblaw has many strengths, not the least of which is its sheer size—it is the largest grocery company in Canada. Just how big is it?[64]

- It is ranked as one of the best Canadian brands. Its President's Choice and no name brands are among the best in Canada. It is not only known for groceries but also for banking, MasterCard services, car and home insurance, and long distance calling through its PC Financial Services business unit.

- Its stores are well positioned within their markets and are more modern than competitors' stores.

EXHIBIT | **4.8** | Scenario Planning Process

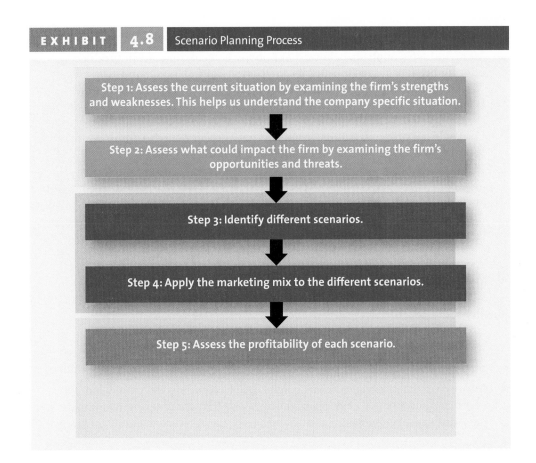

Step 1: Assess the current situation by examining the firm's strengths and weaknesses. This helps us understand the company specific situation.

Step 2: Assess what could impact the firm by examining the firm's opportunities and threats.

Step 3: Identify different scenarios.

Step 4: Apply the marketing mix to the different scenarios.

Step 5: Assess the profitability of each scenario.

- Its sales in 2007 were over $29.3 billion, with $330 million in profits, and assets worth over $13.5 billion.

- Its workforce is more than 134,000 people across Canada.

- It has 670 corporate stores, 402 franchised stores, and 470 associate stores. It operates under the following banners: Loblaws, Provigo, Maxi, Dominion (in Newfoundland and Labrador), Cash and Carry, Zehrs Markets, The Real Canadian Superstore, The Real Canadian Wholesale Club, Atlantic Superstore, and Extra Foods, No Frills, SuperValue, Valu-mart, Fortinos, Lucky Dollar Foods, Atlantic SaveEasy, Extra Foods, Shop Easy Foods, and Your Independent Grocer.

- It distributes food to approximately 8000 independent stores in addition to its own corporate, franchised and associated stores.

However, being big isn't always strength; a huge company sometimes suffers from its sluggish reactions to change and cumbersome hierarchical decision making. But size has generally been one of Loblaw's key strengths, perhaps because it has been able to develop inventory and distribution systems rapidly, expand into new retail businesses, and negotiate with vendors better than most of its rivals.

Loblaw is the largest grocery company in Canada.

Weaknesses   Although Loblaw's weaknesses are few, they are potentially serious.

- Many industry analysts believe that Loblaw is weak in its fresh produce offering because it lags most of its competitors in this merchandising area. "Fresh" is now the biggest buzzword in Canadian grocery retailing and Loblaw must improve or face stiff competition.[65] It seems that analysts are right given that Wal-Mart's foray into the Canadian grocery business is targeted at Loblaw's apparent weakness. It opened new grocery supercentres, bannered as Your Fresh Market, in 2007 in London and Hamilton, Ontario.

- Another weakness relates to its failed attempt to compete successfully in non-food categories such as home and kitchen accessories, bed and bath, and electronics. Its attempt to transform itself from just a grocery chain to a one-stop retailer did not go as planned due to supply chain challenges, poor choice, or lack of customer acceptance.

Step 2: Assess Opportunities and Threats

In the second half of the SWOT analysis, we assess the firm's opportunities and threats.

Opportunities   Consider some potential opportunities for Loblaw:

- Substantially improve its fresh produce offering to make it more competitive.

- Improve its operational efficiency to be able to compete with Wal-Mart and other competitors (e.g., Shopper's Drug Mart) that are entering the already crowded grocery market.

- Expand its drug store and beauty division to compete with the likes of Shopper's Drug Mart, PharmaPlus, London Drugs, and others in this lucrative market.

- Revamp its non-food merchandising strategy and supply chain for these products to become more competitive.

- Diversify into other areas such as having outpatient medical clinics in its stores.

- Expand in-store financial services to make Loblaw even more of a one-stop shopping experience.

Threats   Like any firm, Loblaw also faces several formidable threats:

- Wal-Mart's foray into the Canadian grocery business, particularly targeting the fresh produce offering, where Loblaw seems to be weak, will be a major challenge over the next few years. With Wal-Mart's deep pockets, efficient supply chain system, global experience, and its ability to negotiate with vendors better than most rivals, Loblaw may be unable to compete with Wal-Mart on price.

- In addition to Wal-Mart, other entrants such as Shopper's Drug Mart will intensify competition in the grocery industry exerting further pressure on Loblaw's dominance in the industry.

- Small but nimble local retailers eat into its market in certain categories. Some such retailers can beat Loblaw on assortment and service but usually not on price.

Step 3: Identify Different Scenarios

On the basis of the analysis performed in Steps 1 and 2, executives can identify some alternative scenarios that might happen in the next five years. Two of the scenarios could be as follows:

- Loblaw expands its non-food category (apparel, home appliances, electronics, etc.) to compete with the likes of Wal-Mart, Staples Business Depot, and Future Shop.

- Loblaw changes its store formats to offer various other services such as medical clinics, gas bars, and eyewear and optical services to create a truly one-stop shopping experience for customers. It could also consider changing its store hours for some urban stores to have them open 24 hours a day.

Each of these alternative scenarios requires careful consideration and reflection to assess the risks, benefits, and costs of that move. To determine which are the best opportunities, it is useful to try to match the firm's competencies with the opportunity's attractiveness. Clearly, if the firm has a high competency to engage in an opportunity and the opportunity is attractive, it represents a likely opportunity to pursue.

Loblaws could examine the attractiveness of changing its apparel assortment. This would allow head-on competition in the apparel area with Wal-Mart and Zellers. Also, a change in store formats would enable its customers not only to shop while they waited to see a doctor, but then fill their prescription afterwards. The cost of these changes would be substantial and could lead Loblaws away from its core business and strength. Thus, Loblaw would need to carefully examine the market to see how Canadians feel about buying electronics or clothing at Loblaws.

Step 4: Apply the Marketing Mix to the Different Scenarios

In this step, the firm develops a potential strategy for each of the different scenarios created in Step 3. For simplicity, let's just consider the option of Loblaw changing its store format and hours of operation. It provides an intriguing yet straightforward option for several reasons. Because Loblaw already has over 1000 stores in cities and neighbourhoods all across Canada, its stores have a pharmacy and it has a trusted and well recognized brand, consumers are likely to see it as a good one-stop experience and will likely visit the store and shop more often. Lengthening its store hours will also cater to customers who find it difficult to shop at regular store hours. The two potential problems for Loblaw with this option are making the right choice in its expansion strategy and customer acceptance of its new format.

Step 5: Assess the Profitability of Each Scenario

After developing strategies for several options, as in Step 3, and applying the marketing mix as in Step 4, managers must finally assess the profitability of each option. In so doing, they weigh the expected revenues against the expected costs. The projects with the highest expected profit are the best to pursue. Therefore, if Loblaw finds that the expected revenues from expanding into new categories of merchandise or store formats exceed its expected costs, then the scenario is a viable option.

Loblaws must identify different scenarios to determine how best to compete against Wal-Mart and Sobeys.

Learning Objectives Review

1) Explain how a firm's core competencies, customers, and partners influence its marketing strategy

2) Identify and explain the factors in a firm's macroenvionment

3) Understand how marketers use scenario planning to make marketing decisions and strategies

1) Successful marketing firms focus their efforts on satisfying customer needs that match their core competencies. Everything a firm does should utilize its strengths and revolve around the customer; without the customer, nothing gets sold. Firms must discover their customers' wants and needs and then be able to provide a valuable product or service that will satisfy those needs. If there were only one firm and many customers, a marketer's life would be a piece of cake. But because this setup rarely occurs, firms must monitor their competitors to discover how they might be appealing to their customers. Marketing life certainly would be difficult, if not impossible, without corporate partners. Good marketing firms work closely with their suppliers, marketing research firms, consultants, and transportation firms to coordinate the extensive process of discovering what customers want and getting it to them when and where they want it. Each of these activities—identifying corporate strengths, discovering customer needs, and working with corporate sponsors—helps add value to firms' products and services.

2) To be successful, marketers must understand fully what is going on outside their firm. For instance, what are the chances that a fast-food hamburger restaurant would be successful in a predominantly Hindu neighbourhood? Right—not very good. Marketers must be sensitive to such cultural issues to be successful, and then they must also consider competitors as well as customer demographics—age, income, market size, education, gender, and ethnicity—to identify specific customer groups. In any society, major social trends influence the way people live. Understanding these trends—such as green market-

ing, privacy issues, and the time-poor society—can help marketers serve their customers better. Furthermore, in no other time in history has technology moved so rapidly and had such a pervasive influence on the way we live. Not only do marketers help develop technologies for practical, everyday uses, but technological advances also help marketers provide consumers with more products and services more quickly and efficiently. In addition, the general state of the economy influences how people spend their disposable income. When the economy is healthy, marketing grows relatively easy. But when the economy gets bumpy, only well-honed marketing skill can yield long-term successes. Naturally, all firms must abide by the law, but many legal issues also affect marketing directly. These laws can be broken into those that pertain to competitive practices, such as antitrust legislation, and those designed to protect consumers from unfair or dangerous practices, such as warning labels on cigarette packages.

3) Scenario planning integrates information on how the macroenvironment impacts a company, its competition, its corporate partners, and its customers as a means to understand the potential outcomes of different applications of a firm's marketing mix. Scenario planning is performed in five steps. In the first two steps, it assesses its strengths, weaknesses, opportunities, and threats (SWOT) in light of its macroenvironment in relation to its competition, corporate partners, and customers. Third, it identifies different scenarios. Fourth, it applies the marketing mix to the different scenarios. Finally, it assesses the profitability of each scenario. The scenario(s) with the highest potential are considered for implementation.

Key Terms

- baby boomers, 91
- competitive intelligence (CI), 88
- country culture, 98
- culture, 98
- demographics, 89
- economic situation, 100
- foreign currency fluctuations, 100
- generation X, 91

- generation Y, 92
- generational cohort, 90
- green marketing, 96
- inflation, 100
- interest rates, 100
- just-in-time (JIT) inventory system, 85
- macroenvironmental factors, 86

- political/regulatory environment, 102
- scenario planning, 103
- seniors, 90
- technological advances, 99
- tweens, 93

Concept Review

1. List the two elements a firm must assess before looking externally, i.e., the microenvironment.

2. List and describe the elements of a firm's macroenvironment.

3. List five ways in which baby boomers, generation X, and generation Y are different.

4. If a store permanently offers extended shopping hours, what macroenvironmental factor(s) are they appealing to?

5. List some of the important social and cultural trends affecting the Canadian market.

6. Besides language, explain why using the same advertisement for Ontario and for Quebec wouldn't be equally successful.

7. Why do marketers care about the new technologies consumers are using in their homes?

8. What is meant by scenario planning? List three benefits of scenario planning.

9. Describe each of the five steps of the scenario planning process.

10. What is the difference between a firm's strengths and its opportunities?

Marketing Applications

1. Assume you are going to open a new store. Describe it. Who are your competitors? What would you do to monitor your competitors' actions?

2. In which generational cohort do you belong? What about your parents? How do you approach buying a car differently than your parents would? What about buying an outfit to wear to a party? How can firms use their knowledge of generational cohorts to market their products and services better?

3. How can firms use customer demographics like income, market size, education, and ethnicity to market to their customers better?

4. Identify some of the changes in the gender landscape. Describe how they might affect the marketing practices of (a) men's apparel retailers, (b) do-it-yourself home improvement retailers, and (c) upscale salon services.

5. Identify some recent technological innovations in the marketplace and describe how they have affected consumers' everyday activities.

6. Do you feel as if firms are invading or could invade your privacy? Why or why not?

7. Why should Canadian companies selling goods in the United States care about the value of the U.S. dollar?

8. Time-poor consumers have adopted various approaches to "buy" themselves more time, such as (a) voluntarily simplifying their complex lives, (b) using new technologies for greater empowerment and control, (c) using their time productively when travelling or commuting, and (d) multitasking. Identify and describe some products and services that consumers use to implement each of these strategies.

9. Identify a company that you believe does a particularly good job of marketing to different cultural groups. Justify your answer.

10. You have recently been hired by a major department store in its marketing department. Your boss informs you that you are going to supervise a field research study being conducted. You arrive at your assigned store and find that the study consists of shadowing customers. The store has set up a "private" shopping event for store credit card holders. All who attend must swipe their card to receive the special discount coupon book. The shadow shoppers (who were hired by the store manager) are given handheld devices loaded with a specific customer's information and past purchase behaviour. Thus each shadow shopper knows the name, address, income, family size, and spending patterns for the customer she or he is observing. You begin to feel uncomfortable about this study since the consumers have no idea that they are being tracked or the level of confidential information about them that a stranger has access to. You are also concerned that the shadow customers are not regular employees or employees of an established marketing research provider. What if anything would or should you do about your concerns?

Net Savvy

1. Seventh Generation is the leading brand of nontoxic, environmentally safe household products in Canada (e.g., sold at Home Depot). Visit its website (www.seventhgeneration.com), and review the philosophy behind the business. Next, review the site to identify the products that the company offers. Briefly summarize some of the consumer trends you note, and describe the ways in which its products address the wants and needs of its customers.

2. The Internet has been a double-edged sword for consumers. On the one hand, it provides easy access to many businesses and sources for information. On the other hand, consumers must give up some of their privacy to access this information. The Privacy Rights Clearinghouse provides information to consumers about privacy and opt-out strategies. Visit its website (www.privacyrights.org) and review the privacy survival guide. From that document, select and describe three actions you might take to protect your own privacy.

Chapter Case Study

SIMPLY AUDIOBOOKS:[66] CHANGING THE WAY WE READ BOOKS

Overview

Simply Audiobooks is a Toronto-based online audiobook rental business targeted to travellers and commuters. Customers can rent fiction and non-fiction titles on CDs, which they can listen to while in transit, whether on holiday or commuting to work. It saves the price of buying the book or waiting to borrow a copy from the library. The company which was founded in 2003 by Sean Neville and Sanjay Singhal began shipping audiobooks in mid-2003 out of Sean's basement. Sean is the company's president and CEO and Sanjay is the company's chairman and chief marketing officer (CMO). Today, Simply Audiobooks has more than 50 employees and revenues in excess of $6 million. It was named one of the Top 50 retailers on the Internet, won Ernst and Young entrepreneurial company of the year in 2005, and placed 6th on Profit Hot 50 rankings of Canada's emerging growth companies. Simply Audiobooks is the most successful independent player in the online audiobook rental market.

The People and the Concept

Sean and Sanjay studied for their MBAs at Cornell University, but at different times. As part of their MBA program, they had both taken a course in entrepreneurship where they had to write a business plan for a start-up company. As they learned from their class experience, it is generally easier to start a new business by taking an existing, proven business model and adapting it to another industry. This is exactly what Sean and Sanjay did for Simply Audiobooks. Sean, 32, was a vice-president of sales and marketing at a plastics firm in Toronto. He always wanted to get into business for himself and was looking around for a small business that he could buy—one that is not doing very well or where the owners were about to retire or just wanted to get out of the business. Sanjay, 41, who also has a master's degree in engineering, had been involved in three other start-ups, but only one involving voicemail technology was successful. He had just sold his interest in Toronto-based Mpathix Inc. and was looking for another business opportunity to get into.

Simply Audiobooks, the brainchild of Sean, was conceived while commuting to his job at the plastics plant near Toronto's Pearson International Airport. During his long commute, he often found himself stuck in bumper-to-bumper traffic on Highway 401 in the rush hour traffic. In his car, he wanted to listen to Jim Collins' popular business title "Good to Great," but was unwilling to pay the cost to buy it. His local library did not have the title in stock and Sean had no time to drive around searching for it. Sean's dilemma and his knowledge of U.S.-based Netflix Inc., North America's largest on-line movie rental firm, business model sparked the idea for an online shopping/home delivery audiobook rental business, which became Simply Audiobooks. The lesson he had learned in his entrepreneurship class about adapting a business model suddenly became more real and exciting to him. In addition, his experience listening to an audiobook on cassettes for the Canadian Securities course he was taking made him realize that Netflix's distribution model had to be tweaked to adapt to the varying weights of audiobooks. Sean immediately went into research mode carefully analyzing Netflix's business model and the industry for audiobooks. He realized that imitating someone else's business model is not without risk—Netflix could sue him for infringement of their business model. This possibility aside, Sean quit his job as vice-president of sales and marketing to launch Simply Audiobooks. But he needed money and someone who had real experience with a start-up and is connected with the venture capital market. Enter Sanjay Singhal.

Simply Audiobooks built a solid business by understanding and acting on the environmental factors that were key to its success.

The threat of Netflix filing a lawsuit against Simply Audiobooks, as it did against Blockbuster in 2006, didn't dissuade Sean and Sanjay. "We went ahead with it, kind of thinking 'Damn all the torpedoes; we'll deal with that if and when it happens.' But I'd learned enough in [a] law course to know that the patent was quite likely nondefensible," says Singhal. Regardless, Sean and Sanjay found valuable background information for their venture by sifting through 10K filings by U.S. public companies such as Netflix, and also Audible Inc., which sells downloadable audiobooks. They realized that no one else was involved in the rent-by-mail model, thus their opportunity to enter this niche.

Originally, they targeted corporate sales in Canada but within a few quick months of launching, they discovered that their best prospects were consumers in the United States. The U.S. market represents 94 percent of sales, with audiobooks shipped from offices in Buffalo and Las Vegas. The Canadian and U.K markets account for 4 percent and 2 percent of sales respectively.

The Business Model

Each subscriber is sold a membership plan that allows them to rent up to four titles at any given time, depending on their membership plan. Membership plans cost from $11.95 per month of one title at a time to $36.95 per month for four titles at a time. Books are automatically shipped in order of availability and priority. That means every time the company receives a selection back from a customer, they are able to send out that customer's top next available pick the same day. Inventory effectiveness is maximized by splitting longer books into "selections." The policy was designed so that they could ship the most books to the most members, while keeping costs affordable for customers. Membership plans can be cancelled at any time with no fees or penalties.

When customers order a title, the company pays the shipping costs and includes a postage-paid return package, so that the customers can easily get and return their rental for free. Once they are done with the selection, they just pop it back in the box and drop it into the mail. There is no postage, handling or late fees charged to customers and they can keep their audiobooks as long as they like. Fulfilment is completed via first class mail and most orders are delivered in two to five business days.

The Market

"Audiobooks are ideal for commuters," says Sean. "The average one-way commute in North America takes 24 minutes. Therefore, the average commuter can listen to one audiobook (about four hours) in five days of commuting." According to Sanjay, the ideal customer is older middle-age people, living in big cities or the suburban, with above average education and income and who loves to read while travelling or commuting. For these people, unlimited rental of audiobooks would be more appealing than either buying the titles or waiting on their library to get them. Originally, the plan was for Simply Audiobooks to be a Canadian company, serving Canada. A pilot program to test the U.S. market convinced Sanjay and Sean to do otherwise.

The market for audiobooks is intensely competitive. It consists of about 10 independent players plus mainstream book publishers like Random House and offline mom-and-pops operating in brick-and-mortar locations. The independent players include Recorded Books, Books Free, Jigger Bug, Audio-to-Go, Books in Motion, Kitabe, and Audible (a public trade company that is 10 times the size of Simply Audiobooks). According to Sanjay, Simply Audiobooks is the same size of all of these independent players (except for Audible) combined. The company's executives attribute their success to their agility and deep advertising budget. We understand that acting quickly to stay ahead of the competition is crucial. "When a series of processes converge to create a new business possibility, like YouTube, it happens for everyone at the same time. If you're not first or significantly better than everyone else, you'll get trampled. Within six months, we had people cutting and pasting from our home page," says Sanjay. After about a year in operation, Simply Audiobooks had enough scale that it could outspend competitors on advertising and marketing, further lengthening its competitive lead.

As an Internet business, domain names are a major consideration since a good name can either drive traffic to a company's website or to its competitors' website. Simply Audiobooks found this out the hard way. Simply Audiobooks missed registering simplyaudio.com, a short-form of its domain name. That domain name was picked up by a U.S. competitor, Jiggerbug, which entered the same business a year later. "There was a fair bit of traffic that was going to jiggerbug.com that was really looking for us," Sanjay recalled. Fortunately, they discovered that Jiggerbug forgot to register a domain containing a misspelling of its name with only one "g," and managed to do a trade. Mr. Singhal took the CEO of Jiggerbug out for a steak dinner in Las Vegas, and swapped domain names.

Success Drivers

A major factor accounting for Simply Audiobooks success is the growing trend among consumers toward temporary ownership of products rather than outright ownership. According to Reinier Evers, founder of trendwatching.com, a consumer trends company, "There's an increased interest in anything that has to do with temporary ownership, as ownership of goods is less of a status symbol these days, and renting goods is seen as smart. Consumers also like to try out as many new 'experiences/goods' as possible, which means the Netflix model appeals." In 2005, the Audio Publishers Assn. (APA) estimated the size of the total audiobook market at $871 million, up 4.7 percent from the previous year. Another estimate puts this market in the US$2 billion range. The APA also found almost 25 percent of the U.S. population listens to audiobooks. Another factor accounting for Simply Audiobooks' success is Netflix's popularity which made it easier for customers to envision how they can rent audiobooks online. Netflik's success also drove traffic to Simply Audiobooks' website. Interestingly, although Internet technologies played a huge role in the creation and growth of the company, audiobook technology itself has had little impact on the company's success. The majority of audiobooks are still available through cassette tapes and CDs rather than downloadable books and consumers seem to have a preference for these formats. According to Sanjay, three other key factors that contribute to Simply Audiobooks success are (1) the highly complementary skills and personalities of the initial three employees they hired and those that were hired subsequently, (2) their ability to raise close to half-million dollars early in the business because that provided the capital needed to manage the venture and adequately advertise, and (3) their business model of pre-paid subscription which allows them to borrow customer's money in order to run the business, thus, the company was always adequately capitalized.

The Future

The company wants to stick to its core strength in audiobooks and become the 800-pound gorilla of the industry rather than branching out into movie and game rentals and become unfocused. The idea is that Simply Audiobooks will give customers whatever audiobooks they want, whenever they want them. Nonetheless, the company sells cassette tapes and CDs through its website and offers downloads of audiobooks for MP3 players or cellphones. This is currently a small part of the business. In addition to its core online rental business, the company recently opened its first bricks-and-mortar store by buying Spoken Word, Canada's largest audiobook only retail shop, and opened another store in Oakville, Ontario. It also expanded overseas with a new office in Manchester, England and is looking at opportunities in countries such as Australia, New Zealand, and India. Both Sean and Sanjay believe that the physical store is just another way to introduce more consumers to the audiobook world, and draw them to the on-line service. The company has not ruled out extending its product line to other rental products but not movies or video games.

Chief Marketing Officer, Sanjay Singhal, suggests that although most online rental companies have shunned physical storefronts, we strongly believe that these physical stores offer a huge growth possibility. Our plan is not just to use them for selling traditional books on tape and CDs but to offer discounted downloads of audiobooks onto portable electronic devices such as iPod and MP3 players. These people would prefer to come to our store and pay us to download our selections on their iPod for them instead of going online to do it themselves. Sanjay's positive outlook for the physical store success is based on his observation that the market for audiobooks is very different from DVDs. One key difference is that about 30 percent of audiobook sales are still in the form of cassette tapes, leaving CDs and DVDs a life expectancy of at least 10 years.

Questions

1. Briefly explain how knowledge of the macroenvironment and the circumstances of Sean and Sanjay helped influence the decision to pursue the idea behind Simply Audiobooks.

2. List the factors in Simply Audiobooks' microenvironment that you think are responsible for their success.

3. Identify and describe the macroenvironmental factors that influence the creation and growth of Simply Audiobooks.

CHAPTER 5

LEARNING OBJECTIVES

After studying this chapter, you should be able to:

LO **1** Explain how marketers use information systems to create value for customers

LO **2** Discuss ethical issues firms encounter when conducting marketing research

LO **3** Describe the necessary steps to conduct marketing research

LO **4** Explain the differences between primary and secondary data, and determine when each should be used

LO **5** Explain the differences between exploratory and conclusive research

Marketing Research and Information Systems

As one of the largest casino operators in the world, Harrah's Entertainment runs more than 50 casinos in 13 U.S. states and five countries under a variety of brand names. Its facilities typically include hotel and convention space, restaurants, and entertainment facilities.[1] For example, Casino Windsor, a Harrah's property, offers a four-diamond hotel, a luxurious entertainment centre with top performers, and several world-class restaurants.

While you may not agree with or like gambling, many consumers do enjoy the entertainment it provides. And, in Ontario, 20 percent of gross gaming revenues generated by Casino Windsor accrue to the government and are used to support programs such as health care and education.

Harrah's has become successful by understanding the needs and wants of its customers. To do this, it collects a vast amount of information about its millions of customers' preferences and gaming activities. In a move to provide greater value to customers and earn their loyalty and their business, Harrah's assigned its managers to comb through this collected information using sophisticated analytical techniques called data mining. Contrary to the conventional wisdom, what they found when they looked at the data wasn't that the high rollers had the greatest lifetime value; it was average, middle-aged working people and seniors, like school teachers, machinists, and bankers, who meant the most to Harrah's bottom line. Analysis of the data revealed that these customers, who represent 26 percent of Harrah's customer base, bring in the lion's share (82 percent) of its revenues.

Then the analysis revealed that these customers weren't interested in the typical gaming incentives, like free rooms, food, and nongaming entertainment. So Harrah's developed a three-tiered incentive program that provides different levels of service to different customer segments, designated according to their level of play as Total Gold, Total Platinum, or Total Diamond program players. The Total Rewards program was introduced at Casino Windsor in June 2007. Customers can earn reward credits toward vacations, sporting events, and merchandise. But they also get more of what they want, namely, better service through shorter waits in line. While competing casino operators are trying to lure in customers by adding amenities like luxury spas, upscale shopping centres, and fabulous shows, Harrah's is garnering a very loyal following by catering to those who prefer to drop by after work to play the slots.

Data mining techniques revealed that Harrah's most profitable customers were average middle aged working people and seniors like 84 year old Josephine Crawford who won more than $10 million at a Harrah's slot machine in Atlantic City, New Jersey.

The Total Gold customers must stand in regular lines at the reception desk and restaurants, whereas Total Platinum customers are directed into shorter lines, and the privileged Total Diamond customers bypass most lines altogether. The entire three-tier promotion, of course, was made very conspicuous, which made customers more interested in rising to the higher tiers. Harrah's use of marketing research was a real winner! With the recent acquisition of Caesars Entertainment Inc., Harrah's will have plenty of opportunity to expand its Total Rewards Program, customer information database and, of course, its revenue.[2]

marketing research
A set of techniques and principles for systematically collecting, recording, analyzing, and interpreting data that can aid decision makers involved in marketing goods, services, or ideas.

As the Harrah's example shows, **marketing research** is a key prerequisite to successful decision making; it consists of a set of techniques and principles for systematically collecting, recording, analyzing, and interpreting data that can aid decision-makers involved in marketing goods, services, or ideas.[3] When marketing managers attempt to develop their strategies, marketing research can provide valuable information that will help them make segmentation, positioning, product, place, price, and promotion decisions. Marketing research is also key to understanding topics such as consumer and B2B buying behaviour (Chapters 6 and 7), global marketing and cultural differences (Chapter 17), new product development, branding and customer service (Chapters 9 to 11), and for assessing the effectiveness of pricing, promotions, and product and service delivery strategies (Chapters 12 to 16).

As shown by our chapter roadmap, we examine how marketing information systems create value for firms and their customers. We also discuss some of the ethical implications of using customer information marketing, followed by a detailed discussion of the marketing research process and its various elements.

Firms invest millions of dollars in marketing research every year. Canada's market research industry is valued at just under a half-billion dollars. Some of the major

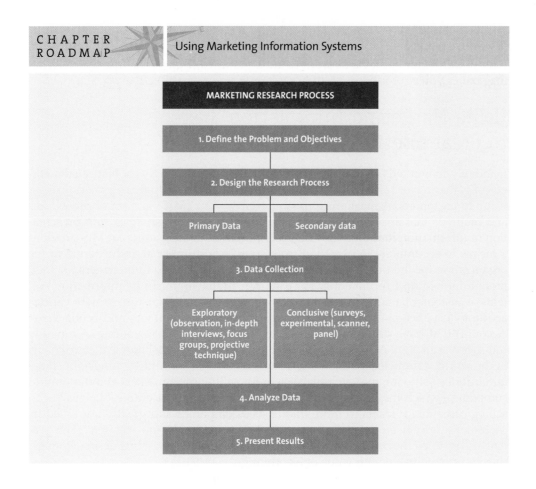

Canadian players in Canada's multi-million dollar market research and polling industry include Angus Reid, COMPAS, Decima Research, EKOS Research Associates, Ipsos-Reid, Leger Marketing, Pollara, and the Strategic Research Council. In addition, there are foreign-owned firms with offices in Canada such as ACNielsen Canada and Forrester Research. According to a *Marketing News* report, the top 25 market research firms in the world, with combined 2003 revenues of US$11.7 billion (CAD$15.2 billion), control about 62 percent of the worldwide spending on research services.[4] Why do marketers find this research valuable? First, it helps reduce some of the uncertainty under which they constantly operate. Successful managers know when research might help their decision making and then take appropriate steps to acquire the information they need. Second, marketing research provides a crucial link between firms and their environments, which enables them to be customer oriented because they build their strategies using customer input and continual feedback. Third, by constantly monitoring their competitors, firms can respond quickly to competitive moves. Fourth, ongoing marketing research can identify emerging opportunities and new and improved ways of satisfying consumer needs and wants from changes in the external environment.

If you think market research is only applicable to private companies, think again. Nonprofit organizations and governments also use research to serve their constituencies better. Political parties have been slicing and dicing the voting public for decades to determine relevant messages for different

Politicians and nonprofit organizations do research to understand their constituencies.

demographics. Politicians desperately want to understand who makes up the voting public to determine how to reach them. But not only do they want to know your political views; they also want to understand your media habits, such as what magazines you subscribe to, so they can target you more effectively.[5]

LO ① Using Marketing Information Systems to Create Better Value

marketing information system (MIS)
A set of procedures and methods that apply to the regular, planned collection, analysis, and presentation of information that then may be used in marketing decisions.

data warehouses
Large computer files that store millions and even billions of pieces of individual data.

Loews Cineplex used a marketing information system to learn the impact of group sales to the corporation.

In today's networked business world, marketers use increasingly sophisticated methods of gathering and employing marketing information to help them provide greater value to customers. A **marketing information system (MIS)** is a set of procedures and methods that apply to the regular, planned collection, analysis, and presentation of information that then may be used in marketing decisions. An MIS provides a means to accumulate information from sources both internal and external to the organization for the purpose of making it routinely available to managers for their more informed decision making. For example, Scotiabank uses its information systems of customer banking transactions to segment and target customers with various accounts (e.g., Scotia One, Scotia Powerchequing, Basic Banking, and Scotia Value Account) that have different features and fees based on their volume of monthly transactions. In another way, Loews Cineplex, one of the largest movie theatre chains in the world, contracted with Siebel, a leading provider of multichannel e-business applications software, to develop a system for selling group tickets at a discount to companies, which they can use as employee rewards and incentives. Loews began selling discounted tickets to more than 16,000 companies and greatly improved its customer service, yielding a 17-percent sales growth from its top accounts.[6] This system also enabled the company to better meet the needs of its best business customers, thus improving the overall value of its offering.

Although an MIS can be expensive, if used properly, it can be a valuable investment. Nowadays, companies usually find it necessary to use their marketing information

systems for more than just routine reports; many use it to generate customized analyses or for individual marketing research projects. For example, Harrah's might be interested in comparing the number of guests drawn in by two different promotions targeted to the same specific geographic region of the country. By initiating a query of the number of guests from the set of postal codes that constitute the targeted area, an analyst could compare the effectiveness of each marketing program or take the analysis one step further and determine the total revenue generated from those guests, broken down into the amount they spent on gambling, accommodations, and other hotel services like restaurants, cocktail lounges, gift shops, and massage services. In this way, the MIS helps the company determine which promotion addressed which aspects of the Harrah's experience that customers valued most.

Since the use of MIS has become more widespread, organizations of all types have vast amounts of data available to them. One of the most valuable resources such firms have at their disposal is their rich cache of customer information and purchase history. However, it can be difficult to make sense of the millions and even billions of pieces of individual data, which are stored in large computer files called **data warehouses**. For this reason, firms find it necessary to use data mining techniques to extract valuable information from their databases. Data mining uses a variety of statistical analysis tools to uncover previously unknown patterns in the data or relationships among variables. Through data mining, for example, Harrah's found out that its most profitable customers weren't the high rollers whom they expected had the highest value. A gardening retailer might learn through its data mining that 25 percent of the time that customers buy a garden hose, they also purchase a sprinkler. Data mining provides American Express with invaluable insights into purchasing behaviour by its credit cardholders, allowing it to implement database marketing programs, for example, promoting luggage to cardholders who travel frequently. Data mining can be used by a broad range of organizations, both public and private, for-profit and nonprofit.

Marketers use data mining techniques to study consumers' purchase behaviours.

The Ethics of Using Customer Information

LO **2**

As we noted in Chapter 3, upholding strong business ethics requires more than a token nod to ethics in the mission statement. A strong ethical orientation must be an integral part of a firm's marketing strategy and decision making. In Chapter 3, we discussed how marketers have a duty to understand and address the concerns of the various stakeholders in the firm—recall Exhibit 3.5, an example of how various stakeholders' needs should be included in the decision process of a marketing research firm.

data mining
The use of a variety of statistical analysis tools to uncover previously unknown patterns in the data stored in databases or relationships among variables.

As technology continues to advance rapidly, especially in terms of a firm's ability to link data sets and build enormous databases that contain information on millions of customers, marketing researchers must be careful to not abuse their ability to access these data, which can be very sensitive. Recent security breaches at the Canadian Imperial Bank of Commerce (CIBC), Winners and HomeSense, and Club Monaco have shown just how easily this stored data can be abused. CIBC reported in January 2007 that it has lost a file containing the personal details of 470,000 accounts of current and former clients of Talvest Mutual Funds, which are managed by CIBC Asset Management. The file went missing in late December 2006 when it was being transported from Montreal to Toronto. It contained information including client names and addresses, signatures, dates of birth, bank account numbers, and social insurance numbers. CIBC contacted police, the privacy commissioner, and financial services regulators as soon as the security breach became apparent. The bank also contacted affected Talvest clients by letter to advise them of this issue and to detail the steps they are taking to safeguard their information. CIBC said it will compensate clients for any monetary loss arising from the security breach and will provide a free credit-monitoring service to catch potentially fraudulent transactions. The bank has also set up a dedicated website and call centre for customer inquiries.[7] Thus, the lesson for marketing researchers is to respect and protect the privacy of individual customers absolutely. From charitable giving to medical records to Internet tracking, consumers are more anxious than ever about preserving their fundamental right to privacy.

More and more, consumers want to be assured that they have control over the information that has been collected about them through various means, such as a website or product registration or rebate form. Consumers' anxiety has become so intense that the Canadian government has promulgated various regulations, such as the Privacy Act that governs the collection, use, disclosure, and retention of personal information by federal government institutions and the Personal Information Protection and Electronics Documentation Act (PIPEDA), which governs the collection, use, disclosure, and retention of personal information by certain parts of the private sector.[8] When conducting marketing research, researchers must assure respondents that the information they provide will be treated as confidential and used solely for the purpose of research. Without such assurances, consumers will be reluctant to either provide honest responses to marketing research inquiries or even agree to participate in the first place.

Many firms use data mining in B2B markets as well. For example, IMS Canada uses data mining to uncover the prescription profiles and habits of physicians, which are then sold to pharmaceutical companies. Basically, IMS Canada gets the data from over 4000 Canadian retail pharmacy outlets through agreements with the head offices of the pharmacy chains and through suppliers of software used in pharmacies. The prescription information that IMS compiles includes the drug manufacturer, medication strength, form of the medication, new versus refill prescription, prescription size, transaction location, authorized repeats, a physician-identifying number and the third-party payer, if available. Identifiable patient data are not collected as part of this detailed prescription information database. Pharmaceutical companies often use this information to target physicians with their own drugs. Although many doctors and consumers are unaware of this practice, the Canadian Medical Association has voiced serious concerns about the ethics of providing physicians' prescription profiles to pharmaceutical companies. IMS Canada claims that they basically use the data to develop and evaluate their marketing strategies.[9]

These examples show that it is extremely important to adhere to ethical practices when conducting marketing research. The Canadian Marketing Association, for example, provides three guidelines for conducting marketing research: (1) It prohibits selling or fundraising under the guise of conducting research, (2) it supports maintaining research integrity by avoiding misrepresentation or the omission of pertinent research data, and (3) it encourages the fair treatment of clients and suppliers. Numerous codes of conduct written by various marketing research societies all reinforce the duty of the researcher to respect the rights of the subjects in the course of their research. The bottom line: Marketing research should be used only to produce unbiased, factual information.

The Marketing Research Process

LO 3

While Whirlpool chose to pursue a "World Washer" strategy in Europe that was contrary to its own research findings, its European competitors continued to innovate by responding to preferences in different regions.

Managers consider several factors before embarking on a marketing research project. First, will the research be useful; will it provide insights beyond what the managers already know and reduce uncertainty associated with the project? Second, is top management committed to the project and willing to abide by the results of the research? Related to both of these questions is the value of the research. Marketing research can be very expensive, and if the results won't be useful or management does not abide by the findings, it represents a waste of money.

Consider Whirlpool's approach to the European market for washing machines.[10] Although the findings of a major marketing research program indicated that there were significant regional differences in consumer preferences, managers stayed committed to their strategy of introducing the "World Washer," which could be sold in all EU markets. However, offering the same machine to different regions failed to address those different preferences in the marketplace, like Britons' preference to wash laundry more frequently using quieter machines than their neighbours in the rest of Europe. While the company maintained its "World Washer" strategy, its European competitors continued to innovate by responding to preferences in different regions. Although Whirlpool considered the research to be a worthwhile project, it was not particularly valuable to the firm because it chose to pursue a strategy that was contrary to its own research findings.

Whirlpool Corporation
Building unmatched loyalty
one customer at a time.

Because research is both expensive and time consuming, it is important to establish in advance exactly what information is required to answer specific research questions, and how that information should be obtained. Researchers assess the value of a project through a careful comparison of the benefits of answering some of their questions and the costs associated with conducting the research. For instance, going back to Whirlpool's European washing machine study, suppose the company had a choice of conducting in-depth interviews with several hundred washing machine owners at a cost of $200 per interview or doing an online survey with the same number of respondents but at a cost of only $2 per questionnaire. Which data collection method should Whirlpool use? Clearly the questionnaires are much less expensive, but the in-depth interviews provide richer information that would be virtually impossible to access through questionnaires. As this simple example shows, there are always value trade-offs in marketing research. Researchers can always design a more expensive study and eke out more and better information, but in the end, they should choose the method that will provide them with the information they need at the lowest cost.

The marketing research process itself can be divided into five steps as shown in Exhibit 5.1. Although the stages of the marketing research process are shown as a step-by-step progression, of course, research doesn't always happen this way. Sometimes, researchers go back and forth from one step to another as the need arises. For example, marketers may establish a specific research objective, which they follow with data collection and preliminary analysis. If they uncover new information during the data collection step or if the findings of the analysis spotlight new research needs, they might redefine their objectives and begin again from a new starting point. A major automobile manufacturer once set out to identify consumer responses to its new company logo, only to discover in preliminary focus groups that some of the respondents thought the company had gone out of business! Clearly, those researchers had to regroup and set out in a different direction with an entirely different objective.

Another important step when embarking on a research project is to plan the entire project in advance. For example, when setting up a questionnaire, marketers should consider the data collection process and anticipate the types of analyses that might produce meaningful results for decision-makers. For example, open-ended questions on a questionnaire can slow down the coding process and make it difficult to run some sophisticated statistical analyses. If the decision-makers want a sophisticated analysis fast, a questionnaire filled with open-ended questions may not be the best choice. By planning the entire research process well in advance of starting the project, researchers can avoid unnecessary alterations to the research plan as they move through the process. Now let us examine each step of the research process in more detail.

Step 1: Define the Problem and Objectives

Correctly defining the marketing problem is one of the most important elements of the marketing research process. Why? If you define the problem incorrectly, you will more than likely end up with the wrong solution even though the rest of the process is done perfectly. On the other hand, if you define the problem correctly but fail to carry out the rest of the process correctly, you may end up with results which may be useless or even misleading. Once the research problem is defined, marketers must specify the research objectives or questions to be answered. Marketing research efforts and resources can be wasted if the research objectives are poorly defined.[11] Poor design arises from three major sources:

The major advantage of using primary data like focus groups for market research is that it can be tailored to fit the pertinent research questions. But it usually is more expensive and takes longer to collect than secondary data.

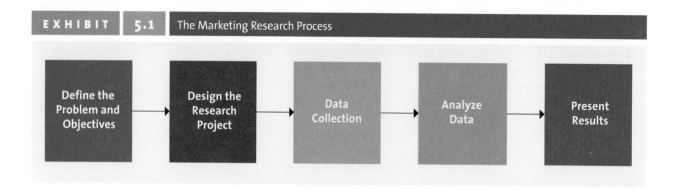

Define the Problem and Objectives → Design the Research Project → Data Collection → Analyze Data → Present Results

basing research on irrelevant research questions, focusing on research questions that marketing research cannot answer, or addressing research questions to which the answers are already known. However, timely and focused marketing research could help companies refine their marketing efforts and campaigns. Thus, market researchers devote considerable effort to defining the problem and trying to separate the symptoms of a problem from the actual problem.

For example, Wendy, the owner of a small clothing store in downtown Ottawa catering to girls between the ages of 10 to 16 years, thought that the declining sales she was observing in her store were due to inadequate or poor advertising. Thus, she increased her advertising and promotions in order to boost sales and regain her lost customers. Unfortunately, this provided only temporary benefits since the declining sales continued after the promotions ended. After hiring a marketing researcher, she realized that the declining sales were just a symptom of the real problem—outdated merchandise. She learned that the current group of 10- to 16-year-olds is quite different from their predecessors.

The objective of Superior Razor's research project is to evaluate its position in the marketplace relative to its competitors.

Step 2: Design the Research Project

The second step in the marketing research project involves design. In this step, researchers identify the type of data needed and determine the type of research necessary to collect it. Recall that the objectives of the project drive the type of data needed, as outlined in Step 1. Let's look at how this second step works using a hypothetical example about marketing disposable razors.

Superior Razors, a marketer of a national brand of men's shaving products, sets out to evaluate its position in the marketplace relative to its competitors. The specific purpose of the marketing research is twofold: to determine current market share and to assess how that position will change in the next few years.

Identifying the type of data needed for the first purpose—determining market share—is fairly straightforward. It requires finding the company's sales during a particular time frame relative to total industry sales.

Identifying the type of data needed for the second purpose—assessing the extent to which the firm's market position will improve, stay the same, or deteriorate—is not as easy to obtain. For instance, the company's marketers might want to assess customers' brand loyalty, because if the company enjoys high levels of loyalty, the future looks rosier than if loyalty is low. Superior Razor's market share in relation to that of its competitors over time can also shed light on the future of its market position. The firm will want to know which firms have been gaining market share and which are losing.

Thus, after the firm has identified its specific objectives and needs, it must consider whether the data required to make a decision are secondary or primary in nature.

Secondary data **Secondary data** are pieces of information that have already been collected from other sources and usually are readily available. Census data, the company's sales invoices, information from trade associations, the Internet, books, and journal articles are all readily available, free (or inexpensive) sources of secondary data. Exhibit 5.2 provides a sample list of secondary sources for marketing data.

In addition, marketers can purchase **syndicated data**, which are data available for a fee from commercial research firms such as Information Resources Inc. (IRI), National Purchase Diary Panel, ACNielsen, and Leger Marketing. (Exhibit 5.3 contains information about various firms that provide syndicated data.) This type of information, in our hypothetical razor example, might include the prices of various razors, sales figures, growth or decline in the category, and advertising and promotional spending. Consumer packaged goods firms that sell to wholesalers may not

secondary data
Pieces of information that have already been collected from other sources and usually are readily available.

syndicated data
Data available for a fee from commercial research firms such as Information Resources Inc. (IRI), National Purchase Diary Panel, and ACNielsen.

LO 4

EXHIBIT **5.2**	Sample List of Sources for Secondary Data

GUIDES, INDEXES AND DIRECTORIES	**STATISTICS CANADA and OTHER GOVERNMENT PUBLICATIONS**
Business Periodical Index	Annual Retail Trade
Canadian Almanac and Directory	Canadian Economic Observer
Canadian Business Index	Canada Yearbook
Canadian News Index	Family Expenditure Guide
Canadian Periodical Index	Market Research Handbook
Canadian Trade Index	Statistics Canada Catalogue
Directory of Associations in Canada	Western Economic Diversification Canada
Fraser's Canadian Trade Directory	Ontario Ministry for Economic Development and Trade
Predicasts Index	Department of Foreign Affairs and Trade
Scott's Directories	U.S. Census
Standards Periodical Directory	Stat-USA

PERIODICALS AND NEWSPAPERS	**TRADE SOURCES**
Advertising Age	Aberdeen Research
Adweek	ACNielsen
American Demographics	Conference Board of Canada
Business Horizons	Dun & Bradstreet Canada
Canadian Business	Financial Post Publishing
Canadian Consumer	Find/SVP
Forbes	Gale Research
Fortune	Interactive Advertising Bureau
Harvard Business Review	Jupiter Research
Journal of Advertising	Forrester Research
Journal of Marketing Management	MacLean Hunter Research Bureau
Journal of Personal Selling and Sales Management	MapInfo Canada
	Predicasts International
Journal of Small Business	
LexisNexis	**DATABASES**
Marketing Magazine	CANSIM (Statistics Canada)
Marketing & Media Decisions	CompuServe
Marketing News	Dialog
Progressive Grocer	Dow Jones
Sales and Marketing Management	Factiva
The Globe and Mail	Infoglobe
The Financial Post	Infomart
The Financial Post Magazine	Information Resources Inc.
The Wall Street Journal	SEDAR
	The Source

Source: Adapted from Crane, Kerin, Hartley, Berkowitz, Rudelius, *Marketing*, 6th Canadian ed. (Whitby ON: McGraw-Hill Ryerson, 2007).

EXHIBIT 5.3	Syndicated Data Providers in Canada and the U.S. and Their Services
Ipsos Canada, decimal Research, Leger Marketing, Angus Reid, SES Research, EKOS Research Associates, The Strategic Counsel, Pollara, and COMPAS	Provides polling services and marketing research on all aspects of marketing including loyalty, branding, media analysis, pricing, position, image enhancement, customer satisfaction, focus groups, online panels, surveys, etc. across many industries.
Bureau of Broadcasting Measurement	Provides broadcast measurement and consumer behaviour data, as well as intelligence to broadcasters, advertisers and agencies on audience behaviours during and after broadcasts.
Print Measurement Bureau	Provides single-source data on print readership, non-print media exposure, product usage and lifestyles of Canadians. It uses an annual sample of 24,000 to measure the readership of over 115 publications and consumer usage of over 2500 products and brands.
ACNielsen (www.acnielsen.com)	With its *Market Measurement Services*, the company tracks the sales of consumer packaged goods, gathered at the point of sale in retail stores of all types and sizes.
J.D. Power and Associates (www.jdpower.com)	Widely known for its automotive ratings, it produces quality and customer satisfaction research for a variety of industries.
Mediamark Research Inc. (www.mediamark.com)	Supplies multimedia audience research pertaining to media and marketing planning for advertised brands.
National Purchase Diary Panel (www.npd.com)	Tracking services provide information about product movement and consumer behaviour in a variety of industries.
NOP World (www.nopworld.com)	The *mKids US* research study tracks mobile telephone ownership and usage, brand affinities, and entertainment habits of American youth between 12 and 19 years of age.
Research and Markets (www.researchandmarkets.com)	Promotes itself as a "one-stop shop" for market research and data from most leading publishers, consultants, and analysts.
Ropercentre for Public Opinion Research (www.ropercenter.uconn.edu)	The *General Social Survey* is one of the nation's longest running surveys of social, cultural, and political indicators.
Simmons Market Research Bureau (www.smrb.com)	Reports on the products American consumers buy, the brands they prefer, and their lifestyles, attitudes, and media preferences.
Yankelovich (www.yankelovich.com)	The *MONITOR* tracks consumer attitudes, values, and lifestyles shaping the American marketplace.

have the means to gather pertinent data directly from the retailers that sell their products to the consumer, which makes syndicated data a valuable resource for them. Some syndicated data providers also offer information about shifting brand preferences and product usage in households, which they gather from consumer panels. Adding Value 5.1 describes the valuable information Leger Marketing provides to its Canadian and U.S. customers.

A marketing research project often begins with a review of the relevant secondary data such as the company's own records, prior research studies undertaken by the company, newspapers, magazines, and other published sources listed in Exhibits 5.2 and 5.3. Generally, secondary data can be quickly accessed at a relatively low cost. For example, Statistics Canada data on retail trade provides data about sales of different types of retail establishments either free or very inexpensively. These patterns may be the only accurate sources available to a small new business that wants to determine the size of its potential market. For such a firm, gathering accurate and comprehensive data on its own would be quite difficult. Researchers must ensure that the secondary data, especially from external sources are current, relevant and can shed light on the research problem or objectives.

Adding Value | 5.1 | Leger Marketing: Speeding Strategic Decision Making[12]

Did you ever wonder how companies find out how people feel about a television show, a new product, or the wireless telecommunications industry? Chances are the information came from surveys conducted by Leger Marketing. One of the largest Canadian-owned independent marketing research and polling firms operating in Canada and the U.S., Leger Marketing offers its clients a team of 115 professionals with expertise in the pharmaceutical, financial, telecommunications, communications and media, retail, electronic commerce, and public affairs sectors. It also boasts an impressive operational capacity of four call centres and 200 state-of-the-art CATI stations in Montreal, Winnipeg, Edmonton, and Calgary, and can conduct telephone surveys across Canada and the United States within very short timeframes. In addition, it offers seven focus-group rooms and a 40-seat auditorium specially designed for advertising tests.

Leger Marketing offers its clients strategic advice in a wide array of areas including media and advertising analysis, marketing planning, market research, product launch, segmentation analysis, positioning, customer satisfaction and loyalty strategies, pricing and packaging strategies, mystery shopper, and image assessment. It also offers website analytics, which marketers can use to evaluate and improve the performance of their websites. It offers these services through various tools such as: BUILD UP for simulating new product launch, EFFICOM and EFFIPUB for measuring advertising effectiveness and impact, POSITION OPTIMZER, for assessing a brand's positioning, WEB PERFORM for evaluating website performance, and 48 HOURS for businesses wishing to receive reliable information quickly.

Finally, Leger Marketing has an online panel of 350,000 people that represents various consumer segments of the Canadian population. This impressive panel makes it possible for Leger to complete surveys among the general public and more specific consumer segments. It is therefore hardly surprising that Leger Marketing can offer marketers a 48-hour service—a solution for businesses and decision-makers who wish to receive reliable information quickly from a large representative sample of consumers regarding their marketing campaigns, products, and brands.

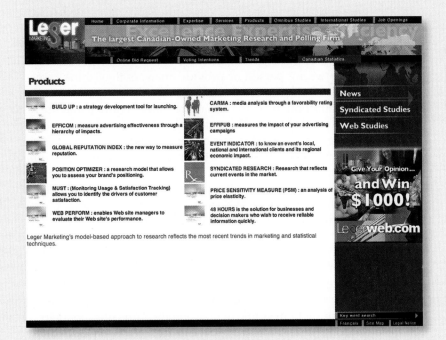

Leger Marketing offers marketers research information in 48 hours.

At other times, however, secondary data are not adequate to meet researchers' needs. Because the data initially were acquired for some purpose other than the research question at hand, they may not be completely relevant. For instance, the Statistics Canada Census is a great source for demographic data about a particular market area, and it can be easily accessed at a low cost. However, the data are collected only every 10 years, so they quickly become outdated. For example, if a firm were interested in opening a retail flooring store in 2009, it would have to rely on Statistics Canada Census data collected in 2006—three years old. If it hoped to locate in an area where housing starts are projected to grow rapidly in the next several years, these data would be too old to provide much in the way of insights. Researchers must also pay careful attention to how the secondary data were collected; despite the great deal of data available on the Internet, easy access does not ensure that the data are trustworthy.

Internet Marketing 5.1 shows how marketers are beginning to use Radio Frequency Identification (RFID) to gather additional types of information.

primary data
Data collected to address specific research needs.

Primary Data   In many cases, the information researchers need is available only through **primary data**, or data collected to address specific research needs. Marketers collect primary data using a variety of means such as observing consumer behaviour, conducting focus group interviews, or surveying customers using the mail, telephone, in-person interviews, or the Internet. Primary data collection can help eliminate some of the problems inherent to secondary data.

A major advantage of primary research is that it can be tailored to fit the pertinent research questions, though it also has its own set of disadvantages. For one thing, it is usually more costly to collect primary than secondary data, and the collection typically takes longer. Furthermore, marketers often require sophisticated training and experience to design and collect primary data that are unbiased, valid, and reliable. (For a summary of the advantages and disadvantages of each type of research, see Exhibit 5.4 on page 128.) Biased data results when, for example, the sample does not represent the entire population, researchers inject their own biases by the way they ask questions or try to get respondents to answer in specific ways, or the respondents may be the wrong person or provide answers they think researchers want to hear. Reliability and validity are described next.

Data collection through primary research requires that the researcher makes several important decisions. These decisions include which methods to use (see Exhibit 5.5 on page 129 for a list of various methods), what types of sampling plan is best given the research objective, what types of research instruments (questionnaire, observation, etc.) to use, how should the research instrument be designed (described below), and how best to contact potential respondents (telephone, online, in-person, or by mail). Improper execution of any of these important aspects of primary data collection could seriously reduce the reliability and validity of the research study.

reliability
The extent to which the same result is achieved when a study is repeated under identical situations.

Simply put, **reliability** is the extent to which you will get the same result if the study is repeated under identical situations.[13] For example, on a Saturday in August you randomly stop shoppers in a mall and ask them to fill out a short questionnaire about why they shop at that particular mall. Let's say your data analysis shows that the reason they shop at that mall is because they get very good deals, Now, if you were to repeat the study in the same mall, using the same questionnaire, on another Saturday, and randomly ask shoppers to fill out the questionnaire, you should find the same result—people shop at the mall because they get good deals. If you found otherwise, then the reliability of your study is called into question. **Validity** is the extent to which

validity
The extent to which a study measures what it is supposed to measure.

the study actually measures what it is supposed to measure.[14] For example, suppose you want to measure consumers' trust in online retailers using a questionnaire. Validity seeks to determine whether the questions you asked on the questionnaire actually measure online trust or if it measures some other construct. It is important to note that a market research study must be both reliable and valid for it to be useful.

Internet Marketing   5.1   RFID—My Underwear Is Reporting My Whereabouts?[15]

How would you like it if, for instance, one day you realized your underwear was reporting on your whereabouts? Sounds too far-fetched? Well, not quite. Radio Frequency Identification (RFID) technology is a chip enclosed inside a paper label that can be placed on products. Unlike barcode readers, which scan a visual image of a barcode to collect data, RFID readers pick up a signal from a tiny RFID tag that is smaller than an ant's head. RFID tags consist of a silicon data chip, an antenna for data transmission and an enclosure that provides the outside casing of the tag. The RFID tag can automatically be read from several metres away and does not have to be in the line of sight of the reader. RFID tags can be attached to or incorporated into a product, animal, or person for the purpose of identification using radio waves. Currently, the main driving force behind the use of RFID is to increase the efficiency of supply chain management for large enterprises. RFID increases the speed and accuracy with which inventory can be tracked and managed thereby saving money for the business. Wal-Mart, the world's largest retailer, is a major proponent of this technology. In November, 2003 Wal-Mart notified its top 100 suppliers that as of January 2005 they had to use RFID technology if they wanted to do business with Wal-Mart.

Apart from supply chain and inventory management, RFID has other significant applications in numerous contexts such as in passports, transit payments, product tracking, automotive, animal identification, human implants, libraries, student ID cards, drivers' licences, and even in sporting events to track championship times in running races, marathons, triathlons, cycling, mountain biking competitions, in-line skating, and cross-country skiing. For example, RFID technology is already being used in Canada for transit payments in Montreal, product tracking by the Canadian Cattle Identification Agency, and by Toyota in its 2007 Toyota Camry with smart keys/smart start option—the car starts automatically while the key is still in the driver's purse or pocket once the driver comes within 1 metre of the car.

In spite of RFID's tremendous benefits in logistics and supply chain tracking and in reduced costs and improved profitability for businesses, the use of the technology has engendered considerable controversy and even product boycotts by consumer privacy advocates, some of whom describe RFID tags as "spychips." The four main privacy concerns regarding RFID are: (1) the purchaser of an item will not necessarily be aware of the presence of the tag or be able to remove it. The tag may still be used later for returns, recalls, or recycling, hence you can be tracked as long as the tag is on the item; (2) the tag can be read at a distance without the knowledge of the individual; (3) if a tagged item is paid for by credit card or in conjunction with use of a loyalty card, then it would be possible to tie the unique ID of that item to the identity of the purchaser; and (4) the Electronic Product Code global system of tags create globally unique serial numbers for all products. Essentially, we can be tracked across the globe without our knowledge or consent and without knowing who is doing the tracking, who has access to the information, who it's being shared with, and how it's being used. The following two recent applications serve to highlight the sinister use of RFID. In once case, Gillette used RFID in a pilot program to conduct a "smart shelf" test at a Tesco store in Cambridge, England. They automatically photographed shoppers taking RFID-tagged safety razors off the shelf, to see if the technology could be used to deter shoplifting. Once consumers became aware of this trial, they boycotted Gillette and Tesco. In another incident, uncovered by the *Chicago Sun-Times*, shelves in a Wal-Mart in Broken Arrow, Oklahoma, were equipped with readers to track the Max Factor Lipfinity lipstick containers stacked on them. Webcam images of the shelves were viewed 1200 km away by Procter & Gamble researchers in Cincinnati, Ohio, who could tell when lipsticks were removed from the shelves and observe the shoppers in action. Some industry professionals believe that this technology has the potential to revolutionize the way marketers undertake market research. Can you describe some possible scenarios where RFID could revolutionize the conduct of market research?

Product tracking
Technologies, such as RFID, provide realtime data collection and detection of product in the pipeline. Sends automated messages to the event engine.

RFID

Tag

Antenna

Reader

RFID tags can automatically be read from several metres away and do not have to be in the line of sight of the reader.

| EXHIBIT 5.4 | Advantages and Disadvantages of Secondary and Primary Data |

Type	Examples	Advantages	Disadvantages
Secondary Research	• Census data • Sales invoices • Internet information • Books • Journal articles • Syndicated data	• Saves time in collecting data because they are readily available • Reduces data collection costs	• May not be precisely relevant to information needs • Information may not be as timely as needed • Sources may not be original and therefore usefulness is an issue • Methodologies for collecting data may not be relevant or may contain bias in the subject matter
Primary Research	• Observed consumer behaviour • Focus group interviews • Surveys	• Specific to the immediate data needs and topic at hand • Offers behavioural insights generally not available from secondary research	• Usually more costly to collect • Typically takes longer to collect • Often requires more sophisticated training and experience to design and collect unbiased, valid, reliable data

sample
A segment or subset of the population that adequately represents the entire population of interest.

sampling
The process of picking a sample.

One very important aspect of market research that can affect the reliability and validity of a study is the sampling plan. Often it is too difficult, impractical, or costly to study the entire group of consumers, so marketers usually select a **sample**, a segment or subset of the population that adequately represents the entire population of interest. For example, if you are interested in studying the loyalty of Canadian teenage boys to brand name clothing, then your population is all Canadian teenage boys and your sample is the small subset of boys selected for your study. How you select the sample is also very important. Three important questions that must be answered are: (1) who should be surveyed, (2) how big should the sample be, and (3) what types of **sampling** procedure to use, for example, simple random sampling, convenience sampling, stratified sampling, cluster sampling, and so on. More details on the sampling procedure are provided in the Online Learning Centre at www.mcgrawhill.ca/olc/grewal. Each of these sampling procedures has their advantages and disadvantages and the decision as to which one to use will depend on the research objectives of the study. Although there is a formula in statistics to calculate required sample size, as a rule of thumb, sample sizes should be large enough to ensure the reliability of the study. Generally, larger samples tend to yield more reliable results up to a certain point.

Step 3: Data Collection Process

Data collection begins only after the research design process. Depending on the nature of the research problem, the collection can employ either exploratory or conclusive research.

exploratory research
Attempts to begin to understand the phenomenon of interest; also provides initial information when the problem lacks any clear definition.

As its name implies, **exploratory research** attempts to begin to understand the phenomenon of interest; it also provides initial information when the problem lacks any clear definition. Exploration can include informal methods, like reviewing available secondary data, or more formal methods that encompass qualitative research, such as observation techniques, in-depth interviews, focus groups, and projective techniques (see Exhibit 5.5).

conclusive research
Provides the information needed to confirm preliminary insights, which managers can use to pursue appropriate courses of action.

If the firm is ready to move beyond preliminary insights, it likely is ready to engage in **conclusive research**, which provides the information needed to confirm those insights and which managers can use to pursue appropriate courses of action. For marketing researchers, because it is often quantitative in nature, conclusive research offers a means to confirm implicit hunches through surveys, formal studies such as specific experiments, scanner and panel data, or some combination of these. (See Exhibit 5.5 right side.) In the case of formal research, it also enables the researcher

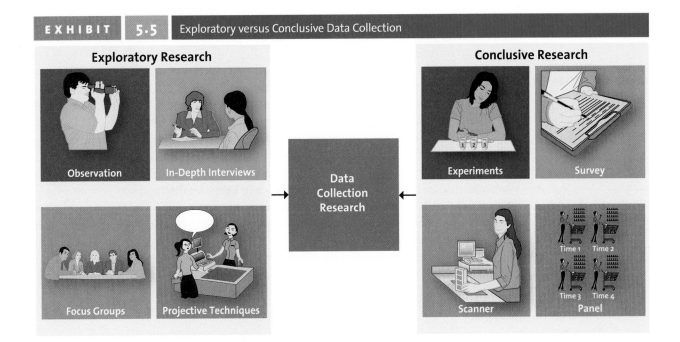

EXHIBIT 5.5 Exploratory versus Conclusive Data Collection

Exploratory Research

Observation

In-Depth Interviews

Focus Groups

Projective Techniques

Data Collection Research

Conclusive Research

Experiments

Survey

Scanner

Panel

Time 1   Time 2   Time 3   Time 4

to test his or her predictions or **hypothesis**, which is a statement or proposition predicting a particular relationship among multiple variables that can be tested through research such as experiments and survey research. An example of a hypothesis is: customer satisfaction leads to or is positively related to customer loyalty.

Many research projects use exploratory research as the first phase of the research process and follow it up with conclusive research. Let's attempt to understand this progression by studying both methods in detail.

Exploratory Research Methods

Managers commonly use several exploratory research methods: observation, in-depth interviewing, focus group interviews, and projective techniques (Exhibit 5.5 left side).

Observation   An exploratory research method, **observation** entails examining purchase and consumption behaviours through personal means or the use of technology such as video camera or other tracking devices. For example, researchers might observe customers while they shop or when they go about their daily lives, during which processes they use a variety of products. Observation can last for a very brief period of time (e.g., two hours watching teenagers shop for clothing in the mall), or it may take days or weeks (e.g., researchers live with families to observe their use of products). When consumers are unable to articulate their experiences, observation research becomes particularly useful; how else could researchers determine which educational toys babies choose to play with or confirm purchase details that consumers might

hypothesis
A statement or proposition predicting a particular relationship among multiple variables that can be tested through research.

LO **5**

observation
An exploratory research method that entails examining purchase and consumption behaviours through personal or video camera scrutiny.

This family is being observed cooking.

not be able to recall accurately? As Ethical Dilemma 5.1 describes, observational research can even be used to understand the differences among consumers when they shop in retail stores.

ethnography
An observational method that studies people in their daily lives and activities in their homes, work, and communities.

Ethnography is an observational method that studies people in their daily lives and activities in their homes, work, and communities. It is often used when market researchers believe that potential respondents may be unable to articulate in a useful way their experiences with a product or service. This type of research yields insights and intimate details that respondents may not want to reveal. It is increasingly being used by companies (e.g., Unilever, Procter & Gamble, and Miller Lite). Ethnographic studies require highly trained and experienced researchers. They often use video cameras, audio recording devices, and diaries to keep detailed records of their observations. Analysis of ethnographic data requires very experienced and knowledgeable market researchers to make sense of hours of video tapes, audio tapes, or volume of notes from the researcher's diary.

Procter & Gamble sends video crews to households around the world to gain insights into life's daily routines.[16] This exercise yields priceless insights into consumer behaviour that could not be captured using traditional methods such as interviews or focus groups. For example, people have selective memories and might tell a market researcher that they brush their teeth three times a day for two minutes each time. Camera crews capture a different picture though, sometimes leading to new products. Watching people sort laundry showed researchers piles of clothes that never went into the washing machine, resulted in the creation of Dryel, a home dry cleaning kit.[17]

in-depth interview
A research technique in which trained researchers ask questions, listen to and record the answers, and then pose additional questions to clarify or expand on a particular issue.

In-Depth Interviews   An **in-depth interview** is an exploratory research technique in which trained researchers ask questions, listen to and record the answers, and then pose additional questions to clarify or expand on a particular issue. For instance, in addition to simply watching teenagers shop for apparel, interviewers might stop them one at a time in the mall to ask them a few questions, such as: "We noticed that you went into and came out of Abercrombie & Fitch very quickly and without buying anything. Why was that?" If the subject responds that no one had bothered to wait on her, the interviewer might ask a follow-up question like, "Oh? Has that happened to you before?" or "Do you expect sales assistance there?" The results often provide insights that help managers better understand the nature of their industry, as well as important trends and consumer preferences, which can be invaluable for developing marketing strategies.

focus group interview
A research technique in which a small group of persons (usually 8 to 12) comes together for an intensive discussion about a particular topic, with the conversation guided by a trained moderator using an unstructured method of inquiry.

In-depth interviews provide quite a few benefits. They can provide a historical context for the phenomenon of interest, particularly when they include industry experts or experienced consumers. They also can communicate how people really feel about a product or service at the individual level, a level that rarely emerges from other methods that use group discussions. Finally, marketers can use the results of in-depth interviews to develop surveys.

A consumer is being interviewed.

Focus Group Interviews   In **focus group interviews**, a small group of persons (usually 8 to 12) comes together for an intensive discussion about a particular topic. Using an unstructured method of inquiry, a trained moderator guides the conversation on the basis of a predetermined general outline of the topics of interest. Researchers usually record

Ethical Dilemma ✋ | 5.1 Getting Up Close and Personal with Shoppers[18]

Successful marketing starts with knowing your customers—the more intimately you know them, the more likely you will be able to serve them. The key to learning about consumers is to get into their heads—a terribly difficult, if not impossible feat, but this is the challenge marketers face, especially in a fiercely competitive world where competition is global. Marketing professionals and researchers alike also know that often there is

Do you believe it is ethical for a firm to record the movements and activities of customers as they shop in a store? Would your opinion be different if the customers were informed that they were being watched?

a huge disconnect between what consumers tell you in surveys and focus groups and what they actually do when shopping in stores. Thus, many companies conduct in-store research such as mall intercepts, distributing in-store trials, free samples, store displays, and simply just observing consumers shop in order to get a better understanding of their attitudes and behaviours. Recently, Frito-Lay Canada placed GPS devices on grocery carts to determine consumers shopping patterns as they move through the store. The device basically tracks the aisles they visited, the time they spent at particular spots, etc. Frito-Lay then translated that information into actionable game plans to go to their retailers and implement merchandising tactics that responded to those findings. Indeed, the use of other observational research methods where consumers may be unaware that they are being studied in their natural habitat is on the rise.

In some cases researchers obtain consent from the consumers they are watching and videotaping, and in other cases do not. The ethical dilemma for marketing researchers centres around whether using observational techniques in which the subjects are not informed that they are being studied, like viewing customers in a mall or a retail store, violates the rule of fair treatment. Observing uninformed consumers very well may lead to important insights that would not otherwise be discovered. But do the results justify the methodology?

---

the interactions by video- or audiotape so they can carefully comb through the interviews later to catch any patterns of verbal or nonverbal responses.

In particular, focus groups gather qualitative data about initial reactions to a new or existing product or service, opinions about different competitive offerings, or reactions to marketing stimuli, like a new ad campaign or point-of-purchase display materials.

Lexus, for example, used focus groups to develop an advertising campaign for its ES 300 model. Finding the right message and determining the right medium to convey that message was imperative for the vehicle launch. Using extensive focus group testing with both current ES owners and owners of competitive models, Lexus set out to determine what "luxury" meant for consumers in their car purchases. Lexus owners saw luxury as "a personal oasis of tranquility and freedom." Armed with this information, Lexus initiated a targeted newspaper campaign that built on its "relentless pursuit of perfection" theme for the ES 300 launch.[19]

Virtual focus groups have started to make inroads into the market researchers' toolkit. Lego, for instance, invited over 10,000 kids to participate in a virtual focus group to get ideas for new products.[20] The participants saw short lists of proposed toys and clicked on the ones they liked. They ranked their choices and even suggested new ideas. These ideas were fed, in turn, to other potential customers and were rated against the ideas from Lego's own toy creators. The new suggestions, in turn, got creative juices flowing among still other potential customers. The resulting product, the Star Wars Imperial Destroyer, was different from anything else in Lego's 73-year history—it was Lego's largest and most expensive set ever, at 3100 parts and a $300 price tag. Its first production run, planned to last a year, sold in less than five weeks.

Projective Technique   A **projective technique** is a type of qualitative research in which subjects are provided a scenario and asked to express their thoughts and feelings about it. For example, consumers may be shown a cartoon that has a consumer looking at a shelf display in a supermarket with a text box above the consumer. The respondent would write in their thoughts on the issue in the text box. Thus, the cartoon allows the respondent to visualize the situation and project his/her thoughts or feelings by filling out the text box.

One question that must be going through your mind at this stage is which of these primary qualitative data collection techniques are used more frequently. Generally, focus groups and in-depth interviews are used more frequently than personal observations, especially ethnographic studies. Deciding which technique to use depends on several important considerations such as the objective of the research, the cost to undertake the research, time required to undertake the research, how soon the results are needed, and whether the marketer has the research expertise in-house or has to hire a market research firm to do the research, especially with methods such as ethnography and projective techniques. Normally, marketers have to make a trade-off between these considerations in order to get the results in a timely and cost-effective manner. Often a company may use several methods together in order to get actionable results.

Conclusive Research Methods

Conclusive research is intended to verify insights and to aid decision makers in selecting a specific course of action.[21] Conclusive research can be descriptive in nature—such as when it profiles a typical user or nonuser of a particular brand according to a survey. It can also be experimental—such as when a soft-drink producer conducts a taste test to determine which formulation of a green, high caffeine drink is preferred by customers. Conclusive research can also be collected from the merchandise that is scanned at a store, or from a group of customers, known as a panel, who record all of their purchases. In this section, we will discuss each of these conclusive research techniques—survey, experiment, scanner, and panel.

Survey Research   A **survey** is a systematic means of collecting information from people that generally uses a questionnaire. A **questionnaire** is a form that features a set of questions designed to gather information from respondents and thereby accomplish the researchers' objectives. Survey questionnaires can take different forms: phone, mail, or fax, delivered via the Internet or even conducted in person, for example, mall intercepts. Individual questions on a questionnaire can be either unstructured or structured. **Unstructured questions** are open-ended and allow respondents to answer in their own words. An unstructured question like "What are the most important characteristics for choosing a brand of shampoo?" yields an unstructured response. However, the same question could be posed to respondents in a structured format by providing a fixed set of response categories, like price, fragrance, ability to clean, and dandruff control, and then asking respondents to rate the importance of each. **Structured questions** thus are closed-ended questions for which a discrete set of response alternatives, or specific answers, is provided for respondents to evaluate (see Exhibit 5.6).

Developing a questionnaire is part art and part science. The questions must be carefully designed to address the specific set of research questions. Moreover, for

projective technique
A type of qualitative research in which subjects are provided a scenario and asked to express their thoughts and feelings about it.

Lego's Star Wars Imperial Destroyer, with 3100 parts and a $300 price tag was designed with the help of virtual focus groups.

survey
A systematic means of collecting information from people that generally uses a questionnaire.

questionnaire
A form that features a set of questions designed to gather information from respondents and thereby accomplish the researchers' objectives; questions can be either unstructured or structured.

unstructured questions
Open-ended questions that allow respondents to answer in their own words.

structured questions
Closed-ended questions for which a discrete set of response alternatives, or specific answers, is provided for respondents to evaluate.

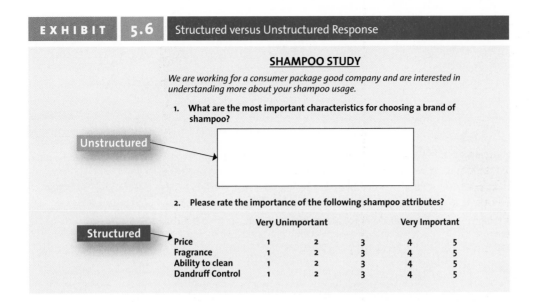

EXHIBIT | **5.6** | Structured versus Unstructured Response

SHAMPOO STUDY

We are working for a consumer package good company and are interested in understanding more about your shampoo usage.

1. **What are the most important characteristics for choosing a brand of shampoo?**

Unstructured

2. **Please rate the importance of the following shampoo attributes?**

	Very Unimportant				Very Important
Price	1	2	3	4	5
Fragrance	1	2	3	4	5
Ability to clean	1	2	3	4	5
Dandruff Control	1	2	3	4	5

Structured

a questionnaire to produce meaningful results, its questions cannot be misleading in any fashion (e.g., open to multiple interpretations), and they must address only one issue at a time. Furthermore, they must be worded in vocabulary that will be familiar and comfortable to those being surveyed. More specifically, the questions should be sequenced appropriately: general questions first, more specific questions next, and demographic questions at the end. Finally, the layout and appearance of the questionnaire must be professional and easy to follow, with appropriate instructions in suitable places. For some tips on what *not* to do when designing a questionnaire, see Exhibit 5.7.

Marketing surveys can be conducted either online or offline, but online marketing surveys offer researchers the chance to develop a database quickly with many responses, whereas offline marketing surveys provide a more direct approach that includes interactions with the target market.

Web surveys have steadily grown as a percentage of all quantitative surveys. Although the Internet has not proven effective for online focus groups, online surveys have a lot to offer managers with tight deadlines,[22] including the following benefits:

- **Response rates are relatively high.** Typical response rates run from 1 to 2 percent for mail and 10 to 15 percent for phone surveys. For online surveys, in contrast, the response rate can reach 30 to 35 percent, or even higher in business-to-business research.

- **Respondents may lie less.** Respondents lie in any medium. Have you ever wondered, for example, how many administrative assistants fill out mail surveys for their bosses? And what sort of answers they might give? Because the Internet has a higher perception of anonymity than telephone or mail contacts, respondents are more likely to be more truthful.

- **It is inexpensive.** An average 20-minute phone interview can cost $30 to $40, compared with $7 to $10 for an online interview. Costs likely will continue to fall more as users become more familiar with the online survey process.

Online marketing surveys enable researchers to develop a database quickly with many responses at a relatively low cost.

EXHIBIT 5.7	What Not to Do When Designing a Questionnaire	
Issue	**Good Question**	**Bad Question**
Avoid questions the respondent cannot easily or accurately answer.	When was the last time you went to the grocery store?	How much money did you spend on groceries last month?
Avoid sensitive questions unless they are absolutely necessary.	Do you take vitamins?	Do you dye your hair?
Avoid double-barreled questions, which refer to more than one issue with only one set of responses.	1. Do you think Stephane Dion would make a good prime minister? 2. Do you think Jack Layton would make a good prime minister?	Do you think that Stephane Dion or Jack Layton would make a good prime minister?
Avoid leading questions, which steer respondents to a particular response, irrespective of their true beliefs.	Please rate how safe you believe a Volvo is on a scale of 1 to 10, with 1 being not safe and 10 being very safe.	Volvo is the safest car on the road, right?
Avoid one-sided questions that present only one side of the issue.	To what extent do you feel fast food contributes to adult obesity? 1: Does not contribute, 5: Main cause	Fast food is responsible for adult obesity: Agree/Disagree
Avoid questions with implicit assumptions, which presume the same point of reference for all respondents.	Should children be allowed to drink Coca-Cola in school?	Since caffeine is a stimulant, should children be allowed to drink Coca-Cola in school?
Avoid complex questions and those that may seem unfamiliar to respondents.	What brand of wristwatch do you typically wear?	Do you believe that mechanical watches are better than quartz watches?

Source: Adapted from A. Parasuraman, Dhruv Grewal, and R. Krishnan, *Marketing Research,* 2nd ed. (Boston, MA: Houghton Mifflin, 2007), Ch. 10.

- **Results are processed and received quickly.** Reports and summaries can be developed in real time and delivered directly to managers in simple, easy-to-digest reports, complete with colour, graphics, and charts. Traditional phone or mail surveys require laborious data collection, tabulation, summary, and distribution before anyone can grasp their results.

- **Greater use of multimedia elements**. Online surveys allow marketers to show their products with graphics, sounds, and movement and then ask questions based on the images shown. This gives marketers greater flexibility in asking questions, which tends to increase response rates and generate more truthful answers.

The Internet can also be used to collect data other than that available from quantitative surveys. If consumers give a firm permission to market to them, the firm can collect data about their usage of its website and other Internet applications. In addition, open-ended questionnaires can be used to collect more in-depth qualitative data.

Survey research is widely used for descriptive research to study consumers' attitudes, preferences, behaviours, and knowledge about products and brands. It is generally more cost-effective than other methods for reaching a large sample of consumers. Survey questionnaires usually yield quantitative data that can be easily analyzed using sophisticated statistical methods to analyze the relationships among variables. However, it suffers from a few shortcomings. Consumers may be unable to answer some of the questions on the questionnaire, cannot recall the information, or may even interpret the questions differently from what the researchers intended. Some may even try to answer the questions according to what they think the researchers want. Another big problem, especially in the data analysis phase, is when respondents answer some but not all the questions on the questionnaire. Incomplete data makes the analysis and interpretation of the data more complicated and tricky.

Experimental research is a type of quantitative research that systematically manipulates one or more variables to determine which variable(s) have a causal effect on another variable. For example, suppose Cheesecake Factory is trying to determine the most profitable price for a new menu item. They put the item on the menu at four different prices in four different markets. In general, the more expensive the item, the less it will sell. But by running this experiment, they determine that the most profitable item is the second most expensive item. Evidently, some people believed the most expensive item was too expensive, so they didn't buy it. The two least expensive sold fairly well, but Cheesecake didn't make as much money on each item sold. In this experiment, we believe that the changes in price caused the changes in quantities sold, and therefore impacted profitability.

experimental research
A type of quantitative research that systematically manipulates one or more variables to determine which variable has a causal effect on another variable.

Scanner research is a type of quantitative research that uses data obtained from scanner readings of UPC codes at check-out counters. Whenever you go into your local grocery store, your purchases are rung up using scanner systems. The data from these purchases are likely to be acquired by leading marketing research firms, such as Information Resources Inc. or AC Nielsen. They use this information to help leading consumer package good firms (e.g., Kellogg's, Pepsi, and Sara Lee) assess what is happening in the marketplace. For example, a firm can determine what would happen to sales if they reduced their price by 10 percent in a given month. Did it increase, decrease, or stay the same?

scanner research
A type of quantitative research that uses data obtained from scanner readings of UPC codes at checkout counters.

Panel research is a type of quantitative research that involves collecting information from a group of consumers (the panel) over time. The data collected from the panellists may be from a survey, or a record of purchases. This data provides consumer package good firms with a comprehensive picture of what individual consumers are buying or not buying. Thus, one key difference between scanner research and panel research is the nature of aggregation. Scanner research typically focuses on weekly consumption of a particular product at a given unit of analysis (e.g., individual store, chain, and region); whereas panel research focuses on the total weekly consumption of a particular person or group of people. Exhibit 5.8 highlights some of the differences between exploratory and conclusive research methods.

panel research
A type of quantitative research that involves collecting information from a group of consumers (the panel) over time; data collected may be from a survey or a record of purchases.

EXHIBIT 5.8	Differences Between Exploratory and Conclusive Research	
Research Project Components	**Exploratory Research**	**Conclusive Research**
Research purpose	General: to generate insights about a situation	Specific: to verify insights and aid in selecting a course of action
Data needs	Vague	Clear
Data sources	Ill defined	Well defined
Data collection form	Open-ended, rough	Usually structured
Sample	Relatively small, often not randomly drawn; subjectively selected to maximize generalization of insights	Relatively large and randomly drawn; objectively selected to permit generalization of findings
Data collection	Often flexible; no set procedure	Generally rigid; well-laid-out procedure
Data analysis	Informal; typically nonquantitative	Formal; typically quantitative
Inferences/ recommendations	More tentative than final	More final than tentative

Source: A. Parasuraman, Dhruv Grewal, and R. Krishnan, *Marketing Research*, 2nd ed. Copyright © 2007 by Hougton Mifflin Company. Adapted with permission.

Regardless of how they do it though, collecting data can be an expensive process for entrepreneurs working on a shoestring budget. Entrepreneurial Marketing 5.1 suggests a host of avenues that they might pursue.

Like exploratory data collection methods, the choice of conclusive data collection methods also depends foremost on the marketing research objectives, which are balanced by other considerations such as cost, timeliness, and usefulness of the results. Surveys using questionnaires are the most commonly used conclusive research methods.

Step 4: Analyze Data

data
Raw numbers or other factual information of limited value.

information
Data that has been organized, analyzed, and interpreted, and converted into a useful form for decision makers.

The next step in the marketing research process—analyzing and interpreting the data—should be both thorough and methodical. To generate meaningful information, researchers analyze and make use of the collected data. In this context, **data** can be defined as raw numbers or other factual information that, on their own, have limited value to marketers. However, when the data are interpreted, they become **information,** which results from organizing, analyzing, and interpreting data and puts the data into a form that is useful to marketing decision-makers. For example, a checkout scanner in the grocery store collects sales data about individual consumer purchases. Not until those data are categorized and examined do they provide information about which products and services were purchased together or how an in-store promotional activity translated into sales. For example, a certain department store ran a special Christmas promotion on a brand of men's white shirt and tie, which were sold together at a discounted price if paid for with the store's credit card. Subsequent analysis of the raw scanner data revealed that the shirt and tie promotion, although targeted to men, was purchased mainly by women. Armed with this information, the store then sent personalized letters in the mail thanking the women for their purchases and informing them of a Valentines' special on a blazer for their loved ones, which will make a perfect fit with the shirt and tie they bought in December.

The purpose of converting data to information is to describe, explain, predict, and/or evaluate a particular situation. For example, Wendy, the downtown Ottawa-based retailer of tweens clothing learned that her core customers live in various suburbs around the outskirts of the downtown. This piece of data takes on new meaning when she learns that none of these customers were drawn to her store by a clever and expensive direct mail campaign. By analyzing data she collected through a survey, she discovered that her core customers are working professionals who are drawn to the store when they walk by it on their way to and from work, not people from the upscale apartments in the downtown region that she targeted with her direct mail advertisements.

Coinstar, a worldwide leader of self-service coin counting machines, uses sophisticated regression models to identify and rank potential locations for its machines.

Data analysis might be as simple as calculating the average purchases of different customer segments or as complex as forecasting sales by market segment using elaborate statistical techniques. Coinstar, a worldwide leader in self-service coin counting, has begun analyzing marketing research in increasingly sophisticated ways. The company operates machines in more than 10,000 supermarkets in Canada, the United States, and the United Kingdom; consumers use the machines, which can count up to 600 coins per minute, to process large volumes of change that they exchange for a voucher good for cash or groceries. Since it was founded in

1991, the company has tried to identify new and profitable locations on an ongoing basis as demand for its services continues to grow. When the company was small, coming up with "best guesses" of prime locations based on intuition worked out well, but Coinstar researchers recently developed regression models to identify and rank potential locations where it could locate its "green machines." This approach greatly improved Coinstar's ability to find prospective locations and forecast those that had the best potential for growth and profitability. The company can now capitalize on the estimated $7.7 billion in coins sitting in people's homes, waiting to be converted to paper money or grocery purchases.[23]

It is important for market researchers to analyze and interpret the data in an objective manner and do not try to hide or colour coat findings that are different from what they had hoped for. Misinterpreting the findings or manipulating the statistics in a way to suit the researcher's hunch or prediction could lead to the wrong decision, which could have serious consequences for marketers. The temptation to lie with statistics is something market researchers have to always be aware of and try to avoid.

Step 5: Present Results

In the final phase in the marketing research process, the analyst prepares the results and presents them to the appropriate decision-makers. A typical marketing research report includes an executive summary, the body of the report (which discusses the research objectives, methodology used, and detailed findings), the conclusions, the limitations, and appropriate supplemental tables, figures, and appendixes. To be effective, a written report must be short, interesting, methodical, precise, lucid, and free of errors.[24] Furthermore, the reports should use a style appropriate to the audience and devoid of technical jargon and include recommendations that managers can actually implement.

For example, when eBrain, a marketing research firm in Arlington, Virginia, surveyed 1522 women regarding their consumer electronics experiences, the researchers found that they needed to report some rather startling results. Approximately three-quarters of those surveyed stated that they had received better service when they shopped with a man; 40 percent even claimed that they typically would only shop with men in tow. One of their biggest gripes was that service personnel were consistently condescending to them. Reporting these findings in a straightforward manner allowed the consumer electronics managers who received the report to implement some meaningful programs that acknowledged that women account for more than half of the $97 billion in consumer electronic sales each year and, beyond that figure, influence three-quarters of electronics purchases.

Several retailers responded accordingly.[25] Target paired up with Sony to offer a line of consumer electronics branded "Liv" that would attract the store's core market of women between the ages of 25 and 40 years. SoundTrack stores retrained its staff to stress product benefits rather than features and began to designate its delivery service as "Red Carpet" treatment, which meant literally that the deliverers would protect floor surfaces in consumers' homes. Circuit City opened two pilot stores under the name "Iris" that it intended to be more appealing to women, and Best Buy tailored its stores to appeal to its female customers. The Source started offering health and relaxation products, known as its "Lifeline" product mix. Home Depot and Rona widened their aisles and made their stores more women-friendly.

Entrepreneurial Marketing

5.1   Marketing Research on a Shoestring Budget

Imagine your company needs some research conducted but has a relatively small budget. Fortunately, marketing research does not have to have a high price tag, though it always takes drive and knowledge. Here are some ways to uncover the information you and your company might need without breaking the bank.

Objective: What is it that you need to know?

- **Network.** Use your phone directory on your cell phone and call friends and professional colleagues. In most cases, researchers probably already know people in the industry who will be able to share their knowledge. They can help marketers determine what their objectives should be in upcoming research projects.

Customer Analysis: Who are your customers, and what do they want?

- **Customers.** Talk with current and prospective customers. Ask them the right questions, and they will provide the necessary answers. This approach is remarkably cheap because it entails only the researcher's labour, though it will require a large time commitment. Marketers need to take care how they ask the questions though; people tend to provide answers that they think the questioner wants or that seem socially acceptable.

- **Online.** Use a search engine like Google by simply typing in some appropriate keywords.

- **Statistics Canada.** Statistics Canada is an important source of information. At www.statcan.ca, industry, demographic, and economic reports are all accessible for free. Although not known for its ease of use, the website offers a wealth of information.

Competitive Analysis: What are your competitors doing?

Secondary Sources: Many are listed in Exhibit 5.2 in this chapter.

- **Websites.** Visit competitors' websites, if they have them. Learn about their products and services, pricing, management team, and philosophies. Read their press releases. You can even infer what part of the business is thriving through reading their career pages.

- **SEC Filings.** If competitors are public, they are required to file 10K forms annually with the Securities Exchange Commission (SEC). Search for SEC filings using www.finance.yahoo.com or http://

moneycentral.msn.com/home.asp, both of which provide sales and expense numbers, in addition to other important information in the footnotes.

- **University Libraries Electronic Databases.** Most Canadian universities subscribe to several electronic business databases that provide information on Canadian companies. These databases are usually accessible remotely by students, staff, and alumnus at no cost to users. A sample of these databases include Canadian Business Resource, Canadian Business & Current Affairs, Factiva, Financial Post databases, MarketResearch.com, Mergent Online, Mergent WebReports, Proquest Asian Business, and Proquest European Business. Many of these databases provide company profiles, financial data, contact information, and short stories or case studies on company successes, failures, and innovations.

- **Go There.** If competitors are smaller mom-and-pop stores, visit them. Hang out in front of the store armed with a pad and paper and count the number of people who walk in, then the percentage of people that walk out having purchased something. Use logic and judgment. Have the customers purchased items that appear to have higher profit margins? Find out where and what competitors are advertising.

- **NAICS Codes.** For a wider view of the competitive industry, review the North American Industry Classification System (NAICS) codes. The NAICS identifies companies operating in an industry sector with a six digit code. The government's website at strategis.ic.gc.ca and www.statcan.ca help pinpoint the correct NAICS code and can generate an industry-specific report. For example, if you want to identify women's clothing stores, you would go to number 44812. The first two digits, 44, identify merchandise retailers (as would 45). The third digit breaks down the merchandise retailers further. For example, retailers selling clothing and clothing accessories are in classification 448, while general merchandise retailers are in classification 452. The fourth digit subdivides clothing and accessory retailers (448) into clothing stores (4481), shoe stores (4482), and jewellery and luggage stores (4483). The fifth digit provides a further breakdown into men's clothing stores (44811) and women's clothing stores (44812). The sixth digit (not shown here) is used to capture differences in the three North American countries using the classification scheme, the United States, Mexico, and Canada.

Classification by Type of Merchandise

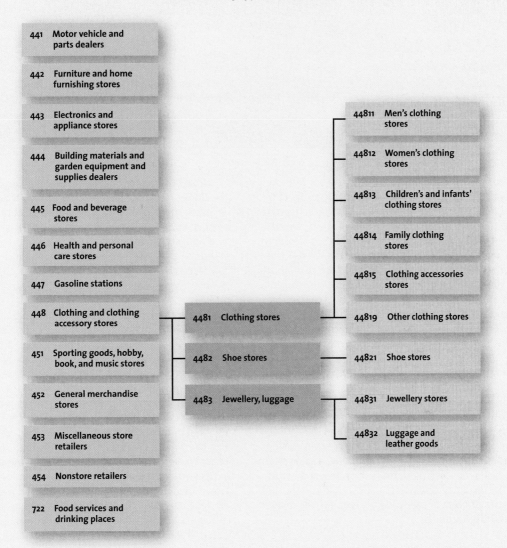

Focus Groups, Surveys, and Analyst Reports: What detailed information can you gather?

- **Be Specific.** Determine precisely what information is required; it is very costly to pay for research that does not assist in a decision or provide strategic direction.

- **Surveys.** Determine what form will provide the most value. Phone surveys cost about $40 per interview, mailings average from $5000 to $15,000 for 200 responses, and e-mail and Web-based surveys usually are much cheaper.

- **Focus Groups.** Although focus groups can be more expensive, there are ways to cut corners. Develop the questions in-house, and don't outsource the moderator or facility. It is important, however, to find the right participants.

- **Analyst Reports.** Prewritten reports, covering a broad price range and a wide variety of questions, are available for purchase from the hundreds of companies that write and sell reports. Two of the best known are www.forrester.com and www.hoovers.com.

Learning Objectives Review

1) Explain how marketers use information systems to create value for customers

2) Discuss ethical issues firms encounter when conducting marketing research

3) Describe the necessary steps to conduct marketing research

4) Explain the differences between primary and secondary data, and determine when each should be used

5) Explain the differences between exploratory and conclusive research

1) A marketing information system (MIS) is a set of procedures and methods for the regular, planned collection, analysis, and presentation of information that marketers can use to make marketing decisions. An MIS provides a means to accumulate information from sources both internal and external to the organization, which then makes that information routinely available to managers for their informed decision making. In turn, an MIS enables firms to understand what customers want better through analyses of their purchases. This specialized knowledge can translate into purchasing and promotion programs that are tailor-made for customers.

2) Marketing researchers have obligations to their subjects and to society to behave in an ethical manner. This responsibility means that marketing researchers must take every precaution to ensure the confidentiality of the data they collect from consumers and the privacy of study participants. Researchers should never misrepresent the purpose of a study; for example, a sales pitch should never be cast as a marketing research study. Finally, the results of research studies should be reported fully. If data or parts of the study are ignored, the results might be misinterpreted.

3) There are five steps in the marketing research process. The first step is to define the problem and research objectives and research needs, which sounds so simple that managers often gloss over it. But this step is crucial to the success of any research project because, quite basically, the research must answer those questions that are important for making decisions. In the second step, designing the research project, researchers identify the type of data that are needed, whether primary or secondary, on the basis of the objectives of the project from Step 1, and then determine the type of research that enables them to collect those data. The third step involves deciding on the data collection process and collecting the data. Depending on the research objectives and the findings from the secondary data search, researchers will choose either exploratory or conclusive research. Exploratory research usually involves observation, in-depth interviews, or projective techniques, whereas if the project calls for conclusive research, the researchers may perform a survey, an experiment, or use scanner, and panel data. The fourth step is to analyze and interpret the data, and the fifth and final step is to prepare the findings for presentation. Although these steps appear to progress in a linear fashion, researchers often work backward through the process as they learn at each step.

4) Secondary data are pieces of information that have been collected from other sources, such as the Census, internal company sources, the Internet, books, articles, trade associations, or syndicated data services. Primary data are data collected to address specific research needs, usually through observation, focus groups, interviews, surveys, or experiments. Research projects typically start with secondary research, which provides a background for what information is already known and what research has been done previously. Also, compared with primary research, secondary research is quicker, easier, and less expensive, and it requires less methodological expertise. However, secondary research likely was collected for reasons other than those pertaining to the specific problem at hand, which means the information may be dated, biased, or simply not specific enough to answer the research questions. Primary research, in contrast, can be designed to answer very specific questions, but it also can be expensive and time consuming.

5) Many managers use exploratory research methods as the first phase of the research process in order to get a deeper insight into the situation. Exploratory research methods include observation, in-depth interviewing, focus groups, and projective techniques. Conclusive research is used to verify the insights gained from exploratory research and aid in choosing a course of action. Conclusive research methods involve experiments, surveys, scanner, and panel research. With both exploratory and conclusive research methods, the specific methods managers choose depends foremost on the marketing research objectives, which must be balanced by other considerations such as costs, timeliness, and usefulness of the results.

Key Terms

- conclusive research, 128
- data, 136
- data mining, 119
- data warehouses, 118
- ethnography, 130
- experimental research, 135
- exploratory research, 128
- focus group interview, 130
- hypothesis, 129
- in-depth interview, 130

- information, 136
- marketing information system (MIS), 118
- marketing research, 116
- observation, 129
- panel research, 135
- primary data, 126
- projective technique, 132
- questionnaire, 132
- reliability, 126

- sample, 128
- sampling, 128
- scanner research, 135
- secondary data, 123
- structured questions, 132
- survey, 132
- syndicated data, 123
- unstructured questions, 132
- validity, 126

Concept Review

1. What is a marketing information system? Explain how a marketing information system could help a company create better value for its customers and itself.

2. Briefly describe the steps in the marketing research process. Explain why it is important to clearly define the problem and research objectives from the very outset of the process.

3. What is the difference between secondary and primary data? What are some of the advantages of each type of data? When should each type of data be used?

4. In data collection methods, researchers may choose between exploratory research methods or conclusive research methods or use both methods. What considerations guide their choice of data collection methods?

5. Today, information and communications technologies (ICT) including the Internet are not only changing the way marketing is practised but how market research is conducted. In response, many companies are using a wide variety of observational methods (GPS, RFID, video camera, audio devices, ethnography, etc.) to gather customer data. Discuss the ethical issues underlying the increasing use of observational research methods using technology.

6. Marketing research is designed to help marketers make better decisions on various aspects of their businesses. The quality of research findings is as good as the quality of the data on which they are based. What are some things marketers could do to ensure that they obtain the best quality data?

7. Explain the main advantages and disadvantages of using the Internet for marketing research versus conventional offline methods.

8. Identify and explain the ways in which the design of a market research study could reduce the reliability and validity of the study. Can a market research study that has high reliability lack validity? Can a study that has high validity lack reliability? Explain your answers.

9. What do you think are some of the differences between exploratory data collection methods, which are mainly qualitative, and conclusive research methods, which are more quantitative in nature? Which type of method should a research prefer and why?

10. Explain some of the problems and challenges market researchers face in the data analysis and interpretation stage of the marketing research process. Should they report these problems when presenting their research report? Why or why not?

Marketing Applications

1. A large department store collects data about what its customers buy and stores these data in a data warehouse. If you were the store's buyer for children's clothing, what would you want to know from the data warehouse that would help you be a more successful buyer?

2. Identify a nonprofit organization that might use marketing research, and describe one example of a meaningful research project that it might conduct. Discuss how this project would be useful to the organization.

3. Marketing researchers do not always go through the steps in the marketing research process in sequential order. Provide an example of a research project that might not follow this sequence.

4. A new men's clothing store is trying to determine if there is a significant market for its type of merchandise in a specific location where it is considering putting a store. Would it be most likely to use primary or secondary data, or a combination of the two, to answer this question?

5. A high-tech firm has just developed a new technology to correct bad vision without surgery or contact lenses. The company needs to estimate the demand for such a service. Would it use primary or secondary data, or a combination of the two?

6. A bank manager notices that by the time customers get to the teller, they seem irritated and impatient. She wants to investigate the problem further, so she hires you to design a research project to figure out what is bothering the customers. What type of research method would you recommend? Is it an exploratory or conclusive method?

7. Snapple has developed a new beverage, and it wants to determine if it should begin to market it throughout Canada. The company used two separate studies for the advertising campaign:

   - A focus group to identify the appropriate advertising message for the new beverage, and
   - A survey to assess the effectiveness of the advertising campaign for the new Snapple beverage.

   Which study was exploratory and which was conclusive?

8. What other studies would you recommend Snapple undertake?

9. Suppose your university wants to modify its course scheduling procedures to better serve students. What are some secondary sources of information that might be used to conduct research into this topic? Describe how these sources might be used. Describe a method you could use to gather primary research data about the topic. Would you recommend a specific order in obtaining each of these types of data? Explain your answer.

10. Tony is planning to launch a new shampoo and is trying to decide what features and price would interest consumers. He sends a request for proposal to four marketing research vendors, and three respond, as described in the table below. Which vendor should Tony use? Explain your rationale for picking this vendor over the others.

Vendor A	Vendor B	Vendor C
The vendor that Tony has used in the past, it estimates it can get the job done for $200,000 and in two months. The vendor plans to do a telephone-based survey analysis and use secondary data.	Tony's key competitor has used this vendor, which claims that it can get the job done for $150,000 and in one month. This vendor plans to do a telephone-based survey analysis and use secondary data. During a discussion pertaining to its price and time estimates, the vendor indicates it will draw on insights it has learned from a recent report prepared for one of Tony's competitors.	This well-known vendor has recently started to focus on consumer packaged good clients. It quotes a price of $180,000 and a time of one month. The vendor plans to conduct a Web-based survey analysis and use secondary data.

Net Savvy

1. Go to the website of either Decima Research (www. decima.com) or Ipsos Canada (www.ipsos.ca), which administers public opinion polls. Search the site for results from any recent survey that is available for free. Print out the results. Identify the objective(s) of the survey. Discuss one of the major findings, and provide an interpretation of the data.

2. Visit the Eopinions.com website (www.eopinions.com), a clearinghouse for consumer reviews about different products and services. Think of a particular business with which you are familiar, and review the ratings and comments for that business. Discuss the extent to which this site might be useful to a marketer for that company who needs to gather market research about the company and its competitors. Identify the type of research this process involves—secondary or primary? Exploratory or conclusive?

Chapter Case Study

RESEARCH BOOSTS IAMS SALES[26]

No longer just man's best friend, Canadians are spending more time with their pets than they did three years ago. Over 50 percent of Canadian households have pets.[27]

Recently there's been a big increase in the amount of money people are willing to spend on their pets. According to Louis McCann, executive director of the Ottawa-based Pet Industry Joint Advisory Council of Canada (PIJAC), the thriving pet industry has grown from a value of about $3.5 billion in 2001 to $4.5 billion today.[28]

More than ever, pet owners view their pet as a member of the family. One survey showed that 50 percent of people chose their pet as the one companion they would want on a desert island.[29]

And so, when the world's number one maker of household products, Procter & Gamble, was on the lookout for acquisitions, the pet industry was attractive. It purchased The Iams Company in 1999, adding it to its Health Care global business unit. Founded by animal nutritionist Paul Iams in 1946,[30] the brand was well recognized and well respected even though it was only available at specialty outlets such as PetSmart and Petcetera and through veterinarians.

Under P&G's ownership, distribution channels were dramatically expanded to mass retailers and grocery store channels, such as Loblaws, Wal-Mart, and Costco. After analyzing the first round of sales results, P&G discovered that awareness for the Iams brand was very high—over 85 percent of pet owners knew about it. Nicolas Lopez, brand manager for Iams at the time, says that existing consumers were extremely loyal. However, the number of pet households that had tried the brand was low with only 25 percent of pet owners ever purchasing the product.

Research was needed to determine how to get more customers to try the product. Lopez says research efforts started with in-depth interviews, intercepting pet owners in parks. These interviews provided an opportunity to understand why some consumers were buying Iams as well as talk to pet owners who weren't currently buying it.

In talking to people who had not yet tried Iams, the focus was on understanding the barriers to trying the product. Through these interviews, Lopez learned that people loved their pets so much they were willing to pay much more if it was the right thing for their pet. This insight became very useful later when a new marketing campaign was developed.

Following these interviews, P&G conducted observational research, spending time with consumers in their homes. The goal was to watch how people interacted with their pets and gain a better understanding of how the Iams brand made a difference in their pets' lives. Lopez says they witnessed firsthand the trend of "pet humanization," pets being given a much more prominent role in the household. In some cases, pets were considered and treated like children.

Naturally these pet owners wanted to know they'd made the right decision about every aspect related to their pet, including food. The research team took note when customers commented on the changes they saw in their pets after feeding them Iams, for example, shinier coats, better digestion, better health, more energy. People claimed their dogs seemed healthier.

Armed with the insights gleaned from in-depth interviews and observation, the Iams team talked to P&G's scientists about the product formula and learned more about the proven technology behind each benefit pet owners cited. This knowledge led the team to develop a marketing campaign geared at consumers that more tightly linked the science behind the brand with the benefits pets would experience after a few weeks of transitioning into Iams, for example, tartar control. The campaign revolved around the concept of "Iams provides visible signs of a healthier pet after only four weeks." P&G focused on five main signs of health: digestion, skin and coat, muscle tone, sparkle in their eyes, and activity levels.

As part of the campaign, P&G provided Iams to radio personalities to feed their dogs, asking them to look for the five signs of health in their pet. These radio personalities then talked about the results on-air.

The research efforts paid off. The marketing campaign was a success and Iams market share increased by 2.5 percent over three years.

Observing pet owners interacting with their pets led P&G to focus on the visible health benefits in its advertising campaigns.

Questions

1. How did P&G define the problem for Iams in the first step of the research process?

2. What type of research method—exploratory or conclusive—did P&G use? Propose other research methods besides in-depth interviews and observational studies that would enable P&G to answer the same research questions. Which method(s) would you use?

3. Why would secondary data not have been very useful in helping P&G understand how to convince consumers to switch to Iams?

CHAPTER 6

Consumer
Behaviour

Sony released its first ever Walkman, the blue-and-silver model shown in the picture, in Japan on July 1, 1979. Not to be undone, by the late 1980s, the Walkman faced stiff competition from the likes of the Walky (Toshiba) and the CassetteBoy (Aiwa). The Walkman not only won the battle, but the name Walkman became a generic term to describe mobile music devices in much the same way as Rollerblade became the generic term for inline skates. However, by the 1990s, the cassette-based Walkman was approaching technological obsolescence, so Sony introduced its Discman. It gradually replaced the cassette-based Walkman and kept Sony as the leader in mobile music. By 2000 Sony had produced over 150 million Walkmans in over 300 different models covering all segments of the market from the cradle to the grave and from the adventurous to the couch potato. But the Walkman's iconic status and dominance was soon to be tested when Apple, a newcomer to the mobile music business, introduced its iPod in October 2001.[1]

During the first quarter of its launch, Apple sold more than 14 million iPods, a figure that could have even been much higher had Apple not underestimated consumer demand. iPods sold out as fast as they came in. Millions of consumers dumped their Walkman and MP3 players for iPods. Just five years after its launch, Apple announced that it had sold over 100 million iPods worldwide. This made the iPod the best-selling music player in history. By 2007, the iPod had close to 80 percent market share in the US and over 55 percent in Canada for all types of mobile players. Even in Japan, the home of the Sony Walkman, the iPod had close to 50 percent market share compared to just about 20 percent for the Walkman. Sony officials acknowledged they had lost to the iPod, not only in overseas markets but also in Japan. Like Sony's Walkman, Apple's iPod became synonymous with all types of MP3 players, except in a much shorter time.

The iPod had far reaching effects on both consumers and businesses, spawning a completely new industry around it—iPod covers, accessories, speakers, adapters, etc. Levi Strauss announced iPod compatible jeans in 2006. BMW released the first iPod automobile interface, allowing drivers of newer BMW vehicles to control their iPod using either the built-in steering wheel controls or the radio head-unit buttons. Some independent stereo manufacturers including JVC, Pioneer, Kenwood, and Alpine, have iPod-specific integration solutions. Beginning in mid-2007, four major airlines, United, Continental, Delta, and Emirates reached agreements to install iPod seat connections. The free service allows passengers to power and charge their iPod, and view their video and music libraries on individual seat-back displays. Even competitors such as Sony Ericsson, Nokia, and Microsoft are modifying their products to work better with the iPod format.

The word podcast, derived from the term iPod, was named 'word of the year' in 2005 by the *New Oxford American Dictionary*. Not only is podcasting an industry in its own right, but it is beginning to challenge conventional radio's broadcasting and business model. Many radio stations (e.g., CBC, CTV) have responded by offering their content as a podcast. Even professors and other professional trainers and organizations are using podcasts to deliver academic and training courses.

Okay, so the iPod has produced revolutionary changes in much the same way as Google did with online search. Can it ever be dethroned? Despite all the talk of iPod killers from the likes of Sony, Microsoft, Creative Design, and others, the iPod is still ahead of the pack. Why? Because it delivers real value to consumers. Apple figures that consumers want a functional music device that is aesthetically pleasing, stylish, and can connect with them at an emotional level—and that is exactly what iPod delivers. Apple delivers value through its marketing communications—the white earphones or "earbuds" that ship with all iPods have become symbolic of the brand. Advertisements feature them prominently, often contrasting the white earphones (and cords) with people shown as dark silhouettes. Apple also delivers value in its pricing and distribution strategy—priced competitively to show its difference in the marketplace and distributed at selected resellers.

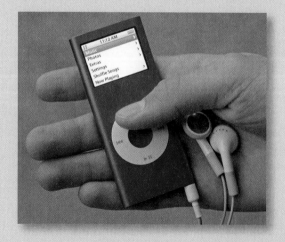

Walkman model TPS-L2, went on sale July 1, 1979. iPod launched in October 2001.

Who has ever bought or received something from others? All of us have, of course; we are all consumers at one time or another. But we are also complex and irrational creatures who cannot always explain our own actions. This trait makes the job of marketing managers even more difficult because without a deep understanding of consumers' behaviour, they will not be able to properly satisfy the needs and wants of their customers. Using theories from sociology, anthropology, and psychology, marketers have been able to decipher many consumer actions and develop basic strategies for dealing with their behaviour.

To understand consumer behaviour, we must ascertain why people buy products or services. Generally, people buy one product or service instead of another because they perceive it to be the better value for them; that is, the ratio of benefits to costs is higher for that product or service than for any other.[2] Consider the tens of thousands of Canadians who purchased Apple's iPod on the very first day it was released in Canada. In making the decision to abandon or replace their MP3 players or Walkmans with the iPod, they must have asked themselves

- What is the best overall value I am getting for price I am paying for the iPod?
- What would friends, family, and co-workers think about my latest gadget?

In this chapter, we explore the process that consumers go through when buying products and services. We also discuss how the consumer buying decision process changes based on the type of buying situations. Then we discuss the psychological, social, cultural, and situational factors that influence this consumer decision process. Throughout the chapter, we illustrate what firms can do to influence consumers to purchase their products and services. The chapter roadmap outlines the major topics covered in this chapter.

The Consumer Decision Process

LO **1**

The consumer decision process model represents the steps that consumers go through before, during, and after making purchases. Because marketers often find it difficult to determine how consumers make their purchasing decisions, it is useful for us to

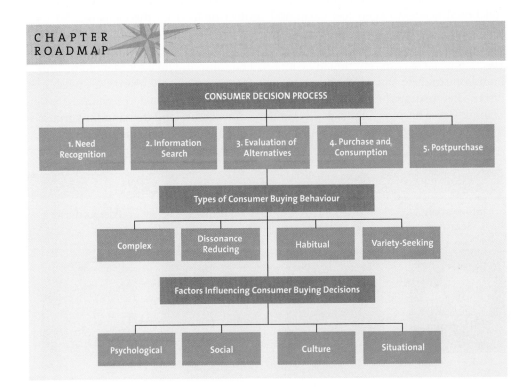

Sarah Jessica Parker's character, Carrie, on HBO's Sex and the City *made Manolo Blahnik's brand of expensive shoes a "must have" in some circles.*

need recognition
The beginning of the consumer decision process; occurs when consumers recognize they have an unsatisfied need and want to go from their actual, needy state to a different, desired state.

break down the process into a series of steps and examine each individually,[3] as in Exhibit 6.1.

Step 1: Need Recognition

The consumer decision process begins when consumers recognize they have an unsatisfied need and want to go from their actual, needy state to a different, desired state. The greater the discrepancy between these two states, the greater the **need recognition** will be. For example, your stomach tells you that you are hungry, and you would rather not have that particular feeling. If you are only a little hungry, you may pass it off and decide to eat later. But if your stomach is growling and you cannot concentrate, the need—the difference between your actual (hungry) state and your desired (not hungry) state—is greater, and you'll want to eat immediately to get to your desired state. Consumer needs like these can be classified as functional, psychological, or a combination of both.[4]

functional needs
Pertain to the performance of a product or service.

Functional Needs   **Functional needs** pertain to the performance of a product or service. For years, materials like GORE-TEX, Polartec, and Thinsulate have been viewed as functionally superior to others that might be used in rugged, high-performance outerwear. Knowing that consumers seek out these materials, high-end outdoor manufacturers such as North Face prominently display the material content on each piece of clothing and equipment they offer. Even mass merchandisers have jumped on this bandwagon.

psychological needs
Pertain to the personal gratification consumers associate with a product or service.

Psychological Needs   **Psychological needs** pertain to the personal gratification consumers associate with a product and/or service. Shoes, for instance, provide a functional need—to keep feet clean and protect them from the elements. So why would anyone pay $500 to $2000 for shoes that may do neither? Because they are seeking a way to satisfy psychological needs. Sarah Jessica Parker's character Carrie on HBO's *Sex and the City*, continually confessed her undying love for Manolo Blahnik's brand of exquisite shoes. Episode after episode, fans not only heard the stylish cast discuss his creations but also were treated to glimpses of his masterpieces. As a result, Blahniks have become a household name in some circles, and demand far surpasses the 15,000 pairs per month that four factories outside Milan can manufacture.[5]

EXHIBIT 6.1   The Consumer Decision Process

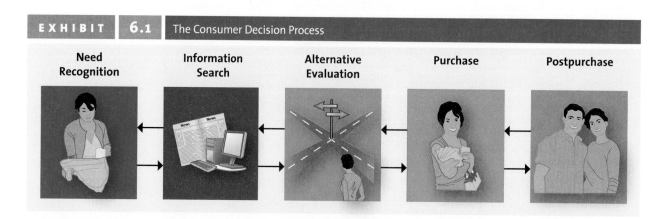

| Need Recognition | Information Search | Alternative Evaluation | Purchase | Postpurchase |

These examples highlight that the vast majority of products and services are likely to satisfy both functional and psychological needs. Whereas the functional characteristics of GORE-TEX are its main selling point, it also maintains a fashionable appeal for mountain climber "wannabes." In contrast, Manolo Blahnik shoes satisfy psychological needs that overshadow the functional needs they serve. For instance, you can get a $15 haircut at First Choice Haircutters or spend $80 or more to get basically the same thing at an upscale salon. Are the two haircuts objectively different? The answer might vary depending on which you believe represents a good haircut and good value. One person might value getting a really good deal; another might enjoy the extra attention and amenities associated with a fancy salon. A key to successful marketing is determining the correct balance of functional and psychological needs that best appeals to the firm's target markets. Harley-Davidson, for instance, produces motorcycles that do much more than get their riders to the mall and back. Harleys are a way of life for motorcycle enthusiasts who want to ride and have fun, as we discuss in Adding Value 6.1.

Step 2: Search for Information

LO **2**

The second step, after a consumer recognizes a need, is to search for information about the various options that exist to satisfy that need. The length and intensity of the search are based on the degree of perceived risk and costs associated with

---

Adding Value   6.1   H.O.G. Heaven[6]

It seems as though everybody wants a piece of H.O.G. Heaven these days. For years, Harley-Davidson motorcycles have been the premier form of two-wheeled transportation for motorcycle enthusiasts, and demand has exceeded supply. Even though other manufacturers, such as BMW, Yamaha, Suzuki, Honda, and Kawasaki offer functional, dependable, fast motorcycles, they cannot compete with the Harley mystique.

A rich history, rider support, and its protected brand have contributed to Harley's cultlike following. Ten short years after William S. Harley and Arthur Davidson assembled their first motorcycles in a wooden shed in 1903, the company had opened a Milwaukee factory, won several racing awards, incorporated and introduced its first V-twin–powered motorcycle, and patented the classic "Bar and Shield" logo. It then went on to supply the U.S. military with motorcycles during World War I. Since 1916 Harley's magazine, *Enthusiast*, has featured such notables as Elvis Presley atop Harleys during its run as the longest continually published motorcycle magazine.

Perhaps the single most important event in Harley-Davidson's history came in 1983 when the company formed the Harley Owner's Group (H.O.G.)—the largest factory-sponsored motorcycle club in the world, whose more than 800,000 members' sole mission is "to ride and

Everyone wants to own a Harley, even Jay Leno.

have fun." Not only do H.O.G. members receive copies of the *Enthusiast* and *Hog Tales*, H.O.G.'s official publication, but they also can take part in the Fly & Ride program, through which members get to fly to nearly 40 locations in the United States, Canada, Europe, and Australia, pick up a Harley at the local dealership, and tour the countryside. The best part about H.O.G. membership, though, is the camaraderie with like-minded devotees. In their local chapters, supported by their local dealers, and during special events throughout the world, H.O.G. members have been able to share their love of Harleys as a community.

In addition to remarkable rider support, Harley-Davidson has taken great care to create and protect its global brand. Ranked among the top 50 most recognized global brands, Harley offers a full range of branded parts, accessories, and apparel through various outlets, including retail stores, dealerships, and online. The look, feel, and sound of a Harley are unmistakable—the company even tried to patent the "distinctive" exhaust sound made by its V-twin engines in 1994.

Although Harley-Davidson encourages the idea that its riders are "rugged individualists" who can customize their Hogs to reflect their individual tastes, the company actually has created a band of brand loyalists who believe function is more than two wheels and a motor. It's art, it's history, and it's community.

purchasing the product or service. If the way your hair is cut is important to your appearance and self-image, you may engage in an involved search for the right salon and stylist. Alternatively, an athlete looking for a short "buzz" cut might go to the closest, most convenient, and cheapest barber shop. Regardless of the required search level, consumers rely on two key types of information: internal and external.

internal search for information
Occurs when the buyer examines his or her own memory and knowledge about the product or service, gathered through past experiences.

In an **internal search for information**, the buyer examines his or her own memory and knowledge about the product or service, gathered through past experiences. For example, every time Brad, who likes to shop online and loves action movies, wants to watch a movie, he orders it on zip.ca. He relies on his memory of past experiences when making this purchase decision. On the other hand, in an **external search for information**, the buyer seeks information outside his or her personal knowledge base to help make the buying decision. Consumers might fill in their personal knowledge gaps by talking with friends, family, or a salesperson; search the Internet; look-up *Consumer Reports*, or peruse sponsored media such as magazines, television, or radio.

external search for information
Occurs when the buyer seeks information outside his or her personal knowledge base to help make the buying decision.

Factors Affecting Consumers' Search Processes   It is important for marketers to understand the many factors that affect consumers' search processes. Among them are the following:

- *The perceived benefits versus perceived costs of search.* Is it worth the time and effort to search for information about a product or service? For instance, most families spend a lot of time researching the automobile market before they make a purchase because cars are a relatively expensive and important purchase with significant safety implications, whereas they likely spend little time researching which inexpensive plastic toy car to buy for the youngest member of the family.

internal locus of control
Refers to when consumers believe they have some control over the outcomes of their actions, in which case they generally engage in more search activities.

- *The locus of control.* People who have an **internal locus of control** believe they have some control over the outcomes of their actions, in which case they generally engage in more search activities. With an **external locus of control**, consumers believe that fate or other external factors control all outcomes. In that case, they believe it doesn't matter how much information they gather; if they make a wise decision, it isn't to their credit, and if they make a poor one, it isn't their fault. For example, if Brad believes he can get a better deal when buying his first car, he will conduct an extensive search for information and try to use the information when negotiating his purchase. However, if Brad feels that regardless of what information he has, there is little he can do to influence the outcome of the deal, he will not engage in an extensive search.

external locus of control
Refers to when consumers believe that fate or other external factors control all outcomes.

- *Actual or perceived risk.* Three types of risk associated with purchase decisions can delay or discourage a purchase: performance, financial, and psychological. The higher the risk, the more likely the consumer is to engage in an extended search.

performance risk
Involves the perceived danger inherent in a poorly performing product or service.

    Performance risk involves the perceived danger inherent in a poorly performing product or service. An example of performance risk might be the possibility that Brad's sports car does not start or breaks down on the day he is supposed to take his girlfriend out for a drive to show off his new car.

financial risk
Risk associated with a monetary outlay; includes the initial cost of the purchase, as well as the costs of using the item or service.

    Financial risk is risk associated with a monetary outlay and includes the initial cost of the purchase, as well as the costs of using the item or service. Car manufacturers, for instance, recognize that extended warranties help alleviate financial risk because consumers fear extensive postpurchase repair costs. For example, Brad bought two additional years of warranty over the manufacturer's standard "3-year, 60,000 kilometre" coverage for his sports car in order to reduce his financial risk within the first five years of buying the car.

psychological risk
Associated with the way people will feel if the product or service does not convey the right image.

    Finally, **psychological risks** are those risks associated with the way people will feel if the product or service does not convey the right image. For example, Brad looked up reviews of the various sports cars and asked his friends because he wanted people to perceive his choice as a really good one.

- *Type of product or service.* Another factor that affects the depth and type of search a consumer undertakes is the type of product or service—specifically, whether it is a specialty, shopping, or convenience product.

Soda and bread are generally considered convenience goods (left). Shoes and t-shirts are shopping goods (middle). Products made by designers like Polo/Ralph Lauren are specialty goods (right).

Specialty goods/services are products or services toward which the customer shows a strong preference and for which he or she will expend considerable effort to search for the best suppliers. Because Brad wants the best sports car for his money, he searches carefully on the Internet for reviews and talks to friends who own sports cars before he starts shopping.

Shopping goods/services are products or services for which consumers will spend time comparing alternatives, such as apparel, fragrances, and appliances. When Brad decides to buy a new pair of sneakers for himself, he will go from store to store shopping—trying shoes on, comparing alternatives, and chatting with salespeople.

Convenience goods/services are those products or services that the consumer is not willing to spend any effort to evaluate prior to purchase. They are frequently purchased, usually with very little thought. Items such as pop, bread, and soap typically fall into this category.

Consumers can spend considerable time searching for both specialty and shopping goods or services; the difference lies in the kind of search. In some cases, the consumer's specific perceptions and needs help define the kind of search—and the type of product. For Brad, getting a haircut is a convenience purchase, so he visits the fastest, most convenient location. Brad's girlfriend, however, has tried various salons, each time comparing the haircut she received with her previous experiences. For her, a haircut is a shopping service. Finally, Brad's dad patronizes their neighbourhood barber shop because he perceives it to be the best in town. He often waits a few days for an appointment and pays a bit more than similar barber shops. For him, getting a haircut is a specialty service.

specialty goods/services
Products or services toward which the customer shows a strong preference and for which he or she will expend considerable effort to search for the best suppliers.

shopping goods/services
Those for which consumers will spend time comparing alternatives, such as apparel, fragrances, and appliances.

convenience goods/services
Those for which the consumer is not willing to spend any effort to evaluate prior to purchase.

Step 3: Evaluation of Alternatives

Once a consumer has recognized a problem and explored the possible options, he or she must sift through the choices available and evaluate the alternatives. Alternative evaluation often occurs while the consumer is engaged in the process of information search. For example, a vegetarian consumer might learn about a new brand of yogurt that he or she can immediately rule out as a viable alternative because it contains some animal byproducts. Consumers forgo alternative evaluations altogether when buying habitual products; you'll rarely catch a loyal skim milk drinker buying a carton of 4-percent milk.

When consumers begin to evaluate different alternatives, they often base their evaluations on a set of important attributes or evaluative criteria. **Evaluative criteria**

evaluative criteria
Consist of a set of salient, or important, attributes about a particular product.

When you get your hair cut, do you consider it to be a convenience, shopping, or specialty purchase?

What evaluative criteria would you consider when choosing one of these shampoos?

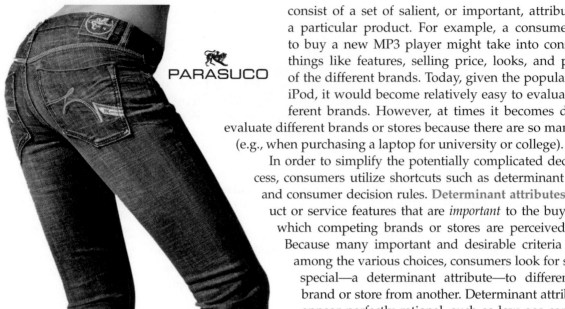

PARASUCO

The distinctive stitching and label on these Parasuco jeans are a determinant attribute that distinguishes the product from other brands.

determinant attributes
Product or service features that are important to the buyer and on which competing brands or stores are perceived to differ.

consumer decision rules
The set of criteria that consumers use consciously or subconsciously to quickly and efficiently select from among several alternatives.

compensatory decision rule
At work when the consumer is evaluating alternatives and trades off one characteristic against another, such that good characteristics compensate for bad ones.

consist of a set of salient, or important, attributes about a particular product. For example, a consumer looking to buy a new MP3 player might take into consideration things like features, selling price, looks, and popularity of the different brands. Today, given the popularity of the iPod, it would become relatively easy to evaluate the different brands. However, at times it becomes difficult to evaluate different brands or stores because there are so many choices (e.g., when purchasing a laptop for university or college).

In order to simplify the potentially complicated decision process, consumers utilize shortcuts such as determinant attributes and consumer decision rules. **Determinant attributes** are product or service features that are *important* to the buyer and on which competing brands or stores are perceived to *differ*.[7] Because many important and desirable criteria are equal among the various choices, consumers look for something special—a determinant attribute—to differentiate one brand or store from another. Determinant attributes may appear perfectly rational, such as low gas consumption per mileage for a sports car, or they may be more subtle and psychologically based, such as the shapes, colour, and look of the car.

Consumer decision rules are the set of criteria that consumers use consciously or subconsciously to quickly and efficiently select from among several alternatives. These rules take several different forms: compensatory, noncompensatory, or decision heuristics.

Compensatory   A **compensatory decision rule** assumes that the consumer, when evaluating alternatives, trades off one characteristic against another, such that good characteristics compensate for bad characteristics.[8] For instance, when Brad was looking to buy a new car he considered several factors such as mileage, style, price, and accessories. Even if the car is priced a little higher than Brad was planning to spend, the superb mileage offsets, or *compensates* for, the higher price.

Although Brad probably would not go through the formal process of making the purchasing decision based on the model described in Exhibit 6.2, it illustrates how a compensatory model would work. Brad assigns weights to each factor depending on their importance to him. These weights must add up to 1.0. So, for instance, mileage is the most important with a weight of .4 and style is least important with a weight of .1. Then he assigns weights to how well each of the cars might perform, with 1 being very poor, and 10 being very good. For instance, he thinks Toyota has the best mileage, so he assigns it a 10. Brad multiplies each performance rating by its importance

EXHIBIT	6.2	Compensatory versus Noncompensatory Choices for Buying a Car			
	Mileage	**Style**	**Price**	**Accessories**	**Overall Score**
Importance Weight	0.4	0.1	0.3	0.2	
Toyota	10	8	6	8	8.2
Honda	8	9	8	3	7.1
Saturn	6	8	10	5	7.2

Evaluations are based on a 1 (Very Poor) to 10 (Very Good) scale.

Compensatory: Toyota has the highest score.

Noncompensatory (Based on Price): Saturn has best evaluation of Price.

rating to get an overall score for each car. The rating for Toyota in this example is the highest of the three cars $((.4 \times 10) + (.1 \times 8) + (.3 \times 6) + (.2 \times 8) = 8.2)$.

Noncompensatory Sometimes, however, consumers use a **noncompensatory decision rule**, in which they choose a product or service on the basis of a subset of its characteristics, regardless of the values of its other attributes.[9] Thus, Brad might find a car with a lot of accessories with great mileage that costs considerably more than he is willing to spend. Brad rejects the car simply on the basis of price. He rated the price of a Toyota as 6 on the 10 point scale. That is, the strength of the good points does not compensate for its biggest weakness—a high ticket price.

Decision Heuristics Some consumers use other **decision heuristics**, which are mental shortcuts that help them narrow down their choices. Some examples of these heuristics include these:

- *Price.* Consumers can choose the more expensive option, thinking they are getting better quality along with the higher price ("You get what you pay for"), or they might buy the one priced in the middle of the alternatives, neither the most expensive nor the cheapest, thinking that it is a good compromise between the two extremes.[10]

- *Brand.* Always buying brand name goods allows some consumers to feel safe with their choices. Purchasing a national brand, even if it is more expensive, gives many consumers the sense that they are buying a higher quality item.[11] For example, many consumers buy the more expensive Tylenol or Advil pain relief tablets over Shopper's Drug Mart's Life brand pain tablets because they believe it is a higher quality product despite identical ingredients.

- *Product presentation.* Many times, the manner in which a product is presented can influence the decision process. For example, two similar homes that are comparably priced will be perceived quite differently if one is presented in perfectly clean and uncluttered condition, with fresh flowers and the smell of chocolate chip cookies wafting through, whereas the other appears messy, has too much furniture for the rooms, and emits an unappealing smell. Consumers want to see that some effort has been put into the selling process, and just the way the product is presented can make or break a sale.[12]

Once a consumer has considered the possible alternatives and evaluated the pros and cons of each, he or she can move toward a purchase decision. Internet Marketing 6.1 on page 157 illustrates how Expedia.ca has created value for Canadian consumers by making travel alternatives readily available, as well as how consumers evaluate different travel options.

Step 4: Purchase and Consumption

Value is a strong driver of consumers' purchase decisions. Customers seek out and purchase the products and services that they believe provide them with the best value. Several situational factors (payment options, delivery, store atmospherics, etc.) that influence whether a consumer buys the product immediately or later are discussed below. Then, after consumers have access to the product or service, they usually consume it.

A special type of consumption is called **ritual consumption**, which refers to a pattern of behaviours tied to life events that affect what and how we consume. These behaviours tend to have symbolic meanings and vary greatly by culture. For instance, they might take the form of everyday rituals such as Brad going to Tim Hortons for his daily morning coffee or brushing your teeth, or they can be reserved for special occasions, such as rites of passage or holiday rituals. Many firms try to tie their products and services to ritual consumption; just imagine, where would Hallmark be without holidays?

noncompensatory decision rule
At work when consumers choose a product or service on the basis of a subset of its characteristics, regardless of the values of its other attributes.

decision heuristics
Mental shortcuts that help consumers narrow down choices; examples include price, brand, and product presentation.

ritual consumption
Refers to a pattern of behaviours tied to life events that affect what and how people consume.

Step 5: Postpurchase

The final step of the consumer decision process is postpurchase behaviour. Marketers are particularly interested in postpurchase behaviour because it entails actual, rather than potential, customers. Marketers hope to create satisfied customers who become loyal, purchase again, and spread positive word of mouth, and so are quite important. On the other hand, dissatisfied customers are not likely to patronize the store again and spread negative word of mouth. Generally, there are three possible positive postpurchase outcomes: increased customer satisfaction, decreased postpurchase dissonance, and increased customer loyalty.

Customer Satisfaction   Setting unrealistically high consumer expectations of the product through advertising, personal selling, or other types of promotion may lead to higher initial sales, but it eventually will result in dissatisfaction when the product fails to achieve these high performance expectations. This failure can lead to dissatisfied customers and the potential for negative word of mouth. For example, Starbucks recognized that it should worry when its market research suggested that it was not meeting customer expectations in terms of speed of service. With higher-than-average coffee cup prices, customers expect fast and precise service.[13]

But setting customer expectations too low is an equally dangerous strategy. Many retailers, for instance, don't "put their best foot forward"; no matter how good their merchandise and service may be, if their store is not clean and appealing from the entrance, customers are not likely to enter.

Marketers can take several steps to ensure postpurchase satisfaction, such as these:

- Build realistic expectations: not too high and not too low, and deliver on those expectations.
- Demonstrate correct product use—improper usage can cause dissatisfaction.
- Stand behind the product or service by providing money-back guarantees and warranties.
- Encourage customer feedback, which cuts down on negative word of mouth.
- Periodically make contact with customers to show that the company cares about their business and wants them to be satisfied. It also provides an opportunity to correct any problems. Customers appreciate human contact, though it is more expensive for marketers than e-mail or postal mail contacts.

postpurchase dissonance
The psychologically uncomfortable state produced by an inconsistency between beliefs and behaviours that in turn evokes a motivation to reduce the dissonance; buyers' remorse.

Consumers often feel dissonance when purchasing products or services. It is that uncomfortable feeling of mixed emotions—the movie makes me sad, but I love Bogart and Bergman.

Postpurchase Dissonance   Sometimes, if expectation levels are not met and customers are in some way dissatisfied with the product or service, **postpurchase dissonance** results. Postpurchase dissonance, also known as buyers' remorse, is the psychologically uncomfortable state produced by an inconsistency between beliefs and behaviours that in turn evokes a motivation to reduce the dissonance. Postpurchase dissonance generally occurs when a consumer questions the appropriateness of a purchase after his or her decision has been made.

Postpurchase dissonance is especially likely for products that are expensive, infrequently purchased, and is associated with high levels of risk. Aware of the negativity involved with postpurchase dissonance, some marketers even direct efforts at consumers after the purchase is made to address the issue.

For example, after Brad bought his Pontiac Solstice, GM sent him a letter thanking

Internet Marketing   **6.1**   **Evaluating Travel Alternatives with Expedia**[14]

To illustrate how we evaluate alternatives in a buying decision, consider Expedia.ca, Canada's leading full-service online travel agency. Expedia.ca is a subsidiary of U.S.-based Expedia.com, the world's leading online travel service and the fourth-largest travel agency in the United States. Expedia.ca is well aware that Canadian travellers have high expectations in the competitive world of travel. Expedia's website (www.expedia.ca) makes alternative evaluation easy through a variety of innovations. It allows customers to plan their travel by date, by price, by interest, or by activity. Travellers can book flights, hotel accommodations, car rentals, cruises, and vacation packages with the click of a mouse. The site also offers travel tools, such as travel alerts, flight status checks, seat selectors, airport information, currency converters, driving directions, weather reports, and passport information.

Consumers can use Expedia to narrow their search from a universal set—all airlines—to their evoked set—say, only Air Canada, WestJet, and American Airlines. They can also search according to determinant attributes, such as the lowest price or shortest flight. Some flyers use a noncompensatory decision rule; they will only fly Air Canada for international flights, no matter what the alternatives are, because they are members of the airline's frequent flyer program or prefer to support a Canadian airline. Others will use a compensatory decision rule, so they will fly WestJet from Ottawa to Calgary, depending on which airline has the best combination of the lowest price, shortest flight, and minimum number of stops. Finally, some travellers choose an airline on the basis of key product signals, such as legroom, number of in-flight movie options, or quality of the food.

Expedia makes every travel customer their own travel agent.

him for his purchase and positively reinforcing the message that he made a wise decision by mentioning the high quality that went into the product's design and production. Included with the letter was a customer satisfaction survey (CSI) that asks about his satisfaction with the dealership, salesperson, and other aspects of his purchase experience. Brad also received additional information about GM services available to Solstice owners. To reduce the dissonance, Brad can take several actions:

- Pay attention to positive information about the Solstice, such as looking up reviews by owners and car-buffs on the Internet (e.g., the "Pontiac Pulse" community zone website (www.pontiacpulse.ca)).

- Get positive feedback from friends about his new sports car.
- Seek negative information about sports cars he did not buy. Reading these reviews makes him feel more comfortable with his purchase decision.

Loyalty   In the postpurchase stage of the decision-making process, marketers attempt to solidify a loyal relationship with their customers. They want customers to be satisfied with their purchase and buy from the same company again. Loyal customers will only buy certain brands and shop at certain stores, and they do not consider other brands or firms in their decision. As we explained in Chapter 2, such customers are therefore very valuable to firms, and marketers have designed customer relationship management (CRM) programs specifically to retain them.

Undesirable Consumer Behaviour   Although firms want satisfied, loyal customers, sometimes they fail to attain them. Passive consumers are those that don't repeat purchase or fail to recommend the product to others. More serious and potentially damaging, however, is negative consumer behaviour, such as negative word of mouth and rumours.

negative word of mouth
Occurs when consumers spread negative information about a product, service, or store to others.

Negative word of mouth occurs when consumers spread negative information about a product, service, or store to others. When customers' expectations are met or even exceeded, they often don't tell anyone about it. But when consumers believe that they have been treated unfairly in some way, they usually want to complain, often to many people. One study shows that satisfied customers tell only three people about their experience while dissatisfied customers complain to nine people.[15] To lessen the impact of negative word of mouth, firms provide customer service representatives—whether online, on the phone, or in stores—to handle and respond to complaints. If the

---

Ethical Dilemma   **6.1**   Dissatisfied Customers Use Ihate[company].com[16]

Dissatisfied consumers are taking to the Internet for vindication, and it's working. From rude customer service associates to misrepresented agreements, complaints proliferate online. *Forbes* has even ranked the best corporate complaint sites, including Allstate, PayPal, and American Express. According to some experts, Internet hate sites such as **Ihate[insert company name].com** have helped resolve more consumer complaints than any other method.

Some companies have tried to fight hate sites but with little success. Legal recourse is available only if the hate site uses the offending firm's trademarks, brand names, or other intellectual property in a way that might confuse the public. For the most part though, consumers who set up these sites are protected under freedom of speech and expression laws and have argued that no reasonable person would confuse **Ihate[company].com** with the company's actual site, as in **[your company].com.**

For consumers, the question is why they have to resort to posting a complaint to a website? The answer is simple: there is a breakdown in customer service or in the business's communication with customers. For firms the question is how to protect themselves from these sites. The solution is once again simple: provide better, more timely customer service and complaint resolution.

The best strategy for marketers in dealing with hate sites is to stay on top of them and address their complaints immediately. If a company addresses a problem quickly, the originator may remove the site once his or her need to vent frustration has been satisfied. This disappearance, in turn, discourages new postings by other disgruntled customers. Companies can post their resolution on the site to show customers they are concerned and want to rectify a negative situation.

Even though companies have attempted to curb cyber griping by buying domain names such as **Ihate[their company name].com**, consumers will find a way to share their thoughts online. For example, Canadian Tire lost its legal bid to buy the domain name crappytire.com from Mick McFadden of Ontario who owns the name. In addition to the numerous communities and websites, aggregators like TheComplaintStation.com offer a central repository for consumer complaints, with pages dedicated to specific companies. Similarly, TheVault.com creates a forum for current and previous employees to share their insider views of a company. Should companies show support for these sites by responding to posted complaints, ignore them altogether, or challenge these sites in court if they find the complaints to be posted by people other than customers?

customer believes that positive action will be taken as a result of the complaint, he or she is less likely to complain to family and friends or through the Internet and certain websites, which are a great source of negative word of mouth (see Ethical Dilemma 6.1 on the previous page). Marketers should encourage customers to complain to them directly since this could help them improve their product and service—an essential element of the evaluation control aspect of the marketing plan.

Types of Consumer Buying Decisions   LO ③

Generally, all consumer buying decisions may be described along a continuum from those requiring little or no effort (e.g., buying a cup of coffee on the way to class) to those requiring considerable effort (e.g., buying a new car or a house). Marketers who understand the consumer buying decisions situations are more likely to develop strategies that will help consumers make their purchase experience easier. Exhibit 6.3 classifies consumers' buying behaviour into four types based on the extent of their involvement in the purchase decision and the degree of differences among brands.[17] Involvement refers to the time and effort a buyer invests searching and evaluating information when buying a product or service. Let's examine these four types of buying behaviour more closely.

Complex Buying Behaviour

Complex buying behaviour occurs when a consumer is highly involved in the purchase and perceives significant differences among the available brands. This is usually the case when the product or service is expensive, risky, bought infrequently, and is highly self-expressive. In this situation, the consumer will spend a considerable amount of time and effort searching and evaluating information about the specific product and product class in order to reduce the perceived risks. For example, consider Brad, a new grad with a major in finance, who has landed a high-paying job with a top-tier financial institution and is looking to buy his first car. Brad wants to buy

complex buying behaviour Consumers are highly involved in the purchase and perceive significant differences among available brands.

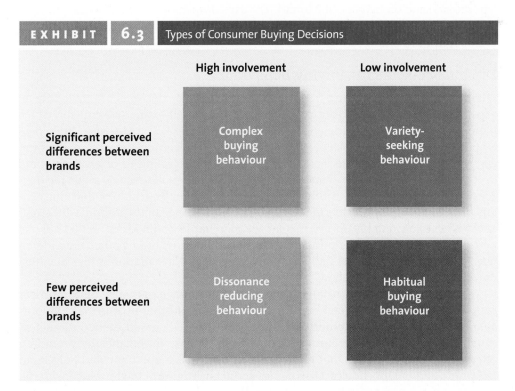

EXHIBIT 6.3 Types of Consumer Buying Decisions

	High involvement	**Low involvement**
Significant perceived differences between brands	Complex buying behaviour	Variety-seeking behaviour
Few perceived differences between brands	Dissonance reducing behaviour	Habitual buying behaviour

Source: Assael Henry, "Types of Buying Behavior," in *Consumer Behavior and Marketing Action* (Boston: Kent Publishing Company, 1987) p. 87.

Buying a used sports car is a complex buying decision. Consumers often research Kelley Blue Book, which provides extensive information on used cars, trucks, and vans.

a sports car and since there are many brands to choose from, he will probably spend a lot of time and effort learning about sports cars in general, and then more specifically about the particular brands he is interested in buying. The potential risks associated with Brad's decision regarding buying his car include financial (did I pay too much?), performance (will it keep me safe in an accident?), and psychological (will my friends think I look cool?). To reduce his perceived risk, Brad will spend a lot of effort searching for information about cars and will carefully study the dealer's guarantee and warranty policies before he actually makes his purchase. Complex buying behaviour is considered a form of extended problem solving since the purchase decision entails a lot of risk.

Marketers who sell high-involvement products such as cars, homes, and computers must understand the information-gathering and evaluation process of consumers like Brad in order to help them learn about the key attributes of the product class (sports cars) and of their specific brand. The car salesperson should provide information about sports cars in general and differentiate their brand along the key attributes of importance to Brad.

Dissonance-Reducing Buying Behaviour

dissonance-reducing buying behaviour
Consumers perceive few differences among brand when buying expensive, infrequent, or risky products.

Dissonance-reducing buying behaviour occurs when a consumer wants to buy an expensive, infrequent, or risky product that is very self-expressive but for which there are few perceived differences among the brands. Few perceived differences among brands create some level of tension, anxiety, and second-guessing in consumers' minds and thus they seek ways of reducing these feelings. For example, Brad is considering installing hardwood flooring in his parent's house as a gift for their 25th wedding anniversary. Within a certain price range, Brad thinks that the various brands of hardwood flooring are quite similar, so he shops around a little and decides relatively quickly on a particular brand of hardwood flooring. With very few perceived brand differences among the hardwood flooring, Brad's purchase decision may be influenced by price, delivery, convenience, and installation rather than just the quality of the wood itself.

After purchasing and installing the floor, Brad may experience discomfort or *postpurchase dissonance*, when he hears family, friends or other people make favourable comments about the brands he did not buy. As discussed earlier, marketers could help consumers like Brad overcome postpurchase dissonance by providing after-sale communications that reinforce their choice as a good one and help them feel proud about their choices. Dissonance-reducing buying behaviour is considered a form of extended problem solving since the purchase is expensive and entails a fair bit of risk.

Habitual Buying Behaviour

Habitual buying behaviour is characterized by low consumer involvement and little perceived brand difference. Thus, consumers make their decision with little thought or conscious effort. For example, every morning Brad stops by the Tim Hortons on his way to work to pick up his coffee and a muffin. He doesn't ponder the potential benefits of going to Second Cup, Timothy's, or Starbucks even though they are all on his way to work; Brad engages in habitual decision making. Marketers strive to attract and maintain habitual purchasers by creating strong brands and store loyalty (see Chapters 9 and 10) because these customers don't even consider alternative brands or stores. Price, sales promotion, and advertising that reinforces the brand are effective for habitual purchase behaviour.

> **habitual buying behaviour**
> Consumers make purchase decisions with little or no thought.

Variety-Seeking Buying Behaviour

Variety-seeking buying behaviour is characterized by low consumer involvement but significant perceived differences among brands. For example, Brad loves Haagen-Dazs ice cream but will switch to Ben & Jerry's not out of dissatisfaction but just out of a desire to try something new or different. Brad may have spent a moderate amount of time and effort looking and evaluating the other available brands of ice cream at the grocery store before selecting Ben & Jerry's. Customers engage in this type of buying process when they have had some prior experience with the product or service and the perceived risk is moderate. Variety-seeking buying behaviour is a form of limited problem solving because consumers rely on past experience more than on external information but may pay attention to new varieties shown in advertising, promotional offers, and point-of-purchase displays.

> **variety-seeking buying behaviour**
> Consumers have low-involvement but perceive significant differences among brands.

With variety-seeking products, marketers of leading brands should focus on getting consumers to engage in habitual buying behaviour by dominating shelf space and running advertising aimed at reminding consumers of the benefits of their brands. Challenger brands should focus on getting consumers to switch by using strategies such as special offers, price discounts, coupons, free samples, in-store trials, and advertising that will encourage trial of their brands.

Factors Influencing Consumer Buying Decisions LO

Consumer buying decisions can be influenced by several factors, as illustrated in Exhibit 6.4. Of course the elements of the marketing mix affect these decisions. We discuss these elements throughout this book. Four other factors are discussed here. First are psychological factors, which are influences internal to the customer, such as motives, attitudes, perception, and learning. Second, we examine social factors, such as family and reference groups. Third, cultural factors also influence the decision process. Fourth, there are situational factors, such as the specific purchase, a particular shopping situation, or the time of day, that affect the decision process.

Every decision people make as consumers will take them through some form of the consumer decision process. But, like life itself, this process does not exist in a vacuum.

Psychological Factors

Although marketers themselves can influence purchase decisions, a host of psychological factors affects the way people receive marketers' messages. Among them are motives, attitudes, perception, and learning. In this section, we examine how such psychological factors can influence the consumer decision process.

Motives In Chapter 1, we argued that marketing is all about satisfying customer needs and wants. When a need such as thirst, or a want such as a Diet Coke, is not satisfied, it motivates us, or drives us, to get satisfaction. So, a **motive** is a need or want that is strong enough to cause the person to seek satisfaction.

> **motive**
> A need or want that is strong enough to cause the person to seek satisfaction.

EXHIBIT 6.4 Factors Affecting the Consumer Decision Process

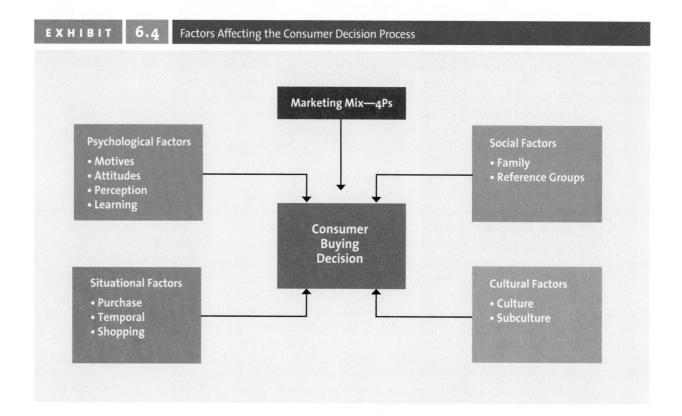

PSSP hierarchy of needs
Argues that when lower-level, more basic needs (physiological and safety) are fulfilled, people turn to satisfying their higher-level human needs (social and personal).

physiological needs
Those relating to the basic biological necessities of life: food, drink, rest, and shelter.

safety needs
Pertain to protection and physical well-being.

social needs
Relate to one's interactions with others.

personal needs
Relate to ways people satisfy their inner desires.

People have several types of motives. One of the best known paradigms for explaining these motive types was developed by Abraham Maslow more than 30 years ago.[18] A variation on the paradigm, called the **PSSP hierarchy of needs**, argues that people are motivated to satisfy higher-level human needs as the lower-level needs are taken care of.[19] As illustrated in Exhibit 6.5, PSSP stands for Physiological, Safety, Social, and Personal needs. As our more basic needs (physiological and safety) are fulfilled, we turn to satisfying our more advanced needs (social and personal).

Physiological needs deal with the basic biological necessities of life—food, drink, rest, and shelter. Although for most people in developed countries these basic needs are generally met, there are those in both developed and less-developed countries who are less fortunate. However, everyone remains concerned with meeting these basic needs. Marketers seize every opportunity to convert these needs into wants by reminding us to eat at Taco Bell, drink milk, sleep on a Sleep Country's Beautyrest mattress, and stay at a Marriott.

Safety needs pertain to protection and physical well-being. The marketplace is full of products and services that are designed to make you safer, such as airbags in cars and burglar alarms in homes, or healthier, such as vitamins and organic meats and vegetables.

Social needs relate to our interactions with others. Haircuts and makeup help you look more attractive, the iPod Nano makes you look cool, and deodorants prevent odour. Greeting cards help you express your feelings toward others.

Finally, **personal needs** allow people to satisfy their inner desires. Yoga, meditation, health clubs, and many books appeal to people's desires to grow or maintain a happy, satisfied outlook on life.

Which of the PSSP needs applies when a consumer purchases a magazine? Magazines such as *Weight Watchers,* for instance, help satisfy *physiological* needs like how to eat healthy, but also *personal* needs like how to be happy with one's life. Magazines like *Canadian Home & Country,* on the other hand, provide tips on how to make the home a *safer* place to live. Finally, magazines such as *Weddings* help satisfy *social* needs since it

EXHIBIT **6.5** PSSP Hierarchy of Needs

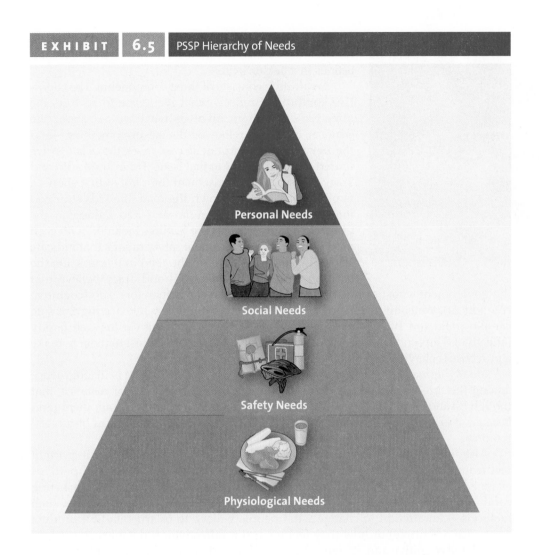

- Personal Needs
- Social Needs
- Safety Needs
- Physiological Needs

provides instructions on topics such as how to prepare invitations so friends and family will be properly informed and no one will be offended. Many of these magazines can fulfill several PSSP needs simultaneously. Good marketers add value to their products or services and thereby nudge people up the PSSP hierarchy.

Attitude We have attitudes about almost everything. For instance, we don't like this class, but we do like the instructor. We like where we live, but we don't like the weather. An **attitude** is a person's enduring evaluation of his or her feelings about and behavioural tendencies toward an object or idea. Attitudes are learned and long lasting, and they might develop over a long period of time, though they can also abruptly change. For instance, you might like your instructor for much of the semester—until she returns

attitude
A person's enduring evaluation of his or her feelings about and behavioural tendencies toward an object or idea; consists of three components: *cognitive*, *affective*, and *behavioural*.

Which PSSP needs do these magazines fulfill?

People buy Volvos because they believe they are safe (cognitive component of an attitude), because they like them (affective), and because they have many convenient dealerships to visit (behavioural).

cognitive component
A component of *attitude* that reflects what a person believes to be true.

affective component
A component of *attitude* that reflects what a person feels about the issue at hand—his or her like or dislike of something.

behavioural component
A component of *attitude* that comprises the actions a person takes with regard to the issue at hand.

perception
The process by which people select, organize, and interpret information to form a meaningful picture of the world.

your first exam. The one thing attitudes have in common for everyone is their ability to influence all decisions and actions in a person's life.

An attitude consists of three components. The **cognitive component** reflects what we *believe* to be true, the **affective component** involves what we *feel* about the issue at hand—our like or dislike of something—and the **behavioural component** comprises the *action(s)* we undertake with regard to that issue. For example, Ed and Tracy Lee see an advertisement for a Volvo that shows a family of five driving down the road, the kids strapped into their car seats and mom and dad talking in the front. An announcer lists the features included with each model, as well as government safety ratings that indicate Volvo is the safest brand on the road in its class. On the basis of this advertisement, Ed and Tracy believe that the government statistics must be true and that the car is therefore safe (cognitive component). Watching the happy family looking comfortable while driving this safe car allows Ed and Tracy to feel that they would like to have this car for their family (affective). Thus encouraged, they go to the Volvo dealership closest to them to make a purchase (behavioural).

Ideally, agreement exists among these components. When there is incongruence among the three however, cognitive dissonance occurs. Suppose, for instance, that though Ed and Tracy believe the Volvo is safe and like the car, they buy another brand because it is cheaper. It is likely that they will experience the discomfort of buyers' remorse.

Although attitudes are pervasive and usually slow to change, the important fact from a marketer's point of view is that they can be influenced and perhaps changed through persuasive communications and personal experience. Marketing communication—through salespeople, advertisements, free samples, or other such methods—can attempt to change what people believe to be true about a product or service (cognitive) or how they feel toward it (affective). If the marketer is successful, the cognitive and affective components work in concert to affect behaviour. Continuing with our example, suppose that prior to viewing the ad, Ed and Tracy thought that a Toyota Camry was the safest car on the road, but they liked the looks of the Volvo. The ad positively influenced the cognitive component of their attitude toward Volvo, making it consistent with the affective component.

Perception Another psychological factor, **perception,** is the process by which we select, organize, and interpret information to form a meaningful picture of the world. Perception influences our acquisition and consumption of goods and services because it assigns meaning to such things as colour, symbols, taste, and packaging. Culture, tradition, and our overall upbringing determine our perceptual view of the world. For instance, Tracy has always wanted a Volvo because her best friend in college had one, and they had a great time driving across the country together one summer. However, based on his past experiences, Ed has a different perception. Ed thinks Volvos are slow, stodgy, unfashionable, and meant to be driven by little old ladies with grey hair—though they are safe! Volvo has worked hard in recent years to overcome this long-standing, negative perceptual bias that Ed and many others hold by creating faster cars with more stylish designs and using promotion to reposition the brand to portray a more positive image.

In trying to influence perceptions, marketers must understand and focus on the four components of perception: *selective exposure, selective attention, selective comprehension, and selective attention.* A person who looks at the news and sports channels only, but not the comedy or women's television network channels, is engaged in selective exposure because they are excluding other programmes or channels. Similarly, consumers who only listen to messages that are consistent with their beliefs, and not others, are practising selective attention. For instance, although someone may look at the sports channel, they may watch hockey, soccer, or baseball but not boxing or wrestling because these may be too violent for their tastes. Selective comprehension occurs when consumers interpret a marketing message in a way that is different from what the marketer intends. For example, a Dolce and Gabbana ad was intended to be edgy and sexual but consumers felt that it reinforced stereotypes about rape and degraded women. Knowing this, marketers can target

their communications in those media that maximize exposure to their target market and create messages that are consistent with their beliefs and attitude so that they will pay attention to the messages and interpret them in the intended way. Finally, selective retention describes the situation where consumers do not remember all the information they see, read or hear. Marketers can provide the information in various other forms such as print, online, and other displays to reinforce their message.

D&G was criticized for one of its ads which was intended to be edgy and sexy, but consumers felt that it reinforced stereotypes about rape and degraded women.

learning
Refers to a change in a person's thought process or behaviour that arises from experience and takes place throughout the consumer decision process.

Learning   Learning refers to a change in a person's thought process or behaviour that arises from experience and takes place throughout the consumer decision process. For instance, after Brad recognized that he needed a sports car, he started looking for ads and searching for reviews and articles on the Internet. He learned from each new piece of information, so that his thoughts about sports cars were different than before he had read anything. In addition, Brad liked the salesperson at the dealership who served him. Brad learned from this experience, and it became part of his memory to be used in the future, possibly so he would recommend the dealership or salesperson to his friends.

Learning affects both attitudes and perceptions. Throughout the buying process, Brad's attitudes shifted. The cognitive component changed for him when he learned that the dealership offers various additional services at low costs to Solstice owners. Once he started getting the additional services (e.g., free car washes, special rates for car detailing), he realized how much he liked the service, which indicates the affective component, then subscribed to it—the behavioural component. Each time Brad was exposed to information about the service, he learned something different that affected his perception of the dealership. Before he tried it, Brad hadn't realized how friendly and helpful the people at the dealership were; thus, his perception of the dealership service changed through learning.

A person's perceptions and ability to learn are affected by their societal experiences, which we discuss next.

Social Factors

Exhibit 6.4 illustrates that the consumer decision process is also influenced by the external, social environment, which consists of the customer's family and reference groups.[20]

Family   Many purchase decisions are made about products or services that the entire family will consume or use. Thus, firms must consider how families make purchase decisions and understand how various family members might influence these decisions.

Family members often influence buying decisions.

When families make purchase decisions, they often consider the needs of all the family members. In choosing a restaurant, for example, all the family members may participate in the decision making. In other situations, however, different members of the family may take on different roles. For example, Brad recalled that when he was a kid, his dad and two older brothers were the ones who looked through car magazines and *Consumer Reports* to search for information about a new car. But once the family arrived at the dealership, his dad not his brothers, decided which model and colour to buy, and his mom negotiated the final deal.

Despite that example, children and adolescents play an important role in family buying decisions. For instance, the tween segment alone in Canada spent close to $3 billion in 2005 on personal items such as snacks, soft drinks, electronics, and apparel. Kids in Canada directly influence the purchase of billions of dollars more on items such as food, snacks, beverages, toys, health and beauty aids, clothing, accessories, gifts, and school supplies. Their indirect influence on family spending on big ticket items such as recreation, vacations, technology, and even the family car is even higher.[21]

Influencing a group that holds this much spending power is vitally important. Traditional food retailers are already caught in a squeeze between Wal-Mart, which lures low-end customers, and specialty retailers like Whole Foods, which target the high end. Knowing how children influence food buying decisions is a strategic opportunity for traditional supermarkets and their suppliers to exploit. Getting this group to prefer one store, chain, or product over another can make a difference in the bottom line, as well as in the chances for survival in a difficult marketplace.[22]

reference group
One or more persons whom an individual uses as a basis for comparison regarding beliefs, feelings, and behaviours.

Reference Groups   A reference group is one or more persons an individual uses as a basis for comparison regarding beliefs, feelings, and behaviours. A consumer might have various reference groups, including family, friends, coworkers, or famous people the consumer would like to emulate. These reference groups affect buying decisions by (1) offering information, (2) providing rewards for specific purchasing behaviours, and (3) enhancing a consumer's self-image.

Reference groups provide information to consumers directly through conversation or indirectly through observation. For example, when Apple launched its iPod in 2001, the advertisement featured the most popular music at the time and some of the world's biggest stars such as Eminem. That alone was enough to draw the attention from millions of kids all over the world who then continued to add iPods to their wish list for Christmas or birthdays. Thus, as mentioned in the opening vignette, it was hardly surprising that Apple sold 14 million iPods in the first three months and could not keep up with demand.

Some reference groups also influence behaviours by rewarding behaviour that meets with their approval or chastising those who engage in behaviour that doesn't. For example, smokers are often ostracized by their friends and made to smoke outside or in restricted areas.

By identifying and affiliating with reference groups, consumers can create, enhance, and maintain their self-image. Customers who want to be seen as "earthy" might buy Birkenstock sandals, whereas those wanting to be seen as "high fashion" might buy Manolo Blahnik shoes, as we discussed previously in this chapter. A recent survey of Canadian and American teenagers showed that Hollister, American Eagle, West Coast Brands, and Abercrombie & Fitch are the most popular brands among this group.[23]

Some stores, like Abercrombie & Fitch, play on these forms of influence and hire sales associates they hope will serve as a reference group for customers who shop there. These hip, attractive, and somewhat aloof employees are encouraged to wear the latest store apparel—thereby serving as living mannequins to emulate.

Culture

We defined **culture** in Chapter 4 as the shared meanings, beliefs, morals, values, and customs of a group of people passed on from one generation to another. Your cultural group might be as small as your reference group at school or as large as the country in which you live or the religion in which you participate. For instance, the culture at Brad's college evokes a "high-achiever" attitude. This reputation influences, to some extent, the way he spends his leisure time, the types of people he hangs out with, and the kinds of products he buys. Culture is one of the most pervasive factors influencing consumer behaviour. Therefore, marketers must work hard to understand how it is different not only in Canada but in those countries to which they plan to market their products. Marketing strategies that may work in Canada or North America may not work well in Japan or India because consumers in those countries are culturally different as discussed in Chapter 17 on Global Marketing. Additionally, even within Canada, there are cultural differences between various sub-groups or subcultures. A subculture is a group of people whose beliefs and values are different from the rest of the larger society in which they live. Examples of subcultures in Canada include French-Canadian subculture, Chinese-Canadian subculture, South-Asian subculture, and Acadian subculture. Research has shown that Chinese and Asian Canadians prefer to do business with marketers who truly understand their culture and needs rather than those who have very superficial ways of acknowledging their community, which a lot of people in the community actually find irritating.[24]

culture
The set of values, guiding beliefs, understandings, and ways of doing things shared by members of a society; exists on two levels: visible artifacts (e.g., behaviour, dress, symbols, physical settings, ceremonies) and underlying values (thought processes, beliefs, and assumptions).

Situational Factors

Psychological and social factors typically influence the consumer decision process the same way each time. For example, your motivation to quench your thirst usually drives you to drink a Pepsi, and your reference group at the workplace coerces you to wear appropriate attire. But sometimes, **situational factors,** or factors specific to the situation, override, or at least influence, psychological and social issues. These situational factors are related to the purchase and shopping situation, as well as to the temporal state, as illustrated in Exhibit 6.4. Entrepreneurial Marketing 6.1 on page 169 describes a rental car company that is desirable only in certain situations.

situational factors
Factor affecting the consumer decision process; those that are specific to the situation that may override, or at least influence, psychological and social issues.

Purchase Situation Customers may be predisposed to purchase certain products or services because of some underlying psychological trait or social factor, but these factors may change in certain purchase situations. For instance, Priya Persaud, a Vancouverite, considers herself a thrifty, cautious shopper—someone who likes to get a good deal. But her best friend is getting married, and she wants to buy the couple a silver tray. If the tray were for herself, she would probably go to Stokes, Bowring, or possibly even Wal-Mart. But since it is for her best friend, she went to Birks. Why? To purchase something fitting for the special occasion of a wedding.

Shopping Situation Consumers might be ready to purchase a product or service but be completely derailed once they arrive in the store. Marketers use several techniques to influence consumers at this choice stage of the decision process. Consider the following techniques:

- *Store atmosphere.* Some retailers and service providers have developed unique images that are based at least in part on their internal environment, also known as their atmospherics.[25] Research has shown that, if used in concert with other aspects of a retailer's strategy, music, scent, lighting, and even colour can positively influence the decision process.[26] For example, Abercrombie & Fitch

Rainforest Cafe has developed internal environments that are not only pleasant but also consistent with their food and service.

aggressively positions itself as a lifestyle brand called "Casual Luxury." Its stores are plastered with photos of physically attractive young models, blasted with loud dance music through powerful speakers, and pumped full of the company's signature cologne, Fierce. The stores are also staffed with attractive models, young salespeople who embody the Abercrombie & Fitch lifestyle: attractive, athletic, popular, enthusiastic, and outgoing.[27] Restaurants such as The Rainforest Cafe have developed internal environments that are not only pleasant but also consistent with their food and service.

- *Salespeople*. Well-trained sales personnel can influence the sale at the point of purchase by pointing out the advantages of one item over another and encouraging multiple purchases. The salesperson at Birks, for instance, explained to Priya why one platter was better than the next and suggested some serving pieces to go with it.

- *Crowding*. Customers can feel crowded because there are too many people, too much merchandise, or lines that are too long. If there are too many people in a store, some people become distracted and may even leave.[28] Others have difficulty purchasing if the merchandise is packed too close together. This issue is a particular problem for shoppers with mobility disabilities. However, too few customers in store may also dissuade customers from entering or shopping since they may feel that something is wrong with the store. For example, many students want to go to bars that are popular and crowded than those that are empty or deserted.

- *In-store demonstrations*. The taste and smell of new food items may attract people to try something they normally wouldn't. Similarly, some fashion retailers offer "trunk shows," during which their vendors show their whole line on a certain day. During these well-advertised events, customers are often enticed to purchase that day because they get special assistance from the salespeople and can order merchandise that the retailer otherwise does not carry.

- *Promotions*. Retailers employ various promotional vehicles to influence customers once they have arrived in the store. For instance,

In-store demonstrations entice people to buy.

Entrepreneurial Marketing

6.1 Zipcar—The Urban Rent-a-Car[29]

Estimates show that car ownership is 68 percent in Canada and 99.8 percent in the U.S., that is, there are as many cars on the roads as there are Americans old enough to drive.[30] And whether it's your basic "A to B" functional car or a luxury status symbol, we all seem to believe that a car is a necessity for daily life. So why is it that in cities such as Toronto, Vancouver, Seattle, Boston, and Washington, DC, consumers are skipping the car payments, forgoing car insurance, and choosing to share cars with their neighbours?

During a trip to Berlin, Zipcar founder Robin Chase observed cars, parked around the city, that could be rented by the hour. When she returned to Boston, a city notorious for its parking congestion, Chase designed and instituted a similar concept. Keeping the specific needs of Boston consumers in mind, Chase employed Internet and wireless data transmission to ease reservation headaches and placed Zipcars at strategically chosen spots around the city. The Zipcar concept was quickly exported to Canada, in Toronto and Vancouver because of their green bias and the environmental focus of many residents in these cities. Zipcar Toronto has over 160 cars and Vancouver has more than 100. Membership in Zipcar costs a $25 one-time application fee and a $55 annual

Zipcar president Scott Griffins says people can pay by the hour to use a car in the city.

fee. Rates are between $8.30–$14.75 an hour and $59 per day (any 24-hour period), with gas, parking, and insurance included. Every Zipcar reservation includes 150 free kilometres. Members simply make online reservations through the website, and within approximately two minutes, the information is transmitted via a wireless network to a chip inside the car. At the car, the member swipes a membership card over the windshield to unlock the doors and retrieve the key, which is tethered to a wire beside the ignition. Zipcar uses 11 makes and models of vehicles that range from standard sedans to small SUVs and luxury vehicles.

Supporters of the concept say it's a lot cheaper than owning a car and better for the environment because it also encourages people to take transit, walk, or bike. In Toronto, Zipcar competes with AutoShare, a private company and in Vancouver, with the Cooperative Auto Network, a nonprofit co-op.

Worldwide, Zipcar continues to see 100 percent+ annual increases in members and vehicles and became the first car sharing service in North America to attain profitability in all of its established markets. Zipcar has the largest active membership base of any car sharing service, with more than 90,000 members and 2500 vehicles.

an unadvertised price promotion can alter a person's preconceived buying plan. Multi-item discounts, such as "buy 1, get 1 free" sales, are popular means to get people to buy more than they normally would. Finally, because many people regard clipping coupons from the newspaper as too much trouble, some stores make coupons available in the store.

- *Packaging.* It is difficult to make a product stand out in the crowd when it competes for shelf space with several other brands. This problem is particularly difficult for consumer packaged goods, such as groceries and health and beauty products. Marketers therefore spend millions of dollars designing and updating their packages to be more appealing and eye catching.

Temporal State   Our state of mind at any particular time can alter our preconceived notions of what we are going to purchase. For instance, some people are "morning people," whereas others function better at night. In turn, a purchase situation may have different appeal levels depending on the time of day and the type of person the consumer is. Mood swings can even alter consumer behaviour. Suppose Priya received a parking ticket just prior to shopping at Birks. It is likely that she would be less receptive to the salesperson's influence than if she came into the store in a good mood. Her bad mood may even cause her to have a less positive postpurchase feeling about the store.

As we've seen, people's lives are lived in different contexts, humans are not machines, and consumer decisions simply are not made in vacuums. Marketers who understand this are better positioned to serve their target consumers i.e., develop marketing mixes that are consistent with their customers' expectations.

Learning Objectives Review

1) Describe the steps a customer goes through when buying a product or service

2) Discuss what determines how much time consumers will search for information before buying a product or a service

3) Understand how the level of customer involvement in the buying decision varies with the types of buying decisions

4) Discuss how psychological, social, cultural, and situational factors influence consumers' buying behaviour

1) Consumers generally start their decision process by recognizing that they must buy something to satisfy a need or want. Sometimes the needs are simple; I need food because I am hungry. Often, however, they become more complex; I want to buy my girlfriend an engagement ring.

Once they recognize the need, consumers start searching for information. Generally, the more important the purchase, the more time and effort the consumer will spend on the search process. Firms facilitate this search by providing promotional materials and personal selling. Once they have enough information, consumers can evaluate their alternatives and make a choice.

In the next step of the decision process, consumers purchase and use the product or service. But the process doesn't simply stop there. After the sale, the consumer is either satisfied with the purchase or experiences postpurchase dissonance. Every marketer wants satisfied customers, but when instead they are confronted with dissatisfied customers who are in some way unsure about their purchase, marketers must proactively turn the situation around. If they don't, the customer may be gone for good.

2) A variety of factors affect consumers' searches for information about a potential purchase. First, they consider the time and effort associated with searching versus the benefits derived from the search. Second, people who have an internal locus of control—those who believe they have control over the outcomes of their actions—are more likely to spend time searching for information than those with an external locus of control. Third, consumers who perceive a high performance, financial, or psychological risk associated with the purchase will spend relatively more time searching for information than those who do not. Finally, consumers will spend more time searching for information for specialty goods than for shopping or convenience goods, respectively.

3) How much time a consumer spends making a purchasing decision depends on the product or service being purchased. Some purchasing decisions require limited problem solving because the perceived risk of the purchase is low or the consumer has previous experience purchasing the product or service. Impulse and habitual purchases fall in this category. Sometimes, however, consumers enter into complex buying behaviour because the perceived risk of the purchase is great.

4) First and foremost, firms must design their products and services to meet their customers' wants and needs, but understanding certain aspects of consumer behaviour can help as well. For instance, it is important to understand people's motives (i.e., what drives them to buy), their attitudes (i.e., how they feel about a product or service), and their perceptions (i.e., how information about that product or service fits into their worldview). Knowledge about these psychological characteristics helps firms design and provide products and services that their customers want and need.

In addition, people don't live in a vacuum. Consumers are influenced by their family, their reference groups, and their culture. Understanding these social groups and people's roles within them provides important insights into consumers' buying behaviour. Finally, though consumers already carry a host of psychological and social factors along with them on a shopping expedition, certain other factors can influence a purchase at the point of sale. For instance, customers might change their buying behaviour because the purchase situation is different than the one they are used to. Also, things can happen to customers, both positive and negative, once they are in a store that might alter their preconceived notion of what they plan to purchase. Finally, people can be just plain finicky, and being in an unusually good or extremely bad mood can also alter a purchase decision. The more firms understand these psychological, social, cultural, and situational factors, the more likely they will be to influence purchase decisions.

Key Terms

- affective component, 164
- attitude, 163
- behavioural component, 164
- cognitive component, 164
- compensatory decision rule, 154
- complex buying behaviour, 159
- consumer decision rules, 154
- convenience goods/services, 153
- culture, 167
- decision heuristics, 155
- determinant attributes, 154
- dissonance-reducing buying behaviour, 160
- evaluative criteria, 153

- external locus of control, 152
- external search for information, 152
- financial risk, 152
- functional needs, 150
- habitual buying behaviour, 161
- internal locus of control, 152
- internal search for information, 152
- learning, 165
- motive, 161
- need recognition, 150
- negative word of mouth, 158
- noncompensatory decision rule, 155
- perception, 164
- performance risk, 152

- personal needs, 162
- physiological needs, 162
- postpurchase dissonance, 156
- PSSP hierarchy of needs, 162
- psychological needs, 150
- psychological risk, 152
- reference group, 166
- ritual consumption, 155
- safety needs, 162
- shopping goods/services, 153
- situational factors, 167
- social needs, 162
- specialty goods/services, 153
- variety-seeking buying behaviour, 161

Concept Review

1. Give three reasons why it is important for marketers to understand the factors that influence consumers' purchasing decisions.

2. List the five steps of the consumer buying decision process. What should be the primary focus of marketing strategy at the alternative evaluation stage? The purchase stage?

3. What are the primary factors that affect consumers' search processes? What marketing strategies can marketers employ to ensure that customers get the information they need in order to make their shopping decisions?

4. Briefly explain the four types of consumer buying behaviour and describe four strategies marketers could use to facilitate consumer purchasing in each case. Give examples of products you would classify as complex buying and dissonance-reducing choices. In what ways are they different or related?

5. Identify and briefly explain the four psychological factors that influence consumer buying decisions.

6. What marketing tactics could be used to break through customers' selective perception i.e., selective exposure, selective attention, selective comprehension, and selective interpretation?

7. How can marketers use the PSSP model to develop successful marketing programs for their target market?

8. Briefly explain how social and situational considerations influence customer buying decisions.

9. Perceived risks are a key determinant of consumer buying decisions. Explain what is meant by perceived risks and identify tactics marketers could use to mitigate these risks.

10. Culture is one of the most important but least understood influences on consumer buying decisions. Explain how marketers can ensure that their marketing efforts are suited to their culturally diverse target market. What are the challenges involved in developing such efforts?

Marketing Applications

1. Describe two products: one you just purchased without much thought and one that took some deliberation on your part. Why did you spend a different amount of time and effort deciding on your purchases of the two products?

2. Assume you are in the market to buy a new car. What kind of car would you consider? What type of need(s) would you be satisfying if you purchased that particular type of car?

3. Explain the factors that affect the amount of time and effort that a consumer might expend when choosing an optometrist for contact lenses. How would your answer change if the consumer were looking for contact lens cleaning solution?

4. When evaluating different alternatives for a Saturday night outing at a fine restaurant, explain how a consumer would use decision heuristics to narrow down the choice of restaurants. Give examples of heuristics such as price, brand, and presentation in your answer.

5. What can retailers do to make sure that they have satisfied customers after the sale is complete?

6. Tazo makes a blend of exotic green teas, spearmint, and rare herbs to create a tea called Zen. Using the PSSP hierarchy of needs, explain which need(s) are being fulfilled by this tea.

7. Identify and describe the three social factors that influence the consumer decision process. Provide an example of how each of these might influence the purchase of the necessary products and services for a family vacation.

8. Nike has developed a new shoe for long-distance runners designed to minimize wear and tear on the joints and tendons. Develop a theme for an advertising strategy that ensures all three components of attitude are positively covered.

9. What can a marketer do to positively influence a situation in which a consumer is ready to buy but has not yet done so?

10. You were recently hired by a retail and catalogue company that promotes itself as a Canadian firm selling only Canadian made goods. The products featured in advertising and in the catalogues tell the stories of the firms that produced the goods in Canada. The sales response to the firm's Made in Canada position has been incredible and growth has been impressive. One day while speaking to a vendor, you find out a shipment of merchandise will be delayed since the product is coming from overseas and is late. A few days later you hear a similar story. As it turns out, the firm just barely earns the Made in the Canada label. Although technically the products meet a standard to be classified as Canadian made, you worry that the firms is not being truthful to its customers. You decide to write a letter to the VP of marketing detailing your concerns. What would you put in the letter?

Toolkit

CONSUMER BEHAVIOUR

Jill is trying to decide, once and for all, which soft drink company is her favourite. She has created a chart to help her decide. She has rated Coca-Cola, Pepsi-Cola, and Jones Soda in terms of price, taste, variety, and packaging. She has also assessed how important each of these four attributes is in terms of her evaluations. Use the toolkit provided at www.mcgrawhill.ca/olc/grewal to determine which cola Jill will choose using a compensatory model. Which cola would she choose using a noncompensatory model? If you were Jill, which model would you use, the compensatory or the noncompensatory. Why?

Net Savvy

1. Visit the Harley-Davidson website (www.harley-davidson.com) and review the information provided about its Harley Owners Group (H.O.G.). Describe the efforts the company makes to maintain customer loyalty through its programs. What are the benefits to H.O.G. members? Discuss how these measures might be effective in creating value for members.

2. Customers use a variety of methods to provide feedback to companies about their experiences. Planetfeedback.com was developed as one such venue. Visit its website (www.planetfeedback.com) and identify the types of feedback that customers can provide. Look over the feedback about Ford, and summarize some of the most recent comments. What is the ratio of positive to negative comments about Ford during the last year or so? Describe the effect these comments might have on customer perceptions of Ford.

Chapter Case Study

THE SMART CAR PREPARES TO ENTER THE U.S. MARKET[31]

All the rage in crowded cities in Western Europe, the smart car brand will finally make its way across the Atlantic. Although various models are available elsewhere, an entirely new model is being introduced into the U.S. market: the smart SUV. According to Scott Keogh, General Manager at smart USA, the company expects to sell 25,000 smart cars to U.S. consumers in its first year.

Company Background[32]

The smart car was conceived in 1994 through a joint venture between Mercedes-Benz and SMH, the Swiss manufacturer of Swatch watches, and named for "**S**watch, **M**ercedes, and **art**." Engineered with the environment in mind, the car originally was to use electric power or hybrid technology but ultimately was produced to consume either gasoline or diesel power, though it still achieves "green" status because of its anticorrosion undercoat and the powder coating on its steel body, which avoid polluting with wastewater and solvents. The body also features already coloured, moulded plastic panels to eliminate the need for paint booths and their resulting emissions.

The smart car was designed as a part of an overall transportation strategy for Europe's bustling big cities. To support efforts to reduce congestion, the smart car was to be used to reach local destinations, whereas longer trips would rely on rail and air transportation. For example, the Swiss have integrated smart cars into their transportation system to the point that consumers can have smart cars, rather than taxis, awaiting them at 40 different train stations.

EXHIBIT c6.1 Smart Models Available in the U.K.

The World Market for smart

Wholly owned by DaimlerChrysler, smart cars are currently sold in 30 countries, including Germany, Italy, Switzerland, Australia, Canada, Hong Kong, Israel, Japan, Lebanon, Mexico, South Africa, Taiwan, Turkey, and the United Kingdom. Because it manufactures a variety of models, the company provides a user-friendly smart configuration tool on its website (www.smart.com) so potential buyers can design their own cars. (See Exhibit C6.1 above for an example of the smart configuration tool for the U.K. market.)

As the world's smallest car, smart has earned the affectionate nicknames the electric razor on wheels, a glorified go-cart, high fashion by Hot Wheels, and a rolling backpack, to cite a few. Driving it has been likened to driving in a telephone booth, though some view it more as a high-tech toy whose cabin is part cockpit, part playpen. An article in *Money* magazine told readers to "Think of it as the T-shirt of cars: cute, comfy and cheap."[33] But beyond the teasing, the smart car has also been referred to as "an environmentalist's own rolling Kyoto treaty"[34] because of its ability to get 100 km per litre, its low emissions, and the recyclability of 85 percent of the materials used in its production. In markets in which gasoline costs upwards of $5 a gallon, the car has real appeal, especially among the eclectic crowd, with its hip, cool image. According to Keogh, the smart car is "a unique car for people who really want to stand out."[35] (See Exhibit C6.2 for an example of how the company conveys its hip image.)

One of the hallmarks of the smart car is its size. Its dimensions—2.5 m long, 1.5 m wide, and 1.5 m tall—puts it 1.5 m shorter and 0.3 m narrower than the Volkswagen Beetle. Originally the smart car was intended only for the narrow streets of crowded European cities, where two-seaters are common, parking spaces are very scarce, and these cars navigate tight spots and squeeze into the tiniest of parking spots. When pulled in nose-to-curb, three of them can fit into one parallel parking space.

EXHIBIT c6.2 Smart Car—A Hip Image

Although it only sports a three-cylinder, 50- to 60-horsepower engine, the smart car is reported to purr like a kitten and offer some spunk. In addition to front and optional side airbags, air conditioning, remote central locking, and electric windows, smart car buyers can change their car's colours if they purchase interchangeable snap-on body panels. When the mood hits, the owner pulls off the black panels, snaps on the red, and makes a whole new fashion statement.

The Canadian Market[36]

The Mercedes-Benz Canada smart car was launched in Canada in September 2004. On October 24, 2004, the Government of Canada held a ceremony on Parliament Hill where the then Transport Minister, Jean Lapierre, received the keys to a Mercedes-Benz smart car. The smart fortwo, shown in picture with Minister Lapierre, was adopted as part of Transport Canada's vehicle fleet. According to Mr. Lapierre, "This purchase demonstrates the Government of Canada's commitment to reducing greenhouse gas emissions and encouraging a more sustainable transportation system." The Government of Canada demonstrated its readiness to embrace the smart car but were Canadians ready to embrace the 2.5 m long, 800cc three-cylinder diesel engine that gives 4.7 litres per 100 kilometres at a cost of between $16,500 for the base and $22,500 for the loaded version?

Normally, new car launches are big events for automotive manufacturers where the primary goal is to generate buzz through millions of dollars advertising, media events, and promotional activities. However, unlike the normal practice, when Mercedes-Benz Canada launched its smart car in Canada, there was no national marketing campaign—no big advertising push, no television spots in prime time, or full page ads in newspapers. Why? It's because the smart car, the smallest car in Canadian history, was already sold out before it was launched and many customers had to wait several months for delivery—some until March 2005 because Mercedes-Benz Canada had none in stock. Mercedes-Benz's smart assembly plant initially allocated 800 vehicles for Canada from its plant in France for the fourth quarter of 2004. But the orders with deposits started coming in February when Mercedes announced the smart car would arrive in showrooms in October. When orders quickly exceeded supply, Mercedes gained a further 200 from the factory. That didn't come close to satisfying demand and the waiting times grew longer. Incredible success beyond the wildest imagination of Mercedes-Benz Canada! But let's go back to our neighbour to the South.

The U.S. Market

In the recent past, small cars have had a difficult time making big inroads into the U.S. automobile market. American consumers like the luxury and safety provided by their large, massive horsepower cars, SUVs, and trucks—even when fuel prices skyrocket—partly because they are accustomed to a more sparsely populated geography, except for those U.S. consumers who live in sprawling metropolitan areas. Although uniquely styled cars like the PT Cruiser, Volkswagen Beetle, and Mini Cooper have managed to get a piece of the limelight, they appeal only to small niches in the market.

Rumours have abounded for years about the possible introduction of smart cars to the U.S. market. Various issues prevented the sale of the original models, such as the fear that they would never sell in sufficient numbers to be viable, their high price tag by American standards, and the difficulty of making them compliant with EPA regulations. In addition, U.S. auto safety advocates voiced serious concerns about the crashworthiness of the small vehicles in a market in which big vehicles rule the road.

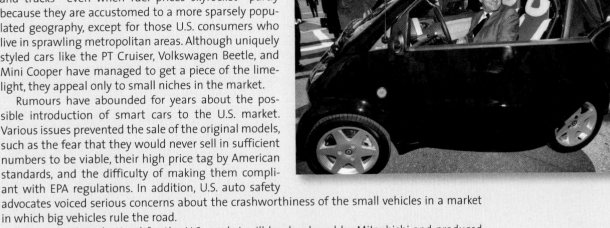

| EXHIBIT | c6.3 | The smart fortwo, shown in picture with Minister Lapierre |

The smart SUV destined for the U.S. market will be developed by Mitsubishi and produced in DaimlerChrysler's Juiz de Fora, Brazil, manufacturing facility. A cross between a car and an SUV (though a particularly small SUV by American standards), the smart will sport permanent all-wheel drive. The jury remains out about how well it will be accepted because the features demanded by Americans may differ drastically from those demanded by Europeans and Asians. Selected Mercedes-Benz dealerships throughout the United States will sell the smart cars from separate showrooms they are required to build to market the car.

Questions

1. Identify and discuss the type of decision process that consumers go through when purchasing this type of product. How have smart cars created value?

2. Identify the determinant attributes that might set the smart car apart from competing makes and models (e.g., the Ford Focus TDCi, Toyota Prius, Honda Insight, PT Cruiser Diesel, and Honda Diesel Wagon). What attributes might be of concern to consumers?

3. What are some differences between the Canadian market and U.S. that might make it tougher to sell the smart car to U.S. consumers? Why do you think that the smart car destined for the U.S. market is a cross between a car and an SUV?

4. Explain why you think the smart car was such a huge success with Canadian consumers. Do you think Canadian consumers will buy smart SUVs or smart cars that are larger and use gasoline rather than diesel? Why?

Business-to-Business Marketing

Think about the jeans in your closet. You probably bought them from a store in the course of a business-to-consumer (B2C) transaction. But from whom did the company that manufactured your jeans, say Seven for All Mankind, buy the components needed to get those jeans ready for you? Seven needed to buy the raw materials, like denim and thread. It also had to buy sewing machines to make the jeans and washers and dryers to help give them that popular vintage look. To age your new jeans further, the company even had to buy little rocks to put into the dryers, along with some knives and sanders. When the company purchased these materials, they were shipped to the Seven factory on trucks or by rail. These very transactions—purchasing the materials and transportation, designing the patterns for cutting and manufacturing the fabric—are managed by computer systems that were developed by and purchased from software engineers and consultants. Then, once the jeans have been produced, they must be transported to and sold by retailers. In each of these transactions, one business sells to another, which makes each a B2B transaction. B2C transactions only occur when a business, typically a retailer, sells to a consumer.

In this chapter, we will look at the different types of B2B markets and examine the B2B buying process with an eye toward how it differs from the B2C buying process, which we discussed in Chapter 6. Several factors influence the B2B buying process, and we discuss these as well. Finally, the chapter concludes with a discussion about the role of the Internet and its influence on the way B2B marketing is conducted. The sequence of topics is outlined in the chapter roadmap.

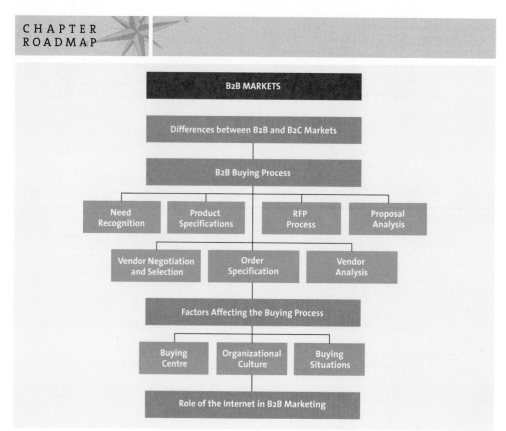

CHAPTER
ROADMAP

business-to-business (B2B) marketing
The process of buying and selling goods or services to be used in the production of other goods and services, for consumption by the buying organization, or for resale by wholesalers and retailers.

Imagine how many B2B transactions took place before Jessica Simpson was able to buy these destroyed denim jeans.

Business-to-business (B2B) marketing refers to the process of buying and selling goods or services to be used in the production of other goods and services, for consumption by the buying organization, and/or for resale by wholesalers and retailers. Therefore, B2B marketing involves manufacturers, wholesalers, retailers, and service firms that market goods and services to other businesses but not to the ultimate consumer. The distinction between a B2B and a B2C transaction is not the product or service itself; rather, it is the ultimate purchaser and *user of* that product or service. Had your jeans been sold to an industrial supply firm, which then sold them to a custodial firm whose employees would wear them on the job, the transaction would still be a B2B transaction because the jeans are being purchased and used by a business rather than by an individual household consumer.

B2B Markets

LO 1

In our jeans example in the opening vignette, we described two types of B2B organizations: manufacturers/producers and resellers. However, institutions and governments also may be involved in B2B transactions. We now describe each of these B2B organizations and how the government classifies them. (See Exhibit 7.1.)

Manufacturers or Producers

Some of the biggest business-to-business buyers are manufacturers and producers. They buy raw materials, components, and parts that allow them to manufacture their own goods. For example, Hewlett-Packard (HP) uses a variety of components to make its computer products, including plastic for its exterior cases, interior components, and packaging. Given its high sales volume, HP must manage its supply and demand chains closely to minimize any shortages or overages. Therefore, HP created a private Internet (intranet) that connects the company with its plastics suppliers so it can consolidate plastic purchases and efficiently communicate with other supply chain areas.[1] The improvement in the information flow engendered by this intranet has cut 25 percent off the time it takes HP to receive the merchandise, 30 percent off plastic costs, and a significant portion off its internal administrative costs.[2]

Corporate Couriers uses Telus' business solutions to enter and track customers' packages through the Internet or by telephone through a customer service representative.

EXHIBIT	7.1	B2B Markets

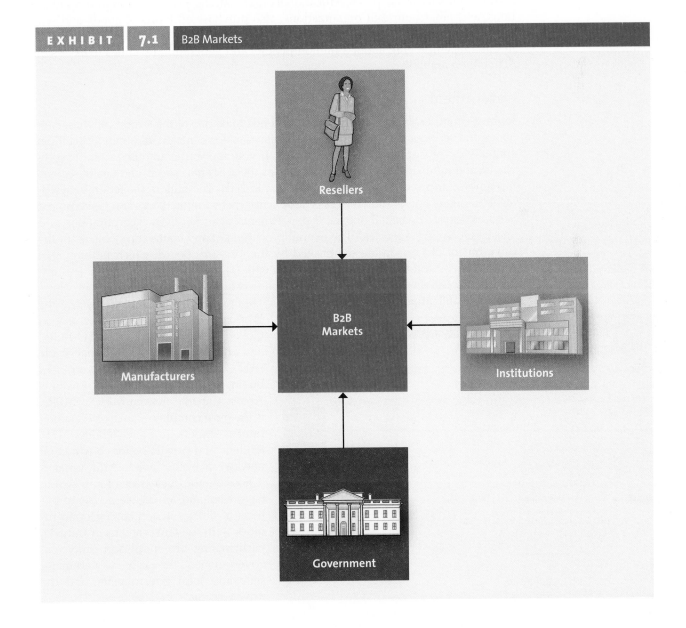

Resellers

Resellers are marketing intermediaries that resell manufactured products without significantly altering their form. For instance, wholesalers and distributors buy jeans from Seven for all Mankind and sell them to retailers—a B2B transaction, and retailers in turn resell those same jeans to the ultimate consumer—a B2C transaction—wholesalers, distributors, and retailers are all resellers. The Retail Council of Canada estimates that there were about 235,000 retail establishments in Canada, which employ about 2 million Canadians and generated revenues of over $390 billion in 2006. In fact, the retail trade provides more than 12 percent of all jobs in every community across the country and represents Canada's second-largest labour force.[3] Similarly, the wholesale sector employs about 740,000 Canadians and generated sales close to $500 billion in 2006, representing 6.7 percent of Canada's gross domestic product (GDP).[4] The role of wholesalers, retailers, and other intermediaries involved in the distribution of goods are discussed in greater detail in Chapters 13 and 14.

Institutions

Institutions, such as hospitals, educational organizations, prisons, religious organizations, and other nonprofit organizations, also purchase all kinds of goods and services for the people they serve. For instance, there are 80,000 nonprofit organizations in Canada, employing about 2 million people, and generating revenues in excess of $110 billion annually.[5]

Government

In most countries, the central government tends to be one of the largest purchasers of goods and services. For example the Canadian Government spends about $240 billion annually on procuring goods and services. If you add in the amounts spent by provincial and municipal governments as well as the academic, social, and health sectors, this amount increases to close to $450 billion in 2006. The bulk of the federal government buying of goods and services is done centrally by Public Works and Government Services Canada on behalf of over 85 departments, agencies, Crown corporations, and Special Operating Agencies.[6] The overall procurement and contracting policies of the Government of Canada are established by the Treasury Board, which requires that contracting be conducted in a manner that will: (1) stand the test of public scrutiny, increase access, encourage competition, and reflect fairness; and (2) comply with Canada's trade obligations under the North American Free Trade Agreement (NAFTA), the World Trade Organization Agreement on Government Procurement (WTO-AGP), and the Agreement on Internal Trade (AIT). Information about government buying can be obtained from Business Access Canada or from MERX.[7] MERX is the most complete source of Canadian public tenders, private tenders, U.S. tenders, and private-sector construction news available in Canada. MERX makes it possible for businesses of any size to have easy and affordable access to billions of dollars in contracting opportunities with the Government of Canada, participating provincial and municipal governments, the U.S. Government, state and local governments, and the private sector.[8]

MERX is the most complete source of public tenders, private tenders, U.S. tenders, and private-sector construction news available in Canada.

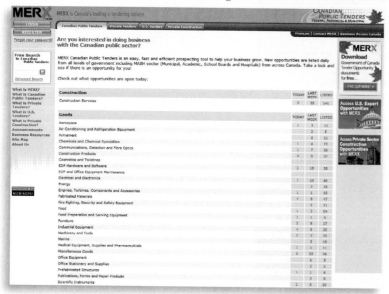

B2B Classification System and Segmentation

LO **2**

Statistics Canada collects data about business activity in Canada through its classification scheme, which categorizes all firms into a hierarchical set of six-digit **North American Industry Classification System (NAICS) codes.**[9] The NAICS was developed jointly by Canada, the United States, and Mexico to provide comparable statistics about business activity in all of North America. The NAICS code replaces the Standard Industrial Classification (SIC) system that was in use since the 1930s. NAICS 2007 groups economic activity into 20 sectors and 928 Canadian industries. The NAICS 6-digit numerical system works as shown in Exhibit 7.2. The first two digits represents the sector in the economy (e.g., 41 is the Wholesale sector), the third digit represents the subsector (e.g., 414 is Personal and Household Goods Wholesalers), the fourth digit represents the industry group, the fifth digit represents a specific subgroup within the industry, and the full 6-digits refer to the country-level or national industry, which in our example is Clothing and Clothing Accessories Wholesalers. The NAICS system is revised periodically to add new industries or to consolidate or delete others. The last update was done in 2007.

North American Industry Classification System (NAICS) codes
A classification scheme that categorizes all firms into a hierarchical set of six-digit codes.

The NAICS classification system can be quite useful to B2B marketers for analyzing market shares, demand for goods and services, import competition into the Canadian market, and for segmenting and targeting markets. Suppose, for instance, that a high-tech telecommunications components manufacturer has developed a new product that will significantly speed data transmission. Which of the types of firms listed under NAICS classification 51721 (wireless telecommunication) would be the most worthwhile to pursue as customers? To answer this question, the components manufacturer would first do research, probably using interviews conducted by company sales representatives, to determine which types of firms would find the new component most useful for their products. Then, using the NAICS data collected by Statistics Canada or the U.S. Census Bureau, the manufacturer could assess the number, size, and geographical dispersion of firms within each type, which might indicate both the product's potential and the types of firms that constitute the target market.

B2B firms, like B2C firms, focus their marketing efforts on serving specific target markets to create value for those customers.[10] For instance, Telus has dedicated business units that serve business customers within each of its targeted markets, which are segmented by account size (e.g., small, medium, and large companies). The products geared toward small businesses offer basic voice services, packaged plans, and no long-term contracts. For its

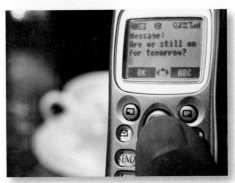

Which NAICS codes are used for these products?

EXHIBIT	7.2	Wholesale: NAICS Codes

2007 NAICS Code	Level
41	Wholesale Trade (National Economy or all of Canada)
414	Personal and Household Goods Wholesalers
4141	Textile, Clothing and Footwear Wholesalers
41411	Clothing and Clothing Accessories Wholesalers
414110	Clothing and Clothing Accessories Wholesalers (National Economy or all of Canada)

Source: www.bundesbank.de/download/meldewesen/bankenstatistik/kundensystematik/naics_2007_canada.pdf. Accessed December 4, 2007.

largest customers, Telus provides everything from professional services to corporate calling cards.[11] Companies may also segment their business customers according to end use application depending on the different ways customers use their products. For example, universities and large research companies purchase basic computers for their office and administrative use, more sophisticated computers for science and engineering research, and even more sophisticated computer system for medical research. Computer manufacturers such as Dell, HP, and IBM segment these business customers based on end use application and may target only one end use segment. Companies may also segment their business customers based on their geographic location such as U.S., Europe, China, India, and Latin America. Finally, B2B marketers segment their markets based on the benefits sought by their customers.

Let us now explore in a little more detail, some of the unique characteristics of B2B markets that distinguish them from B2C markets. Exhibit 7.3 lists the key characteristics of B2B and B2C buying behaviour.

LO **3**

Differences between B2B and B2C Markets

Market Characteristics   In B2C markets, consumers buy goods to satisfy their own individual or household needs and are heavily influenced by price, personal tastes, brand reputation, or personal recommendations of friends and family. In B2B markets, demand for goods and services is derived from B2C sales in the same supply chain. More specifically, **derived demand** is the linkage between consumers' demand for a company's output and its purchase of necessary inputs to manufacture or assemble that particular output. For instance, the demand for raw denim used to make Seven for All Mankind jeans is derived from the sale of the jeans to consumers. Thus, demand for raw material and semi-finished goods purchased by business firms tend to fluctuate more, and more frequently. In addition, demand in many business markets is inelastic, that is, the total demand for goods is not affected much

derived demand
The linkage between consumers' demand for a company's output and its purchase of necessary inputs to manufacture or assemble that particular output.

EXHIBIT	**7.3**	Characteristics of Business-to-Business Buying and B2C

Market Characteristics
- Demand for business products is derived
- Fewer customers, more geographically concentrated, and orders are larger
- Demand is more inelastic, fluctuates more, and more frequently

Product Characteristics
- Products are technical in nature and purchased based on specifications
- Mainly raw and semi-finished goods are purchased
- Heavy emphasis is placed on delivery time, technical assistance, after sale service, and financing assistance

Buying Process Characteristics
- Buying decision is more complex
- Buying may involve competitive bidding, negotiated pricing, and complex financial arrangements
- Qualified, professional buyers who follow a more formalized buying process
- Buying criteria and objective are specified as are procedures for evaluating and selecting vendors and products
- Multiple people with varied interests participate in purchase decisions
- Reciprocal arrangements exists and negotiations between buyers and sellers are common
- Buyers and sellers usually work closely to build close long-term relationships
- Online buying over the Internet is common

Marketing Mix Characteristics
- Direct selling is the primary form of selling and physical distribution is often essential
- Advertising are technical in nature and promotions emphasize personal selling
- Price is often negotiated, inelastic, frequently affected by trade and quantity discounts. Price usually includes a service or maintenance component

by price changes in the short run. For instance, a small increase in the price for raw denim will not cause a huge drop in the demand for denim in the apparel industry in the short-run. Another characteristic of B2B markets is that the number of business buyers is substantially fewer than in B2C markets and are more concentrated in big cities, towns, and industrial areas. Also, the sizes of the orders are substantially larger than consumer purchases. For example, Bombardier announced that Lufthansa placed an order for 15 Bombardier CRJ900 Jets worth US$584 million.[12]

Product Characteristics   In B2B markets, the products ordered are primarily raw materials and semi-finished goods that are processed or assembled into finished goods for the ultimate consumers. For example, Dell orders all the computer components from different suppliers and then assembles the computers before shipping to the final consumer. In certain B2B markets (e.g., aerospace, medical, pharmaceutical, shipping, defence, etc.) the products are very technical and sophisticated in nature and must conform to technical standards specified by the buyer. Thus, the raw materials, components, and semi-finished goods undergo rigorous testing before shipping. Also, orders must be delivered on the dates agreed to by both buyers and sellers. Technical services and financing assistance are important aspects of B2B buying behaviour. Companies such as Nortel Networks and Bombardier often provide vendor financing—a practice where a company provides a loan to its customer that is used to buy goods from the company.[13] In B2C markets, consumers buy finished goods for their own personal consumption.

Buying Process Characteristics   Generally, for routine purchases or small dollar value purchases, only one or a few individuals within a department or the company may be responsible for the buying decision. However, for purchases of highly technical or complex products involving thousands or millions of dollars, the buying effort is much more structured, formalized, and professional. More people are usually involved in complex buying decisions, they are usually technically trained and qualified professionals, and represent different interests (e.g., managerial, technical, and departmental) within the organization. The group of people involved in the buying decision is often referred to as the buying centre, which is described in detail below. Most companies have formal policies and procedures to guide buying decisions that must be closely followed by the people involved in the buying decisions. Examples of such procedures include rules governing competitive bidding, negotiated pricing, complex financial arrangements, buying criteria, and objectives as well as procedures for evaluating competitive bids.

Another major difference between B2B and B2C buying lies in the nature of the relationship between the firm and its suppliers. Generally, the buying decision is based on negotiations, which for complex purchases could be quite extended. The negotiated contract normally covers a range of concerns including price, delivery, warranty, technical specifications, and claim policies. In B2B markets, buyers and sellers strive to develop close relationships with each other and so will often provide help or advice in order to ensure a win-win situation for both parties. For example, Shepherd Thermoforming and Packaging (discussed in Entrepreneurial Marketing 7.1) noted that their customers often choose to come in and work with their engineering staff to create the desired look and product functionality that they need.[14]

In addition, some firms may engage in reciprocal buying arrangements—a practice where two firms agree to buy each other's products and services. Clearly, reciprocal buying has both negative and positive consequences for the both buying and selling firms involved as well as for other suppliers. Two such consequences are that it excludes other vendors from participating in the buying process and may limit the firms to each other's products, which may not be the best thing.

Marketing Mix Characteristics   Another major difference between the typical B2B and B2C transaction is the role of the salesperson. While salespeople are an important component of the communications mix for B2C transactions like real estate, insurance, jewellery, consumer electronics, and high-end apparel, most fast moving consumer goods (FMCG) found in grocery and discount stores are not sold with the aid of salespeople. On the other hand, in most B2B sales, the salesperson is an integral component of the transaction. As discussed later in Ethical Dilemma 7.1, pharmaceutical manufacturers rely primarily on sales representatives to promote their drugs to doctors. Also, many manufacturers provide trade and quantity discounts to resellers for carrying their products.

The Business-to-Business Buying Process

The B2B buying process (Exhibit 7.4) parallels the B2C process, though it differs in many ways. Both start with need recognition, but the information search and alternative evaluation steps are more formal and structured in the B2B process. Typically, B2B buyers specify their needs in writing and ask potential suppliers to submit formal proposals, whereas B2C buying decisions are usually made by individuals or families and sometimes are unplanned or impulsive. In contrast, B2B buying decisions often are made by committees after a great deal of consideration. Finally, in B2C buying situations, customers evaluate their purchase decision and sometimes experience postpurchase dissonance. Formal performance evaluations of the vendor and the products sold generally do not occur, as they do in the B2B setting. As discussed in greater detail in the section below on buying situations, it is worth noting

---

Entrepreneurial Marketing 7.1 Shepherd Thermoforming and Packaging Inc.— Forming the Future through Innovation[15]

From your hot tub to your chocolate tray, Tylenol package, smoke detector cover, and other plastic accoutrement in your homes and cars, chances are they were manufactured by Brampton-based Shepherd Thermoforming and Packaging. The company manufactures heavy gauge plastic for automotive, bathware, appliance, and other industries and thin gauge plastic for packaging, trays, and a number of other thermoformed products. This $10-million-a-year business is the brainchild of Barry Shepherd, who started the business in 1985. Currently, Shepherd Thermoforming and Packaging enjoys an annual growth rate in revenues of about 12 percent and employs 40 workers. Back in 1985, did Barry Shepherd ever dream of becoming so successful? Hardly! His idea was very simple—create a one-man business selling packaging manufactured by third parties.

With the help of his wife, he began in a small office, provided by his then employer, selling packaging products for his former company as an independent supplier on commission. Twenty years later, Shepherd Thermoforming and Packaging is housed in a 40,000-square metre state-of-the-art facility with several thermoforming and packaging machines, equipment, and tools. Barry Shepherd transformed his business from a small reseller operation into a multi-million dollar design, manufacturing, and marketing operation. His customers include both large and small businesses in the consumer packaging, material handling, and automotive industries as well as OEMs (original equipment manufacturers).

His move from a reseller to a manufacturer is due in part to his financial success as a reseller—within three years of start up, Barry Shepherd was earning revenues in excess of $1 million. But Barry also saw that the demand for thermoforming and packaging products was growing steadily as consumers were buying more products—from toys to toothbrushes—that were wrapped in plastic packaging. Thus, he invested in his first machinery and ever since, his business just keeps growing as demand increases and he strengthens his company's capabilities. Shepherd Thermoforming and Packaging Inc. works closely with its customers in order to ensure they get the products they want while keeping costs down and minimizing delays. Barry notes that most customers choose to come in and work with his engineering staff to create the desired look and product functionality that they need. They bring their computer-aided design (CAD) files that assist in producing the thermoformed part quickly and accurately.

Despite his more than 20 years of success, Barry Shepherd must now contend with two new trends—globalization (which brings competition from low-cost producers in other countries such as China, India, and Brazil) and the growing trend among consumers to use more environmentally friendly products and packaging. It seems that he will truly need to rely on the company's slogan—forming the future through innovation—in order to form the future of Thermoforming and Packaging. Is he up for the challenge?

Toyota recognized the need to change tire suppliers when customers complained that their current supplier's tires did not perform adequately on snowpacked and off-the-road surfaces.

that not all B2B purchases go through each stage or go through each stage with the same intensity. For example, a routine purchase of office stationery will likely not go through all the stages of the buying decision process. However, the purchase of a computerized call centre system for the company will likely go through all the stages more rigorously than buying a few replacement computers for office use. Let's examine all six stages within the context of Toyota purchasing tires for its vehicles from Goodyear, Dunlop, and Firestone.[16]

Stage 1: Need Recognition

In the first stage of the B2B buying process, the buying organization recognizes, through either internal or external sources, that it has an unfilled need. For instance, Toyota's design teams might realize that their suppliers have increased the prices of the types of tires they use. At the same time, customers have complained that the tires they are currently using do not work very well on their all-wheel-drive vehicles. Toyota's own driving tests on snow-packed and off-the-road surfaces also indicate the need for a change. Through suppliers' salespeople, tradeshow demonstrations, ads in trade journals, Internet searches, and white papers, the company also has become aware of the benefits of different tire manufacturers.

EXHIBIT 7.4   Business-to-Business Buying Process

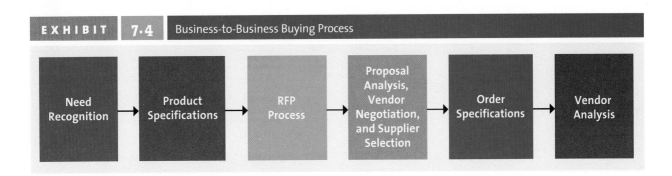

Need Recognition → Product Specifications → RFP Process → Proposal Analysis, Vendor Negotiation, and Supplier Selection → Order Specifications → Vendor Analysis

Stage 2: Product Specifications

After recognizing the need, the organization considers alternative solutions and comes up with potential specifications that suppliers might use to develop their proposals to supply the product. Because a significant share of Toyota vehicles are made and sold in North America, the company has made a strong commitment to engaging in long-term, mutually beneficial relationships with North American suppliers. In 2004, for instance, it spent nearly $13 billion for parts and materials from hundreds of North American suppliers and business partners.[17] Rather than working in a vacuum to determine its specifications for the new tires, Toyota's design teams and engineers actually go on site to vendors' plants to develop the specifications for prototypes with their experts.

Stage 3: RFP Process

request for proposals (RFP)
A process through which buying organizations invite alternative suppliers to bid on supplying their required components.

The **request for proposals (RFP)** is a common process through which buying organizations invite alternative suppliers to bid on supplying their required components. The purchasing company may simply post its RFP needs on its website, work through various B2B linkages (which we discuss later in this chapter), or contact potential suppliers directly. Toyota, for example, has set up ToyotaSupplier.com so current and

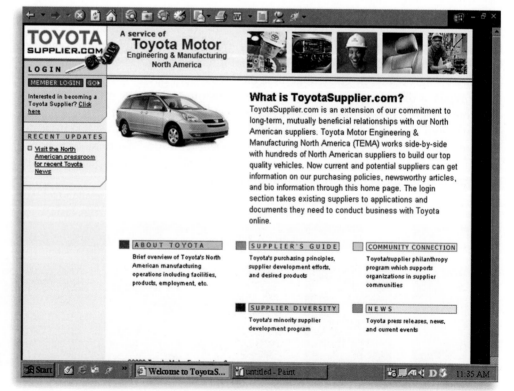

*ToyotaSupplier.com is
used to post RFPs so
current and potential
suppliers can get
information on its
purchasing policies and
relevant news articles.*

potential suppliers can get information on its purchasing policies and relevant news articles.[18]

Stage 4: Proposal Analysis, Vendor Negotiation, and Supplier Selection

The buying organization, in conjunction with its critical decision-makers, evaluates all the proposals it receives in response to its RFP. Firms are likely to narrow the process to a few suppliers, often those with which they have existing relationships, and discuss key terms of the sale, such as price, quality, delivery, and financing. Some firms have a policy that requires them to negotiate with several suppliers, particularly if the product or service represents a critical component or aspect of the business. This policy keeps suppliers on their toes; they know that the buying firm can always shift a greater portion of its business to an alternative supplier if it offers better terms. For example, because Toyota negotiates with Dunlop and Firestone as well, Goodyear knows that it cannot grow lax in the benefits it offers. In the end, Toyota decides to purchase from Goodyear because it has the best combination of strength of brand, ability to deliver, product quality, and ease of ordering.

In Step 4: Proposal Analysis, Vendor Negotiation, and Supplier Selection, Toyota decides to purchase from Goodyear because it has the best combination of strength of brand, ability to deliver, product quality, and ease of ordering.

Stage 5: Order Specifications

In the fifth stage, the firm places its order with its preferred supplier (or suppliers). The order will include a detailed description of the goods, prices, delivery dates, and, in some cases, penalties if the order is not filled on time. The supplier then will send an acknowledgement that it has received the order and fill it by the specified date. For Toyota, this description includes the specific sizes and number of tires it wants, the price it will agree to pay for those tires, the date it expects to receive them, and the result if the wrong tires are delivered or delivered after the due date.

Stage 6: Vendor Analysis

Just as occurs in the consumer buying process, firms analyze their vendors' performance so they can make decisions about their future purchases. The difference is that, in a B2B setting, this analysis is typically more formal and objective. Let's consider how Toyota might evaluate Goodyear's performance, as in Exhibit 7.5, using the following steps:

1. The buying team develops a list of issues that it believes are important to consider in the evaluation of the vendor.
2. To determine how important each of these issues (in column 1) is, the buying team assigns an importance score to each (column 2.) The more important the

| EXHIBIT | 7.5 | Evaluating a Vendor's Performance |

(1) Key Issues	(2) Importance Score	(3) Vendor's Performance	(4) Importance Performance
Strength of brand	.30	5	.15
Meets delivery dates	.20	4	.8
Product quality	.40	5	2.0
Ease of ordering	.10	3	.3
Total	1.0		4.6

issue, the higher a score it will receive, but the importance scores must add up to 1. In this case, the buying team believes that product quality and strength of brand are most important, whereas meeting the delivery dates and the ease of ordering are less important.

3. In the third column, the buying team assigns numbers that reflect its judgments about how well the vendor performs. Using a five-point scale, where 1 equals "poor performance" and 5 equals "excellent performance," the buying team decides that Goodyear has fairly high performance on all issues except ease of ordering.

4. To get the overall performance of the vendor, in the fourth column, the team combines the importance of each issue and the vendor's performance scores by multiplying them together. Note that Goodyear performed particularly well on the most important issues. As a result, when we add the importance/performance scores in column 4, we find that Goodyear's overall evaluation is quite high—4.6 on a 5-point scale!

Factors Affecting the Buying Process   LO 4

The six-stage B2B buying process may be influenced by three factors within the purchasing organization: the buying centre, the buying organization's philosophy or corporate culture, and the buying situation.

The Buying Centre

In most large organizations, several people typically are responsible for the buying decisions. These **buying centre** participants can range from employees who have a formal role in purchasing decisions (e.g., the purchasing or procurement department) to members of the design team that is specifying the particular equipment or raw material needed to employees who will be using a new machine that is being ordered. All these employees are likely to play different roles in the buying process, which vendors must understand and adapt to in their marketing and sales efforts.

We can categorize six different buying roles within a typical buying centre. One or more people may take on a certain role, or one person may take on more than one of the following roles: "(1) **initiator**, the person who first suggests buying the particular product or service; (2) **influencer**, person whose views influence other members of the buying centre in making the final decision; (3) **decider**, the person who ultimately determines any part of or the entire buying decision—whether to buy, what to buy, how to buy, or where to buy; (4) **buyer**, the person who handles the paperwork of the actual purchase; (5) **user**, the person(s) who consumes or uses the product or service; and (6) **gatekeeper**, the person(s) who controls information or access, or both, to decision makers and influencers."[19]

To illustrate how a buying centre operates, consider purchases made by a hospital. Where do hospitals obtain their X-ray machines, syringes, and bedpans? Why

buying centre
The group of people typically responsible for the buying decisions in large organizations.

initiator
The buying centre participant who first suggests buying the particular product or service.

influencer
The buying centre participant whose views influence other members of the buying centre in making the final decision.

decider
The buying centre participant who ultimately determines any part of or the entire buying decision—whether to buy, what to buy, how to buy, or where to buy.

buyer
The buying centre participant who handles the paperwork of the actual purchase.

user
The person who consumes or uses the product or service purchased by the buying centre.

gatekeeper
The buying centre participant who controls information or access to decision makers and influencers.

Many people are involved in making B2B purchasing decisions.

are some medical procedures covered in whole or in part by insurance, whereas others are not? Why might your doctor recommend one type of allergy medication instead of another?

The Initiator—Your Doctor   When you seek treatment from your physician, he or she *initiates* the buying process by determining the products and services that will best address and treat your illness or injury. For example, say that you fell backwards off your snowboard and, in trying to catch yourself, shattered your elbow. You require surgery to mend the affected area, which includes the insertion of several screws to hold the bones in place. Your doctor promptly notifies the hospital to schedule a time for the procedure and specifies the brand of screws she wants on hand for your surgery.

The Influencer—The Medical Device Supplier, the Pharmacy   For years, your doctor has been using ElbowMed screws, a slightly higher-priced screw. Her first introduction to ElbowMed screws came from the company's sales representative, who visited her office to demonstrate how ElbowMed screws were far superior to those of its competition. Your doctor recognized ElbowMed as good value. Armed with empirical data and case studies, ElbowMed's sales rep effectively *influenced* your doctor's decision to use that screw.

The Decider—The Hospital   Even though your doctor requested ElbowMed screws, the hospital administrators ultimately is responsible for *deciding* whether to buy ElbowMed screws. The hospital supplies the operating room, instrumentation, and surgical supplies, and therefore, the hospital administrators must weigh a variety of factors to determine if the ElbowMed screw is not only best for the patients but also involves a cost that is reimbursable by various insurance providers.

The Buyer   The actual *buyer* of the screw will likely be the hospital's materials manager, who is charged with buying and maintaining inventory for the hospital in the most cost-effective manner. Whereas ElbowMed screws are specific to your type of procedure, other items, such as gauze and sutures, may be purchased through a group purchasing organization (GPO), which obtains better prices through volume buying.

The User—The Patient   Ultimately though, the buying process for this procedure will be greatly affected by the *user*, namely, you and your broken elbow. If you are uncomfortable with the procedure or have read about alternative procedures that you prefer, you may decide that ElbowMed screws are not the best treatment.

The Gatekeeper—The Insurance Company   Your insurer may believe that ElbowMed screws are too expensive and that other screws deliver equally effective results and therefore refuse to reimburse the hospital in full or in part for the use of the screws.

In the end, the final purchase decision must take into consideration every single buying centre participant. Ethical Dilemma 7.1 examines how the "influencer" (the pharmaceutical sales representative and pharmaceutical companies) influences the "decider" (the physician) on purchases made by the "user" (the patient.)

Organizational Culture

A firm's **organizational culture** reflects the set of values, traditions, and customs that guide its managers and employees' behaviour. The firm's culture often comprises a set of unspoken guidelines that employees share with one another through various work situations. For example, a new employee might be told that the workday begins at 9:00 a.m.; however, in observing coworkers, he or she learns that most arrive at 8:30 a.m. and thus decides to start arriving earlier.

organizational culture Reflects the set of values, traditions, and customs that guide a firm's employees' behaviour.

Ethical Dilemma

7.1   How Does the Doctor Know Best?

The pharmaceutical industry is constantly introducing new drugs and new uses for existing drugs. Thus doctors have to constantly update their knowledge of pharmaceuticals and what they are prescribed for. One of the key information sources for doctors on changes in the pharmaceutical industry is the sales representatives who visit with the doctors. A recent study found that doctors want detailed information about drug safety, pricing, and prescribing in addition to information about new drugs. The doctors also want to understand the difference between the new drug and the old drug.

Unfortunately the study found that the sales representatives often do not provide all of this data to the doctors. The sales reps instead focus on the benefits of their new drugs while not volunteering pricing information, side effect data, or comparisons with existing products. Even safety data was found to be skewed toward placing the new drugs in a favourable light. To make matters worse, the

study found that when competitors' products were mentioned to doctors they were generally discussed in unfavourable terms.

Perhaps an even more troubling finding of the study was that doctors who were frequently visited by sales representatives often chose to treat patients with drug therapies and not alternative nondrug therapies even if researchers consider the nondrug therapy superior. These doctors were also less likely to prescribe the generic equivalents to costly branded drugs. In other words, the sales representatives are having a dramatic impact on the doctors' choice in treatment of their patients.[20]

What, if anything, should be done about the behaviour of pharmaceutical sales representatives? What incentives could doctors or the medical community provide to encourage pharmaceutical companies to provide doctors with the desired information, while limiting their influence over patient care?

From an ethical perspective, what information should pharmaceutical sales representatives provide to doctors?

---

autocratic buying centre
A buying centre in which one person makes the decision alone, though there may be multiple participants.

democratic buying centre
A buying centre in which the majority rules in making decisions.

consultative buying centre
A buying centre in which one person makes the decision but he or she solicits input from others before doing so.

consensus buying centre
A buying centre in which all members of the team must reach a collective agreement that they can support a particular purchase.

Organizational culture can have a profound influence on purchasing decisions, and corporate buying centre cultures might be divided into four general types: autocratic, democratic, consultative, and consensus, as illustrated in Exhibit 7.6. Knowing which buying centre culture is prevalent in a given organization helps the seller decide how to approach that particular client, how and to whom to deliver pertinent information, and to whom to make the sales presentations.

In an **autocratic buying centre**, though there may be multiple participants, one person makes the decision alone, whereas the majority rules in a **democratic buying centre**. **Consultative buying centres** use one person to make a decision but solicit input from others before doing so. Finally, in a **consensus buying centre**, all members of the team must reach a collective agreement that they can support a particular purchase.[21]

Cultures act like living, breathing forces that change and grow, just as organizations do. Even within some companies, culture may vary by geography, by division, or by functional department. Whether you are a member of the buying centre or a supplier trying to sell to it, it is extremely important to understand its culture and the roles of the key players in the buying process. Not knowing the roles of the key players in that case would waste a lot of time—both yours and the buying centre's—and could even alienate the real decision maker. Adding Value 7.1 on page 192 examines how Volkswagen works with their suppliers to put a Volkswagen together.

Buying Situations

The type of buying situation also affects the B2B decision process. Most B2B buying situations can be categorized into three types: new buys, modified rebuys, and straight rebuys. (See Exhibit 7.7 on page 193.) To illustrate the nuances between these

EXHIBIT | **7.6** | Organizational Buying Culture

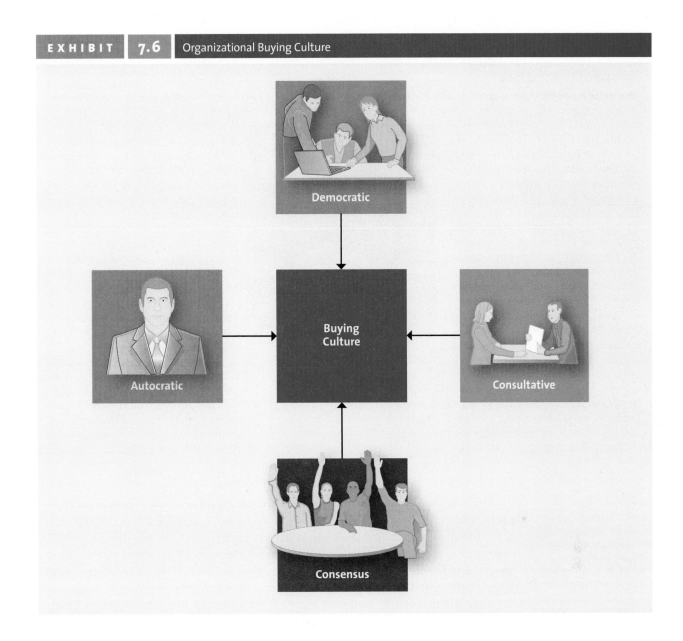

three buying situations, we portray how Dell Inc. develops relationships with some of its business customers after first targeting them.

Dell has been very successful in the B2B market, primarily because it is flexible, maintains a customer focus, and provides complete product solutions at value prices. Dell uses strong sales relationships and database marketing to understand what its customers want and how to fulfill those wants. First, Dell advertises heavily to educational and government institutions during the second and third quarters of the year, which coincide with the start of their buying cycle. Second, Dell's salespeople understand the financial and resource constraints that these groups face, so it offers complete packages of software, hardware, and IT services and provides installers who not only set up the equipment but also remove old hardware. Third, Dell works closely with its buyers to obtain feedback and solicit help from its product development teams so that production is geared toward customer needs. Fourth, Dell divides its accounts into three categories: acquisition, development, and retention. Working with key decision-makers, the company maintains consistent contact with each account and maximizes every dollar it allocates toward technology spending.[22]

Adding Value   7.1   Putting a Volkswagen Together[23]

The German-based Volkswagen Group, which owns and distributes the Audi, Bentley, Bugatti, Lamborghini, Seat, Skoda, VW, and VW Commercial brands, noted at one point that its purchasing agents spent 70 percent of their time searching for, analyzing, validating, and forwarding information about parts and components. That meant that they had only about 30 percent of their time to devote to activities that would add value to the firm, which was an unacceptable limitation. What could VW do? It recognized that its purchasing process needed to be made far more efficient.

Volkswagen now manages its own Internet-based private network—intranet—that links more than 5000 suppliers of roughly $77 billion worth of components, automotive parts, and indirect raw materials—equal to 70 percent of Volkswagen's annual revenue. With its new integrated software system iPAD, or Internal Purchasing

Volkswagen's software system, iPad, has cut order processing time from two hours to nine minutes since VW's purchasing agents receive product descriptions directly from suppliers online.

Agent Desk, Volkswagen has cut processing time dramatically. With iPAD, purchasing agents receive product descriptions directly from suppliers online, so the search process, which used to take two hours, is now complete in nine minutes. Moreover, whereas agents used to spend, on average, 60 minutes per order, they now spend only 20.

In addition to improving its internal processes, Volkswagen has maintained a strong relationship with its suppliers by setting up online tools to track invoices and payments and allowing suppliers to log on to its secure "Supplier Cockpit" website to find information pertinent to their products. Other online tools, including a catalogue, auction, and request for proposals (RFP), are readily available. Perhaps most important though, Volkswagen focuses on continually promoting its close partnerships and collaboration with its vendors.

---

new buy
In a B2B setting, a purchase of a good or service for the first time; the buying decision is likely to be quite involved because the buyer or the buying organization does not have any experience with the item.

modified rebuy
Refers to when the buyer has purchased a similar product in the past but has decided to change some specifications, such as the desired price, quality level, customer service level, options, or so forth.

straight rebuy
Refers to when the buyer or buying organization simply buys additional units of products that had previously been purchased.

In a **new buy** situation, a customer purchases a good or service for the first time,[24] which means the buying decision is likely to be quite involved because the buyer or the buying organization does not have any experience with the item. In the B2B context, the buying centre is likely to proceed through all six steps in the buying process and involve many people in the buying decision. Typical new buys might range from capital equipment to components that the firm previously made itself but now has decided to purchase instead. For example, the University of Ottawa bought its first videoconferencing equipment and facility in 1993 in order to enhance its distance education capability. Prior to this, it relied mainly on its audiographics network, which carried the voices of professors, students, and teaching aides over two telephone lines—one for voice and one for the graphics portion of the course over the Internet.

In a **modified rebuy**, the buyer has purchased a similar product in the past but has decided to change some specifications, such as the desired price, quality level, customer service level, options, or so forth. Current vendors are likely to have an advantage in acquiring the sale in a modified rebuy situation, as long as the reason for the modification is not dissatisfaction with the vendor or its products. A few years ago, many universities across Canada replaced their huge CRT monitors in their students' labs with flat screen LCD monitors.

Straight rebuys occur when the buyer or buying organization simply buys additional units of products that had previously been purchased. A tremendous amount of B2B purchases are likely to fall in the straight rebuy category. For example, after the purchase of its first videoconferencing facility in 1993, the University of Ottawa has bought a few more. Currently, the university has five videoconferencing rooms that can seat between 18 and 88 students.

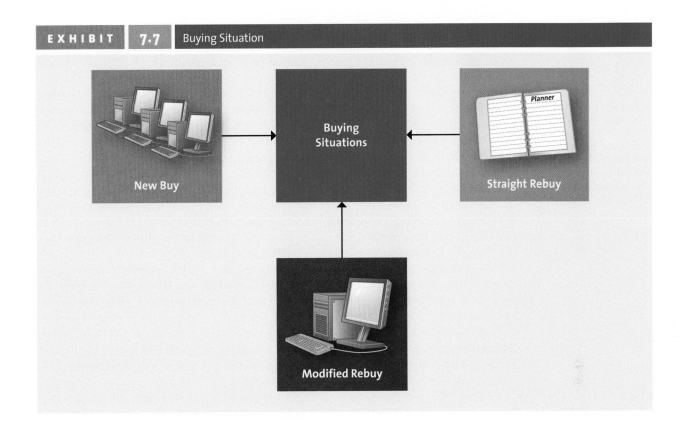

These varied types of buying situations call for very different marketing and selling strategies. The most complex and difficult is the new buy because it requires the buying organization to make changes in its current practices and purchases. As a result, several members of the buying centre will likely become involved, and the level of their involvement will be more intense than in the case of modified and straight rebuys. In new buying situations, buying centre members also typically spend more time at each stage of the B2B buying process, similar to the extended decision making process that consumers use in the B2C process. In comparison, in modified rebuys, the buyers spend less time at each stage of the B2B buying process, similar to limited decision making in the B2C process (see Chapter 6).

In straight rebuys, however, the buyer is often the only member of the buying centre involved in the process. Similar to a consumer's habitual purchase, straight rebuys often enable the buyer to recognize the firm's need and go directly to the fifth step in the B2B buying process, skipping the product specification, RFP process, and proposal analysis and supplier selection steps.

Regardless of the situation, more and more firms have begun to use the Internet to help facilitate buying for both buyers and sellers. Let's look at the various ways in which the Internet has transformed B2B marketing.

Role of the Internet in Business-to-Business Marketing

LO **5**

As consumers, we often use the Internet to research products and buy them for ourselves, our family, and our friends. In a similar fashion, the B2B market has been radically altered in recent years through Internet technologies. For instance, the Internet has become the communication mode of choice, and sometimes of necessity, for connecting divisions and employees located in dispersed locations. Consider a salesperson on a sales call far from his or her company headquarters. By logging in to the company's database, the salesperson can quickly find information about product availability and order status and even consult with his or her supervisors about important negotiating points, such as price and discounts.

The Internet is equally useful for communications between businesses through private exchanges and auctions. (See Exhibit 7.8.) A **private exchange** occurs when a specific firm (either buyer or seller) invites others to participate in online information exchanges and transactions. These exchanges help streamline procurement or distribution processes. Like Toyota with its ToyotaSource.com, as discussed earlier in this chapter, IBM, General Motors, Ford, General Electric, Wal-Mart, and other large firms have formed private exchanges and included their key suppliers. Some, such as IBM and GE, even have mandated that their suppliers must deal with them primarily through such online exchanges. These private exchanges, such as the one described in Internet Marketing 7.1, provide tremendous cost savings through the elimination of periodic negotiations and routine paperwork, as well as the ability to form a supply chain that can respond quickly to the buyer's needs.

For example, as we said earlier in this chapter, Dell's suppliers derive their demand from the sales information Dell provides to them. The suppliers in turn can provide needed component orders quickly and without requiring extensive inventory stockpiles.[25] Because products and the prices of computer parts change rapidly through continuous innovation, the lack of an extensive inventory helps Dell keep its finished computer prices in sync with the declining prices of the component parts. These savings can be passed on to consumers as lower prices, which provides Dell with a very competitive position in the marketplace.

At another level, manufacturers and suppliers can work together to design better products.[26] Manufacturers and retailers collect detailed information about their customers' preferences and other market trends, which they can share with those key suppliers involved in product design. This collaborative design process results in products that more closely match customer needs, thus creating and delivering higher customer value.

Private exchanges have also formed on the manufacturer-to-retailer side of the supply chain. For example, P&G's private network collects information from the cash register (the point of sale) and electronically transfers it back through P&G's distributors to corporate headquarters.[27] By analyzing this information, P&G can track sales of its numerous products to determine the exact demand for each. This demand information then can be transmitted back to suppliers so that the supply side is coordinated as well.

Furthermore, B2B transactions have increasingly turned to online auctions, whether English or reverse. In an **English auction**, goods and services are simply sold to the highest bidder. Thus, if a PC manufacturer has a number of unsold PCs, it can auction them through an exchange (perhaps even through eBay) and sell them to the buyer that bids the highest price for them. In the **reverse auction**, however, the buyer provides specifications to a group of sellers, who then bid down the price until

private exchange
Occurs when a specific firm, either buyer or seller, invites others to join to participate in online information exchanges and transactions; can help streamline procurement or distribution processes.

English auction
Goods and services are simply sold to the highest bidder.

reverse auction
The buyer provides specifications to a group of sellers, who then bid down the price until the buyer accepts a specific bid.

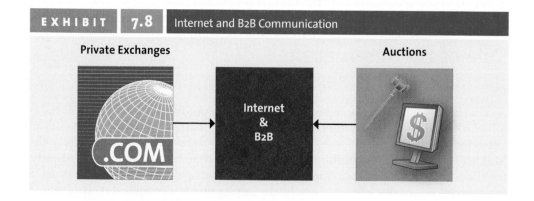

EXHIBIT | **7.8** | Internet and B2B Communication

Private Exchanges — .COM → Internet & B2B ← **Auctions** — $

Internet Marketing | 7.1 | Covisint—Where People, Information, and Applications Come Together[28]

Covisint was created in February 2000 by a consortium of five major automobile manufacturers—Ford, General Motors, DaimlerChrysler, and Renault-Nissan, later joined by Peugeot Citroen—who ponied-up $200 million to coordinate trading processes with a large universe of suppliers in the automotive industry. The idea was to make *Covisint the central hub where original equipment manufacturers (OEMs) and suppliers of all sizes come together to do business in a single business environment using the same tools and user interface, plus one user id and password.* The goal of Covisint was to act as a solution aimed at transforming all key business processes within the automotive industry. The plan was that Covisint's solutions would allow companies to harness the power of the Internet to unlock significant value and efficiency through collaboration, visibility, and integration. This way they can help companies save time, money, and free organizations from non-value added tasks. Some of the problems facing the automotive industry that Covisint was expected to address include: (1) poor quality control caused by the auto industry supply chain system, (2) managing, tracking, and controlling supplier's performance and status, (3) identifying potential supplier problems earlier for effective preventive actions, (4) communicate requirements and changes to the supply chain in a timely manner, and (5) spend less time filing, managing, and shuffling through paper submissions and status reports. Covisint promised to give organizations access to information

in real time, so that they can monitor actual consumption, inventory levels, and thus respond quickly and efficiently to the changes. Covisint enables companies of any size, location, or technical sophistication to securely share vital business information, applications, and processes across their trading partner network. As a provider of interoperability solutions and services, Covisint helps businesses speed decision-making, reduce cost (transportation, travel, and paperwork), increase efficiency, collaborate, and improve responsiveness in serving customers.

Today, Covisint services extend beyond the automotive industry to include health care, financial services, and public sector organizations. Through its Web-based platform, Business Now, Covisint supports over 266,000 users, representing more than 30,000 organizations in over 96 countries in seven languages in the global automotive industry. It also supports over 15,000 users, representing more than 450 organizations across the North American healthcare continuum—health systems, commercial payers, physician groups/practices, home health agencies, third-party administrators, extended care facilities, and home medical equipment providers—as well as nine Medicaid programs. Within Covisint's first year of operations, GM reported that it has spent $200 million for indirect goods through Covisint's catalogue system and sold $2 billion worth of materials and machinery through Covisint's online auctions.

the buyer accepts a specific bid. Firms like Dell, HP, Motorola, Palm, and Sun have lowered their procurement and component costs by using reverse auctions.[29]

Thus, in various ways, B2B marketing both differs from and mirrors the process we detailed in Chapter 6, on consumer behaviour (B2C). The market segmentation process in B2B selling reflects the collective nature of the consumers in this field, whether they be manufacturers, resellers, institutions, or governments. Furthermore, though the buying process should look familiar and markedly similar to that in Chapter 6, it contains some unique aspects in its six stages, which makes sense considering the many factors that come into play in the B2B buying process. The constitution of the buying centre (autocratic, democratic, consultative, or consensus), the culture of the purchasing firm, and the context of the buying situation (new buy, modified rebuy,

straight rebuy) all influence the B2B buying process in various ways, which means that sellers must be constantly aware of these factors if they want to be successful in their sales attempts. Finally, just as it is seemingly everywhere we look, the Internet has radically changed some elements of the B2B world, increasing the frequency of both private electronic exchanges and auctions.

Using reverse auctions, firms like Dell are able to lower their procurement and component costs since they provide specifications to a group of sellers, who then bid down the price until Dell accepts a specific bid.

Learning Objectives Review

1) Describe the nature and composition of B2B markets

2) Explain the ways B2B firms segment their markets

3) Explain the key differences between B2B buying and consumer buying behaviour

4) Describe the factors that influence the B2B buying process

5) Discuss how the Internet has enhanced B2B marketing

1) The B2B market is comprised of four groups of organizations: manufacturers/producers, resellers, governments, and institutions. Manufacturers such as HP and Dell spend huge amounts to buy raw materials and parts for the computers, printers and other products they produce. Similarly, farmers spend huge amounts to buy fertilizers, seeds, and other agricultural products for their crops. Resellers are mainly wholesalers, distributors, and retailers who distribute the goods of manufacturers. In Canada, wholesale and retail trades are among the largest sectors of the economy. The government sector—federal, provincial, and municipal—in Canada and in most other countries is the largest buyer in a country. Institutions such as non-profit organizations, universities, prisons, etc., also spend millions of dollars buying finished products for their organizations and clients. The B2B market is substantially larger than the B2C market in terms of both volume and value of their purchases.

2) The basic principles behind market segmentation remain the same for both B2B and consumer markets. Specifically, B2B firms want to divide the market into groups of customers with different needs, wants, or characteristics and that therefore might appreciate products or services geared especially toward them. On a broad level, B2B firms divide the market into four types: manufacturers or producers, resellers, institutions, and government. Manufacturers purchase materials to make other objects or to help run their businesses, such as computer and telephone systems. Resellers are primarily wholesalers, distributors, or retailers that sell the unchanged products. Institutions typically include nonprofit organizations such as hospitals, schools, or churches. Finally, governments purchase all types of goods and services and are the largest buyer in Canada. To assist in their market segmentation, B2B businesses can use the NAICS, developed by Canada, the U.S. and Mexico, to identify potential customers by type and then develop marketing strategies to reach them. Businesses may also segment B2B markets by account size and end use application.

3) B2B markets are different from B2C markets in terms of (1) the characteristics of market demand; (2) the types, value and volume of products bought; (3) the nature of the buying process, which is more formalized, professional, and involve more people; and (4) the nature of the marketing mix—personal and online selling is more prevalent and prices are negotiated and inelastic in the short-run. At first glance, the B2B buying process looks similar to the consumer process described in Chapter 6. It starts with need recognition and ends with an evaluation of the product's or service's performance. But it is really quite different, primarily because of its formality. For instance, in the second stage, product specifications, the buying group spells out very specific requirements for the products or services it wants to purchase. Then, in the RFP process of the third stage, the buying firm announces its need for a product or service and solicits formal proposals. In the fourth stage, buyers analyze the various proposals and negotiate a deal. Unlike the consumer process, the fifth stage, in which the B2B firm places the order, is very formal and spells out every detail of the sales contract.

4) In B2B situations, it is likely that several people, organized into a buying centre, will be involved in making the purchase decision. The vendor must understand the relationships among the participants of the buying centre to be effective. A firm's organizational culture can also influence the decision process. For instance, if a firm is trying to sell to a young, high-tech computer component manufacturer, it might be advised to send salespeople who are fluent in technology-speak and can easily relate to the customer. Finally, the buying process depends to a great extent on the situation. If a firm is purchasing a product or service for the first time, the process is much more involved than if it is engaging in a straight rebuy.

5) The Internet has done more to change the way B2B marketing is conducted than any previous innovation. Not only has the Internet made it easier for people to communicate within firms, it also facilitates the transfer of information among companies. Buyers can purchase products and services over the Internet through private exchanges, which are set up by one firm that invites other participants, and through B2B Internet auctions. These exchanges and auctions have created opportunities to streamline the procurement process, opened up markets to new buyers and sellers, and provided for more competitive market pricing.

Key Terms

- autocratic buying centre, 190
- business-to-business (B2B) marketing, 178
- buyer, 188
- buying centre, 188
- consensus buying centre, 190
- consultative buying centre, 190
- decider, 188
- democratic buying centre, 190

- derived demand, 182
- English auction, 194
- gatekeeper, 188
- influencer, 188
- initiator, 188
- modified rebuy, 192
- new buy, 192
- North American Industry Classification System (NAICS) codes, 181

- organizational culture, 189
- private exchange, 194
- request for proposals (RFP), 186
- resellers, 180
- reverse auction, 194
- straight rebuy, 192
- user, 188

Concept Review

1. Explain how marketers may use NAICS Codes to segment B2B markets. List two other ways marketers may use it to segment B2B markets. Support your answer with appropriate examples.

2. List and discuss the unique characteristics of B2B markets relative to B2C markets.

3. What are the major differences between the consumer buying process discussed in Chapter 6 and the B2B buying process discussed in this chapter?

4. Explain why all B2B purchases may not go through all the stages of the B2B buying decision process and why some may go through the process in a more systematic and rigorous manner. Give examples of buying situations to support your answer.

5. What are the key bases for distinguishing between new buy, modified buy, and straight rebuys? Support your answer with three clear examples.

6. List five specific ways in which the Internet has enhanced B2B buying and decision making.

7. Explain the concept of the buying centre. What factors may influence the behaviour of the buying centre? What is the role of gatekeepers in buying centres and how do they influence the buying decision?

8. Explain how understanding the role, structure, and behaviour of a buying centre may help a marketer sell to B2B buyers.

9. In the text, it is claimed that the six-step B2B buying process is similar to the five-step B2C buying process. How would you go about reclassifying the B2B process to fit the B2C process?

10. How does understanding the organizational culture and buying centre's culture of a potential B2B customer help a salesperson who is targeting that organization?

Marketing Applications

1. Provide an example of each of the four key types of B2B organizations.

2. Mazda is trying to assess the performance of two manufacturers that could supply music systems for its vehicles. Using the information below, determine which manufacturer Mazda should use.

Performance Evaluation of Brands

Issues	Importance Weights	Manufacturer A's Performance	Manufacturer B's Performance
Sound	0.4	5	3
Cost	0.3	2	4
Delivery time	0.1	2	2
Brand cache	0.2	5	1
Total	1		

Notes: Performance is rated on a scale of 1–5, where 1 = poor and 5 = excellent.

3. Assume you have written this textbook and are going to attempt to sell it to your school. Identify the six members of the buying centre. What role would each play in the decision process? Rank them in terms of how much influence they would have on the decision, with 1 being most influential and 6 being least influential. Will this ranking be different in other situations?

4. Provide an example of the three types of buying situations that the bookstore at your school might face when buying textbooks.

5. Describe the organizational culture at your school or job. How is it different than the one at the last school you attended or the last job you had?

6. Nike manufactures shoes and sportswear. How has the Internet changed the way this company communicates with its suppliers and retail customers?

7. You have just started to work in the purchasing office of a major oil processing firm. The purchasing manager has asked you to assist in writing an RFP for a major purchase. The manager gives you a sheet detailing the specifications for the RFP. While reading the specifications you realize that they have been written to be extremely favourable to one bidder. How should you handle this situation?

8. You have recently been hired by Cognos, Canada's premier business intelligence solution provider, as a salesperson for its suite of business intelligence applications, Pick one prospective company you plan to sell to and explain how you would go about identifying the persons in the different roles in the buying centre for the chosen company. How would you try to target the needs of the different members in the buying centre?

9. Cognos has developed a new business intelligence application that they would like to sell to some of their existing customers. You are part of the sales team. How would your approach to selling to an existing customer be different than selling to a new customer?

10. You are the owner of a mid-sized company (about 450 employees) that has a call centre that specializes in providing 24 hours a day technical support for individual computer owners. One day a sales rep from either Dell, HP, or Lenovo approaches you with a business proposal that goes something like this: If you buy all of your computer supplies from us, we will make you our exclusive call centre operator for all of Ontario and Quebec. Assume that all the conditions of the offer made to you are favourable. Will you accept the offer? Do you think that accepting such an offer is ethical?

Toolkit

B2B VENDOR ANALYSIS

Help David evaluate two software vendors. He has created a chart to help him decide which one to pick. He has rated the two vendors on brand strength, timeliness of deliveries, product quality, and ease of ordering. His firm is generally most interested in quality and then in timeliness. Reputation is somewhat important. The ease of ordering is least important. Use the toolkit provided at www.mcgrawhill.ca/olc/grewal to specify the importance weights and help David pick the best software vendor.

Net Savvy

1. Browse Public Works and Government Services Canada website (www.pwgsc.gc.ca) to learn more about how you may sell goods and services to the federal government. Using the information on the website, describe the buying process used by the federal government and explain how the electronic tendering system supports buying and selling between Canadian companies and the Government of Canada.

2. Mark's Works Warehouse, a Canadian company that currently operates mainly in the B2C market, has hired you as their government-business relations officer with the primary task of helping the company move into the B2B marketplace selling its merchandise primarily to government departments. Explain how you would go about getting Mark's Works Warehouse ready to do business with the Canadian government. Hint: you will find loads of helpful information on the website of Public Works and Government Services Canada (www.pwgsc.gc.ca), Business Access Canada (http://contractscanada.gc.ca), and Strategis Canada (http://strategis.ic.gc.ca/).

Chapter Case Study

THE TELFER SCHOOL MOVES INTO THE DESMARAIS BUILDING[30]

For over 25 years, the School of Management at the University of Ottawa was housed in Vanier Hall, an old building that was increasingly becoming unsuited for a modern business school. In 2007, the School of Management at the University of Ottawa received the largest-ever naming endowment for a business school in Canada—a $25-million gift from one of its alumni, mining magnate, Ian Telfer. Thus, the School is now called The Telfer School of Management. In 2007, the Telfer School moved into a brand new home—the $15-million Desmarais building. The Telfer School of Management occupies six of the 12 floors of the new Desmarais building.

The move into a new building meant that numerous purchase decisions had to be made: new furniture, furnishings, fixtures, equipment, and other items, many of which had not been purchased at all or in such large quantities for the past 25 years. The Telfer School's administration wanted to ensure that new purchases conformed to modern workplace standards for ergonomically and aesthetically pleasing furniture, fixtures, and equipment. Examples of these items include office desks and chairs for professors and staff, meeting tables and chairs in professors' offices, tables and chairs for meeting rooms, desks and chairs for classrooms, filing cabinets, and audio visual equipment such as television sets, LCD monitors for students' case rooms, overhead projectors, and videoconferencing services. In addition, many computers, printers, as well as computer desks and chairs were bought for student computer labs. Millions of dollars and considerable efforts were spent purchasing these items for the approximately 4000 students, professors, and staff of the Telfer School.

So exactly how were these purchases made? Who was involved in the purchase decisions and what was the buying process used to make the purchases? Decisions regarding the people who needed to be involved in the buying decisions as well as what buying process should be used were determined by the nature of the buying situation, that is, whether the purchase was a new buy, a modified rebuy, or a straight rebuy. For example, let's consider the purchase of furniture for professors' offices, e.g., desk, chairs, filing cabinets, shelving for books, and tables and chairs for meeting with students and visitors. The people involved in the purchase decisions were:

- one interior designer representing the architect of the building, Moriyama-Teshima
- two interior designers from the University's Physical Resources
- two representatives from the University's Materials Management Department
- two representatives from the Telfer School (its Manager of Services and the Associate Dean, Strategy, Planning and Management.)

Input was initially sought from a sample of the School's professors and staff about the types of furniture to be purchased. The University also sought the services of a professional interior design firm to provide ideas and advice on how to outfit the interior of the building.

The architects at Moriyama-Teshima had their own interior designer suggest a colour and finishes palette that fit with their vision of the building; it was presented to the University Physical Resources and the Telfer School and was accepted.

Generally, at the University of Ottawa, some purchase decisions are centralized at the University level while others are decentralized at the level of the Faculties and Services. Usually, all purchases over $5000 go through a competitive bidding process where the University Materials Management Service—the University's centralized procurement service—work with individual faculty or the services purchasing unit to develop the specifications of the purchases. The decentralized process is generally used with respect to purchases of less than $5000 (straight rebuys or modified rebuys) if it does not involve a change in the University's approved suppliers. The University maintains a shortlist of pre-approved vendors, which it uses for most of its ongoing purchases.

The centralized purchasing process at the University is as follows:

- A need is defined, usually by the faculty or services purchasing unit.
- The appropriate number of quotes is requested depending on the estimated cost, or a formal tendering process for bids is set in motion for purchase above $10,000.
- The evaluation of the quotes is completed and a winning supplier is selected.

- The Faculty or Services Department enters a purchase requisition in the University's financial system.
- Materials Management Service converts the requisition into a Purchase Order and formally places the order with the supplier.
- The goods are received and the invoice is sent to the University's financial service for payment.

The decentralized purchasing process at the University is as follows:

- A need is defined, usually by the Faculty or Services Department purchasing unit.
- The appropriate number of quotes is requested (verbal or written) depending on the estimated cost.
- The evaluation of the quotes is completed and a winning supplier is selected.
- The Faculty or Services Department contacts the winning supplier with an "order number" and the order is formally placed.
- The goods are received and the invoice is processed for payment at the Faculty or Services Department that ordered the goods.

When it came to buying furniture, once the architect, interior designers, and the University agreed on a particular interior design, that design was used to develop the specifications for the office furniture, e.g., workstations, professors' chairs, visitors' chairs and tables, filing cabinets, and shelving. The furniture specifications were used to develop a request for proposal (RFP) using the University of Ottawa tendering process. This process requires that interested vendors or suppliers submit sealed bids, which were evaluated by the University. In an attempt to get the best possible deal—not necessarily the lowest price but the best value for money—the University allowed vendors to either submit a bid to supply *all* of furniture needs, e.g., workstations (office table and overhead cupboards), chairs for professors and staff, tables and chairs for visitors, filing cabinets, and shelving *or* submit separate bids for each individual item. That is, one firm could bid on the shelving part of the RFP only or the filing cabinets only, and so on. The rationale was that a firm whose core business is cabinets and shelving would provide a better deal than a firm that specializes in workstations and chairs and may have to sub-contract with another firm for cabinets and shelving. On the other hand, a firm that submitted one bid for all the furniture needs may be able to provide a better deal for the University.

Because the University wanted to establish a five-year plan for furniture purchases for all faculties, Schools, and Services across the campus, the purchase decision was primarily a centralized purchase decision. Thus, the Telfer School and other academic units occupying the Desmarais building were consulted, but would likely not have had much say in the final decision.

In the end, the University selected five vendors and offered each of them five-year contracts to supply all its furniture needs over the duration of the contract. These five vendors have now become part of the University's shortlist of approved furniture vendors from whom any academic unit or service across the campus can place an order for furniture. Modified rebuys or straight rebuys, which are decentralized can be easily placed with any one of these vendors.

It is important to note that the price that vendors quote for large purchases is usually lower than for re-ordering a small quantity or a single unit. And for that reason the University always reserves the right to go out to tender for larger than usual quantities of a tender item such as chairs. For example, while a vendor may quote a price of $300 for a chair for professors or staff for orders placed in large quantities, the identical chair may cost $350 or more when only one or two chairs are re-ordered.

Now let's consider the purchase of audio visual (AV) equipment for the School. Generally, the purchase of AV equipment for all faculties and services is done centrally through the University's central AV department in conjunction with the Materials Management Service. The central AV department also maintains a shortlist of approved vendors for all of the University's audio visual needs. They generally resist attempts by individual units and departments to purchase AV equipment from non-approved vendors. The School wanted to replace all its old tube televisions with either LCD or plasma televisions as well as purchase LCD monitors for the MBA students' case rooms and other meeting rooms—a purchase that the School had never made before.

However, since the School was paying for these purchases, it was cost conscious and realized that if it were to go with the AV department's list of pre-approved vendors and process, it likely would get the technology needed, however, at a far higher price. Recognizing the challenges of bypassing the central AV department, the Manager of Services and the Associate Dean, Strategy, Planning & Management, and two other senior administrators at the Telfer School worked closely with the University's AV department and the Materials Management Service for this purchase. Ultimately, the School was able to purchase the equipment and technologies it needed through a supplier that is not on the University's pre-approved list using a modified centralized purchasing process. This arrangement resulted in considerable savings to the School.

The additional computers needed for the new students' labs were bought from Lenovo with whom the University has an ongoing contract. Regular scheduled revisions to the contract are made following recommendations by the University's IT group in consultation with IT representatives from the Faculty or Services Department.

The contract with Lenovo requires that all the University's desktop and laptop computer needs must be supplied by Lenovo. The only exception to this arrangement is that professors can purchase their computers from any other vendor (Dell, HP, Future Shop, Apple, SUN, etc.) if it is being paid for from the professor's research funds.

Questions

1. What are the main differences between the buying decision process described in this case and the consumer buying decision process described in Chapter 6, Consumer Behaviour?

2. Identify the members of the buying centre for the office furniture purchases. What roles did each play? How did their roles influence the ultimate purchase decision?

3. In what ways does the buying decision process described in this case for the furniture and fixtures conform or depart from the buying process depicted in Exhibit 7.4.

4. Using the concept of the three buying situations, i.e., new buy, modified rebuy, and straight rebuy, how would you classify the various purchase decisions described in the case? Explain the rationale for your answer.

5. As noted in the case, the interior design firm, Moriyama-Teshima, was chosen by the University based on the recommendation of the architect of the Desmarais building rather than going through a tendering process. Discuss in what ways this arrangement benefits the University and to what extent it may raise ethical concerns. Can the University actually know if it got a better deal from Moriyama-Teshima without getting bids from other vendors? Explain.

CHAPTER 8

LEARNING OBJECTIVES

After studying this chapter, you should be able to:

LO **1** Describe the STP process

LO **2** Describe the bases marketers use to segment a market

LO **3** Discuss the criteria for determining the attractiveness of a segment and whether it is worth pursuing (targeting)

LO **4** Explain how a firm decides what type of segmentation strategy to use—undifferentiated, differentiated, concentrated, or micromarketing

LO **5** Explain what positioning is and describe how firms do it

Segmentation, Targeting, and Positioning

The daily hair care category in Canada, as measured by ACNielsen, is valued at $694 million.[1] Although the market is characterized by high competition, frequent innovation, and heavy media investment, it is one of the largest and most dynamic categories for retailers. There are over 45 brands in the category, with the top 10 brands accounting for just over half of the total market dollars.

Into this competitive market, Unilever launched Sunsilk in Canada in June 2006. Sunsilk joined a portfolio that also includes Dove, Thermasilk, Suave, and Salon Selectives.[2]

To win with this new brand, a meaningful consumer proposition was essential. Unilever conducted in-depth interviews with women in the target market to better understand their attitudes and the relationship they have with their hair. From this information, a persona was developed for use in marketing efforts.

Personas are biographies of fictional customers that inform and drive business decisions on product design, development, and marketing strategy. Although the persona is fictional, almost every detail in the story is based upon actual observation of real customers in their normal working environments.

The Sunsilk target consumer's persona is affectionately named and described as a 25-year-old going through a "quarter-life crisis" and for whom life is a series of dramas. She is living an emotional roller coaster: living the natural tensions of the beginning of adulthood and also having the greatest time of her life. Highly social, she is creating her own life, making her own choices and deciding on her own adventures. Her hair is very important to how she feels about herself, and if it is "off," it becomes one of her many dramas—she may even "wig out."

Segmentation work helped identify an attractive target market. Developing an in-depth understanding of the target consumer led to Sunsilk's positioning as problem-solving products tailor-made for each hair problem. The persona work paid big dividends. The Sunsilk launch in Canada was a huge success.

Some people like conditioning shampoo, while others like a volumizing shampoo. Some people want a natural product; others care primarily about how well the product cleans. Still other people demand affordable shampoo, whereas some prefer it to be salon quality. More likely though, a group of people desires a shampoo that conditions, is affordable, and contains natural ingredients; whereas another group demands a shampoo that is salon quality, deep cleansing, and volumizing. There are many combinations of these three product attributes; each potentially appeals to a different group of people.

In Chapter 1, we learned that marketing is about satisfying consumers' wants and needs. A company could make one type of shampoo and hope that every shampoo user would buy it, but that's the kind of mistake that has been leading the hair care industry into decline. Or, as we described in Chapter 2, shampoo manufacturers could analyze the market to determine the different types of shampoo people want and then make several varieties that cater to the wants of specific groups. It is not enough just to make the product, however. Shampoo manufacturers such as Unilever must position their shampoos in the minds of their target market so those consumers understand why a particular shampoo meets their needs better than competitive brands do.

In Chapter 2, we described the steps involved in a marketing plan: The manager first defines the firm's mission and objectives and then performs a situation analysis. The third step of the marketing plan is to identify and evaluate opportunities by performing an STP (segmentation, targeting, and positioning) analysis—which makes up the topic of this chapter. In Chapters 3 and 4 we discussed how understanding the marketing environment and conducting systematic, rigorous research is crucial in giving marketers a better knowledge and understanding of their consumers, which is subsequently used to develop effective STP strategies to better serve their customers.

In the opening vignette, Unilever identified a group of shampoo users that would respond similarly to the firm's marketing efforts. Groups like this one are also known as market segments. Those who like natural, affordable, conditioning shampoos are one market segment; people who prefer salon quality, deep cleansing, and oil-reducing shampoos constitute a different segment. After evaluating the attractiveness of different market segments, Unilever decided to concentrate its new product line on one group—its target market—because it believes it could satisfy this group's needs better than its competitors could. As we noted in Chapter 2, the process of dividing the market into groups of customers who have different needs, wants, or characteristics and who therefore might appreciate products or services geared especially for them is called market segmentation.

Once the target market was identified, Unilever had to convince the targeted group that when it comes to hair care products, their choice should be Sunsilk. It is achieving this task by defining the marketing mix variables so that the target customers have a clear, distinctive, desirable understanding of what the product or services do or represent, relative to competing products—a process we described in Chapter 2 as market positioning. To achieve its market positioning, Unilever designed a lifestyle advertising campaign that has positioned Sunsilk as the choice of women who need "hairapy," or therapy for hair. The idea is to get customers to recall Sunsilk at the need recognition stage of the consumer buying process described in Chapter 6. It has also made sure that the shampoo is available almost anywhere its customers would want to buy it.

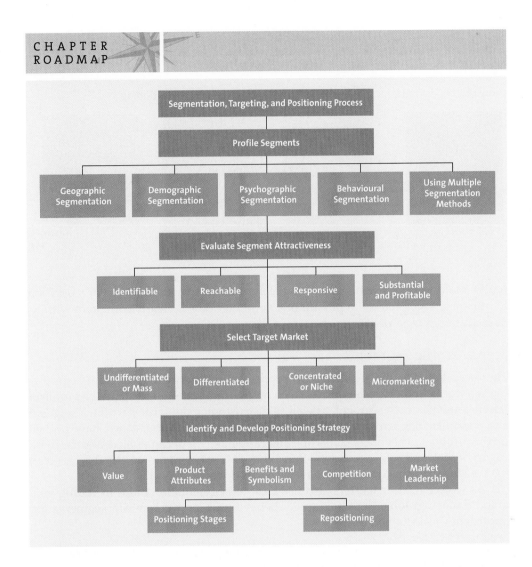

CHAPTER
ROADMAP

In this chapter, we discuss how a firm conducts a market segmentation or STP analysis. As shown in our chapter roadmap, we'll first discuss market segmentation, or how a segmentation strategy fits into a firm's overall strategy and objectives and which segments are worth pursuing. Then we discuss how to choose a target market or markets by evaluating each segment's attractiveness and, on the basis of this evaluation, choosing which segment or segments to pursue. Finally, we describe how a firm develops its positioning strategy. The segmentation, targeting, and positioning process is shown in Exhibit 8.1.

Step 1: Establish Overall Strategy or Objectives

LO ①

As discussed in Chapter 2, the first step in the planning process is to articulate the vision or the objectives of the company's marketing strategy clearly. The segmentation strategy must then be consistent with and derived from the firm's mission and objectives, as well as its current situation—its strengths, weaknesses, opportunities, and threats (SWOT). Unilever's objective, for instance, is to increase sales in a competitive industry. The company recognized its strengths were its globally recognized brand name and its ability to place new products on retailers' shelves. Identifying this potentially large and profitable market segment before many of its mainstream competitors offered a great opportunity, though following through on that oppor-

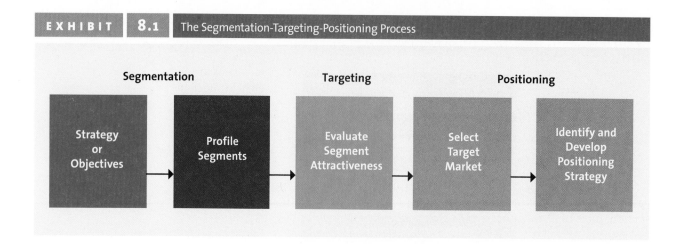

EXHIBIT 8.1 The Segmentation-Targeting-Positioning Process

Segmentation — Strategy or Objectives → Profile Segments

Targeting — Evaluate Segment Attractiveness → Select Target Market

Positioning — Identify and Develop Positioning Strategy

tunity could lead to a significant threat: competitive retaliation. Unilever's decision to pursue a target market in pursuit of a good hair day, is clearly consistent with its overall strategy and objectives.

LO **2**

Step 2: Profile Segments

The second step in the segmentation process is to describe the different segments (needs, wants, and characteristics), which helps firms better understand the profile of the customers in each segment, as well as the customer similarities within a segment and dissimilarities across segments. Soft-drink marketers, for instance, have broken up the carbonated beverage landscape into caffeinated or decaffeinated, regular (with sugar) or diet, and cola versus something else. This segmentation method is based on the benefits that consumers derive from the products.

As we see next, marketers also use various segmentation bases including geographic, demographic, psychographic, behavioural, and composite segmentation approaches—see Exhibit 8.2.

geographic segmentation
The grouping of consumers on the basis of where they live.

Geographic Segmentation   Geographic segmentation organizes customers into groups on the basis of where they live. Thus, a market could be grouped by country (Canada, Germany, China), region (Atlantic Canada, Western Canada), areas within

EXHIBIT 8.2 Methods for Segmenting Markets

Segmentation Method	Sample Segments
Geographic	Country, region, province, city, urban, rural, climate Continent: N. America, Asia, Europe, Africa Within U.S.: Pacific, mountain, central, south, mid-Atlantic, northeast
Demographic	Age, gender, income, education, occupation, race, marital status, family size, family life cycle, religion, ethnic background (e.g. white, Black, Asian, Indian, German, Irish, Arab), and generational cohort (e.g. Baby Boomer, Gen X, Gen Y), home ownership
Psychographic	Personality (innovators, thinkers, achievers, experiencers, believers, strivers, makers, survivors), lifestyle (conservative, liberal, adventuresome, outgoing, health- and fitness-conscious), and social class (upper class, middle class, working class)
Behavioural	Benefits sought (convenience, economy, prestige, quality, speed, service), usage (heavy, moderate, light, non-user, ex-user, potential user, first-time user), and loyalty (not loyal, somewhat loyal, completely loyal)

a region (province, city, neighbourhoods, area codes), or by climate and topography (warm, cold and snowy, mountainous). Not surprisingly, geographic segmentation is most useful for companies whose products satisfy needs that vary by region.

Firms can provide the same basic goods or services to all segments even if they market globally or nationally, but better marketers make adjustments to meet the needs of smaller geographic groups. For instance, a national grocery store chain like Safeway or Loblaws runs similar stores with similar assortments in various locations across Canada. Within those similar stores though, a significant percentage of the assortment of goods will vary by region, city, or even neighbourhood, depending on the different needs of the customers who surround each location.

Consider a new superstore in Surrey, British Columbia, designed to cater specifically to the surrounding South East Asian (Punjabi) neighbourhood. In the produce section, piles of shiny, green *pasilla* chiles sit beside paddle-shaped cactus leaves and bumpy, brown yucca roots. At the meat counter, a customer greets a clerk in Punjabi and asks him to marinate some meat.

Demographic Segmentation Demographic **segmentation** groups consumers according to easily measured, objective characteristics such as age, gender, income, education, race, occupation, religion, marital status, family size, family life cycle, and home ownership. These variables represent the most common means to define segments because they are easy to identify and because demographically segmented markets are easy to reach. For instance, if McCain's or Pizza Hut wants to advertise their newest pizza to kids, they can easily determine that the best time for television ads would be during cartoons shown on Saturday morning or after school on weekdays. By considering the viewer profiles of various TV shows, McCain's and Pizza Hut can find the ones that fit its target market's demographic profile.

One demographic variable, sex, plays a very important role in how firms market products and services. For instance, TV viewing habits vary significantly between men and women. Men tend to channel surf—switching quickly from channel to channel—and watch primetime shows more often if they are action oriented and have physically attractive cast members. Women, in contrast, tend to view shows to which they can personally relate through the situational plot or characters and those recommended by friends.[3] Thus, a company like Gillette, which sells razors for both men and women, will consider the appeal of various shows when it buys advertising

demographic segmentation
The grouping of consumers according to easily measured, objective characteristics such as age, gender, income, and education.

Firms like Gillette use an important demographic factor, gender, to sell different types of razors to men (Fusion ad on the left) and women (Venus ad on the right).

time on television. Also, as discussed in Chapter 4, the growth of ethnic Canadians from mainland China, Hong Kong, Taiwan, Philippines, and South East Asia (India, Pakistan, Sri Lanka) have led companies to develop marketing mixes and strategies targeted to these groups.

However, demographics may not be useful for defining the target segments for other companies. For example, demographics are poor predictors of the users of activewear, such as jogging suits and athletic shoes. At one time, firms like Nike assumed that activewear would be purchased exclusively by young, active people, but the health and fitness trend has led people of all ages to buy such merchandise. Furthermore, relatively inactive consumers of all ages, incomes, and education find activewear more comfortable than traditional street clothes. Because it is relatively easy to gather demographic information; demographic variables are often used for segmenting markets. However, depending on the nature of the product and market, marketers may find it more advantageous to combine demographic segmentation with other segmentation bases described below in order to derive a richer understanding of their potential customers. The Nike example shows that stereotyping rather than a deep understanding of market segments could lead to poor STP strategies.

Psychographic Segmentation   Of the various methods for segmenting, or breaking down the market, **psychographics** is the one that delves into how consumers describe themselves. Usually marketers determine (through demographics, buying patterns, or usage) into which segment an individual consumer falls. But psychographics allows people to describe themselves using those characteristics that help them choose how they occupy their time (behaviour) and what underlying psychological reasons determine those choices.[4] For example, a person might have a strong need for inclusion or belonging, which motivates him or her to seek out activities that involve others, which in turn influences the products he or she buys to fit in with the group. If a consumer becomes attached to a group that enjoys literary discussions, he or she is motivated to buy the latest books and spend time in stores such as Chapters. Such self-segmentation by the consumer could be very valuable knowledge for

psychographics
Used in segmentation; delves into how consumers describe themselves; allows people to describe themselves using those characteristics that help them choose how they occupy their time (behaviour) and what underlying psychological reasons determine those choices.

Marketers like Benetton want their ads to appeal to one's self-concept. "I'm like them, so I should buy their products."

bookstore managers trying to find new ways of attracting customers. Determining psychographics involves knowing and understanding three components: self-values, self-concept, and lifestyles.

Self-values are goals for life, not just the goals one wants to accomplish in a day. In this context, they refer to overriding desires that drive how a person lives his or her life. Examples of self-value goals might include self-respect, self-fulfillment, or a sense of belonging. This motivating factor of psychographics enables people to develop self-images of how they want to be and then determine a way of life that will help them arrive at these ultimate goals. From a marketing point of view, the values help determine the benefits the target market may be looking for from a product. Lexus uses the tagline *relentless pursuit of perfection* and BMW *'someday' just arrived* to target these values. In this sense, the underlying, fundamental, personal need that pushes a person to seek out certain products or brands stems from his or her desire to fulfill a goal.

How does that underlying goal affect the individual? It does so through **self-concept**, or the image people have of themselves.[5] A person who has a goal to belong may see, or want to see, himself or herself as a fun-loving, gregarious type whom people wish to be around. Marketers can make use of this image through communications that show their products being used by groups of laughing people who are having a good time. The connection emerges between the group fun and the product being shown and connotes a certain lifestyle. Television commercials for dating services such as Lavalife use this technique to sell their services. L'Oreal uses the tagline, *so it costs a bit more, but I'm worth it*, for its hair colour products.

Lifestyles, the third component of people's psychographic makeup, are the way we live.[6] If values provide an end goal and self-concept is the way one sees oneself in the context of that goal, lifestyles are how we live our lives to achieve goals. Someone with a strong sense of belonging who sees himself as a "people person" will probably live in a well-populated area that allows for many activities. He likely will join clubs or partake in activities that attract like-minded people. Marketers thus have a built-in target group with similar interests and buying desires. Lululemon quickly built a global empire of sportswear clothing and accessories based not on demographics but on the philosophy of a healthy, balanced, fun-filled lifestyle. Similarly, Rollerblade makes different skates for people with different lifestyles—the *Astro ABT* for regular skaters who want comfort, *Crossfire II 4d Air Carbon* for those looking for a perfect blend of speed, versatility, and comfort, and the *Problade 07* for racers.

The most widely used psychographic system is the **VALS**™, owned and operated by SRI Consulting Business Intelligence.[7] On the basis of their answers to the VALS questionnaire, consumers are classified into the eight segments in the two dimensions shown in Exhibit 8.3. On the vertical dimension, segments are described by their resources, including their income, education, health, energy

self-values
Goals for life, not just the goals one wants to accomplish in a day; a component of *psychographics* that refers to overriding desires that drive how a person lives his or her life.

self-concept
The image a person has of him- or herself; a component of *psychographics*.

lifestyles
A component of *psychographics*; refers to the way a person lives his or her life to achieve goals.

VALS™
A psychographic tool developed by SRI Consulting Business Intelligence; classifies consumers into eight segments: innovators, thinkers, believers, achievers, strivers, experiencers, makers, or survivors.

Rollerblade makes different skates for people with different lifestyles ranging from weekend warriors to racers.

Using the VALS™ framework, it is a lot harder to identify "thinkers" (left) as opposed to "makers" (right) because "thinkers" are motivated by ideals, whereas "makers" are prompted to buy based on their need for self-expression.

level, and degree of innovativeness. The upper segments have more resources and are more innovative; those on the bottom have fewer resources and are less innovative.

The horizontal dimension shows the segment's primary motivation. Consumers buy many products and services because of their primary motivations—that is, how they see themselves in the world and how that self-image governs their activities. The three universal primary motives are ideals, achievement, and self-expression. People who are primarily motivated by ideals are guided by knowledge and principles, whereas those who are motivated by achievement look for products and services that demonstrate success to their peers. Exhibit 8.4 provides a description of the VALS types.

Firms are finding that psychographics are often more useful for predicting consumer behaviour than are demographics. For instance, freshman college students and some day labourers may have similar demographics according to their age, education, and income, but they spend their income quite differently because of their very different mindsets. Likewise, baby boomers are made up of five distinctly different VALS types.

There are limitations to using psychographic segmentation however. Psychographics are not as objective as demographics, and it is harder to identify potential customers. With demographics, for example, a firm like Nike can easily identify its customers as, say, men or women and then direct its marketing strategies to each group differently. It is much harder to identify and target thinkers versus makers. For these reasons, psychographic segmentation is often used in conjunction with other segmentation methods.[8]

behavioural segmentation
Group of consumers based on the benefits they derive from products or services, their usage rate, their user status, and their loyalty.

EXHIBIT 8.3   VALS™ Framework

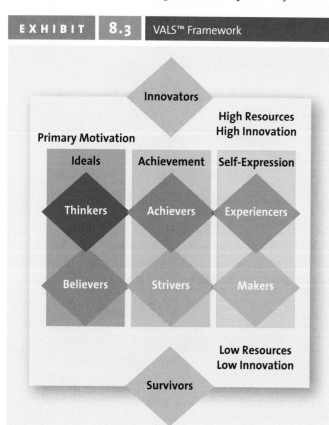

Source: http://www.sric-bi.com/VALS/types.shtml

Behavioural Segmentation Behavioural segmentation groups consumers on the basis of the benefits they derive from products or services,

EXHIBIT 8.4	Description of VALS™ Categories

Innovators	**Thinkers**	**Believers**	**Achievers**
• Successful, sophisticated, take charge people • High self-esteem • Change leaders • Established and emerging business leaders • Very active consumers • Purchases reflect cultivated taste for finer things	• Mature, satisfied, comfortable • Value responsibility • Well-educated, knowledge seekers • Respect for authority • Conservative, practical consumers • Like durability and clear value	• Conservative conventionalists • Concrete beliefs around family, religion, community • Deep rooted moral codes • Established routines • Predictable, loyal consumers • Choose familiar products and established brands	• Goal-oriented lifestyles • Deep commitment to career and family • Respect for authority • Value stability, self-discovery • Active consumers • Favour prestige products that demonstrate their success, time saving products
Strivers	**Experiencers**	**Makers**	**Survivors**
• Trendy and fun loving • Money defines success • Favour stylish products • Active yet impulsive consumers • Shopping is social activity and display of status • Spend as much as they can	• Seek variety and excitement • Active in sports and social activities • Enthusiastic, impulsive consumers • Spend high proportion of income on fashion and entertainment • Want to look good and have cool stuff	• Practical people with constructive skills • Value self sufficiency • Traditional views of family and work • Suspicious of new ideas • Unimpressed by material possessions • Prefer value over luxury	• Believe the world is changing too quickly • Comfortable with familiarity • Concerned with safety and security • Always focused on meeting needs not fulfilling wants • Cautious consumers • Loyal to favourite brands • Love a good deal

Source: The VALS™ Types. Accessed www.sric-bi.com/VALS/types.shtml on December 15, 2007.

their usage rates of products or services, their user status, and their loyalty. Because marketing is all about satisfying consumers' needs and wants, dividing the market into segments whose needs and wants are best satisfied by the product benefits can be very powerful. It is also relatively easy to portray a product's or service's benefits in the firm's communication strategies.

To illustrate benefit segmentation, consider Qoo, a ball-shaped character that dances across television screens in Japan, Korea, Taiwan, and Singapore, as well as a good-tasting health drink owned by Coca-Cola. The iconic Qoo character is a lovable yet mischievous symbol that reminds mothers of their own children while making children laugh. Using a benefit segmentation approach, Coca-Cola designed a product that parents would serve to their kids because it was healthy (the benefit) and their kids would drink because they loved the television character.

Firms have long known that it pays to retain loyal customers. Loyal customers are those who feel so strongly that the firm can meet their relevant needs best that any competitors are virtually excluded from their consideration; that is, these customers buy almost exclusively from the firm.[9] These loyal customers are the most profitable in the long term.[10] In light of the high cost of finding new customers and the profitability of loyal customers, today's companies are using loyalty segmentation and investing in retention and loyalty initiatives to retain their most profitable customers. Canadians are crazy about loyalty cards, with nearly 9 in 10 adults (87 percent) actively participating in at least one loyalty program, whether it's retail or air travel. Loyalty card participation cuts across all demographics, for instance, 96 percent of affluent consumers actively participate in a loyalty program, 78 percent of young adults (18 to 25 years old), 90 percent of seniors (60 years or older), and 95 percent of women (25 to 49) do as well. In the U.S., only 39.5 percent of the general population actively participates in a loyalty program.[11]

benefit segmentation The grouping of consumers on the basis of the benefits they derive from products or services.

loyalty segmentation Strategy of investing in loyalty initiatives to retain the firm's most profitable customers.

Airlines, for instance, definitely believe that all customers aren't created equal. At Air Canada, the customers who have flown the most miles with the company, the "Super Elite," receive a distinctive card, get personalized Air Canada Super Elite luggage tags, special access to Aeroplan Reward seats, priority reservation waitlist, preferred seat selection, Air Canada concierge service, priority airport check-in, extra checked baggage allowance, priority boarding, guaranteed reservations for full-fare tickets, and priority baggage handling among other benefits.[12] None of these special services are available to the occasional flyer.

Usage rate (heavy users, regular users, light users, occasional users) as well as user status (current users, ex-users, potential users) can also be used as segmentation variables. For example, fast food restaurants often use promotional coupons to target occasional visitors to their restaurant or to entice people who have never visited their restaurants to come in and try their food and services.

Using Multiple Segmentation Methods   Although all segmentation methods are useful, each has its unique advantages and disadvantages. For example, segmenting by demographics and geography is easy because information about who the customers are and where they are located is readily available, but these characteristics don't help marketers determine their customer needs. Because "birds of a feather flock

EXHIBIT 8.5	PYSTE Cluster		
Cluster Name	**Urban Lower Middle (U4): Urban Bohemia**	**Suburban Affluent (S1): Suburban Affluence**	**Suburban Affluent (S1): Asian Heights**
Description	From body piercing to tattoos, Urban Bohemia includes a diverse population by design. A neighbourhood with a youthful skew, this cluster occupies itself in a variety of artistic, retail, and generally creative employment. Men and women employed in cultural, artistic, and entertainment-related jobs abound. Household maintainers under age 25, many with college degrees, are also found in this cluster.	This Cluster with a flair for fine living represents both old and new wealth. Because wealth accumulates through life stage, this cluster exhibits an older skew with many empty nests. Suburban Affluence indexes high on managerial and technical employment and are married with children.	Asian ancestries combined with hard work and growing wealth create and mould these upscale neighbourhoods. Asian Heights represents the affirmation of dreams cultivated through generations of immigrants and often through hardship. These families boost local economies as well as family prospects. Asian Heights indexes high on Chinese, Korean, and Japanese immigration as well as households of six or more persons.
Age Household Income	$46,000	$166,000	$96,000

Source: http://tetrad.com/pcensus/can/psyteadv_clusters.pdf .

together," companies use a combination of geographic, demographic and lifestyle characteristics, called **geodemographic segmentation**, to classify consumers.[13] Consumers in the same neighbourhoods tend to buy the same types of cars, appliances, and apparel, shop at the same types of retailers, and behave similarly to media and promotions. One of the most widely used tools for geodemographic segmentation in Canada is **PSYTE cluster** profiles developed by Compusearch. The PSYTE system groups all neighbourhoods in Canada into 60 different lifestyles clusters with specific locations. The information in Exhibit 8.5 on the previous page describes three PSYTE clusters.[14] PRIZMce, another tool developed by Environics Research, groups Canadians into one of 66 lifestyle types—with names like Cosmopolitan Elite, Electric Avenues, Les Chics, and Lunch at Tim's—is also widely used in Canada. The system provides a Canadian segmentation model that has linked geodemographics to psychographics, incorporating "Social Values" data from Environics Research with demographics and product preferences to explain consumer behaviour.[15]

Geodemographic segmentation can be particularly useful for retailers because customers typically patronize stores close to their neighbourhood. Thus, retailers can use geodemographic segmentation to tailor each store's assortment to the preferences of the local community. This kind of segmentation is also useful for finding new locations; retailers identify their "best" locations and determine what type of people live in the area surrounding those stores, according to the geodemographic clusters. They can then find other potential locations where similar segments reside. Geodemographic systems such as PSYTE and PRIZMce, can also help marketers track and compare sales performance among various clusters in different locations.

Knowing what benefits customers are seeking or how the product or service fits a particular lifestyle is important for designing an overall marketing strategy, but such segmentation schemes present a problem for marketers attempting to identify specifically which customers are seeking these benefits. Thus, firms often employ a combination of segmentation methods, using demographics and geography, as discussed above, to identify and target marketing communications to their customers, then using benefits or lifestyles to design the product or service and the substance of the marketing message. Adding Value 8.1 discusses how multiple segmentation methods can combine to develop a richer segmentation strategy for financial markets.

Developing a market segmentation strategy over the Internet usually is somewhat easier than developing it for traditional channels. Internet Marketing 8.1 on page 215 explains why.

Step 3: Evaluate Segment Attractiveness   LO **3**

The third step in the segmentation process involves evaluating the attractiveness of the various segments. To undertake this evaluation, marketers first must determine whether the segment is worth pursuing using several descriptive criteria: Is the segment identifiable, reachable, responsive, and substantial and profitable (see Exhibit 8.6)?

Identifiable Firms must determine who is within their market to be able to design products or services to meet their needs. It is

geodemographic segmentation
The grouping of consumers on the basis of a combination of geographic, demographic, and lifestyle characteristics.

PSYTE clusters
The grouping of all neighbourhoods in Canada into 60 different lifestyles clusters.

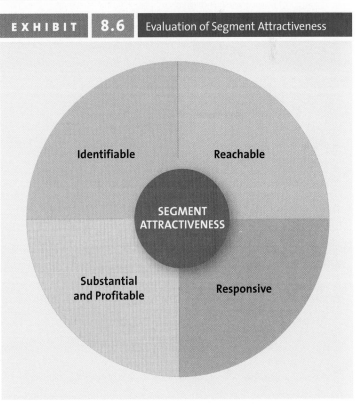

| EXHIBIT | 8.6 | Evaluation of Segment Attractiveness |

Adding Value

8.1   **Segmenting the Financial Services Market Using Demographics and Lifestyles[16]**

LIMRA, a financial services research and consulting organization, which operates in Canada and the U.S., surveyed its consumers to determine their personal financial objectives and the type of lifestyle they wanted when they retired. The survey yielded four identifiable segments for middle-income households, as described in the chart below.

Steve Hall is a financial consultant who is prospecting for new customers. What can he do with combined demographic and lifestyle LIMRA data? The demographic data can identify the type of people in a segment, how firms might reach these people through the media or other selling vehicles, and how profitable the segments may be. For instance, Steve has found a group of "Worker Bees" who are self-employed, over 40, and have relatively

The financial services consulting firm, LIMRA, targets four identifiable segments based on demographics and lifestyle data to best meet the needs of middle-income households getting ready to retire.

high incomes. The lifestyle data then can be used to help design products and promotional messages that are relevant to this group. For instance, Steve historically would study a customer's portfolio and his or her attitude toward taking financial risks before preparing a retirement package for that customer. But knowing the type of lifestyles to which these "Worker Bees" aspire when they retire enables the sales agent to better match customers' lifestyles and the financial planning process. Since the "Worker Bees" are very entrepreneurial and love to work, Steve designs a sales presentation that stresses how much money they need to save over the coming years to maintain their relatively modest lifestyle and enable them to continue to work as long as they wish or are physically able.

Demographic and Retirement Lifestyle Segmentation for the Financial Services Market

	Pragmatic Planners	Worker Bees	Grand Thinkers	Status Quo
DEMOGRAPHIC CHARACTERISTICS	✓ Single ✓ No dependent children ✓ Educated ✓ Moderate income ✓ Have discretionary income ✓ Under 45 years old	✓ Couples ✓ Less formal education ✓ High income ✓ High investable assets ✓ Over 40 ✓ Self-employed	✓ Couples ✓ Broad education levels ✓ Moderate incomes ✓ Broad age ranges	✓ Couples ✓ With dependent children ✓ Less formal education ✓ Broad income range ✓ Over 40
PERCENTAGE OF MIDDLE-MARKET HOUSEHOLDS	30 percent	15 percent	34 percent	21 percent
RETIREMENT LIFESTYLE GOALS	✓ Save to buy home ✓ Eliminate or reduce debt ✓ Save for retirement ✓ Maintain modest but comfortable standard of living ✓ Spend time with family ✓ Enjoy leisure activities	✓ Start or expand business ✓ Save for retirement ✓ Maintain modest but comfortable living standard ✓ Start or run business ✓ Keep working in a capacity similar to today's	✓ Save to buy home ✓ Protect family in case of death ✓ Eliminate or reduce debt ✓ Save for retirement ✓ Maintain modest but comfortable standard of living ✓ Spend time with family ✓ Enjoy leisure activities	✓ Protect family in case of death ✓ Protect family in case of disability ✓ Eliminate or reduce debt ✓ Save for retirement ✓ Maintain modest but comfortable standard of living ✓ Spend time with family

Source: Pete Jacques, "Aspirational Segmentation," *LIMRA's MarketFacts Quarterly* 22 (Spring 2003), p. 2.

Internet-based segmentation facilitates the implementation of segmentation strategies in several ways. First, it offers the possibility to cater to very small segments, sometimes as small as one customer at a time, very efficiently and inexpensively (e.g., mortgage and insurance sites that provide personalized quotes). A personalized website experience can be executed at a significantly lower cost than would be possible in other venues, such as in a retail store or over the phone. For example, frequent fliers of Air Canada are able to check prices and choose special services online at a fraction of the cost that the company would incur for a phone or ticket counter interaction with an agent.[18]

Second, segmentation over the Internet simplifies the identification of customers and provides a great deal of information about them. Cookies, small text files a website places on a visitor's hard drive,[19] provide a unique identification of each potential customer who visits a website and detail how the customer has searched through the site. Marketers also can ask visitors to fill out an online registration form.

Third, through the Internet the company can make a variety of recommendations to customers on the basis of their site visit patterns and how they search the site. For example, Amazon.ca and other e-tailers provide recommendations for related products to customers browsing and/or searching their site, which are based on matching their profiles to those of other customers. This tactic helps to boost sales of similar and complementary products.

Fourth, the marketing strategy can be customized in real time according to known data about the customer. For example, Staples can offer merchandise at different prices in different parts of the country by simply asking customers to enter their postal code.

However, the growth of Internet-based segmentation also has prompted increased consumer concerns and public policy mandates. Consumers are often worried about their privacy, especially when asked to identify themselves through site registrations or even by accepting cookies when visiting a site. Responding to both privacy concerns and industry self-regulation, most Internet sites now include privacy policies that clearly state what types of consumer information are collected and how that information is used. Consumers also are given a choice to "opt out" if they do not want their information shared with third parties or to be part of the firm's future marketing campaigns.

Although cookies themselves do not contain consumer-specific information, the use of consumer site visit information, along with data gathered from other sources, has potential legal consequences and may affect customer relationships. For example, when Amazon tried to offer different prices on the same day for certain DVDs, many observers criticized the practice as discrimination among consumer segments. Amazon argued that the price differences were the result of a pricing test being conducted; however, consumers and participants in chat forums like DVD Talk Forum disagreed. Many observers now contend that charging different prices to different customers is not bad as long as it is used to discount, rather than charge premium, prices.

equally important to ensure that the segments are distinct from one another because too much overlap between segments means that distinct marketing strategies aren't necessary to meet segment members' needs.

The Gap has identified several distinct segments to pursue. Recognizing that many of its core customers had families, The Gap opened GapKids and babyGap. Its research also indicated an opportunity to compete with Victoria's Secret in the women's intimate apparel market, so it opened GapBody. Finally, though The Gap is largely successful with middle-of-the-road customers, it was too expensive for some customers and not fashion-forward enough for others. Its Old Navy and Banana Republic stores appeal better to these markets.

Reachable   The best product or service cannot have any impact if that market cannot be reached (or accessed) through persuasive communications and product distribution. The consumer must know the product or service exists, understand what it can do for him or her, and recognize how to buy it.

La Senza is one of Canada's leading specialty retailers of women's lingerie and apparel. It is composed of La Senza Lingerie, La Senza Girl, La Senza Express, La Senza International, La Senza Spirit, and lasenza.com and it sells through stores and the Internet. However, La Senza Girl does not sell through the Internet but has a straightforward plan for reaching its target customers: girls between 7 and 14 years of

La Senza must ensure any new segment it considers is identifiable, reachable, responsive, substantial, and profitable.

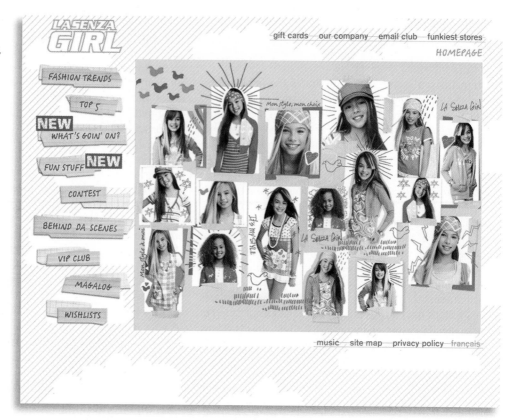

age.[20] The company simply uses its website to attract its targeted customers to explore its merchandise and fashions so that they can be comfortable and knowledgeable when they visit the physical stores to shop. Advertisements appear in media that are consistent with the lifestyle La Senza Girl is trying to portray—lively, attractive, stylish, fun, and cool.

Responsive For a segmentation strategy to be successful, the customers in the segment must react similarly and positively to the firm's offering. If, through the firm's distinctive competencies, it cannot provide products or services to that segment, it should not target it. For instance, suppose La Senza is considering introducing a line of formal dress wear for its large and very lucrative 18 to 35 year-old customer segment. People in this market are currently purchasing formal dress wear at stores like the Bay, Holt Renfrew, and Les Ailes de la Mode (Wings of Fashion). In contrast, La Senza has built a reputation for carrying a full range of intimate, stylish, sexy daywear and sleepwear bras, panties, camisoles, pyjamas, and nightshirts and competes best in this apparel line. Thus, though the formal dress wear segment meets all the other criteria for a successful segment, La Senza should not pursue it because the market probably will not be responsive to it.

Substantial and Profitable Once the firm has identified its potential target markets, it needs to measure their size and growth potential. If a market is too small or its buying power insignificant, it won't generate sufficient profits or be able to support the marketing mix activities. Although The Gap had identified potential new target markets to pursue, it was imperative for the company to determine if the market for women's intimate apparel was relatively small, in which case the company would fit the products into its regular stores. If the market was large, the products would require their own space. The Gap experimented cautiously with the new concept by first placing a section of intimate apparel in some of its stores. Over time, Gap managers realized the potential of the concept and began to roll out GapBody stores.

The Gap has identified several distinct segments to pursue. Two of its brands: Gap (right) and Gap Kids (left) appeal to different target markets.

Marketers must also focus their assessments on the potential profitability of each segment, both current and future. Some key factors to keep in mind in this analysis include market growth (current size and expected growth rate), market competitiveness (number of competitors, entry barriers, product substitutes), and market access (ease of developing or accessing distribution channels and brand familiarity). Some straightforward calculations can help illustrate the profitability of a segment:[21]

Segment profitability = Segment size

multiply by Segment adoption percentage

multiply by Purchase behaviour

multiply by Profit margin percentage

minus Fixed costs,

where

Segment size	=	Number of people in the segment.
Segment adoption percentage	=	Percentage of customers in the segment who are likely to adopt the product.
Purchase behaviour	=	Purchase price × number of times the customer would buy the product or service during a given time period.
Profit margin percentage	=	((Selling price – variable costs) ÷ selling price).
Fixed costs	=	Fixed costs (e.g., advertising expenditure).

Several segments may appear to be equally profitable according to this formula. In some cases however, it is more accurate to evaluate the profitability of a segment over the lifetime of one of its typical customers. That is, through Customer Lifetime Value (CLV)—the total value of purchases of the customer over a lifetime of patronage. For example, Ken Danns has been a loyal Costco customer for the last five years, spending about $300 per week at Costco. He plans to continue patronizing Costco for at least another five more years. To Costco, Ken Danns is not a $300 customer but a $156,000 customer if he patronizes Costco for 10 years ($300 × 52 weeks × 10 years). To address the issue of CLV, marketers consider factors such as how long the customer will remain loyal to the firm, the defection rate (percentage of customers who switch

Which segment will be more profitable to Carhartt, its traditional market for rugged work clothes (right), or the fashion-forward segment (left)?

on a yearly basis), the costs of replacing lost customers (advertising, promotion), whether customers will buy more or more expensive merchandise in the future, and other such factors.[22]

Now that we've evaluated each segment's attractiveness (Step 3), we can select the target markets to pursue (Step 4.)

LO **4**   Step 4: Select Target Market

The fourth step in the STP process is selecting a target market. The key factor likely to affect this decision is the marketer's ability to pursue such an opportunity or target segment. Thus, as we mentioned in Chapter 2, a firm is likely to assess both the attractiveness of the opportunity (opportunities and threats based on the SWOT analysis, profitability of the segment) and its own competencies (strengths and weaknesses based on SWOT analysis) very carefully.

What could be a more undifferentiated market segment strategy than greeting cards? After all, they are available in grocery stores, discount stores, drug stores, and specialty card stores. Ninety percent of households purchase at least one greeting card per year. Everyone needs greeting cards from time to time, right? Then how does Hallmark, a greeting card company with more than $4.4 billion in annual sales and a brand recognized around the globe, segment its market?[23]

First, using a geographic segmentation strategy, Hallmark is continuing its global expansion, particularly to India and China. Also, it is using a benefit segmentation strategy by targeting those seeking the convenience of sending a card over the Internet. The industry was worried that e-cards, which are generally free, would negatively affect traditional card sales, but in fact the availability of e-cards has helped to boost sales. Hallmark has a link on its home page for Free-Cards to promote its brand name via the Internet. Internet users are exposed to traditional advertising, and Hallmark can sell and promote its movies made for the Hallmark Channel and sell gifts, ornaments and other popular personal expression items. Exhibit 8.7 provides an illustration of how a firm like Hallmark might match its competencies with the attractiveness of various alternative segments and use this process to pick the best fit.

Establishing a basic segmentation strategy is not always as easy and clear as it was for La Senza. Exhibit 8.8 illustrates several segmentation strategies. Sometimes it makes sense to not segment at all. In other situations, a firm should concentrate on one segment or go after multiple segments at once. Finally, some firms choose to specialize in their product or service line to meet the needs of very small groups—perhaps even one person at a time. We discuss each of these basic segmentation types next.

EXHIBIT   **8.7**   Hallmark's Assessment of Potential Target Markets

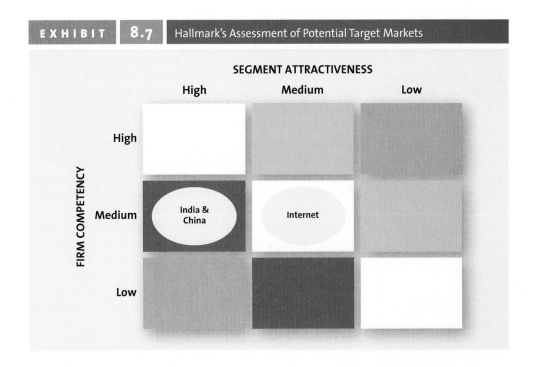

SEGMENT ATTRACTIVENESS

EXHIBIT   **8.8**   Segmentation Strategies

Mass or Undifferentiated

Differentiated

Concentrated

**Micromarketing
One-to-One**

Kettleman differentiates itself with its "no-wall" experience. When customers walk into their bagel shop, the first thing they see is the Kettleman's Bagel Roller working and rolling fresh bagels.

Speedpass, the little black transponder on the key chain, allows you to buy and pay for gas and other products at Esso quickly, hassle-free.

Undifferentiated Segmentation Strategy, or Mass Marketing When everyone might be considered a potential user of its product, a firm uses an **undifferentiated segmentation strategy**. (See Exhibit 8.8.) If the product or service is perceived to provide the same benefits to everyone, there simply is no need to develop separate strategies for different groups. Although not a common strategy in today's complex marketplace, an undifferentiated strategy can be effective for very basic items, such as salt, sugar or greetings cards. However, even those firms that offer salt, sugar, or greeting cards now are trying to differentiate their products as is the case with Hallmark.

An undifferentiated strategy also is common among smaller firms that offer products or services that consumers perceive to be indistinguishable, such as a neighbourhood bakery. But again, more marketing-savvy entrepreneurs typically try to differentiate themselves in the marketplace. The corner bakery thus becomes "Kettleman's Bagel" or "The Great Canadian Bagel." By making their commodity-like products appear special, they add value for the customer and differentiate themselves from their competition.

What about gasoline? Everyone with a car needs it. Yet gasoline companies have vigorously moved from an undifferentiated strategy to a differentiated one by segmenting their market into low-, medium-, and high-octane gasoline users. Esso even uses its Speedpass to differentiate its quick service to consumers—with just a swipe at the pump with Speedpass, you are ready to pump gas—no need to swipe cards, enter personal information, or sign receipts plus customers earn Esso Extra points or Aeroplan Miles on every eligible purchase made at Esso. Points can be redeemed for gas, car washes, snacks, and travel rewards.

undifferentiated segmentation strategy (mass marketing) A marketing strategy a firm can use if the product or service is perceived to provide the same benefits to everyone, with no need to develop separate strategies for different groups.

differentiated segmentation strategy A strategy through which a firm targets several market segments with a different offering for each.

Differentiated Segmentation Strategy Firms using a **differentiated segmentation strategy** target several market segments with a different offering for each (see Exhibit 8.8). La Senza, for instance, employs three store formats—La Senza, La Senza Girl, and La Senza Express—to appeal to three different segments respectively—(1) confident, fashion-forward, 18- to 35 year-old women; (2) younger girls; and (3) women looking for the ultimate destination for bras and panties for everyday and trend-forward styles.[24] In a similar fashion, Adidas Group appeals to various segments through its various companies, including Adidas Reebok, Rockport, and TaylorMade-Adidas Golf lines of clothing and footwear.

Firms embrace differentiated segmentation because it helps them obtain a bigger share of the market and increase the market for their products overall. The more retail formats La Senza develops to reach different market segments, the more apparel and accessories it can and will sell. Offering several different lingerie lines enable La Senza to appeal to more customer segments than if it had just one line. Furthermore, providing products or services that appeal to multiple segments helps diversify the business thereby lowering the company's overall risk. For example, if a line directed toward one segment is performing poorly, the impact on the firm's profitability can be offset by revenue from another line that is doing well.

But a differentiated strategy can be expensive. Consider La Senza's investment in accessories alone. The firm must develop, manufacture, transport, store, and promote the accessories separately for each of its store concepts.

Concentrated Segmentation (Niche) Strategy   When an organization selects a single, primary target market and focuses all its energies on providing a product to fit that market's needs, it is using a **concentrated or niche segmentation strategy** (see Exhibit 8.8). Entrepreneurial start-up ventures often benefit from using a concentrated strategy, which allows them to employ their limited resources more efficiently. The story of BALMSHELL in Entrepreneurial Marketing 8.1 is an example of this strategy since it plays in a single segment in the beauty market. Gennum Corporation of Burlington Ontario is another example of a niche strategy—it is the world's leading innovator in microcircuitry for hearing aids—a niche market.

Have you ever shopped at Christopher & Banks?[25] Well, if you aren't 48 years old and the mother of two, live in a small town or the suburbs, and like polyester jumpers, flowered cardigans, and embroidered animals, then you aren't part of its target

> **concentrated segmentation strategy**
> A marketing strategy of selecting a single, primary target market and focusing all energies on providing a product to fit that market's needs.

Entrepreneurial Marketing   **8.1**   BALMSHELL—Lip-Gloss with a Difference![26]

Born and raised in Toronto, identical twin sisters Jennifer and Fiona Lees have it all. At just 20-something, the twin duo are CEOs and creators behind the new and exciting lip-gloss with a difference—BALMSHELL. The two self-confessed makeup junkies always wanted to create a non-sticky and conditioning lip-gloss without the use of sweeteners, petroleum jelly, or mineral oil and saw a market opportunity for high quality lip-gloss. BALMSHELL lip-gloss can be found in 10 different shades at Holt Renfrew for a cool $25, much more than even Clinique's and Estee Lauder's highest priced lip glosses, which sell for about $20. You can pick up BALMSHELL at Sephora, Sephora.com in Canada, and at all 200 Sephora stores in France.

BALMSHELL differentiates its high quality lip-gloss from competitors through unique packaging.

Since its launch in September 2006, BALMSHELL has received rave reviews from fashion magazines such as *Marie Claire*, Canada's *Fashion* and *Flare*. With no experience in the cosmetic industry, only a love of lip-gloss, the sisters decided to take on the industry. With their determination, hard work, and stylish outlook, they turned their dream into a reality. Following their entrepreneurial instinct, the duo developed what they considered to be the perfect lip-gloss. After years of working with a cosmetic manufacturer they developed a formula using only the finest ingredients to produce a high-shine, moisturizing lip-gloss that looks and feels fabulous.

What sets their product apart from competitors is unique packaging inspired by a float-art pen from a kitschy shop in Yorkville. The packaging features colourful illustrations and amusing stories about colour names like Shopaholic and Sleep-in Beauty. Their design mandated no visible or tangible seam on the canister and the plastic had to feel as much like glass as possible. The thread on the lid had to be long and tight to keep it from getting sticky. When the lip-gloss has been used up, the handle can be unscrewed and the float-art attached to a key chain, which comes with the lip-gloss. Customers can't get enough of the super sheer gloss.

This success led to BALMSHELL's big break—they were asked to participate in the 2007 Oscar Nominee Gift Bag and the 2007 Grammy gift bags, for which they produced a limited edition, Red Carpet Ready shade. With A-list celebrities having BALMSHELL lips, what more can the twins ask for? Today, BALMSHELL is expanding its lip-gloss line and may expand into other product lines.

Do you want to be BALMSHELL ready for your next event?

Firms like Lands' End are engaged in mass customization since they provide custom-made products to the masses.

market. Christopher & Banks, a little-known chain of almost 500 stores that utilizes a very concentrated segmentation strategy, understands that its customers don't shop at The Gap, Chico's, or Ann Taylor.

To better understand its customers, Christopher & Banks asks women in focus groups where they eat, what cars they drive, and what their daily routines are. The responses have yielded some important insights. Customers want clothes that can be worn both at work and to a child's baseball game after work. To save time shopping, these women want merchandise that is designed to mix and match. Focus groups even look at photos of women and decide which one best represents the chain's target customer.

Micromarketing[27]   Take a look at your collection of belts. Have you ever had one made to match your exact specifications? (If you're interested, try www.leathergoodsconnection.com.) When a firm tailors a product or service to suit an individual customer's wants or needs, it is undertaking an extreme form of segmentation called **micromarketing** or **one-to-one marketing** (see Exhibit 8.8). Small producers and service providers generally can tailor their offering to individual customers more easily, whereas it is far more difficult for larger companies to achieve this degree of segmentation. Nonetheless, companies like Dell and Lands' End have capitalized on Internet technologies to offer "custom-made" computers, dress shirts, chinos, and jeans. Firms that interact on a one-to-one basis with many people to create custom-made products or services are engaged in **mass customization**, providing one-to-one marketing to the masses. Prior to the Internet era, micromarketing was almost impossible to achieve except for probably small, entrepreneurial firms. However, the Internet has made it possible for firms of all sizes and markets to engage in micromarketing.

Nike and its many customers seem to have taken this concept to heart. The success of its online make-your-own-shoe feature and a tiny SoHo studio that has seen a steady stream of celebrities customizing their kicks, led Nike to take its ID program mainstream. A new NikeID "lab" is now open at Niketown on 57th Street in Manhat-

micromarketing or one-to-one marketing
An extreme form of segmentation that tailors a product or service to suit an individual customer's wants or needs.

mass customization
The practice of interacting on a one-to-one basis with many people to create custom-made products or services; providing one-to-one marketing to the masses.

tan, where consumers make an appointment to sit down at a computer and put their own stamp on a pair of sneakers. Three to four weeks later, custom sneakers arrive at their doorstep. There are more features at this studio than the online version, which attracts 3 million unique visitors each month. There also are consultants assigned to each "designer" to help them realize their shoe fantasies. Customers pick everything from colour and materials to the fit. They can also add a "signature" on the back of the shoe. Nike looks to the ID program as a way to ramp up its personal connection with customers, and the offerings, including apparel, will continue to expand.

The degree to which firms should segment their markets—from no segmentation to one segment to multiple segments to one-to-one segments—depends on the balance the firm wants to achieve between the added perceived customer value that segmentation can offer and its cost.

Sometimes firms' target market selection also can raise serious ethical concerns. Ethical Dilemma 8.1 examines the issue of marketing certain foods to children.

Step 5: Identify and Develop Positioning Strategy

LO **5**

The last step in developing a market segmentation strategy is **positioning**. Positioning is the mental picture or perception—the thoughts, feelings, and impressions—that people have about a company, its products and brands relative to competing products, brands, or companies. This mental picture is formed from multiple sources such as friends, family, relatives, reference groups, published articles in magazines and newspapers, reports and stories from radio, television, and the Internet, as well as the customer's own experience. Regardless, of whether companies want it or not, consumers form their own ideas and feelings about a product or brand, and it is those very ideas and emotions that drive them toward or away from a brand or company. Basically, positioning is what determines consumers' *preference* for a company's products or brands. Preference is when consumers *want* a company's brand and will not accept competitors' substitutes. For example, Internet surfers prefer Google over Yahoo! for online searching and Apple's iPod over Sony's Walkman MP3 players for mobile music. Preference drives market share and revenues—both Apple and Google are the dominant players in their space. Recognizing the strategic importance of positioning, many companies

positioning
The mental picture that people have about a company and its products or services relative to competitors.

Ethical Dilemma | 8.1 | The Junk Food Wars[28] Targeting Kids

The global rise in obesity among children has led to intense scrutiny of high fat, salt, sugar (HFSS) food products producers that market to young children. For example, carbonated soft drinks are an extremely popular HFSS product among tweens and teens. Average consumption of carbonated soft drinks is about 400 cans per person per year. The nonprofit Center for Science in the Public Interest (CSPI) has labelled these products "liquid candy."

The CSPI recently called for new labelling requirements on HFSS foods so that consumers would realize that their overconsumption can contribute to a variety of health concerns, including obesity, diabetes, tooth decay, and osteoporosis. The CSPI is just one of many organizations now demanding changes to the way marketers of junk food target the young children market segment.

In response, many manufacturers have begun altering their product mix to focus on the health benefits of their products. For instance, General Mills has changed all of its cereals to whole grains, including its Trix and Lucky Charms children's brand cereals. Kraft Foods has identified products that it believes are nutritionally sound and grouped them together under the umbrella of its "Sensible Solutions" program. Sensible Solutions products are the only ones that will be targeted toward children and advertised during children's traditional viewing hours. Traditional Kraft favourites such as Oreos, Lunchables, and some Post cereals will not appear in ads during those times. In addition, Kraft is expanding its traditional lines with healthier sugar-free versions, such as sugar-free double chocolate and caramel creamy pudding, and vitamin fortified SuperMac & Cheese.

Whether these changes will have any impact on the problem of childhood obesity is unknown. Should marketers deny this very profitable market segment with products that have been successful and are demanded by them to appease organizations like CSPI? Shouldn't these young children be allowed to choose the foods they want to eat?

work very hard to shape consumers' perceptions of their brands. Positioning is one of the most important but difficult and least understood aspects of marketing strategy development. Why?

It is difficult because it is not easy to shape consumers' perceptions in the way marketers may want. It is also difficult because while marketers must keep their positioning fresh in order to keep abreast with the ever changing marketplace, consumers' perceptions are enduring and do not change easily. It's very risky for marketers because if it is not done correctly, the brand may not succeed in the marketplace. Effective positioning, therefore, requires that marketers not only shape their customers' thinking and feelings but also to evolve these feelings as they reposition their products and brands to keep up with the dynamic marketplace. For example, HP successfully repositioned itself from a boring, stodgy printer company to a consumer electronics powerhouse. It is now the leading computer company.

Market positioning involves a process of defining the marketing mix variables so that target customers have a clear, distinctive, desirable understanding of what the product does or represents in comparison with competing products. Effective positioning is about letting consumers know what the company's unique value proposition is and for whom it is intended. Clarity of this message is crucial for successful positioning. For example, Abercrombie & Fitch offer casual luxury to young, sexy, athletic- and cheerleading-type college students. Their advertising messages, models, store design, and merchandise all reinforce this message. They do not make clothing for overweight, fat, or obese people because they do not want to be perceived as being all things to all people. Rather, they determine their target market needs and wants and try to deliver the best value to their customers.

EXHIBIT 8.9	Positioning Strategies	
Positioning Strategy	**Company**	**Examples of Ad Jingles**
Value Price/Quality	Gillette Häagen Dazs Advanced Micro Devices Dell Buy.com Tiger Direct Wal-Mart West Jet	"The best a man can get" "Made like no other" "Smarter choices" "To deliver the most energy-efficient products in the industry" "Canada's low price Internet superstore" "The best computer and electronics deals anywhere" "Always low prices" "No frill, low-fare, air travel in Canada"
Product Attributes Leadership	Energizer KFC American Express Toyota Lexus RX 330 Intel	"It keeps going and going" "Finger Lick'n Good" "Don't leave home without it" "Stunning combination of style, technology and luxury" "Leap ahead"
Benefits/Symbolism	Abercombie & Fitch 3M HP Toyota L'Oréal (self-concept) Canon (self-expression) Kodak (personal meaning)	"Casual luxury" "3M Innovation" "HP Invents" "Relentless Pursuit of Excellence" "Because I'm worth it" "Express yourself" "Share moments. Share life"

Competition
  Head to Head
  Differentiation
	Avis
	ING Direct
	Capital One
		"We try harder"
		"The unmortgage, save your money"
		"Hands in your Pocket"

From the preceding discussion, it is obvious that a firm's positioning strategies must focus on the value a product or service offers the target consumer, or how it is better than competitors' products and services. When positioning against competitors, the objective is to play up how the brand being marketed provides the desired benefits better than those of competitors. Positioning strategies are realized by communicating particular messages (i.e., the **positioning statement**) in persuasive communications through different media. Usually, firms position their products and services according to value, product attributes, benefits and symbolism, and against competition (see Exhibit 8.9 on the previous page). Let's explore each of these in a bit more detail.

positioning statement
Expresses how a company wants to be perceived by consumers.

Value   Value is a popular positioning method because the relationship of price to quality is among the most important considerations for consumers when they make a purchase decision. Value positioning may open up avenues to attract new customer segments that the company previously had neglected. For example, while Proctor & Gamble's (P&G's) competitors, such as Unilever and Colgate, found success with lower-priced "value" products like Suave shampoo and Alberto VO5, P&G seemed to ignore that 80 percent of the world could not afford its products. In an attempt to correct this oversight, P&G company managers are now working globally to understand "price-sensitive customers" in various regions and sharing strategies to promote P&G products. For example, they've taken flagship products like Ivory soap and dropped the price 10–15 percent below that of rivals such as Dial. In the kids' toy market, Mega Bloks uses a low-price, value-based strategy whereas its competitor, Lego, relies on a high-price positioning strategy.

Other value-based positioning strategies emphasize that consumers are offered the best product or service but must pay a premium price to cover the additional cost. Air Canada's Super Elite flyer program described earlier in this chapter is an example of this type of positioning. BALMSHELL lip-gloss described in the entrepreneurial box of this chapter is another example—it was introduced at Holt Renfrew, a high-end retailer, at a premium price relative to existing lip-gloss. Or a company may go after a competitor by offering a comparable product at a lower price. This strategy is often observed for high-end products or luxury brands such as hotels and sports cars. Some companies claim that they are offering the same value for much less money. This type of positioning is common among wireless service providers (e.g., Roger's, Bell, Telus), cable/satellite TV and radio providers (Sirius, Roger's), electronics retailers (Future Shop), and department stores (Zellers). Companies like Internet Superstore, Buy.com, and Tiger Direct, emphasize that consumers are getting the best computer deals anywhere but at much lower prices. Finally, companies may use value positioning that lets consumers know they are getting much less but they are also paying much less. WestJet, dollar stores (e.g., Buck or Two, Dollar Daze, Dollar Store, etc.), and countless retailers targeting cost-conscious consumers commonly use this strategy.

Product Attributes   This positioning strategy focuses on those attributes of the product that are most important to the target market. For example, Volvo, the car company traditionally positioned for the safety-conscious driver, wants to stretch its

Can Volvo reposition its cars to be more exciting with higher performance without losing its traditional position that appeals to safety-conscious drivers?

safety image to one focused on driving performance and excitement. The company expects the positioning adjustment to be difficult but achievable, because so many of Volvo's boxier vehicles remain on the road today, which reinforces its more conservative image. Volvo's goal is not to abandon the safety perception associated with the brand but rather to expand its image to compete with other top luxury brands.[29] Positioning strategies that are based on product attributes tend to focus on product leadership emphasizing dimensions such as innovation, quality, performance, design, and reliability. 3M and HP focus on their innovations while Rockport focuses on comfort and a wide selection of shoes for all occasions. A product attributes success story, BALMSHELL is able to compete in the highly competitive lip-gloss market by attracting a target market that wants quality, long-lasting, and good looking lip-gloss. (See Entrepreneurial Marketing 8.1.)

Benefits and Symbolism   This type of positioning emphasises the benefits of the brand as well as the psychological meaning of the brand to consumers. For example, Jacob Connexion is about comfort in a casual, modern style and Jacob lingerie is about femininity, European elegance, and unparalleled comfort. La Senza Express is the ultimate destination dedicated to bras & panties and Abercrombie & Fitch is all about casual luxury.[30] The meanings created by these brands are often the reasons why consumers buy them rather than lesser known brands that sometimes offer similar benefits or quality. For established companies, a well-known symbol can also be used as a positioning tool, especially to appeal to loyal customers. What comes to mind when you think of Colonel Sanders, the Jolly Green Giant, the Gerber Baby, or Tony the Tiger? Or consider the Texaco star, the Nike swoosh, or the Ralph Lauren polo player. These symbols are so strong and well known that they create a position for the brand that distinguishes it from its competition.

Competition   Firms can choose to position their products or services *head-to-head* against a specific competitor or an entire product/service classification on similar attributes within the target market. Using head-to-head positioning, Avis positioned itself alongside Hertz with its message "Avis is only no. 2 in rent a cars. So why go with us? We try harder (When you're not the biggest, you have to.)."[31] Head-to-head positioning often leads to price wars such as the "cola wars" and "airline wars," which are good for consumers but bad for businesses. Marketers must be careful that they don't position their product too closely to their competition because they risk confusing customers or face legal challenges. If, for instance, their package or logo looks too much like a competitor's, they might be opening themselves up to a trademark infringement lawsuit. Numerous store brands have been challenged for having packaging confusingly similar to that of national brands. McDonald's, for example, sues anyone who uses the "Mc" prefix. It sued Quality Inns International when it named its no-frills chain McSleep Inns.[32] On the other hand, courts have allowed parody jeans for full figured women to be sold under the Lardashe label, despite the objections of Jordache jeans.

Firms can also choose a *differentiation* strategy by going after a less competitive, smaller market niche.[33] For instance, 7-Up positioned its product as "the Uncola" to differentiate it from caramel-coloured cola beverages like Pepsi and Coke. Goodrich tires were promoted as "the other guys," or the ones without the blimp, to set them apart from Goodyear tires. McDonalds, which is historically known as the world's #1 beef burger joint has responded to industry critics and health-conscious consumers by improving the "health of its menu" with more healthy choices—salads and chicken sandwiches. In doing so, it tried to avoid competition with arch rivals Wendy's and Burger King while minimizing the impact of cannibalization of its existing menu items. Thus, McDonald's carefully picked and named its new salads and chicken sandwiches. This move paid off brilliantly for McDonald's because it has for the first time in its 52-year history, overtaken the #1 chicken joint—Kentucky Fried Chicken—when it racked up chicken sales of $5.2 billion in the 12 months through March 2007.[34]

Market Leadership Instead of positioning head-to-head, companies, especially market leaders, may emphasize their leadership position within their industry. Canadian companies such as the Royal Bank, Loblaw, Canadian Tire, and global companies such as Amazon, Intel, HP, Google, and eBay play up their status as market leaders in their respective industry. Each of these companies is the leader in their industry and so consumers often perceive them as setting the standards of their industry.

Now that we have identified the various methods by which firms position their products and services, we discuss the actual stages they go through in establishing that position.

Positioning Stages

When developing a positioning strategy, firms go through five important stages. Before you read about these stages though, examine Exhibit 8.10, a hypothetical perceptual map of the soft drink industry. A **perceptual map** displays, in two or more dimensions, the position of products or brands in the consumer's mind. We have chosen two dimensions for illustrative purposes: strong versus light taste (vertical) and fun versus healthy (horizontal). Also, though this industry is quite complex, we have simplified the diagram to include only a few players in the market. The position of each brand is denoted by a small circle, and the numbered asterisks denote consumers' **ideal points**—where a particular market segment's ideal product would lie on the map.

To derive a perceptual map such as this, marketers follow five steps.

1. **Determine consumers' perceptions and evaluations of the product or service in relation to competitors'.** Marketers determine their brand's position by asking consumers a series of questions about their and competitors' products.

perceptual map
Displays, in two or more dimensions, the position of products or brands in the consumer's mind.

ideal point
The position at which a particular market segment's ideal product would lie on a *perceptual map.*

| EXHIBIT | 8.10 | Perceptual Map for the Soft Drink Industry |

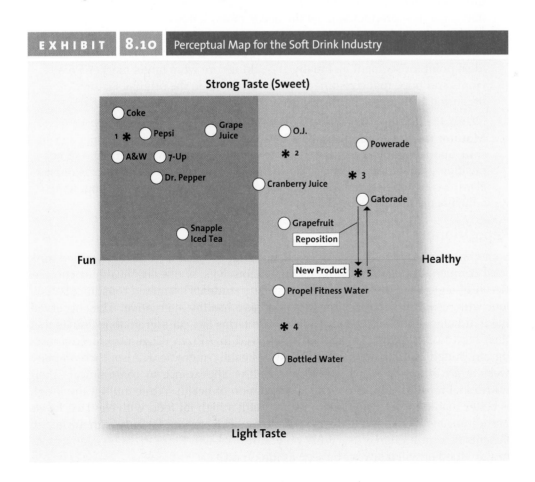

For instance, they might ask how the consumer uses the existing product or services, what items the consumer regards as alternative sources to satisfy his or her needs, what the person likes or dislikes about the brand in relation to competitors, and what might make that person choose one brand over another.

2. **Identify competitors' positions.** When the firm understands how its customers view its brand relative to competitors', it must study how those same competitors position themselves. For instance, POWERade ("Liquid Hydration") positions itself closely to Gatorade ("Is It In You?"), which means they appear next to each other on the perceptual map and appeal to target market 3. They are also often found next to each other on store shelves, are similarly priced, and are viewed by customers as sports drinks. Gatorade also knows that its sports drink is perceived to be more like POWERade than like its own Propel Fitness Water (located near target market 4), Coca-Cola (target market 1), or Sunkist orange juice (target market 2).

3. **Determine consumer preferences.** The firm knows what the consumer thinks of the products or services in the marketplace and their positions relative to one another. Now it must find out what the consumer really wants, that is, determine the "ideal" product or service that appeals to each market. For example, a huge market exists for traditional Gatorade, and that market is shared by POWERade. Gatorade also recognizes a market, depicted as the ideal product for segment 5 on the perceptual map, of consumers who would prefer a less sweet, less calorie-laden drink that offers the same rejuvenating properties as Gatorade. Currently, no product is adequately serving market 5.

4. **Select the position.** Continuing with the Gatorade example, the company has three choices to appeal to the "less sweet sports drink" target market 5. It could develop a new product to meet the needs of market 5. Alternatively, it could adjust or reposition its marketing approach—its product and promotion—to sell original Gatorade to market 5 (arrow pointing down from Gatorade to the ideal point for segment 5). Finally, it could ignore what target market 5 really wants and hope that consumers will be attracted to the original Gatorade because it is closer to their ideal product than anything else on the market (arrow pointing up from the ideal point for segment 5 to Gatorade).

5. **Monitor the positioning strategy.** Markets are not stagnant. Consumers' tastes shift, and competitors react to those shifts. Attempting to maintain the same position year after year can spell disaster for any company. Thus, firms must always view the first three steps of the positioning process as ongoing, with adjustments made in step four as necessary.

Repositioning

Sometimes firms try to change their positioning. For example, many so-called junk food companies are trying to reposition themselves as offering healthier choices. Recently, a group of Wilfrid Laurier University students examined consumer behaviour with respect to repositioning junk food as a healthy alternative. They observed the trend among junk food companies to use terms like multigrain to insinuate that their food was healthy.[35] The students observed that Pizza Pizza introduced a multigrain dough that contains omega-3 fat, a healthy ingredient. Also, the company website advertising has a natural and healthy appearance to communicate their nutritional repositioning and create a perception of health. While multigrain dough is better than typical white dough, pizza is still a high fat food with elevated levels of sodium, and toppings like pepperoni, cheese, and sausage far outweigh the health benefits of a multigrain crust. What do you think—will Pizza Pizza be ever seen as healthy food or will it always be seen as junk food?

Good marketers constantly re-evaluate their brand's position in order to determine when to reposition it. Companies should reposition their brands to keep up with changes in the marketplace or to put a fresh spin to their stale and stodgy brand. Many companies that operate on the idea, "if ain't broke, then don't fix it" often find out too late that their brand needs a serious make over. The result is that their positioning is so badly damaged that it takes years and huge budgets to rebuild. A familiar example is Yahoo! In the early days of the Internet, Yahoo! successfully positioned itself as the largest Web portal and consumers used Yahoo! as their portal of choice. Then came Google, which positioned itself as the best search engine. Yahoo! tried to go head-to-head with Google as a search engine but failed miserably. Yahoo! is still seen as a Web portal whether they want that image or not. Companies that are proactive in protecting their positioning, change or tinker with their positioning to keep up with market dynamics. For example, for most of GE's history, its positioning was based on product—*we bring good things to life*—which has served GE very well. Recently, GE replaced that positioning with one that focuses on its rich history of innovation—*imagination at work.*

As the Yahoo! example described above shows, repositioning is not an easy task because consumers' perceptions do not change readily even though the marketplace is changing rapidly. One disadvantage of repositioning is that if it's not done well, the company risks alienating its core customers while simultaneously failing to attract new customers. A major advantage of successful repositioning is that it strengthens the brand in the marketplace thereby allowing the company to keep its core customers satisfied while drawing new customers to the brand. For example, Cadbury successfully repositioned from a leading brand for older customers to a brand for a younger (25- to 35-year-olds) target market because customer loyalty among its older customers have been dropping. To do this, Cadbury refreshed its brand by (1) updating the look of its packaging, displays, and marketing communications to portray a more cheerful and lively appearance, and (2) launched an advertising campaign that depicted the product being enjoyed in a work environment. The result is that Cadbury was able to increase its customer loyalty rating by 5 percent in 2005 over 2004. On the other hand, McDonald's Arch Deluxe failed when it was positioned as the Adult Hamburger in much the same way as how Happy Meals are positioned for children. This move actually alienated kids and their happy meals, and failed to secure an adult audience. The $100-million campaign was abandoned and some store sales declined—not surprisingly it is called the McFlop.

Brand repositioning refers to a strategy in which marketers change a brand's focus to target new markets or realign the brand's core emphasis with changing market preferences.[36] As manufacturers were driving prices of appliances down and steel was pushing material costs up, Whirlpool Corporation ("Whirlpool") began to see its appliances become a commodity. The company needed an innovation that would justify higher prices and increase its market share. The design chief of Whirlpool fought against traditional mind sets and brought in usability researchers, graphic artists, and engineers to design new appliances. *The Duet® laundry pair* is a result of one of these teams (photo on next page). It is a matching set of stylish washers and dryers that demands the highest price in the front-loading washer/dryer market and owns 20 percent of the front-loading washer/dryer market. Whirlpool has brought appliances into a realm that previously didn't exist. Appliances can be "cool"—Paris's Louvre Museum has exhibited the Whirlpool next-generation concept products and the Smithsonian awarded Whirlpool its annual National Design Award in corporate achievement.[37]

GE repositioned itself from a manufacuterer of excellent products to an innovator in keeping with marketing trends where innovation is seen as the basis of competitive advantage.

brand repositioning (rebranding)
A strategy in which marketers change a brand's focus to target new markets or realign the brand's core emphasis with changing market preferences.

New marketing opportunities also may spur firms to reposition their brands. The growing youth segment, its purchasing power, and its increasing influence on household purchasing decisions has made firms in various industries sit up and take notice. Since buying the Elizabeth Arden unit from Unilever in 2000, FFI Fragrances has repositioned several of the firm's cosmetics lines to attract younger consumers, using celebrities such as Kate Beckinsale, Kirsten Dunst, Sarah Jessica Parker, and Catherine Zeta-Jones in its advertisements.[38] Some magazines have also been repositioned, moving from the overcrowded young teen segment to slightly older teens, such as *YM*'s repositioning of its publication to cater to 19-year-olds.[39]

Repositioning can change the quality image of the brand too. Canada's Wonderland enhanced its image as Canada's premier theme park after research revealed that consumers liked the fact that the park had been purchased by Paramount Pictures. It redefined itself as a Hollywood brand[40] and launched new rides based on blockbuster movies including Canada's first inverted coaster—Top Gun and a flying coaster—Tomb Raider: The Ride. WestJet repositioned itself from a "no frills" low cost leader to a considerably higher quality airline by adding luxuries like leather seats and seat-back LCD television screens.

Repositioning also breathes life into old brands. Such revitalization sometimes can result from changing the packaging and/or altering the characteristics of the brand.[41] Aqua Velva aftershave lotion changed its packaging to a more convenient bottle, and Arm & Hammer started advertising a variety of uses for its baking soda, including deodorizing refrigerators.[42]

Although repositioning can improve the brand's fit with its target segment or boost the vitality of old brands, it is not without costs and risks. Firms often need to spend tremendous amounts of money to make tangible changes to the product and packages, as well as intangible changes to the brand's image through advertising. These costs may not be recovered if the repositioned brand and messages are not credible to the consumer or if the firm has mistaken a fad for a long-term market trend.

Whirlpool has successfully repositioned its washer/dryer market with the newly designed Duet® *line. It is so stylish that it has been displayed in Paris's Louvre Museum and has won a design award from the Smithsonian.*

Learning Objectives Review

1) Describe the STP process

2) Describe the bases marketers use to segment a market

3) Discuss the criteria for determining the attractiveness of a segment and whether it is worth pursuing (targeting)

4) Explain how a firm decides what type of segmentation strategy to use—undifferentiated, differentiated, concentrated, or micromarketing

5) Explain what positioning is and describe how firms do it

1) The STP process is a systematic process consisting of five stages. First, marketing managers establish the overall objectives of their marketing strategy. Next, they identify the various market segments and develop a profile for each segment. Then the segments are evaluated to determine their attractiveness and fit with the company's competencies. This information is then used to select the segment(s) they would like to serve—targeting. Finally, marketing managers develop a positioning strategy that is consistent with the target market in order to communicate their unique value proposition.

2) There is really no one "best" method to segment a market. Firms choose from various segmentation bases depending on the type of product/service they offer and their goals for the segmentation strategy. For instance, if the firm wants to identify its customers easily, geographic or demographic segmentation likely will work best. But if it is trying to dig deeper into why customers might buy its offering, then lifestyle, benefits, or loyalty segmentation work best. Geodemographic segmentation provides a nice blend of geographic, demographic, and psychographic approaches. Typically, a combination of several segmentation methods is most effective.

3) Marketers use several criteria to assess a segment's attractiveness. First, the customer should be *identifiable*—companies must know what types of people are in the market so they can direct their efforts appropriately. Second, the market must be *reachable*—the firm must be able to reach the segment through effective communications and distribution. Third, the firm must be *responsive* to the needs of customers in a segment. It must be able to deliver a product or service that the segment will embrace. Finally, the market must be *substantial* enough to be worth pursuing. If relatively few people appear in a segment, it is probably not cost effective to direct special marketing mix efforts toward them. Additionally, the segment must be *profitable*, both in the near term and over the lifetime of the customer.

4) Most firms use some form of segmentation strategy. An undifferentiated strategy is really no segmentation at all and only works for products or services that most consumers consider to be commodities. The difference between a differentiated and a concentrated strategy is that the differentiated approach targets multiple segments, whereas the concentrated targets only one. Larger firms with multiple product/service offerings generally use a differentiated strategy; smaller firms or those with a limited product/service offering often use a concentrated strategy. Firms that employ a micromarketing or one-to-one marketing strategy tailor their product/service offering to each customer—that is, it is custom made. In the past, micromarketing was reserved primarily for artisans, tailors, or other craftspeople who would make items exactly as the customer wanted. Recently however, larger manufacturers and retailers have begun experimenting with custom-made merchandise as well. Service providers, in contrast, are largely accustomed to customizing their offering. Hair salons could not flourish if every customer got the same cut.

5) Positioning is the "P" in the STP (segmentation, targeting, and positioning) process. It refers to how customers think about a product, service, or brand in the market relative to competitors' offerings. Firms position their products and services according to several criteria. Some focus on their offering's *value*—customers get a lot for what the product or service costs. Others determine the most *important product attributes* for customers and position their offering on the basis of those attributes. *Benefits and symbols* can also be used for positioning, though few products or services are associated with symbols that are compelling enough to drive people to buy. Companies may also use their dominant position in their market—*market leadership*—to position their products or services. Finally, *competition* is one of the most common positioning methods and relies on the favourable comparison of the firm's offering with the products or services marketed by competitors (head-to-head). Companies may also choose to compete by differentiating their value proposition.

Key Terms

- behavioural segmentation, 210
- benefit segmentation, 211
- brand repositioning (rebranding), 229
- concentrated segmentation strategy, 221
- demographic segmentation, 207
- differentiated segmentation strategy, 220
- geodemographic segmentation, 213
- geographic segmentation, 206
- ideal point, 227
- lifestyles, 209
- loyalty segmentation, 211
- mass customization, 222
- micromarketing, 222
- one-to-one marketing, 222
- perceptual map, 227
- positioning, 223
- positioning statement, 225
- psychographics, 208
- PSYTE clusters, 213
- self-concept, 209
- self-values, 209
- undifferentiated segmentation strategy (mass marketing), 220
- VALS™, 209

Concept Review

1. How do segmentation, targeting, and positioning add value to a company's value proposition?

2. Outline the steps in the STP process. What are some of the key decisions marketers have to make at each step?

3. List the bases that can be used to segment a market for a product or service. Which of these bases is considered to be the most difficult to use and which is the easiest? Why?

4. Describe the segmentation bases you think Unilever used to develop its target segment. What kinds of products do you think this segment was buying before Unilever introduced its Sunsilk brand? Thinking back to the consumer buying decision process, what kind of strategies do you think were necessary to get this segment to switch to Sunsilk?

5. List the four types of targeting strategies companies can use to serve selected market segments. What are the main points to consider before selecting one or some combination of these strategies? What are the advantages and disadvantages of each strategy and how can competitors influence the strategy a company chooses?

6. Explain the difference between positioning and a positioning statement. Why do you think marketers find market positioning one of the most difficult aspects of the STP process? How can marketers try to influence the positioning of their products or services in the market place?

7. List four types of strategies companies could use to position their products or services in the marketplace. When Home Depot says, "you can do it, we can help," what type of positioning is it striving for?

8. What is a perceptual map? How is it used in developing positioning strategies or to identify market opportunities?

9. Why should marketers consider repositioning their brand? Explain what is meant by repositioning and what are the major challenges and risks inherent in repositioning.

10. A news article on the Internet suggests that Sony is thinking of repositioning its PlayStation 2 game console as a computer. Do you think that Sony can do this successfully? Give reasons. Do you think consumers will ever see the PlayStation as a computer? Why or why not?

Marketing Applications

1 . You have been asked to identify various strategies for segmenting a market, which then will be used to choose one strategy for your sporting goods shop. List and discuss each of the overall strategies that can be used to develop a segmentation approach. Provide an example of each of the four strategies the sporting goods shop might use.

2. What overall segmentation strategy would you suggest for a small entrepreneur starting a business? Justify why you would recommend that particular approach.

3. The concept of "mass customization" seems like a contradiction in terms. How and why would a retailer use mass customization?

4. Various methods are used to segment markets. Identify the typical customer for each of the four methods discussed in the text.

5. You have been asked to evaluate the attractiveness of several potential market segments. What criteria should you use to evaluate those segments? Why are these appropriate criteria?

6. A small-business owner is trying to evaluate the profitability of different segments. What are the key factors he or she must consider? For how long should the business owner conduct the evaluation?

7. Think about the various hotel brands that you know (e.g., Marriott, Holiday Inn, Super 8). How do those brands position themselves in the market?

8. Put yourself in the position of an entrepreneur who is developing a new product to introduce into the market. Briefly describe the product. Then, develop the segmentation, targeting, and positioning strategy for marketing the new product. Be sure to discuss (a) the overall strategy, (b) characteristics of the target market, (c) why that target market is attractive, and (d) the positioning strategy. Provide justifications for your decisions.

9. Think of a specific company or organization that uses various types of promotional material to market its offerings. (The Web, magazine ads, newspaper ads, catalogues, newspaper inserts, direct mail pieces, and flyers might all be sources of promotional materials.) Locate two or three promotional pieces for the company and use them as a basis to analyze the segment(s) being targeted. Describe the basic segmentation strategy reflected in these materials, and describe characteristics of the target market according to the materials. Be sure to include a copy of all the materials used in the analysis.

10. You have been hired recently by a large bank in its credit card marketing division. The bank has relationships with a large number of colleges and universities and prints a wide variety of credit cards featuring college and university logos, images, and the like. You have been asked to oversee the implementation of a new program targeting the freshman class at the schools with which the bank has a relationship. The bank has already purchased the names and home addresses of the incoming freshman class. You have been told that no credit checks will be required for these cards as long as the student is over 18 years of age. The bank plans a first day of school marketing blitz that includes free hats, t-shirts, and book promotions, as well as free pizza, if the students simply fill out an application. Do you think it is a good idea to offer this program to these new students?

Toolkit

MARKET POSITION MAP ANALYSIS

Assume you are a brand manager for a major manufacturer. You have identified a number of market segments and are trying to understand how its products are positioned relative to other manufacturers'. Use the toolkit provided at www.mcgrawhill.ca/olc/grewal to conduct a Market Position Analysis.

Net Savvy

1 . Go to L'Oréal Canada website (www.lorealparis.ca/en/home.html) and try to describe the segmentation approach they use to group customers. Try to apply the vocabulary presented in this chapter to describe their segmentation strategy. Then click on "Skincare," then "brand portfolio," and finally "ReFinish"—who do you think is the target market for their "ReFinish Micro-Dermabrasion system"? How would you describe L'Oréal's product positioning in Canada?

2. Suppose you want to open a specialty coffee and treats shop near the campus of your university and so you thought it would be helpful as a starting point to collect some demographic data. Your first hunch is StatsCan but from your experience you realize this would be difficult and take a long time. Help is on the way. Go to SRC's Free Demographics website at www.freedemographics.com/ and register to use this free service. Use this site to generate a report on the demographics of the area you want to locate your coffee shop. How helpful is this site?

Chapter Case Study

M&M MEAT SHOPS—USING DEMOGRAPHICS TO DRIVE DECISIONS[43]

Known as the store with hundreds of meal ideas but only one aisle, M&M Meat Shops is Canada's largest retail chain of specialty frozen foods with over 470 locations coast to coast. The demand for ready-to-heat food is increasing as home-cooked meals become more difficult in time-strapped households, an important demographic for the company.

The first store opened in October 1980 based on a consumer insight by founders Mark Nowak and Mac Voisin that it was not possible to buy restaurant quality steaks in retail outlets. Neither Nowak, a lawyer, nor Voisin, an engineer, had much marketing experience. However, when the company started offering franchises, they recognized the need to have a segmentation methodology to help them assess potential new locations.

M&M Meat Shops uses demographics as well as a segmentation system, MOSAIC, to gain insights into their trade areas, their customers, and to help refine M&M Meat Shops' understanding of who has the best lifestyle fit for the company.

The M&M Max Card allows the company to track 94 percent of all sales transactions gathering valuable information about consumer shopping habits.

Demographic data helps the company understand if a trade area has potential or not. It is demographics that highlight if an area is, for example, experiencing growth or decline in population, if the area is home to more apartment dwellers than home owners, as well as what the dominant language is. Segmentation systems pick up where uni-variate demographics leave off and help define neighbourhoods more thoroughly. Two neighbours with similar incomes, religious backgrounds, and housing can have very different lifestyles and buying habits and it's vitally important for a marketer to be able to identify these differences.

Although their Head Office personnel have worked with PSYTE Canada Advantage (described earlier in this chapter), today they use a sophisticated segmentation, MOSAIC, that classifies their customer data into one of 150 different lifestyle clusters. The MOSAIC system incorporates thousands of variables from as many areas as possible (such as occupation dwellings, ethnicity, mobility, house value, household income, language, etc.), which provides M&M Meat Shops with a more precise look at their trade areas and helps to define their customer base.

In Ontario, one of the top clusters for M&M Meat Shops is known as "Wine with Dinner." This group is university-educated, athletic, and lives in single-detached homes with larger than average families. They have an average household income of $70,000 and spend a lot of money on home decor and gardening.

Using information produced through segmentation analysis efforts, M&M Meat Shops selects which target markets to pursue. Its target customer is typically a woman (35 years +) with a family with a very active family life that includes two or more children. These consumers are time-starved and need convenient food options. Having identified the best target markets, the company turns its efforts to finding more consumers who fit the profile and reaching them with relevant campaigns.

As the country becomes much more multicultural, ongoing analysis is conducted to understand the changing Canadian population. According to the 2006 Census, the face of Canada continues to change at a fairly rapid pace. In the five years between the 2001 and 2006 Censuses, 1.6 million new residents called Canada home, of which 1.2 million, or 75 percent of those residents, were new immigrants. These new Canadians are a potentially huge market for retailers, one that is anticipated to grow. By 2017, 1 in 5 Canadians are expected to be a member of a visible minority. Armed with such insights, M&M Meat Shops has begun to research the complexities of ethnic marketing.

Although M&M Meat Shops is predominantly a suburban chain, it is starting to launch a new urban concept called M&M Meat Shops Uptown. The first location is in downtown Toronto and features edgier décor than the suburban outlets. This new concept is designed to fit the urban lifestyle with extended hours of operation as well as the inclusion of specialty products such as indoor grills and computer kiosks to help customers create their own menus and download recipes.[44]

Other expansion plans for M&M Meat Shops include a foray into the U.S. Determining where to open the first U.S. stores is a massive undertaking. One step in this research is to compare the company's top Canadian MOSAIC clusters to U.S. MOSAIC clusters to check for similarities in lifestyle. (The Canadian and U.S. clusters are totally different.) Because these lifestyle systems are a combination of demographic and psychographic information, they help to identify areas in the U.S. that have very similar lifestyles to M&M Meat Shops' strongest Canadian markets.

Knowing it pays to retain loyal customers, the company's MAX program rewards its most loyal customers. The program also provides the company with valuable consumer insights. M&M Meat Shops says that 94 percent of all sales transactions are tracked through the program and that 93 percent of customers, or 5.7 million Canadians, have a MAX card. Data collected from the card, such as postal codes, are used to understand how far customers travel to outlets—useful information when determining locations of new stores. It also helps more narrowly focus advertising efforts to reach the core customer profile.

Segmentation data and loyalty program data are provided to franchisees to help them to increase market penetration in their trade areas and even to determine what mix of products to stock. M&M's approach adds value to franchisees, helping them to first attract and then keep their best customers.

M&M Meat Shops uses census data combined with its MAX card loyalty program to better serve growing ethnic markets. For example, butter chicken was featured in sales flyers during Diwali celebrations.

Questions

1. Describe the type of segmentation strategy M&M Meat Shops use to serve its suburban markets. Provide support for your answer.

2. Why would a different strategy be needed for its Uptown urban store locations?

3. Why do companies like M&M Meat Shops need to use a combination of segmentation approaches when identifying potential target markets?

4. What are some key demographic differences M&M Meat Shops should consider for their entry into the U.S. market?

5. Besides adapting their advertising to reflect different cultural holidays, what are some other ways M&M Meat Shops could reach out to Canada's growing ethnic population?

CHAPTER 9

LEARNING OBJECTIVES

After studying this chapter, you should be able to:

LO **1** Describe how firms adjust their product lines to changing market conditions

LO **2** Understand why brands are valuable to firms

LO **3** Discuss how firms implement different branding strategies

LO **4** Explain how a product's packaging and label contribute to a firm's overall strategy

Product, Branding, and Packaging Decisions

Since its debut in 1957, Dove has grown to become a global brand sold in over 80 countries. Launched as a beauty bar that wouldn't dry skin the way soap did, Dove is now the world's top cleansing brand.[1] Dove products can be found in one of every four homes in Canada.[2]

At the heart of the brand is the original Dove beauty bar. Containing 1/4 moisturizing cream, Dove's brand promise is to gently cleanse skin while moisturizing. This simple benefit positioning has been successfully leveraged in multiple personal care categories. After more than four decades of building a strong brand, Unilever extended the brand into new product lines including moisturizing body wash, antiperspirant and deodorant, face care, shampoos and conditioners, and styling aids.

Some brand extensions fail because there isn't a strong fit with the core brand, for example, Ben-Gay Aspirin, Vaseline Aftershave, or 7-Up lip balm. New Dove products fit well with the core brand. And, Unilever had organizational competencies in the new product categories. For instance, it already had expertise in face care (Ponds), hair care (Therma Silk, Salon Selectives, Finesse), and antiperspirants (Degree.)

Consumer insights were used to drive brand extension ideas. The deodorant extension was based on consumer research that identified a need for a mild moisturizing product that would not irritate razor burn from shaving underarms. Brand consistency was achieved across new products because all extensions supported the moisturization functional attribute.

This brand consistency has helped develop solid brand associations. The Dove brand image has always been associated with moisture and mildness. Feminine imagery is often used to convey the properties of the brand. The logo, an abstract image of a dove, connotes universal feminine attributes such as peace, mildness, and softness. The image is further exemplified in packaging where curved bottle shapes and lines are used. Even the core product, the Dove beauty soap bar, is curved so that it contours to the shape of a woman's body.

The simple Dove value proposition has remained unchanged for over 50 years: its brand promise of mildness and moisturization still relevant and compelling to consumers. Dove built a strong brand by continually delivering on its brand promise, making it a trusted brand not only with consumers but also professionals—Dove is the number one dermatologist recommended cleansing bar.

By staying true to the brand promise, Dove not only created a valued product, it also built strong brand equity, high customer awareness and intense loyalty.

Unilever successfully leveraged the brand equity created in the Dove beauty soap bar to extend the brand in new product categories such as those shown here.

product
Anything that is of value to a consumer and can be offered through a voluntary marketing exchange.

As a key element of a firm's marketing mix (4Ps) strategies, product strategies are central to the creation of value for the consumer. A **product** is anything that is of value to a consumer and can be offered through a marketing exchange. In addition to *goods*, such as toothpaste, or *services*, such as a haircut, products might also be *places* (e.g., Whistler, B.C.), *ideas* (e.g., "stop smoking"), *organizations* (e.g., Canadian Blood Services), *people* (e.g., Avril Lavigne), or *communities* (e.g., Facebook.com) that create value for consumers in their respective competitive marketing arenas.

As shown in our chapter roadmap, this chapter begins with a discussion of how firms adjust their product lines to meet and respond to changing market conditions. Then we turn our attention to branding—why are brands valuable to the firm, and what are the different branding strategies firms use? We also never want to underestimate the value of a product's packaging and labelling in product strategies and promotion. Packaging and labelling must send out a strong message from the shelf: Buy me! The final section of this chapter examines packaging and labelling issues.

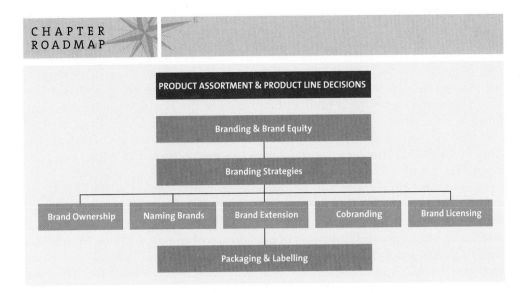

CHAPTER
ROADMAP

PRODUCT ASSORTMENT & PRODUCT LINE DECISIONS

Branding & Brand Equity

Branding Strategies

| Brand Ownership | Naming Brands | Brand Extension | Cobranding | Brand Licensing |

Packaging & Labelling

Product Assortment and Product Line Decisions

The complete set of all products offered by a firm is called its **product assortment** or **product mix**. Colgate-Palmolive's product assortment is shown in Exhibit 9.1. The product assortment typically consists of various **product lines**, which are groups of associated items, such as items that consumers use together or think of as part of a group of similar products. Colgate-Palmolive's product lines include oral care, personal care, household care, fabric care, and pet nutrition.

product assortment (product mix)
The complete set of all products offered by a firm; also called the *product mix*.

product lines
Groups of associated items, such as those that consumers use together or think of as part of a group of similar products.

EXHIBIT 9.1   Colgate-Palmolive Product Assortment

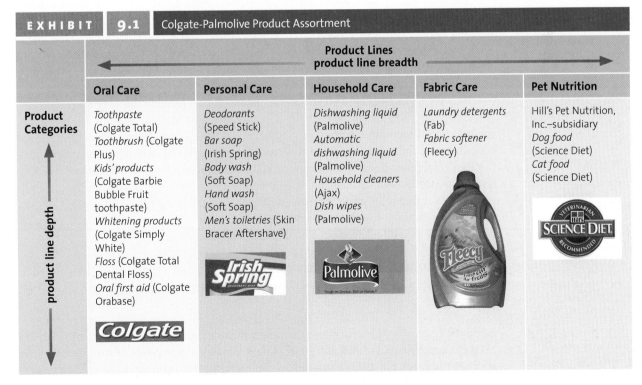

	Oral Care	Personal Care	Household Care	Fabric Care	Pet Nutrition
Product Categories	*Toothpaste* (Colgate Total) *Toothbrush* (Colgate Plus) *Kids' products* (Colgate Barbie Bubble Fruit toothpaste) *Whitening products* (Colgate Simply White) *Floss* (Colgate Total Dental Floss) *Oral first aid* (Colgate Orabase)	*Deodorants* (Speed Stick) *Bar soap* (Irish Spring) *Body wash* (Soft Soap) *Hand wash* (Soft Soap) *Men's toiletries* (Skin Bracer Aftershave)	*Dishwashing liquid* (Palmolive) *Automatic dishwashing liquid* (Palmolive) *Household cleaners* (Ajax) *Dish wipes* (Palmolive)	*Laundry detergents* (Fab) *Fabric softener* (Fleecy)	Hill's Pet Nutrition, Inc.–subsidiary *Dog food* (Science Diet) *Cat food* (Science Diet)

Product Lines
product line breadth

product line depth

Source: www.colgate.com.

product category
An assortment of items that the customer sees as reasonable substitutes for one another.

brand
The name, term, design, symbol, or any other features that identify one seller's good or service as distinct from those of other sellers.

product line breadth
The number of product lines, or variety, offered by the firm.

product line depth
The number of categories within a product line.

stock keeping units (SKUs)
Individual items within each product category; the smallest unit available for inventory control.

category depth
The number of stock keeping units (SKUs) within a category.

Within each product line, there are often multiple product categories. A **product category** is an assortment of items that the customer sees as reasonable substitutes for one another. For example, in the oral care product line, Colgate-Palmolive offers several categories with a variety of offerings to choose from in each: toothpaste, whitening products, toothbrushes, kid's oral care products, floss, and oral first aid. Each category within a product line may use the same or different **brands**, which are the names, terms, designs, symbols, or any other features that identify one seller's good or service as distinct from those of other sellers.[3] For instance, Colgate-Palmolive offers several brands of toothbrushes (e.g., 360, Whitening, Massager, Navigator).

Product assortments can also be described in terms of their breadth and depth. A firm's **product line breadth** (sometimes also referred to as variety) represents the number of product lines offered by the firm; Colgate-Palmolive has five. **Product line depth**, in contrast, is the number of categories within a product line. Within Colgate-Palmolive's oral care line, for example, there are several categories—toothpaste, toothbrushes, kids' products, and so forth. Its pet nutrition product line, however, comprises fewer categories and therefore has less depth.

Within each product category are a number of individual items called **stock keeping units (SKUs)**, which are the smallest unit available for inventory control. For instance, within the toothpaste category, Colgate-Palmolive offers 49 Colgate SKUs that represent various sizes, flavours, and configurations of Colgate Herbal White, Colgate Total, and Colgate Fresh Confidence.[4] Each individual product is a unique SKU. The 100-ml size of Colgate Total Clean Mint is one SKU, while the 100-ml package of Colgate Total Whitening Paste is a second SKU. The same size package of Colgate Total Advanced Fresh Gel represents a third SKU. The **category depth** is the number of SKUs within a category. Each SKU has its own unique product code (UPC) code as well.

The decision to expand or contract product lines and categories depends on several industry-, consumer-, and firm-level factors. Among the industry factors, firms expand their product lines when it is relatively easy to enter a specific market (entry barriers are low) and/or when there is a substantial market opportunity.[5] When firms add new product categories and brands to their product assortments, they often earn significant sales and profits, as was the case with Doritos' Cool Ranch product line, Ford's Explorer line, and Chrysler's minivans.[6]

However, unchecked and unlimited product line extensions may have adverse consequences. Too much variety in the product assortment is often too costly to maintain, and too many brands may weaken the firm's brand reputation.[7] In the past several years, for example, Heinz has gone through a major restructuring, consolidating its global operations and increasing concentration on those products and markets that were doing well. In Europe, it reduced the number of different Heinz ketchup options (as indicated by the bottle designs available) from 24 to 12.[8]

Now let's look at why firms change their product mix's breadth, depth, or number of SKUs, as well as product line decisions for services.

LO ① Change Product Mix Breadth

Firms may change their product mix breadth by either adding to or deleting product lines.

Increase Breadth   Firms often add new product lines to capture new or evolving markets, increase sales, and compete in new venues. After years of simply watching sports-utility vehicle (SUV) sales increase steadily, Porsche decided to add a new product line when it entered the SUV market with its Porsche Cayenne. The vehicle, which debuted in 2003, attempts to live up to the performance standards and sporty image Porsche sports cars enjoy. Porsche's decision to extend its brand name to a new product line was no surprise, given that approximately 40 percent of Porsche sports car owners were buying SUVs as their second automobiles.[9]

Decrease Breadth   Sometimes it is necessary to delete entire product lines to address changing market conditions or meet internal strategic priorities. A few years ago, SC Johnson sold off many products in its skin care line, including its successful Aveeno brand, to Johnson & Johnson.[10] The firm no longer competes in the skin care business, though it remains a strong competitor in its original product lines, such as home cleaning (Pledge, Windex), air care (Glade), and home storage (Saran, Ziploc).[11]

Change Product Mix Depth

As with product line breadth, firms occasionally either add to or delete from their product line depth.

Increase Depth   Firms may add new products within a line to address changing consumer preferences or pre-empt competitors while boosting sales. In 2003, Levi-Strauss introduced its Signature line of low-cost jeans to be sold through Wal-Mart. The Signature line is priced at only $21 to $23 a pair, almost half the price of the popular Levi's 505 and 501 brands (the "red tab" line) sold through department stores.[12] The firm's decision was an attempt to get a much-needed sales boost in the face of tough competition from the likes of Diesel and Parasuco and reach new target markets by selling through other retailers. A firm may also add new products to its product line in order to serve new target segments. For instance, Seiko developed the Seiko LaSalle watch for a lower market segment who wants to wear a Seiko watch but cannot afford its luxury brand.

Decrease Depth   From time to time it is necessary to delete product categories to realign resources. The decision to delete products is never taken lightly. Generally, substantial investments have been made to develop the brand and manufacture the products. Consumer goods firms, such as Procter & Gamble and Unilever, make

Do you really need 450 hp to pick up diapers?
You ever run out of diapers?

The Cayenne Turbo

Porsche increased its product mix breadth by adding the Cayenne SUV. It was a natural extension since 40 percent of Porsche sports car owners were buying SUVs as their second car.

pruning decisions regularly to eliminate unprofitable items and refocus their marketing efforts on more profitable items. For example, when executives at consumer goods giant Unilever noted flat sales and declining profits in 1999, they recognized they were carrying a lot of excess baggage. The company took decisive action to divest in 400 core brands, like Ragu pasta sauces, and reduce its portfolio of 1600 brands. This move made Unilever more competitive with rivals like Procter & Gamble and freed up resources for future acquisitions, such as Ben & Jerry's Homemade Ice Cream.[13]

Change Number of SKUs

A very common and ongoing activity for many firms is the addition or deletion of SKUs in existing categories to stimulate sales or react to consumer demand. Fashion manufacturers and their retailers, for instance, change their SKUs every season. Generally, these changes are minor, such as a different colour or fabric. Sometimes though, the change is more drastic, such as when jeans manufacturers lowered the waistline and flared the legs of their products.

Product Line Decisions for Services

Many of the strategies used to make product line decisions for physical products can also be applied to services. For instance, a service provider like a bank typically offers different product lines for its business and retail (consumer) accounts; those product lines are further divided into categories based on the needs of different target markets.

On the retail side, banks offer savings and chequing accounts to individual consumers. The different types of accounts thus are equivalent to SKUs. The Royal Bank of Canada (RBC) is Canada's largest bank as measured by assets and serves more than 14 million personal, business, public sector, and institutional clients through offices in North America and 34 countries around the world.[14] It offers a variety of chequing account products to meet the needs of its different target markets. For example, the RBC VIP account has high monthly fees and offers an all inclusive package covering multiple accounts, unlimited transactions and a free premium Visa card. Students can take advantage of an RBC No Limit Banking for Students account with unlimited debits, a no fee credit card, and moderate monthly fees. For customers who use fewer than 15 transactions per month, the RBC Day to Day Banking account offers very low monthly fees. Seniors benefit from 25 percent off monthly banking fees on all accounts.[15]

Branding

Branding provides a way for a firm to differentiate its product offerings from those of its competitors and can be used to represent the name of a firm and its entire product assortment (General Motors), one product line (Chevrolet), or a single item (Corvette). Brand names, logos, symbols, characters, slogans, jingles, and even distinctive packages constitute the various brand elements firms use,[16] which they usually choose to be easy for consumers to recognize and remember. For example, most consumers are aware of the Nike Swoosh logo and would recognize it even if the word "Nike" did not appear on the product or in an advertisement. Exhibit 9.2 summarizes these brand elements.

LO ❷ ### Value of Branding for the Customer and the Marketer

Brands add value to merchandise and services beyond physical and functional characteristics or the pure act of performing the service.[17] Let's examine some ways in which brands add value for both customers and the firm. (See Exhibit 9.3.)

EXHIBIT 9.2	What Makes a Brand?
Brand Element	**Description**
Brand name	The spoken component of branding, it can either describe the product or service/product characteristics and/or be composed of words invented or derived from colloquial or contemporary language. Examples include Comfort Inn (suggests product characteristics), Saturn (no association with the product), or Accenture (invented term).
URLs (uniform resource locators) or domain names	The location of pages on the Internet, which often substitutes for the firm's name, such as Yahoo! and Amazon.
Logos and symbols	Logos are visual branding elements that stand for corporate names or trademarks. Symbols are logos without words. Examples include the Nike Swoosh and the Mercedes star.
Characters	Brand symbols that could be human, animal, or animated. Examples include the Pillsbury Doughboy and the Jolly Green Giant.
Slogans	Short phrases used to describe the brand or persuade consumers about some characteristics of the brand. Examples include State Farm's "Like A Good Neighbour" and Tim Hortons "Always Fresh."
Jingles	Audio messages about the brand that are composed of words or distinctive music. Examples are Intel's four-note sound signature that accompanies the "Intel Inside" slogan.

Adapted from: Kevin Lane Keller, *Strategic Brand Management*, 2d ed. (Upper Saddle River, NJ: Prentice Hall, 2003).

Brands Facilitate Purchasing　Brands are often easily recognized by consumers and, because they signify a certain quality level and contain familiar attributes, brands help consumers make quick decisions.[18] Imagine how much time it would take to buy groceries if there were no recognizable brands on the shelves! This would also be the case for purchases such as cars. When consumers see a brand like Honda, they immediately know what it is, its level of quality and engineering, its relative status, how much it generally costs, and, most important, whether they like it and want to buy it. Brands enable customers to differentiate one firm or product from another. Without branding, how could we easily tell the difference between a Honda and a Toyota without looking very closely?

Brands Establish Loyalty　Over time and with continued use, consumers learn to trust certain brands. They know, for instance, that Band-Aid bandages always perform in the exact same way. Many customers become loyal to certain brands in much the same way that you or your friends likely have become loyal to your college or university. They wouldn't consider switching brands and, in some cases, feel a strong affinity to certain brands. For instance, Coca-Cola drinkers don't drink Pepsi, and wouldn't touch a Dr Pepper.

Brands Protect from Competition and Price Competition　Strong brands are somewhat protected from competition and price competition. Because such brands are more established in the market and have a more loyal customer base, neither competitive pressures on price nor retail-level competition is as threatening to the firm. For instance, Chemise Lacoste is known for its polo shirts. Although many similar brands are available and some retailers offer their

EXHIBIT 9.3　Value of Branding

The fact that consumers are familiar with Lululemon as a brand helps the company reduce marketing costs.

own brands, Lacoste is perceived to be of superior quality, garners a certain status among its users, and can therefore command a premium price.

Brands Reduce Marketing Costs   Firms with well-known brands can spend relatively less on marketing costs than firms with little-known brands because the brand sells itself. People have become familiar with Lululemon's white stylized "A" logo, so its advertisements don't need to explain who the company is or what it does. People just know.

Brands are Assets   Brands are also assets that can be legally protected through trademarks and copyrights and thus constitute a unique ownership for the firm. Firms sometimes have to fight to keep their brands "pure." Rolex and other Swiss watch companies are ever watchful to ensure that the value of their brands is not diluted with counterfeit merchandise or sales through unauthorized dealers.

Brands Impact Market Value   Having well-known brands can have a direct impact on the company's bottom line. The value of a brand can be calculated by assessing the earning potential of the brand over the next 12 months;[19] as some examples, Canada's most valuable brands appear in Exhibit 9.4.

Brand Equity

To understand branding, we look at three areas: brand equity, brand ownership, and brand names as illustrated in Exhibit 9.5 on page 246. The value of a brand translates into **brand equity**, or the set of assets and liabilities linked to a brand that add to or subtract from the value provided by the product or service.[20] Coca-Cola ranks number one on the best global brands list with a value of $67 billion while McDonald's is ninth with a value of just over $27 billion.[21] Like the physical possessions of a firm, brands are assets the firm can build, manage, and harness over time to increase its

brand equity
The set of assets and liabilities linked to a brand that add to or subtract from the value provided by the product or service.

EXHIBIT	9.4	Canada's 10 Most Valuable Brands	
Rank	**Brand**	**Sector**	**2006 Brand Value-CAD$M**
1	RBC Financial Group	Banks/Financial Services	3,989.6
2	TD Canada Trust	Banks/Financial Services	3,167.9
3	Petro-Canada	Energy	3,064.0
4	Bell	Telecom	2,914.9
5	Shoppers Drug Mart	Retail	2,830.6
6	Tim Hortons	Restaurant	1,878.2
7	BMO Financial Group	Banks/Financial Services	1,854.6
8	Canadian Tire	Retail	1,634.2
9	Scotiabank	Banks/Financial Services	1,378.7
10	Telus	Telecom	1,079.3

Source: The Business Week/Interbrand Annual Ranking of the 2006 Best Global Brands, http://www.ourfishbowl.com/images/surveys/Interbrand_BCB2006.pdf

Ingeniously designed to help protect the things that need protecting.

 At Honda, we continue to show our commitment to "Safety for Everyone" by developing new technologies designed to help protect you and your family in the event of an accident. Regardless of the size or price of your Honda.* By studying the dynamics of collisions between vehicles, our engineers created the

ACE helps absorb frontal-collision energy.

Advanced Compatibility Engineering™ (ACE™) body structure. It's a unique design that helps spread the energy of a frontal collision throughout the body. ACE is only from Honda and comes standard on the all-new Civic. In the future, ACE will come standard on many of our models as they evolve. After all, we made a promise to help keep all of our drivers and passengers safe.

Safety for Everyone. **HONDA**
The Power of Dreams

*Does not include specialty vehicles: Honda Insight, Honda S2000 and Acura NSX. © 2005 American Honda Motor Co., Inc. safety.honda.com

---

revenue, profitability, and overall value. Firms spend millions of dollars on promotion, advertising, and other marketing efforts throughout a brand's life cycle. These marketing expenditures, if done carefully, result in greater brand recognition, awareness, and consumer loyalty for the brand.

Polo/Ralph Lauren has mastered the art of building brand equity by defining its own version of value. The name Polo/Ralph Lauren, the ubiquitous polo player, and associated brands like Polo/Ralph Lauren Purple Label, RLX, and Polo Jeans Co. have engendered a loyal following throughout North America and the rest of the world. Ralph Lauren merchandise can command prices 50 to 100 percent higher than similar-quality merchandise from lesser known and appreciated designers and manufacturers. The brand, under the tight control of its parent company, has been licensed for tabletop, bed and bath, furniture, paints, broadloom, and gift items.[22] These licensed products are manufactured and distributed by firms other than Polo/Ralph Lauren, but the brand association earns them greater value.

How do we know how "good" a brand is, or how much equity it has? Experts look at four aspects of a brand to determine its equity: brand awareness, perceived value, brand associations, and brand loyalty.

Brand Awareness   **Brand awareness** measures how many consumers in a market are familiar with the brand and what it stands for, and have an opinion about that brand. The more aware or familiar customers are with a brand, the easier their decision-making process will be. Familiarity matters most for products that are bought without much thought, such as soap or chewing gum. However, brand awareness

When customers see an ad for Honda, they immediately make associations with familiar attributes, like safety, to help them make quick decisions.

brand awareness
Measures how many consumers in a market are familiar with the brand and what it stands for; created through repeated exposures of the various brand elements (brand name, logo, symbol, character, packaging, or slogan) in the firm's communications to consumers.

| EXHIBIT | 9.5 | Brand Overview |

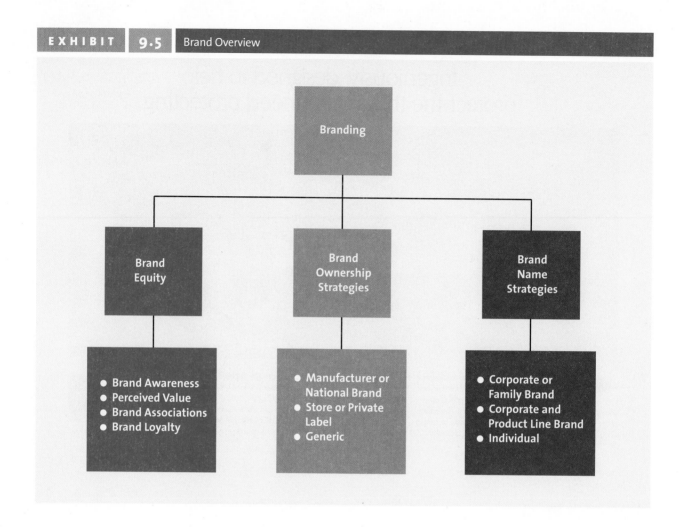

Branding

Brand Equity
- Brand Awareness
- Perceived Value
- Brand Associations
- Brand Loyalty

Brand Ownership Strategies
- Manufacturer or National Brand
- Store or Private Label
- Generic

Brand Name Strategies
- Corporate or Family Brand
- Corporate and Product Line Brand
- Individual

These brands have such predominance in their product market that the brand name is used as the generic product category.

is also important for infrequently purchased items or items the consumer has never purchased before. If the consumer recognizes the brand, it probably has attributes that make it valuable.[23] For those who have never purchased a Toyota, for instance, just being aware of the brand can help facilitate a purchase. Certain brands gain such predominance in a particular product market over time that they become synonymous with the product itself; that is, the brand name starts being used as the generic product category. Examples include Kleenex tissue, Clorox bleach, Xerox copiers, Band-Aid adhesive bandages, and Rollerblade skates. Companies must be vigilant in protecting their brand names, because if they are used so generically, over time, the brand itself can lose its trademark status. Thermos, trampoline, linoleum, and yoyo are all examples of brands that lost their trademark status. Aspirin has become a generic brand in the U.S.; however remains a registered trademark in Canada.[24]

Marketers create brand awareness through repeated exposures of the various brand elements (brand name, logo, symbol, character, packaging, or slogan) in the firm's communications to consumers. Such communication media include advertising and

promotions, personal selling, sponsorship and event marketing, publicity, and public relations[25] (see Chapters 15 and 16). Because consumer awareness is one of the most important steps in creating a strong brand, firms are willing to spend tremendous amounts of money advertising the brand, including more than $2.5 million for just one 30-second spot on television during the Super Bowl.

First Choice Haircutters, a national haircutting chain, provides its customers with great value because the haircut is better than good and the price is more than reasonable.

Perceived Value Brand awareness alone does not ensure a strong brand. Consumers could be aware of a brand but have a negative opinion of its value or of the firm's reputation. **Perceived value**, therefore, is the relationship between a product or service's benefits and its cost. Customers usually determine the offering's value in relationship to that of its close competitors. If they feel an inexpensive brand is about the same quality as a premium brand, the perceived value of the cheaper choice is high.

perceived value
The relationship between a product or service's benefits and its cost.

Good marketing raises customers' quality perceptions relative to price; thus, it increases perceived value. Many customers tend to associate higher prices with higher quality, but they also have become more informed and perceptive in recent years. Retailers like Zellers and Giant Tiger specialize in providing great value. Certainly, merchandise at these stores is not always of the highest possible quality, and the apparel is not the most fashion-forward. But customers don't necessarily want to buy a wastebasket or paring knife that will last for 50 years and be suitable for display in a living room, nor do they need to show up at school looking like they came from a fashion-show runway. Instead, they want products to do what they were designed to do and be available at a reasonable price. First Choice Haircutters, a national haircutting chain, provides "affordable, professional haircare"—usually at one-half to one-third salon prices. Its customers perceive the chain to be a great value because the haircut is better than good and the price is more than reasonable.

Brand Associations **Brand associations** reflect the mental links that consumers make between a brand and its key product attributes, such as a logo, slogan, or famous personality. These brand associations often result from a firm's advertising and promotion efforts. For example, Wal-Mart conveys its low prices with advertising that stresses price cuts and the slogan "Always Low Prices." Associations with specific attributes help create differentiation between the brand and its competitors, as when Volvo stresses that its cars are made with consumer safety in mind. Firms also attempt to create specific associations for their brands with positive consumer emotions, such as fun, friendship, good feelings, family gatherings, and parties. As mentioned in the opening vignette, the Dove brand image has always been associated with moisture and mildness.

brand associaition
The mental links that consumers make between a brand and its key product attributes; can involve a logo, slogan, or famous personality.

Firms sometimes even develop a personality for their brands, as if the brand were human. **Brand personality** refers to such a set of human characteristics associated with a brand,[26] which has symbolic or self-expressive meanings for consumers.[27] Brand personality elements include male, female, young, old, fun-loving, and conservative, as well as qualities such as fresh, smooth, round, clean, or floral.[28] McDonald's has created a fun-loving, youth-oriented brand personality with its golden arches, brightly lit and coloured restaurants, exciting and youthful packaging and advertising, and spokesperson and mascot Ronald McDonald, the clown.

brand personality
Refers to a set of human characteristics associated with a brand, which has symbolic or self-expressive meanings for consumers.

Dove rewards consumers for their loyalty with double points at Shoppers Drug Mart.

brand loyalty
Occurs when a consumer buys the same brand's product or service repeatedly over time rather than buying from multiple suppliers within the same category.

Brand Loyalty   **Brand loyalty** occurs when a consumer buys the same brand's product or service repeatedly over time rather than buying from multiple suppliers within the same category.[29] Therefore, brand-loyal customers are an important source of value for firms. First, such consumers are often less sensitive to price. In return, firms sometimes reward loyal consumers with loyalty or customer relationship management (CRM) programs, such as points customers can redeem for extra discounts or free services, advance notice of sale items, and invitations to special events sponsored by the company. Second, the marketing costs of reaching loyal consumers are much lower because the firm does not have to spend money on advertising and promotion campaigns to attract these customers. Loyal consumers simply do not need persuasion or an extra push to buy the firm's brands. Internet Marketing 9.1 illustrates some ways that companies use the Internet to build strong and profitable relationships with customers through strong brands. Third, a high level of brand loyalty insulates the firm from competition because, as we noted in Chapter 2, brand-loyal customers do not switch to competitors' brands, even when provided with a variety of incentives.

Firms can manage brand loyalty through a variety of CRM programs. They create associations and clubs to provide a community feeling among loyal customers,[30] like Harley-Davidson's Harley Owners Group (HOG), which the company formed in 1983 so Harley owners could meet with other owners in their communities. As we described in Chapter 4, more than 1000 HOG chapters worldwide host a total of almost 1 million members. Other firms, like airlines, hotels, long-distance telephone providers, credit card companies, and retailers, have developed frequent buyer/user programs to reward their loyal customers. The better CRM programs attempt to maintain some continuous contact with loyal customers by sending them birthday cards or having a personal sales associate contact them to inform them of special events and sales.

Adding Value 9.1 on page 250 illustrates some of the difficulties in building and protecting a brand.

LO ❸ Branding Strategies

Firms institute a variety of brand-related strategies to create and manage key brand assets, such as the decision to own the brands, establishing a branding policy, extending the brand name to other products and markets, cooperatively using the brand name with that of another firm, and licensing the brand to other firms.

Brand Ownership

manufacturer brands (national brands)
Brands owned and managed by the manufacturer.

Brands can be owned by any firm in the supply chain, whether manufacturers, wholesalers, or retailers. There are three basic brand ownership strategies: manufacturer or national brands, private label or store brands, and generic brands. (See Exhibit 9.6.) **Manufacturer brands** are owned and managed by the manufacturer, are also known as **national brands**, and include Nike, Mountain Dew, KitchenAid, and Marriott. The majority of the brands marketed in Canada are manufacturer brands. Manufacturing firms spend millions of dollars each year to promote their brands. For example, Procter & Gamble spends about $100 million in media expenditures annually to promote its Tide brand of liquid and powdered detergents.[31] By owning their brands, manufacturers retain more control over their marketing strategy, are able to choose the appropriate market segments and positioning for the brand, and can build the brand and thereby create their own brand equity.

Internet Marketing 9.1 Branding on the Net

For marketers, the Internet is more than just the information highway or a place to transact with customers; it is the ultimate channel for branding the company and its products. Marketers use the Internet to:

- Create awareness and hype for new brands or marketing campaigns,
- Teach consumers more about the company and their products,
- Educate them as to which products best suit their needs,
- Help customers decide which products to buy by giving them tools to help them compare price, features, and quality,
- Encourage sampling of their brands, and
- Project a positive image of the brand to consumers.

In short, marketers use the Internet to build strong, lasting, and profitable relationships with customers through strong brands. But how do they actually use the Internet to do this?

Savvy marketers rely on a wide array of online tools and strategies to build strong brands. Interactive websites that allow customers to play games, contests or quizzes, chat, and share their experiences are provided not just for fun but also to build consumer trust and develop positive associations with the brand. Sounds, music, shapes, colours, images of people, places, products and packaging, plus the overall look and feel of the website affect our mood and attitude. Marketing research has shown that customers who have a very positive attitude toward a site

and brand are more likely to shop at the site or purchase the brand. Some may even spread positive word of mouth with no incentives from the company. This is precisely how eBay has built its brand reputation.

Many companies use many of the techniques mentioned above to reinforce their brand. Nike (www.nike.com) uses rock music along with a dark background and combines ordinary people and celebrities to reinforce its brand message—Just do it! For example, on the Nike Women website (www.nike.com/nikewomen/) choreographer Jamie King teaches women all the moves for a perfect Caribbean workout. Barbie (www.barbie.ca) uses music, colours, and a variety of interactive features targeted at tween girls to get them to play and learn more about Barbie and related products. Abercrombie and Fitch (www.abercrombie.ca) uses black and white images of its well sculpted male and beautiful female models to reinforce its brand of casual luxury targeted to good looking young people. Many high fashion websites such as Christian Dior (www.dior.com) have developed very artistic and appealing websites that speak of sophistication and exclusivity, which is consistent with their brand perception in the marketplace. Gillette's Venus website (www.gillettevenus.com) uses soft, feminine colours, interactive features and product displays consistent with their brand message—reveal the Goddess in you. Many visitors to these websites develop strong emotional attachments and report feelings of happiness and satisfaction with their experiences on the sites.

EXHIBIT 9.6 Brand Ownership Strategies

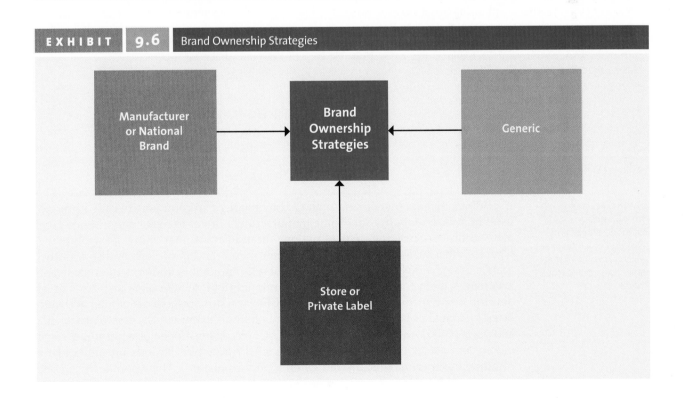

Adding Value

9.1 Ambush Marketing Threatens 2010 Winter Games

The Olympic brand is one of the world's most valuable and recognizable brands; it brings huge economic value added to cities that host the Olympics and companies that sponsor the Olympic Games. The Olympic Games are an international forum for athleticism. Every four years a new city hosts the Winter Games, and well before the athletes arrive or tickets are sold, a new brand must be created, promoted, strengthened, and protected by the hosting city. This is vital to the success of fundraising for the massive endeavour. Sponsoring companies expect to derive substantial benefits from their sponsorship money.

When Vancouver first announced its Olympic Games' bid, some criticisms were voiced. Anti-Olympic groups in Vancouver stressed that spending in preparation for the Olympic Games was a contradiction to reduced spending on social, health, and education programs.[32] Critics said that the costs and benefits had not been properly analyzed. Many feared that Vancouver would be portrayed in a negative light, focusing on its increasing homelessness and traffic congestion.[33]

Despite the critics, Vancouver was awarded the bid. The task at hand is for the Vancouver Organizing Committee (VANOC) to develop and strengthen the 2010 Winter Games Olympic Brand. Multiple brands have been created consisting of the names, phrases, marks, logos, and designs relating to the Olympic Movement and the 2010 Olympic and Paralympic Winter Games and even the furry mascots: Quatchi, a sasquatch, the sea-bear Miga, and Sumi, a spirit animal that flies.

For the upcoming Games the VANOC has chosen images featuring the breathtaking coast, forests, and mountain peaks in Vancouver. The abstract artistry and digital elements are meant to represent Canada's modern cities and leading-edge technology and innovation. These branding elements will help portray Vancouver in a positive and inviting way, adding value to the brand by promoting natural beauty and cultural heritage.[34]

So how do you protect such a high profile brand? By eliminating ambush marketing: when businesses intentionally, or inadvertently, exploit the goodwill of the brand.

The 2010 Olympic Games in Vancouver results in the creation of multiple brands including furry mascots Quatchi, Miga, and Sumi.

For example, retailers could infer they are official sponsors by setting up an Olympic display in their store window. Consumers may think the company is a legitimate sponsor and choose to patronize the store, believing they are supporting the Olympic Games and Canadian athletes. A team is in place at VANOC to monitor inappropriate use of the 2010 Winter Games' brand and enforce its proper use.[35] As well, new legislation is being considered that would make it easier to prevent ambush marketing by reducing the evidence required to prove it.[36]

Protecting the Olympic brand is important because the brand generates significant revenues that are essential in helping to offset the great cost of hosting and staging the 2010 Winter Games. Developing a strong brand increases the value that sponsors receive. This is important to all Canadians as it helps bring income to Canadian athletes and ensures the success of the Olympic Games in the world's view.

For more information on how the Olympic brand is protected see www.vancouver2010.com/en/LookVancouver2010/ProtectingBrand/OlympicBrandFAQs.

---

private-label brands (store brands)
Brands developed and marketed by a retailer and available only from that retailer; also called *store brands.*

Brands that are owned and managed by retailers, in contrast, are called **private-label** brands or **store brands**. Some manufacturers prefer to make only private-label merchandise because the costs of national branding and marketing are prohibitive, whereas other firms manufacture both their own brand and merchandise for other brands or retailers. For instance, Whirlpool sells appliances under its own name and also makes them for Sears under the Kenmore brand. Wholesalers also sometimes develop private-label brands. President's Choice, a private label developed and marketed by Canada's largest food distributor, Loblaw, is extremely successful in Canada and parts of the United States.[37] President's Choice is positioned as a premium, high-quality private label with moderate prices.[38] Private-label brands are particularly common in supermarkets, discount stores, and drug stores. Their popularity among consumers depends on several factors, including consumer preferences for a lower-cost brand and the trust consumers have in the store and its brand. Such private-label brands, especially those marketed by large chains such as Wal-Mart and Costco, are fast gaining in popularity and consumer loyalty. President's Choice Decadent Chocolate Chip Cookies has become Canada's best-selling brand of cookies.[39]

President's Choice, a private label developed and marketed by Canada's largest food distributor, Loblaw Companies, is successfully positioned as a premium, high-quality private label with moderate prices.

Private-label brands have also gained popularity in apparel and other categories found in department and specialty stores. The Bay, for instance, provides several store brands, including Beaumark, Mantles, Truly, and Togo. Specialty retailers, such as The Gap and Victoria's Secret, stock only their own labels and rank among the top 20 most recognized apparel and accessory brands.[40]

Generic products are those sold without brand names, typically in commodities markets. For instance, shoppers can purchase unbranded salt, grains, produce, meat, or nuts in grocery stores. Hardware stores often sell unbranded screws, nuts, and lumber. However, even in these markets, the popularity and acceptance of generic products has declined. Consumers question the quality and origin of the products, and retailers have found better profit potential and the ability to build brand equity with manufacturer and store brands. For example, many fruits and vegetables sold through supermarket chains now carry either the manufacturer's brand name (e.g., Dole bananas) or the store's.

generic
A product sold without a brand name, typically in commodities markets.

Naming Brands and Product Lines

Firms use several very different strategies to name their brands and product lines. (See Exhibit 9.7.)

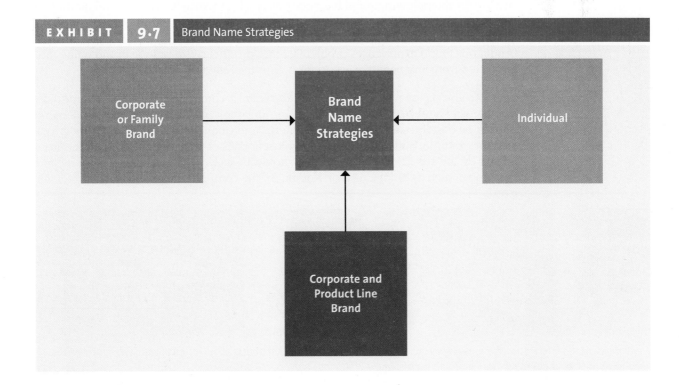

EXHIBIT	9.7	Brand Name Strategies

Corporate or Family Brand → Brand Name Strategies ← Individual

Corporate and Product Line Brand ↑ Brand Name Strategies

imagination at work

Corporate or Family Brand A firm can use its own corporate name to brand all its product lines and products, such as the General Electric Company (GE), which brands its appliances prominently with the GE brand name. Similarly, all products sold through The Gap stores (Gap, GapKids, babyGap, GapMaternity, GapBody) bear only The Gap brand name. When all products are sold under one **corporate brand** or **family brand**, the individual brands benefit from the overall brand awareness associated with the family name.

Corporate and Product Line Brands A firm also could use combinations of the **corporate and product line brands** to distinguish its products. For example, Kellogg's uses its family brand name prominently on its cereal brands (e.g., Corn Flakes, Froot Loops, Rice Krispies) helping to maintain its powerhouse status on grocery store shelves. In other cases, the individual brand's name is more prominently displayed on the package than the Kellogg's name, as in the case of Pop-Tarts, Eggo, and Nutri-Grain. In addition, Kellogg's owns non-cereal and breakfast food brands, such as Cheez-It and Famous Amos, that are not overtly associated with the family brand.

Individual Brands A firm can use **individual brand** names for each of its products. For example, in its house and home products line, Procter & Gamble markets various detergent products (Tide, Gain, Cheer, Downy, Febreze), paper products (Bounty, Charmin), household cleaners (Mr. Clean, Swiffer), and dishwashing products (Cascade, Dawn, Joy). Furthermore, it markets brands in various other product lines, such as personal and beauty products (Olay, Old Spice, Secret, Cover Girl), health and wellness products (Pepto Bismol, Oral B, Puffs), baby products (Pampers, Luvs), and pet nutrition and care products (Iams).[41] Similarly, Loblaw operates across Canada under the following brands: Atlantic Superstore, Dominion, Extra Foods, Fortinos, Loblaws, Maxi, No Frills, Provigo, Your Independent Grocer, and Zehrs. Sobeys operates under the following retail banners: Sobeys, IGA Extra, IGA, Foodland, and Price Chopper. Individual brands allow a company to compete within one category, for example, laundry detergent, offering a variety of products to different target markets. And if one brand experiences problems, other products with unique brand names are protected from any negative association with the failed brand.

Choosing a Name What's in a name? When it comes to naming new products, companies should consider the following desirable qualities: 1) The brand name should be descriptive, suggestive of benefits and qualities associated with the product, for example, Sunkist. The name evokes images of oranges ripening on the trees kissed by the sun. 2) The brand name should be easy to pronounce, recognize, and remember such as Tide, Crest, or Kodak. 3) The company should be able to register

Depending on the brand, sometimes Kellogg's uses its family brand name prominently on its cereal brands, while other times the individual brand's name is more prominently displayed on the package.

the brand name as a trademark and legally protect it. 4) For companies looking to global markets, the brand name should be easy to translate into other languages.

Did you know that Research In Motion bounced around the idea of PocketLink as a name for what later became BlackBerry? While PocketLink was descriptive, RIM wanted something catchier. The company got help from Lexicon Branding, which briefly considered strawberry—the keyboard looked like seeds on a strawberry to them—but discarded it as being too slow a word. BlackBerry rolled off the tongue much faster, used alliteration, was comprised of two short five-letter words, and had an image of being playful and friendly. [42]

Sometimes a change of name is in order. Vancouver's Backwoods Brewery had been selling its beer to restaurants and bars for nearly a decade when it decided to rebrand as Dead Frog. Competing against whacky wine names like Fat Bastard and Cat's Pee on a Gooseberry Bush, beer marketing had been pretty conservative. The company wanted a memorable but irreverent name that would appeal to a younger audience. [43]

Brand Extension

A **brand extension** refers to the use of the same brand name for new products being introduced to the same or new markets.[44] The dental hygiene market, for instance, is full of brand extensions; Colgate, Crest, and Butler all sell toothpaste, toothbrushes, and other dental hygiene products. Roots has extended its brand from athletic clothing to leather bags, yoga wear and accessories, and even a line of baby clothes. Brand extensions are also common in global expansions. For example, Coca-Cola, Nike, and Levi's are sold the world over under the same name. In some cases, firms use the same wording and lettering in their logos when extending their brands globally.

There are several advantages to using the same brand name for new products. First, because the brand name is already well established, like the Dove example discussed in the opening vignette, the firm can spend less in developing consumer brand awareness and brand associations for the new product.[45] Gillette's Braun brand started selling kitchen appliances (coffeemakers, toasters, food processors, blenders, juicers), then extended into various other product categories, including shaving (dry razors, beard care), beauty care products (cordless hair stylers), oral care products (power toothbrushes), and steam irons.[46]

Second, if the brand is known for its high quality, that perception will carry over to the new product. Following its success in the PC market, Dell extended its brand name to monitors, printers, handheld computers, digital juke boxes, LCD televisions, servers, and network switches, among other products.[47]

Third, the marketing costs for a new product by an established brand are lower because consumers already know and understand the brand. Moreover, consumers who have adopted the core brand are more likely to try the extension.

Fourth, when brand extensions are used for complementary products, a synergy exists between the two products that can increase overall sales. For example, Frito-Lay markets both chips and dips under its Frito-Lay and Doritos brand names.[48] When people buy the chips, they tend to buy the dips as well.

Fifth, successful brand extensions can result in cross category trial and boost sales because adopters of the new extended brand may try other products in the brand family they are not

brand extension
The use of the same brand name for new products being introduced to the same or new markets.

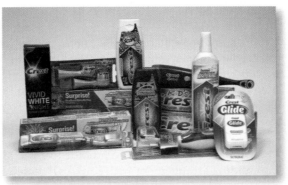

Crest uses a brand extension strategy since they use the same brand name for many related products.

already using. For example, consumers who had not used the Neutrogena brand before trying the Neutrogena On-the-Spot Acne Patch might be encouraged to try Neutrogena moisturizing lotion, especially if their experience with the acne patch has been positive.[49]

Not all brand extensions are successful, however. Some can dilute brand equity.[50] **Brand dilution** occurs when the brand extension adversely affects consumer perceptions about the attributes the core brand is believed to hold.[51] For example, Cadbury's association with fine chocolates and candy was weakened when the company extended its brand name to mainstream food products such as mashed potatoes and soups.[52] If the brand extension is very similar to the core brand, it even could cause cannibalization of sales from the core brand. Entrepreneurial Marketing 9.1 examines the rise and extension of Sir Richard Branson's brand, Virgin.

To prevent the potentially negative consequences of brand extensions, firms must consider the following caveats:

brand dilution
Occurs when a brand extension adversely affects consumer perceptions about the attributes the core brand is believed to hold.

- Marketers should carefully evaluate the fit between the product class of the core brand and that of the extension.[53] If the fit between the product categories is high, consumers will consider the extension credible, and the brand association will be stronger for the extension.

- Firms should carefully evaluate consumer perceptions of the attributes of the core brand and seek out similar attributes for the extension because brand-specific associations are very important for extensions.[54] For example, if HP printers were associated with reliability, performance, and value, consumers would expect the same brand-specific attributes in other products that carried the HP brand name.

- Firms should refrain from extending the brand name to too many products and product categories to avoid diluting the brand and damaging brand equity.

- Firms should consider whether the brand extension will be distanced from the core brand, especially if the firm wants to use some but not all of the existing brand associations. When Marriott introduced its budget line of hotels, it downplayed the Marriott name, calling the new chain Fairfield Inn. And did you even know that Marriott International owns 99 percent of the Ritz-Carlton chain of luxury hotels? Not many people do, and that ignorance is by the company's design. The information is buried on the Ritz-Carlton's Web page.[55]

Cobranding

cobranding
The practice of marketing two or more brands together, on the same package or promotion.

Cobranding is the practice of marketing two or more brands together, on the same package or promotion. Primarily due to credit card companies, such as Visa and MasterCard, the practice has greatly increased in the past decade. Airlines were among the first to cobrand with credit card companies (such as the CIBC Aeroplan Visa Card), but recently, firms in other industries, such as banking, retail, and restaurants, have begun forming similar alliances resulting in cards like BMO Mosaic MasterCard, TD Gold Visa, and President's Choice MasterCard to name a few. Starbucks was the first in the quick-service restaurant industry to offer its own Starbucks credit card in alliance with Visa.[56]

Cobranding enhances consumers' perceptions of product quality[57] by signalling otherwise unobservable product quality through links between the firm's brand and a well-known quality brand. For example, NutraSweet's claim to be a sugar substitute that was safe and left no aftertaste got a boost after both Coca-Cola and Pepsi started offering products that contained it. The cobranding of Intel, with its "Intel Inside" logo, helped boost the brand reputations of PC manufacturers that chose to use Intel chips.

Cobranding can also be a prelude to an acquisition strategy. FedEx entered into a cobranding arrangement with Kinko's, whereby it provided FedEx delivery services

Entrepreneurial Marketing

9.1 | Exploring Virgin Territories

Sir Richard Branson's first business venture was a magazine called *Student*, launched in 1968 when he was only 17.[58] Two years later, he started a mail-order record company called Virgin, but the business was adversely affected by a postal strike the very next year. He then opened his first Virgin record store, followed by a recording studio and a record label. In 1984, Branson started Virgin Atlantic Airways. The Virgin label can now be found on a broad array of product categories and markets, including health clubs (Virgin Active), book publishing (Virgin Books), travel and tourism (Virgin Holidays, Virgin Express, Virgin Limobike, Virgin Trains), cell phones (Virgin Mobile), and cosmetics (Virgin Cosmetics), to name a few. These product categories currently enjoy group sales of over $8 billion and maintain approximately 35,000 employees.[59]

The Virgin name has been placed on products and product categories far removed from its core businesses: air travel and music stores (the firm sold its record business to Thorn EMI in 1992). These developments have challenged the conventional wisdom that successful brand extensions must

Sir Richard Branson has successfully extended the Virgin brand beyond its core businesses of air travel and music stores. One of his latest ventures is Virgin Home Loans.

occur in similar product categories. However, Virgin's core emphasis on value has made most of its extensions successful. Some believe that the success of the Virgin brand extensions is due not to the quality of any particular Virgin product but to the characteristics associated with the family brand—being irreverent, entertaining, and unconventional.

Although it may appear that there are no limits to extending the Virgin brand name, the firm has experienced some failures, especially in the alcoholic and cola beverages markets. Its brand of vodka was a failure, and Virgin Cola was never introduced in Canada, failed in the United States, and achieved only a 3-percent market share in the United Kingdom. The primary risk that Virgin runs from extending its brand too far is not being able to satisfy all its customers of all its brands. As long as the customer has a nice flight on Virgin Atlantic, he or she may try Virgin Mobile. But if that same person has a bad experience with his or her cell phone contract, Virgin Atlantic—and the other Virgin brands—may lose a customer forever.

at Kinko's retail outlets.[60] Then in early 2004, FedEx acquired Kinko's for an estimated $2.4 billion and has begun rebranding Kinko's as FedEx Kinko's.[61]

However, there are, of course, some risks to cobranding, especially when customers for each of the brands are vastly different. For example, the Burger King and Häagen-Dazs cobranding strategy failed because the customer profiles for each brand were too different.[62] Cobranding may also fail if the brands' owners cannot resolve financial disputes about revenue or royalty sharing.[63] Finally, the firms that own the brands may change their priorities, as a result of which the cobranded product may no longer be available. In this scenario, the customer relationships and loyalty created with the cobranded product would be lost.[64]

Brand Licensing

Brand licensing is a contractual arrangement between firms, whereby one firm allows another to use its brand name, logo, symbols, and/or characters in exchange for a negotiated fee.[65] Brand licensing is common for toys, apparel, accessories, and entertainment products, such as video games; in the United States, it generates more than $100 billion in retail sales per year.[66] The firm that provides the right to use its brand (licensor) obtains revenues through royalty payments from the firm that has obtained the right to use the brand (licensee). These royalty payments sometimes take the form of an upfront, lump-sum licensing fee or may be based on the dollar value of sales of the licensed merchandise.

brand licensing
A contractual arrangement between firms, whereby one firm allows another to use its brand name, logo, symbols, or characters in exchange for a negotiated fee.

Several aspects of a brand can be licensed. Popular apparel designers, such as Ralph Lauren, Calvin Klein, and Eddie Bauer, and luxury goods manufacturers often license the right to use their brand name on a variety of products. The Porsche name is used by Grundig radios and also appears on watches, luggage sets, and tennis racquets. The computer world has even capitalized on the Porsche brand name with the game *Need for Speed: Porsche Unleashed*. Canadian Tire has built on the growing popularity of NASCAR racing to become the official automotive retailer of NASCAR in Canada.[67] One very popular form of licensing is the use of characters created in books and other media. Such entertainment licensing has generated tremendous revenues for movie studios like Disney, Lucas Films (think of the *Star Wars* memorabilia), and New Line (licensor of *Lord of the Rings* toys and collectibles), as well as for comic book publishers such as Marvel Entertainment Inc. (*Spider-Man*). A long-standing staple of licensing has been major league sports teams that play in the NBA, NFL, or NHL, as well as various collegiate sports teams.

Licensing is an effective form of attracting visibility for the brand and thereby building brand equity while also generating additional revenue. There are, however, some risks associated with it. For the licensor, the major risk is the dilution of its brand equity through overexposure of the brand, especially if the brand name and characters are used inappropriately.[68]

Consider, for instance, the famous—or possibly infamous—alligator shirt. In 1933, the company founded by Frenchman David Lacoste (the licensor), famous as a tennis player and for his nickname "the alligator," entered into a licensing agreement with Andre Gillier (the first licensee) to produce a high-quality, white, knit shirt with a ribbed collar, short sleeves, and a crocodile emblazoned on the left breast. The line expanded to include other casual apparel items, and in 1966, the Lacoste name was licensed to American manufacturer Izod (the second licensee). Alligator-emblazoned apparel could be found in better department stores and country club golf and tennis shops into the late 1980s. But Izod also began to sell the alligator apparel in discount stores, and quality and sales suffered. The alliance continued until 1992, when Lacoste severed its ties with Izod. Lacoste has since regained its prestigious image and can be found in boutiques and exclusive specialty department stores around the world.[69]

Licensors also run the risk of improperly valuing their brand for licensing purposes or entering into the wrong type of licensing arrangement. For example, Marvel Entertainment Inc.'s previous deals with movie studios for the use of its comic book characters were "undervalued," because the firm took lump-sum licensing fees upfront rather than pegging its royalty fees to sales. As a result, the firm probably left money on the table for deals on the first *X-Men* and *Blade* films.[70] In entertainment licensing, both licensors and licensees run the risk that characters based on books and movies will be only a fad. Moreover, the success or failure of merchandise based on movies is directly affected by the success or failure of the movie itself.[71]

The famous tennis player Rene "the alligator" Lacoste (top in 1927 photo) co-founded a firm that made a white, knit shirt, with an alligator emblazoned on the left breast. The brand is still sold today (bottom) at Lacoste boutiques and stores like Neiman Marcus.

Packaging

LO **4**

Packaging is an important brand element with more tangible or physical benefits than the other brand elements because packages come in different types and offer a variety of benefits to consumers, manufacturers, and retailers. Consumers typically seek convenience in terms of storage, use, and consumption.

But packaging also serves to protect products. Wrappers and exterior cartons protect eggs from being broken and help to prevent tampering with products such as toothpaste. Packaging provides the UPC label used by retail scanners as well as contents, directions, and other additional product information. The package can also be an important marketing tool for the manufacturer if it is used to convey the brand's positioning. Cosmetics giant Estée Lauder considers the packaging to be primarily about brand image, so its packages portray a modern, sophisticated look that is immediately recognizable.[72] Packaging is considered by many marketers to be the last frontier in advertising because of its role in promoting products to consumers at the point of purchase. Packaging may also affect consumers' emotions and drive impulse buying. The shapes of fragrance, perfume, and deodorant bottles and containers are good examples of marketers extending the use of packaging beyond a distribution function to encourage purchase and differentiation. Many children also pressure their parents to buy products, like breakfast cereal, more because of the packaging than for the product. In these instances, packaging acts as a point of differentiation and makes consumers feel proud to own the brand.

Coca-Cola's Fridge Packs boosted sale. Consumers were able to store 12 cans in their refrigerators conveniently making it easy to grab a cold drink whenever they wanted one.

Retailers' priorities for packaging, however, differ: They want convenience in terms of displaying and selling the product. For customers, Coca-Cola's Fridge Pack of 12 cans offers a compact shape and convenience when carrying it home and storing it in their refrigerators; for retailers, the packaging offers the means to easily stack the packages on their shelves.

In addition, items may often be packed into larger cartons, pallets, or containers to facilitate shipment and storage from the manufacturer to the retailer. These shipping packages benefit the manufacturer and the retailer in that they protect the shipment during transit; aid in loading, unloading, and storage; and allow cost efficiencies due to the larger order and shipment sizes.

Because packaging is critical to the firm's brand positioning and shelf appeal, many innovations in design and materials have occurred in the past few decades. Some examples include[73]

- **Stand-up, reclosable zipper pouches.** Capri Sun's stand-up pouch juice drink took the lead; now a variety of products and pouch types are available, including pouches with reclosable zippers. You can even buy tuna in a stand-up pouch.
- **Aluminum beverage cans.** First introduced in 1965, cans dominated the beverage market by 1985. Even some water and energy drink brands now are available in aluminum cans.
- **Aseptic drink bottles.** TetraPak and IP provided designs and machinery that increased the shelf life of beverages without refrigeration. They are used primarily by juice marketers but also by some soup companies.
- **Child-resistant/senior-friendly packages.** Products that are harmful to children under the age of five years, such as drugs and medicines, solvents, chemicals, and pesticides, now are packaged with child-resistant tops. Seniors appreciate packages that are light, easy to handle, easy to read, and easy to

Innovative packages can enhance a product's positioning and shelf appeal. Consider: reclosable packages, child-resistant/senior-friendly packages, ring-pull aluminum cans, aseptic drink bottles, and twist-off tops.

open. Responding to consumer feedback, McNeil Consumer Healthcare in Canada developed the E-Z Open cap, a non-child resistant closure specifically targeted to customers with arthritis.[74]

- **Green and biodegradable packaging.** Today's environmentally conscious consumers are demanding less packaging and want to be able to easily recycle it. Vancouver-based Earthcycle launched compostable palm fibre-based packaging for items like takeout food and produce. Palm fibre takes about 90 days to decompose and is being used by Loblaw and Wal-Mart.[75] And Procter & Gamble converted all of its liquid laundry brands (such as Tide, Gain and Cheer) to a concentrated formula in containers half the previous size. Retailers appreciated the storage and shelf-space savings of the smaller packages.[76]

Product Labelling

Labels on products and packages provide information the consumer needs for his or her purchase decision and consumption of the product. In that they identify the product and brand, labels are also an important element of branding and can be used for promotion. The information required on them must comply with general and industry-specific laws and regulations, including the constituents or ingredients contained in the product, where the product was made, directions for use, and/or safety precautions.

Many labelling requirements stem from various laws, including the Competition Act, the Consumer Packaging and Labelling Act and Regulations, the Food and Drugs Act, and the Hazardous Materials Act. Several federal agencies, industry groups, and consumer watchdogs carefully monitor product labels. The Food and Drugs Act regulates the information on food, drugs, and cosmetics package labels. The Consumer Packaging and Labelling Act covers food products and ensures that the claims made by the manufacturer are true and that labels accurately reflect ingredients and quantities. All this has to be done in both of Canada's official languages, French and English.

The label for Dannon Yogurt highlights seven specific benefits.

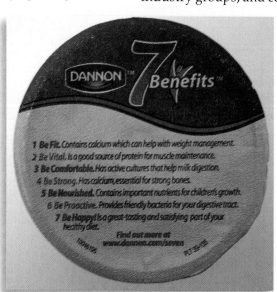

Manufacturers' claims on labels also can be subject to criticisms by various consumer groups. In the United Kingdom, the consumer watchdog group ITC ruled that Danone's Shape yogurt was not "virtually fat free," as its label claimed. The Dairy Industry Federation guidelines state that only products containing less than 0.3 grams of fat per every 100 grams could be called "virtually fat free," but Danone's Shape yogurt contained three times that amount.[77]

Ethical Dilemma 9.1 illustrates some of the problems companies face in promoting the types of ingredients they use in their products, as well as the associated labelling concerns. These concerns are further compounded when the products are sold across international borders.

A product label is much more than just a sticker on the package; it is a communication tool. Many of the elements on the label are required by laws and regulations (i.e., ingredients, fat content, sodium content, serving size, calories), but other elements of the label remain within the control of the manufacturer. How manufacturers use labels to communicate the benefits of their products to consumers varies by the product. For example, the label for Dannon yogurt highlights the fact that yogurt contains calcium. Many other products highlight other specific ingredients, vitamin content, or nutrient content (e.g., iron). This focus signals to consumers that the product offers these benefits. Although often overlooked, the importance of the label as a communication tool should not be underestimated.

Ethical Dilemma   9.1   What's Behind a Seal of Approval?

Today's shoppers want to buy more nutritious foods and avoid those that are unsound. With consumers becoming increasingly focused on healthy eating, many companies have jumped on the bandwagon, putting "seals of approval" on their products. For example, Kraft Foods introduced Sensible Solution, a green flag currently used on over 500 products, promoted as a way for consumers to more easily choose great-tasting foods that are better for them. Smart Spot is PepsiCo's better-for-you signal to consumers. Even restaurants are getting into game, seizing the opportunity to market select menu items as healthy fare. Swiss Chalet promotes the Heart and Stroke Foundation's Health Check symbol on entrees and side dishes that meet the program's nutrient criteria.

But what's in a seal? To bear the Smart Spot symbol, products must meet the following criteria:

- contain at least 10 percent of the Daily Value of a targeted nutrient (i.e., protein, fibre, calcium, iron, vitamin A, vitamin C) and meet limits for fat, saturated fat, trans fat, cholesterol, sodium, and added sugar, or
- are formulated to have specific health or wellness benefits, or
- are reduced in calories or nutrients such as fat, sodium, or sugar.[78]

Sound good? It might until you dig a little deeper. Diet Pepsi sports a Smart Spot label because it has no sugar, no calories, and no carbs. However, nutritionists argue that people should drink juice, water, or milk if they really want to make a healthy choice. Plus there's the matter of the aspartame sweetener to consider. Baked Cheetos get the nod because they have no cholesterol, no trans fats, and are baked. But they are still high in calories (130 calories for 34 Cheetos, 45 of which are from fat) and contain no fibre, vitamins, or minerals.

As for what's cooking in Kraft's kitchens, their Oreo Thinsations are packaged in convenient 100-calorie pack-

Have you seen these better-for-you labels on products in grocery stores? Would you buy Organic Candy Floss?

ages. While they are lower in fat than conventional Oreo cookies, in the end, those 100 calories are still empty and sugary.

Does Swiss Chalet fare any better? Menu items marked with the Health Check symbol appear to be very nutritious and a good choice for consumers who are concerned about their health. However, there are very few menu items that earn the symbol and some, like salads, must be eaten without dressing in order to qualify.

A recent twist to the health labelling trend is seen in companies promoting organic junk food. To some consumers the organic label has become a seal of approval. Yet, are organic Pop Tarts any better for you than regular ones? What about Pure Fun Organic Cotton Candy? Critics claim it's just a way to give health conscious consumers an excuse to eat junk food.[79]

While most of these companies are working hard to provide consumers with healthier choices, you have to question whether these better-for-you labels are just a marketing ploy. What do you think? Are health symbols self-serving or sincere?

Learning Objectives Review

1) Describe how firms adjust their product lines to changing market conditions

2) Understand why brands are valuable to firms

3) Discuss how firms implement different branding strategies

4) Explain how a product's packaging and label contribute to a firm's overall strategy

1) Market conditions change. New opportunities arise, others mature and die. Competition may become more intense or competitors may move on to pursue other opportunities. Firms grow their product lines by adding either new product categories or new SKUs within a product category. The decision to add products should be made carefully. Excessive product line expansions can confuse consumers and dilute the appeal of the brand's core products. Sometimes, products or product lines become unprofitable, the firm's priorities change, or consumer preferences shift. When this happens, firms must prune their product lines by deleting items or possibly even entire product categories.

2) Brands facilitate the consumer search process. Some customers are loyal to certain brands, which essentially protects those brands from competition. In addition, brands are valuable in a legal sense, in that trademarks and copyrights protect firms from counterfeiters and knockoff artists. Firms with well-known brands can spend relatively less on marketing because the brand and its associations help sell the product. Finally, brands have real market value as a company asset.

3) Firms use a variety of strategies to manage their brands. First, they must decide whether to offer national, private-label, or generic brands. Second, they have a choice of using an overall corporate brand or a collection of product line or individual brands. Third, to reach new markets or extend their current market, they can extend their current brands to new products. Fourth, firms can cobrand with another brand to create sales and profit synergies for both. Fifth, firms with strong brands have the opportunity to license their brands to other firms. Sixth and finally, as the marketplace changes, it is often necessary to reposition a brand.

4) Like brands, packaging and labels help sell the product and facilitate its use. The package holds the product, and its label provides product information. The package also provides additional consumer information on its label and facilitates transportation and storage for both retailers and their customers. Labels have become increasingly important to consumers because they supply important safety, nutritional, and product usage information.

Key Terms

- brand, 240
- brand association, 247
- brand awareness, 245
- brand dilution, 254
- brand equity, 244
- brand extension, 253
- brand licensing, 255
- brand loyalty, 248
- brand personality, 247
- category depth, 240

- cobranding, 254
- corporate and product line brands, 252
- corporate brand (family brand), 252
- generic, 251
- individual brands, 252
- manufacturer brands (national brands), 248
- perceived value, 247

- private-label brands (store brands), 250
- product, 238
- product assortment (product mix), 239
- product category, 240
- product line breadth, 240
- product line depth, 240
- product lines, 239
- stock keeping units (SKUs), 240

Concept Review

1. Explain the differences between product mix breadth and product mix depth. Why is understanding this difference important?

2. Explain why branding is important to marketers. What value do customers derive from purchasing and using brand name products?

3. What is brand equity? Describe the strategies marketers could employ to increase the value of their brand equity.

4. Differentiate between a national brand, generic brand, and store brand. Should retailers carry all three types of brands? Why?

5. Describe the desirable qualities companies should consider when choosing product names.

6. What are the advantages of using the same brand name and extending it to new products?

7. Explain how brand licensing differs from co-branding.

8. What is co-branding? When does it make sense for a company to use a co-branding strategy?

9. Explain how marketers increase the value of their product offering through packaging. Discuss the ethical issues surrounding product packaging and labelling? How might some of these issues be resolved?

10. Explain how labelling could be used as a marketing weapon rather than just providing legally required information.

Marketing Applications

1. Prepared foods at Whole Foods Market, the world's largest retailer of organic foods, are very profitable. To make them even more profitable, suggest two strategies that would alter the product mix breadth and depth.

2. Visit a grocery store and look for Colgate Total toothpaste on the shelves. How many different SKUs (include all sizes and flavour variations) are sold at the store? What are the advantages and disadvantages of having so many different variations?

3. Suppose you have just been hired by a jewellery manufacturer as a marketing consultant. The manufacturer has been making private-label jewellery for 75 years but is thinking about developing its own brand of jewellery. Discuss the advantages and disadvantages of such a strategy.

4. Identify a specific brand that has developed a high level of brand equity. What specific aspects of that brand establish its brand equity?

5. Are you loyal to any brands? If so, pick one and explain why you believe you are loyal, beyond that you simply like the brand. If not, pick a brand that you like and explain how you would feel and act differently toward the brand if you were loyal to it.

6. Ford Motor Company owns several brands: Ford, Lincoln, Mercury, Mazda, Volvo, Jaguar, Land Rover, and Aston Martin. Within each brand are many models, each of which has a unique identifying name. Wouldn't it be easier to just identify them all as Fords? Justify your answer.

7. Unlike Ford, BMW has only one brand and gives each car it makes a number instead of a name, for example, the BMW Series 3, Series 5, or Series 7. What are the advantages to BMW of this approach?

8. Identify a specific company that has recently introduced a new brand extension to the marketplace. Discuss whether you believe the brand extension example you provided will benefit or harm the firm.

9. Do you think all food sold in a grocery store should have an ingredient and nutrition label? Consider the perspectives of consumers, the manufacturer, and the store.

10. You are hired by a small bakery that is interested in distributing its product through supermarkets. The market for the bakery's products has been steadily growing and it is time to expand distribution now that the bakery has expanded its production capacity. You have an appointment with the manager of a local grocery chain. The manager is familiar with the bakery's products and is excited about the possibility of having them in the store. He has asked you to come up with a plan to package your products in a way that makes them attractive to shoppers, keeps baked goods fresh, and uses the least amount of packaging possible to satisfy even the most stringent environmentalist. You've never had to deal with this issue before. At the bakery, goods are packed in paper bags after being selected from protective glass displays. Come up with a package that works for the retailer and is affordable for the bakery.

Net Savvy

1. Visit the Procter & Gamble website (www.pg.ca). Identify and briefly describe its different *product lines*. Now identify one of its *product categories*, and discuss the *product line breadth* of that particular category. Be sure to justify your answers.

2. Interbrand Corporation is a leading brand consultancy firm headquartered in New York that conducts research on the monetary value of different brands. Visit the company's website (www.interbrand.com) and access the most recent "Best Global Brands" survey. Identify the top five brands, their brand values, and their countries of origin. Describe changes in the rankings of these firms from the previous year. Why do you think the rankings changed? Identify the brands with the greatest increase and the greatest decrease in terms of percentage change in brand value from the previous year.

Chapter Case Study

BAND-AID® BRAND PRODUCTS:[80] BUILDING ON THE VALUE OF THE BRAND[81]

Part of global giant Johnson & Johnson's Consumer Products Company, Band-Aid® is widely known as a leader in the wound care market. With its dominant share of the market, the brand is widely recognized and respected by consumers and health care professionals alike. Known as an innovator of wound care products, the company continues to introduce new products that exploit creative technologies, one of which led *Good Housekeeping* magazine to name Band-Aid® Brand Liquid Bandage a "Good Buy" award winner. From its early beginnings to today, the company has excelled at providing value to its customers and demonstrated that people across the world can trust the brand.

The Brand Begins

Necessity is the mother of invention, and in the case of Band-Aid® the saying applies. Back in 1920, when Earl Dickson came home from his cotton-buying job at Johnson & Johnson, he would always find a hot meal that his wife Josephine had prepared for him. He also found visible burns and cuts on Josephine from her kitchen labours, which prompted Earl to piece together gauze squares and adhesive tape to cover her wounds. Soon, Earl decided to prepare ready-made bandages in this fashion, with pieces of gauze at intervals along the tape so that Josephine could cut the premade strip and tend to her wounds throughout the day. When the product was first launched in the market, the bandages were made by hand, were not sterile, and had annual sales of just $3000.

The Company Today

Today, Band-Aid® products are machine-made and completely sterile. A visit to the company's website (www.bandaid.com) reveals the distance Band-Aid® has come from the early tape and gauze product, as well as the modern demand for over-the-counter first-aid products in a variety of categories.

In keeping with its long history of product innovations, the company continues to invest in new product development and marketing (Exhibit C9.1). Band-Aids® come in a host of styles, including those with popular characters for kids; uniquely shaped bandages for various parts of the body; antibiotic Band-Aids® to help fight germs; waterproof products with aloe to treat burns; scar-healing strips; bandages in clear plastic, stretchy cloth, and round and square shapes; and treated and untreated pads. Moreover, the Band-Aid® franchise has expanded to include various ointments, gauze, tapes, and kits for a plethora of first-aid needs. For example, One-Step Cleansing + Infection Protection Foam antiseptic cleans and heals wounds without the need for antibiotic ointment; Calamine Spray dries rashes from poison ivy; Bug-Bite Relief Patches relieve itching and prevent scratching; and FIRST AID TO GO!® Mini First-Aid Kits include essential travel-sized products.

EXHIBIT	C9.1	Examples of Band-Aid® Product Innovations

Year	Product Innovation
1920	Band-Aid® brand adhesive bandages—3" wide and 18" long—introduced to the market
1924	First machine-made, sterile bandages
1940	Packaging adds red strings to open bandage packages
1951	Plastic strips
1956	Decorated bandages
1958	Sheer vinyl bandages
1994	Sport-strip bandages
1997	Antibiotic adhesive bandages with ointment on the pad
2000	Advanced healing strips for wound care
2001	Liquid bandage that promotes fast healing
2003	Scar-healing technology that fades red and raised scars

Source: www.bandaid.com.

But new product introductions by Band-Aid® don't come cheap; of the $28-million marketing budget for 2003, $17 million was earmarked for three new product extensions. Advanced Healing Blister Block, a round, waterproof cushioning strip to heal and prevent foot blisters, received $7 million in marketing support to tout its ability to promote fast, natural healing. Finger Care Tough Strips obtained a marketing budget of $5 million and was rolled out as an extension of regular finger care products. Finally, Extra Large Tough Strips were also supported with $5 million for marketing.[82] Previous years' launches were similarly supported, including Liquid Bandages ($7 million), Water Block Bandages ($8 million), and Hurt-Free Antiseptic Wash ($5 million).

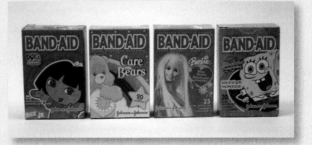

The company is in an enviable position. People around the world see the value of Band-Aid® products to heal, prevent, and repair minor nicks, cuts, scrapes, wounds, and bruises. Continued product innovations and line expansions likely will help the company continue to be the most recognized name in tape, bandages, and gauze.

Band-Aids come in a variety of sizes and styles. These packages are made for children.

Questions

1. Visit the company's website (www.bandaid.com) and identify and describe the different product lines that it markets. How would you describe its product line breadth?

2. Review the different product categories in each of the company's product lines. Which has the greatest breadth? Which has the least?

3. Look at the new products that the company offers. Identify which are extensions of the Band-Aid® brand name and which are not. Discuss the extent to which the brand extensions might dilute brand equity.

4. Review the company's products designed for children. To what extent do these use manufacturer (national) branding? Private-label (store) branding? Licensed branding? Justify your answers. What added value do these products offer compared with regular Band-Aid® protection products?

CHAPTER 10

LEARNING OBJECTIVES

After studying this chapter, you should be able to:

LO 1 Understand how firms create value through innovation

LO 2 Explain the diffusion of innovation theory, and how managers can use it to make product line decisions

LO 3 Describe the process that firms go through to create new products and services

LO 4 Discuss the product life cycle, and how how it is used to make product line decisions

Developing New Products

For 125 years, E. D. Smith has provided Canadian consumers with delicious, high quality jams and spreads. But in order to stay ahead in the highly competitive jam market, they needed to solicit feedback from consumers to make their products even better. Many companies turn to consumer focus groups and survey feedback from customers for this data. But E. D. Smith did even better than that: they went face-to-face with customers in the jam aisle. In co-operation with its research company, they polled over 3000 consumers all across the country to better understand how to improve existing products, and how to market them effectively.

The team feels strongly about talking directly with consumers. Interacting right in the aisle generates more genuine comments, and by talking to shoppers who are about to buy jam, researchers can uncover real insights and help get at what's really on grocery shoppers' minds at the point of purchase. The results are more real and more emotional responses than a survey or questionnaire. And customers get to test the products! On-the-spot taste tests helped the research team at E. D. Smith to learn that most consumers found jams to be far too sweet. Promotional tools were also investigated. Consumers said they were most likely to take advantage of a coupon as a way to try a new product.

Acting on its new research findings, E. D. Smith made big changes to stay competitive. Three new product lines were introduced into the market: reduced sugar jams, triple fruit spreads with reduced sugar, and even a no-sugar added line of Spa-inspired jams.[1] As well, packaging was redesigned to clearly communicate the no-sugar feature. Coupons, at store shelf level, encourage trial of these innovative products. Using the information from the grocery store studies to develop new products has helped E. D. Smith retain its leadership in the jam aisle.

None of these products were available a few years ago.

Imagine living 200 years ago. You cook your meals on a stove fueled by coal or wood. As a student, you do your homework by hand, illuminated only by candlelight. You get to school on foot, by horseback, or in a horse-drawn carriage, if you're really fortunate. Your classroom is small and basic, and you have very few classmates. The professor simply lectures and writes on a chalkboard.

Fast forward to today. You finish your homework on a personal computer with word-processing software that appears to have a mind of its own and can correct your spelling automatically. Your climate-controlled room has ample electric light. While you work on your computer, you can also be talking with a friend using the hands-free headset of your wireless phone. On your way to school, in your car, you pick up fast food from a convenient drive-through window while listening to a mixture of songs recorded recently and more than 40 years ago, which are broadcast through the air from a satellite. When you arrive at university, you sit in a 200-person classroom in which you can plug in your laptop and take notes on your computer while the professor lectures with the aid of PowerPoint presentations.

Our lives are defined by the many new products and services developed through scientific and technological advances and refined either with the help of outside idea generation companies or by firms' internal product development teams. Whereas scientific research opens up the world of ideas, technological research transforms these ideas into interesting and useful services, tangible products, and processes.

This is the second chapter that deals with the first P in the marketing mix: product. (Refer to the chapter roadmap.) Continuing our discussion from the preceding chapter, we explore how companies add value to firms' product and service offerings through innovation in products and services. We also look at the process firms go through to develop new products and services. We conclude the chapter with an examination of how new products and services are adopted by the market and how firms change their marketing mix as the product or service moves through its life cycle.

Innovation and Value

LO

innovation
The process by which ideas are transformed into new products and services that will help firms grow.

Innovation is the process by which ideas are transformed into new products and services that will help firms grow. Without innovation and its resulting new products and services, firms would have only two choices: continue to market current

CHAPTER
ROADMAP

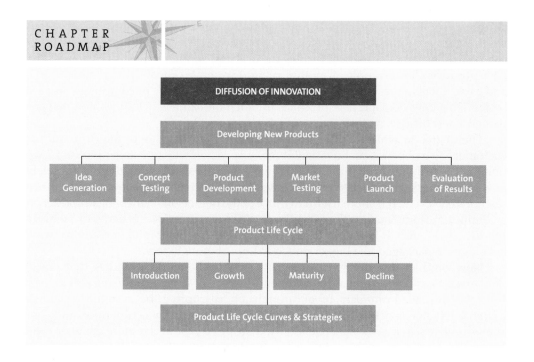

products to current customers or take the same product to another market with similar customers.

Although innovation strategies may not work in the short run, overriding long-term reasons compel firms to introduce new products and services. First, as they add new products to their offerings, firms can create and deliver value more effectively by satisfying the changing needs of their current and new customers or simply by keeping customers from getting bored with the current product or service offering. For example, Unilever's Dove Beauty Bar product line successfully extended the brand into hair, face, and skin care lines, all under the Dove umbrella. Today, Dove loyalists can enjoy not only bar soap but also antiperspirants and deodorants, moisturizing lotions, cleansers, toners, shampoo, conditioner, and much more.[2]

Second, the longer a product exists in the marketplace, the more likely it is that the market will become saturated. Without new products or services, the value of the firm will ultimately decline.[3] Suppose, for instance, that Reebok adopted a strategy of producing the same sneakers year after year. Because many people don't actually wear out their shoes within a year, they would have no incentive to buy new ones. But people tend to get tired of the same old shoes and seek variety.[4] By introducing new lines several times a year, Reebok is able to sustain its growth.

Third, the portfolio of products that innovation can create helps the firm diversify its risk and therefore enhances firm value better than a single product can.[5] If some products in a portfolio are doing poorly, others may be doing well. As we saw in the opening vignette, E.D. Smith has a product portfolio that includes jams and spreads, but it also makes pie fillings, syrup, ketchup, and salsa. Firms with multiple products are better able to withstand external shocks, including changes in consumer preferences or intensive competitive activity. For this reason, firms like 3M demand that a specific

By adding new products, Unilever's Dove brand creates and delivers value more effectively by satisfying the changing needs of its current and new customers or simply by keeping customers from getting bored with its current product offerings.

percentage of their sales each year must come from new products introduced within the previous few years.

Fourth, in some industries, such as the arts and software, most sales come from new products. For example, a motion picture generates most of its theatre, DVD, and cable TV revenues within a year of its release. Consumers of computer software and video games demand new products in much the same way that fashion mavens demand new apparel styles.

The degree to which a new product or service adds value to the firm and for customers also depends on how new it really is. When we say a "new product," we don't necessarily mean that the product has never existed before; these completely new-to-the-market products represent fewer than 10 percent of all new product introductions each year. It is more useful to think of the degree of newness of a product on a continuum from "new-to-the-world"—as WiFi was a few years ago—to "slightly repositioned," such as the repositioning of Kraft's Capri Sun brand of ready-to-drink beverages, repackaged in a bigger pouch to appeal more to teens.

pioneers
New product introductions that establish a completely new market or radically change both the rules of competition and consumer preferences in a market; also called *breakthroughs.*

New product introductions, especially new-to-the-world products that create new markets, can add tremendous value to firms. These new products, services, or processes are called **pioneers**, breakthroughs or "disruptive" because they establish a completely new market or radically change both the rules of competition and consumer preferences in a market.[6] Generally, disruptive products require a higher level of learning from consumers and offer much more benefits than predecessor products (see Exhibit 10.1). For example, consumers have to spend a lot of time learning about the Internet in order to adopt it, but now that they have mastered this, its benefits have changed the way they work, play, and interact with people. On the other hand, Wi-Fi does not require a lot of learning yet offers consumers tremendous flexibility and freedom in the way they work, communicate, and interact—anytime and anywhere once there is a Wi-Fi hot spot or if they subscribe to mobile wireless. Some examples of pioneers include minicomputers, the Intel microprocessor, Canon's desktop photocopiers, Microsoft's Windows operating system, eBay's online auction model, and the PalmPilot.[7]

first movers
Product pioneers that are the first to create a market or product category, making them readily recognizable to consumers and thus establishing a commanding and early market share lead.

Pioneers have the advantage of being **first movers**; as the first to create the market or product category, they become readily recognizable to consumers and thus establish a commanding and early market share lead. As an example, for decades

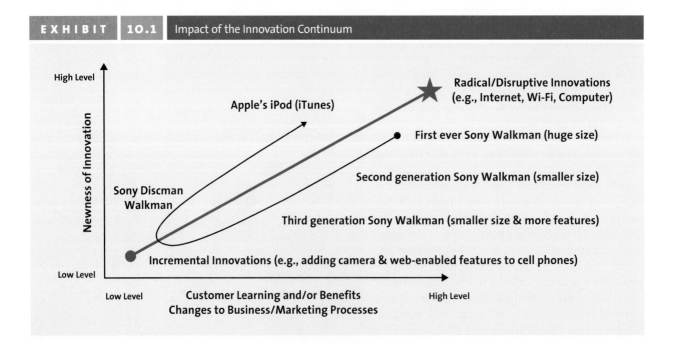

| EXHIBIT | 10.1 | Impact of the Innovation Continuum |

consumers bought and used the Sony Walkman for mobile music, which required them to buy and carry tapes or CDs. Apple's iPod eliminated the need for CDs with its iTunes service—a radically new service associated with a digital mobile device. Freedom and convenience—the ability to carry more than 10,000 songs plus photos and videos and to share these with friends have dramatically changed the concept of mobile music players as first introduced by Sony. Studies also have found that market pioneers can command a greater market share over a longer time period than later entrants can.[8] (Refer back to the opening vignette in Chapter 6, which describes how Apple's iPod has dethroned the Sony Walkman.)

This finding does not imply, however, that all pioneers succeed.[9] In many cases, imitators capitalize on the weaknesses of pioneers and subsequently gain advantage in the market. Because pioneering products and brands face the uphill task of establishing the market alone, they pave the way for followers, which can spend less marketing effort creating demand for the product category and instead focus directly on creating demand for their specific brand. Also, because the pioneer is the first product in the market, it often has a less sophisticated design and may be priced relatively higher, leaving room for better and lower priced competitive products. As the Sony example in Exhibit 10.1 shows, every subsequent generation of the Sony Walkman had increasingly more features but the Apple iPod not only imitated the idea of mobile music, it radically changed the way mobile music is bought, sold and consumed. Even the device—the iPod—offers a revolutionary look and feel compared to the Walkman.

Not all new products succeed in the marketplace. In fact, the majority of new products are failures: As many as 95 percent of all consumer goods fail, and products across all markets and industries suffer failure rates of 50 to 80 percent.[10] Why? There are many reasons but the most common ones include the following: (1) they offer consumers too few benefits compared to existing products; (2) they are too complex or require substantial learning and effort before consumers can use them, and (3) bad timing, that is, they are introduced at a time when consumers are not ready for such new products or services. As the iPod example shows, new products succeed because they offer substantial benefits that customers like and want even though they may not be inexpensive. Other such examples discussed in this text so far include Lululemon clothing, BlackBerry, Dussault jeans, BALMSHELL lip-gloss, and Kicking Horse Coffee.

Have you ever heard of any of these products? No wonder. They all failed. Dr. Care Toothpaste (left) was targeted to young children, however, parents questioned the idea of toothpaste in an aerosol can. Dunk-A-Balls cereal (centre) was shaped like basketballs so children could play with them before eating them. The Garlic Cake (right) was supposed to be served as an hors d'oeuvre. But the company forgot to mention potential usage occasions to consumers, so people wondered why they would want to eat one.

Even if they succeed, new-to-the-world products are not adopted by everyone at the same time. Rather, they diffuse or spread through a population in a process known as diffusion or adoption of innovation.

LO **2**

Adoption of Innovation

diffusion of innovation
The process by which the use of an innovation, whether a product or a service, spreads throughout a market group over time and over various categories of adopters.

The process by which the use of an innovation—whether a product or a service—spreads throughout a market group, over time and over various categories of adopters, is referred to as diffusion of innovation[11] or adoption of innovation. The theory surrounding diffusion or adoption of innovation helps marketers understand the rate at which consumers are likely to adopt a new product or service. It also gives them a means to identify potential markets for their new products or services and predict their potential sales, even before they introduce the innovations.

As the consumer adoption cycle in Exhibit 10.2 shows, the number of users of an innovative product or service spreads through the population over a period of time and generally follows a bell-shaped curve. A few people buy the product or service at first, then increasingly more buy, and finally fewer people buy as the degree of the diffusion slows. For example, it took close to 20 years to get about 90 percent of Canadians to use ATMs (automated teller machines) but within five years over 60 percent of Canadians adopted the Internet. Comparing the iPod and Sony Walkman, Merrill Lynch analyst, Steve Milunovich observes that after nearly 2.5 years, iPod shipments are approximately 1 million units ahead of the Walkman's pace after being on the market for the same period of time back in the 1980s when the Walkman was first released.[12]

Thus, purchasers can be divided into five groups according to how soon they buy the product after it has been introduced.

Innovators

innovators
Those buyers who want to be the first to have the new product or service.

Innovators are those buyers who want to be the first on the block to have the new product or service. These buyers enjoy taking risks, are regarded as highly knowledgeable, and are not price sensitive. You probably know someone who is an innovator—or perhaps you are one for a particular product or service category. For example,

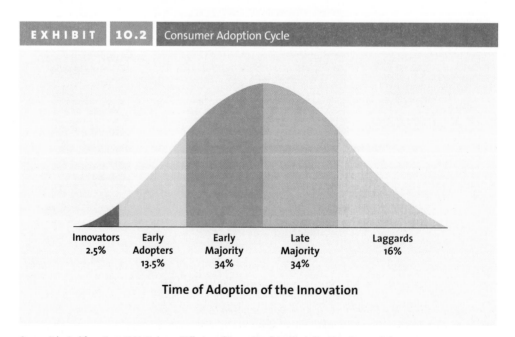

| EXHIBIT | 10.2 | Consumer Adoption Cycle |

Innovators 2.5%   Early Adopters 13.5%   Early Majority 34%   Late Majority 34%   Laggards 16%

Time of Adoption of the Innovation

Source: Adapted from Everett M. Rodgers, *Diffusion of Innovation* (New York: The Free Press, 1983).

the person who stood in line for days to be sure to get a ticket for the very first show-ing of the latest *Harry Potter* movie is an innovator in that context. Firms that invest in the latest technology, either to use in their products or services or to make the firm more efficient, also are considered innovators. Typically, innovators keep themselves very well informed about the product category by subscribing to trade and specialty magazines, talking to other "experts," searching the Internet, and attending product-related forums, seminars, and special events. Typically, innovators represent only about 2.5 percent of the total market for any new product or service.

However, these innovators are crucial to the success of any new product or ser-vice because they help the product gain market acceptance. Through talking and spreading positive word of mouth about the new product, they prove instrumental in bringing in the next adopter category, known as early adopters.

Early Adopters

The second subgroup that begins to use a product or service innovation is the **early adopters**. They generally don't like to take as much risk as innovators but instead wait and purchase the product after careful review. Early adopters tend to enjoy nov-elty and often are regarded as the opinion leaders for particular product categories.

This group, which represents about 13.5 percent of all buyers in the market, acts as opinion leaders who spread the word to the next big groups—early majority and late majority. As a result, early adopters are crucial for bringing the other three buyer categories to the market. If the early adopter group is relatively small, the number of people who ultimately adopt the innovation likely will also be small.

early adopters
The second group of consumers in the diffusion of innovation model, after *innovators*, to use a prod-uct or service innovation; generally don't like to take as much risk as innovators.

Early Majority

The **early majority**, which represents approximately 34 percent of the population, is crucial because few new products and services can be profitable until this large group buys them. If the group never becomes large enough, the product or service typically fails.

The early majority group differs in many ways from buyers in the first two stages. Its members don't like to take as much risk and therefore tend to wait until "the bugs" are worked out of a particular product or service. When early majority custom-ers enter the market, the number of competitors in the marketplace usually also has reached its peak, so these buyers have many different price and quality choices.

early majority
A group of consumers in the diffusion of innovation model that represents ap-proximately 34 percent of the population; members don't like to take much risk and therefore tend to wait until bugs are worked out.

Late Majority

At 34 percent of the market, the **late majority** is the last group of buyers to enter a new product market; when they do, the product has achieved its full market poten-tial. By the time the late majority enters the market, sales tend to level off or may be in decline.

late majority
The last group of buyers to enter a new product market.

Laggards

Laggards make up roughly 16 percent of the market. These consumers like to avoid change and rely on traditional products until they are no longer available.[13] In some cases, laggards may never adopt a certain product or service. For example, some house-holds still use rotary phones versus touchtone models or listen to music on audiocas-settes because they do not own a CD player. Very few companies actively pursue these customers.

laggards
Consumers who like to avoid change and rely on traditional products until they are no longer available.

Using the Adoption Cycle

Using the diffusion of innovation theory or adoption cycle, firms can predict which types of customers will buy their new product or service immediately after

Laggards may never adopt a new product or service.

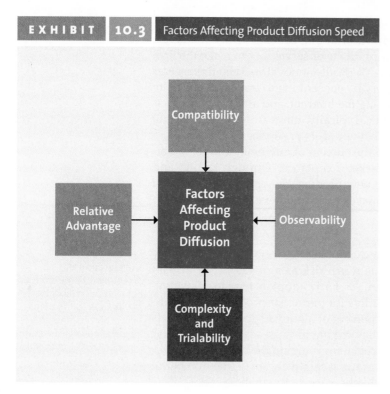

| EXHIBIT | 10.3 | Factors Affecting Product Diffusion Speed |

its introduction, as well as later as the product gets more and more accepted by the market. With this knowledge, the firm can develop effective promotion, pricing, and other marketing strategies to push acceptance among each customer group. However, because different products are adopted at different rates, marketers must understand what the diffusion curve for the new product looks like, as well as the characteristics of the target customers in each stage of the diffusion. The speed with which products are adopted depends on several product characteristics, illustrated in Exhibit 10.3.

Relative Advantage If a product is perceived to be better than substitutes, then the diffusion will be relatively quick. Many believe, for example, that Starbucks' meteoric rise to success is because it is a superior substitute to doughnut or traditional coffee shops. Similarly, the BlackBerry was adopted by business consumers over other devices because it offered substantially more benefits that these consumers needed (refer back to Chapter 1 opening vignette).

Compatibility Most business professionals and executives have to make decisions in a timely fashion and be able to communicate their decisions in a timely manner also—they need real time information in order to do this. The BlackBerry is compatible with this mode of operation and so it is hardly surprising that it is hugely popular. Similarly, the ritual of "having a coffee" is well ingrained in many cultures, including Canadian culture. "Having a coffee" is consistent with people's past behaviour, their needs, and their values. Since people are accustomed to drinking coffee, it has been relatively easy for Starbucks to acquire customers in Canada. The diffusion has been much slower in countries like China and Japan, where tea has been the traditional drink.

Observability The ubiquitous Starbucks logo can be easily seen on cups in and around Starbucks stores. When products are easily observed, their benefits or uses are easily communicated to others, thus enhancing the diffusion process. A botox treatment to reduce wrinkles, on the other hand, is not easily observed by others and therefore has diffused more slowly. Many examples of how the BlackBerry was used to close business deals or to make life-saving decisions are reported in many newspapers and magazines on the Internet. Indeed, you can see the Blackberry being used everywhere from the workplace to the road to sports venues and even in bars. This allows others to easily observe the benefits of the technology when people are working even when they are on the golf course or riding in a taxi.

What has made Starbucks so successful? It has a strong relative advantage *to other coffee venues. It is* compatible *with people's current behaviour. Products and locations are easily* observable *by others. It is* not complex *and is easy to try.*

Complexity and Trialability   Products that are relatively less complex are also relatively easy to try. These products will generally diffuse more quickly than those that are not. Purchasing a tall nonfat latte, for instance, is a lot easier than purchasing a new car with a GPS system. The BlackBerry is very simple to use and business consumers can try it at a minimal cost before adopting it through the entire organization.

The diffusion of innovation theory thus comes into play in the immediate and long-term aftermath of a new product or service introduction. But before the introduction, firms must actually develop those new offerings. Therefore, in the next section, we detail the process by which most firms develop new products and services and how they initially introduce them into the market.

How Firms Develop New Products

LO **3**

The new product development process begins with the generation of new product ideas and culminates in the launch of the new product and the evaluation of its success. The stages of the new product development process, along with the important objectives of each stage, are summarized in Exhibit 10.4. Although this exhibit depicts linear and sequential stages, in reality, the process is iterative, consisting of a number of feedback loops at various stages. Generally the process is a team effort with the new product team comprised of members from various functions: marketing, design, engineering, manufacturing, procurement and finance, all of whom play different roles at different stages of the process. Marketing plays a crucial role in the new product development process by communicating customer needs and wants and marketplace preferences and attitudes to the R&D and engineering group.

Bear in mind that it's not always necessary to take a new product through each stage in the process. Substantially new products will likely follow the process fairly closely while products involving incremental changes such as line extensions, imitating a successful product from a competitor or low development cost, may skip one or more steps. For example, Procter and Gamble launched its Folgers brand of decaffeinated crystal coffee without market testing. Although skipping stages in the new product development process is very risky, companies often do it in order to reduce costs or launch new products quickly.

Idea Generation

To generate ideas for new products, a firm can use its own internal research and development (R&D) efforts, collaborate with other firms and institutions, license technology from research-intensive firms, brainstorm, research competitors' products and services, and/or conduct consumer research. Sometimes new product ideas come from employees, customers, suppliers and partners or are generated by attending trade shows and conferences. Companies also generate ideas using reverse engineering or, in more extreme cases, even digging through a competitor's garbage. See Exhibit 10.5 for an example of how employee ideas resulted in a new product. Firms

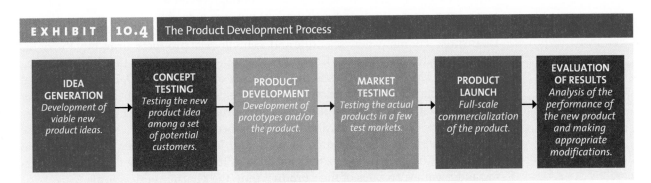

EXHIBIT 10.4   The Product Development Process

IDEA GENERATION	CONCEPT TESTING	PRODUCT DEVELOPMENT	MARKET TESTING	PRODUCT LAUNCH	EVALUATION OF RESULTS
Development of viable new product ideas.	Testing the new product idea among a set of potential customers.	Development of prototypes and/or the product.	Testing the actual products in a few test markets.	Full-scale commercialization of the product.	Analysis of the performance of the new product and making appropriate modifications.

| **EXHIBIT** | **10.5** | Sources of Ideas |

Post-it® Notes were not a planned
product. Spencer Silver was working in the
3M research laboratories in 1970 trying to
find a strong adhesive. He developed a
new adhesive, but it was even weaker than
what 3M already manufactured. It stuck
to objects, but could easily be lifted off.

No one knew what to do with the
adhesive but Silver didn't discard it. Then
one Sunday four years later, another 3M
scientist named Arthur Fry was singing
in the church's choir. He used markers
to keep his place in the hymnal, but they
kept falling out of the book. Remembering
Silver's adhesive, Fry used some to coat his markers. Success! With the weak adhesive, the markers
stayed in place, yet lifted off without damaging the pages. 3M began distributing Post-it ® Notes
nationwide in 1980—10 years after Silver developed the super weak adhesive. Today they are one of
the most popular office products available.

Source: Adapted from Post-It Note History, www.ideafinder.com/history/inventions/postit.htm.

that want to be pioneers rely more extensively on R&D efforts, whereas those that
tend to adopt a follower strategy are more likely to scan the market for ideas. Let's
look at each of these idea sources.

Internal Research and Development   Many firms have their own R&D departments, in which scientists work to solve complex problems and develop new ideas.[14]
Historically, firms such as IBM in the computer industry, Rubbermaid in the consumer goods industry, 3M in the industrial goods industry, and Merck and Pfizer in
the pharmaceuticals industry have relied on R&D development efforts for their new
products. In other industries, such as software, music, and motion pictures, product
development efforts also tend to come from internal ideas and investments. Internet
Marketing 10.1 discusses how the Internet can be used as a new and powerful way to
invite customers into the research lab.

The product development costs for these firms are quite high, and the resulting
new product or service has a good chance of being a technological or market breakthrough. Firms expect such products to generate enough revenue and profits to make
the costs of R&D worthwhile; however, R&D investments generally are considered
continuous investments, so firms may lose money on a few new products. In the long
run though, these firms are betting that a few extremely successful new products,
often known as blockbusters, can generate enough revenues and profits to cover the
losses from other introductions that might not fare so well.

Licensing   For many new scientific and technological products, firms buy the rights
to use the technology or ideas from other research-intensive firms through a licensing
agreement. This approach saves the high costs of in-house R&D, but it means that
the firm is banking on a solution that already exists but has not been marketed. For
example, many pharmaceutical firms license products developed by biotechnology
firms such as Amgen, Biogen, and Genentech. Because most biotechnology firms are
smaller, tend to be very research focused, and lack the resources and expertise to
market their own innovations, they are content to obtain some development financing and royalties on sales of their product from the pharmaceutical firms.[15]

| Internet Marketing | **10.1** | **Making Consumers Co-creators of New Products** |

As more consumers use the Internet as a part of their daily lives, online communities are growing in popularity. In these virtual interest groups, users with similar passions can discuss anything from their favourite import model to how to improve on the design of a car. Companies have always wanted to get customer feedback on products before they actually design and launch them, something that was extremely difficult in the offline world. They used to rely on a few focus groups and product testing. Now the Internet has made it possible for them to capture the insights of millions of customers from all over the world in real time and in a variety of ways. Online communities are a frequently used mechanism to solicit customer input. Having consumers become part of these communities is a goldmine for marketers because it provides a way to invite customers into the research lab, so to speak. Integrating customer views into a company's new product development process can offer an untapped source for new ideas, refinements to existing product designs and features, or even a knowledgeable test market for a prototype—all of this at little or no cost to companies.

Marketers usually try to get consumers to participate in the idea generation stage, concept testing and product development stage, and test market stage. At the idea generation stage, consumer participation could be as simple as asking them for new ideas and product suggestions or to comment on an existing idea or concept. BMW did just this when they conducted an idea competition for driver assistance systems of the future (www.bmw.com/innovationlab). In the concept testing and product development stage, consumers become co-creators. This could be through an open discussion about improving product plans, or a complex real-time drag-and-drop application that allows consumers to alter a product as they see fit. This allows consumers to not only identify wants and needs in a product, but also to use their problem-solving skills and creativity to add value. Peugeot held a design contest where nearly 2800 design enthusiasts from 90 countries showed their proposed car designs (www.peugeot-avenue.com). Finally, community members can be a part of the market testing and product launch stage, in the role of an end-user. Simply blogging about the advantages and challenges of a new product or through e-mailing to a friend would fulfill this stage. Or, it can be more involved. Volvo presented different concept cars (www.conceptlabvolvo.com) and invited visitors to give their feedback after virtual presentations and test simulations. All this information becomes a source of tremendous learning for the company, allowing them to build products that consumers want. Selling products to the very customers who helped co-create them is easier because they already feel very connected to the product.

The Ford-F150 truck and Texas Instrument-TI-92 calculator were instant successes because they used the Internet to generate customer feedback and customers felt ownership of the products. Marketers have learned that even something as complicated as the design of a new car can benefit from the involvement of online consumers. Taking advantage of this wealth of information is important to help companies innovate smartly and ensure products are responding to consumer needs. The next time you are visiting your favourite online forum, consider how your ideas could add value to a new product launch.

Brainstorming   Firms often engage in brainstorming sessions during which a group works together to generate ideas. One of the key characteristics of a brainstorming session is that no idea can be immediately accepted or rejected. The moderator of the session may channel participants' attention to specific product features and attributes, performance expectations, or packaging, but only at the end of the session do the members vote on the best ideas or combinations of ideas. Those four to eight ideas that receive the most votes are carried forward to the next stage of the product development process.

Competitors' Products   A new product entry by a competitor may trigger a market opportunity for a firm, which can use reverse engineering to understand the competitor's product and then bring an improved version to market. **Reverse engineering** involves taking apart a product, analyzing it, and creating an improved product that does not infringe on the competitors' patents, if any exist. This copycat approach to new product development is widespread and practised by even the most research-intensive firms. Copycat consumer goods show up in grocery and drugstore products, as well as in technologically more complex products like automobiles and computers. For example, China Unicom Ltd., the state-controlled telecommunications giant ranked as China's second-biggest mobile operator, launched RedBerry a new product aimed squarely at BlackBerry.[16]

reverse engineering Involves taking apart a competitor's product, analyzing it, and creating an improved product that does not infringe on the competitor's patents, if any exist.

These innovative consumers are called lead users *because they modify existing products according to their own ideas to suit their specific needs.*

Customer Input Listening to the customer is essential for successful idea generation.[17] Prior studies have found that as much as 85 percent of all new business-to-business (B2B) product ideas come from customers.[18] Because customers for B2B products are relatively few in number, firms can follow their use of products closely and survey them often for suggestions and ideas to improve those products. The firm's design and development team then works on these suggestions, sometimes in consultation with the customer. This joint effort between the selling firm and the customer significantly increases the probability that the customer eventually will buy the new product. Internet Marketing 10.1 illustrates how companies use the Internet to solicit and incorporate customer feedback in the new product development process.

In the food and beverage industry, in which new product failure rates are as high as 78 percent, Kraft minimizes its risk through a careful new product development process that includes consumer research. Frito Lay is the third-fastest-growing food company in Canada. Its Lightly Salted Lay's potato chips were developed after research showed that saturated fats and trans fats are at the top of consumers' concerns but that sodium also ranks high. Sales were beyond their expectations.[19] Innovation is the lifeblood of Frito Lay's business. Some years, innovation has accounted for more than 100 percent of its growth in Canada—without it, sales would be flat.[20]

lead users
Innovative product users who modify existing products according to their own ideas to suit their specific needs.

One successful customer input approach is to analyze **lead users**, those innovative product users who modify existing products according to their own ideas to suit their specific needs.[21] These lead users have customized the firm's products; other customers might wish to do so as well. Thus, studying lead users helps the firm understand general market trends that might be just on the horizon. Manufacturers and retailers of fashion products often spot new trends by noticing how trendsetters have altered their clothing and shoes. For instance, designers of high-fashion jeans distress their products in different ways depending on signals they pick up "on the street." One season, jeans appear with whiskers, the next holes, the next paint spots. Products developed by paying attention to lead users include Gatorade, protein-based shampoo, Liquid Paper correction fluid, mountain bikes, chocolate milk, desktop publishing, and the World Wide Web.

At the end of the idea-generation stage, the firm should have several ideas that it can take forward to the next stage: concept testing.

Concept Testing

concepts
Brief written descriptions of a product or service; its technology, working principles, and forms; and what customer needs it would satisfy.

Ideas with potential are developed further into **concepts**, which in this context refer to brief written descriptions of the product; its technology, working principles, and forms; and what customer needs it would satisfy.[22] A concept might also include visual images of what the product would look like.

concept testing
The process in which a concept statement that describes a product or a service is presented to potential buyers or users to obtain their reactions.

Concept testing refers to the process in which a concept statement is presented to potential buyers representative of the target market or users to obtain their reactions. These reactions enable the developer to estimate the sales value of the product or service concept, possibly make changes to enhance its sales value, and determine whether the idea is worth further development.[23] If the concept fails to meet customers' expectations, it is doubtful it would succeed if it were to be produced and marketed. Because concept testing occurs very early in the new product introduction process, even before a real product has been made, it helps the firm avoid the costs of unnecessary product development.

The concept for an electric scooter might be written as follows:

The product is a lightweight electric scooter that can be easily folded and taken with you inside a building or on public transportation. The scooter weights 25 pounds [11 kg]. It travels at speeds of up to 15 miles [24 km] per hour and can go about 12 miles [19 km] on a single charge. The scooter can be recharged in about two hours from a standard electric outlet. The scooter is easy to ride and has simple controls—just an accelerator button and a brake. It sells for $299.[24]

Concept testing progresses along the research techniques described in Chapter 5. The firm likely starts with exploratory research, such as in-depth interviews or focus groups, to test the concept, after which it can undertake conclusive research through Internet or mall-intercept surveys. Video clips on the Internet might show a virtual prototype and the way it works so that potential customers can evaluate the product or service.[25] In a mall-intercept survey, an interviewer would provide a description of the concept to the respondent and then ask several questions to obtain his or her feedback.

The most important question pertains to the respondent's purchase intentions were the product or service made available. Marketers also should ask whether the product would satisfy a need that other products currently are not meeting. Depending on the type of product or service, researchers might also ask about the expected frequency of purchase, how much customers would buy, whether they would buy it for themselves or as a gift, when would they buy, and whether the price information (if provided) indicates a good value. In addition, marketers usually collect some demographic information so they can analyze which consumer segments are likely to be most interested in the product.

Some concepts never make it past this stage, particularly if respondents seem uninterested. Those that do receive high evaluations from potential consumers, however, move on to the next step, product development.

Product Development

Product development or **product design** entails a process of balancing various engineering, manufacturing, marketing, and economic considerations to develop a product's form and features or a service's features. An engineering team develops a product prototype that is based on research findings from the previous concept testing step, as well as their own knowledge about materials and technology. A **prototype** is the first physical form or service description of a new product, still in rough or tentative form, that has the same properties as a new product but is produced through different manufacturing processes—sometimes even crafted individually.[26]

Product prototypes are usually tested through alpha and beta testing. In **alpha testing**, the firm attempts to determine whether the product will perform according to its design and whether it satisfies the need for which it was intended.[27] Rather than using potential consumers, alpha tests occur in the firm's R&D department. For instance, Ben & Jerry's Ice Cream alpha tests all its proposed new flavours on its own employees at its corporate headquarters in Vermont. It may be a great job, but it also sounds rather fattening!

As discussed in Ethical Dilemma 10.1, many people, consumer groups, and governmental agencies are concerned when alpha testing involves tests on animals, particularly when it comes to pharmaceuticals and cosmetics.

In contrast, **beta testing** uses potential consumers, who examine the product prototype in a "real use" setting to determine its

product development (product design)
Entails a process of balancing various engineering, manufacturing, marketing, and economic considerations to develop a product.

prototype
The first physical form or service description of a new product, still in rough or tentative form, that has the same properties as a new product but is produced through different manufacturing processes, sometimes even crafted individually.

alpha testing
An attempt by the firm to determine whether a product will perform according to its design and whether it satisfies the need for which it was intended; occurs in the firm's research and development (R&D) department.

beta testing
Having potential consumers examine a product prototype in a real-use setting to determine its functionality, performance, potential problems, and other issues specific to its use.

Beta testing uses potential consumers who examine a product prototype in a "real use" setting to determine its functionality, performance, potential problems, and other issues specific to its use.

Ethical Dilemma

10.1 Should Cosmetics Firms Test Products on Animals?

Cosmetics testing on animals has been a primary issue for animal right activists for years.[28] As public opposition to animal testing increases, so do many companies' declarations that they "do not test products on animals." However, such statements can be misleading because even though the whole product may not have been tested on animals, the individual ingredients may have been.

One of the founding principles of The Body Shop, and one that has resonated well with its customers is that its products are free of animal testing. While the website for The Body Shop states that it has never tested or commissioned testing of its ingredients or products on animals, many of the ingredients in their products were in fact tested on animals by other companies. The company changed the labels on their products from "not tested on animals" to "against animal testing" because it is impossible to avoid ingredients ever tested on animals.[29] Another major cosmetics manufacturer, Procter & Gamble, has eliminated animal testing on more than 80 percent of its products. It uses a combination of vitro testing, computer modelling, and historical data to determine the safety of new products and ingredients. These methods are more expensive than more traditional methods, but P&G claims that the results are better. If performed correctly, new chemicals can either be dropped from consideration or pushed forward in as little as three days compared to the six months previously required for animal testing.

Animal welfare groups continue to influence the use of animal testing in the cosmetics industry by using propaganda, pressure from consumers, and lobbying legislatures; and the industry continues to push back citing consumer choice, expense, and free trade.

The European Union has passed a ban on animal testing altogether. Beginning in 2009, any cosmetic tested on animals, even in other parts of the world, cannot be sold in the European Union. However, the cosmetic industry is worried that this ban will not only affect their companies' sales, but also their customers' ability to find the products they want. The E.U. cosmetics industry successfully lobbied for an extension on certain areas of toxicity testing to provide more time to find alternatives. The cosmetic industry believes it will be difficult to find alternative testing methods in time, and if they cannot, then they will have fewer ingredients to make the products consumers want.

The issues involved in animal testing for cosmetics are complex. At the broadest level, should firms be allowed to develop products that customers want, even if there is some potential harm to the environment or to those animals that share the environment with humans? More specifically, should firms be allowed to test products on animals, even when those products are not specifically designed to improve the health and well-being of their human users? After all, these products may make their users more attractive, but they will not save their lives. Does the testing that is performed endanger the lives or health of the animals?

functionality, performance, potential problems, and other issues specific to its use. The firm might develop several prototype products that it gives to users, then survey those users to determine whether the product worked as intended and identify any issues that need resolution.

When it comes to these product design details, computer companies have taken great initiatives. Adding Value 10.1 explores the factors that make Research In Motion's BlackBerry Pearl an excellent product design.

Market Testing

The firm has developed its new product or service and tested the prototypes. Now it must test the market for the new product with a trial batch of products, although as mentioned earlier, companies sometimes skip this step due to competitive, timing, or cost pressures. These tests can take two forms: premarket testing or test marketing.

premarket test
Conducted before a product or service is brought to market to determine how many customers will try and then continue to use it.

Premarket Tests   Firms conduct **premarket tests** before they actually bring a product or service to market to determine how many customers will try and then continue to use the product or service according to a small group of potential consumers. One popular proprietary premarket test version is called BASES II, conducted by the research firm ACNielsen. During the test, potential customers are exposed to the marketing mix variables, such as the advertising, then surveyed and given a sample of the product to try.[30] After some period of time, during which the potential customers try the product, they are surveyed about whether they would buy/use the

Adding Value | 10.1 | Designing RIM's BlackBerry Pearl 8100 smartphone[31]

What makes a good industrial product design? Research In Motion's Blackberry Pearl 8100 smartphone has all the properties of good design. It took over three years of researching and testing. The result of all this hard work is a small and stylish phone with every function you'd expect from a BlackBerry product. The BlackBerry Pearl is much more than a typical cell phone: it also sports full e-mail transmission and instant messaging capabilities, a 1.3 mega pixel camera, a calendar and organizer in synch with your desktop computer, and even a navigation system. Furthermore, the BlackBerry Pearl follows the key rules of design

- **Utility.** The product should be safe and easy and intuitive to use. Each feature must convey its function clearly to the user. The navigational pearl in the centre of the keypad is central. The compact design of the BlackBerry Pearl offers an intuitive graphical interface for easy use of the full productivity suite.

- **Appearance.** The form, line, proportion, and colour must be integrated into a pleasing whole. Experts and consumers alike believe the BlackBerry Pearl is a sleek and stylish upgrade in aesthetics from other models.[32]

- **Ease of Maintenance.** Product design must facilitate ease of maintenance and repair. The small device is simple to use, with a standard numerical pad and a QWERTY keypad. Extra accessories, like a carrying case, provide additional protection.

- **Good Value.** The relationship between what customers receive and product cost should be significant and obvious to consumers. The BlackBerry Pearl is not priced at the low end of the communications market. Yet its features work flawlessly and its dependability offers great value to the consumer. The BlackBerry Pearl's base price, when introduced in September 2006, was only $199 with a two-year contract; nearly $200 less than its closest competitor.[33]

- **Communication.** The product should communicate the corporate design philosophy and mission through its visual qualities. Because the BlackBerry Pearl looks like a more stylish version of other models in the BlackBerry product line, it reflects RIM's corporate theme: freedom and connectivity to fit your life.

product again. This second survey indicates an estimation of the probability of a consumer's repeat purchase. From these data, the firm generates a sales estimate for the new product that enables it to decide whether to introduce the product, abandon it, redesign it before introduction, or revise the marketing plan. An early evaluation of this sort—that is, before the product is introduced to the whole market—saves marketers the costs of a nationwide launch if the product fails.

Sometimes firms simulate a product or service introduction,[34] in which case potential customers view the advertising of various currently available products or services along with advertising for the new product or service. They receive money to buy the product or service from a simulated environment, such as a mock Web page or store, and respond to a survey after they make their purchases. This test thus can determine the effectiveness of a firm's advertising as well as the expected trial rates for the new product.

Test Marketing   A method of determining the success potential of a new product, **test marketing** introduces the offering to a limited geographical area (usually a few cities) prior to a national launch. A test marketing effort uses all the elements of the marketing mix: It includes promotions like advertising and coupons, just as if the product were being introduced nationally, and the product appears in targeted retail outlets, with appropriate pricing. On the basis of the results of the test marketing, the firm can estimate demand for the entire market.

test marketing
Introduces a new product or service to a limited geographical area (usually a few cities) prior to a national launch.

Test marketing costs more and takes longer than premarket tests, which may provide an advantage to competitors that could get a similar or better product to market first. For this reason, some firms, such as Newman's Own Organic, launch new products (e.g., its Fig Newmans™) without extensive consumer testing and rely instead on intuition, instincts, and guts.[35]

However, test marketing offers a key advantage: The firm can study actual consumer behaviour, which is more reliable than a simulated test. Canada Post piloted

Petro-Canada is test marketing a new, upscale restaurant and convenience store concept in Southwestern Ontario to gauge consumer response.

Fetch, a service that lets people access advertisers' information via e-mail and cell phones without compromising their privacy, in Calgary. The city has a relatively young demographic profile, precisely the target demographic Canada Post wanted to reach, plus residents tend to be more technically inclined. It turned out to be a good choice and the pilot exceeded expectations.[36] Labatt chose Calgary and Edmonton as the test markets for its new Brazilian Brahma beer. As a test market, Calgary offers an attractive demographic in terms of income levels, lifestyle, and a relatively youthful population.

Other cities are used for test markets for a variety of reasons. London, Ontario is often chosen because its population is reflective of a "typical" Canadian city. Winnipeg is a good location to test shampoos and skin lotions for dry skin because of its cold winters. Petro-Canada is currently testing a new, upscale convenience store and restaurant concept called Neighbours in Oakville, Brampton, and Vaughan, all Ontario cities with slightly higher incomes.

Many firms use BehaviorScan to improve the probability of success during the test marketing phase of a new product introduction. BehaviorScan utilizes consumer panel data collected passively at the point of sale in stores and through home scanning to measure individual household first time trial and repeat purchases. New products are placed in stores within one week of introduction, rather than the typical 8- to 12-week period. Since more sales data are collected in a shorter period of time than conventional test marketing methods, first-year sales can be estimated after just 16 to 24 weeks in the test market.[37] Once the market demand is estimated, the product is released nationally.

However, sometimes test marketing can result in tipping your hand to competitors, who carefully monitor sales and preemptively launch their own products. For instance, Kellogg tracked sales of Toast-Ems during test marketing by General Foods. Noting they were becoming popular, they quickly went national with PopTarts before the test was finished. General Foods invented freeze-dried coffee and was in the midst of test marketing its Maxim brand when Nestle launched Taster's Choice, which went on to become the leading brand.[38]

Product Launch

If the market testing returns with positive results, the firm is ready to introduce the product to the entire market. As noted in Adding Value 10.1, the BlackBerry Pearl was launched after three years of researching and testing. Frito Lay originally launched its Wasabi and Spicy Curry Lay's chips in Toronto and Vancouver, where the largest number of Asian-born Canadians reside. Sales of the curry flavour were three to four times higher than expected[39] and the product has since been launched nationally. However, Wasabi didn't enjoy as much success.

A product launch is the most critical step in the new product introduction and requires tremendous financial resources and extensive coordination of all aspects of the marketing mix. If the new product launch is a failure, it may be difficult for the product—and perhaps the firm—to recover. Some products show great promise through their launches, though, as Exhibit 10.6 describes.

So what does a product launch involve? First, on the basis of the research it has gathered on consumer perceptions and the tests it has conducted, as well as any competitive considerations, the firm confirms its target market(s) and decides how the product will be positioned. Then the firm finalizes the remaining marketing mix variables for the new product, including the marketing budget for the first year.[40]

EXHIBIT 10.6 | Top New Products[41]

	Product	Unique Benefits
	Sun-Rype Fruit Plus Vitamins & Minerals	7 essential vitamins and minerals and a good source of Folate, all in a great-tasting 100 percent juice.
	Neilson The Ultimate Chocolate Milk	All the goodness of low-fat white milk (15 essential nutrients including calcium and Vitamin D), no trans fat and only 2.5 g fat per 250 ml serving.
	Knorr Frozen Entrees	Easy to prepare in the skillet or microwave; simply sauté for 10 minutes.
	Lifestream Organic Whole Grain Pasta	Organic whole wheat durum flour and organic brown flax meal. high in fibre and contains no trans fats
	Becel Topping & Cooking Spray	No calories and no fat. Simply spray on fresh vegetables, popcorn, or a variety of other foods to add delicious flavour.

Source: www.bestnewproducts.ca.

Promotion   The test results help the firm determine an appropriate integrated marketing communications strategy.[42] For products that are somewhat complex or conceptually new, marketers may need to provide for more consumer education about the product's benefits than they would for simpler and more familiar products. For technical products, technical support staff must be trained to answer any customer questions that may arise immediately after the launch. Research In Motion promotes the BlackBerry Pearl as small, smart, and stylish to attract consumer markets and offers troubleshooting tips for top issues via its technical solution centre.

Place   The firm must have an adequate quantity of products available for shipment and to keep in stock at relevant stores. The product offering should also be as complete as possible. For example, a firm launching a new printer should ensure it has an adequate supply of the related cartridges or toners. Interested consumers can purchase a BlackBerry Pearl from any Bell, Rogers, or Telus wireless products location. This not only provides the new product in a convenient location, it also allows the opportunity for tailored customer service and subscription to appropriate service plans.

Price   The firm needs to ensure that they get the price right. It is sometimes easier to start with a higher price and offer promotions (coupons, rebates, etc.) and then over time to lower the price than it is to introduce the new product at a low price and then try to raise it. The BlackBerry Pearl is a premium telecommunications product commanding a fitting price of $445.95 without a service contract. However, carriers entice new buyers by bundling a reduced price for the Pearl if a service plan is included. The price can drop by hundreds of dollars, or even to zero with a long-term contract. [43]

Timing   The timing of the launch may be important, depending on the product.[44] Hollywood studios typically release movies targeted toward general audiences (i.e., those rated G or PG) during the summer when children are out of school. New automobile models traditionally are released for sale during September, and fashion products are launched just before the season of the year for which they are intended.

Evaluation of Results

After the product has been launched, marketers must undertake a critical postlaunch review to determine whether the product and its launch were a success or failure and what additional resources or changes to the marketing mix are needed, if any. Firms measure the success of a new product by three interrelated factors: (1) its satisfaction of technical requirements, such as performance; (2) customer acceptance; and (3) its satisfaction of the firm's financial requirements, such as sales and profits.[45] If the product is not performing sufficiently well, poor customer acceptance will result, which in turn leads to poor financial performance. The new product development process, when followed rationally and sequentially, helps avoid such domino-type failures. The product life cycle, discussed in the next section, helps marketers manage their products' marketing mix during and after its introduction.

The Product Life Cycle   LO

The **product life cycle** (PLC) defines the stages that new products move through as they enter, get established in, and ultimately leave the marketplace and thereby offers marketers a starting point for their strategy planning. Exhibit 10.7a illustrates a typical product life cycle, including the industry sales and profits over time. In their life cycles, products pass through four stages: introduction, growth, maturity, and decline. When innovators start buying the product, the product enters the **introduction stage** of its life cycle. In the **growth stage**, the product gains acceptance, demand and sales increase, and competitors emerge in the product category. In the **maturity stage**, industry sales reach their peak, so firms try to rejuvenate their products by adding new features or repositioning them. If these efforts succeed, the product achieves new life.[46] If not, it goes into the **decline stage** and eventually exits the market.

Not every product follows the same life cycle shape; many products stay in the maturity period for a very long time. For example, "white good" categories, such as clothes washers, dryers, and refrigerators, have been in the maturity stage for a very long time and will remain there indefinitely until a superior product comes along to replace them.

product life cycle
Defines the stages that new products move through as they enter, get established in, and ultimately leave the marketplace and thereby offers marketers a starting point for their strategy planning.

introduction stage
Stage of the product life cycle when innovators start buying the product.

growth stage
Stage of the product life cycle when the product gains acceptance, demand and sales increase, and competitors emerge in the product category.

maturity stage
Stage of the product life cycle when industry sales reach their peak, so firms try to rejuvenate their products by adding new features or repositioning them.

decline stage
Stage of the product life cycle when sales decline and the product eventually exits the market.

The product life cycle also offers a useful tool for managers to analyze the types of strategies that may be required over the life of their products. Even the strategic emphasis of a firm and its marketing mix (4Ps) strategies can be adapted from insights about the characteristics of each stage of the cycle, as we summarize in Exhibit 10.7b.

Let's look at each of these stages in depth.

Introduction Stage

The introduction stage for a new, innovative product or service usually starts with a single firm, and innovators are the ones to try the new offering. Some new-to-the-world products and services that defined their own product category and industry include the telephone (invented by Alexander Graham Bell in 1876), the transistor semiconductor (Bell Laboratories in 1947), the Walkman portable cassette player

EXHIBIT	**10.7a**	Product Life Cycle

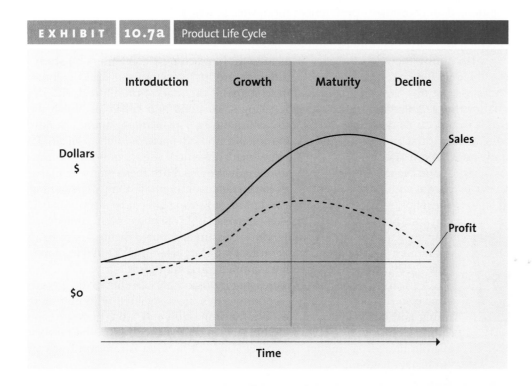

EXHIBIT	**10.7b**	Characteristics of Different Stages of the Product Life Cycle

	Introduction	Growth	Maturity	Decline
Sales	Low	Rising	Peak	Declining
Profits	Negative or low	Rapidly rising	Peak to declining	Declining
Typical consumers	Innovators	Early adopters and early majority	Late majority	Laggards
Competitors (number of firms and products)	One or few	Few but increasing	High number of competitors and competitive products	Low number of competitors and products

(Sony in 1979), the Internet browser (Netscape in 1994), and BlackBerry (Research In Motion in 2003). See Exhibit 10.8 for an example of how BlackBerry has moved from introduction to subsequent stages of the product life cycle. Sensing the viability and commercialization possibilities of this market-creating new product, other firms soon enter the market with similar or improved products at lower prices. The same pattern holds for less innovative products like apparel, some CDs, or even a new soft drink flavour. The introduction stage is characterized by initial losses to the firm due to its high start-up costs and low levels of sales revenue as the product begins to take off. If the product is successful, firms may start seeing profits toward the end of this stage.

Growth Stage

The growth stage of the product life cycle is marked by a growing number of product adopters, rapid growth in industry sales, and increases in both the number of competitors and the number of available product versions.[47] The market becomes more segmented and consumer preferences more varied, which increases the potential for new markets or new uses of the product or service.[48] Innovators start rebuying the product, and early majority consumers enter.

These new-to-the-world products defined their own product category and industry. The telephone (left) was invented in 1876, and the Sony Walkman (right) came out in 1979.

Also during the growth stage, firms attempt to reach new consumers by studying their preferences and producing different product variations—varied colours, styles, or features—which enables them to segment the market more precisely. The goal of this segmentation is to ride the rising sales trend and firmly establish the firm's brand, so as not to be outdone by competitors. For example, there are now several firms that produce DVD players for both broad mass-market applications and specialized markets, such as those in which consumers use them with computers, on the road, or to record homemade movies. With these many available product options, industry sales have risen rapidly; more than 50 percent of households in North America and parts of Europe have now adopted DVD players.[49] Simultaneously, the average price of DVD players has gone down sharply, which provides tremendous consumer value. For the Thanksgiving holiday season sale, for example, Wal-Mart offered DVD players for as little as $29, causing a consumer stampede in some stores.[50]

As firms ride the crest of increasing industry sales, profits in the growth stage also rise because of the economies of scale associated with manufacturing and marketing costs, especially promotion and advertising. At the same time, firms that have not yet established a stronghold in the market, even in narrow segments, may decide to exit in what is referred to as an "industry shakeout."

EXHIBIT 10.8	Product Life Cycle Strategies as illustrated using BlackBerry		
	Introduction	**Growth**	**Maturity**
Product	Basic product offered	New product variations introduced	Diversify brands and models into a full product line
Price	High price	Prices drop slightly	Full complement of price points in product line
Place	Selective distribution	Build distribution outlets, add dealers to reach new business markets	Build more intensive distribution to reach consumer markets
Promotion	Build word of mouth and product awareness among early adopters	Build awareness in broader markets and media channels	Stress brand differences and benefits

Maturity Stage

The maturity stage of the product life cycle is characterized by the adoption of the product by the late majority and intense competition for market share among firms. Marketing costs (e.g., promotion, distribution) increase as these firms vigorously defend their market share against competitors. At the same time, they face intense competition on price as the average price of the product falls substantially compared with the shifts during the previous two stages of the life cycle. Lower prices and increased marketing costs begin to erode the profit margins for many firms. In the later phases of the maturity stage, the market has become quite saturated, and practically all potential customers for the product have already adopted the product. Such saturated markets are prevalent in developed countries; in Canada, most consumer packaged goods found in grocery and discount stores are already in the maturity stage.

Firms may pursue several strategies during this stage to increase their customer base and/or defend their market share, such as entry into new markets and market segments and developing new products. See Exhibit 10.9 for additional strategies for extending the maturity stage of the product life cycle.

Entry into New Markets or Market Segments   Because the market is saturated at this point, firms may attempt to enter new geographical markets, including international markets (as we will discuss in Chapter 17), that may be less saturated. For example, Whirlpool has started manufacturing washing machines for Brazil, China, and India that it prices lower than those it sells in North America to attract the large consumer base of lower-income consumers in these countries.[51] In many developing economies, the large and growing proportion of middle-class households is just beginning to buy the home, kitchen, and entertainment appliances that have been fairly standard in Canadian households for several decades. In India alone, the roughly 487 million middle-class consumers will spend $420 billion on a variety of consumer products in the next four years.[52]

However, even in mature markets, firms may be able to find new market segments. Emerging new trends or changes in consumer tastes may fragment mature markets, which would open new market opportunities. As the popularity of the Internet increased, for example, firms such as Expedia, Orbitz, Priceline, and Travelocity found that they could provide the easy access and convenience of online bookings for air travel, hotel stays, and car rentals. Consumers who prefer such access and convenience, as well as the ability to compare prices across different service providers, increasingly are using the Internet to make their travel plans.

New market opportunities also may emerge through simple product design changes, such as in the market for "wipes." Just a few years ago, baby wipes accounted for most of the sales of personal wipes, but Procter & Gamble's Oil of Olay Facial Cleansing Cloths and Unilever's Ponds Age-Defying wipes have recently gained significant market share.[53] In the household sector, products such as P&G's Swiffer, the electrostatic wipe for mopping floors, have expanded the market greatly. Clorox has added premoistened Armor All wipes to its do-it-yourself car cleaning line[54] and the Clorox® ToiletWand™ for consumers who don't enjoy unsightly and unsanitary toilet brushes hanging around in their bathrooms.[55] Although the household cleaning and cosmetic markets are both well established and mature, marketers working in these product categories saw trends early and moved to create new products that offer value for consumers.

Just a few years ago, baby wipes accounted for most of the sales of personal wipes. Firms have seen the opportunity to enter new markets, so products have proliferated.

Development of New Products   Despite market saturation, firms continually introduce new products with improved features or find new uses for existing products

EXHIBIT	10.9	Strategies for Extending the Product Life Cycle

Strategy	Example
Develop new uses for products	• Baking soda is now promoted for much more than just baking.
Modify the product • change quality • boost performance • alter appearance	• graphite added to tennis racquets and golf clubs • computer chip speed enhanced • introduce new scent, modify packaging, change colours
Increase frequency of use	• Dentyne gum promoted as a way to help clean your teeth when you can't brush after a meal.
Increase the number of users	• Tums have always contained calcium but when this fact was promoted, people concerned about bone density began to purchase the product.
Find new users	• Club Med introduced vacations geared to baby boomers, seniors, golfers, and those looking for cruises after some of their original target market of swinging singles got married and had children.
Reposition product	• Sun tan lotion evolved to become sun screen protection • Vitamin D sold as a cancer deterrent
Tweak marketing strategy	• Greeting cards sold in supermarkets • Upscale cosmetics sold in drug stores

because they need constant innovation and product proliferation to defend market share during intense competition. Firms such as 3M, P&G, and Hewlett-Packard, for instance, continuously introduce new products. Innovations by such firms ensure that they are able to retain or grow their respective market shares.

Sometimes new products are introduced by less-than-famous companies. Even in a product category as old as food, entrepreneurs like Rachna and Mona Prasad keep coming up with new innovations, as we discuss in Entrepreneurial Marketing 10.1.

Decline Stage

Firms with products in the decline stage either position themselves for a niche segment of diehard consumers or those with special needs or they completely exit the market. The few laggards that have not yet tried the product or service enter the market at this stage. Take vinyl long-playing records (LPs) for example. In an age of CDs and Internet-downloaded music in MP3 and other formats, it may seem surprising that vinyl records are still made and sold. Although the sales of vinyl LPs have been declining in the past 15 years, about 2 million are sold in the United States each year. In Canada, vinyl sales declined from $913,000 in 2000 to $608,000 three years later compared to CD sales that same year of $686,976,000.[56] Still, diehard music lovers prefer the unique sound of a vinyl record to the digital sound of CDs and music in other formats. Because the grooves in vinyl records create sound waves that are similar to those of a live performance, and therefore provide a more authentic sound, nightclub DJs, discerning music listeners, and collectors prefer them. Even some younger listeners have been buying vinyl records, influenced perhaps by their parents' collections, the sound, or simply the uniqueness of an LP. In Edmonton, independent and high-profile bands alike are competing for limited record-pressing resources, a sign that vinyl is in vogue again.[57] The nostalgia factor associated with the old albums has given new life to the older medium.

Aiding this continued demand is the fact that there are simply too many albums of music from the predigital era that are available only on vinyl. It may take many years, maybe even decades, for all the music from earlier generations to be digitized.

Entrepreneurial Marketing

10.1 Gourmantra—Spice Business Heats Up

Rachna Prasad invited all her friends to a housewarming party promising them a great home-cooked Indian meal. But she wasn't sure she could actually pull it off so she asked her mother for help. Her mother didn't have time to cook but did come up with a novel solution. She packaged up all the necessary spices for the meal in just the right proportions and gave her daughter detailed preparation instructions. Rachna's friends raved about the meal. When asked for her secret, she gave them the leftover spice blends and cooking instructions from her mother.

Friends regularly requested these spice blends after that, leaving Rachna wondering if a business opportunity could be built around authentic home-cooked Indian meals that required minimal preparation time. To test the market, Rachna, her mother Rekha, and her sister Mona, a part-time student in Wilfrid Laurier University's MBA program, booked a booth at the Markham fair. When their product sold out within hours, they started their company, Rasika.

While still at Laurier, Mona entered the LaunchPad $50K New Venture Competition, hoping to win enough money to buy a commercial grade spice grinder that would allow them to grow the business. She won third place against 400 other competitors. Buoyed by this success, they rebranded the company, changing its name from Rasika to Gourmantra, and hired a graphic designer to create professional packaging. The pre-packaged spice blends, designed to make the cooking process simple, are made with the highest grade of spices and are free of oils, preservatives, artificial colours, and MSG. All consumers need to do is add chicken, lamb, beef, shrimp, chick peas, or vegetables. Four meal flavour kits are currently available: Chana Masala, Korma, Tandoori, and Butter Chicken.

Rachna and Mona have introduced Gourmantra to consumers through sampling programs and fairs in southern Ontario positioning the company to enter the North American market via retailers such as A&P Dominion, Sobeys, Food Basics, Wal-Mart and other large grocery chains. This new line of at-home meal kits is now spicing up the Indian food category by taking the guesswork out of preparing authentic dishes.

Gourmantra's prepackaged spice blends offer convenience to consumers, taking the guesswork out of Indian cooking.

Many collectors are attracted to old albums for their history as evidence by the recent sale of a one-of-a-kind Velvet Underground recording for US$25,200.[58]

The Shape of the Product Life Cycle Curve

In theory, the product life cycle curve is assumed to be bell shaped with regard to sales and profits. In reality, however, each product or service has its own individual shape; some move more rapidly through their product life cycles than others, depending on how different the product or service is from products currently in the market and how valuable it is to the consumer. New products and services that consumers accept very quickly have higher consumer adoption rates very early in their product life cycles and move faster across the various stages.

For example, DVD players and DVDs moved much faster than VCRs across the life cycle curve and have already reached the maturity stage, likely because consumers, who already owned VCRs, were accustomed to recording TV shows and playing prerecorded movies and programs. It also was easy to switch VCR customers to DVD technology because DVDs were more durable and had better resolution than videotapes. Finally, prices for DVDs and DVD players dropped more quickly and drastically than did VCR prices, which made the new technology a better value.

Lastly, as shown in Exhibit 10.10, the type of product affects variations in the shape of the product life cycle curve. When first introduced, microwaves were considered

EXHIBIT 10.10 Variations on the Product Life Cycle Curve

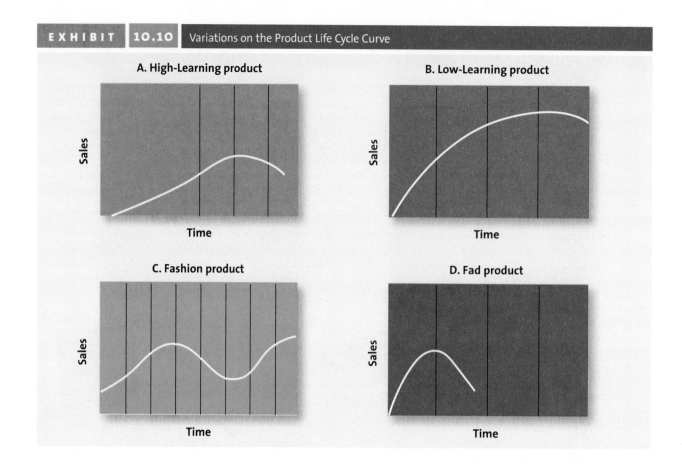

high learning products and spent much longer in the introduction stage than subsequent low learning products like microwave popcorn. Fads move through the stages very quickly while fashion products tend to be cyclical in nature. For example, wide men's ties and suit lapels may be out of style today, but may well become fashionable again in the future.

Strategies Based on Product Life Cycle: Some Caveats

Although the product life cycle concept provides a starting point for managers to think about the strategy they want to implement during each stage of the life cycle of a product, this tool must be used with care. The most challenging part of applying the product life cycle concept is that managers do not know exactly what shape each product's life cycle will take, so there is no way to know precisely what stage a product is in. If, for example, a product experiences several seasons of declining sales, a manager may decide that it has moved from the growth stage to decline and stop promoting the product. As a result, of course, sales decline further. The manager then believes he or she made the right decision because the product continues to follow a predetermined life cycle. But what if the original sales decline was due to a poor strategy or increased competition—issues that could have been addressed with positive marketing support? In this case, the product life cycle decision became a self-fulfilling prophecy, and a growth product was doomed to an unnecessary decline.[59]

Fortunately, new research, based on the history of dozens of consumer products, suggests that the product life cycle concept is indeed a valid idea, and new analytical tools now provide "rules" for detecting the key turning points in the cycle.[60] In the pharmaceutical industry, where breakthrough innovations are few and far between, firms use the product life cycle to identify the consumer promotions needed at each stage to get the most out of their existing brands.[61]

Learning Objectives Review

1) Understand how firms create value through innovation

2) Explain the diffusion of innovation theory, and how managers can use it to make product line decisions

3) Describe the process that firms go through to create new products and services

4) Discuss the product life cycle, and how it is used to make product line decisions

1) New products and services keep current customers coming back for more and induce new customers into the market. Multiple products and services also help diversify the firm's portfolio, thus lowering its overall risk and enhancing its value. Although risky, new-to-the-world products have tremendous potential because they are the first in the market to offer something that has never before been available.

2) The diffusion of innovation theory can help firms predict which types of customers will buy their products or services immediately upon introduction, as well as later as it gains more acceptance in the market. The firm can then develop marketing strategies to encourage acceptance among each customer group. Diffusion of innovation also can help predict sales.

3) When firms develop new products, they go through several steps. First, they generate ideas for the product or service using several alternative techniques, such as internal research and development, licensing, brainstorming, tracking competitors' products or services, or working with customers. Second, firms test their concepts by either describing the idea of the new product or service to potential customers or showing them images of what the product would look like. Third, the design process entails determining what the product or service will actually include and provide; fourth, firms test market their designs. Fifth, if everything goes well in the test market, the product is launched. Sixth, firms must evaluate the new product or service to determine its success.

4) The product life cycle helps firms make marketing mix decisions on the basis of the product's stage in its life cycle. In the introduction stage, companies attempt to gain a strong foothold in the market quickly by appealing to innovators. During the growth stage, the objective is to establish the brand firmly. When the product reaches the maturity stage, firms compete intensely for market share, and many potential customers already own the product or use the service. Eventually, most products enter the decline phase, during which firms withdraw marketing support and eventually phase out the product. Knowing where a product or service is in its life cycle helps managers determine its specific strategy at any given point in time.

Key Terms

- alpha testing, 277
- beta testing, 277
- concepts, 276
- concept testing, 276
- decline stage, 282
- diffusion of innovation, 270
- early adopters, 271
- early majority, 271
- first movers, 268

- growth stage, 282
- innovation, 266
- innovators, 270
- introduction stage, 282
- laggards, 271
- late majority, 271
- lead users, 276
- maturity stage, 282
- pioneers, 268

- premarket test, 278
- product development (product design), 277
- product life cycle, 282
- prototype, 277
- reverse engineering, 275
- test marketing, 279

Concept Review

1. Explain how new product or service innovations add value to the firm.

2. Sketch and describe the diffusion of innovation curve. How can marketers use the information provided by this curve to make marketing strategies and decisions?

3. Identify and discuss the factors that influence the adoption of new products.

4. List the steps in the new product development process. Describe some of the sources companies use to generate ideas for new products at the beginning of this process.

5. Why might a company need to exercise caution during the test marketing stage of the new development process?

6. What other factors besides the product itself does a company need to finalize during the product launch stage?

7. Do all products go through each and every stage of this process? Explain your answer.

8. What is the product life cycle (PLC)? Describe the characteristics of each stage of the PLC in terms of sales, profits, typical consumers, competition, and 4Ps strategies.

9. Describe some of the strategies companies can use to extend the life of a mature product.

10. Explain why the product life cycle is not a fail-proof tool in managing products.

Marketing Applications

1. Some people think that a product should be considered "new" only if it is completely new to the market and has never existed before. Describe or give examples of other types of new products.

2. Apple has introduced the iPhone featuring a touch screen. How quickly do you think this product will diffuse among the Canadian population? Describe the types of people that you expect will be in each of the diffusion of innovation categories.

3. Are there any advantages for companies that are the first to introduce products that create new markets? Justify your answer. If you see advantages, explain why some new products fail.

4. Identify and describe the ways that companies generate new product ideas. Which of these ways involve the

customer? How can firms assess the value of the ideas that customers generate?

5. Describe an example of a new product or service that is targeted at the student market. Using the concept testing discussion in the chapter, describe how you would conduct a concept test for this product or service.

6. A number of portable MP3 players are currently available in the market. How might the design and value provided by MP3 players make this product more appealing to consumers than, say, portable CD players?

7. Mazda is about to introduce a new model and is currently in the market testing phase of the new product development process. Describe two ways that Mazda might conduct initial market testing prior to launching this new model.

8. What shampoo do you use? What stage of the product life cycle is it in? Is the shampoo manufacturer's marketing strategy—its 4Ps—consistent with the product's stage in its life cycle? Explain.

9. In what stage of the product life cycle is a new model of a Palm PDA? Is Palm's marketing strategy—its 4Ps—consistent with the product's stage in its life cycle? How is it different from that of the shampoo in the previous question? Explain.

10. You have recently been hired by a cosmetics company in the product development group. The firm's brand is a top-selling, high-end line of cosmetics. The head of the development team has just presented research that shows the "tween" girls, aged 11 to 15, are very interested in cosmetics and have the money to spend. The decision is made to create a line of tween cosmetics based on the existing adult line. As the product moves through development you begin to notice that the team seems to lean toward a very edgy and sexual theme for the line, including naming the various lines "envy," "desire," "prowess," and "fatal attraction." You begin to wonder, is this concept too much for girls in the targeted age group?

Net Savvy

1. Go to www.bestnewproducts.ca and search for an interesting new product. Is this an innovative, new-to-the-world product? Discuss the extent to which the new product has the properties outlined in Adding Value 10.1 as important for new product design and development.

2. The automotive industry is constantly adding new and different products into cars and trucks. Conduct an Internet or library database search for innovative new automotive technologies. Choose products that fit each stage of the product life cycle, and justify your choices.

Chapter Case Study

MARKETING APPLE'S IPOD:[62] MUSIC TO YOUR EARS[63]

Whether it starts with a dream, an idea, or a thought, the road to marketing success is often long and requires research, planning, product alterations, and creative contemplations, which makes it all the more rare to witness the success of the iPod, the brainchild of Apple founder Steve Jobs, who got his product designed, built, and on shelves in less than a year. The cool product of choice for listening to and trading the latest sounds, the iPod has expanded to various models that music enthusiasts have quickly bought up during its brief existence. Furthermore, its introduction and subsequent acceptance has spawned an entire industry comprised of companies that market compatible accessories. Despite some initial problems with its battery life, the product is going strong, driving the majority of Apple's revenue growth. iPod thus is a prime example of successful marketing.

The Product Concept

Launched in October 2001, iPod was the first portable music player with the capability to download and store thousands of songs digitally. Its sales have reached over 4 million per year. The concept started off in response to consumer wants and in an environment that was ready for a product that would change the tide in the practice of pirating digital forms of music. Jobs saw the need for a good quality player that would allow its users to legally download and customize their music and to trade songs. In less than three years, his invention had already been termed "a cultural phenomenon" by *Brandweek* magazine.

This is not to say the road to success was without hurdles. Jobs had to persuade the major music labels to allow their artists' songs to be downloaded for 99 cents each, or about $9.99 per album. After being burned by sites like Roxio's Napster, which allowed peer-to-peer downloading for free, the music industry was hesitant to open its doors to such a proposal. Jobs sold the idea to the recording industry by making sure it would get its cut and relying on his credibility as a well-known name in computers and the head of Pixar Animation Studios. iPod owners would purchase songs via Apple's iTunes Music Store software, accessed through the iMac. The concept represented a cultural change for how people would access, purchase, and listen to music. The support of the industry soon became overwhelming; iTunes now offers more than 1 million tracks, representing five major music labels and 600 independents.

Making It Happen

Being first in the market with a very desirable product meant Jobs was able to command upward of $400 for the 40GB (10,000 songs stored) iPod model. More than 1000 accessories have been rolled out, including car adapters, custom carrying cases, and home speakers.

When other companies realized the power of the iPod, they began cobranding with Apple so that they could get a piece of the action. Hewlett-Packard, Bose, Volkswagen of America, and BMW—which built adapters into some of its cars' stereo systems—are just a few examples. Other smaller companies marketed iPod accessories, allowing Apple to extend the iPod's reach even further in the retail market. Even U2 got into the game, working with Apple to offer an iPod specific to the band.

The iPod's most distinguishing feature, according to Apple's advertising agency, was the white cord that connects the player to the earphones and that identifies iPod users as they go about their daily business, whether that means walking across campus, dancing down the sidewalk, or driving in their BMWs. Anyone can spot a member of the iPod "club." The introductory multimedia advertising campaign therefore focused on a simple, silhouetted dancing figure with a highlighted iPod and earphones.

The Video iPod can store 15,000 songs, display 25,000 photos on a 6-cm colour screen, and play videos. A new 80GB model allows consumers to watch movies and TV shows, play new iPod games, listen to podcasts or audiobooks, and view photo albums in addition to storing up to 20,000 songs. Customers can purchase music videos, movies like *Pirates of the Caribbean: The Curse of the Black Pearl* and TV shows like *Desperate Housewives* and *Lost*. There is concern among some network affiliates that this "off TV" viewing will hurt ratings and this certainly may ultimately be true, but the video iPod is an example of the paradigm shift that has been developing.

The Future

The iPod has been such a success that some industry analysts claim Apple would be better off as a marketer of entertainment and consumer electronics rather than a computer company. As CEO, Jobs has a reputation in the marketplace for his creative genius and for personally seeing new products successfully from the initial idea to the product launch. He has been credited with an uncanny ability to spot the next revolutionary innovation that will change the landscape of

Anyone can spot a member of the iPod "club."

the marketplace. That's a tough reputation to maintain. Will the company morph into a small electronics marketer? Will it take a different direction in the not-so-distant future? The answer depends on so many factors that it defies speculation. For the time being, Apple will enjoy its recent successes and prepare for the next big thing.

Apple's iPod commands an impressive share of the hard-drive based music player market, hovering around 90 percent. However, iPod is seeing a few serious competitors from other companies. Samsung's Z5, Sony's new Walkman, and Microsoft's Zune have earned some recognition and sales. However, they have some of the same problems other portable players are running into—there are not as many accessories for them as for iPod, their synchronization with the computer to upload songs is not nearly as effortless, and their ease of use is still lagging behind the simple language developed by Apple. Some analysts suggest that the mini player sector will see more competition in the future as it becomes a casual market and price competition begins. But they expect that iPod will still dominate the larger memory portable player market. Its brand recognition is growing each year as more companies are cobranding their products to make iPod easier to use, cooler to own, and more visible than ever.

Questions

1. One critical factor that affects the market potential for a product innovation is the ability to offer a differentiated product that delivers unique and superior value to customers. Discuss the extent to which Apple successfully accomplished this with the iPod and with its subsequent introductions, like the iPod shuffle and the iPod nano.

2. How would you classify the iPod today in terms of its stage in the product life cycle? Why?

3. Provide a description of what you think each type of adopter would be for an iPod. Do you you think we are seeing late majority adopters or laggards yet?

LEARNING OBJECTIVES

After studying this chapter you should be able to:

LO 1 Identify how marketing a service differs from marketing a product and apply the principles of intangibility, inseparability, variability, and perishability

LO 2 Explain why it is important that service marketers understand and manage customer expectations

LO 3 Describe strategies that firms can use to help employees provide better service

LO 4 Identify what firms should do when a service fails

Services:
The Intangible
Product

When you want to get rid of student furniture, ancient appliances, or yard waste, who would you call? According to an Ipsos Reid study, 1-800-GOT-JUNK? is the leading branded junk removal option. It was founded in Vancouver in 1989 by Brian Scudmore as a way to put himself through university. Today the $158-million business operates in 312 cities in Canada, the U.S., and Australia with a goal to become the world's largest junk removal company by 2012, the Starbucks of the trash business.[1]

Careful attention has been paid to branding, right down to the blue and green colours used on trucks. They help add tangibility, a crucial component for services companies who otherwise sell the invisible—Got-Junk consumers end up with no tangible reminder of the service that has been provided except perhaps more space in the garage or basement. The gleaming trucks send a signal of quality and professionalism to customers. Rather than buying top of mind awareness via traditional advertising, Got-Junk builds buzz at the local level with its brightly coloured trucks, lawn signs, and enthusiastic employees. The company's public relations staff has successfully generated over 1000 articles, further raising awareness and communicating their message to millions of consumers through appearances on *Dr. Phil* and *Oprah*. In Ontario, a cost-effective customer acquisition campaign gave consumers who ordered the company's services a $20 gift certificate for The Beer Store. Teaming up with The Beer Store made sense because its large and reliable base of male customers was the main target audience for Got-Junk's service.[2]

Finding and keeping employees who deliver outstanding customer service is another key to success for services companies. Hiring great people and treating them well is a core belief at 1-800-Got-Junk? and results in the ability to deliver an exceptional customer experience. Recruitment became a lot easier after the company was ranked as the number one company to work for in British Columbia two years in a row. The public recognition not only garnered media attention but also helped attract new employees in a tough labour market. Since services businesses rely on employees to act as company ambassadors, Got-Junk provides staff with bright blue fleece shirts emblazoned with the company logo, helping to present a uniform—no pun intended—image to customers. Strategies to keep staff pumped and motivated to stay with the company are critical, so employees are encouraged to submit their suggestions to a "Can you imagine?" wall at head office. Ideas so far include having a toy junk truck in McDonald's Happy Meals and wrapping the logo on a 737 jet.[3]

Got-Junk has big plans to build success along the lines of Starbucks, FedEx, or Southwest Airlines. Their slogan proves they've learned from Nike, too. It's "Just Get It Done."

Brightly coloured trucks and employee uniforms send tangible signals to 1-800-GOT-JUNK? customers that theirs is not the typical junk removal company.

service
Intangible customer benefits that are produced by people or machines and cannot be separated from the producer.

customer service
Specifically refers to human or mechanical activities firms undertake to help satisfy their customers' needs and wants.

1-800-Got-Junk turns trash into cash, an example of a firm that provides services as opposed to products. Whereas a **service** is any intangible offering that involves a deed, performance, or effort that cannot be physically possessed,[4] **customer service** specifically refers to human or mechanical activities that firms undertake to help satisfy their customers' needs and wants. By providing good customer service, firms add value to their products or services.

In this chapter we examine the unique characteristics of services which differentiate them from products. Then, as shown in our chapter roadmap, we discuss how companies can provide great service and use elements in the gaps model to help them meet customer expectations. Lastly, we look at how companies can recover from inevitable service failures.

Exhibit 11.1 illustrates the continuum from a pure service to a pure product. Some firms lie somewhere in the middle and include some service and some product or sell products with an "embedded" service element, for example, restaurants. As we noted in Chapter 2, even those firms that are engaged primarily in selling a product, like an apparel store, typically view service as a method to maintain a sustainable competitive advantage. This chapter moves on to take an inclusive view of services as anything from pure service businesses to a business that uses service as a differentiating tool to help it sell physical products.

Economies of developed countries like Canada have become increasingly dependent on services. For example, the service sector makes up more than 70 percent of Canada's economy, the lion's share of jobs, and is growing far faster than goods-producing industries. This dependence and the growth of service-oriented economies in developed countries have emerged for several reasons.

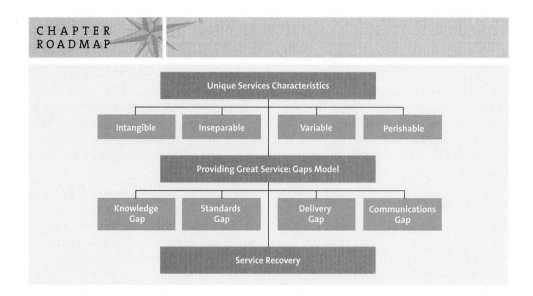

CHAPTER ROADMAP

Unique Services Characteristics

Intangible	Inseparable	Variable	Perishable

Providing Great Service: Gaps Model

Knowledge Gap	Standards Gap	Delivery Gap	Communications Gap

Service Recovery

First, it is generally less expensive for firms to manufacture their products in less-developed countries. Even if the goods are finished in Canada, some of their components likely were produced elsewhere. In turn, the proportion of service production to goods production in Canada, and other similar economies, has steadily increased over time. Second, household maintenance activities, which many people performed by themselves in the past, have become quite specialized. Food preparation, lawn maintenance, house cleaning, laundry and dry cleaning, hair care, and automobile maintenance all are often performed by specialists in the modern economy.

Third, people place a high value on convenience and leisure. Most households have little time for the household maintenance tasks mentioned in the previous point, and many are willing to pay others to do their chores. Fourth, as the Canadian population ages, the need for healthcare professionals—not only doctors and nurses but also assisted living facilities and nursing homes—also increases. Along the same lines, an ever greater number of retirees are travelling more and utilizing various forms of leisure services.

As the population ages, the need for healthcare professionals increases.

EXHIBIT 11.1 The Service–Product Continuum

Doctor	Hotel	Dry Cleaners	Restaurant	Apparel Specialty Store	Grocery Store

◀ **Service Dominant**   **Product Dominant** ▶

LO ① # Services Marketing Differs from Product Marketing

The marketing of services differs from product marketing because of four fundamental differences unique to services: They are intangible, inseparable, variable, and perishable.[5] See Exhibit 11.2. To help remember these differences, it may help to think of them as the 4Is of services in that they are Intangible, Inseparable from their providers, Inconsistent (variable), and cannot be held in Inventory (perishable). These differences make marketing services considerably more challenging than marketing products. This section examines these four differences and discusses how they affect marketing strategies.

Intangible

intangible
A characteristic of a service; it cannot be touched, tasted, or seen like a pure product can.

As the title of this chapter implies, the most fundamental difference between a product and a service is that services are intangible—they cannot be touched, tasted, or seen like a pure product can. When you get a physical examination, you see and hear the doctor, but the service itself is intangible. This intangibility can prove highly challenging to marketers. For instance, it makes it difficult to convey the benefits of services—try describing whether the experience of visiting your dentist was good or bad and why. Healthcare service providers (e.g., physicians, dentists) offer cues

EXHIBIT 11.2 Core Differences between Services and Goods

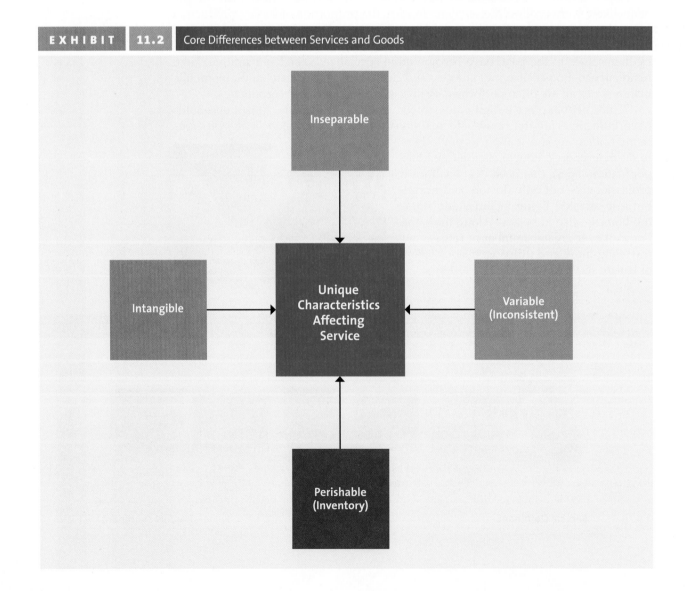

to help their customers experience and perceive their service more positively, such as a waiting room stocked with television sets, computer games and toys for children, upscale beverages, and comfortable chairs to create an atmosphere that appeals to the target market.

Similarly, Starbucks has always enhanced its service offering by providing a comfortable and cozy atmosphere for drinking coffee, working, reading, or chatting with friends and has launched "Hear Music Coffeehouses," fully integrated cafés and music stores. Much like a regular Starbucks, this wholly owned subsidiary is warm and inviting, but in these outlets, customers can buy CDs, have a drink, listen to music, and sift through thousands of songs stored in a computer database to create a personalized, mixed-CD jacket (with liner notes even!). [6]

Furthermore, a service can't be shown directly to potential customers, which also makes it difficult to promote. Marketers must therefore creatively employ symbols and images to promote and sell services, like Walt Disney World does in using its advertising to evoke images of happy families and nostalgic memories of Mickey Mouse and previous visits to the theme park. Likewise, Cirque du Soleil, considered Canada's top cultural export, adds tangibility to its performances with mesmerizingly staged acrobatics, backed by a live orchestra which plays an original score. The entire circus experience is carefully orchestrated to create memorable impressions—the Porta-Potties on its big-top sites even have running water.[7] Professional medical services provide appropriate images of personnel doing their jobs in white coats surrounded by high-tech equipment. Dentists provide patients with tangible evidence of their visits in the form of free toothbrushes. Educational institutions promote the quality of their services by touting their famous faculty and alumni, as well as their accreditations. They also often use images of happy students sitting spellbound in front of a fascinating professor or going on to lucrative careers of their own.

Because of the intangibility of services, the images marketers use reinforce the benefit or value that a service provides. Professional service providers, such as doctors, lawyers, accountants, and consultants, depend heavily on consumers' perceptions of their integrity and trustworthiness. Yet the promotional campaigns some of these professionals use have been criticized by their peers and consumer welfare groups. Tension is created when service providers like personal injury lawyers use aggressive marketing tactics to attract clients to their service but still attempt to maintain a perception of integrity and trustworthiness or when invasion of privacy becomes an issue as discussed in Ethical Dilemma 11.1.

At Starbucks' "Hear Music Coffeehouses," customers can buy CDs, have a drink, listen to music, and create personalized, mixed-CDs.

Since services are intangible, healthcare service providers must create visual images to promote and sell their services.

Inseparable Production and Consumption

Another difference between services and products is that services are produced and consumed at the same time; that is, service and consumption are **inseparable**. Because service production can't be separated from consumption, astute service marketers provide opportunities for their customers to get directly involved in the service. Healthcare providers have found, for instance, that the more control they allow their patients in determining their course of treatment, the more satisfied those patients are.[8]

Because the service is inseparable from its consumption, customers rarely have the opportunity to try the service before they purchase it. And after the service has been performed, it can't be returned. Imagine telling your dentist that you want a "test"

inseparable
A characteristic of a service: it is produced and consumed at the same time; that is, service and consumption are inseparable.

Ethical Dilemma

11.1   Smile, You're On Camera?

Google Maps recently released its latest feature: Street View mapping capabilities. These detailed 360-degree maps of select cities allow users to look at specific items such as individual buildings, parked cars, and even street signs. Some pictures display people sunbathing in their yards or walking their dogs. Critics feel that this is an invasion of privacy while others disagree; what happens in the streets is public information anyway. The online application has spurred the debate about personal privacy—just where is the line drawn between mapping geography and creating surveillance video?

Calgary-based Immersive Media Corporation is behind the technology enabling these detailed street level views. VW Beetles with dodecahedron cameras mounted on top drive all day, recording what they see. Later, computer programs string the images together with the latest 3-D imaging technology.[9] In the future, live video is a possibility.

Static maps have already been created for Toronto, Calgary, Vancouver, Montreal, and Ottawa. According to Myles McGovern, president and CEO of Immersive Media Corp., the true value in these maps is for emergency personnel to survey a venue before arriving at the scene. Other anticipated users include rural engineers, architects, construction managers, and insurance appraisers, who need to see details of a location. This new tool could save companies thousands of dollars in travel and assessment fees. Also, public navigational systems could eventually include landmarks and building descriptions, reducing travel times and eliminating confusing directions. But what about the potential for inappropriate use?

In June 2007, U.S. officials uncovered an alleged plot by a terrorist organization to blow up fuel tanks at John F. Kennedy Airport in New York. A similar tool, Google Earth, was identified as the system that helped formulate this plan. However, experts say these online tools don't provide new information to terrorists: even if Google Earth or Google Maps weren't available, the same information can still be obtained from one of many other sources.

On a smaller scale, the Street View tool could be used for espionage and even stalking. With live video, you could check on your friends who didn't answer your phone call to see if their cars were parked in the driveway. Once captured on a Google Map, your profile would be published for the world to see.

Should Google be allowed to offer this service? While the commercial applications and benefits for business are clear, the problem of citizens' rights remains. Canada's Privacy Commissioner has raised concerns about the service because it could violate federal privacy laws designed to protect citizens from having their personal information easily accessible. Since Google Maps is an online tool, it crosses international borders, making privacy laws complicated and difficult to enforce. Even advanced measures to ensure the safety and security of inhabitants wouldn't rule out foul play. In the end, is Google compromising our safety for the advancement of business, or should public information be made available to everyone, all the time?

Source: Adapted from: www.cbc.ca/thecurrent/2007/200706/20070612.html.

---

cavity filled before he or she starts drilling a real one or asking to try out a new look before your stylist lops several inches off your hair. Because the purchase risk in these scenarios can be relatively high, services sometimes provide extended warranties and 100 percent satisfaction guarantees, such as First Choice Haircutters which promotes "Affordable, Professional Haircare. Guaranteed." Many hotels (e.g., Comfort Inn, Comfort Suites, Quality Inn, Sleep Inn, Clarion) post claims advising guests: "If you are not satisfied with your accommodations or our service, please advise the front desk of a problem right away and give them an opportunity to correct the situation. If the hotel staff is unable to satisfy you, they will give you up to one night's free stay."[10]

Variable (Inconsistent)

variability
A characteristic of a service: its quality may vary because it is provided by humans.

The more humans that are needed to provide a service, the more likely there is to be **variability,** or inconsistency, in the service's quality. A hair stylist may give bad haircuts in the morning because he or she went out the night before, yet that stylist still may offer a better service than the undertrained stylist working in the next station over. A restaurant, which offers a mixture of services and products, generally can control its food quality but not the variability in food preparation or delivery. If a consumer has a problem with a product, it can be replaced, remade, destroyed, or, if it is already in the supply chain, recalled. In many cases, the problem can even be fixed before the product gets into consumers' hands. But an inferior service can't be recalled; by the time the firm recognizes a problem, the damage has been done.

Marketers like Starbucks strive to reduce their service variability through training and standardization. Enterprise Rent-A-Car, for instance, has worked to standardize its service delivery across North America and, to that end, provides extensive training to its associates. Go to any Enterprise outlet at any airport, and chances are you will be greeted in the same personalized way. The airport shuttle drivers will load and unload your bags. When you get off the shuttle, you will be greeted by name, and your car will be ready to go in minutes. This smooth and pleasant service transaction is the result of the company's very specific service standards and excellent training program.

Enterprise Rent-A-Car reduces their service variability through training and standardization. You get the same great service everywhere you go.

Marketers also can use the variable nature of services to their advantage. A micromarketing segmentation strategy can customize a service to meet customers' needs exactly (see Chapter 8). Technology services company, Nerds On Site, will come to your home or office and take care of any repair or service your PC might need—setting up a network, cleaning your hard drive, or designing or hosting your website. Each customer's needs are different, so Nerds On Site employs a cadre of consultants who possess a variety of skills. Clients are matched with their very own "Primary Nerd" on the basis of their needs, which allows for a fully personalized service offering.

Such micromarketing can be expensive to deliver though, particularly for a firm that offers multiple services. Consumers also may get confused or even irritated if they must pay for each little service. Imagine a hotel that charged separately for each bed, towel, bar of soap, use of the TV, and lap in the swimming pool. Instead, service providers usually bundle their services into one package and charge a single price. For example, Club Med resorts offer all-inclusive amenity packages for one price, which includes, for example, a flight from Montreal to Club Med Punta Cana, Dominican Republic and then accommodations, meals, snacks, bar service, and sports and entertainment activities once you arrive for about $1,800 for seven nights—include a friend for $1,000 more![11]

When firms offer multiple services like Club Med, they often bundle the services under one price.

In an alternative approach, some service providers tackle the variability issue by replacing people with machines. For simple transactions like getting cash, using an ATM is usually quicker and more convenient—and less variable—than waiting in line for a bank teller. Adding Value 11.1 describes how some retailers and other service providers have begun to provide additional value with their self-checkout machines.

The technological delivery of services can cause additional problems. Some customers either do not embrace the idea of replacing a human with a machine for business interactions or have problems using the technology. In other cases, the technology may not perform adequately, such as self-checkout scanners that fail to scan all merchandise or ATMs that run out of money or are out of order.

The Internet has reduced service variability in several areas. Prior to the mid-1990s, customers engaged in one-on-one interactions when they purchased travel items (e.g., airlines, hotel, rental car), concert and movie tickets, insurance, mortgages, and merchandise. Today, these purchases can be made directly via the Internet, and if the customer wants more information than is available online, websites provide ways to contact customer service personnel by e-mail or telephone.

Beyond online benefits, the Internet has also reduced service variability. At the William Lutsky YMCA in Edmonton, members can use FitLinxx, a computerized system, to track their workout performance. New users establish goals, workouts, and schedules, and receive detailed workout programs, for example, at least 14 abdominal muscle workouts pop up when users select "abs." FitLinxx learns users' programs, coaches them individually throughout workouts, and tracks progress over time. The system not only has health benefits for users who always get a consistent workout, it has also boosted customer retention and users typically exercise more often than average.[12]

Adding Value   11.1   Adding Convenience through Self-Checkout Machines[13]

Thought of as a gimmick when they were first introduced in 1995, self-checkout machines have gained converts and are heading into more arenas. The machines are multiplying in grocery and discount stores at blistering speed. Canadians are very accustomed to serving themselves and quickly adopt new technology. An Ipsos Reid/NCR study showed that 56 percent of Canadians are more likely to shop at stores with self service than those without.[14]

Self-checkouts are successful and increase customer loyalty because they appeal to those shoppers who want to move through quickly and believe they can zip through their checkouts faster by using the machines. Some experts say the reason customers think self-checkout is faster is that they are active when using it, unlike waiting for a cashier, which leaves customers with nothing to do and may make it seem as though time is dragging. Others contend that self-checkout actually does save between 15 seconds and 15 minutes, depending on the size of an order.

If customers like the machines, so will retailers. Industry experts say each machine costs about $90,000 and handles 15 to 40 percent of the daily transactions of stores that maintain them. Although expensive, the machines reduce labour expenses; one cashier can oversee the operation of four to eight self-checkouts. And the machines don't have to be trained, nor do they ever come to work late or with a bad attitude.

Do self-checkout machines increase or reduce consumers' perception of service?

Perishable (Inventory)

Services are **perishable** in that they cannot be held in inventory or stored for use in the future. You can't stockpile a yoga class like you could a six-pack of beer, for instance. The perishability of services provides both challenges and opportunities to marketers in terms of the critical task of matching demand and supply. As long as the demand for and the supply of the service match closely, there is no problem, but unfortunately, this perfect matching rarely occurs. A ski area, for instance, can be open as long as there is snow, even at night, but demand peaks on weekends and holidays, so ski areas often offer less expensive tickets during off-peak periods to stimulate demand. Airlines, cruise ships, movie theatres, and restaurants confront similar challenges and attack them in similar ways. Airlines offer promotional pricing to encourage people to book flights during the off-season and movie theatres routinely discount matinee showings when demand is typically lower. Looking to increase facility usage and reach new audiences, Cineplex Galaxy started broadcasting NHL games live in five Canadian cities in 2006. For some hockey fans, it's the next best thing to being there, getting to see a team like the Toronto Maple Leafs at a fraction of the cost at $10.95 versus between $23 and $381 to take in a game at the Air Canada Centre.[15]

Balancing the ups and downs of demand and capacity is challenging. As noted earlier, unlike products, services can't be stockpiled in inventory. For services companies, excess demand results in having to turn customers away in peak periods, while excess capacity may mean less desirable expense to revenue ratios. For example dental hygienists, rent, and other expenses still need to be paid even if customers forget their appointments, so dental offices maximize capacity by making advance reminder calls to patients or may charge a cancellation fee if clients do not show-up for their appointments without adequate notice. Hotel reservation systems offer guaranteed late arrivals, ensuring that revenue is not forfeited by holding rooms until very late in the day.

As we have seen, providing great service is not easy, and it requires a diligent effort to analyze the service process piece by piece. In the next section, we examine what is known as the Gaps Model, which is designed to highlight those areas where customers believe they are getting less or poorer service than they should (the gaps) and how these gaps can be closed.

perishability
A characteristic of a service: it cannot be stored for use in the future.

Since services are perishable, service providers like ski areas offer less expensive tickets at night to stimulate demand.

LO ② Providing Great Service: The Gaps Model

service gap
Results when a service fails to meet the expectations that customers have about how it should be delivered.

knowledge gap
Reflects the difference between customers' expectations and the firm's perception of those expectations.

standards gap
Pertains to the difference between the firm's perceptions of customers' expectations and the service standards it sets.

delivery gap
The difference between the firm's service standards and the actual service it provides to customers.

communication gap
Refers to the difference between the actual service provided to customers and the service that the firm's promotion program promises.

Customers have certain expectations about how a service should be delivered. When the delivery of that service fails to meet those expectations, a **service gap** results. The Gaps Model (Exhibit 11.3) is designed to encourage the systematic examination of all aspects of the service delivery process and prescribe the steps needed to develop an optimal service strategy.[16]

As Exhibit 11.3 shows, there are four service gaps:

1. The **knowledge gap** reflects the difference between customers' expectations and the firm's perception of those customer expectations. Firms can close this gap by matching customer expectations with actual service through research.

2. The **standards gap** pertains to the difference between the firm's perceptions of customers' expectations and the service standards it sets. Firms can narrow this gap by setting appropriate service standards and measuring service performance.

3. The **delivery gap** is the difference between the firm's service standards and the actual service it provides to customers. This gap can be closed by getting employees to meet or exceed service standards.

4. The **communication gap** refers to the difference between the actual service provided to customers and the service that the firm's promotion program promises. Generally firms can close this gap if they are more realistic about the services they can provide and manage customer expectations effectively.

As we discuss the four gaps subsequently, we will apply them to the experience that Marcia Kessler had with a motel in Muskoka. She saw an ad for a weekend

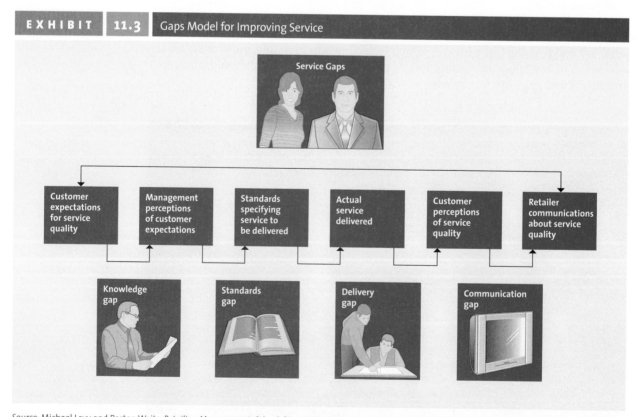

EXHIBIT 11.3 Gaps Model for Improving Service

Source: Michael Levy and Barton Weitz, *Retailing Management*, 6th ed. (Burr Ridge, IL: McGraw-Hill, 2007). Adapted from Valerie Zeithaml, A. Parasuraman, and Leonard Berry, *Delivering Quality Customer Service* (New York: The Free Press, 1990) and Valerie Zeithaml, Leonard Berry, and A. Parasuraman, "Communication and Control Processes in the Delivery of Service Quality," *Journal of Marketing* 52, no. 2 (April 1988), pp. 35–48.

package that quoted a very reasonable daily rate and listed the free amenities available at Paradise Motel: free babysitting services, a piano bar with a nightly singer, a free continental breakfast, a heated swimming pool, and newly decorated rooms. When she booked the room, Marcia discovered that the price advertised was not available during the weekend, and a three-day minimum stay was required. After checking in with a very unpleasant person at the front desk, Marcia and her husband found that their room appeared circa 1950 and had not been cleaned. When she complained, all she got was attitude from the assistant manager. Resigned to the fact that they were slated to spend the weekend, she decided to go for a swim. Unfortunately, the water was "heated" by Georgian Bay, and hovered around 10 degrees. No one was using the babysitting services because there were few young children at the resort. It turns out the piano bar singer was the second cousin of the owner, and he couldn't carry a tune, let alone play the piano very well. The continental breakfast must have come all the way from the continent, because everything was stale and tasteless. Marcia couldn't wait to get home.

What service gaps did Marcia experience while on vacation at the Paradise Motel in Muskoka?

The Knowledge Gap: Knowing What Customers Want

LO **3**

An important early step in providing good service is knowing what the customer wants. While, the motel offered babysitting services, most of its customers did not have kids, had not brought them on their trip, or simply did not want to use the service. However, all guests want their rooms cleaned prior to check-in.

To reduce the knowledge gap, firms must understand the customers' expectations which can be accomplished through customer research and by increasing the interaction and communication between managers and employees.

Understanding Customer Expectations   Customers' expectations are based on their knowledge and experiences.[17] Marcia's expectations were that her room would be ready when she got there, the swimming pool would be heated, the singer would be able to sing, and the breakfast would be fresh.

Expectations vary according to the type of service. Marcia's expectations might have been higher, for instance, if she were staying at a Fairmont rather than the Paradise Motel. At Fairmont, she might expect employees to know her by name, be aware of her dietary preferences, and have placed fresh fruit of her choice and fresh-cut flowers in her room before she arrived.

People's expectations also vary depending on the situation. Marcia may be satisfied with both the preceding hotel properties, depending on the circumstances. If she were travelling on business, the Paradise Motel might be fine, but if she were celebrating her 10th wedding anniversary, she probably would prefer the Fairmont. Regardless of these choices, however, the service provider needs to know and understand the expectations of the customers in its target market.

Evaluating Service Quality   To meet or exceed customers' expectations, marketers must determine what those expectations are. Yet because of their intangibility, the **service quality**, or customers' perceptions of how well a service meets or exceeds their expectations, often is difficult for customers to evaluate.[18] Customers generally use five distinct service dimensions to determine overall service quality: reliability, responsiveness, assurance, empathy, and tangibles (Exhibit 11.4).

If you were to apply the five service dimensions to your own decision-making process when you selected a university—which provides the service of education—you might find results like those in Exhibit 11.5.

service quality Customers' perceptions of how well a service meets or exceeds their expectations.

EXHIBIT   11.4   Building Blocks of Service Quality

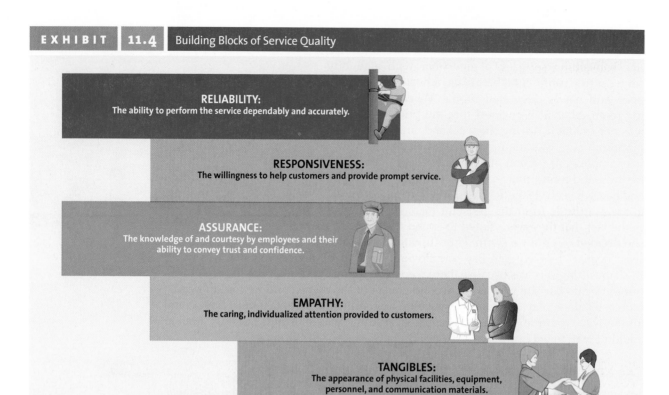

EXHIBIT   11.4   Building Blocks of Service Quality

RELIABILITY:
The ability to perform the service dependably and accurately.

RESPONSIVENESS:
The willingness to help customers and provide prompt service.

ASSURANCE:
The knowledge of and courtesy by employees and their ability to convey trust and confidence.

EMPATHY:
The caring, individualized attention provided to customers.

TANGIBLES:
The appearance of physical facilities, equipment, personnel, and communication materials.

EXHIBIT   11.5   Collegiate Service Dimensions

	University A	University B
Reliability	Offers sound curriculum with extensive placement services and internships.	Curriculum covers all the basics but important courses are not always available. Career placement is haphazard at best.
Responsiveness	Slow to respond to application. Very structured visitation policy. Rather inflexible with regard to personal inquiries or additional meetings.	Quick response during application process. Open visitation policy. Offers variety of campus resources to help with decision making.
Assurance	Staff seems very confident in reputation and services.	Informal staff who convey enthusiasm for institution.
Empathy	Seems to process student body as a whole rather than according to individual needs or concerns.	Very interested in providing a unique experience for each student.
Tangibles	Very traditional campus with old-world look and feel. Facilities are manicured. Dorm rooms are large, but bathrooms are a little old.	New campus with modern architecture. Campus is less manicured. Dorm rooms are spacious with newer bathrooms.

If your expectations include an individualized experience at a state-of-the-art institution, perhaps University B is a better alternative for you. But if you are relying heavily on academic performance and career placement from your university experience, then University A might be a better choice. If a strong culture and tradition are important to you, University A offers this type of environment. What were your expectations, and how did your university choices fall within these service dimensions?

Marketing Research: Understanding Customers   Marketing research (see Chapter 5) provides a means to better understand consumers' service expectations and their perceptions of service quality. This research can be extensive and expensive, or it can be integrated into a firm's everyday interactions with customers. Today, most service firms have developed voice-of-customer programs and employ ongoing marketing research to assess how well they are meeting their customers' expectations.

A systematic **voice-of-customer (VOC) program** collects customer insights and intelligence to influence and drive business decisions. For instance, Dell launched ideastorm.com, an online forum that allows people to submit ideas for improving its products and services. The community votes on the best ideas and if they make sense, the company will act on them. When ideastorm.com contributors wanted Linux pre-installed on their PCs and notebooks Dell surveyed 100,000 customers to get more insights and ended up implementing the idea. Three months after launching ideastorm.com more than 3500 ideas had been posted.[19] Aeroplan uses online surveys and conducts in-person "kitchen table" meetings with selected members asking them everything from what their redemption experience is like to what new services and improvements they'd like to see.[20] Feedback from FedEx's VOC program, involving in-person meetings with business customers, resulted in the development of its intra-Canada deferred (two-day) service.[21] Entrepreneurial Marketing 11.1 provides a glimpse into how voice of the customer insights can be used to instigate change in the modelling industry.

> **voice-of-customer (VOC) program**
> An ongoing marketing research system that collects customer inputs and integrates them into managerial decisions.

Another means to evaluate how well firms perform on the five service quality dimensions (Exhibit 11.4), the concept of the **zone of tolerance** refers to the area between customers' expectations regarding their desired service and the minimum level of acceptable service—that is, the difference between what the customer really wants and what he or she will accept before going elsewhere.[22] To define the zone of tolerance, firms ask a series of questions about each service quality dimension that relate to

> **zone of tolerance**
> The area between customers' expectations regarding their desired service and the minimum level of acceptable service—that is, the difference between what the customer really wants and what he or she will accept before going elsewhere.

- The desired and expected level of service for each dimension, from low to high.
- Customers' perceptions of how well the focal service performs and how well a competitive service performs, from low to high.
- The importance of each service quality dimension.

A very straightforward and inexpensive method of collecting consumers' perceptions of service quality is to gather them at the time of the sale. Service providers can ask customers how they liked the service—though customers often are hesitant to provide negative feedback directly to the person who provided the service—or distribute a simple questionnaire. The company must take care not to lose much of this information, which can happen if there is no effective mechanism for filtering it up to the key decision-makers. Furthermore, in some cases, customers cannot effectively evaluate the service until several days or weeks later. Automobile dealers, for instance, often call their customers a week after they perform a service like an oil change to assess their service quality.

Another excellent method for assessing customers' expectations is making effective use of customer complaint behaviour. Even if complaints are handled effectively to solve customers' problems, the essence of the complaint is too often lost on managers. For instance, a large PC retailer responded to complaints about the lack of service from salespeople and issues with products by providing an e-mail address for people to contact the service department. This proved to be difficult when the problem is that the computer isn't working.[23]

Even firms with the best formal research mechanisms in place must put managers on the front lines occasionally to interact directly with the customers. Unless the managers who make the service quality decisions know what their service providers are facing on a day-to-day basis, and unless they can talk directly to the customers with whom those service providers interact, any customer service program they create will not be as good as it could be.

Entrepreneurial Marketing

11.1   Expanding the Definition of Beauty

When Ben Barry was 14 years old, he became a modelling agent to a beautiful friend who could not land a modelling job. Despite having spent over $3000 on modelling classes and photos, agencies rejected her because her size 8 frame was "too big." Shortly after helping her land glossy magazine gigs, Barry signed on four more models. He took a research trip during spring break in eighth grade, visiting elite modelling agencies and receiving industry advice. The head of Elite Models advised the young entrepreneur of typical model requirements: swan neck, teeny waist, mini hips—all stretched tightly over a 5-foot, 11-inch frame. But Barry didn't like what he was hearing, and continued choosing his models for their personalities and energy, as well as their looks.

When a friend developed an eating disorder it spurred Barry into action. By age 24, he successfully established the Ben Barry Agency Inc. for models, and has secured his reputation as an inspirational entrepreneur in the Canadian fashion and modelling scene. Barry is a driving force behind changing perceptions in the modelling industry. His agency believes that models should reflect the make-up of society with a diversity of ages, sizes, ethnicities, and looks. His many successes range from introducing visible minorities to mall fashion shows, to placing diverse models for the "Real Beauty" campaign run in over 50 countries by Unilever's Dove brand. But despite the enormous 700-percent sales growth from the Dove Campaign for Real Beauty, posh fashion magazines still shun diverse models. There is no research to prove that tall, skinny waifs are good or bad for selling magazines. So Barry has made this his next project.

He is currently pursuing his PhD in innovation and strategy at Cambridge University. His three-year study of marketing in the beauty industry is using consumer consultation to evaluate the effectiveness of model advertising. Based on early findings, and recent decisions like Vogue's choice to feature plus-sized singer Jennifer Hudson on its cover, Barry anticipates major changes in the industry.[24] But rather than affect a paradigm shift to larger models, Barry is more interested in widening the range of accepted sizes.[25] He plans to one day enter the boardroom with top magazines and show them the data that supports diverse beauty.

After a friend was rejected as a model because her size 8 frame was too big, Ben Barry started an agency featuring more realistic models.

Fashioning Reality: A New Generation of Entrepreneurship, Barry's recently released autobiographical book, describes how he is working to change the face of fashion and help alter the public's concept of beauty. Rather than challenge conventions through lobbying and boycotts, Barry says today's smartest activists are inside the system of capitalism, facing tough issues as business people. He hopes the book will inspire other young entrepreneurs to run companies that make a profit by making social change. Instead of waiting until they obtain advanced academic degrees and decades of experience, he hopes to show young people they have all of the knowledge and skills to begin their own businesses today.[26]

The Standards Gap: Setting Service Standards

Say the Paradise Motel in Muskoka set out to determine its customers' service expectations and gained a pretty good idea of them. Its work is still far from over; the next step is to set its service standards and develop systems to ensure high-quality service. How can it make sure that every room is cleaned by 2:00 p.m.? That the food is checked for freshness and quality every day? The firm needs to set high service standards, enforce these standards, and train employees on how to perform their tasks to these standards. Managers must lead by example and demonstrate high service standards, which will permeate throughout the organization.

Achieving Service Goals through Training To deliver consistently high-quality service, firms must set specific, measurable goals based on customers' expectations; to help ensure that quality, the employees should be involved in the goal setting. For instance, although the most efficient process at Paradise Motel would be to start cleaning rooms at 8:00 a.m. and finish by 5:00 p.m., many guests want to sleep late and new arrivals

Service providers, like this housekeeper at a hotel, generally want to do a good job, but they need to be trained to know exactly what a good job entails.

want to get into their room as soon as they arrive. A customer-oriented standard would mandate that the rooms get cleaned between 10:00 a.m. and 2:00 p.m.

Service providers generally want to do a good job, as long as they know what is expected of them. Motel employees should be shown, for instance, exactly how managers expect them to clean a room and what specific tasks they are responsible for performing.

While frontline service employees can be taught specific tasks related to their jobs, it is simply not enough to tell employees to "be nice" or "do what customers want." A quality goal should be specific: Greet every customer you encounter with "good morning/afternoon/evening, Sir or Miss." Try to greet customers by name.

In extreme cases, such training becomes even more crucial. From long ticket lines to cancelled flights to lost baggage, customer service incidents are on the rise in the airline industry. Faced with mounting complaints, airlines are responding with better employee training geared toward identifying and defusing potentially explosive situations. For example, Northwest Airlines has implemented a "Customer First" training program for its ground operations, customer service agents, flight attendants, and pilots that mandates specific performance measures and standardized practices throughout Northwest's service areas. Policies for service during delays, such as providing snacks on board or trucking food out to waiting planes and offering status updates every 15 minutes, have given employees the tools and guidelines they need to better service their customers.[27]

Commitment to Service Quality Service providers take their cues from management. If managers strive for excellent service, treat their customers well, and demand the same attitudes from everyone in the organization, it is likely employees will do the same. Take for example WestJet CEO, Clive Beddoe. Named one of Canada's most respected CEOs in The Tenth Annual 'Canada's Most Respected Corporations Survey,' he's perfectly happy to clean cabins and lend a hand on board flights when he is a passenger. WestJet's legendary reputation for customer service has resulted in revenues of $1.7 billion and record breaking net earnings that grew by 378 percent at the end of 2006.[28] This commitment to service quality has been modelled by company executives from the start. When WestJet launched in 1996, executive vice-president Don Bell spent a lot of time in the airline's call centre fielding questions and booking flights for customers.[29]

Employees, who understand that operating on time is a critical component to service quality and guest experience, work hard to improve on time performance. In 2006, 81.7 percent of flights arrived within 15 minutes of their scheduled time.[30] Sales agents also strive to provide the highest standard of customer service. Their efforts were recognized in 2006 when the Sales Super Centre was named the Best Call Centre in the country in an airline survey conducted by *Canadian Business Magazine's* consumer reports department. An employee profit sharing plan provides rewards beyond public recognition. The vast majority of employees belong to the WestJet Share Purchase Plan making them owners of the company and giving them all the more reason to ensure high levels of service quality.

The Delivery Gap: Delivering Service Quality

The delivery gap is where "the rubber meets the road," where the customer directly interacts with the service provider. Even if there are no other gaps, a delivery gap always results in a service failure. Marcia experienced several delivery gaps at the Paradise Motel: the unclean room, the assistant manager's attitude, the unheated swimming pool, the poor piano bar singer, and the stale food.

Delivery gaps can be reduced when employees are empowered to act in the customers' and the firm's best interests and supported in their efforts so they can do their jobs effectively.[31] Technology can also be employed to reduce delivery gaps. (See Exhibit 11.6.)

Empowering Service Providers In this context, **empowerment** means allowing employees to make decisions about how service is provided to customers. When frontline employees are authorized to make decisions to help their customers, service quality generally improves.[32] Best Buy, for instance, has reengineered its organizational structure to empower employees to be more involved in the day-to-day running of the business and to make adjustments as necessary. The new employee-centric culture has helped Best Buy significantly lower its employee turnover rate. Happy employees make for happy customers.[33]

However, empowering service providers can be difficult and costly. In cases in which the service is very repetitive and routine, such as at a fast-food restaurant, it might be more efficient and easier for service providers to follow a few simple rules. For instance, if a customer doesn't like his hamburger, ask him what he would like instead or offer him a refund. If an exceptional circumstance that does not fit the rules arises, then a manager should handle the issue.

Empowerment becomes more important when price points edge higher and services are more individualized. The Keg Steakhouse & Bar hires the best staff and empowers them through superlative training programs. Staff members are professional—their friendliness, warmth, personality, and enthusiasm are all part of The Keg dining experience. It is because of this that The Keg Steakhouse & Bar was recognized for the fifth year in a row as one of the 50 Best Employers in Canada.[34]

empowerment
In context of service delivery, means allowing employees to make decisions about how service is provided to customers.

The Keg is successful, in part, because it empowers its employees to satisfy customers.

| EXHIBIT | 11.6 | Methods to Reduce Delivery Gaps |

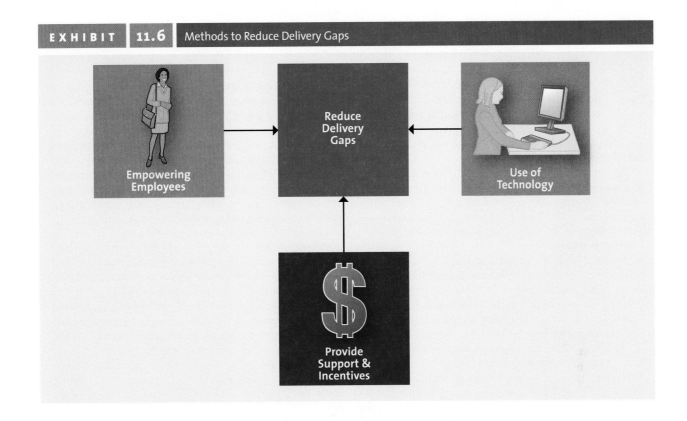

Providing Support and Incentives   A service provider's job can often be difficult, especially when customers are unpleasant or less than reasonable. The old cliché, "Service with a smile," remains the best approach. To ensure that service is delivered properly, management needs to support the service provider.

First, managers and coworkers should provide emotional support to service providers by demonstrating a concern for their well-being and standing behind their decisions. Because it can be very disconcerting when a waiter is abused by a customer who believes her food was improperly prepared, for instance, restaurant managers must be supportive and understanding and work to help employees get through their often emotional reaction to the berating they might experience.[35] When the waiter is empowered to rectify the situation by giving the customer new food and a free dessert, the manager also must stand behind the waiter's decision, not punish her for giving away too much, and thereby provide the needed support.

Second, the support that managers provide must be consistent and coherent throughout the organization. Patients expect physicians to provide great patient care using state-of-the-art procedures and medications, many doctors must squeeze more people into their office hours. These conflicting goals can be so frustrating and emotionally draining on physicians and other healthcare providers that some have found work outside of medicine.

Third, a key part of any customer service program is providing rewards to employees for excellent service. Numerous firms have developed a service reputation by ensuring that their employees recognize the value the firm places on customer service, offering VIP clubs and "Employee of the Month" service awards. Some companies encourage associates or their managers to stand up and recount their great customer service episodes from the past week.[36]

Use of Technology   Technology has become an increasingly important method for facilitating the delivery of services. Since the mid-1990s, with the widespread

Internet Marketing

11.1   Fairmont: Turning Moments Into Memories

Fairmont Hotels & Resorts is the largest luxury hotel company in North America with 38 properties in Canada, the United States, Mexico, and the Caribbean. In order to meet its worldwide expansion objectives, Fairmont recognized the need to build its brand as a provider of unrivalled customer service in all markets.

Inspired by its mission statement, "Turning moments into memories for our guests," Fairmont created an e-business strategy to support its most loyal customers: business visitors. More than 50 percent of Fairmont's customers are mobile professionals attending conventions or business meetings.

Working with Accenture and Cisco, Fairmont developed a new website and online booking engine. The goals were to enhance its ability to market its properties to individual travellers, persuade potential guests to choose Fairmont as their hotel of choice, and provide guests with unmatched online service.

To start, they created a more personalized, transaction-based experience for website visitors. For example, their new online booking system recognizes clients when they log on and preloads information stored in their guest's profile, such as President's Club status (the guest loyalty program) and preferences. Guests can view rooms, rates, availability, and promotional packages offered at each of Fairmont's properties. And they can confirm, update, or cancel their reservations in real time, regardless of their original booking source.

Another part of the e-business solution strengthened guest data warehouse capabilities allowing Fairmont to maintain guest profile information across properties, target guest segments with personalized communications, incentives and discounts, better manage its loyalty program, and acquire new guests and build loyalty. Individual tracking provided the ability to follow visitors globally across the hotel chain, which meant Fairmont could improve its customer service capabilities by better understanding their guests' preferences, booking channels, and spending patterns.

Fairmont's e-business strategy was designed to boost customer loyalty by crafting personalized guest services and picking up nuances in travel habits through self-selected options on the Fairmont website as well as information input by employees at the property level. By leveraging this information, Fairmont was able to gather data that allowed them to personalize and enhance the guest experience and establish targeted marketing campaigns tailored to the preferences of unique market segments.

Fairmont's new website was a finalist for a Webby Business Award and won major hospitality awards. Marketing costs were reduced for its call centre, President's Club fulfillment, promotion, and brochures. New guests were attracted via the Internet and sales increased because of last-minute Web-based promotions. Overall, its e-business strategy resulted in dramatic increases in customer satisfaction rates and customer loyalty by strengthening relationships with travellers via personalized offers.

Source: Adapted from: www6.lexisnexis.com/publisher/EndUser?Action=UserDisplayFullDocument&orgId=616&topicId=12552&docId=l:599387580&start=20, accessed April 20, 2007.

usage of the Internet, firms have invested heavily in technologies that have enabled customers to buy more quickly, more easily, and with more information than in the past. Electronic kiosks, for instance, have found their way into many service venues. Ticketing kiosks at airports allow customers to get boarding passes and seat assignments, often in less than a minute. You can renew your licence plate stickers, order vanity plates, change your address, or pay fines at ServiceOntario kiosks located in major shopping centres in the province. Not only are kiosks convenient, they are open much longer hours than Ministry of Transportation offices and the service experience is much more consistent for users.

Web-enabled services have also changed the way firms do business with other companies. By 2007, 70 percent of all service centres likely will support Web-based service applications. Already, Cisco Systems, the leading supplier of networking equipment and networking management for the Internet, receives in excess of 80 percent of new orders electronically and resolves more than 80 percent of its customer issues through self-service mechanisms.[37]

Using technology to facilitate service delivery can provide many benefits, such as access to a wider variety of services, a greater degree of control by the customer over the services, and the ability to obtain information. Management also benefits from the increased efficiency in service processes through reduced servicing costs, and, in some cases, can develop a competitive advantage over less service-oriented competitors.[38] See Internet Marketing 11.1 on the previous page for examples of how technology can strengthen customer relationships, enhance loyalty, and increase revenue.

The Communications Gap: Communicating the Service Promise

The communications gap pertains to the difference between the service promised and the service actually delivered. A customer of an Internet provider was convinced to cancel her service to sign up with a new one after hearing advertisements for "great service" at a lower cost. During the first three weeks of the service she was only able to access the Internet half a dozen times because of technology failures. She was further disappointed because when she called technology support she had to pay long distance rates since an 800 number was not available to her. When she did call she was told to call back because no one was in that department at the moment. She expected reliable service and helpful customer representatives, but instead received spotty service at best, as well as difficult and expensive technology support.[39]

Although firms have difficulty controlling service quality because it can vary from day to day and provider to provider, they do have control over how they communicate their service package to their customers. If a firm promises more than it can deliver, customers' expectations won't be met. An advertisement may lure a customer into a service situation once, but if the service doesn't deliver on the promise, the customer may never return. Dissatisfied customers also are likely to tell others about the underperforming service, using word of mouth or, increasingly, the Internet, which has become an important channel for dissatisfied customers to vent their frustrations.

The communications gap can be reduced by managing customer expectations. Suppose you need an operation, and the surgeon explains, "You'll be out of the hospital in five days and back to your normal routine in a month." You have the surgery and feel well enough to leave the hospital three days later. Two weeks after that, you're playing tennis again. Clearly, you will tend to think your surgeon is a genius. However, regardless of the operation's success, if you had to stay in the hospital for 10 days and it took you two months to recover, you would undoubtedly be upset.

Promising only what you can deliver, or possibly even a little less, is an important way to control the communications gap.[40] For instance, when Federal Express first issued its next-day delivery guarantee—"absolutely, positively there by 10:30 a.m."—it achieved a competitive advantage until others matched its promise. Now Federal Express often gives next-day service when the customer has paid only for second-day service. If the package arrives on the second day, it meets expectations. If it arrives a day early, it exceeds them.

A relatively easy way to manage customer expectations considers both the time the expectation is created and the time the service is provided. Expectations typically are created through promotions, whether in advertising or personal selling. For instance, if a salesperson promises a client that work can be performed in one day, and it actually takes a week, the client will be disappointed. However, if the salesperson coordinates the work with those responsible for the service delivery, the client's expectations likely will be met.

Customer expectations can also be managed when the service is delivered. For example, recorded messages can tell customers who have telephoned a company how many minutes they will have to wait before the next operator is available.

Service Recovery

 LO 4

Despite a firm's best efforts, sometimes service providers fail to meet customer expectations. When this happens, the best course of action is to attempt to make amends with the customer and learn from the experience. Of course, it is best to avoid a service failure altogether, but when it does occur, the firm has a unique opportunity to demonstrate

When a service failure occurs, like receiving a poor meal at a restaurant, a firm's goodwill can be recovered by giving the customer a free dessert.

its customer commitment.[41] Effective service recovery efforts can significantly increase customer satisfaction, purchase intentions, and positive word of mouth, though customers' post recovery satisfaction levels usually fall lower than their satisfaction level prior to the service failure.[42]

The Paradise Motel in Muskoka could have made amends with Marcia Kessler after its service failures if it had taken some relatively simple, immediate steps: The assistant manager could have apologized for his bad behaviour and quickly upgraded her to a suite and/or given her a free night's lodging for a future stay. The motel could also have given her a free lunch or dinner to make up for the bad breakfast. None of these actions would have cost the motel much money. Yet by not taking action, it lost Marcia, who over the next few years could have been responsible for several thousand dollars in sales, as a customer forever. Furthermore, Marcia is likely to spread negative word of mouth about the motel to her friends and family because of its failure to recover. Quite simply, effective service recovery entails (1) listening to the customer, (2) providing a fair solution, and (3) resolving the problem quickly.[43]

Listening to the Customer

Firms often don't find out about service failures until a customer complains. Whether the firm has a formal complaint department or the complaint is offered directly to the service provider, the customer must have the opportunity to air the complaint completely, and the firm must listen carefully to what he or she is saying.

Customers can become very emotional about a service failure, whether the failure is serious (a botched surgical operation) or minor (the wrong change at a restaurant). In many cases, the customer may just want to be heard, and the service provider should give the customer all the time he or she needs to "get it out." The very process of describing a perceived wrong to a sympathetic listener is therapeutic in and of itself. Service providers therefore should welcome the opportunity to be that sympathetic ear, listen carefully, and appear anxious to rectify the situation to ensure it doesn't happen again.[44]

Finding a Fair Solution

Most people realize that mistakes happen. But when they happen, customers want to be treated fairly, whether that means distributive or procedural fairness.[45] Their perception of what "fair" means is based on their previous experience with other firms, how they have seen other customers treated, material they have read, and stories recounted by their friends.

distributive fairness
Pertains to a customer's perception of the benefits he or she received compared with the costs (inconvenience or loss) that resulted from a service failure.

Distributive Fairness   **Distributive fairness** pertains to a customer's perception of the benefits he or she received compared with the costs (inconvenience or loss). Customers want to be compensated a fair amount for a perceived loss that resulted from a service failure. If, for instance, a person arrives at the airport gate and finds her flight is overbooked, she may believe that taking the next flight that day and receiving a travel voucher is adequate compensation for the inconvenience. But if no flights are available until the next day, the traveller may require additional compensation, such as overnight accommodations, meals, and a round-trip ticket to be used at a later date.[46]

The key to distributive fairness, of course, is listening carefully to the customer. One customer, travelling on vacation, may be satisfied with a travel voucher, whereas another may need to get to the destination on time because of a business appointment. Regardless of how the problem is solved, customers typically want tangible restitution—in this case, to get to their destination—not just an apology. If providing a tangible restitution isn't possible, the next best thing is to assure the customer that steps are being taken to prevent the failure from recurring.

Procedural Fairness With regard to complaints, **procedural fairness** refers to the perceived fairness of the process used to resolve them. Customers want efficient complaint procedures over whose outcomes they have some influence. Furthermore, customers tend to believe they have been treated fairly if the service providers follow specific company guidelines, though rigid adherence to rules can have damaging effects. For example, requiring a manager's approval for every return, no matter how small can take several minutes and therefore can irritate everyone in the checkout line.

When handling returns or other services issues, it is important to use procedures that are perceived to be fair by the customers.

procedural fairness
Refers to the customer's perception of the fairness of the process used to resolve complaints about service.

Consider the local convenience store that sells both cigarettes and alcohol. The storeowner has implemented a policy that everyone under 19 years of age who attempts to purchase these items must show valid identification. If the store clerks comply, the customers see and accept it as part of the purchasing protocol and perceive it as fair for everyone. If a customer clearly looks over 40 years of age, however, it is doubtful that he or she is under 19 years old, and giving the store clerk a little discretion about asking for identification can avoid a service failure.

Resolving Problems Quickly

The longer it takes to resolve a service failure, the more irritated the customer will become and the more people he or she is likely to tell about the problem. To resolve service failures quickly, firms need clear policies, adequate training for their employees, and empowered employees. Health insurance companies, for instance, have made a concerted effort in recent years to avoid service failures that occur because customers' insurance claims have not been handled quickly or to the customers' satisfaction.

Companies should welcome complaints and make it easy for customers to provide feedback listening carefully to what they have to say. Although customers may be complaining, they are nevertheless exhibiting a degree of loyalty and a genuine desire to get their problem fixed. Of customers who do complain, 56 to 70 percent will do business with the company again if the complaint is resolved. That goes up to 96 percent if the complaint is resolved quickly!

It may seem overly simple, but to recover effectively from service failures, firms must not only listen to the customers' complaints but act on them. It is the implementation of this simple rule that offers firms such challenges.

Learning Objectives Review

1) Identify how marketing a service differs from marketing a product and apply the principles of intangibility, inseparability, variability, and perishability

2) Explain why it is important that service marketers understand and manage customer expectations

3) Describe strategies that firms can use to help employees provide better service

4) Identify what firms should do when a service fails

1) First and foremost, services are intangible—they can't be seen or touched—which makes it difficult to describe a service's benefits or promote it to others. Service providers attempt to reduce the impact of the service's intangibility by enhancing its delivery with more tangible attributes, like a nice atmosphere or price benefits. Second, services are produced and consumed at the same time. Third, services are more variable than products, though service providers attempt to reduce this variability through standardization, training, service bundling, and technology. Fourth, because consumers can't stockpile services, marketers provide incentives to stagger demand over time.

2) A knowledge gap occurs when marketers don't understand what their customers want. They may not be providing customers enough or the right service, in which case customers will be disappointed. To understand customer expectations, marketers analyze service quality through comprehensive studies and by interacting with customers.

3) First, firms should provide training to employees regarding how to do their job and interact with customers. Second, they need to demonstrate a strong commitment to service by setting high standards and enforcing these standards, and lead through example. Third, they can empower service providers to solve service issues and problems. Fourth, they should provide employees with both emotional support and the tools they need to do a good job. Fifth, the service program should be consistent throughout the organization. Sixth, service providers need incentives that encourage them to do a good job.

4) In the best-case scenario, the service does not fail in the first place. But failures are inevitable, and when they do happen, the firm must make amends to the customer. Listen carefully to the customer. Let the customer air his or her complaint. Find a fair solution to the problem that not only compensates the customer for the failure but also follows procedures that the customer believes are fair. Resolve the problem quickly.

Key Terms

- communication gap, 304
- customer service, 296
- delivery gap, 304
- distributive fairness, 314
- empowerment, 310
- inseparable, 299
- intangible, 298
- knowledge gap, 304
- perishability, 303
- procedural fairness, 315
- service, 296
- service gap, 304
- service quality, 305
- standards gap, 304
- variability, 300
- voice-of-customer (VOC) program, 307
- zone of tolerance, 307

Concept Review

1. Describe the four dimensions in which services marketing is different from product marketing.

2. Why is intangibility described as the most fundamental difference between products and services?

3. Discuss the actions companies can implement to minimize the potential negative impact of service variability on the delivery of customer service.

4. How can companies deal with the perishability of their services?

5. Identify the components of the Services Gaps Model. Describe each component and explain the strategies companies can implement to reduce the gaps in service delivery.

6. Describe the five dimensions of services quality that consumers often use to judge the quality of a service experience.

7. Explain how the use of technology can help companies deliver higher quality service.

8. Discuss why underpromising and overdelivering is an important way to control the communication gap.

9. What is meant by service recovery? How can companies use service recovery to ensure that a service failure does not lead to a lost customer?

10. Explain the differences between distributive and procedural fairness in the context of service recovery.

Marketing Applications

1. Those companies from which you purchase products and services are not pure sellers of services, nor are they pure sellers of products. What services does a department store provide? What goods does a dentist provide?

2. You have been sitting in the waiting room of your doctor's office for an hour. With the knowledge that products are different than services, develop a list of the things the office manager could do to improve the overall service delivery. Consider how the office might overcome problems associated with the tangibility, separability, variability, and perishability of services.

3. You have conducted a zone of tolerance analysis for a local dry cleaner. You find that the length of the reliability and responsiveness boxes are much greater than those of the other three service quality dimensions. You also find that the dry cleaner is positioned above the zone box on reliability but below the box on responsiveness. What should you tell the manager of the dry cleaner to do?

4. Design a simple system for collecting customer information about the services of your local dry cleaner.

5. Think back to your last job. What training did your employer provide regarding how to interact with customers and provide good customer service? What could your employer have done to prepare you better to interact with customers?

6. Provide a specific situation in which a service provider could have avoided a service failure if he or she had been empowered by an employer to do so. What should that person have done?

7. What types of support and incentives could your university provide advisers to help make them more attentive to students' needs?

8. What technologies do you use that help facilitate your transactions with a specific retailer or service provider? Would you rather use the technology or engage in a face-to-face relationship with a person? How, if at all, would your parents' answer be different to these two questions?

9. A local health club is running a promotional campaign that promises you can lose an inch a month off your waist if you join the club and follow its program. How might this claim cause a communications gap? What should the club do to avoid a service failure?

10. You are hired by a career consulting firm that promises to market new graduates to high-paying employers. The firm provides potential clients with an impressive client list. It charges the clients a fee, and then a separate finder's fee if the client gets a position. The firm aggressively markets its services and has a large client base. You learn that the firm simply takes any submitted résumés and posts them to a variety of online job search engines. The firm never actually contacts any firms on its clients' behalf. The CEO, himself a recent university grad, tells you that the firm never promises that the firm will contact potential employees themselves, only that they have access to and will distribute clients' résumés. What do you think of the career consulting firm's practices?

Toolkit

SERVICES ZONE OF TOLERANCE

Use the Toolkit provided at www.mcgrawhill.ca/olc/grewal to assess the Zone of Tolerance for several service providers.

Net Savvy

1. What services does WestJet offer (www.westjet.com)? Compare its services to those offered by Air Canada (www.aircanada.ca) using the five service quality dimensions (tangibility, responsiveness, reliability, assurance, and empathy).

2. Evaluate the ease with which you can make hotel reservations using Fairmont's (www.fairmont.com) Internet reservation system. Check out the hotel's privacy policy. Are you comfortable with their use of "cookies" to identify visitors when they return to the site?

Chapter Case Study

CANADIAN TIRE—MORE THAN JUST TIRES

You've heard the old adage about Canadian Tire being more than just tires. Well, now you can bank on it—literally. The company, recognized as one of Canada's most successful retailers, has recently made a move into the retail banking world with pilots in Calgary, Alberta, and Kitchener-Waterloo, Ontario.

Canadian Tire has a long history in Canada, dating back to 1922 when two brothers, John and Alfred Billes, combined their savings of $1800 to open Hamilton Tire and Rubber Co. Ltd. on the corner of Gerrard and Hamilton in Toronto. They started out by providing car repairs but also sold tires, batteries, and antifreeze.[47] It didn't take long for the brothers to expand and by 1927 they had three stores, now operating under the name of Canadian Tire.

From these humble beginnings the company has grown to more than 473 dealers operating over 430 stores. Nine out of 10 adult Canadians shop at Canadian Tire at least twice a year and 40 percent of Canadians shop at Canadian Tire every week. Ninety percent of the Canadian population lives within a 15-minute drive of their local Canadian Tire store.[48]

But how will consumers who shop at Canadian Tire stores now feel about banking with the retailer? And how does a primarily product-based company make the move into the services world? Although Canadian Tire is best known for its retail stores, the company does have experience in money matters. It has a long-standing financial services division which offers branded credit cards such as the Canadian Tire Options MasterCard, as well as insurance products and an emergency roadside service. The division also manages the Canadian Tire "Money," On the Card® loyalty program to credit card customers.[49]

Of course, with the venture into online banking, Canadian Tire "Money" takes on a whole new meaning. With 4 million customers using its credit cards and insurance services, Canadian Tire is now hoping it can persuade them to bank with them, too. Visit stores in Calgary or Kitchener-Waterloo and you'll find ATMs and information kiosks encouraging shoppers to make a move into online banking. Consumers can sign up for high interest savings accounts with introductory rates of up to 4.5 percent, open a GIC account, or apply for home mortgages with rates better than the big banks.

The banking pilot is being supported by an advertising campaign that uses "Be nice to your money" as the tag line. Multimedia ads point out, "You're nice to your home. So why not your money?" and promote high interest rate savings accounts with no monthly fees, no minimum balance, and Canadian Tire "Money" to top it all off.[50] Nice indeed.

But unlike rival brick and mortar banks, Canadian Tire's banking operations are all online. When it comes to money, some consumers like the comfort of knowing they can walk into a branch and talk to a bank representative when they have questions. Of course, with online banking, it's a lot easier to reduce variability—computers, unlike their human counterparts, never have to stay up all night with a cranky child, leading to a compromise in service quality. Conventional banks can also send out signals of quality and efficiency through their physical locations whereas online banking is an intangible, invisible service. Convincing shoppers to sign up for a mortgage is infinitely more challenging than providing them with advice about which products to buy for a home renovation or car repair.

Canadian Tire earned the respect of Canadians in the second annual Corporate Reputation survey conducted by Leger Marketing in collaboration with *Marketing*, ranking in the top 10 brands. Lisa Gibson, director of public relations and media relations, feels the loyal customer base, strong product line, integrated marketing, consumer research, and customer service contribute to the high ranking. Plus, she says Canadian Tire is constantly thinking of ways to improve as evidenced by recent initiatives such as new financial services products, better in-store design, improved training for employees, and a focus on women's preferences, without alienating male customers.[51]

Canadian Tire uses promotions featuring high interest savings accounts to attract customers to its banking services.

According to Dean McCann, vice-president, retail banking, Canadian Tire Financial Services, the company did a fair bit of research around the question of "Do you trust Canadian Tire?" and the answer was a resounding yes.[52] Although Canadian Tire money is Canada's most recognized customer loyalty program, whether consumers are ready to bank with the retailer remains to be seen.

Questions

1. How will Canadian Tire's foray into online banking change its position on the service-product continuum shown in Exhibit 11.1?

2. Referring to the core differences between services and goods, how can Canadian Tire overcome the services challenges of intangibility, inseparability, variability, and perishability?

3. Which of the methods to reduce delivery gaps discussed in the chapter will be the most critical to the future success of the banking pilot?

4. In rolling out its banking services, Canadian Tire must pay close attention to customer service quality. What methods can Canadian Tire use to measure its service quality?

CHAPTER 12

Pricing Concepts and Strategies: Establishing Value

When it comes to bread, do you buy the store brand loaf, Wonderbread, Country Harvest, or an ACE Bakery baguette? Each appeals to a different set of consumer preferences and beliefs about pricing. Is it better to spend the extra money to get a better product? Or should you save your money because all brands are basically the same? Is ACE Bakery's bread really that much better? Do you really get what you pay for?

These different philosophies about price reflect the concept of value. Toronto's ACE Bakery was started by Lynda Haynes and Martin Connell in 1993. The fresh baked, high quality artisan breads commanded a premium price; a risky business proposition during the recession of the 1990s. Despite the premium prices they were charging, local foodies sought out what they perceived to be an excellent product. It turned out that customers were cutting back on expensive vacations and big-ticket budget items so they could enjoy great breads and other excellent foods on a more frequent basis. What began in 1993 as a gourmet niche has since grown into the mainstream by identifying and meeting customer needs and wants. The bakery has outgrown two locations and now not only serves "Toronto's Favourite Bread," but also distributes across Canada and the east coast of the U.S. Many regular grocery stores like Longo's, Dominion, and A&P carry ACE favourites, like Rosemary Foccacia and the Classic Baguette. Select products are even available at Costco. ACE Bakery has seemingly found the right price point and offers a great value.[1]

Its founders are passionate about giving back to the community. ACE donates a percentage of its pre-tax profits to food and nutrition programs that assist low-income members of the community, with a specific focus on community kitchen programs that foster healthy programs for children.[2] Consumers are happy to pay a little extra when they know it is helping the less fortunate.

In essence, if consumers value the brand and the benefits a higher price signifies, they likely will buy a loaf of ACE bread. However, a consumer who values lower prices will likely purchase a store brand. Thus, knowing how consumers arrive at their perceptions of value is critical to developing successful pricing strategies. Nonetheless, a good pricing strategy must consider other factors too, so developing this strategy is a formidable challenge to all firms. Do it right, and the rewards to the firm will be substantial. Do it wrong, and failure will be swift and severe. But even if a pricing strategy is implemented well, consumers, economic conditions, markets, competitors, government regulations, and even a firm's own products change constantly—and that means that a good pricing strategy today may not remain an effective pricing strategy tomorrow.

Are you willing to pay more for ACE Bakery's Classic Baguette or Rosemary Foccacia than store brands?

LO **1**   A lot rides on marketers setting the right price, so it's important to understand the role price plays in the marketing mix. As shown in the chapter roadmap, we explain what "price" is as a marketing concept, why it is important, how marketers set pricing objectives, and how various factors influence price setting. Then, we extend this foundation by focusing on specific pricing strategies as well as the psychological aspects of pricing. Lastly, we describe various B2B and consumer pricing tactics and some important legal and ethical issues associated with pricing.

Imagine that a consumer realizes that to save money on a particular item, she will have to drive an additional 20 kilometres. She may judge that her time and travel costs are not worth the savings, so even though the price tag is higher at a nearby store, she judges the overall cost of buying the product there to be lower. To include aspects of price such as this, we define **price** as the overall sacrifice a consumer is willing to make to acquire a specific product or service. This sacrifice usually includes the money that must be paid to the seller to acquire the item, but it also may involve other sacrifices, whether nonmonetary, like the value of the time necessary to acquire the product or service, or monetary, like travel costs, taxes, shipping costs, and so forth, all of which the buyer must give up to take possession of the product.[3]

Consumers judge the benefits a product delivers against the sacrifice necessary to obtain it, then make a purchase decision based on this overall judgment of value. Thus, a great but overpriced product can be judged as low in value and may not sell as well as an inferior but well-priced item. In turn, we cannot define price without referring to the product or service associated with it. The key to successful pricing is to match the product or service with the consumer's value perceptions.

That key raises a related question: If firms can price their products or services too high, can they price them too low as well? Quite simply, yes. A price set too low may signal low quality, poor performance, or other negative attributes about the product

price
The overall sacrifice a consumer is willing to make—money, time, energy—to acquire a specific product or service.

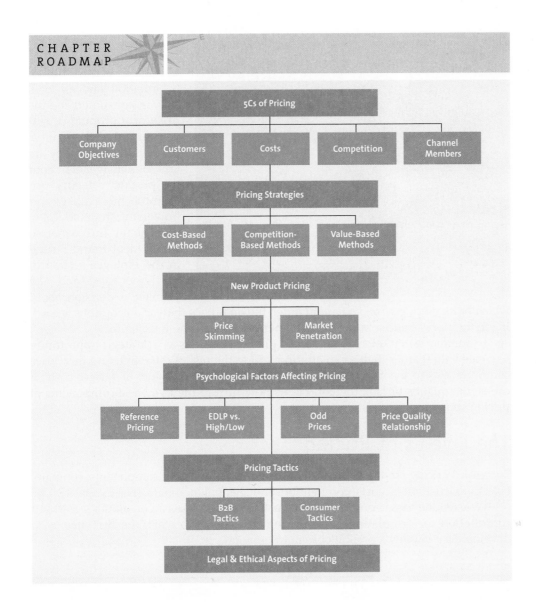

CHAPTER
ROADMAP

or service. Consumers don't necessarily want a low price all the time or for all products. Rather, they want high value, which may come with a relatively high or low price, depending on the bundle of benefits the product or service delivers.

Price is the only element of the marketing mix that generates revenue. Every other element in the marketing mix may be perfect, but with the wrong price, sales simply will not occur. Research has consistently shown that consumers usually rank price as one of the most important factors in their purchase decisions.[4] So, if the firm wants to deliver value and value is judged by the benefits relative to the cost, then pricing decisions are absolutely critical to the effort to deliver value.

Price is the most challenging of the four Ps to manage, partly because it is often the least understood. Historically, managers have treated price as an afterthought to their marketing strategy, setting prices according to what competitors were charging or, worse yet, by adding up their costs and tacking a desired profit on to set the sales price. Prices rarely changed except in response to radical shifts in market conditions. Even today pricing decisions often fail to reflect our current understanding of the role of price in the marketing mix.

Moreover, managers have held an overly simplistic view of the role of price, considering it simply the amount of money a consumer must part with to acquire

When shopping for wine, most of us infer that a higher price means higher quality.

a product or service. We now know that price is not just a sacrifice but an information cue as well. That is, consumers use the price of a product or service to judge its quality,[5] particularly when they are less knowledgeable about the product category. For example, most college and university students know little about fine wine, so if a student found herself in the Vintages section of the liquor store and had to make a decision about which bottle to purchase, she might judge the quality of the various options according to their prices and assume that a higher price means higher quality.

In summary, marketers should view pricing decisions as a strategic opportunity to create value rather than as an afterthought to the rest of the marketing mix. Price communicates to the consumer more than how much a product or service costs; it can signal quality, or lack thereof. Let us now turn to the five basic components of pricing strategies.

LO ② The Five Cs of Pricing

Successful pricing strategies are built through the five critical components: company objectives, customers, costs, competition, and channel members. (See Exhibit 12.1.)

We examine these components in some detail because each makes a significant contribution to formulating good pricing decisions.[6] To start, the first step is to develop the company's pricing objectives.

| EXHIBIT | 12.1 | Five Cs of pricing |

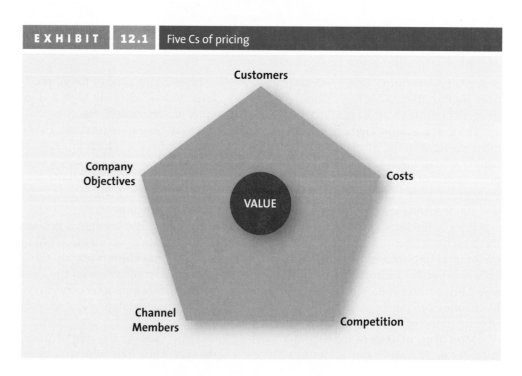

Company Objectives

By now, you know that different firms embrace different goals. Wal-Mart, for example, wants to be seen as a value-based company and so uses every day low pricing (EDLP) whereas Holt Renfrew's high prices reflect its high fashion image.

Each firm then embraces an objective that seems to fit with where management thinks the firm needs to go to be successful, in whatever way they define success. These specific objectives usually reflect how the firm intends to grow. Do managers want it to grow by increasing profits, increasing sales, decreasing competition, or building customer satisfaction?

Company objectives are not as simple as they might first appear; they often can be expressed in slightly different forms that mean very different things. Exhibit 12.2 introduces some common company objectives and examples of their implications for pricing strategies. These objectives are not always mutually exclusive, because a firm may embrace two or more noncompeting objectives.

Profit Orientation   Even though all company objectives may ultimately be oriented toward making a profit, firms implement a **profit orientation** by focusing on target profit pricing, maximizing profits, or target return pricing.

- Firms usually implement **target profit pricing** when they have a particular profit goal as their overriding concern. To meet this targeted profit objective, firms use price to stimulate a certain level of sales at a certain profit per unit.

- The **maximizing profits strategy** relies primarily on economic theory. If a firm can accurately specify a mathematical model that captures all the factors required to explain and predict sales and profits, it should be able to identify the price at which its profits are maximized. Gathering the data on all these relevant factors and coming up with an accurate mathematical model is an extremely difficult undertaking.

- Other firms, less concerned with the absolute level of profits and more interested in the rate at which their profits are generated relative to their investments, typically use **target return pricing** and other pricing strategies designed to produce a specific return on their investment.

Sales Orientation   Firms using a **sales orientation** to set prices believe that increasing sales will help the firm more than increasing profits. For example, a new health club might focus on unit sales or market share and therefore be willing to set a lower membership fee and accept less profit at first. In contrast, a high-end jewellery store might focus on dollar sales and maintain higher prices. This store relies on its prestige image, as well as the image of its suppliers, to generate sales. Even though it sells fewer units, it can still generate high dollar sales levels.

Finally, some firms may be more concerned about their overall market share than about dollar sales per se because they believe that market share better reflects their

profit orientation
A company objective that can be implemented by focusing on *target profit pricing, maximizing profits,* or *target return pricing.*

target profit pricing
A pricing strategy implemented by firms when they have a particular profit goal as their overriding concern; uses price to stimulate a certain level of sales at a certain profit per unit.

maximizing profits strategy
A mathematical model that captures all the factors required to explain and predict sales and profits, which should be able to identify the price at which its profits are maximized.

target return pricing
A pricing strategy implemented by firms less concerned with the absolute level of profits and more interested in the rate at which their profits are generated relative to their investments; designed to produce a specific return on investment, usually expressed as a percentage of sales.

sales orientation
A company objective based on the belief that increasing sales will help the firm more than will increasing profits.

EXHIBIT 12.2	Company Objectives and Pricing Strategy Implications
Company Objective	**Examples of Pricing Strategy Implications**
Profit-oriented	Institute a companywide policy that all products must provide for at least an 18 percent profit margin to reach a particular profit goal for the firm.
Sales-oriented	Set prices very low to generate new sales and take sales away from competitors, even if profits suffer.
Competitor-oriented	To discourage more competitors from entering the market, set prices very low.
Customer-oriented	Target a market segment of consumers who highly value a particular product benefit and set prices relatively high (referred to as premium pricing).

Want to fly from London to Milan? You can do it on Ryan Air for 19€ or about $24.

competitor orientation
A company objective based on the premise that the firm should measure itself primarily against its competition.

competitive parity
A firm's strategy of setting prices that are similar to those of major competitors.

customer orientation
Pricing orientation that explicitly invokes the concept of customer value and setting prices to match consumer expectations.

success relative to the market conditions than do sales alone. A firm may set low prices to discourage new firms from entering the market, encourage current firms to leave the market, take market share away from competitors—all to gain overall market share. For instance, Ireland's discount airline Ryan Air regularly lowers their fares to rates below their competition's prices to gain market share. In all the above cases, profits are of lesser concern; the focus is on increasing sales.

Adopting a market share objective does not always imply setting low prices. Rarely is the lowest-price offering the dominant brand in a given market. Heinz ketchup, Philadelphia brand cream cheese, Crest toothpaste, and Nike athletic shoes have all dominated their markets, yet all are premium-priced brands. Thus, companies can gain market share simply by offering a high-quality product at a fair price as long as they generate high-value perceptions among consumers. Although the concept of value is not overtly expressed in sales-oriented strategies, it is at least implicit because for sales to increase, consumers must see greater value.

Competitor Orientation   When firms undertake a **competitor orientation**, they strategize according to the premise that they should measure themselves primarily against their competition. Some firms focus on **competitive parity**, which means they set prices that are similar to those of their major competitors. Value is only implicitly considered in competitor-oriented strategies, in the sense that competitors may be using value as part of their pricing strategies, so copying their strategy might provide value.

Customer Orientation   A **customer orientation** explicitly invokes the concept of value. Sometimes a firm may attempt to increase value by focusing on customer satisfaction and setting prices to match consumer expectations. Or a firm can use a "no-haggle" price structure to make the purchase process simpler and easier for consumers, thereby lowering the overall price and ultimately increasing value. For example, Saturn has relied on a "no-haggle" price policy since it began selling cars.

It's no secret that most people dread shopping for a car. That's why Saturn retailers are continually finding ways to make buying and servicing your vehicle more pleasant. In addition to the now famous no-hassle, no-haggle sales policy, many Saturn retailers continue to improve the retail experience with additions like family-room-style waiting areas, computer terminals, and children's play areas.

Firms also may offer very high-priced, "state-of-the-art" products or services in full anticipation of limited sales. These offerings are designed to enhance the company's reputation and image and thereby increase the company's value in the minds of consumers. For example, Paradigm, a Canadian speaker manufacturer in Mississauga, produces what many audiophiles consider a high-value product, offering speakers priced as low as $189 per pair. However, Paradigm also offers a very high-end pair of speakers for $6000. Although few people will spend $6000 on a pair of speakers, this "statement" speaker communicates what the company is capable of and can increase the image of the firm and the rest of its products—even that $189 pair of speakers. For an unprecedented 17 years in a row, Paradigm has been rated #1 best price/value by *Inside Track*.[7] Setting prices with a close eye to how consumers develop their perceptions of value can often be the most effective pricing strategy, especially if it is supported by consistent advertising and distribution strategies.

After a company has a good grasp on its overall objectives, it must implement pricing strategies that enable it to achieve those objectives. As the second step in this process, the firm should look toward consumer demand to lay the foundation for its pricing strategy.

Can you tell the difference between the $6000 and the $189 Paradigm speaker?

Customers

The second C of the five Cs of pricing is the most important because it is about understanding consumers' reactions to different prices. Consumers want value, and as you may recall, price is half of the value equation.

To determine how firms account for consumers' preferences when they develop pricing strategies, we must first lay a foundation of traditional economic theory that helps explain how prices are related to demand (consumers' desire for products) and how managers can incorporate this knowledge into their pricing strategies. But first read through Adding Value 12.1, which considers how SABIAN increased its market share by introducing budget priced cymbals.

Demand Curves and Pricing A **demand curve** shows how many units of a product or service consumers will demand during a specific period of time at different prices. Although we call them "curves," demand curves can be either straight or curved, as Exhibit 12.3 shows. Of course, any static demand curve assumes that everything else remains unchanged. For example, marketers creating a demand curve must assume

demand curve
Shows how many units of a product or service consumers will demand during a specific period at different prices.

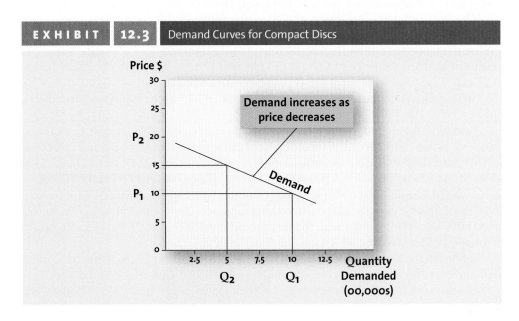

EXHIBIT 12.3 Demand Curves for Compact Discs

Adding Value   12.1   Musicians Look for Cymbals of Success

Fender is possibly the most famous name in electric guitars. And when it comes to cymbals, SABIAN is one of the two biggest names in the business. The company, based in Meductic, New Brunswick, has no lack of celebrity endorsements from the likes of Neil Peart (Rush), Chad Smith (Red Hot Chili Peppers), Tyler Stewart (Barenaked Ladies), Billy Cobham, Phil Collins, Jack DeJohnette, Jeff Watts, and Dave Weckl. Musicians depend on SABIAN to help them deliver the sounds for which they are famous. So do percussionists in major orchestras, including the New York Philharmonic, the Montréal Symphony, and the Philadelphia Orchestra. Even marching bands around the world love that SABIAN crash.[8]

Founded in 1981 by Robert Zildjian, for the sole purpose of producing better cymbals, SABIAN marches to the beat of its own drum. It produces cymbals hand-hammered in the ancient Turkish style and has developed a worldwide reputation for the quality of its products.

SABIAN's impressive double-digit growth has made it the fastest growing

Phil Collins is one of many well-known musicians who uses SABIAN cymbals.

cymbal company in the world, drumming up business in more than 120 countries. Its award-winning marketing and dealer support programs are in tune with the needs of buyers and distributors, and the company has won an export achievement award from the Canadian Manufacturers and Exporters.

Although the company makes cymbals for some of the world's most famous players, it also has introduced low-priced cymbals for students. For example, the XS20, crafted using SABIAN's highly durable premium B20 bronze alloy, is cited as a major breakthrough in the production and pricing of quality B20 bronze cymbals in the budget-priced market.[9] SABIAN's president, Dan Barker, says it's all about great value—performance without the price.[10] With such value, the company not only grabbed a substantial share of the market; it actually helped increase the size of the market, by selling a new product designed for customers who had previously found professional-quality cymbals out of their price range.[11]

---

that the firm will not increase its expenditures on advertising and that the economy will not change in any significant way.

Exhibit 12.3 illustrates the common downward-sloping demand curve in which, as price increases, demand for the product or service decreases. In this case, consumers will buy more CDs as the price decreases. We can expect to uncover a demand curve similar to this one for many, if not most, products and services.

The horizontal axis measures the quantity demanded for the CDs in units and plots it against the various price possibilities indicated on the vertical axis. Each point on the demand curve then represents the quantity demanded at a specific price. So, in this instance, if the price of a CD is $10 per unit ($P_1$), the demand is 1,000,000 units (Q_1), but if the price were set at $15 ($P_2$), the demand would only be 500,000 units (Q_2). The firm will sell far more CDs at $10 each than at $15 each. Why? Because of the greater value this price point offers.

Knowing the demand curve for a product or service enables a firm to examine different prices in terms of the resulting demand and relative to its overall objective. In our preceding example, the music retailer will generate a total of $10,000,000 in sales at the $10 price ($10 × 1,000,000 units) and $7,500,000 in sales at the $15 price ($15 × 500,000 units). In this case, given only the two choices of $10 or $15, the $10 price is preferable as long as the firm wants to maximize its sales in terms of dollars and units. But what about a firm that is more interested in profit? To calculate profit, it must consider its costs, which we cover in the next section.

Interestingly enough, not all products or services follow the downward-sloping demand curve for all levels of price depicted in Exhibit 12.3. Consider **prestige products or services**, which consumers purchase for their status rather than their functionality.

prestige products or services
Those that consumers purchase for status rather than functionality.

| EXHIBIT | 12.4 | Prestige Product Demand Curve |

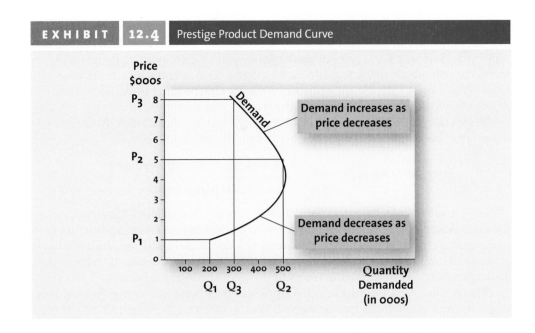

The higher the price, the greater the status associated with it and the greater the exclusivity, because fewer people can afford to purchase it. Most important, in this case, a higher price also leads to a greater quantity sold—up to a certain point. When customers value the increase in prestige more than the price differential between the prestige product and other products, the prestige product attains the greater value overall.

Exhibit 12.4 illustrates a demand curve for a hypothetical prestige service, like a Caribbean cruise. As the graph indicates, when the price increases from $1000 ($P_1$) to $5000 ($P_2$), the quantity demanded actually increases from 200,000 (Q_1) to 500,000 (Q_2) units. However, when the price increases to $8000 ($P_3$), the demand then decreases to 300,000 (Q_3) units after peaking at about 500,000.

Although the firm likely will earn more profit selling 300,000 cruises at $8000 each than 500,000 cruises at $5000 each, we do not know for sure until we consider costs. However, we do know that more consumers are willing to book the cruise as the price increases initially from $1000 to $5000 and that most consumers will choose an alternative vacation as the price increases further from $5000 to $8000.

Price Elasticity of Demand Although we now know something about how consumers react to different price levels, we still need to determine how consumers respond to actual changes in price. Consumers are generally less sensitive to price

Consumers are less sensitive to the price of milk (left) than to steak (right). When the price of milk goes up, demand does not fall significantly because people still need to buy milk. However, if the price of steak rises beyond a certain point, people will buy less because they can turn to the many substitutes for steak.

price elasticity of demand
Measures how changes in a price affect the quantity of the product demanded; specifically, the ratio of the percentage change in quantity demanded to the percentage change in price.

increases for necessary items, like milk, because they have to purchase these items even if the price climbs. When the price of milk goes up, demand does not fall significantly. However, if the price of steak rises beyond a certain point, people will buy less because there are many substitutes. Marketers need to know how consumers will respond to a price increase (or decrease) for a specific product or brand so they can determine whether it makes sense for them to raise or lower prices.

Price elasticity of demand measures how changes in a price affect the quantity of the product demanded. We can calculate it with the following formula:

$$\text{Price elasticity of demand } = \frac{\%\text{ change in quantity demanded}}{\%\text{ change in price}}.$$

elastic
Refers to a market for a product or service that is price sensitive; that is, relatively small changes in price will generate fairly large changes in the quantity demanded.

inelastic
Refers to a market for a product or service that is price insensitive; that is, relatively small changes in price will not generate large changes in the quantity demanded.

In general, the market for a product or service is price sensitive (or **elastic**) when the price elasticity is less than –1, that is, when a 1-percent decrease in price produces more than a 1-percent increase in the quantity sold. In an elastic scenario, relatively small changes in price will generate fairly large changes in the quantity demanded, so if a firm is trying to increase its sales, it can do so by lowering prices.

The market for a product is generally viewed as price insensitive (or **inelastic**) when its price elasticity is greater than –1, that is, when a 1-percent decrease in price results in less than a 1-percent increase in quantity sold. Generally, if a firm must raise prices, it is helpful to do so with inelastic products or services because in such a market, fewer customers will stop buying or reduce their purchases—customers just don't notice or care about the lower price.

Consumers are generally more sensitive to price increases than to price decreases.[12] Also, the price elasticity of demand usually changes at different points in the demand curve unless the curve is actually a straight line, as in Exhibit 12.3. For instance, a prestige product or service, like our Caribbean cruise example in Exhibit 12.4, enjoys a highly inelastic demand curve up to a certain point so that price increases do not affect sales significantly. But when the price reaches that certain point, consumers start turning to other alternatives because the value of the cruise has finally been reduced by the extremely high price.

Travelling to Canada on vacation is much more expensive for Americans. today than it was in 2002 due to significant strengthening of the Canadian dollar.

The Canadian economy has experienced the full force of this elasticity phenomenon during the past few years as the U.S. dollar has lost ground to other major world currencies. In January 2002, the exchange rate was $0.62 for a U.S. dollar. In 2007, the Canadian currency had appreciated significantly, and the exchange rate reached parity by the early fall. Therefore, an American family planning a two-week vacation to Canada in 2002 would have found that a $5000 budget stretched nicely to over $8000 Canadian. However, a repeat visit in the late fall of 2007 would leave that same family with $5000 or less to spend because of currency fluctuations. Not surprisingly, a Consumer Confidence Survey by the U.S. Conference Board indicates that U.S. tourism intentions have softened[13] as Canada is no longer perceived as such a good bargain.

FactorsInfluencingPriceElasticityofDemand   We have illustrated how price elasticity of demand varies across different products and at different points along a demand curve, as well as how it can change over time. What causes these differences in the price elasticity of demand? We discuss a few of the more important factors next.

Income Effect   Generally, as people's income increases, their spending behaviour changes: They tend to shift their demand from lower-priced products to higher-priced alternatives. That is, consumers may buy steak instead of ground beef and splurge on a movie a week instead of one per month. In turn, when the economy is good and consumers' incomes are rising overall, the price elasticity of steak or movies may actually drop, even though the price remains constant. Conversely, when incomes drop, consumers turn to less expensive alternatives or purchase less. This **income effect** refers to the change in the quantity of a product demanded by consumers due to a change in their income.

If there are many close substitutes for a product, customers will be sensitive to small price changes, and the product will be highly price elastic. If, for instance, Skippy raises its price, many customers will switch to another brand.

Substitution Effect The **substitution effect** refers to consumers' ability to substitute other products for the focal brand. The greater the availability of substitute products, the higher the price elasticity of demand for any given product will be. For example, there are many close substitutes for the various brands of peanut butter. If Skippy raises its prices, many consumers will turn to Jif, or President's Choice, or another brand because they can easily find lower-priced substitutes. Extremely brand-loyal consumers, however, are willing to pay a higher price because in their minds, Skippy still offers a better value than the competing brands.

Keep in mind that marketing plays a critical role in making consumers brand loyal, making the price elasticity of demand for some brands very low. For example, Polo/Ralph Lauren sells millions of its classic polo shirt at $65 while shirts of equal quality but without the polo player logo sell for much less. Getting consumers to believe that a particular brand is unique or extraordinary in some way makes other brands seem less substitutable.

Cross-Price Elasticity **Cross-price elasticity** is the percentage change in the quantity of Product A demanded compared with the percentage change in price in Product B. For example, when the price of DVD players dropped rapidly in the years 2000–2004, the demand for DVDs also increased rapidly. We refer to products like DVDs and DVD players as **complementary products**, which are products whose demands are positively related, such that they rise or fall together. In other words, a percentage increase in the quantity demanded for Product A results in a percentage increase in the quantity demanded for Product B.[14] However, when the price for DVD players dropped, the demand for VCRs went down, so DVD players and VCRs are **substitute products** because changes in their demand are negatively related.

Prior to this point, we have focused on how changes in prices affect how much customers buy. Clearly, knowing how prices affect sales is important, but it cannot give us the whole picture. To know how profitable a pricing strategy will be, we must also consider the third C, costs.

Costs

To make effective pricing decisions, firms must understand their cost structures so they can determine the degree to which their products or services will be profitable at different prices. In general, prices should *not* be based on costs because consumers make purchase decisions based on their perceived value; they care little about the firm's costs to produce and sell a product or deliver a service. Consumers use just the price they must pay and the benefits they may receive to judge value; they will not pay a higher price for an inferior product simply because the firm cannot be as cost efficient as its competitors.

If, for instance, a CD were available at both Chapters and Wal-Mart, most consumers would buy it at Wal-Mart, where it likely will be priced lower. But many consumers see additional benefits to shopping at Chapters because it also offers a good selection of books, they can find their choice more easily, or they enjoy buying a CD while sipping a latte they have purchased from the same place. If these consumers did not value these benefits, Chapters would not survive.

income effect
Refers to the change in the quantity of a product demanded by consumers due to a change in their income.

substitution effect
Refers to consumers' ability to substitute other products for the focal brand, thus increasing the price elasticity of demand for the focal brand.

cross-price elasticity
The percentage change in demand for product A that occurs in response to a percentage change in price of product B.

complementary products
Products whose demand curves are positively related, such that they rise or fall together; a percentage increase in demand for one results in a percentage increase in demand for the other.

substitute products
Products for which changes in demand are negatively related; that is, a percentage increase in the quantity demanded for product A results in a percentage decrease in the quantity demanded for product B.

Although companies incur many different types of costs as a natural part of doing business, there are two primary cost categories: variable and fixed.

variable costs
Those costs, primarily labour and materials, that vary with production volume.

Variable Costs   Variable costs are those costs, primarily labour and materials, which vary with production volume. As a firm produces more or less of a good or service, the total variable costs increase or decrease at the same time. Because each unit of the product produced incurs the same cost, marketers generally express variable costs on a per-unit basis. Continuing with our CD example, the variable costs include the labour needed to burn each CD; the costs of the blank CDs, jewel cases, and labels; and royalties paid to the artist. Each of these costs is incurred each time the producer makes a new CD.

In the service industry, variable costs are far more complex. A hotel, for instance, incurs certain variable costs each time it rents a room, including the costs associated with the labour and supplies necessary to clean and restock the room. Note that the hotel does not incur these costs if the room is not booked. Suppose that a particular hotel calculates its total variable costs to be $20 per room; each time it rents a room, it incurs $20 in variable costs. If the hotel rents out 100 rooms on a given night, the total variable cost is $2000 ($20/room × 100 rooms).

Variable costs tend to change depending on the quantity produced. If a record producer creates five CDs, it must pay a set amount for each one. If it makes 500, though, it can probably get the discs at a lower price by buying in bulk. Though not always the case, variable costs per unit may go up or down (for all units) with significant changes in volume.

fixed costs
Those costs that remain essentially at the same level, regardless of any changes in the volume of production.

Fixed Costs   Fixed costs are those costs that remain essentially at the same level, regardless of any changes in the volume of production. Typically, these costs include items such as rent, utilities, insurance, administrative salaries (for executives and higher-level managers), and the depreciation of the physical plant and equipment. Across reasonable fluctuations in production volume, these costs remain stable; whether the producer makes 5 or 500 CDs, the rent it pays for the building in which it burns the CDs remains unchanged.

total cost
The sum of the *variable* and *fixed costs*.

Total Cost   Finally, the total cost is simply the sum of the variable and fixed costs. For example, in one year, our hypothetical hotel incurred $100,000 in fixed costs. We also know that because the hotel booked 10,000 room nights, its total variable cost is $200,000 (10,000 room nights × $20/room). Thus, its total cost is $300,000.

Next, we illustrate how to use these costs in simple analyses that can inform managerial decision making about setting prices.

Break-Even Analysis and Decision Making

A useful technique that enables managers to examine the relationships among cost, price, revenue, and profit over different levels of production and sales is called the break-even analysis. Central to this analysis is the determination of the **break-even point**, or the point at which the number of units sold generates just enough revenue to equal the total costs. At this point, profits are zero.

break-even point
The point at which the number of units sold generates just enough revenue to equal the total costs; at this point, profits are zero.

How do we determine the break-even point? Although profit, which represents the difference between the total cost and the total revenue (total revenue or sales = selling price of each unit sold × number of units sold) can indicate how much money the firm is making or losing at a single period of time, it cannot tell managers how many units a firm must produce and sell before it stops losing money and at least breaks even.

Exhibit 12.5 presents the various cost and revenue information we have discussed in a graphic format.

EXHIBIT | **12.5** | Break-Even Analysis

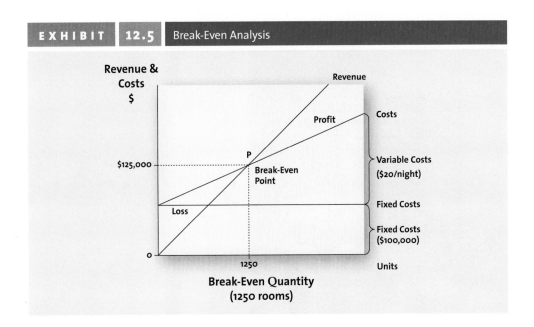

Let's use the hotel example to illustrate the breakeven analysis. Recall that the fixed costs are $100,000 and the variable costs are $20/room rented. If the rooms rent for $100 per night, how many rooms must the hotel rent over the course of a year to break even? If we study the graph carefully, we find the break-even point at 1250, which means that the hotel must rent 1250 rooms before its revenues equal its costs. If it rents fewer rooms, it loses money; if it rents more, it makes a profit. To determine the break-even point in units mathematically, we must consider fixed costs and the **contribution per unit**, which is the price less the variable cost per unit. We use the following formula to calculate the breakeven point in units.

$$\text{Break-even point (units)} = \frac{\text{Fixed costs}}{\text{Contribution per unit}}.$$

contribution per unit Equals the price less the variable cost per unit. Variable used to determine the break-even point in units.

In this case,

$$\text{Break-even point (units)} = \frac{\$100,000}{100 - 20 = \$80} = 1250 \text{ room nights.}$$

When the hotel has crossed that break-even point of 1250 rooms, it will then start earning profit at the same rate of the contribution per unit. So if the hotel rents 2500 rooms—1250 rooms more than the break-even point—its profit will be $100,000 (1250 rooms × $80 contribution per unit).

Although a break-even analysis cannot actually help managers set prices, it does help them assess their pricing strategies because it clarifies the conditions in which different prices may make a product or service profitable. It becomes an even more powerful tool when performed on a range of possible prices for comparative purposes. For example, the hotel management could analyze various prices, not just $100, to determine how many hotel rooms it would have to rent at what price to make a $200,000 profit.

Naturally, however, there are limitations to a break-even analysis. First, it is unlikely that a hotel has one specific price that it charges for each and every room, so the price it would use in its break-even analysis probably represents an "average" price that attempts to account for these variances. Second, prices often get reduced as quantity increases because the costs decrease, so firms must perform several break-even analyses at different quantities.

In a hotel, the cost of the physical structure (left) is fixed—it is incurred even if no rooms are rented. The costs of towels and sheets (right) are variable—the more rooms that are rented, the more the costs.

Third, a break-even analysis cannot indicate for sure how many rooms will be rented or, in the case of products, how many units will sell at a given price. It only tells the firm what its costs, revenues, and profitability will be given a set price and an assumed quantity. To determine how many units the firm actually will sell, it must bring in the demand estimates we discussed previously.

Competition

Because the fourth C, competition, has a profound impact on pricing strategies,[15] we use this section to focus on its effect, as well as on how competitors react to certain pricing strategies. There are three levels of competition—oligopolistic, monopolistic, and pure—and each has its own set of pricing challenges and opportunities.

oligopolistic competition
Occurs when only a few firms dominate a market.

When a market is characterized by **oligopolistic competition**, only a few firms dominate. Firms typically change their prices in reaction to competition to avoid upsetting an otherwise stable competitive environment. Often cited examples of oligopolistic markets include the banking industry and the retail gasoline industry.

price war
Occurs when two or more firms compete primarily by lowering their prices.

Sometimes reactions to prices in oligopolistic markets can result in a **price war**, which occurs when two or more firms compete primarily by lowering their prices. Price wars often appear in the airline industry when a low-cost provider enters a market in which established carriers already exist. But what motivates firms to enter price wars?[16] In the airline example, the new entrants might want to gain market share, whereas the established airlines drop their prices to preserve their market share. Other reasons include avoiding the appearance of being insensitive to consumers and simply overreacting to a price decrease offered by competitors. In many cases, companies do not need to respond to price cuts with price cuts of their own[17] because consumers do not buy solely on the basis of price. Better service, higher quality, and brand loyalty might be used as competitive strategies instead.

monopolistic competition
Occurs when there are many firms that sell closely related but not homogeneous products; these products may be viewed as substitutes but are not perfect substitutes.

Monopolistic competition occurs when there are many firms competing for customers in a given market but their products are differentiated. When so many firms compete, product differentiation rather than a strict pricing competition tends to appeal to consumers. Thus, when Apple entered the hotly contested MP3 player market, it not only priced the iPod at a premium level, but its positioning focused on the product's smart design, cool looks, and convenience.

pure competition
Occurs when different companies sell commodity products that consumers perceive as substitutable; price usually is set according to the laws of supply and demand.

With **pure competition**, different companies that consumers perceive as substitutable sell commodity products. In such markets, price usually is set according to the laws of supply and demand. For example, wheat is wheat, so it does not matter to a commercial bakery whose wheat it buys. However, the secret to pricing success in a pure competition market is not necessarily to offer the lowest price because doing so might create a price war and erode profits. Instead, some firms have brilliantly decommoditized their products. For example, coffee beans used to be regarded as all the same, and then Juan Valdez and the Colombian Coffee Growers Association made their "100 percent Colombian" coffee special, ensuring that coffee drinkers now know the difference between their beans and everything else. In some cases, pure competition opens the market to new players who are able to charge higher prices based on the convenience they offer, as demonstrated in Ethical Dilemma 12.1.

When a commodity can be differentiated somehow, even if simply by a sticker or logo, there is an opportunity for consumers to identify it as distinct from the rest, and in this case, firms can at least partially extricate their product from a pure competitive market.

The Colombia Coffee Growers Association invented Juan Valdez to decommoditize their product in the face of pure competition.

Channel Members

Channel members—manufacturers, wholesalers, and retailers—can have different perspectives when it comes to pricing strategies. Consider a manufacturer that is focused on increasing the image and reputation of its brand but working with a retailer that is primarily concerned with increasing its sales. The manufacturer may desire to keep prices higher to convey a better image, whereas the retailer wants lower prices and will accept lower profits to move the product, regardless of consumers' impressions of the brand. Unless channel members carefully communicate their pricing goals and select channel partners that agree with them, conflict will surely arise.

Channels can be very difficult to manage, and distribution outside normal channels does occur. A **grey market**, for example, employs irregular but not necessarily

grey market
Employs irregular but not necessarily illegal methods; generally, it legally circumvents authorized channels of distribution to sell goods at prices lower than those intended by the manufacturer.

 Ethical Dilemma | **12.1** | White-Label ABM Fees Red-Flagged

It's Friday night and you're at a bar with friends. As usual, you didn't bring along enough cash. No problem. There's an automated banking machine (ABM) in the lobby. Just pop in your bank card and withdraw $20. It's easy. It's convenient. And, it's expensive. Depending on the type of ABM machine you used, that $20 transaction could cost you a whole lot more. While you could withdraw money from your own bank's ABM for little or nothing, machines run by independents use a pricing approach that adds surcharges varying between $1.50 and $6.15.

Today in Canada, about two-thirds of cash machines are white-label, that is privately owned, as opposed to being owned by the banks.[18] The machines have multiplied dramatically in the past decade springing up in bars, convenience stores, movie theatres, and truck stops across the country. Critics charge that the white-label industry has grown outside the strict federal laws that govern the banks. The lack of restrictions has attracted entrepreneurs only too happy to seize the opportunity for profits inherent in white-label fees. There are currently between 200 to 250 companies involved in Canada's white-label industry representing 35,000 non-bank machines that handle about 135 million transactions a year.[19]

With few barriers to entry—a used ABM can be purchased on eBay for as low as $1500—the appeal of white-label machines is attractive. What's more, Canadians don't seem to mind the high fees, relishing the convenience of having ready cash close at hand. However, with a largely unregulated market, the RCMP has recently raised questions about a possible link between privately owned ABM and money laundering. Even though Canada is in the midst of tightening laws against money laundering, it won't affect new ABM rules.[20] Machines stocked with dirty money aren't the only concern though. ABMs could be an ideal way to disperse counterfeit funds, a problem that's captured the attention of Bank of Canada officials. In light of this scrutiny, it's interesting to note that the birth of the white-label business is a direct result of the Competition Bureau's 1996 decision to force Interac to open up the market to non-financial institutions.[21]

In the meantime, Canadians were charged over $420 million last year to access their own money.[22] Even if customers are willing to pay these fees, should the white-label industry be allowed to charge what the market would bear or should it be regulated and fees capped?

Television sets and other consumer electronics are commonly sold in the grey market.

illegal methods; generally, it legally circumvents authorized channels of distribution to sell goods at prices lower than those intended by the manufacturer.[23] Many manufacturers of consumer electronics therefore require retailers to sign an agreement that demands certain activities (and prohibits others) before they may become authorized dealers. But if a retailer has too many high-definition TVs in stock, it may sell them at just above its own cost to an unauthorized discount dealer. This move places the merchandise on the street at prices far below what authorized dealers can charge, and in the long term, it may tarnish the image of the manufacturer if the discount dealer fails to provide sufficient return policies, support, service, and so forth.

To discourage this type of grey market distribution, some manufacturers, such as Fujitsu, have resorted to large disclaimers on their websites, packaging, and other communications to warn consumers that the manufacturer's product warranty becomes null and void unless the item has been purchased from an authorized dealer. [24]

LO ③ Other Influences on Pricing

Thus far, we have focused mainly on product- and firm-specific factors—the five Cs—that influence pricing. Now we turn to broader factors that have a more sweeping effect on pricing in general: the Internet and economic factors.

The Internet

The shift among consumers to acquiring more and more products, services, and information online has made them more price sensitive and opened new categories of products to those who could not access them previously. Gourmet foods, books, music, movies, electronics, and even prescription drugs (see Internet Marketing 12.1) are just a few of the product categories that present a significant online presence. Because they have gained access to rare cheeses, breads, meats, spices, and confections, consumers are demanding more from their local grocery stores in terms of selection and variety and have become more sensitive about prices. Furthermore, consumers' ability to buy electronics at highly discounted prices online has pushed bricks-and-mortar stores to attempt to focus consumers' attention on prepurchase advice and expertise, consulting services, and after-sales service—and away from price.

The Internet also has introduced search engines that enable consumers to find the best prices for any product quickly, which again increases their price sensitivity and reduces the costs associated with finding lower-price alternatives.[25] Not only do consumers know more about prices, they know more about the firms, their products, their competitors, and the markets in which they compete.

Another implication of the Internet for prices has been the growth of online auction sites such as eBay. Gone are the days when sellers had to offer their unwanted items to local buyers at "fire sale" prices. Although there certainly are good deals to be had on eBay, many items can fetch a premium price because bidders tend to get caught up in the bidding process. Also, unique and special interest items, which previously required professional appraisals before their value could be established, now have millions of potential bidders clearly articulating a value for everything from a

| Internet Marketing | **12.1** | **Canadian Internet Pharmacies Serve U.S. Customers** |

Each year more than 1 million Americans buy their drugs from Canadian pharmacies at an estimated value of more than US$1 billion per year. Prior to the Internet, much of the sale of Canadian drugs happened through mail-order and by cross-border visits. However, the Internet has created a new channel for these transactions. By 2005, there were close to 60 Internet pharmacies operating in Canada that sold about $420 million of prescription drugs to Americans. In Manitoba alone, the online dispensaries have created about 2000 jobs and pumped $400 million into its economy.

The big question is why are Americans turning to Canada for their prescription medication? According to the *Canadian Medical Association Journal* (CMAJ), the answer lies in two words: Price and Profitability! Both are inextricably linked. Simply put, without health insurance or a prescription drug benefit plan, many Americans cannot easily afford their medications. They are forced to choose between buying prescriptions and paying for basic necessities. Price is the deciding factor for these consumers, and the Canadian retail prices for brand name prescription drugs are a real bargain. One study, which compared the prices of brand name medications in Canada to major U.S. drug chain pharmacies, found that 41 of the 44 drugs examined were substantially less expensive in Canada. Americans can save anywhere from 24 percent to 70 percent per pill. Many American policymakers are not happy about such pharmacies dedicated to serving American patients.

Why is it that the U.S. government is worried about the online pharmaceutical buyers? Many are from the most vulnerable segment of the Americans—people without drug coverage. Is it because of the safety and quality of Canadian drugs? Hardly, according to CMAJ, Americans who buy Canadian drugs are mainly re-importing American-made drugs with Canadian packaging. The bulk of these drugs are produced in large plants in the U.S. Rather, it is about protecting U.S. drug manufacturers who have become increasingly concerned about their losses of domestic sales and profitability. American manufacturers are trying to curb attempts by state and city governments to make large-scale purchase of cheaper Canadian drugs by filing law suits in the U.S. In Canada, one major pharmaceutical manufacturer, GlaxoSmithKline, has stopped supplying its products to Canadian Internet pharmacies that sell to Americans. Many Americans, especially older ones without drug coverage benefit, consider GlaxoSmithKline's move as a declaration of war and have staged protests in several cities and have boycotted the company's non-prescription products.

However, the cross-border trend isn't without its challenges. In 2006, sales of drugs to Americans through the Internet dropped by almost 50 percent to reach $211 million. In addition, the number of Internet pharmacies operating in Canada has also dwindled to roughly 30 from 55. The surging loonie, the availability of cheaper generic drugs in the U.S., and better U.S. government health insurance have helped to erode the price gap. Will these environmental changes have a lasting impact or can Canadian Internet pharmacies come up with new pricing strategies to stay in business?

Sources:

Sue Cavallucci, "Canadian Internet Pharmacy Sales to the United States Down 50 percent in 2006," www.imshealthcanada.com/web/content/0,3148,77303623_63872702_77770096_80533284,00.html, accessed June 17, 2007;

Tom Scheck, "Some Canadians Worry About American Interest in Pharmacies," Minnesota Public Radio, http://news.minnesota.publicradio.org/features/2003/11/13_scheckt_rxwinnipeg/, accessed June 17, 2007;

Bradley S. Quon, MD, MBA; Rafael Firszt, MD, MBA; and Mark J. Eisenberg, MD, MPH, "A Comparison of Brand-Name Drug Prices between Canadian-Based Internet Pharmacies and Major U.S. Drug Chain Pharmacies," www.annals.org/cgi/content/abstract/143/6/397, accessed June 17, 2007;

Krys Kirton, "50-Plus Consumers Find Price Relief in Canada; Internet Fuels the Trend," Canadian International Pharmacy Association, www.ciparx.ca/index2.php?option=com_content&do_pdf=1&id=17, accessed June 17, 2007;

Steven Morgan and Jeremiah Hurley, "Internet Pharmacy: Prices on the Up-and-Up," *Canadian Medical Association Journal*, March 16, 2004, 170 (6), www.cmaj.ca/cgi/content/full/170/6/945, accessed June 17, 2007.

seven-carat canary diamond engagement ring selling for $189,000 to a 1960 Porsche 356 Roadster selling for $86,500. Today, many consumers use eBay's prior auction section to determine the prices at which products have sold in the past and establish a value for new offerings.

Economic Factors

Two interrelated trends that have merged to impact pricing decisions are the increase in consumers' disposable income and status consciousness. Some consumers appear willing to spend money for products that can convey status in some way. For example, when Holt Renfrew introduced the limited-edition I Am Not a Plastic Bag cotton tote by

Limited-edition cotton totes by British designer Anya Hindmarch sold out in less than an hour at $18 each at Holt Renfrew stores.

cross-shopping
The pattern of buying both premium and low-priced merchandise or patronizing both expensive, status-oriented retailers and price-oriented retailers.

British accessories designer Anya Hindmarch, people camped out in front of the Bloor flagship store to buy one. A total of 3000 bags were received at Holt Renfrew stores across Canada and sold out in less than an hour at $18 each.[26] Products once considered only for the very rich, such as Rolex watches and Mercedes-Benz cars, are now owned by more working professionals. Although such prestige products are still aimed at the elite, more and more consumers are making the financial leap to attain them.

At the same time, however, a countervailing trend finds customers attempting to shop cheap. The popularity of everyday low price retailers like Wal-Mart and Giant Tiger among customers who can afford to shop at department and specialty stores illustrates that it is cool to save a buck. Retailers like H&M and Loblaws, with its Joe Fresh line of clothing, have introduced disposable chic and cross-shopping into Canadians' shopping habits. In this context, **cross-shopping** is the pattern of buying both premium and low-priced merchandise or patronizing both expensive, status-oriented retailers and price-oriented retailers. These stores offer fashionable merchandise at great values—values so good that if items last for only a few wearings, it doesn't matter to the customers. The net impact of these contradictory trends on prices has been that some prestige items have become more expensive, whereas many other items have become cheaper.

Finally, the economic environment at local, regional, national, and global levels influences pricing. Starting at the top, the growth of the global economy has changed the nature of competition around the world. Many firms maintain a presence in multiple countries—products get designed in one country, the parts are manufactured in another, the final product assembled in a third, and after-sales service is handled by a call centre in a fourth. By thinking globally, firms can seek out the most cost-efficient methods of providing goods and services to their customers.

On a more local level, the economy still can influence pricing. Competition, disposable income, and unemployment all may signal the need for different pricing strategies. For instance, rural areas are often subjected to higher prices because it costs more to get products there and because competition is lower. Similarly, retailers often charge higher prices in areas populated by people who have more disposable income and enjoy low unemployment rates.

LO ④ Pricing Strategies

Coming up with the "right" price is never easy. If Research In Motion had decided to price BlackBerry Pearl at a low point initially, how would it have affected future sales—both its own and of potential competitors? Firms embrace different objectives, face different market conditions, and operate in different manners; thus, they employ unique pricing strategies that seem best for the particular set of circumstances in which they find themselves. Even a single firm needs different strategies across its products and services and over time as market conditions change. The choice of a pricing strategy thus is specific to the product/service and target market. Although firms tend to rely on similar strategies when they can, each product or service requires its own specific strategy because no two are ever exactly the same in terms of the marketing mix. Cost-based, competitor-based, and value-based strategies are discussed in this section.

1. Cost-Based Methods

As their name implies, **cost-based pricing methods** determine the final price to charge by starting with the cost. Cost-based methods do not recognize the role that consumers or competitors' prices play in the marketplace. Although relatively simple, compared with other methods used to set prices, cost-based pricing requires that all costs can be identified and calculated on a per-unit basis. Moreover, the process assumes that these costs will not vary much for different levels of production. If they do, the price might need to be raised or lowered according to the production level. Thus, with cost-based pricing, prices are usually set on the basis of estimates of average costs.

cost-based pricing method Determines the final price to charge by starting with the cost, without recognizing the role that consumers or competitors' prices play in the marketplace.

2. Competitor-Based Methods

Most firms know that consumers compare the prices of their products with the different product/price combinations competitors offer. Thus, using a **competitor-based pricing method**, they may set their prices to reflect the way they want consumers to interpret their own prices relative to the competitors' offerings. For example, setting a price very close to a competitor's price signals to consumers that the product is similar, whereas setting the price much higher signals greater features, better quality, or some other valued benefit.

competitor-based pricing method An approach that attempts to reflect how the firm wants consumers to interpret its products relative to the competitors' offerings.

Another competitor-based method is **premium pricing**, which means the firm deliberately prices a product above the prices set for competing products to capture those consumers who always shop for the best or for whom price does not matter. For example, whether or not a $250,000 Ferrari is that much better than a $230,000 Ferrari, some consumers will pay the additional $20,000 to get what they perceive as the very best.

This Ferrari Scaglietti uses premium pricing.

premium pricing A competitor-based pricing method by which the firm deliberately prices a product above the prices set for competing products to capture those consumers who always shop for the best or for whom price does not matter.

3. Value-Based Methods

Value-based pricing methods include approaches to setting prices that focus on the overall value of the product offering as perceived by the consumer. Consumers determine value by comparing the benefits they expect the product to deliver with the sacrifice they will need to make to acquire the product. Of course, different consumers perceive value differently. So how does a manager use value-based pricing methods? We consider two key approaches.

value-based pricing method Focuses on the overall value of the product offering as perceived by consumers, who determine value by comparing the benefits they expect the product to deliver with the sacrifice they will need to make to acquire the product.

Improvement Value Method With this method, the manager must estimate the improvement value of a new product or service. This **improvement value** represents an estimate of how much more (or less) consumers are willing to pay for a product relative to other comparable products. For example, suppose a major telecommunications company has developed a new cell phone. Using any of a host of research methods—such as

improvement value Represents an estimate of how much more (or less) consumers are willing to pay for a product relative to other comparable products.

Is the improvement value on the new iPhone sufficiently greater than competitive products that Apple can charge a higher price for it?

consumer surveys—the manager could get customers to assess the new product relative to an existing product and provide an estimate of how much better it is, or its improvement value.

Exhibit 12.6 illustrates how to calculate the improvement value. Consumers evaluate how much better (or worse) the new cell phone is than an existing product on five dimensions: clarity, coverage, security, battery life, and ease of use. According to the respondents to the survey, the new cell phone has 20 percent more clarity than the comparison phone. These consumers also weight the importance of the five attributes by allocating 100 points among them to indicate their relative importance; for the clarity dimension, this weighting is .40. When the manager multiplies the improvement weight by the relative importance percentage, clarity (20 percent × 0.40) emerges with a weighted factor of 8 percent. The marketer repeats the process for each benefit and sums the weighted factors to arrive at an approximation of the improvement value of the new product from customers' point of view. In this illustration, the improvement value is equal to 21 percent, so if the other cell phone costs $100, the firm should be able to charge customers a value-based price as high as $121 ($100 × 1.21).

Cost of Ownership Method   Another value-based method for setting prices determines the total cost of owning the product over its useful life. Using the **cost of ownership method**, consumers may be willing to pay more for a particular product because, over its entire lifetime, it will eventually cost less to own than a cheaper alternative.[27]

| cost of ownership method A value-based method for setting prices that determines the total cost of owning the product over its useful life. |

Consider, for example, a carpet manufacturing company that needs to set a price for its new high-grade commercial carpet.[28] Its conventional commercial carpeting has an average lifespan of two years, and the costs per square metre are as follows:

$10.00 per square metre

+ 2.00 installation

+ 1.00 removal of old carpet

$13.00 every two years.

The newly introduced carpet lasts for six years; the installation and removal costs are the same. Because the conventional carpet requires installation and removal three times in six years, its total cost over that time is $39.00 per metre. However, we must also discount the payments over the six years by the prevailing interest rate (because the consumer does not have to spend the money immediately, this discount represents the time value of money), which in our example is 10 percent. Therefore, the consumer's discounted spending becomes $32.62 over the six years. Because the new carpet requires the $2.00 installation and $1.00 removal only once in the six years and the time value of money does not come into play (the customer must pay all the money

EXHIBIT 12.6	Improvement Value		
Incremental Benefits	**Improved Value**	**Benefit Weight**	**Weighted Factor**
Clarity	20 percent	0.40	8 percent
Range	40 percent	0.20	8 percent
Security	10 percent	0.10	1 percent
Battery	5 percent	0.20	1 percent
Compatibility	30 percent	0.10	3 percent
Overall		1.00	21 percent

immediately), the company can charge as much as $29.62 per metre ($32.62 − 3.00) for the new carpet. But it might choose to charge less and pass some of the savings on to customers as an incentive to buy the new carpet.

Although value-based pricing strategies can be quite effective, they also necessitate a great deal of consumer research to be implemented successfully. Sellers must know how consumers in different market segments will attach value to the benefits delivered by their products. They also must account for changes in consumer attitudes because the way customers perceive value today may not be the way they perceive it tomorrow. For instance, when first introduced in 2007, iPhones sold for $599. While early adopters lined up to buy them, within months the price dropped to $399.

New Product Pricing

Developing pricing strategies for new products is one of the most challenging tasks a manager can undertake. When the new product is just another "me-too" product, similar to what already appears on the market, this job is somewhat easier because the product's approximate value has already been established. But when the product is truly innovative, or what we call "new to the world," determining consumers' perceptions of its value and pricing it accordingly becomes far more difficult.

Consider, for example, the value to consumers of innovations like air bags. They can prevent serious life-long disabilities and even save lives. So how do car manufacturers attach value to benefits like those? To make it even more complex, automobile companies have to consider the value of an air bag that never deploys. Good marketing research can uncover the value of an innovation in the eyes of the consumer. Let's turn our attention to two distinct pricing strategies for new products: skimming and penetration.

Price Skimming

In many markets, and particularly for new and innovative products or services, innovators and early adopters (see Chapter 10) are willing to pay a higher price to obtain the new product or service. This strategy is known as **price skimming.** Do you recall, among your friends, who owned the first cell phone that had the ability to take pictures, send e-mail and instant messages, and maintain MP3 storage? That person was likely in the top segment of the cell phone market, which made him or her willing to pay the very highest prices when these product enhancements were first introduced. After this high-price market segment becomes saturated and sales begin to slow down, companies generally lower the price to capture (or skim) the next most price sensitive market segment, which is willing to pay a somewhat lower price. This process can continue until the demand for the product has been satisfied, even at the lowest price points. Luxury products are often an exception. For example, Louis Vuitton does not lower the price of its bags, but rather, keeps prices high to support its prestige image.

For price skimming to work, the product or service must be perceived as breaking new ground in some way, offering consumers new benefits currently unavailable in alternative products. Firms use skimming strategies for a variety of reasons. Some may start by pricing relatively high to signal high quality to the market. Others may decide to price high at first to limit demand, which gives them time to build their production capacities. Similarly, some firms employ a skimming strategy to try to quickly earn back some of the high research and development investments they made for the new product. Finally, firms employ skimming strategies to test consumers' price sensitivity. A firm that prices too high can always lower the price, but if the price is initially set too low, it is almost impossible to raise it without significant consumer resistance.

For a skimming pricing strategy to be successful, competitors cannot be able to enter the market easily; otherwise, price competition will likely force lower prices

price skimming
A strategy of selling a new product or service at a high price that *innovators* and *early adopters* are willing to pay in order to obtain it; after the high-price market segment becomes saturated and sales begin to slow down, the firm generally lowers the price to capture (or skim) the next most price sensitive segment.

The publishers of the Harry Potter novels use a price skimming strategy: They set the price high when the book is first introduced, then lower the price significantly to maintain sales.

market penetration pricing
A pricing strategy of setting the initial price low for the introduction of the new product or service, with the objective of building sales, market share, and profits quickly.

experience curve effect
Refers to the drop in unit cost as the accumulated volume sold increases; as sales continue to grow, the costs continue to drop, allowing even further reductions in the price.

and undermine the whole strategy. Competitors might be prevented from entering the market through patent protections, their inability to copy the innovation (because it is complex to manufacture, its raw materials are hard to get, or the product relies on proprietary technology), or the high costs of entry.

Skimming strategies also face a significant potential drawback in the relatively high unit costs often associated with producing small volumes of products. Therefore, firms must consider the trade-off between earning a higher price and suffering higher production costs.

Price skimming also can cause some discontent for consumers. Those who purchase early and pay a higher price may feel somewhat cheated when the prices drop. For instance, when first introduced, *Harry Potter and the Deathly Hallows*, the last book in the series, sold millions of copies for $45.00. One month before it was even released, it could be purchased for half price on Amazon.ca.[29] To avoid negative responses, some firms differentiate their products in some way. For example, publishers generally release a new book first in hard cover and later in soft cover at a lower price.

Market Penetration Pricing

Instead of setting the price high, firms using market penetration pricing set the initial price low for the introduction of the new product or service. Their objective is to build sales, market share, and profits quickly. In direct opposition to a skimming strategy, the low market penetration price encourages consumers to purchase the product immediately rather than waiting for the price to drop. With price skimming, profits are generated through margin, whereas penetration pricing, profits flow through volume. Although it is not always the case, many firms expect the unit cost to drop significantly as the accumulated volume sold increases, an effect known as the experience curve effect. With this effect, as sales continue to grow, the costs continue to drop, allowing even further reductions in the price.

In addition to offering the potential to build sales, market share, and profits, penetration pricing discourages competitors from entering the market because the profit margin is relatively low. Furthermore, if the costs to produce the product drop because of the accumulated volume, competitors that enter the market later will face higher unit costs, at least until their volume catches up with the early entrant.

A penetration strategy also has its drawbacks. First, the firm must have the capacity to satisfy a rapid rise in demand—or at least be able to add that capacity quickly. Second, low price does not signal high quality. Of course, a price below their expectations decreases the risk for consumers to purchase the product and test its quality for themselves. Third, firms should avoid a penetration pricing strategy if some segments of the market are willing to pay more for the product; otherwise, the firm is just "leaving money on the table."

Psychological Factors Affecting Value-Based Pricing Strategies

Understanding the psychology underlying the way consumers arrive at their perceptions, make judgments, and finally invoke a choice is critical to effective pricing strategies, so marketers must examine some of the more important psychological processes that influence consumers' reactions to and use of price. When consumers are exposed to a price, they assign meaning to it by placing it into a category, like "expensive," "a deal," "cheap," "overpriced," or even "fair."

In this section, we examine some of the factors that influence this psychological process of adding meaning to, or evaluating, price.[30] But first, let's look at how one man with incredible vision started a type of retailing that is based on very inexpensive merchandise in Entrepreneurial Marketing 12.1.

Consumers' Use of Reference Prices

A **reference price** is the price against which buyers compare the actual selling price of the product and that facilitates their evaluation process. In some cases, the seller itself provides an **external reference price**, a higher price to which the consumer can compare the selling price to evaluate the deal.[31] Typically, the seller labels the external reference price as the "regular price" or an "original price." When consumers view the "sale price" and compare it with the provided external reference price, their per-

reference price
The price against which buyers compare the actual selling price of the product and that facilitates their evaluation process.

external reference price
A higher price to which the consumer can compare the selling price to evaluate the purchase.

Entrepreneurial Marketing	12.1	**Giant Tiger Stakes its Territory**

On May 13 1961, Gordon Reid opened his first Giant Tiger store in Ottawa, the Nation's Capital. The business concept was very simple—keep the cost of operation low and sell a large volume of merchandise at everyday low prices. The large general merchandise store aimed to offer everything a customer could need, all under one roof. This all-Canadian company has now grown to 190 stores, employing over 6500 people who all work in support of that same original idea.[32]

The main thrusts of Giant Tiger's roaring success are maintaining low rent, efficient transportation, and keeping the cost of store operations low. Tiger Trucking is the private fleet that transports merchandise for the chain to the majority of stores, which are in Ontario and Quebec. In store, employees work directly with customers on the store floor. Many stores don't even advertise a phone number, because having an employee answer the phone would increase costs and would take them away from helping customers![33] Their refund policy is clear: if you present a receipt, you get your money back, no matter how many days have passed.[34]

Each store offers a large assortment of casual clothing and footwear, everyday needs in groceries, cleaning supplies, housewares, stationery, toys and health and beauty products. The identical quality and fashion items offered by major chain stores are sold at Giant Tiger at lower prices. Discontinued items and one-offs are available frequently for special deals on a store-by-store basis. Beyond the Giant Tiger brand, the GT Boutique (www.gtboutique.com/) has been developed to showcase new fashions and trends. A deep-rooted commitment to the community shows that Giant Tiger truly cares about its customers. Along with contributing funds to local charities and supporting fundraising events, many store fronts feature murals that not only beautify but also bring attention to political issues.[35]

People love to shop at Giant Tiger stores because its merchandise is inexpensive, the stores are conveniently located and easy-to-shop, and treasures are found every day among the basics.

The success shows no signs of slowing. A franchise agreement with NorthWest Co. Inc. in 2002 to open 72 new stores made a big impact, with the first 20 stores in cities like Regina, Winnipeg, Edmonton, and Calgary bringing a flood of success for Giant Tiger.[36] Also, 2005 brought expansion stores in and around the Greater Toronto Area. The 2006 federal government announcement to lower the Goods and Services Tax to 6 percent was even made from an Ottawa-area Giant Tiger store! Press coverage of events like this, and returning loyal customers have helped keep Giant Tiger's bottom line remain strong. Despite tough competitors like Wal-Mart and Zellers, Giant Tiger is a home-grown retailer that Canadians continue to loyally support.

In this ad, Sears provides an external reference price of $24.99 in small print, to reflect the regular price of Lee jeans.

ceptions of the value of the deal will likely increase.[37] In the advertisement shown to the left, Sears has provided an external reference price, in smaller print and labelled "Reg.," to indicate that $24.99 is the regular price of Lee jeans. In addition, the advertisement highlights the current "sale" price of $21.99. Thus, the external reference price suggests to consumers that they are getting a good deal and will save money.

Consumers may also rely on an **internal reference price** to judge a price offering by accessing price information stored in their memory—perhaps the last price they paid or what they expect to pay.[38] For instance, when a consumer has been seated in a restaurant and first views the price of a large pepperoni pizza, she only has her internal reference price for comparison. If the price of the pizza on the menu is $12 and the consumer's internal reference price is $10 because she recalls that as the price she usually pays for a large pepperoni pizza at another restaurant, she may judge the menu price as high.

A more complex element of reference prices is the relationship among them. That is, external reference prices influence internal reference prices.[39] When consumers are repeatedly exposed to higher reference prices, their internal reference prices shift toward the higher external reference prices, assuming their initial internal reference price was not too far away from it. The net effect is that consumers will perceive the product or service in question to have a relatively lower selling price, and it therefore becomes a better deal in their perceptions.

Everyday Low Pricing (EDLP) versus High/Low Pricing

internal reference price
Price information stored in the consumer's memory that the person uses to assess a current price offering—perhaps the last price he or she paid or what he or she expects to pay.

everyday low pricing (EDLP)
A strategy companies use to emphasize the continuity of their retail prices at a level somewhere between the regular, nonsale price and the deep-discount sale prices their competitors may offer.

high/low pricing
A *pricing* strategy that relies on the promotion of sales, during which prices are temporarily reduced to encourage purchases.

With an **everyday low pricing (EDLP)** strategy, companies stress the continuity of their retail prices at a level somewhere between the regular, nonsale price and the deep-discount sale prices their competitors may offer.[40] By reducing consumers' search costs, EDLP adds value; consumers can spend less of their valuable time comparing prices, including sale prices, at different stores. For example, Wal-Mart relies on EDLP to communicate to consumers that, for any given group of often purchased items, its prices are lower than those of any other company in that market. This claim does not necessarily mean that every item that consumers may purchase will be priced lower at Wal-Mart than anywhere else—in fact, some competitive retailers will offer lower prices on some items. However, on average, Wal-Mart's prices tend to be lower overall.

Alternatively, some retailers prefer a **high/low pricing** strategy, which relies on the promotion of sales, during which prices are temporarily reduced to encourage purchases. In the end, which consumers prefer which strategy depends on how those consumers evaluate prices and quality. Some prefer not to expend the time to find the lowest price and favour EDLP as an efficient way to get low prices. Alternatively, other consumers may relish the challenge of getting the lowest price or be so price sensitive that they are willing to expend the time and effort to seek out the lowest price every time.

But even this categorization gets more complicated, in that it needs to include quality perceptions as well. Some consumers perceive that stores that use EDLP carry lower quality goods, whereas high/low pricing stores tend to carry better quality items. In part, this perception forms because consumers view the initial price at a high/low store as the reference price. In the end, however, the consumer's decision, once again and as always, comes down to value.

Odd Prices

Have you ever wondered why prices rarely end in round amounts, like $3.00 or $23.00? In various product categories, odd prices, or those that end in odd numbers, usually 9, are very common, such as $3.99, $11.99, and $7.77. Although not documented, most marketers believe that odd pricing got its start as a way to prevent sales clerks from just pocketing money. Because the price was odd, the clerk would have to open the cash register for change, which required that the sale be rung up on the register.

Today, it seems that odd pricing may be so traditional that sellers are afraid to round off their prices for fear that consumers will respond negatively. Also, some sellers may believe that consumers mentally truncate the actual price, making the perceived price appear lower than it really is. For example, if the price is $21.99, consumers may focus more on the $21 than on the 99 cents, which may cause them to perceive the price as significantly lower than $22.00, even though that difference is only a penny. The main finding from research on the odd pricing approach is that odd prices signal to consumers that the price is low.[41] The bottom line is that if sellers want to suggest a deal is to be had, odd prices may be appropriate.

Odd prices signal to consumers that the price is low.

odd prices Prices that end in odd numbers, usually 9, such as $3.99.

The Price–Quality Relationship

Imagine that you have an important date tonight, and you are cooking a special, romantic, Italian dinner. You go to the grocery store to buy the food and realize that your recipe for the antipasto appetizer calls for Lupini beans (a large bean usually imported from Italy). You've never even heard of Lupini beans, much less purchased or used them in a recipe. Luckily, the store has three different brands of Lupini beans. But how do you choose which brand to buy? The three choices are priced at $3.99, $3.79, and $3.49. Are you going to risk the success of this dinner to save a mere $.50 on a can of beans? Probably not. Without other information to help you make a choice, you will likely go for the $3.99 can of beans because, like most consumers, you believe that they must be of higher quality because they cost more.

But not all consumers rely on price to judge quality. When consumers know the brands, have had experience with the products, or have considerable knowledge about how to judge the quality of products objectively, price becomes less important.[42] The store, brand name, product warranties/guarantees, and where the product was produced also represent information consumers use to judge quality. Nonetheless, price generally plays a critical role in consumers' judgments of quality.[43] Given these various psychological pricing factors that come into play for consumers, marketers must consider how they function when they set prices. In the next section, we discuss how to apply psychological factors in the pricing decisions for new products.

Pricing Tactics

It is important to distinguish clearly between pricing strategies and pricing tactics. A *pricing strategy* is a long-term approach to setting prices broadly in an integrative effort (across all the firm's products) based on the five Cs (company objectives, customers, costs, competition, and channel members) of pricing. **Pricing tactics**, in contrast, offer short-term methods to focus on select components of the five Cs. Generally, a pricing tactic represents either a short-term response to a competitive threat (e.g., lowering price temporarily to meet a competitor's price reduction) or a broadly accepted method of calculating a final price for the customer that is short-term in nature. We separate our discussion of pricing tactics into those aimed at intermediaries in a business-to-business (B2B) setting and those directed at end consumers.

pricing tactics Short-term methods, in contrast to long-term pricing strategies, used to focus on company objectives, customers, costs, competition, or channel members; can be responses to competitive threats (e.g., lowering price temporarily to meet a competitor's price reduction) or broadly accepted methods of calculating a final price for the customer that is short term in nature.

Business-to-Business Pricing Tactics and Discounts

The pricing tactics employed in B2B settings differ significantly from those used in consumer markets. Among the most prominent are seasonal and cash discounts, allowances, quantity discounts, and uniform delivered versus zone pricing. (See Exhibit 12.7.)

seasonal discount
Pricing tactic of offering an additional reduction as an incentive to retailers to order merchandise in advance of the normal buying season.

Seasonal Discounts   A **seasonal discount** is an additional reduction offered as an incentive to retailers to order merchandise in advance of the normal buying season. For instance, Lennox may offer its air conditioning dealers an additional seasonal discount if they place their orders and receive delivery before April 1, prior to the warm months when air conditioner sales are highest. If it can ship earlier in the season, Lennox can plan its production schedules more easily and lessen its finished goods inventory. Its dealers, however, must weigh the benefits of a larger profit because of the discount versus the extra cost of carrying the inventory for a longer period of time.

cash discount
Tactic of offering a reduction in the invoice cost if the buyer pays the invoice prior to the end of the discount period.

Cash Discounts   A **cash discount** reduces the invoice cost if the buyer pays the invoice prior to the end of the discount period. Typically, it is expressed in the form of a percentage, such as 3/10, n/30, or "3 percent, 10 days, net 30," all of which means the buyer can take a 3-percent discount on the total amount of the invoice if the bill is paid within 10 days of the invoice date; otherwise the full, or net, amount is due within 30 days. Why do B2B sellers offer cash discounts to customers? By encouraging early payment, they benefit from the time value of money. Getting money earlier rather than later enables the firm to either invest the money to earn a return on it or avoid borrowing money and paying interest on it. In both instances, the firm is better off financially.

advertising allowance
Tactic of offering a price reduction to channel members if they agree to feature the manufacturer's product in their advertising and promotional efforts.

listing allowances
Fees paid to retailers simply to get new products into stores or to gain more or better shelf space for their products.

Allowances   Another pricing tactic that lowers the final cost to channel members is allowances, such as advertising or listing allowances, offered in return for specific behaviours. An **advertising allowance** offers a price reduction to channel members if they agree to feature the manufacturer's product in their advertising and promotional efforts. **Listing allowances** are fees paid to retailers simply to get new products into stores or to gain more or better shelf space for their products. Some argue that slotting allowances are unethical because they put small manufacturers that cannot readily afford allowances at a competitive disadvantage. Demanding large listing allowances could be considered a form of bribery—"paying off" the retailer to get preferential treatment.

EXHIBIT 12.7	Business to Business Pricing Tactics
Tactic	
Seasonal discounts	An additional reduction offered as an incentive to retailers to order merchandise in advance of the normal buying season.
Cash discounts	An additional reduction that reduces the invoice cost if the buyer pays the invoice prior to the end of the discount period.
Allowances	Advertising or listing allowances (additional price reductions) offered in return for specific behaviours. **Advertising allowances** are offered to retailers if they agree to feature the manufacturer's product in their advertising and promotional efforts. **Listing allowances** are offered to get new products into stores or to gain more or better shelf space.
Quantity discounts	Providing a reduced price according to the amount purchased.
Uniform delivered versus zone pricing	**Uniform delivered price:** shipper charges one rate, no matter where the buyer is located. **Zone price:** different prices depending on the geographical delivery area.

Quantity Discounts   A **quantity discount** provides a reduced price according to the amount purchased. The more the buyer purchases, the higher the discount and, of course, the greater the value.

A **cumulative quantity discount** uses the amount purchased over a specified time period and usually involves several transactions. This type of discount encourages resellers to maintain their current supplier because the cost to switch must include the loss of the discount. For example, automobile dealers often attempt to meet a quota or a sales goal for a specific time period, such as a quarter or a year. If they meet their quotas, they earn discounts on all the cars they purchased from the manufacturer during that time period in the form of a rebate cheque. For this very reason, you will often find good deals on cars at the end of a quarter or fiscal year. If the dealership can just sell a few more cars to meet its quota, the rebate earned can be substantial, so taking a few hundred dollars less on those last few cars is well worth the opportunity to receive a rebate worth many times the amount of the losses.

A **noncumulative quantity discount**, though still a quantity discount, is based only on the amount purchased in a single order. It therefore provides the buyer with an incentive to purchase more merchandise immediately. Such larger, less frequent orders can save manufacturers order processing, sales, and transportation expenses. For example, a jeans store might get a 40 percent discount off the manufacturer's suggested retail price for placing a $500 order; a 50-percent discount for an order of $501–$4999, and a 60-percent discount for an order of greater than $5000.

Uniform Delivered versus Geographic Pricing   These pricing tactics are specific to shipping, which represents a major cost for many manufacturers. With a **uniform delivered pricing** tactic, the shipper charges one rate, no matter where the buyer is located, which makes things very simple for both the seller and the buyer. **Geographic pricing**, however, sets different prices depending on a geographical division of the delivery areas. For example, a manufacturer based in Montreal might divide Canada into five different zones and use different shipping rates for each zone to reflect the average shipping cost for customers located therein. This way, each customer in a zone is charged the same cost for shipping. Zone pricing can be advantageous to the shipper because it reflects the actual shipping charges more closely than uniform delivered pricing can.

Pricing Tactics Aimed at Consumers

When firms sell their products and services directly to consumers, rather than to other businesses, the pricing tactics they use naturally differ. In this section, we analyze some tactics for products and services aimed directly at consumers: price lining, price bundling, and leader pricing. (Exhibit 12.8.)

Price Lining   When marketers establish a price floor and a price ceiling for an entire line of similar products and then set a few other price points in between to represent distinct differences in quality, the tactic is called **price lining**.

quantity discount
Pricing tactic of offering a reduced price according to the amount purchased; the more the buyer purchases, the higher the discount and, of course, the greater the value.

cumulative quantity discount
Pricing tactic that offers a discount based on the amount purchased over a specified period and usually involves several transactions.

noncumulative quantity discount
Pricing tactic that offers a discount based on only the amount purchased in a single order.

uniform delivered pricing
The shipper charges one rate, no matter where the buyer is located.

geographic pricing
The setting of different prices depending on a geographical division of the delivery areas.

price lining
Consumer market pricing tactic of establishing a price floor and a price ceiling for an entire line of similar products and then setting a few other price points in between to represent distinct differences in quality.

EXHIBIT 12.8	Pricing Tactics Aimed at Consumers
Tactic	
Price Lining	Establishing a price floor and a price ceiling for an entire line of similar products and then setting price points in between to represent distinct differences in quality.
Price Bundling	Pricing of more than one product for a single, lower price.
Leader Pricing	Building store traffic by aggressively pricing and advertising a regularly purchased item, often priced at or just above the store's cost.

Consider the specific price lines used by Moores Clothing for Men. The firm prices its sports jackets at different price points. For example, its house brand, Joseph & Feiss, sells for around $119. Move up to a middle range price point and you can buy an Alfred Sung jacket for between $159 and $199. At the top end of the line, you can find a pure wool Pronto Umo sports jacket for $229.

While it may be difficult to determine which is the better jacket, having options at different price points means Moores can satisfy a range of tastes and budgets.

Price Bundling   When firms are stuck with a slow moving item, to encourage sales, they sometimes will "bundle" it with a faster moving item and price the bundle below what the two items would cost separately. Sometimes, however, firms bundle products together just to encourage customers to stock up so they won't purchase competing brands, encourage trial of a new product, or provide an incentive to purchase a less desirable product or service to obtain a more desirable one in the same bundle. This practice of selling more than one product for a single, lower price is called **price bundling**.

We present a price bundling example in Exhibit 12.9. Imagine we have four different offerings for sale: home phone line, long distance, Internet, and satellite TV services. Customers use combinations of these products and services differently, and each customer has unique needs. Subscribing to each service separately is the most expensive option, as shown in the first line. However, if customers bundle together three or more services, they can take advantage of lower prices.

Now let's look at how Bell uses price bundling to add value for its customers. For example, a student away at university on a tight budget may elect to subscribe to only the essentials: Internet and a home phone line. Regular price for these items would be $54.35/month. Through their bundled service offering, Bell can entice the student to also sign up for long distance by reducing the price of the Internet service when the long distance service is added. The company benefits from enhancing the relationship with the customer as well as by collecting additional revenue. While the student's monthly bill will rise slightly to $59.30, he will save $60.00/year from the unbundled service prices and should now be able to make long distance calls home to his or her parents from time to time!

price bundling
Consumer pricing tactic of selling more than one product for a single, lower price than what the items would cost sold separately; can be used to sell slow-moving items, to encourage customers to stock up so they won't purchase competing brands, to encourage trial of a new product, or to provide an incentive to purchase a less desirable product or service to obtain a more desirable one in the same bundle.

EXHIBIT 12.9	An Illustration of Price Bundling					
	Internet	**Home Phone**	**Long Distance**	**Television**	**Total**	**Annual Savings**
Regular Price	36.00	18.35	14.95	71.00	140.30	
Bundled Price	31.00	18.35	9.95	66.00	125.30	360.00
Regular Student Price	36.00	18.35			54.35	
Full Price with Added Service	36.00	18.35	9.95		64.30	
Student Bundled Price	31.00	18.35	9.95		59.30	60.00
Regular Family Price	36.00			71.00	107.00	
Full Price with Added Service	36.00	18.35		71.00	125.35	
Family Bundled Price	31.00	18.35		66.00	115.35	120.00

Prices from "Bell Bundle," www.bellbundle.com/en/on/home/calculate-your-bundle, accessed June 20, 2007.

Similarly, a family could be currently subscribing to television and Internet service through Bell for $107.00/month, while obtaining their home phone service from another provider. Again, by bundling the services, Bell can entice the family to switch its residential phone service to Bell by reducing the price of the other services. Adding the new service increases the monthly fee to $115.35 but the family saves $120.00/year compared to the regular priced services and will also enjoy the convenience of receiving a single bill each month.

Bell's "Build a Bundle, Save a Bundle" offering lets customers bundle services together to save money.

Leader Pricing **Leader pricing** is a tactic that attempts to build store traffic by aggressively pricing and advertising a regularly purchased item, often priced at or just above the store's cost. The rationale behind this tactic argues that, while in the store to get the great deal on, say, milk, the consumer will also probably pick up other items he or she needs. The store has priced

leader pricing
Consumer pricing tactic that attempts to build store traffic by aggressively pricing and advertising a regularly purchased item, often priced at or just above the store's cost.

these items at higher profit margins, so their purchase will more than cover the lower markup on the milk. Imagine the marketing potential of various combinations of products; the store uses leader pricing on cocktail sauce, which gives employees the perfect opportunity to ask, "How about a pound of fresh shrimp to go with the cocktail sauce you're purchasing?"

Consumer Price Reductions

The final price a customer pays for a product or service often has been adjusted from the original price because marketers have used various techniques designed to enhance value. Some of these techniques include markdowns, quantity discounts, coupons, and rebates.

Markdowns **Markdowns** are the reductions retailers take on the initial selling price of the product or service.[44] An integral component of the high/low pricing strategy we described previously, markdowns enable retailers to get rid of slow moving or obsolete merchandise, sell seasonal items after the appropriate season, and match competitors' prices on specific merchandise. Retailers must get rid of merchandise that isn't selling because holding on to such items hurts the retailer's image and ties up money in inventory that could be used more productively elsewhere.

markdowns
Reductions retailers take on the initial selling price of the product or service.

Retailers also use markdowns to promote merchandise and increase sales. Particularly when used in conjunction with promotions, markdowns can increase traffic into the store, which many retailers view as half the battle. Once customers are in the store, retailers always hope they will purchase other products at regular prices.

Customers get a size discount for buying larger sizes. With Cheerios, the larger the box, the less it costs per gram.

size discount
The most common implementation of a quantity discount at the consumer level; the larger the quantity bought, the less the cost per unit (e.g., per gram).

coupon
Provides a stated discount to consumers on the final selling price of a specific item; the retailer handles the discount.

rebate
A consumer discount in which a portion of the purchase price is returned to the buyer in cash; the manufacturer, not the retailer, issues the refund.

Quantity Discounts for Consumers   We have already discussed how firms use quantity discounts in the B2B marketplace, but the most common implementation of a quantity discount at the consumer level is the **size discount**. For example, there are three sizes of General Mills' popular cereal Cheerios—425-, 575-gram, and 1.5-kilogram boxes priced at approximately $4.19, $4.49, and $6.89, respectively. The larger the quantity, the less the cost per gram, which means the manufacturer is providing a quantity discount. Most grocery stores now post the price per 100 grams on the shelves so consumers can easily compare value for money. The goal of this tactic is to encourage consumers to purchase larger quantities each time they buy. In turn, these consumers are less likely to switch brands and often tend to consume more of the product, depending on the product usage characteristics. Typically, buying a larger package of toilet tissue does not mean consumers will use it faster, but buying a larger box of cereal may encourage them to eat more of it or eat it more often.[45]

Seasonal Discounts   Seasonal discounts are price reductions offered on products and services to stimulate demand during off-peak seasons. You can find hotel rooms, ski lift tickets, snowmobiles, lawn mowers, barbeque grills, vacation packages, flights to certain destinations, and Christmas cards at discounts during their "off" seasons. Some consumers even plan their buying around these discounts, determined to spend the day after Christmas stocking up on discounted wrapping paper and bows for the following year.

Coupons and Rebates   Coupons and rebates both provide discounts to consumers on the final selling price. However, for the **coupon**, the retailer handles the discount, whereas the manufacturer issues the refund in the case of the **rebate**, which is defined as a portion of the purchase price returned to the buyer in the form of cash.

The goal of coupons is to prompt consumers to try a product, reward loyal customers, or encourage repurchases. By saving the consumer money, firms add value to their products. Whereas a coupon provides instant savings when presented, a rebate promises savings, usually mailed to the consumer at some later date. The "hassle factor" for rebates is higher than for coupons; the consumer must first buy the item during a specified time period, then mail in the required documentation—which usually includes the original sales receipt—and finally wait four to six weeks (or more!) for a cheque to arrive. Although consumers may believe this process adds value when the potential rebate is $50, they might question whether a rebate for a couple of dollars is worth their time and effort. From the marketer's viewpoint, however, rebates offer greater control than coupons and provide valuable customer information. Coupons and rebates are considered to be sales promotion tools as well as pricing tactics so you'll read more about them in Chapter 16.

With so many different pricing strategies and tactics, it is no wonder that unscrupulous firms find ample opportunity to engage in pricing practices that can hurt consumers. We now take a look at some of the legal and ethical implications of pricing.

LO ⑤ Legal Aspects and Ethics of Pricing

Prices tend to fluctuate naturally and respond to varying market conditions. Thus, though we rarely see firms attempting to control the market in terms of product quality or advertising, they often engage in pricing practices that can unfairly reduce competition or harm consumers directly through fraud and deception. A host of laws and regulations at both the federal, provincial and municipal levels attempt to prevent unfair pricing practices, but some are poorly enforced, and others are difficult to prove.

Deceptive or Illegal Price Advertising

Although it is always illegal and unethical to lie in advertising, a certain amount of "puffery" is typically allowed (see Chapter 16). But price advertisements should never deceive consumers to the point of causing harm. For example, a local car dealer's advertising that it had the "best deals in town" would likely be considered puffery. In contrast, advertising "the lowest prices, guaranteed" makes a very specific claim and, if not true, can be considered deceptive.

Deceptive Reference Prices Previously, we introduced external reference prices, which create reference points for the buyer against which to compare the selling price. If the reference price is bona fide, the advertisement is informative. If the reference price has been inflated or is just plain fictitious, however, the advertisement is deceptive and may cause harm to consumers. The Competition Bureau fined Suzy Shier $1 million after an investigation revealed that the company placed price tags on garments showing a 'regular' price and a 'sale' price when in fact the clothes had not been sold in any significant quantity for any reasonable time at the 'regular' price.[46] But it is not easy to determine whether a reference price is bona fide. What standard should be used? If an advertisement specifies a "regular price," just what qualifies as regular? How many units must the store sell at this price for it to be a bona fide regular price—half the stock? A few? Just one? Finally, what if the store offers the item for sale at the regular price but customers do not buy any? Can it still be considered a regular price? In general, if a seller is going to label a price as a regular price, the Better Business Bureau suggests that at least 50 percent of the sales have occurred at that price.[47]

Is this a legitimate sale, or is the retailer using deceptive reference prices?

Loss Leader Pricing As we discussed previously, leader pricing is a legitimate attempt to build store traffic by pricing a regularly purchased item aggressively but still above the store's cost. **Loss leader pricing** takes this tactic one step further by lowering the price below the store's cost. No doubt you have seen "buy one, get one free" offers at grocery and discount stores. Unless the markup for the item is 100 percent of the cost, these sales obviously do not generate enough revenue from the sale of one unit to cover the store's cost, which means it has essentially priced the total for both items below cost.

Bait and Switch Another form of deceptive price advertising occurs when sellers advertise items for a very low price without the intent to really sell any. This **bait-and-switch** tactic is a deceptive practice because the store lures customers in with a very low price on an item (the bait), only to aggressively pressure these customers into purchasing a higher-priced item (the switch) by disparaging the low-priced item, comparing it unfavourably with the higher-priced model, or professing an inadequate supply of the lower-priced item. Again, the laws against bait-and-switch practices are difficult to enforce because salespeople, simply as a function of their jobs, are always trying to get customers to trade up to a higher-priced model without necessarily deliberately baiting them. The key to proving deception centres on the intent of the seller, which is also difficult to prove.

Predatory Pricing

When a firm sets a very low price for one or more of its products with the intent to drive its competition out of business, it is using **predatory pricing**. Predatory pricing is illegal under the Competition Act because it constrains free trade and represents a form of unfair competition. It also tends to promote a concentrated market with a few dominant firms (an oligopoly).

loss leader pricing
Loss leader pricing takes the tactic of *leader pricing* one step further by lowering the price below the store's cost.

bait-and-switch
A deceptive practice of luring customers into the store with a very low advertised price on an item (the bait), only to aggressively pressure them into purchasing a higher-priced item (the switch) by disparaging the low-priced item, comparing it unfavourably with the higher-priced model, or professing an inadequate supply of the lower-priced item.

predatory pricing
A firm's practice of setting a very low price for one or more of its products with the intent to drive its competition out of business; illegal under the Competition Act.

Is this price discrimination illegal?

price discrimination
The practice of selling the same product to different resellers (wholesalers, distributors, or retailers) or to the ultimate consumer at different prices; some, but not all, forms of price discrimination are illegal.

price fixing
The practice of colluding with other firms to control prices.

horizontal price fixing
Occurs when competitors that produce and sell competing products collude, or work together, to control prices, effectively taking price out of the decision process for consumers.

vertical price fixing
Occurs when parties at different levels of the same marketing channel (e.g., manufacturers and retailers) collude to control the prices passed on to consumers.

But again, predation is difficult to prove. First, one must demonstrate intent, that is, that the firm intended to drive out its competition or prevent competitors from entering the market. Second, the complainant must prove that the firm charged prices lower than its average cost, an equally difficult task.

Price Discrimination

There are many forms of price discrimination, but only some of them are considered illegal under the Competition Act. When firms sell the same product to different resellers (wholesalers, distributors, or retailers) at different prices, it can be considered **price discrimination**; usually, larger firms receive lower prices.

We have already discussed the use of quantity discounts, which is a legitimate method of charging different prices to different customers on the basis of the quantity they purchase. The legality of this tactic stems from the assumption that it costs less to sell and service 1000 units to one customer than 100 units to 10 customers. But quantity discounts must be available to all customers and not be structured in such a way that they consistently and obviously favour one or a few buyers over others. Still, some marketers have found ways to get around these rules, for example, offering 'preferred member' pricing. The Competition Act only requires companies to demonstrate that their price discounts do not restrict competition. While quantity discounts may be a grey area, it is perfectly legitimate to charge a different price to a reseller if the firm is attempting to meet a specific competitor's price. In addition, a barter agreement, in which buyers and sellers negotiate a mutually agreed upon price, is commonplace and absolutely legal in retail settings such as car sales and collectibles markets.

Price Fixing

Price fixing is the practice of colluding with other firms to control prices. Recently, the five largest music companies—Universal Music, Sony Music, Warner Music, BMG Music, and EMI—and three of the largest music retailers—Musicland Stores, Trans World Entertainment, and Tower Records—agreed to pay $67.4 million and distribute $75.7 million in CDs to public and nonprofit groups to settle a lawsuit for alleged price fixing during the late 1990s.[48]

This particular case of price fixing is especially interesting because it includes both horizontal and vertical price fixing. **Horizontal price fixing** occurs when competitors that produce and sell competing products collude, or work together, to control prices, effectively taking price out of the decision process for consumers. In this particular case, prosecutors alleged that horizontal price fixing had occurred among the record companies, which specified pricing terms associated with the sale and distribution of CDs. **Vertical price fixing** occurs when parties at different levels of the same marketing channel (e.g., manufacturers and retailers) collude to control the prices passed on to consumers. In the music industry case, prosecutors alleged that the music companies colluded with music retailers to maintain retail prices for CDs.

As these legal issues clearly demonstrate, pricing decisions involve many ethical considerations. In determining both their pricing strategies and their pricing tactics, marketers must always balance their goal of inducing customers, through price, to find value and the need to deal honestly and fairly with those same customers. Whether another business or an individual consumer, buyers can be influenced by a variety of pricing methods; it is up to marketers to determine which of these methods works best for the seller, the buyer, and the community.

Learning Objectives Review

1) Explain what price is and its importance in establishing value in marketing

2) Discuss how the 5Cs—company objectives, customers, costs, competition, and channel members—influence pricing decisions

3) Explain how firms set prices for their goods and services

4) Discuss various pricing strategies and tactics and their use in marketing (e.g., cost-based pricing, competition-based pricing, value-based pricing, psychological pricing, new product pricing, and pricing tactics targeted to consumers and channel members)

5) Explain the legal and ethical issues involved in pricing

1) Price is the only element of the marketing mix that generates revenues. It is also half the value equation. Although costs and other factors should be taken into consideration when setting prices, the most important factor is how the customer views the price in relationship to what he or she receives.

2) Successful pricing strategies are built on the 5Cs—company objectives, customers, costs, competition, and channel members. Company goals and objectives set the framework for pricing strategies. Companies focusing on image set high prices, while those that focus on value tend to use every day low prices. Understanding customers' reactions to different prices help marketers set prices that are consistent with their customers' attitudes and preferences. The demand curve and price elasticity of demand are two related tools that markers use to gauge customers' sensitivity to prices changes. Customers' income and the availability of substitute products also influence customers' reaction to price changes. The third C, costs, is a major determinant of pricing. Cost of producing a good helps marketers determine the possible prices they can charge and the levels of profitability they can expect. Break-even analysis is a helpful tool that is used to help marketers determine the price level at which the number of units sold exactly covers the cost of producing the good. The fourth C, competition, influences pricing because a firm usually pays close attention and reacts to a competitor's moves. Intense competition may produce price wars. The level of competition is usually determined by the market structure of the industry. That is, whether the industry structure is oligopolistic, monopolistic, or pure competition. The final, C, channel members—manufacturers, wholesalers, retailers—influence prices because they play a key role in getting the product to the final consumer,

and they are independent and usually have their own objectives and competitive situation to deal with. The company may want to set a certain price level for its products in order to reflect quality and value but retailers may decide they want to move more volume and so reduce the price, hence the possibility for conflict. Also, manufacturers may give discounts to channel members, which may influence the price the ultimate consumer pays.

3) The various methods of setting prices each have their own set of advantages and disadvantages. The fixed percentage and markup approaches are quick and easy but fail to reflect the competitive environment or consumer demand. Although it is always advisable to be aware of what competitors are doing, using competitor-based pricing should not occur in isolation without considering consumers' reactions. Taking a value-based approach to pricing, whether the improvement value or the total cost of ownership, in conjunction with these other methods provides a nicely balanced method of setting prices.

4) Companies tend to use different pricing strategies and tactics for different products or different markets. Pricing strategies are a long-term approach to pricing products, whereas price tactics focus more on the short-term aspects of the 5Cs of pricing. The various pricing strategies can be grouped into three broad categories—cost-based strategies, value-based strategies, and competition-based strategies. Cost-based strategies are based on the firm ascertaining the cost of producing and marketing the product, and then adding some mark-up for profit. Competition-based pricing is based on a firm understanding what competitors are doing and reacting accordingly. Firms may choose to set prices below, at or above competitors' prices. Value-based pric-

ing is based on a firm understanding consumers' perceptions of value as reflected in the price of the product (cheap, expensive, bargain, etc.). Consumers' assessments of value may be influenced by their reference prices of similar products or may use marketers' prices to infer a price-quality relationship. Marketers often use price skimming or penetration pricing when they introduce new products in the marketplace based on the nature of the product and their marketing goals, for example, whether they want to gain market share, show price leadership, or signal innovation.

Companies may use a wide variety of pricing tactics from two categories: (1) business-to-business pricing tactics and discounts, and (2) pricing tactics aimed at consumers. Business-to-business pricing tactics and discounts usually include seasonal discounts, cash discounts, quantity discounts, allowances, and geographic pricing. Pricing tactics aimed at consumers include quantity discounts, markdowns, seasonal discounts, and coupons and rebates.

5) There are almost as many ways to get into trouble by setting or changing a price as there are pricing strategies and tactics. Three of the most common legal issues pertain to advertising deceptive prices. Specifically, if a firm compares a reduced price with a "regular" or reference price, it must actually have sold that product or service at the regular price. Advertising the sale of products priced below the retailer's cost constitutes an unfair competitive practice, as does bait-and-switch advertising. Charging different prices to different customers is sometimes, but not always, illegal, whereas any collusion among firms to fix prices is always illegal.

Key Terms

- advertising allowance, 346
- bait-and-switch, 351
- break-even point, 332
- cash discount, 346
- competitive parity, 326
- competitor orientation, 326
- competitor-based pricing method, 339
- complementary products, 331
- contribution per unit, 333
- cost of ownership method, 340
- cost-based pricing method, 339
- coupon, 350
- cross-price elasticity, 331
- cross-shopping, 338
- cumulative quantity discount, 347
- customer orientation, 326
- demand curve, 327
- elastic, 330
- everyday low pricing (EDLP), 344
- experience curve effect, 342
- external reference price, 343
- fixed costs, 332
- geographic pricing, 347

- grey market, 335
- high/low pricing, 344
- horizontal price fixing, 352
- improvement value, 339
- income effect, 331
- inelastic, 330
- internal reference price, 344
- leader pricing, 349
- listing allowances, 346
- loss leader pricing, 351
- markdowns, 349
- market penetration pricing, 342
- maximizing profits strategy, 325
- monopolistic competition, 334
- noncumulative quantity discount, 347
- odd prices, 345
- oligopolistic competition, 334
- predatory pricing, 351
- premium pricing, 339
- prestige products or services, 328
- price, 322
- price bundling, 348
- price discrimination, 352

- price elasticity of demand, 330
- price fixing, 352
- price lining, 347
- price skimming, 341
- price war, 334
- pricing tactics, 345
- profit orientation, 325
- pure competition, 334
- quantity discount, 347
- rebate, 350
- reference price, 343
- sales orientation, 325
- seasonal discount, 346
- size discount, 350
- substitute products, 331
- substitution effect, 331
- target profit pricing, 325
- target return pricing, 325
- total cost, 332
- uniform delivered pricing, 347
- value-based pricing method, 339
- variable costs, 332
- vertical price fixing, 352

Concept Review

1. Explain the importance of pricing in the marketing mix from the perspective of the firm and the consumer.

2. List the 5Cs of pricing. Which one do you consider to be the most important and why?

3. Explain how companies try to determine consumers' sensitivity to price changes. What factors influence their price sensitivity?

4. Why is it important for firms to determine costs when setting prices?

5. Why does a company need to understand a product's break-even point?

6. How has the Internet changed the way some people use price to make purchasing decisions?

7. What is the major difference between pricing strategies and pricing tactics? Give three examples of each.

8. Explain how psychological factors may influence a firm's pricing strategy.

9. In what conditions should a price skimming strategy be used? When is it appropriate to use a market penetration strategy?

10. Explain the four types of illegal or unethical pricing practices.

Marketing Applications

1. You and your two roommates are starting a pet grooming service to help put yourself through university. There are two other well-established pet services in your area. Should you set your price higher or lower than that of the competition? Justify your answer.

2. One roommate believes the most important objective in setting prices for the new pet grooming business is to generate a large profit, while keeping an eye on your competitors' prices; the other roommate believes it is important to maximize sales and set prices according to what your customers expect to pay. Who is right and why?

3. Assume you have decided to buy an advertisement in the local newspaper to publicize your new pet grooming service. The cost of the ad is $1000. You have decided to charge $40 for a dog grooming, and you want to make $20 for each dog. How many dogs do you have to groom to break even on the cost of the ad? What is your break-even point if you charge $50 per dog?

4. On your weekly grocery shopping trip, you notice that the price of ground beef has gone up 50 cents a kilogram. How will this price increase affect the demand for ground beef, ground turkey, and hamburger buns? Explain your answer in terms of the price elasticity of demand.

5. Zinc Energy Resources Co., a new division of a major battery manufacturing company, recently patented a new battery that uses zinc-air technology. The unit costs for the zinc-air battery are: The battery housing is $8, materials are $6, and direct labour is $6 per unit. Retooling the existing factory facilities to manufacture the zinc-air batteries amounts to an additional $1 million in equipment costs. Annual fixed costs include sales, marketing, and advertising expenses of $1 million; general and administrative expenses of $1 million; and other fixed costs totalling $2 million. Please answer the following questions.

   a. What is the total per-unit variable cost associated with the new battery?

   b. What are the total fixed costs for the new battery?

   c. If the price for the new battery was set at $35, what would the break-even point be?

6. How do pricing strategies vary across markets that are characterized by monopolistic, oligopolistic, and pure competition?

7. Though not illegal, many firms operating over the Internet have been experimenting with charging different consumers different prices for the same product or service. Since stores in different parts of the country might have different prices, some websites require postal code information before providing prices. Why would retailers charge different prices in different markets or postal codes? Is it ethical for retailers to do so? Is it a good business practice?

8. Suppose you have been hired as the pricing manager for a grocery store chain that typically adds a fixed percentage onto the cost of each product to arrive at the retail price. Evaluate this technique. What would you do differently?

9. Coupons and rebates benefit different channel members. Which would you prefer if you were a manufacturer, a retailer, and a consumer? Why?

10. Imagine that you are the newly hired brand manager for a T-shirt company whose new line is about to come out. Because of a major fashion magazine's very positive review of the line, the company wants to reposition the brand as a premium youth brand. Your boss asks what price you should charge for the new T-shirt line. The current line, considered mid-range retail, is priced at $20. What steps might you undertake to determine what the new price should be?

Toolkit

BREAK-EVEN ANALYSIS

A shoe manufacturer has recently opened a new manufacturing plant in Asia. The total fixed costs are $50 million. They plan to sell the shoes to retailers for $50, and their variable costs (material and labour) are $25 per pair. Calculate the break-even volume. Now see what would happen to the break-even volume if the fixed costs were increased to $60 million due to the purchase of new equipment, or the variable costs were decreased to $20 due to a new quantity discount provided by the supplier. Use the toolkit provided at www.mcgrawhill.ca/olc/grewal to experiment with changes in fixed cost, variable cost, and selling price to see what happens to break-even volume.

Net Savvy

1. Several different pricing models can be found on the Internet. Each model appeals to different customer groups. Go to www.ebay.com and try to buy this book. What pricing options and prices are available? Do you believe that everyone will choose the least expensive option? Why or why not? Now go to www.amazon.ca. Is there more than one price available for this book? If so, what are those prices? If you had to buy another copy of this book, where would you buy it, and why would you buy it there?

2. Prices can vary depending on the market being served. Because Dell sells its computers directly to consumers all around the world, the Dell website makes it easy to compare prices for various markets. Go to www.dell. com. Begin on the Dell Canada site and determine the price of a Dimension 3000 desktop computer. Next go to the Dell United Kingdom website and another country of your choice to find the price of the same computer. (If you need to convert currency, go to www.xe.com.) How does the price of the desktop computer vary? What would account for these differences in price?

Chapter Case Study

FINDING THE BEST PRICE: BIZRATE VERSUS EBAY[49]

Economists point to auction websites such as eBay as the best means to represent the value of any given product, because the price is determined solely by the value that the consumer attaches to it. That is, the value of the item is accurately reflected in the price paid. Thus, the prices paid for items on eBay must be some of the lowest prices available, right?

Recently, various Internet search engines, such as www.shopzilla.com, www.pricegrabber. com, and www.pricecanada.ca, have gained popularity. Perhaps one of the most popular is www. bizrate.com.

Do auction websites or price search engines really give consumers the lowest price? To address this question, we performed searches using both Bizrate and eBay for two specific products: a Sony model DCR-DVD 101 DVD camcorder and a Yamaha receiver, model HTR 5790. At bizrate.com, we found 17 stores that sold the Yamaha receiver at prices ranging from a high of $719 to a low of $495. For the Sony camcorder, we found 51 stores offering it at prices from $800 to $449.

At eBay, the prices for the Yamaha receiver started at $550 and moved down to $495; the Sony camcorder prices ranged from $774 to $480.

	Bizrate		eBay	
Product	**Low**	**High**	**Low**	**High**
Yamaha receiver	$495	$719	$495	$550
Sony DVD camcorder	$449	$800	$480	$774

Thus, it appears from analyzing these two products alone that the lowest prices are available through both channels, but the high-end prices are lower at eBay. eBay displays similar products together on the same page, which may explain why the range of prices found on eBay is narrower than that on Bizrate.

Questions

1. How has the Internet changed price competition for well-known, branded products?

2. Would the nature of price competition on the Internet be different if we had looked for commodities or esoteric luxury products?

3. Do you think this accessibility to detailed price comparisons has reduced price competition, such that all sellers price at the same level?

4. What assumptions do you tend to make about a product that seems priced very low? Very high?

CHAPTER 13

LEARNING OBJECTIVES

After studying this chapter you should be able to:

LO **1** Understand the importance of distribution and the interrelationships between distribution channels, supply chain management, and logistics management

LO **2** Explain how distribution channels add value to businesses and consumers

LO **3** Describe distribution channel design and management decisions and strategies

LO **4** Explain how logistics and supply chain management affect distribution strategy

Marketing Channels: Distribution Strategy

Zara International, Inc. (www.zara.com), a fast-growing Spanish apparel retailer and an inexpensive but chic subsidiary of Inditex (Industria de Diseño Textil, Galicia, Spain), operates about 820 fashionable clothing stores in 60 countries, including nine in Canada.[1] The chain takes in annual sales of more than $3 billion—an impressive number for a company founded only 30 years ago. The first Zara shop opened its doors in 1975 in La Coruña in the northwestern region of Spain's Galicia. Nearby is Zara's ultramodern headquarters and its 500,000 square metre distribution centre that supplies all its stores.

In a tribute to Zara's "with it" image, according to *Vogue*, even French customers of Zara stores identify Zara as being of French origin. Various fashion pages continue to feature celebrities like Cindy Crawford shopping at a Zara store in Canada; Chelsea Clinton visiting the Zara store in Ankara, Turkey; the children of the Spanish royal family purchasing regularly at the Zara store on Madrid's upscale Velazquez Street; and tourist buses making sightseeing stopovers at the Zara store on Paseo de Garcia in Barcelona. Today Zara shops can be found in upscale neighbourhoods such as New York's 5th Avenue, Paris's Champs Elysées, London's Regent Street, and Tokyo's Shibuya Shopping Centre.

Inditex (www.inditex.com), which owns and operates Zara, is made up of almost 100 companies that all deal with activities related to textile design, production, and distribution. Inditex also operates seven other chains: Kiddy's Class, Pull and Bear, Massimo Dutti, Bershka, Stradivarius, Oysho, and Zara Home. But Zara International is the largest and the oldest of its chains, providing close to 80 percent of its revenues.

Although Zara competes with local retailers in most of its markets, analysts consider its three closest competitors to be The Gap, Sweden's Hennes & Mauritz (H&M), and Italy's Benetton. There are, however, important differences in the ways the four firms operate. The Gap and H&M own most of their stores but outsource all their manufacturing. In contrast,

Zara's advanced supply chain and information systems enable it to get its relatively inexpensive high fashion apparel to stores in New York (left) and Paris (right) in a matter of a few weeks.

Benetton has invested relatively heavily in manufacturing, but licensees run its stores. Zara not only owns a majority of its stores, it also produces a majority of its own clothes, mostly at its ultramodern manufacturing complex in northwestern Spain. In another departure from the pack, Zara makes over 40 percent of its own fabric—far more than most of its rivals.

From its base in Spain, Zara also operates its own worldwide distribution network. Controlling the supply chain gives Zara flexibility that its competitors can only dream about. It also allows Zara to operate with minimal inventory buildups because its stores get deliveries twice a week, and newly supplied items rarely remain on the retail shelves for more than a week. In this sense, Zara has one of the most sophisticated supply chains of any apparel retailer. Zara takes only four to five weeks to design a new collection and then about a week to manufacture it. Its competitors, by comparison, need an average of six months to design a new collection and another three weeks to manufacture it. How does Zara do it?

The company derives its competitive advantage from an astute use of information and technology. All its stores are electronically linked to the headquarters in Spain. Store managers, together with a fleet of sharp-eyed, design-savvy trend spotters on Zara's staff, routinely prowl fashion hot spots such as university campuses and happening nightclubs. Their job is to function as the company's eyes and ears, to spot the next wave. Using wireless handheld devices, they send images back to corporate headquarters so that designers can produce blueprints for close-at-hand manufacturers to start stitching, resulting in garments that will be hanging in Zara stores within weeks.

In effect, Zara's designers have real-time information when they make decisions, with the commercial team, about the fabric, cut, and price of a new line of garments. This combination of real-time information sharing and internalized production means that Zara can work with almost no stock and still have new designs in its stores twice a week. Customers love the results of this high-velocity operation: They queue up in long lines at Zara's stores on designated delivery days, a phenomenon dubbed "Zaramania" by the press.

In this chapter, we discuss the third P, place, which includes all activities required to get the right products to the right customer when that customer wants it. Students of marketing often overlook or underestimate the importance of place in the marketing mix simply because it happens behind the scenes. Yet distribution channels, or place, add value for customers because they get products to customers efficiently—quickly and at low cost.

As shown in our chapter roadmap, we begin by understanding the importance of distribution, what distribution channels are, how they add value and how they are designed. Then we move to a discussion of supply chain and the critical role it plays in distribution strategy. Lastly we end the chapter by examining how logistics management integrates activities from the efficient flow of raw materials through to the delivery of finished goods.

The Importance of Distribution   LO **1**

So far in this textbook, we've examined how companies conduct in-depth market research, gain insights into consumer and business behaviour, carefully segment markets and select the best target markets, develop new products and services, and set prices that signal good value. However, even if they execute these activities flawlessly, if they are unable to secure appropriate distribution channels that reach prospective customers, their products and services are unlikely to ever meet their revenue targets.

Convincing intermediaries, such as wholesalers and retailers, to carry new products can prove to be more difficult than you might think. For example, a typical grocery store may carry between 30,000 and 40,000 different items. But a good number of these would have to be cleared off the shelves to make room for all the new foods, beverages, household goods, pet products, and other miscellaneous items launched

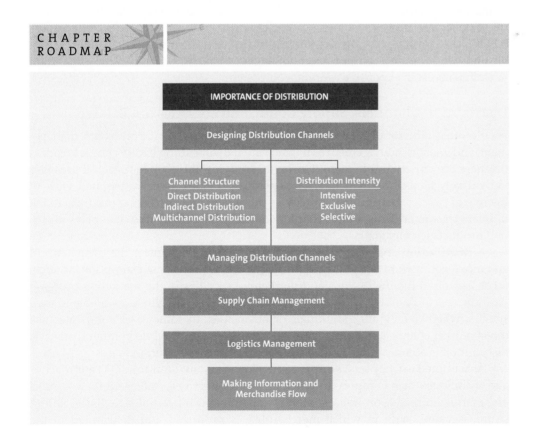

CHAPTER
ROADMAP

The Royal Canadian Mint released the world's first coloured circulation featuring the poppy, at Tim Hortons outlets to ensure broad distribution in time for Remembrance Day.

each year. With dozens of new products being introduced each day, the fight for shelf space is fierce. For many companies, distribution is not only difficult, it's expensive and involves paying listing fees to get shelf space as we discuss later in the chapter.

All goods and services organizations need a well thought out distribution strategy—even organizations that physically make money. On October 21, 2004, the Royal Canadian Mint released the world's first coloured circulation coin, a quarter that featured a red poppy to pay homage to the 117,000 Canadians who died in battle.[2] Normally coins are distributed through banks. However, very few consumers receive coins at banks. The Mint needed a distribution partner that could get its coins into circulation quickly as Remembrance Day was fast approaching. It chose Tim Hortons because of its many outlets across the country and its ability to reach so many Canadians. And since consumers could only pay in cash at that time, they were almost certain to get some poppy quarters along with their Double Doubles.

A good distribution strategy, well integrated with other elements of the marketing mix, can result in increased revenues. For example, Brick Brewing Co. in Waterloo, Ontario prides itself on being an industry innovator. It introduced 473-ml brown plastic bottles, that chill faster, stay cold longer, are lightweight and unbreakable, making it the first Canadian company to put beer in plastic bottles.[3] While this might sound like a product or packaging decision, the plastic bottle was closely tied to distribution strategy, because it allowed Brick to expand its sales to outlets where glass bottles were prohibited, such as university residences, sports events, and concert venues. It also let the company compete against canned beer distribution without having to invest in expensive canning equipment.

Distribution Channels, Supply Chain, and Logistics are Related

People often talk about distribution channel management, supply chain management, and logistics management as if they were the same thing because these business practices are closely interrelated. However, studying these three business practices individually as well as their interrelationships provides a very integrated view of the role of *place* or distribution strategy in producing and delivering products to the ultimate consumer. Thus, in this chapter we study the unique role each plays in getting products to consumers.

A **distribution channel** is the set of institutions that transfer the ownership of and move goods from the point of production to the point of consumption; as such, it consists of all the institutions and marketing activities in the marketing process.[4] As indicated in Exhibit 13.1, distribution channels make products available to consumers, whether they are individuals or businesses. In some cases companies use direct market channels to deliver their goods to consumers while in other instances, distribution is accomplished indirectly through the use of intermediaries.

As we noted in Chapter 1, **supply chain management** refers to a set of approaches and techniques firms employ to efficiently and effectively integrate their suppliers, manufacturers, warehouses, stores, and transportation intermediaries into a seamless value chain in which merchandise is produced and distributed in the

distribution channel
The institutions that transfer ownership of and move goods from the point of production to the point of consumption.

supply chain management
Refers to a set of approaches and techniques firms employ to efficiently and effectively integrate their suppliers, manufacturers, warehouses, stores, and transportation intermediaries into a seamless value chain in which merchandise is produced and distributed in the right quantities, to the right locations, and at the right time.

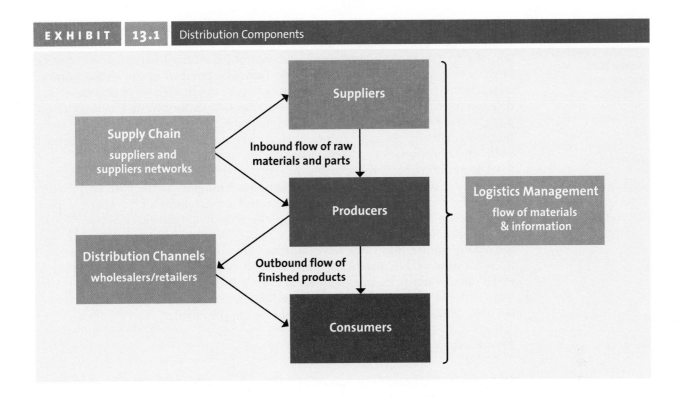

EXHIBIT 13.1 Distribution Components

right quantities, to the right locations, and at the right time, as well as to minimize systemwide costs while satisfying the service levels their customers require.[5] As we learned in the opening vignette, Zara employs a completely integrated supply chain because the company owns or at least has considerable control over each phase. As a result, it is able to conceive of, design, manufacture, transport, and ultimately sell high-fashion apparel much more quickly and efficiently than any of its major competitors.

A simplified supply chain would be one where manufacturers make products and sell them to intermediaries such as retailers or wholesalers. This becomes much more complicated if we include suppliers of materials to manufacturers and all of the manufacturers, wholesalers, and stores in a typical supply chain. **Wholesalers** are firms that buy products from manufacturers and resell them to retailers, and **retailers** sell products directly to consumers. Manufacturers ship to a wholesaler, or, in the case of many multistore retailers, to the retailer's distribution centre or directly to stores. The more intermediaries that are involved in the supply chain, the greater the complexity and number of transactions involved for a company to reach consumers directly.

Although the above discussion reflects the typical flow of manufactured goods, many variations to this supply chain exist. Some retail chains, like Home Depot and Costco, function as both retailers and wholesalers; they act as retailers when they sell to consumers directly and as wholesalers when they sell to other businesses, like building contractors or restaurant owners. When manufacturers such as Dell or Avon sell directly to consumers, they are performing both production and retailing activities. When Dell sells directly to a university or business, it becomes a business-to-business (B2B) transaction, but when it sells to the students or employees individually, it is a B2C (business-to-consumer) operation.

Supply chain management focuses on the relationships among members of the supply chain and distribution channel and the need to coordinate efforts to provide customers with the best value.

wholesalers
Those firms engaged in buying, taking title to, often storing, and physically handling goods in large quantities, then reselling the goods (usually in smaller quantities) to retailers or industrial or business users.

retailers
Sell products directly to consumers.

logistics management
The integration of two or more activities for the purpose of planning, implementing, and controlling the efficient flow of raw materials, in-process inventory, and finished goods from the point of origin to the point of consumption.

Logistics management is that element of supply chain management that concentrates on the movement and control of the physical products. It describes the integration of activities to plan, implement, and control the efficient flow of raw materials, in-process inventory, and finished goods from the point of origin to the point of consumption. These activities may include, but are not limited to, customer service, demand forecasting, distribution communications, inventory control, materials handling, order processing, parts and service support, plant and warehouse site selection, procurement, packaging, return goods handling, salvage and scrap disposal, traffic and transportation, and warehousing and storage.[6]

Distribution channel management, supply chain management, and logistics management are related but have been handled differently in the past. Distribution channel management traditionally has been the responsibility of marketing departments, under the direction of a marketing vice president. Logistics was traditionally the responsibility of operations, under a vice president of operations. Although their goals were similar, they often saw solutions differently, and sometimes they worked at cross-purposes. For instance, the marketing department's goal might have been to make sales, whereas logistics wanted to keep costs low. Firms have come to realize there is tremendous opportunity in coordinating marketing and logistics activities not only within a firm but also throughout the supply chain.

LO ② Designing Distribution Channels

Distribution channels are composed of various entities that are buying, such as retailers or wholesalers; selling, such as manufacturers or wholesalers; or helping facilitate the exchange, such as transportation companies. Like interactions between people, these relationships can range from close working partnerships to one-time arrangements. In almost all cases though, they occur because the parties want something from one another. For instance, Home Depot wants hammers from Stanley Tool Company, Stanley wants an opportunity to sell its tools to the public, and both companies want UPS to deliver the merchandise.

Each channel member performs a specialized role. If one member believes that another isn't doing its job correctly or efficiently, it usually can replace that member. So, if Stanley isn't getting good service from UPS, it can switch to Fed Ex. Likewise, if Home Depot believes its customers don't perceive Stanley tools to be a good value, it may buy from another tool company. Home Depot could even decide to make its own tools or use its own trucks to pick up tools from Stanley. However, even if a channel member is replaced, the function it performed remains, so someone needs to complete it.

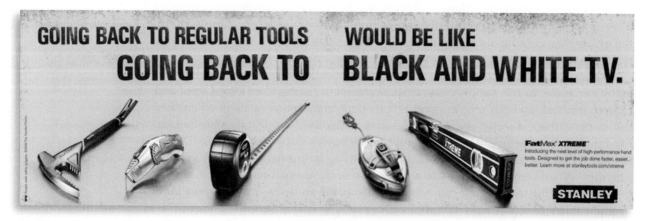

The Home Depot and Stanley Tool Company have a mutually beneficial partnership. The Home Depot buys tools from Stanley because their customers find value in Stanley products. Stanley sells tools to Home Depot because they have established an excellent market for its products.

Distribution channels perform a variety of transactional, logistical and facilitating functions as noted in Exhibit 13.2. One important role played by intermediaries is to reduce the number of marketplace contacts, resulting in more efficient systems. Intermediaries also match the requirements of individual consumers to the goods that manufacturers produce, handle physical distribution and storage of goods making them available for customers to purchase, facilitate searches by both buyers and sellers, and standardize exchange transactions. While channel functions may shift from one intermediary or channel member to another, it's important to recognize that they cannot be eliminated. As noted in the Home Deport example above, these functions must be completed by some organization in order to get the right products to the right customers when they want them.

In this section, we examine how distribution channels are structured, as well as the appropriate level of distribution intensity.

Distribution Channel Structure

LO **3**

When a firm is just starting out or entering a new market, it doesn't typically have the option of designing the "best" distribution channel structure—that is, choosing from whom it buys or to whom it sells. A new retailer selling children's clothing, for instance, will be primarily concerned about getting the right assortment and needs to scout the market to get just the right mix. Some manufacturers won't want to sell to this new retailer initially because its credit isn't established or the manufacturers already have enough of their products represented by other retailers in the area. The problem can be equally daunting for manufacturers entering a new market, whose primary concern will be to find retailers that want to take a chance on their line. Every company must develop a distribution strategy for how it will sell goods to consumers. The distribution system may take the form of direct distribution, indirect distribution, and multichannel distribution, or some combination of these forms.

Direct Distribution   As shown in Exhibit 13.3, direct distribution channels allow manufacturers to deal directly with consumers. Many products and services are distributed this way. For decades Dell's distribution strategy was based exclusively on using direct channels. This strategy has only very recently changed with its decision to begin selling select personal computers at Wal-Mart stores. Other companies, such as Avon and Tupperware, continue to use a direct only model. Direct distribution also plays a significant role in business to business dealings with companies such as IBM selling its mainframe computers directly to its largest customers in the public sector (government,) and private sector (banking and insurance) industries. Lastly,

EXHIBIT	**13.2**	Functions Performed by Intermediaries

Transactional Function

Buying—purchase goods for resale to other intermediaries or consumers
Risk Taking—ownership of inventory that can become outdated
Promotion—promote products to attract consumers
Selling—transact with potential customers

Logistical Function

Physical Distribution—transport goods to point of purchase
Storing—maintain inventory and protect goods

Facilitating Function

Gather Information—share competitive intelligence about customers or other channel members
Financing—extend credit and other financial services to consumers

some companies may be forced to distribute their goods directly because they are unable to secure shelf space in retail outlets or are unable to pay the high listing fees demanded by retailers for the shelf space. For example, many large grocery store chains charge listing fees that cover their costs in rearranging the store shelves and the warehouse, plus the administration costs associated with adding a new product. Ethical Dilemma 13.1 examines the issue of listing fees in more depth.

Indirect Distribution   With indirect distribution channels, one or more intermediaries work with manufacturers to provide goods and services to consumers. In some cases, there may only be one intermediary involved. Many automotive manufacturers, such as Ford, General Motors and Daimler Chrysler use indirect distribution with dealers acting as the retailer, as shown in Exhibit 13.3. Typically only one intermediary is used in the case of large retailers such as The Bay. Wholesalers are often used when a company does not buy in sufficient quantity to make it cost effective for a manufacturer to deal directly with a retailer. The use of wholesalers is quite common for low-cost or low-unit value items such as candy and chips as shown in the last example in Exhibit 13.3.

When developing its distribution strategy, a company may choose to use a push strategy or a pull strategy. With a push strategy, a manufacturer focuses its promotional efforts, for example personal selling or sales promotion, on channel members to convince them to carry its product. This strategy literally pushes the product through distribution channels to end consumers. Sometimes, if channel members are reluctant to stock new products, manufacturers may use a pull strategy. In this case, promotional efforts are directed at consumers in order to build demand for products which, in turn may convince retailers to carry them. Consumers who see television commercials or print advertisements or who receive direct mail information or coupons regarding new products may approach local retailers and request that they stock these products, thus pulling them through the distribution channels.

Multichannel Distribution   Today, many companies are embracing a multichannel, or hybrid, approach to distribution. As shown in Exhibit 13.4, companies such as Sony are better able to reach both consumers and business customers by using a combination of both direct and indirect distribution channels. In very large cities, Sony may sell directly via its own branded stores, while in other areas it may sell indirectly through retailers like Best Buy and Future Shop. Some companies engage a sales force to deliver products to customers while others pursue a direct marketing approach through the

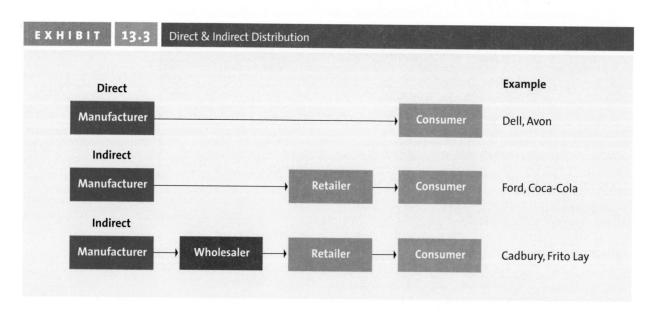

EXHIBIT 13.3   Direct & Indirect Distribution

					Example
Direct					
Manufacturer	→			Consumer	Dell, Avon
Indirect					
Manufacturer	→	Retailer	→	Consumer	Ford, Coca-Cola
Indirect					
Manufacturer	→ Wholesaler →	Retailer	→	Consumer	Cadbury, Frito Lay

Ethical Dilemma

13.1 | Listing Fees: Needless or Necessary?

Most consumers never think about how products make it to grocery store shelves. Often they don't realize that suppliers can pay thousands of dollars in listing fees to have their products stocked. In the world of grocery marketing, shelf space and position are critical. Listing fees can determine whether an item gets placed at eye level or down on a bottom shelf where it's harder to find.

In Canada, listing fees can range from a few hundred dollars, to $25,000 per item per store to $1 million per grocery chain. When it comes to getting listed, Val Laidlaw, director of customer marketing at Dare Foods of Kitchener says the first task is to get retailers on side and convince them your product will do well. Retailers don't care if your product helps you gain market share. They only care if it will help them by growing a category, bringing new consumers to the category, or adding to their profit.

Many large grocery store chains charge listing fees to cover their costs in rearranging the store shelves and the warehouse to accommodate the new product. Plus there are administration costs associated with adding a new product. The fee depends on many variables, including potential sales volume, trade allowances, product promotion offered (e.g., samples, in-store demos, promotional pricing, co-op advertising), product category, and com-

pany size. Grocery retailers know that large companies like Christies or Colgate Palmolive can afford listing fees. However, some category leaders don't have to pay them because retailers know they simply must stock popular products like Coke and Tide. Also, if there is high consumer demand for the product, there may be no listing fee.

The size of the category within a store plays an important role in obtaining space, too. With products such as cookies and crackers, offering enough money in listing fees will likely get you on the shelves since consumers are likely to try new products in these categories. However, the frozen food section of a grocery store is very expensive to expand, making it very tough to get new products listed. SKUs that don't perform well are de-listed within six months of hitting the shelves. Based on the AC Nielsen definition of a successful new product, failure rates can range up to 70 percent.

Grocery stores have a right to be selective when choosing from 100,000 plus items if they only have room for 40,000 items. However, critics say listing fees curb fair access to the market and erode consumer choice since small companies can't afford the fees. And the fees ultimately get passed on to consumers in the form of higher prices. What do you think? Are listing fees needless or necessary?

Adapted from Shirley Lichti, "Listing Fees Can Decide A Food Product's Fate," www.marketingmagic.ca/articles/ListingFees.htm, accessed July 3, 2007.

EXHIBIT | 13.4 | Multichannel Distribution

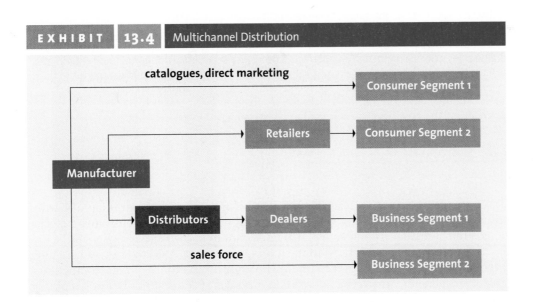

use of catalogues. Sears Canada sells directly at its retail stores as well as online and through the use of catalogues. See Internet Marketing 13.1 to read examples of companies that elect to use a multichannel approach to distribution.

When choosing which channels and retailers through whom to sell, the manufacturer should consider where the end customer expects to find the product, as well as some important retailer characteristics.

Internet Marketing

13.1 Integrated Multichannel Retailing: The Future of Distribution

Not long ago, many so-called Internet "gurus," futurists, and technology writers were predicting that the Internet would lead to the demise of physical stores. The mantra of the day was that the Internet offered convenience, something today's busy consumers crave. Companies were urged to get online or risk going out of business. Thousands of Internet businesses sprang up almost daily while many traditional retailers dismissed Internet shopping as a passing fad. This era, aptly referred to as the dot.com bubble, was fuelled by Internet successes such as Amazon, Dell, Yahoo!, and eBay. Reputable bricks-and-mortar companies such as Procter & Gamble and K-Mart hedged their bets, creating online stores as independent units with names that were distinctly different from their physical businesses. P&G created reflect.com and K-Mart created bluelight.com. Many companies feared that if they embraced the Internet and it failed, their brand reputation would be tarnished—a risk they were not prepared to take. In mid-2001, when the dot.com bubble burst, it seemed that many of these traditional retailers had made the right decision not to integrate their offline and online brands. However, Victoria's Secret and JC Penney were two traditional retailers that recognized the long-term potential of the Internet and created websites closely integrated with their offline brands. These pioneers demonstrated the true potential of the Internet to add value to a company's business through integrated multichannel distribution.

In the years that followed the dot.com bust, many businesses, especially large retailers, saw their online sales increase exponentially. The growth of online sales continued to increase at over 25 percent per year. However, in 2006, the growth rate of online sales slowed significantly, a trend analysts predict will continue for the rest of the decade. Online sales seem to have reached a plateau at around 5 percent of all sales. Although the Internet is seen as a key distribution channel and the way to manage supply chains and logistics, many companies still have not fully integrated their online and offline operations. Those that have are reaping huge returns. Recently Dell, which mastered the art of online selling, opened kiosks in shopping malls and is now selling its computers through Wal-Mart. Once the number one computer company in the world, Dell realized that in order to compete with HP, its chief rival, it must offer consumers multichannel retailing. Dell is not alone. Expedia, the largest online travel company, had hoped to eliminate the travel agent business model with its Internet only operations. However, it has come to the sober realization that it must do more to better serve its consumers. Thus, Expedia has almost tripled the number of travel ticketing kiosks in hotel lobbies and other locations to attract tourists.

The fact is some consumers like an interactive experience while others prefer the atmosphere of shopping in malls and stores. Most consumers mix it up depending on the occasion, product, and motivation. They are neither truly online or offline consumers—they are both. These new hybrid consumers use technology to their advantage while still enjoying the pleasure of physical shopping. Today's consumers want to order online but pick-up or return at physical stores, or view products in physical stores and order online. Although this sounds simple, it cannot happen without a seamlessly integrated distribution, supply chain and logistics management system. Best Buy, Sears, and numerous other big-box retailers are now jumping on this trend offering consumers exactly this type of service. The Internet is the perfect platform for companies to integrate physical stores, catalogue operations, mail-order businesses, and purely online operations. It is also the perfect platform for seamlessly integrating and coordinating ALL the institutions, processes, activities, and technologies required to create high quality products and to deliver these to consumers in a cost-effective, efficient, and timely manner, when and how consumers want to get them.

Adapted from "Online Sales Lose Steam," Matt Richtel and Bob Tedeschi, www.nytimes.com/2007/06/17/technology/17ecom.html?ex=1183694400&en=701e359b8f74485b&ei=5070, accessed January 4, 2008.

Customer Expectations Distribution channel management is an integral part of any marketing strategy. A key part of any strategy is to determine customer expectations. From a retailer's perspective, it is important to know from which manufacturers its customers want to buy. Manufacturers, in contrast, need to know where their target market customers expect to find their products and those of their competitors. Customers generally expect to find certain products at some stores but not at others. For instance, children's apparel manufacturer OshKosh B'Gosh would not choose to sell to Holt Renfrew or Giant Tiger because its customers would not expect to shop at those stores for children's clothing. Instead, Holt Renfrew might carry imported clothing from France, and Giant Tiger will probably offer bargain closeouts. But OshKosh's customers would definitely expect to find its clothing offerings at major department stores such as The Bay or Sears.

Companies need to stay abreast of changes in where customers buy products and change their distribution strategies accordingly. As an example, when country singer

Garth Brooks realized that the majority of his CDs were purchased at Wal-Mart, he signed an exclusive distribution deal with the retailer that eliminated his record label. Similarly, 70's Rock & Roll Hall of Fame band The Eagles released "Long Road out of Eden," its first new studio album in 28 years, exclusively at Wal-Mart. Although decisions like these may limit distribution to just one retailer, artists benefit from increased promotion and an increased share of the profits.

Channel Member Characteristics   Several factors pertaining to the channel members themselves will help determine the distribution structure. Generally, the larger and more sophisticated the channel member, the less likely that it will use intermediaries. A small specialty toy manufacturer will probably use a group of independent salespeople to help sell its line, whereas a large manufacturer like Mattel will use its own sales force. In the same way, an independent grocery store might buy merchandise from a wholesaler, but Wal-Mart, the world's largest grocer, only buys directly from the manufacturer. Larger firms often find that by performing the distribution functions themselves, they can gain more control, be more efficient, and save money. As discussed in Adding Value 13.1, large national convenience store chains prefer to deal with one regional supplier when it comes to buying products like ice.

Distribution Intensity

When setting up distribution for the first time or introducing new products, firms decide the appropriate level of **distribution intensity**—the number of channel members to use at each level of the supply chain. Distribution intensity commonly is divided into three levels: intensive, exclusive, and selective. (See Exhibit 13.5.)

distribution intensity The number of supply chain members to use at each level of the supply chain.

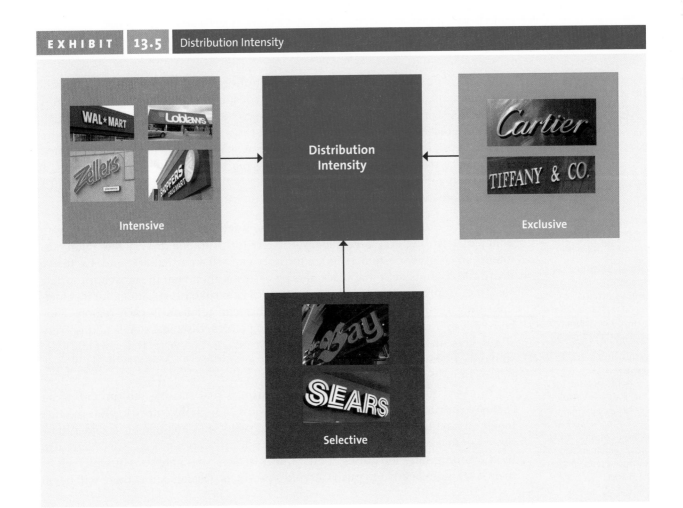

EXHIBIT   13.5   Distribution Intensity

Adding Value | 13.1 | Arctic Glacier: Heating Up the Ice Industry

The next time you are enjoying a few frosty beers on a camping trip with friends, stop to think about the ice that chilled your beverage. Chances are it's Arctic Glacier Premium Ice, from Canada's largest ice cube maker.[7] Arctic Glacier Inc. is a leading producer, marketer, and distributor of high-quality packaged ice to consumers across North America, adding value to water by freezing it. A simple concept, yet the company has excelled in the ice industry mainly because of its excellent distribution. Wherever it sells its ice, Arctic Glacier tends to have about 50 to 60 percent of the market share.[8]

It is estimated that the fragmented North American ice industry is comprised of over 2000 companies, most of which are small, independent, family-owned businesses operating as monopolies in local markets. Two main barriers keep new competitors from entering: 1) extremely high start up costs for ice production and 2) seasonality of the business combined with the high costs of transporting ice. In manufacturing and selling ice, high costs are incurred from refrigerated storage and delivery equipment associated with the business.[9]

Arctic Glacier believes that there are significant growth opportunities through the acquisition of well-run, regional and local ice companies. From a marketing channel perspective, the consolidation of corner stores into national conven-

The Arctic Glacier bag is a familiar one across North America. The Winnipeg-based company has become a market leader, adding value to water by turning it into ice.

ience store chains like Couche-Tard, Mac's, and 7-11 helps to create fewer, larger customers. These customers generally prefer dealing with one regional ice supplier which gives further support to Arctic Glacier's strategy.[10] Leveraging its strong relationship with retailers, Arctic Glacier can really benefit from the summer sun. When it's hot and you need ice, it's likely you won't even care what the price is—and this translates into profits for Canada's king of cool.[11]

---

marketing channel
The set of institutions that transfer the ownership of and move goods from the point of production to the point of consumption; consists of all the institutions and marketing activities in the marketing process.

intensive distribution
A strategy designed to get products into as many outlets as possible.

exclusive distribution
Strategy of granting exclusive rights to sell to one or very few retail customers so no other customers can sell a particular brand.

exclusive geographic territories
Territories granted to one or very few retail customers by a manufacturer using an exclusive distribution strategy; no other customers can sell a particular brand in these territories.

Intensive Distribution An **intensive distribution** strategy is designed to get products into as many outlets as possible. Most consumer packaged goods companies, such as Pepsi, Procter & Gamble, Kraft, and most other nationally branded products found in grocery and discount stores, strive for and often achieve intensive distribution. Pepsi, for instance, wants its product available everywhere—grocery stores, convenience stores, restaurants, and vending machines. Timex watches, starting at around $60, can also be found in many locations. The more exposure these products get, the more they sell.

Exclusive Distribution Manufacturers also might use an **exclusive distribution** policy by granting **exclusive geographic territories** to one or very few retail customers so no other customers in the territory can sell a particular brand. Exclusive distribution can benefit manufacturers by assuring them that the most appropriate customers represent their products. Cosmetics firms like Estée Lauder, for instance, limit their distribution to a few select, higher-end retailers in each region. They believe that if they sell their products to drug stores, discount stores, and grocery stores, this distribution would weaken their image. Likewise, Rolex watches are sold only by high end jewellers and a few retail outlets in keeping with their prestigious brand image.

In cases of limited supply or when a firm is just starting out, providing an exclusive territory to one customer helps ensure enough inventory to offer the customer an adequate selection. For instance, Cervélo is a Canadian bicycle manufacturer that makes light weight racing bikes. It selects its authorized dealers carefully. By controlling sales territories, it guarantees dealers adequate supply, which gives them a strong incentive to push Cervélo's products. Dealers know there will be no competing retailers to cut prices, so their profit margins are protected, which also gives them an incentive to carry more inventory and use extra advertising, personal selling, and sales promotions.

Selective Distribution   Between the intensive and exclusive distribution strategies lies **selective distribution**, which uses a few selected customers in a territory. Similar to exclusive distribution, selective distribution helps a seller maintain a particular image and control the flow of merchandise into an area, so many shopping goods manufacturers use it. Recall that shopping goods are those products for which consumers are willing to spend time comparing alternatives, such as most apparel items, home items like branded pots and pans or sheets and towels, branded hardware and tools, and consumer electronics. Seiko uses a selective distribution strategy for its watches to match its more upscale image and pricing. Retailers still have a strong incentive to sell the products but not to the same extent as if they had an exclusive territory.

Managing Distribution Channels

If a distribution channel is to run efficiently, the participating members must cooperate. Oftentimes, however, channel members have conflicting goals. For instance, Stanley wants Home Depot to carry all its tools but not those of its competitors so that Stanley can maximize its sales. But Home Depot carries a mix of tool brands so it can maximize the sales in its tool category. When channel members are not in agreement about their goals, roles, or rewards, **channel conflict** results. For example, in England, singer and songwriter Prince infuriated retailers with his decision to have a newspaper, *The Mail,* include free copies of his new Planet Earth CD. After the giveaway was announced, Columbia Records' corporate parent, Sony Music, said it would not release the CD for retail sale in the U.K.[12]

Most consumer packaged goods companies, such as Pepsi (top), strive for intensive distribution—it wants to be everywhere. But cosmetics firms like Estée Lauder (bottom) use an exclusive distribution strategy by limiting their distribution to a few select, higher-end retailers in each region.

Channel conflict can be resolved through good negotiations. But when the issues can't be worked out, relationships can fall apart, and the firms may go their separate ways. In other cases, conflict may lead to a stronger supply chain. In the mid-1980s, Procter & Gamble was having trouble selling to Wal-Mart; in their relationship, there was no sharing of information, no joint planning or sales forecasting, and no systems coordination. So Sam Walton ventured out on a canoe trip with Lou Pritchett, P&G's vice president of sales. On this trip, they started a process of examining how the two firms could mutually profit by working together. The conflict thus ultimately resulted in a much stronger partnership between the two firms in which they currently work together to establish sales forecasts and determine how to best restock P&G merchandise on Wal-Mart's shelves. All parties benefit. Customers get lower prices and high product availability, and because P&G produces according to demand, there is less need for inventory, so its salespeople spend less time in the stores. Finally, Wal-Mart achieves higher sales and lower inventory costs.[13]

Companies can manage distribution channels by developing strong relationships with supply chain partners. Or they can coordinate the channel using a vertical marketing system.

selective distribution
Lies between the intensive and exclusive distribution strategies; uses a few selected customers in a territory.

channel conflict
Results when supply chain members are not in agreement about their goals, roles, or rewards.

Managing Channels through Vertical Marketing Systems

Although conflict is likely to occur in any distribution channel, it is generally more pronounced when the channel members are independent entities. Distribution channels that are more closely aligned, whether by contract or ownership, share common goals and therefore are less prone to conflict.

In an independent distribution channel (the left panel of Exhibit 13.6), the several independent members—a manufacturer, a wholesaler, and a retailer—each attempt to satisfy their own objectives and maximize their own profits, often at the expense of the other members. None of the participants has any control over the others.

For instance, the first time Zara purchases cotton fabric from Tessuto e Colore in Northern Italy, both parties try to extract as much profit from the deal as possible, and after the deal has been consummated, neither party feels any responsibility to the other. Over time, Zara and Tessuto might develop a relationship in which their transactions become more routinized and automatic, such that Zara depends on Tessuto for fabric, and Tessuto depends on Zara to buy a good portion of its output. This scenario represents the first phase of a **vertical marketing system** (the right panel of Exhibit 13.6) in which the members act as a unified system because they realize that each party can maximize their individual benefits by working together to make the distribution system more efficient rather than individually or at cross-purposes. There are three types, or phases, of vertical marketing systems, each with increasing levels of formalization and control. The more formal the vertical marketing system, the less likely conflict will ensue.

vertical marketing system A supply chain in which the members act as a unified system; there are three types: *administrated, contractual,* and *corporate.*

Administered Vertical Marketing System
The Zara/Tessuto channel relationship offers an example of an **administered vertical marketing system**. In an administered vertical marketing system, there is no common ownership and no contractual relationships, but the dominant channel member controls the channel relationship. In our example, because of its size and relative power, Zara imposes some control over Tessuto; it dictates, for instance, what Tessuto should make and when it should be delivered. Zara also has a strong influence over the price. If either party doesn't like the way the relationship is going, however, it can simply walk away.

administered vertical marketing system A *supply chain* system in which there is no common ownership and no contractual relationships, but the dominant channel member controls the channel relationship.

Contractual Vertical Marketing System
Over time, Zara and Tessuto may formalize their relationship by entering into contracts that dictate various terms, such as how much Zara will buy each month, at what price, and the penalties for late deliveries. In **contractual vertical marketing systems** like this, independent firms at different levels

contractual vertical marketing system A system in which independent firms at different levels of the supply chain join together through contracts to obtain economies of scale and coordination and to reduce conflict.

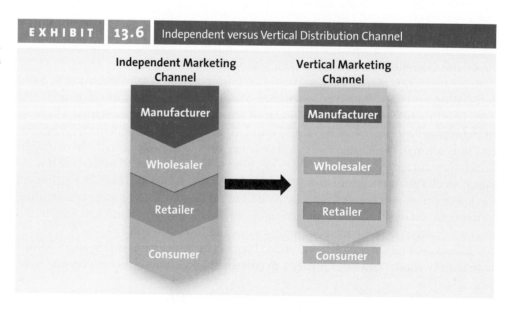

EXHIBIT **13.6** Independent versus Vertical Distribution Channel

Independent Marketing Channel

Manufacturer
Wholesaler
Retailer
Consumer

Vertical Marketing Channel

Manufacturer
Wholesaler
Retailer
Consumer

of the supply chain join together through contracts to obtain economies of scale and coordination and to reduce conflict.[14]

Franchising is the most common type of contractual vertical marketing system; franchising companies and their franchisees account for $90 billion in Canadian retail sales—an astonishing 26 percent of all retail sales in this country—and employ more than 1 million people.[15] **Franchising** is a contractual agreement between a franchisor and a franchisee that allows the franchisee to operate a retail outlet using a name and format developed and supported by the franchisor. Exhibit 13.7 lists some of Canada's favourite franchises.

In a franchise contract, the franchisee pays a lump sum plus a royalty on all sales in return for the right to operate a business in a specific location. The franchisee also agrees to operate the outlet in accordance with the procedures prescribed by the franchisor. The franchisor typically provides assistance in locating and building the business, developing the products or services sold, management training, and advertising. To maintain the franchisee's reputation, the franchisor also makes sure that all outlets provide the same quality of services and products.

A franchise system combines the entrepreneurial advantages of owning a business with the efficiencies of vertical marketing systems that function under single ownership (a corporate system, as we discuss next). Franchisees are motivated to make their stores successful because they receive the profits, after they pay the royalty to the franchisor. The franchisor is motivated to develop new products, services, and systems and to promote the franchise because it receives royalties on all sales. Advertising, product development, and system development are all done efficiently by the franchisor, with costs shared by all franchisees. Entrepreneurial Marketing 13.1 discusses the approach to franchising used by M&M Meat Shops.

Zara and Tessuto e Colore in Northern Italy might develop a vertical marketing system in which transactions have become routinized and automatic, such that Zara depends on Tessuto for fabric, and Tessuto depends on Zara to buy a good portion of its output.

franchising
A contractual agreement between a *franchisor* and a *franchisee* that allows the franchisee to operate a business using a name and format developed and supported by the franchisor.

Rank	Franchise	Type	Start-Up Costs	Number of Outlets
EXHIBIT 13.7		Canada Franchise Favourites		
1	Extreme Pita	Pita, salads	$60K	143
2	Subway	Submarine sandwiches & salads	$73,700	2259
3	Booster Juice	Smoothies & juice bar	$175K	75
4	Domino's Pizza	Pizza	$197K	230
5	Living Lighting	Interior & exterior lighting	$200K	29
6	Buck or Two	Retail merchandise	$250K	200
7	Dairy Queen	Soft serve ice cream, hamburgers, hot dogs	$300K	590
8	M&M Meat Shops	Specialty frozen foods	$300K	340
9	Tim Hortons	Coffee, doughnuts, sandwiches	$500-800K	2724
10	McDonald's	Hamburgers, chicken, salads	$500K–1.6M	1400

Source: http://www.franchisedirectory.ca/

Entrepreneurial Marketing

13.1   Fire Up the Grill

After graduating with a degree in mechanical engineering, Mac Voisin couldn't find a job, so he started selling real estate and eventually became a builder. A few years later, he and his brother-in-law, Mark Nowak, were barbecuing and lamenting the fact that the quality of steaks they bought from grocery stores never seemed to be as good as the ones they got at nice restaurants. Why was it, they wondered, that restaurants could consistently deliver a great product? They soon discovered that restaurants sourced choice cuts of meat and aged it between 21 to 28 days to make it more tender.

This insight led Mac and Mark to form M&M Meat Shops. They opened their first store in October 1980 with the goal of giving customers the certainty of great products every time. They bought high quality frozen foods in bulk and waited for customers to roll in. The first few months of business were dismal. Their products were packaged in very large boxes intended for restaurants, not consumers, and came without cooking instructions. However, the two persevered, learning and making changes.

Sales continued to be slow until a local business reporter for *The Record*, Kitchener-Waterloo's daily newspaper, wrote an article about their store. They went from virtually no customers to being deluged overnight. To continue the sales momentum, M&M Meat Shops staff offered samples, wore crazy hats, carried purchases out to customers' cars, thanked them and asked them to come back—anything to build customer loyalty.

Nine months after the first store was opened, a friend in Cambridge asked about getting a franchise. Today M&M Meat Shops has over 465 stores across Canada, opening about 35 new stores each year. For Mac Voisin, franchising was ideal because it offered speed to market, quickly penetrating new markets. This was important in the early days of the business because the company's concept could easily be duplicated. In fact, over 150 copycat stores opened in Ontario over the next 10 years. Today only about half a dozen are still in business. Voisin jokes that many other companies took the approach that if you had a pulse and a pocketbook, you could buy a franchise. M&M Meat Shops didn't subscribe to this philosophy. Instead, they invited the right people to join the team, people who could be both business partners and friends. Some franchisees invest their life savings (a typical store costs about $325,000) and so M&M Meat Shops wants them to be successful. As a result, potential franchisees are carefully screened and given personality profiling to see if they are team players. And while entrepreneurial skills might be considered an asset elsewhere, Voisin says they raise a red flag for M&M Meat Shops because such franchisees typically want to do things their own way instead of sticking to the corporate formula.

M&M Meat Shop co-founder, Mac Voisin.

Over the years, companies like Wal-Mart, Zellers, and Esso have asked to carry M&M Meat Shops products. These retailers would have dramatically expanded the company's distribution reach, however, Voisin decided against it sensing the move would ultimately hurt the brand—M&M Meat Shops prides itself on offering high quality whereas retailers like Wal-Mart focus on low price. Other people have asked why the company didn't expand vertically by raising its own chickens or starting its own trucking firm. Voisin says M&M Meat Shops knew it couldn't do everything well and so made a conscious decision to focus on its core business.

Today the chain has sales of $480 million with each store approximately 1400 square feet in size. With over 465 stores, Voisin figures the Canadian market will reach saturation at between 600 to 700 stores. As a result, plans are currently underway for expansion to the midwestern United States using their proven franchising strategy of getting the right people to the right place at the right time.

Corporate Vertical Marketing System   Because Zara deals with "fast fashion," it is imperative that it have complete control over the most fashion-sensitive items. So Zara manufactures these items itself and contracts out its less fashionable items to other manufacturers.[16] The portion of its supply chain that Zara owns and controls is called a **corporate vertical marketing system**. Because Zara's parent company Inditex owns the manufacturing plants, warehouse facilities, retail outlets, and design studios, it can dictate the priorities and objectives of that supply chain, and thus conflict is lessened.

corporate vertical marketing system
A system in which the parent company has complete control and can dictate the priorities and objectives of the supply chain; it may own facilities such as manufacturing plants, warehouse facilities, retail outlets, and design studios.

Supply Chains Add Value   LO 4

Why would a manufacturer want to use a wholesaler or a retailer? Don't these supply chain members just cut into their profits? Wouldn't it be cheaper for consumers to buy directly from manufacturers? In a simple agrarian economy, the best supply chain may in fact follow a direct route from manufacturer to consumer: The consumer goes to the farm and buys food directly from the farmer. But how will the food get cooked? The consumer doesn't know how to make a stove, nor does she have the materials to do so. The stove maker who has the necessary knowledge must buy raw materials and components from various suppliers, make the stove, and then make it available to the consumer. If the stove maker isn't located near the consumer, the stove must be transported to where the consumer has access to it. To make matters even more complicated, the consumer may want to view a choice of stoves, hear about all their features, and have the stove delivered and installed.

How many companies are involved in making and getting a stove to your kitchen?

Each participant in the supply chain thus adds value. The components manufacturer helps the stove manufacturer by supplying parts and materials. The stove maker then turns the components into the stove. The transportation company gets the stove to the retailer. The retailer stores the stove until the customer wants it, educates the customer about product features, and delivers and installs the stove. At each step, the stove becomes more costly but also more valuable to the consumer.

Exhibits 13.8A and B show how using supply chain partners can provide value overall. Exhibit 13.8A shows three manufacturers, each of which sells directly to three consumers in a system that requires nine transactions. Each transaction costs money—for example, the manufacturer must fill the order, package it, write up the

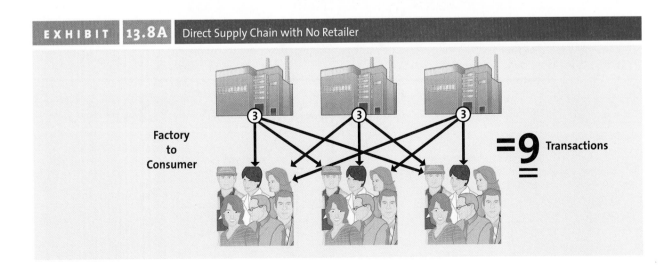

EXHIBIT 13.8A   Direct Supply Chain with No Retailer

Factory to Consumer

=**9** Transactions

paperwork, and ship it—and each cost is passed on to the customer. Exhibit 13.8B shows the same three manufacturers and consumers, but this time they go through a single retailer. The number of transactions falls to six, and as transactions are eliminated, the supply chain becomes more efficient, which adds value for customers by making it more convenient and less expensive to purchase merchandise.

Supply Chain Management Streamlines Distribution

Supply chain management offers the 21st century's answer to a host of distribution problems faced by firms. As recently as the early 1990s, even the most innovative firms needed 15 to 30 days—or even more—to fulfill an order from the warehouse to the customer. The typical order-to-delivery process had several steps: order creation, usually using a telephone, facsimile, or mail; order processing, using a manual system for credit authorization and assignment to a warehouse; and physical delivery. Things could, and often did, go wrong. Ordered goods were not available. Orders were lost or misplaced. Shipments were misdirected. These mistakes lengthened the time it took to get merchandise to customers and potentially made the entire process more expensive and frustrating, a familiar scenario for many of us.

Faced with these predicaments, firms began stockpiling inventory at each level of the supply chain (retailers, wholesalers, and manufacturers), but keeping inventory where it is not needed becomes a huge and wasteful expense. Take, for instance, the troubled U.S. airline industry. Bankrupt US Airways took drastic steps to reduce its spare inventory of replacement parts by more than $100 million, or 24 percent of its annual maintenance budget. Prior to the cut, the firm was carrying $500 million in extra inventory to support its 279 mainline jets and spending $130 million annually on new parts or parts repair. Similarly, Delta Airlines decreased its maintenance costs by roughly 51 percent by implementing an inventory management system. Between 2001 and 2002, Delta's maintenance expenses dropped 11 percent, saving the company $90 million.[17]

Supply Chain Management Affects Marketing

Every marketing decision is affected by and has an effect on the supply chain. When products are designed and manufactured, how and when the critical components

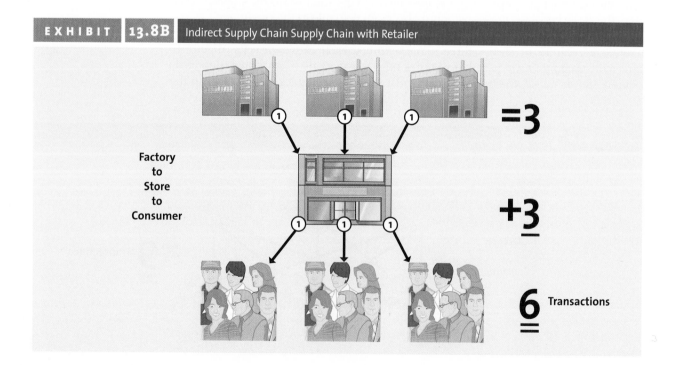

EXHIBIT 13.8B Indirect Supply Chain Supply Chain with Retailer

Factory to Store to Consumer

=3

+3

6 Transactions

reach the factory must be coordinated with production. The sales department must coordinate its delivery promises with the factory or distribution centres. A **distribution centre**, a facility for the receipt, storage, and redistribution of goods to company stores or customers, may be operated by retailers, manufacturers, or distribution specialists.[18] Furthermore, advertising and promotion must be coordinated with those departments that control inventory and transportation. There is no faster way to lose credibility with customers than to promise deliveries or run a promotion and then not have the merchandise when the customer expects it. Entrepreneur Michael Dell got into the computer business and developed his firm into one that provides better value to customers with great supply chain management. The company builds roughly 50,000 made-to-order computers a day and carries just four days' worth of parts inventory. Online sales account for nearly half of its orders. Using state-of-the-art technology, Dell monitors every aspect of the supply chain, including supplier report cards that compare individual performance to preset criteria.

Michael Dell makes made-to-order computers on this assembly line.

Five interrelated activities emerge in supply chain management: designing distribution channels, making information flow (discussed earlier in this chapter), managing the relationships among supply chain partners, making merchandise flow, and managing inventory. In the next few sections, we examine these remaining activities.

Making Information Flow

Information flows from the customer to stores, to and from distribution centres, possibly to and from wholesalers, to and from product manufacturers, and then on to the producers of any components and the suppliers of raw materials. To simplify our discussion and because information flows are similar in other supply chain links and B2B channels, we shorten the supply chain in this section to exclude wholesalers, as well as the link from suppliers to manufacturers. Exhibit 13.9 illustrates the flow of information that starts when a customer buys a Sony DVD player at Future Shop. The flow follows these steps:

distribution centre
A facility for the receipt, storage, and redistribution of goods to company stores or customers; may be operated by retailers, manufacturers, or distribution specialists.

- **Flow 1 (Customer to Store):** The sales associate at Future Shop scans the **universal product code (UPC)** tag, the black-and-white bar code found on most merchandise, on the DVD player packaging, and the customer receives a receipt.

- **Flow 2 (Store to Buyer):** The point-of-sale (POS) terminal records the purchase information and electronically sends it to the buyer at Future Shop's corporate office. The sales information is incorporated into an inventory management system to aid in planning future purchases and promotions.

- **Flow 3 (Store to Manufacturer):** The purchase information from each Future Shop store is typically aggregated by the retailer as a whole, which creates an order for new merchandise and sends it to Sony. The buyer at Future Shop may also communicate directly with Sony to get information and negotiate prices, shipping dates, promotional events, or other merchandise-related issues.

- **Flow 4 (Store to Manufacturer):** If the merchandise is reordered frequently, the ordering process can become automatic and virtually bypass the buyer.

- **Flow 5 (Store to Distribution Centre):** Stores also communicate with the Future Shop distribution centre to coordinate deliveries and check inventory status.

universal product code (UPC)
The black-and-white bar code found on most merchandise.

In Flow 3, the retailer and manufacturer exchange business documents through a system called electronic data interchange (EDI).

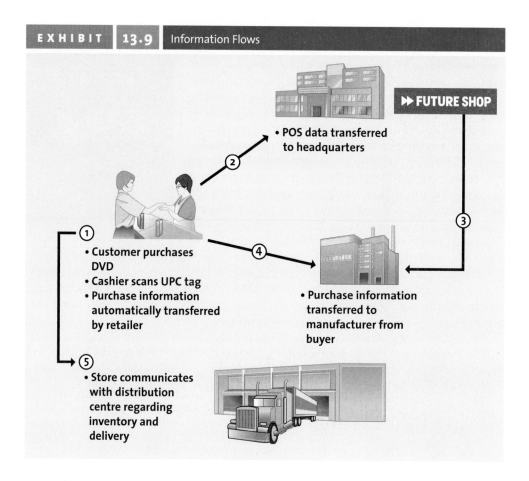

EXHIBIT 13.9 Information Flows

FUTURE SHOP

2. POS data transferred to headquarters

1.
• Customer purchases DVD
• Cashier scans UPC tag
• Purchase information automatically transferred by retailer

4. • Purchase information transferred to manufacturer from buyer

3.

5. • Store communicates with distribution centre regarding inventory and delivery

Electronic Data Interchange

electronic data interchange (EDI)
The computer-to-computer exchange of business documents from a retailer to a vendor and back.

Electronic data interchange (EDI) is the computer-to-computer exchange of business documents from a retailer to a vendor and back. In addition to sales data, purchase orders, invoices, and data about returned merchandise can be transmitted back and forth.

Many retailers now require vendors to provide them with notification of deliveries before they take place using an **advanced shipping notice**, an electronic document that the supplier sends the retailer in advance of a shipment to tell the retailer exactly what to expect in the shipment. If the advanced shipping notice is accurate, the retailer can dispense with opening all the received cartons and checking in merchandise. In addition, EDI enables vendors to transmit information about on-hand inventory status, vendor promotions, and cost changes to the retailer, as well as information about purchase order changes, order status, retail prices, and transportation routings.

advanced shipping notice
An electronic document that the supplier sends the retailer in advance of a shipment to tell the retailer exactly what to expect in the shipment.

Typically, EDI is transmitted over the Internet through either intranets or extranets. **Intranets** are secure communication systems contained within one company, such as between buyers and distribution centres. In contrast, an **extranet** is a collaborative network that uses Internet technology to link businesses with their suppliers, customers, or other businesses. These extranets are typically private and secure, in that they can be accessed only by certain parties. Thus, some but not all manufacturers would have access to a retailer's extranet.

intranet
A secure communication system contained within one company, such as between the firm's buyers and distribution centres.

Especially through extranets, EDIs have gone beyond merely communicating order and shipping information. Suppliers, through the Internet, can describe and show pictures of their products, and buyers can issue requests for proposals. The two parties then can electronically negotiate prices and specify how the product will be made and how it should look.

extranet
A collaborative network that uses Internet technology to link businesses with their suppliers, customers, or other businesses.

Toy giant Hasbro, for example, launched an EDI initiative to improve its order processing. Before this, roughly 70 percent of all incoming orders filtered through 100 vendors in Asia. Each order was sent from the vendor to the appropriate manufacturer, and the manufacturer manually reviewed all vendor requests. When exceptions or delays occurred, the process became laborious because of the numerous faxes and phone calls needed to resolve any issue. After Hasbro implemented EDI for its manufacturers, 80 percent of the orders needed no human interaction at all. As a result, the Asian operations were able to handle a 100-percent increase in their order volume without any additional resources.[19]

Hasbro makes toys and games like this "Risk Star Wars—Clone Wars Edition," but they communicate efficiently with their vendors with EDI.

Managing Supply Chains through Strategic Relationships

There is more to managing supply chains than simply exercising power over other members in an administered system or establishing a contractual or corporate vertical marketing system. There is also a human side.

In a conventional distribution channel, relationships between members often are based on the argument over the split of the profit pie—if one party gets ahead, the other party falls behind. Sometimes this type of transactional approach is acceptable if the parties have no interest in a long-term relationship. If Harry Rosen sees a trend for very narrow white belts, it would be interested in purchasing from a vendor in which an ongoing relationship would be built. Harry Rosen would not purchase from a vendor on a one-time basis just to get a one-time good price. This is because long-term relationship building is important to the company's business practices.

More often than not, firms seek a **strategic relationship**, also called a **partnering relationship**, in which the supply chain members are committed to maintaining the relationship over the long term and investing in opportunities that are mutually beneficial. In a conventional or administered supply chain, there are significant incentives to establishing a strategic relationship, even without contracts or ownership relationships. Both parties benefit because the size of the profit pie has increased, so both the buyer and the seller increase their sales and profits. These strategic relationships are created explicitly to uncover and exploit joint opportunities, so members depend on and trust each other heavily; share goals and agree on how to accomplish those goals; and are willing to take risks, share confidential information, and make significant investments for the sake of the relationship. Successful strategic relationships require mutual trust, open communication, common goals, and credible commitments.[20]

strategic relationship (partnering relationship) A supply chain relationship that the members are committed to maintaining long term, investing in opportunities that are mutually beneficial; requires mutual trust, open communication, common goals, and credible commitments.

Harry Rosen grew from a single 500-square foot Toronto tailor shop to a national upscale menswear chain. It works hard to develop strategic partnerships with its suppliers based on mutual trust, open communications, common goals, and credible commitments.

Mutual Trust Mutual trust holds a strategic relationship together. When vendors and buyers trust each other, they're more willing to share relevant ideas, clarify goals and problems, and communicate efficiently. Information shared between the parties thus becomes increasingly comprehensive, accurate, and timely. With trust, there's also less need for the supply chain members to constantly monitor and check up on each other's actions because each believes the other won't take advantage, even given the opportunity. RFID systems that enable sealed cartons to be checked into a distribution centre without being opened would be impossible without mutual trust.

Open Communication To share information, develop sales forecasts together, and coordinate deliveries, Harry Rosen and its suppliers maintain open and honest communication. This maintenance may sound easy in principle, but most businesses don't tend to share information with their business partners. But open, honest communication is a key to developing successful relationships because supply chain members need to understand what is driving each other's business, their roles in the relationship, each firm's strategies, and any problems that arise over the course of the relationship.

Common Goals Supply chain members must have common goals for a successful relationship to develop. Shared goals give both members of the relationship an incentive to pool their strengths and abilities and exploit potential opportunities together. For example, Harry Rosen and its local suppliers recognize that it is in their common interest to be strategic partners. Harry Rosen needs the quick response local manufacturers afford, and those manufacturers recognize that if they can keep Harry Rosen happy, they will have more than enough business for years to come. So if Harry Rosen needs a special production run to make an emergency shipment, suppliers will work to meet the challenge. If one of Harry Rosen's suppliers has difficulty getting a particular fabric or financing its inventory, it is in Harry Rosen's best interest to help it because they are committed to the same goals in the long run.

Credible Commitments Successful relationships develop because both parties make credible commitments to, or tangible investments in, the relationship. These commitments involve spending money to improve the products or services provided to the customer.[21] For example, if Harry Rosen makes a financial commitment to its suppliers to help them develop state-of-the-art manufacturing facilities and computer systems for improved communication, it is making a credible commitment—putting its money where its mouth is.

Just like many other elements of marketing, managing the supply chain can seem like an easy task at first glance: Put the merchandise in the right place at the right time. But the various elements and actors involved in a supply chain create unique and compelling complexities and require that firms work carefully to ensure they are achieving the most efficient and effective chain possible.

Logistics Management: Making Merchandise Flow

To illustrate the different types of merchandise flows consider the following scenario.[22] Merchandise is shipped from Sony to Future Shop's distribution centres or from Sony directly to stores. If the merchandise goes through distribution centres, it is then shipped to stores and then to the customer.

Inbound Transportation

dispatcher
The person who coordinates deliveries to distribution centres.

Because its distribution centres typically are quite busy, a **dispatcher**—the person who coordinates deliveries to Future Shop's distribution centres—assigns a time slot for each shipment of DVD players to arrive. If the truck misses the time slot, it is fined. Although many manufacturers pay transportation expenses, some retailers negotiate with their vendors to absorb this expense. These retailers believe they can lower net merchandise cost and control their merchandise flow better if they negotiate directly with truck companies and consolidate shipments from many vendors.

Receiving and Checking

Receiving refers to the process of recording the receipt of merchandise as it arrives at a distribution centre or store. Checking is the process of going through the goods upon receipt to ensure they arrived undamaged and that the merchandise ordered was the merchandise received.

RFID tags make receiving and checking merchandise accurate, quick, and easy.

Today, many distribution systems use EDI designed to minimize, if not eliminate, these processes. The advance shipping notice tells the distribution centre what should be in each box. The recipient scans the UPC label on the shipping carton or the radio frequency identification (RFID) tag, which identifies the carton's contents, and those contents then are automatically counted as being received and checked. **Radio frequency identification (RFID) tags** are tiny computer chips that automatically transmit to a special scanner all the information about a container's contents or individual products.

radio frequency identification (RFID) tags Tiny computer chips that automatically transmit to a special scanner all the information about a container's contents or individual products.

Storing and Cross-Docking

There are three types of distribution centres: traditional, cross-docking, and combinations. A traditional distribution centre is a warehouse in which merchandise is unloaded from trucks and placed on racks or shelves for storage. When the merchandise is needed in the stores, a worker goes to the rack, picks up the item, and places it in a bin. A conveyor system or other material-handling equipment transports the merchandise to a staging area, where it is consolidated and made ready for shipment to stores.

The second type, called a cross-docking distribution centre, is one to which vendors ship merchandise prepackaged in the quantity required for each store. The merchandise already contains price and theft detection tags. Because the merchandise is ready for sale, it goes straight to a staging area rather than into storage. When all the merchandise going to a particular store has arrived in the staging area, it is loaded onto a truck, and away it goes.

Most modern distribution centres combine the two previous approaches. It is difficult for a firm to operate without some storage facilities, even if merchandise is stored for only a few days. For instance, some merchandise, such as tent stakes at Mountain Equipment Co-op, has relatively slow sales but must be carried because it rounds out an assortment. These items are good candidates for storage in a distribution centre, even if the rest of the merchandise is cross-docked. Also, no matter how good a sales forecasting system may be, sometimes the merchandise arrives before it is needed in the stores. In these cases, the retailer must have a system to store the merchandise temporarily.

In a cross-docking distribution centre, merchandise moves from vendors' trucks to the retailer's delivery trucks in a matter of hours.

Getting Merchandise Floor-Ready

Floor-ready merchandise is merchandise that's ready to be placed on the selling floor immediately. Getting merchandise floor-ready entails ticketing, marking, and, in the case of apparel, placing garments on hangers. Ticketing and marking refers to creating price and identification labels and placing them on the merchandise. It is more efficient for a retailer to perform these activities at a distribution centre than in its stores because the work is time consuming and messy. Some retailers force their suppliers to ship merchandise floor-ready, thus totally eliminating this expensive, time-consuming process for themselves.

Shipping Merchandise to Stores

Shipping merchandise to stores is quite complex for multistore chains. A Future Shop distribution centre will run approximately 100 trucks to its stores per day. To handle such complex transportation problems, distribution centres use a sophisticated routing and scheduling computer system that considers the rate of sales in the store, road conditions, and transportation operating constraints to develop the most efficient routes possible. As a result, stores receive an accurate estimated time of arrival, and the supply chain maximizes vehicle use. In Canada, different shipping methods are chosen depending on the nature of the goods, costs, location of customers relative to manufacturers, and needs of the customers. These methods include air (e.g., Air Canada), rail (e.g., Canadian Pacific Railway), land (e.g., Challenger Motor Freight), and sea (e.g., SEA-CAN.)

Inventory Management through Just-In-Time Systems

just-in-time (JIT) inventory systems
Inventory management systems designed to deliver less merchandise on a more frequent basis than traditional inventory systems; the firm gets the merchandise "just in time" for it to be used in the manufacture of another product; also known as *quick response (QR) systems* in retailing.

quick response
An inventory management system used in retailing; merchandise is received just in time for sale when the customer wants it.

lead time
The amount of time between the recognition that an order needs to be placed and the arrival of the needed merchandise at the seller's store, ready for sale.

Customers demand specific SKUs, and they want to be able to buy them when needed. At the same time, firms can't afford to carry more than they really need of an SKU, because to do so is very expensive. Suppose, for instance, a shoe store carries $1 million worth of inventory at its own expense. Experts estimate that it would cost between 20 and 40 percent of the value of the inventory, or $20,000 to $40,000 per year, to hold that inventory! So firms must balance having enough inventory to satisfy customer demands with not having more than they need.

To help reconcile these seemingly conflicting goals, many firms have adopted just-in-time (JIT) inventory systems. **Just-in-time inventory systems**, also known as **quick-response** (QR) systems in retailing, are inventory management systems designed to deliver less merchandise on a more frequent basis than traditional inventory systems. The firm gets the merchandise "just-in-time" for it to be used in the manufacture of another product, in the case of parts or components, or for sale when the customer wants it, in the case of consumer goods. The benefits of a JIT system include reduced **lead time** (by eliminating the need for paper transactions by mail and overnight deliveries), increased product availability, and lower inventory investment. JIT systems lower inventory investments, but product availability actually increases.

To illustrate a JIT system, consider Procter & Gamble's five-step process. Managers start with demand data, which they obtain directly from their retailers. They work closely with these retailers to develop sales forecasts and shipping schedules that better align P&G's production with demand at the retail store. This effort reduces both excess inventory and out-of-stock situations. Most importantly, P&G produces just enough to meet demand. To achieve this balance, the company has moved from producing every product once a month to a system in which it produces every item every day, which it then delivers to the customer the following day.[23]

Learning Objectives Review

1) Understand the importance of distribution and the interrelationships between distribution channels, supply chain management, and logistics management

2) Explain how distribution channels add value to businesses and consumers

3) Describe distribution channel design and management decisions and strategies

4) Explain how logistics and supply chain management affect distribution strategy

1) Companies cannot take the distribution of products for granted. Appropriate distribution channels must be identified and channel members need to be convinced to carry these new products, both of which are integral to a successful distribution strategy. A distribution channel is the set of institutions and marketing activities that transfer the ownership of and move goods from the manufacturer or producer to the consumer. Supply chain management refers to the effort to coordinate suppliers, manufacturers, warehouses, stores, and transportation intermediaries so that the merchandise the customer wants is produced in the right quantities and sent to the right locations at the time the customer wants it. In this sense, the supply chain is considered to be longer and covers more aspects of the distribution strategy since it extends backwards to include suppliers. Logistics concentrates on the physical movement and control of the products, whereas supply chain management includes the managerial aspects of the process as well.

2) Without distribution channels, consumers would be forced to find raw materials, manufacture products, and somehow get them to where they could be used, all on their own. Each channel member adds value to the product by performing one of these functions. Supply chain management creates value for each firm in the chain and helps bind together many company functions, including manufacturing, inventory management, transportation, advertising, and marketing.

3) Sometimes, particularly when firms are starting out, companies cannot choose their ideal partners but instead take any partners they can get to obtain the materials or customers they need. In general, the larger and more sophisticated the company, the more likely it will perform some supply chain activities itself rather than using third-party intermediaries. When deciding on the distribution channel structure, firms can choose from direct, indirect, and multichannel distribution. Firms that want as much market exposure as possible use intensive distribution, whereas firms that either want to maintain an exclusive image or are not large enough to sell to everyone tend to use an exclusive distribution strategy. Somewhere in the middle lies a selective distribution strategy.

4) For a supply chain to operate properly, the flow of information and merchandise must be coordinated, and supply chain members must work together to their mutual benefit. In more sophisticated supply chains, information flows seamlessly between supply chain members through EDI. Many of the best supply chains use a JIT or QR inventory management system, which provides the right amount of inventory just when it is needed. The JIT systems thus improve product availability and reduce inventory investments. The increasing use of RFID technology is expected to have a revolutionary impact on distribution channels, supply chain management, and logistics management in the future. The expectation is that the overall system of producing and delivering will become much more sophisticated and efficient.

The more closely aligned the supply chain members are with each other, the less likely there will be significant conflict. An administered supply chain occurs when a dominant and powerful supply chain member has control over the other members. In a contractual supply chain (e.g., franchising), coordination and control are dictated by contractual relationships between members. Corporate supply chains can operate relatively smoothly because one firm owns the various levels of the chains. Supply chains also can be effectively managed through strong relationships developed with supply chain partners. To create such relationships, the partners must trust each other, communicate openly, have compatible goals, and be willing to invest in each other's success.

Key Terms

- administered vertical marketing system, 372
- advanced shipping notice, 378
- channel conflict, 371
- contractual vertical marketing system, 372
- corporate vertical marketing system, 375
- dispatcher, 380
- distribution centre, 377
- distribution channel, 362
- distribution intensity, 369
- electronic data interchange (EDI), 378
- exclusive distribution, 370
- exclusive geographic territories, 370
- extranet, 378
- franchising, 373
- intensive distribution, 370
- intranet, 378
- just-in-time inventory systems, 382
- lead time, 382
- logistics management, 364
- marketing channel, 370
- quick response, 382
- radio frequency identification (RFID) tags, 381
- retailer, 363
- selective distribution, 371
- strategic relationship (partnering relationship), 379
- supply chain management, 362
- universal product code (UPC), 377
- vertical marketing system, 372
- wholesaler, 363

Concept Review

1. Explain why having a well thought out distribution strategy is important to a company's success.

2. Explain the factors that must be considered when designing a distribution strategy.

3. Explain the differences between direct, indirect, and multichannel distribution systems. What role do technologies and consumer behaviour play in the rise of multichannel distribution?

4. Describe the functions performed by intermediaries. Why would companies choose to have intermediaries fulfill these functions rather than perform them themselves?

5. Explain how customer expectations and channel member characteristics impact a company's distribution strategy.

6. Explain intensive, selective, and exclusive distribution intensity. Under what circumstances would it be best to use each of these strategies?

7. Describe how companies manage distribution channels using vertical marketing systems.

8. Explain how supply chain management and logistics management add value to a company's consumer offerings.

9. Explain how supply chain management improves marketing activities.

10. What are the major elements of a logistics management system? Explain the benefits of a well-run just-in-time inventory management system.

Marketing Applications

1. Explain distribution strategy and identify the major activities that distribution channels, supply chain, and logistics management involve. Identify several ways that supply chain management adds value to a company's offerings, with regard to both consumers and business partners.

2. You are hired by a small bakery that is interested in distributing its product through supermarkets. The market for the bakery's products has been steadily growing and it is time to expand distribution now that the bakery has expanded its production capacity. You have an appointment with the manager of a local grocery chain. The manager is familiar with the bakery's products and is excited about the possibility of having them in the store. He presents the contract and you notice a $10,000 fee for stocking the product. When you ask about the fee, you are told it is simply the cost of doing business and that the bigger bakeries are not in favour of adding your product line to the chain. You know that the bakery cannot afford to pay the fee. What should you do now?

3. Discuss the advantages and disadvantages of Dell's decision to change from using a direct distribution strategy to a multichannel approach to distribution.

4. Research the "160-kilometre diet" trend and discuss how growing consumer awareness of shipping costs and environmental concerns has led to a push for more locally produced foods.

5. Give an example of a retailer that participates in an independent (conventional) supply chain and one involved in a vertical marketing system. Discuss the advantages and disadvantages of each.

6. In what ways can the flow of information be managed in the supply chain? How can the ready flow of information increase a firm's operating efficiencies?

7. Describe how B2B transactions might employ EDI to process purchase information. Considering the information discussed in Chapter 7 about B2B buying situations, determine which buying situation (new task, modified rebuy, or straight rebuy) would most likely align with the use of EDI technology. Justify your answer.

8. Discuss the advantages to a retailer like SportChek of expending the time and effort to get merchandise floor-ready at either the point of manufacture or in the distribution centre rather than having retail store staff members do it in the stores. Provide the logic behind your answer.

9. Why would a big company like Nike want to develop strategic partnerships with locally owned running stores? Describe what Nike would have to do to maintain such relationships.

10. You are hired as an assistant brand manager for a popular consumer product. One day in an emergency meeting, the brand manager informs the group that there is a problem with one of the suppliers and that he has decided to send you over to the manufacturing facilities to investigate the problem. When you arrive at the plant you learn that a key supplier has become increasingly unreliable in terms of quality and delivery. You ask the plant manager why they don't switch suppliers since this is becoming a major problem for your brand. He informs you that the troubled supplier is his cousin whose wife has been very ill, and he just can't switch right now. What course of action should you take?

Net Savvy

1. Dell is considered exemplary in its ability to manage its supply chain efficiently. Log on to the company's website (www.dell.com) and go through the process of configuring a computer to purchase. Print out a copy of the computer system you have designed, making note of the delivery date and price. Describe how Dell has revolutionized computer sales and delivery. Is there any indication that Dell has partnered with other companies to sell peripheral equipment like printers or scanners? How would this partnership add value to customers?

2. The opening vignette for this chapter highlighted ways that Zara International, a division of Inditex, successfully manages its supply chain. Visit Inditex's website (www.inditex.com) and review the company's commitment to social responsibility, particularly the section that pertains to its code of conduct. Considering the discussion in this chapter about strategic relationships, how does Inditex address the factors necessary for mutually beneficial partnerships according to its code of conduct?

Chapter Case Study

WAL-MART: PIONEER IN SUPPLY CHAIN MANAGEMENT[24]

Wal-Mart dominates the retailing industry in terms of its sales revenue, its customer base, and its ability to drive down costs and deliver good value to its customers. After all, the world's largest corporation takes pride in having received numerous accolades for its ability to continuously improve efficiency in the supply chain while meeting its corporate mandate of offering customers Always Low Prices.

Tight inventory management is legendary at Wal-Mart through its just-in-time techniques, some of which are homegrown, that allow the firm to boast one of the best supply chains in the world. Wal-Mart has not only transformed its own supply chain but influenced how vendors throughout the world operate. For example, retailers everywhere are now placing much more emphasis on vendors' on-time and accurate deliveries. To meet these requirements, vendors have had to upgrade their inventory management and delivery systems to ensure they are doing business the way their large retailer customers prefer.[25] Recognized for its ability to obtain merchandise from global sources, Wal-Mart also pioneered the strategy of achieving high levels of growth and profitability through its precision control of manufacturing, inventory, and distribution. Although the company is not unique in this regard, it is by far the most successful and most influential corporation of its kind and has put into practice various innovative techniques.

And when Wal-Mart does something, it does it on a massive scale. Wal-Mart's computer system, for example, is second only to that of the Pentagon in storage capacity. Its information systems analyze more than 10 million daily transactions from point-of-sale data and distribute their analysis in real time both internally to its managers and externally via a satellite network to Wal-Mart's many suppliers, who use the information for their production planning and order shipment.

Much of the popularity of supply chain management has been attributed to the success of Wal-Mart's partnership with Procter & Gamble. During the 1980s, the two collaborated in building a software system that linked P&G to Wal-Mart's distribution centres, taking advantage of advances in the world's telecommunications infrastructure. When a Wal-Mart store sold a particular P&G item, the information flowed directly to P&G's planning and control systems. When the inventory level of P&G's products at Wal-Mart's distribution centre got to the "reorder point," the system automatically alerted P&G to ship more products; this information in turn helped P&G plan its production. Wal-Mart was also able to track when a P&G shipment arrived at one of its distribution warehouses, which enabled it to coordinate its own outbound shipments to stores. Both Wal-Mart and P&G realized savings from the better inventory management and order processing, savings that in turn were passed on to Wal-Mart's consumers through its always low prices.

Wal-Mart's Innovations

Wal-Mart has pioneered many innovations in the purchase and distribution processes of the products it sells. As many as 20 years ago, Wal-Mart drove the adoption of UPC bar codes throughout the retail industry; it also pioneered the use of electronic data interchange (EDI) for computerized ordering from vendors. Its hub-and-spoke distribution network ensures goods are brought to distribution centres around the country and then directed outward to thousands of stores, each of which are within a day's travel. Through the use of cross-docking, one of its best-known innovations, goods get trucked to a distribution centre from suppliers and then are immediately transferred to trucks bound for stores, without ever being placed into storage.[26] In addition, Wal-Mart uses a dedicated fleet of trucks to ship goods from warehouses to stores in less than 48 hours, as well as to replenish store inventories about twice a week. Thus, with flow-through logistics, the company speeds the movement of goods from its distribution centres to its retail stores around the world.

Today the retail giant continues to push the supply chain toward greater and greater efficiency. It has well-established systems for the continuous replenishment of merchandise, vendor-managed inventory, cross-docking, strategic collaborations with producers in the manufacturing planning cycle, order and delivery, and direct shipments from manufacturers. It also strives to apply new technologies. For example, by the end of 2006, Wal-Mart had all suppliers place RFID (radio frequency identification) tags on all pallets and cases it received.[27] Its continuous use of innovations thus leads to lower inventory and operating costs, which enables Wal-Mart to keep its costs in check.

Wal-Mart furthermore has made an art of managing the flow of products and information among its suppliers, distribution centres, and individual stores through technology, the application of which allows for precision control of logistics and inventory. It's this type of innovation that has put Wal-Mart at the top of the retailing game. Not all organizations can pull this approach off so well; Wal-Mart is a unique case in which a single, very powerful firm took primary responsibility for improving performance across its own supply chain. By developing a superior supply chain management system, it has reaped the rewards of higher levels of customer service and satisfaction, lower production and transportation costs, and more productive use of its retail store space. Fundamentally, it boils down to Wal-Mart's ability to link together suppliers, manufacturers, distributors, retail outlets, and, ultimately, customers, regardless of their location. Although operational innovation isn't the only ingredient in Wal-Mart's success, it has been a crucial building block for its strong competitive position.

Questions

1. How does an individual firm like Wal-Mart "manage" a supply chain, particularly considering that supply chains include multiple firms with potentially conflicting objectives? Describe some of the conflicts that could arise in such a circumstance.

2. What are some of the ways that Wal-Mart's supply chain management system has provided it the benefits of higher levels of product availability and lower merchandise acquisition and transportation costs? Provide specific examples of each benefit.

LEARNING OBJECTIVES

After studying this chapter, you should be able to:

LO **1** Explain what will make retailers successful in the future

LO **2** Describe how retailers create value for customers

LO **3** Discuss the forms of non-store retailing

LO **4** Explain how the Internet has changed the way consumers shop

Retailing

Established in 1973 as a natural footwear company, Roots is Canada's leading lifestyle brand and is known around the world for its wide range of quality leather goods, clothing and accessories.[1] Co-founders Michael Budman and Don Green started out with a single store in Toronto selling the Roots Negative Heel Shoe and have since grown the company to more than 125 stores in Canada and the U.S. plus 20 locations in Asia.[2] Privately owned, Roots makes an estimated $300 million in annual sales[3] with a product line that has expanded far beyond its beginnings in footwear to include not only leisure and athletic wear, but also golf wear, yoga wear, leather bags, luggage, music and electronics, necklaces, watches, and body sprays.

Having built a company that is thoroughly Canadian, right down to its beaver logo, Roots has been a long-time supporter of amateur athletes. It was only natural for the company to take this tradition to a higher level. In 1998, Roots began its formal Olympic involvement, outfitting the Canadian team for the Winter Games in Nagano, Japan.[4] Being a part of the international Olympic showcase has had a tremendous impact on Roots' brand equity and sales. The Roots outfits created a stir in the international sports community and beyond. Puff Daddy, Celine Dion, Pamela Anderson, and Prince Charles have been seen sporting the red beret of the Canadian team.[5] This unprecedented success allowed Roots to build on the momentum, pursuing a marketing mix focused on a strategic retail presence outside of Canada. Although the company recently lost the rights to dress Canada's Olympic team to the Hudson's Bay Company, Roots continues to be the official outfitter of the USA Olympic Team.

To succeed in the global market companies need a point of differentiation. For Roots this is health, natural living, and environmental sustainability.[6] Budman considers innovation and

constant renewal as two secrets of Roots' success and finds inspiration all around him. For example, when he noticed a huge number of Asian customers in one of his Toronto stores during a Boxing Day sale, he immediately decided to do something to give back to the Asian community and created leather Chinese prosperity bags to celebrate Chinese New Year.[7] Budman's instincts were worthy of a gold medal—the bags flew off the shelves.

Ross Rebagliati, seen here wearing Roots' gear, made Olympic history at the Nagano Winter Games winning Canada's first ever gold medal for snowboarding.

retailing
The set of business activities that add value to products and services sold to consumers for their personal or family use; includes products bought at stores, through catalogues, and over the Internet, as well as services like fast-food restaurants, airlines, and hotels.

wholesalers
Those firms engaged in buying, taking title to, often storing, and physically handling goods in large quantities, then reselling the goods (usually in smaller quantities) to retailers or industrial or business users.

Retailing sits at the end of the supply chain, where marketing meets the consumer. Regardless of how strong a firm's strategy is or how great the product or service is, if it isn't available when the customer wants it, where he or she wants it, at the right price, and in the right size, colour, and style, it simply won't sell. It is primarily the retailer's responsibility to make sure that these customers' expectations are fulfilled.

In this chapter and as shown in our roadmap, we explain how retailing has evolved into its current structure. Then, we examine how retailers create value by implementing marketing strategies, which leads us to a discussion of how the Internet has transformed the way some retailers do business. We follow this with a discussion of the various types of retailers and non-store retailing. We conclude with a look at how to develop a retailing strategy and positioning.

Retailing is defined as the set of business activities that add value to products and services sold to consumers for their personal or family use. Our definition of retailing includes products bought at stores, through catalogues, and over the Internet, as well as services like fast-food restaurants, airlines, and hotels. Some retailers claim they sell at "wholesale" prices, but if they sell to customers for their personal use, they are still retailers, regardless of how low their prices may be. **Wholesalers**

CHAPTER
ROADMAP

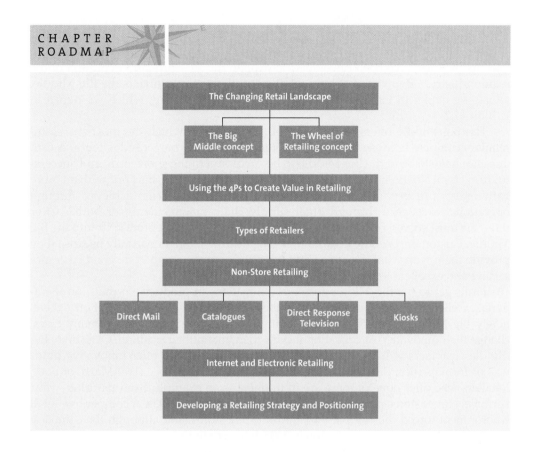

(see Chapter 13), in contrast, are those firms engaged in buying, taking title to, often storing, and physically handling goods in large quantities, then reselling the goods (usually in smaller quantities) to retailers or industrial or business users.

Retailing today is changing, both in Canada and around the world. No longer do manufacturers rule many marketing channels, as they once did. Retailers like Wal-Mart, Carrefour (a French hypermarket), Home Depot, Loblaws, and Metro (a German retail conglomerate)[8]—the largest retailers in the world—dictate to their suppliers what should be made, how it should be configured, when it should be delivered, and, to some extent, what it should cost. These retailers are clearly in the driver's seat.

Retailing in the aggregate is a big business. Virtually every penny you spend, except for taxes, goes to retailers. Food, rent, clothing, tuition, insurance, and haircuts are all either retail services or goods provided by retailers. Even nonprofit organizations like the Salvation Army, Goodwill Industries, and the Ontario Science Centre have retail operations. Canadian retail sales in 2006 were $390 billion, representing more than 227,000 retail establishments. Retailing is Canada's third largest industry by size, employing approximately 2 million people.[9]

Even nonprofit organizations like Goodwill Industries have retail operations.

LO ① The Changing Retail Landscape

Various theories have been developed to explain the structure and evolution of the retail industry.[10] Two views of how retail institutions may evolve is the Big Middle, which we depict in Exhibit 14.1[11] and the Wheel of Retailing, which we depict in Exhibit 14.2.

The Big Middle refers to that part of the market in which the most successful retailers compete because the biggest potential customer base resides there. A firm does not have to be in the Big Middle to be successful in the short term, and successful firms typically do not start there. Great new retailers often start out with an innovative format or products, offer a low-price advantage (usually achieved through operational excellence through great supply chain management), or both.[12] Over time, the most successful "innovative" and "low-price" competitors drift into the Big Middle. Customers become loyal to these Big Middle retailers partially because they provide them with what they need and what they are accustomed to: good customer service and excellent loyalty programs.

Firms get to the Big Middle through innovations in products, formats, or operational excellence or some combination of these that lead to great value. But once there, newly Big Middle retailers must constantly monitor, fine tune, and, in many cases, change their innovative or operational skills to maintain their position. Over time, Big Middle customers will be lured away by other retailers that offer innovative products or formats (Best Buy, Home Depot, The Gap), a lower price (Wal-Mart), or both. Retailers who offer none of these are in trouble. As an example, Saan (Surplus Army, Airforce, Navy) stores peaked at over 350 stores in the late 1990s. A competitive retail environment forced the company to shrink to 142 stores, and although the company emerged from bankruptcy protection in 2005, it has continued to struggle.[13] Many other retailers that focused on low prices have disappeared from the Canadian scene including Bargain Harold's, Consumers Distributing, Robinson's, Kresge, and BiWay.

The retail-market structure shown in Exhibit 14.1, containing Innovative, Big Middle, and Low-Price segments, has remained constant throughout the decades, but the retail players in each segment have changed. For instance, in the 1980s, the Big Middle contained primarily traditional department stores like Eatons, The Bay, and Sears. The innovative stores were Best Buy, Home Depot, and The Gap, and the

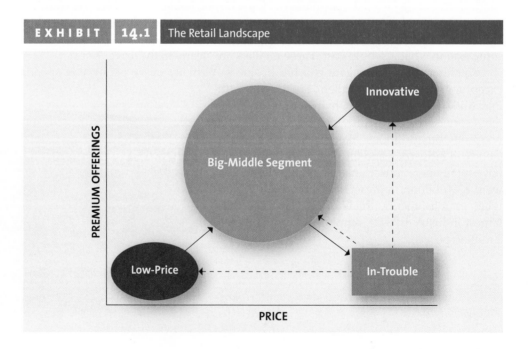

EXHIBIT 14.1 The Retail Landscape

EXHIBIT **14.2** The Wheel of Retailing

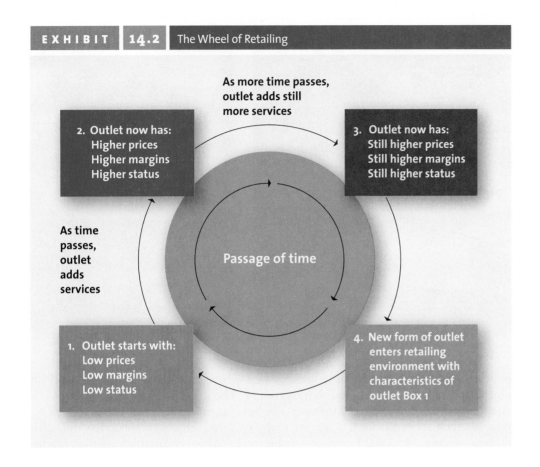

As more time passes, outlet adds still more services

2. Outlet now has:
Higher prices
Higher margins
Higher status

3. Outlet now has:
Still higher prices
Still higher margins
Still higher status

As time passes, outlet adds services

Passage of time

1. Outlet starts with:
Low prices
Low margins
Low status

4. New form of outlet enters retailing environment with characteristics of outlet Box 1

low-price stores included Wal-Mart, Kmart, and Saan. Today, customers have shifted and retailers have changed. Now, the Big Middle encompasses the 1980s' "low-price" leaders Wal-Mart and Zellers, while Kmart, Woolco, Robinson's, and Eatons have not only been forced out of the Big Middle but have disappeared completely from the Canadian retail landscape. At the same time, Home Depot, Best Buy, and The Gap, although still innovative, have moved into the Big Middle.

To maintain their positions in the Big Middle, retailers must understand their strengths and weaknesses, continually keep an eye on their target segments and competition, and do anything and everything they can to retain and grow loyal customers. If they don't, someone else will.

The Wheel of Retailing (shown in Exhibit 14.2) offers a second view of how new forms of retail outlets compete in the market. Generally, retailers enter with low prices, low margins and low status. Over time, they add more and more service and other improvements and thus, are able to raise prices, earn higher margins and achieve higher status with consumers. For example, the first menu at McDonald's offered only hamburgers, french fries and milk shakes for take out. Today, McDonald's has a wide and varied menu, upscale coffee, indoor seating, WiFi access and play areas for children. There's even a door man and a grand piano in the Manhattan location. And in Europe, the company is experimenting with a more restaurant-like, sit down experience. In Wolfratshausen, Germany, McDonald's has a fireplace, leather sofas, wooden floors, vases with flowers, and a McCafe serving pastry, tiramisu and cappuccino.[14]

In some Canadian McDonald's outlets, garish plastic is being replaced by appealing colours and natural materials, fireplaces, flat screen TVs, leather chairs, and modern lighting fixtures. Stores are being redesigned featuring up to four different zones geared to the needs of different target markets, for example, a high-traffic zone for

McDonald's redesigned restaurant in Scarborough (right) has moved it further along the Wheel of Retailing compared to early restaurants (left).

people on the go, a comfortable seating area where customers can linger, and an area specifically for families and large groups.[15] The retrofit is linked to McDonald's strategy to gain a large part of the specialty beverage market which is dominated by retailers such as Starbucks and Second Cup. By introducing upscale coffee and comfortable seating, McDonald's progresses along the Wheel of Retailing earning higher margins and gaining higher status. These innovations in products and formats have enabled McDonald's to continue to serve its existing loyal customers and reach out to new target segments while charging competitive prices—key factors for successful retailing. Thus, it is hardly surprising that McDonald's continues to dominate its industry and stave off competition from new entrants.

In the Wheel of Retailing concept, as stores add services and improvements expand the mix of merchandise carried and upgrade their facilities, it generally adds to their costs, which results in higher prices. This opens up opportunities for new lean, mean entrants at the beginning of the wheel. For example, as a discount store, Wal-Mart entered the Canadian market and undercut established department stores like Zellers, Kmart, and Woolco. Later, extreme value retailers such as Dollarama entered the market undercutting existing discount stores like Wal-Mart.

How Do Retailers Create Value?

Moores Clothing for Men creates value by helping men put it all together. Their wardrobe consultants provide fashion advice, and their tailors make sure everything fits properly.

Imagine trying to buy a suit for a job interview without being able to visit a retailer. You would have to figure out exactly what size, colour, and style of suit you wanted. Then you'd have to contact various manufacturers, whether in person, by phone, or over the Internet, and order the suit. Assuming it fit you reasonably well, you might still need to take it to a tailor to have the sleeves shortened. Then you'd have to go through the same process for a shirt or blouse, accessories, and shoes. It would not be very convenient.

Retailers like Moores Clothing for Men create value by pulling it all together for you. The store offers a broad selection of suits, shirts, ties, and other accessories that it has carefully chosen in advance. You can see, touch, feel, and try on each item

Costco attracts people of all ages and income brackets as consumers shift to value retailers.

while in the store. You can buy one suit or shirt at a time or buy several shirts to go with your new suit. Finally, the store provides a salesperson to help you coordinate your outfit and a tailor to make the whole thing fit perfectly.

Now and in the future, success for retailers will mean learning how to compete in a value-driven world. Remember, value doesn't just mean low price. It means getting more benefit for the money. Retailers that provide great value, like Costco, were once known largely as a destination for monthly stock-up trips only. But today, it has penetrated the weekly shopping routine. Consumers of all ages, nearly all income groups, and practically all segments have undertaken the "shift to value." Consumers have fundamentally changed their reference points for both price and quality, such that they have been trained to expect significantly lower prices from many retailers. As an example, Suzy Shier is known for offering current fashion trends at very affordable prices. In addition, as many people's lifestyles have become more casual, consumers have begun to redefine quality from "good" to just "good enough" for particular items and occasions, such as their casual weekend wardrobe. As their definition of quality changes, so does their definition of value.

Value retailers—those in the Big Middle—continue to improve their "shopability," providing more convenient store layouts and shopping experiences that make the task faster and easier. Value retailers are rapidly expanding, bringing more types of retailers and store locations under fire. The majority of regional and national retailers have not yet felt the full force of the value retailers. But the most vulnerable, the smaller, undifferentiated regional chains, have consistently lost out to value retailers when they arrive in the local market.

Using the Four Ps to Create Value in Retailing   LO ②

Like other marketers, retailers perform important functions that increase the value of the products and services they sell to consumers in their target markets. We now examine these functions, classified into the four Ps.

You can only get House & Home private-label bedding at The Bay.

Product

A typical grocery store carries 30,000 to 40,000 different items; a regional department store might carry as many as 200,000. Providing the right mix of merchandise and services that satisfies the needs of the target market is one of retailers' most fundamental activities. Offering assortments gives customers choice. But to reduce transportation costs and handling, manufacturers typically ship cases of merchandise to retailers, such as cartons of mayonnaise or boxes of blue shirts. Because customers generally don't want or need to buy more than one of the same item, retailers break the cases and sell customers the smaller quantities they desire.

Manufacturers don't like to store inventory because their factories and warehouses are typically not available to customers. Consumers don't want to store more than they need because it takes up too much space. Neither group likes to store inventory that isn't being used because doing so ties up money that could be used for something else. Retailers thus provide value to both manufacturers and customers by performing the storage function, though many retailers are beginning to push their suppliers to hold the inventory until they need it. (Recall our discussion of JIT inventory systems in Chapter 13.)

It is difficult for retailers to distinguish themselves from their competitors through the merchandise they carry because competitors can purchase and sell many of the same popular brands. So many retailers have developed **private-label brands** (also called store brands), which are products developed and marketed by a retailer and available only from that retailer. For example, if you want House & Home bedding, you have to go to The Bay. Ethical Dilemma 14.1 deals with the outsourcing challenges faced by private-label retailers.

private-label brands Brands developed and marketed by a retailer and available only from that retailer; also called *store brands.*

Price

Price helps define the value of both the merchandise and the service, and the general price range of a particular store helps define its image. Although both Banana Republic and Old Navy are owned by The Gap, their images could not be more different. Banana Republic prices its merchandise to attract young professionals, whereas Old Navy aims to satisfy trendy, price-sensitive consumers.

Price must always be aligned with the other elements of the retail mix: product, promotion, place, personnel, and presentation. For instance, you would not expect to pay $20 for a candy bar sold in your local grocery store, but a limited-edition candy bar, made of fine Belgian dark chocolate, packaged in a gold-plated keepsake box, sold at Holt Renfrew, might be a real steal at $20.

Promotion

Retailers know that good promotion, both within their retail environments and throughout the mass media, can mean the difference between flat sales and a growing consumer base. Advertising in traditional media such as newspapers, magazines, and television continues to be important to get customers into the stores. (Entrepreneurial Marketing 14.1 on page 399 describes how Please Mum will flex its promotional muscle having secured the rights to retail sales of Olympic-themed children's clothing for the 2010 Winter Games.) Once in the store, however, retailers use displays and

Ethical Dilemma

14.1 A Swipe at Sweatshops[16]

Retailers must provide good customer value and still make a profit. Increased competition, homeland labour costs, and energy and material costs have forced many retailers to contract with manufacturers in countries with lower cost structures to make their private-label merchandise. But it is difficult to control what goes on in a factory that the firm doesn't own in a country thousands of kilometres away from the firm's home office. Let's consider some of the problems facing Wal-Mart.

In a class-action lawsuit covering 100,000–500,000 workers spanning six countries, such as China, Nicaragua, and Bangladesh, Wal-Mart has been accused of overlooking substandard work conditions at suppliers' factories, such as pay withholdings, beatings, and firings based on employees' suspected union activity. Wal-Mart's logo, "Always Low Prices," spans its corporate culture, not just its signage, which means constant pressure to slash costs and prices has demanded that its suppliers lower their costs even further. But the bad publicity arising from this lawsuit has taken a toll on Wal-Mart's image. Wal-Mart retaliated with an advertising campaign that attempted to repair the damage, but critics point out that the retail giant monitors its own plants without assistance from Social Accountability International (SAI), a nonprofit international organization whose mission is to promote human rights for workers around the world,[17] or any other antisweatshop groups involved in enforcing labour standards. These critics freely express their skepticism that Wal-Mart can police itself. Despite all the controversy, Wal-Mart refuses to release its labour reports or the names of the factories in which its products are made.

Retailers must address some key questions:

- Is a Canadian-based retailer responsible for human rights violations that take place in a factory it does not own and in a country in which it does not operate?

- What can retailers do to ensure that the merchandise they purchase is made in factories that are safe and clean and that the employees of those factories are treated humanely and paid a fair wage?

---

signs, placed at the point of purchase or in strategic areas such as the end of aisles, to inform customers and stimulate purchases of the featured products.

Store credit cards and gift cards are more subtle forms of promotion that also facilitate shopping. Retailers also might offer pricing promotions—such as coupons, rebates, in-store or online discounts, or perhaps buy-one-get-one-free offers—to attract consumers and stimulate sales. These promotions play a very important role in driving traffic to retail locations, increasing the average purchase size, and creating opportunities for repeat purchases. But retail promotions also are valuable to customers; they inform customers about what is new and available and how much it costs.

In addition to more traditional forms of promotion, many retailers are devoting more resources to their overall retail environment as a means to promote and showcase what the store has to offer. Their displays of merchandise, both in the store and in windows, have become an important form of promotion. For example, Shoppers Drug Mart has redesigned its cosmetics counters as Beauty Boutiques. Since many shopping activities can be rather mundane, those retailers who can distinguish themselves with unusual and exciting store atmospherics add value to the shopping experience. G.A.P. Adventures™, founded by Calgarian Bruce Poon Tip, has opened concept stores in Vancouver, Toronto, Calgary, Melbourne, and New York City where visitors can watch G.A.P. Adventures™ documentaries featuring travellers on expeditions around the world.[18] These features enhance customers' visual experiences, provide them

Shoppers Drug Mart redesigned its cosmetic counters as Beauty Boutiques to better display and promote merchandise.

Concept Stores by G.A.P. Adventures provide prospective travellers with a visual and educational experience before they book their trips.

with educational information, and enhance the store's sales potential by enabling customers to "try before they buy."

A variety of factors influence whether customers will actually buy once they are in the store, some of which are quite subtle. Consumers' perceptions of value and their subsequent patronage are heavily influenced by their perceptions of the store's "look and feel." Consider the difference between having coffee at Tim Hortons versus Second Cup. Which outlet would you rather spend time socializing with your friends? Music, colour, scent, and crowding can also significantly impact the overall shopping experience.[19] Therefore, the extent to which stores offer a more pleasant shopping experience fosters a good mood, resulting in greater spending.

Personal selling and customer service representatives are also part of the overall promotional package. Retailers must provide services that make it easier to buy and use products, and retail associates, whether in the store, on the phone, or over the Internet, provide customers with information about product characteristics and availability. They can also facilitate the sale of products or services that consumers perceive as complicated, risky, or expensive, such as an air conditioning unit or a diamond ring. In some retail firms, these salesperson and customer service functions are being augmented, or even replaced, by technology used through in-store kiosks, the Internet, or self-checkout lanes.

The knowledge retailers can gain from their store personnel and customer relationship management (CRM) databases is key for developing loyal customers and operating loyalty programs. Traditionally, retailers treated all their customers the same way, but today, the most successful retailers concentrate on providing more value to their best customers. Using direct salesperson contact, targeted promotions, and services, they attempt to increase their **share of wallet**—the percentage of the customer's purchases made from that particular retailer—with their best customers. For instance, Internet retailers can use consumer information to provide a level of personal service that previously was available only through expensive salespeople in the best specialty stores.

share of wallet
The percentage of the customer's purchases made from a particular retailer.

Place

Retailers already have realized that convenience is a key ingredient to success, and an important aspect of this success is convenient locations.[22] As the old cliché claims, the three most important things in retailing are "location, location, location." Many customers choose stores on the basis of where they are located, which makes great locations a competitive advantage that few rivals can duplicate. For instance, once Starbucks saturates a market by opening in the best locations, it will be difficult for a new competitor to break in to that same market—where would it put its stores?

To offer more convenience, some Shoppers Drug Mart stores are open 24 hours a day so customers can pick up prescriptions or other items any time.

In pursuit of better and better locations, retailers are experimenting with different options to reach their target markets. Canada's largest drugstore retailer, Shoppers Drug Mart®, now has some stores that are open 24 hours a day so customers can pick up prescriptions and other items any time.

Types of Retailers

In the next few sections, we examine the various types of retailers, identify some major players, and discuss some of the issues facing each type.

Food Retailers

Not too long ago, people shopped for food primarily at traditional grocery stores. Today, however, you can buy food at **drugstores**, discount stores, warehouse clubs, and convenience stores. Pharmacy chains like Shoppers Drug Mart offer milk, bread, and even

drugstore
A specialty store that concentrates on health and personal grooming merchandise, though pharmaceuticals may represent more than 60 percent of its sales.

conventional supermarket
Offers groceries, meat, and produce with limited sales of nonfood items, such as health and beauty aids and general merchandise, in a self-service format.

big-box food retailer
Comes in three types: supercentre, hypermarket, and warehouse club; larger than *conventional supermarket*; carries both food and nonfood items.

general merchandise retailer
May be a *discount store, specialty store, category specialist, department store, drugstore, off-price retailer,* or *extreme value retailer;* may sell through multiple channels, such as the Internet and catalogues.

discount store
Offers a broad variety of merchandise, limited service, and low prices.

specialty store
Concentrates on a limited number of complementary merchandise categories in a relatively small store.

fresh fruit in some locations. Wal-Mart and the Real Canadian Superstore all provide supercentres whose product mix contains 30 to 40 percent food items. Food sales represent about 50 percent of the total sales in warehouse clubs like Costco and Sam's Club. Convenience stores now offer more than a Slurpee and gasoline, for example, Petro-Canada Neighbours stores provide upscale sandwiches and salads. And retailers such as Zellers and Ikea have in-store restaurants making it easy for customers to shop longer. And of course, restaurants also compete for consumers' food dollars. The characteristics of the three major categories of food retailers—**conventional supermarkets**, **big-box food retailers**, and convenience stores—are summarized in Exhibit 14.3.

All this competition can mean trouble for traditional grocery stores. Yet some continue to thrive because they offer their target customers great value—they are conveniently located, make shopping easy, have fair prices, and find special products and services that are important to their customers. Adding Value 14.1 describes how Pete's Frootique effectively competes on selection and service.

General Merchandise Retailers

The main types of **general merchandise retailers** are discount stores, specialty stores, category specialists, department stores, drugstores, off-price retailers, and extreme value retailers. Many of these general merchandise retailers sell through multiple channels, such as the Internet and catalogues, as we discussed previously in this chapter.

Discount Stores   A **discount store** offers a broad variety of merchandise, limited service, and low prices. Wal-Mart and Zellers dominate the discount store industry in Canada and vie for similar target markets. But because their competencies are slightly distinct, they both can survive. Wal-Mart pioneered the everyday low-price concept, and its efficient operations have allowed it to offer the lowest-priced basket of merchandise in every market in which it competes—which doesn't necessarily mean that Wal-Mart has the lowest price on every item in every market. But it does try to be the lowest across a wide variety. Zellers, in contrast, has concentrated on merchandising. Opting for quality and style, Zellers offers exclusive lines by Martha Stewart and Hilary Duff, providing good value without being cheap.

Specialty Stores   **Specialty stores** concentrate on a limited number of complementary merchandise categories in relatively small stores. For example, Payless ShoeSource is the largest specialty family footwear retailer in the western hemisphere. Payless stores

EXHIBIT 14.3	**Food Retailer Characteristics**	
Category	**Description**	**Examples**
Conventional Supermarket	Offer groceries, meat, and produce with limited sales of nonfood items, such as health and beauty aids and general merchandise, in a self-service format.	Safeway is a popular supermarket in western Canada; Sobey's is common on the East Coast.
Big-Box Food Retailers	Come in three types: supercentres, hypermarkets, and warehouse clubs. Larger than conventional supermarkets, they carry both food and nonfood items.	Supercentres and warehouse clubs are popular in Canada, whereas hypermarkets tend to flourish in Europe and South America. Hypermarkets (Carrefour) and warehouse clubs (Costco) generally carry a greater percentage of food.
Convenience Stores	Provide a limited number of items at convenient locations in small stores with speedy checkout.	Stores such as 7-Eleven generally charge higher prices than most other types of food stores. Most convenience stores also sell gasoline, which accounts for more than 55 percent of their annual sales.

Adding Value   14.1   Pete's Frootique—A Food Adventure

Most produce found at grocery stores is somewhat of a commodity item. A Granny Smith apple at one store is the same as at any store, for the most part. Convenient locations and price have traditionally been the two most important criteria for choosing where to shop for groceries. However, one Halifax-area vendor is taking a unique approach to fresh and healthy. Pete's Frootique, named after famed Canadian food expert Pete Luckett, is making grocery shopping an exciting experience.

Pete's Frootique began as a tiny market with $300 of produce in Saint John, New Brunswick. Today, there are two vibrant and colourful 18,000-square-foot locations in eastern Canada. The bright, open-concept markets are filled with glowing pyramids of succulent fruit, vegetables and signs everywhere that tempt you to have a sample before you buy. Knowledgeable staff offer you information about the selection of produce, storage and cooking tips, all with a smile.[23] If you have a nutrition question, look no further

than the on-staff registered dietitian who will help you understand which foods can re-energize your health.[24] You can also visit the in-house fresh juice bar, take-out foods shop, European delicatessen, and gourmet butcher shop all while listening to live entertainment.[25] You are also invited to stay and have a bite to eat in the funky dining area. Their dynamic website offers a definitive guide to fresh produce along with tasty recipes and information about the stores. The value-added extras like product sampling help customers make informed purchase decisions and also convey the high level of expertise of the staff.

The unique approach to shopping isn't going unnoticed. The stores have won numerous grocery awards including best Independent Specialty Grocery Store in Canada three times.[26] The entertainment value of the market, combined with high quality product, helps to keep customers coming back. Each trip to Pete's Frootique is a dynamic grocery experience!

---

feature fashionable, quality footwear and accessories for women, men, and children at affordable prices in a self-selection format.

Category Specialists A **category specialist** offers a narrow variety but a deep assortment of merchandise. Some are like large specialty stores, such as Paderno (home and kitchen tools) or Chapters/Indigo (books); others resemble discount stores in appearance and have similar low prices but offer a more concentrated assortment of goods, such as Future Shop (consumer electronics) or RONA (home improvement). Most category specialists use a self-service approach, but some, like Home Depot, provide extensive customer service. Because category specialists offer such an extensive assortment in a particular category, they can so overwhelm the category that other retailers have difficulty competing; in these cases, the specialists are frequently called **category killers**.

Stores like Home Depot are known as category specialists because they offer a narrow variety but a deep assortment of merchandise.

Department Stores Department stores refer to those retailers that carry many different types of merchandise (broad variety) and lots of items within each type (deep assortment), offer some customer services, and are organized into separate departments to display their merchandise. Department stores often resemble a collection of specialty shops, including women's, men's, and children's clothing and accessories; home furnishings and furniture; and kitchenwares and small appliances.

With the demise of Eatons, the largest remaining department store chains in Canada are Sears and The Bay. Other store chains are very diverse. Some, like Zellers, carry relatively inexpensive products and compete closely with discount stores, whereas others, like Holt Renfrew, sell expensive, exclusive merchandise and compete with high-end specialty store chains.

category specialist
Offers a narrow variety but a deep assortment of merchandise.

category killer
Offers an extensive assortment in a particular category, so overwhelming the category that other retailers have difficulty competing.

Department stores have lost market share to specialty stores, discount stores, and category specialists in recent years. They seem to have gotten stuck in the middle, between those retailers that provide a better value at lower prices and those that offer more complete and fashionable assortments and better customer service, according to consumer perceptions. But they are fighting back with a vengeance. The Bay has begun placing a greater emphasis on high-fashion, private-label merchandise than in the past.

Drugstores Drugstores are specialty stores that concentrate on health and personal grooming merchandise, though pharmaceuticals often represent more than 60 percent of their sales. The largest drugstore chains in Canada—Shoppers Drug Mart® (Pharmaprix^MD in Quebec), Jean Coutu, PharmSave and London Drugs[27]—face a major challenge because of the low margins they earn on prescription drugs; health insurance companies and government programs pay most of the cost of many prescriptions, and the health insurance companies negotiate substantially lower prices with drugstores. These drugstores therefore are attempting to make up for their lost profits on prescriptions by concentrating their efforts on nonpharmaceutical products. General merchandise has long been a staple in drugstores, but food, and particularly, fresh food like milk and fruit, are relatively new additions to their assortment.[28]

off-price retailer
A type of retailer that offers an inconsistent assortment of merchandise at relatively low prices.

Off-Price Retailers Off-price retailers, such as Winners, Designer Depot, and HomeSense, offer an inconsistent assortment of merchandise at relatively low prices. They typically buy from manufacturers or other retailers with excess inventory or at the end of a season for one-fourth to one-fifth the original wholesale price. Because of the way these retailers buy, customers can never be confident that the same type of merchandise will be in stock each time they visit the store. Different bargains also will be available on each visit. To improve their offerings' consistency, some off-price retailers complement their opportunistically bought merchandise with merchandise purchased at regular wholesale prices. In addition to their low prices, the key to off-price retailers' success is the treasure hunt environment they create.

extreme value retailer
A general merchandise discount store found in lower-income urban or rural areas.

Extreme value retailers are a subset of off-price retailers and one of the fastest growing retailing segments. Extreme value retailers, such as Dollarama, are general merchandise discount stores found in lower-income urban or rural areas. They are much smaller than traditional discount stores, usually less than 9000 square feet.

LO ③ Non-Store Retailing

Non-store retailing, often called direct marketing or direct response marketing, plays a significant role in marketing products and services. With annual growth rates that outstrip retail sales, it has become one of the fastest-growing forms of retailing. Through non-store retailing formats such as direct mail, catalogues or direct response television ads, consumers can learn about new products and purchase them from the comfort of their homes. The Canadian Marketing Association reports that $51 billion in annual sales are generated through direct marketing activities in Canada and that the industry employs over 480,000 people.[29] Although often considered a promotional tool, direct marketing is a also form of retailing which is why it is discussed in this chapter. For many marketers, direct marketing is rapidly becoming the medium of choice for reaching consumers.

Direct marketing has four defining characteristics: it is targeted, motivates an action, is measurable and can provide information for the development of a marketing database.[30] It is an information-driven process that enables marketers to narrowly target the appropriate audiences. For example, a company selling a health supplement can use direct marketing to reach only people who subscribe to health related magazines in an effort to motivate them to take action such as calling a 1-800 number, visiting a website, or placing a mail order. They can easily measure the response for each magazine using uniquely assigned coded coupons, 1-800 numbers, or Internet microsites. The use of response generating direct marketing forms, such as direct mail, direct response television, or telemarketing can provide meaningful results and allow the evaluation of a marketing campaign in a timely manner.[31]

Direct marketing offers benefits to both buyers and sellers. Companies that use direct marketing campaigns appreciate the ability to sell to a much wider target audience than could be reached with traditional marketing channels. In comparison to personal selling or mass media advertising, the cost of reaching consumers is much lower with direct marketing. As mentioned earlier, one of the defining characteristics of direct marketing is its measurability—campaigns can be closely monitored to track results. Measurability means marketers know who responds to their campaigns, allowing them to build rich databases that can be used to cross-sell, tailor offers, and create specific promotions geared to individual customers in future campaigns.

Consumers appreciate direct marketing for its convenience and ease of use. Shoppers can browse through catalogues, read a direct mail offer, or access a company's website any time they like. Online forms of direct marketing provide access to a wide range of products from both Canadian and international companies.

As shown in Exhibit 14.4, there are a number of forms direct marketing can take including direct mail, catalogues, direct response television, kiosks, online marketing, telemarketing, and personal selling. We focus on the first four forms here, followed by a discussion of Internet and electronic retailing. Personal selling and telemarketing are addressed later in Chapter 16.

EXHIBIT **14.4** Forms of Non-Store Retailing

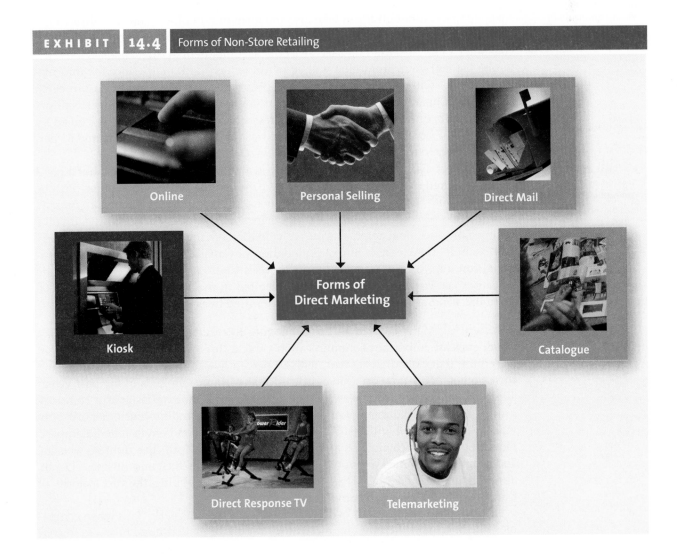

The Heart and Stroke Foundation of Canada uses direct mail to promote its lottery, which funds research that results in breakthrough medical advances, social change, and health education.

direct mail
A targeted, printed form of communication sent to a prospective customer's mailbox.

Direct Mail Although it can take also the form of e-mail, we consider **direct mail** primarily as a targeted, printed form of communication distributed to a prospective consumer's mailbox. Mailing lists are a critical component of direct mail. Choose the wrong list and your promotion will be perceived as "junk mail" since the information and offer will not be targeted to the appropriate audience. Canada Post research shows that Canadian households receive an average of 27 pieces of direct mail per week. In spite of such high volumes, addressed mail continues to be welcomed by Canadians—83 percent spend time with addressed direct mail every day and 63 percent are likely to read it as soon as it is received.[32]

For direct mail to be effective, not only is a good contact list a must, but a good offer is required to compel consumers to take immediate action. Good offers must be relevant to both consumers and to the product, and are important whether a company is promoting products to consumers or businesses. But offers don't always involve selling a product. Registered charities rely on direct mail in their fundraising efforts. For example, the Heart & Stroke Foundation of Canada, which receives no operational funding from government sources, uses direct mail extensively to promote its cause. The Foundation's efforts have resulted in the recruitment of over 140,000 volunteers and 13 million donors[33] and have raised over $125 million in donations.[34]

Catalogues Many companies use catalogues to strategically build their business. Catalogues are important communication vehicles for retail outlets. They represent a medium that Canadians accept, with 80 percent welcoming retail catalogues into their homes. More than half have ordered items from catalogues in the past year.[35] Typically catalogues have been mailed, which can become an issue as a company grows. Although Mountain Equipment Co-op has 2.6 million customers, it only mails catalogues to about 200,000 of them due to the cost and environmental impact. However, it makes catalogues available for download as pdf files from its website. Today, most companies with physical catalogues, such as Ikea and Business Depot, also offer online catalogues. Despite the ease of online shopping, the vast majority of Canadians still prefer hard copy catalogues.

Catalogue marketing has evolved dramatically from its early days when companies like Sears and the now defunct Eatons regularly mailed huge missives to con-

sumers. Although Sears still produces large catalogues, many companies are opting for much thinner versions. The Sears *Wish Book* holds fond memories for many adults who remember leafing through its pages as children in anticipation of gifts they might receive. It is such a tradition in Canada that the Sears *Wish Book* was recently integrated into a pre-holiday season episode of *Corner Gas*, a popular television show.

Catalogues are particularly important for companies with no bricks-and-mortar locations. Ottawa-based cooking tool company, Ashton Green, has never had a physical store. It started out as a mail order business selling only from its catalogue. As the company grew, it took its catalogue online and added e-commerce capabilities, extending its reach and its sales.

Direct response television Direct **response television** (DRTV) refers to television commercials or infomercials, with a strong call to action usually via 1-800 number, return mail address, or website. Although many people may question the effectiveness of this form of direct marketing, DRTV and the Shopping Channel are the two most welcome forms of direct marketing among Canadians.[36] DRTV now accounts for 25 percent of all television commercials with the top purchases being exercise product, diet/health/weight merchandise, videos and beauty/cosmetics.[37]

Most DRTV ads are short 60 and 120 second formats or much longer 30 minute infomercials. For many people, the very term 'infomercial' conjures up images of late night TV pitchman telling them how their product slices and dices better than

direct response television Television commercials or infomercials with a strong call to action.

The George Foreman Grill is promoted and sold using DRTV infomercials.

anything on the market. Most seem to be selling products that seem too good to be true—fitness routines that promise to melt the pounds away, miracle knives so sharp you'll never have to buy another, or rejuvenating face creams that magically erase the wrinkles. Almost everyone has heard of the George Foreman Grill but not nearly as many people recognize Foreman as a heavyweight boxing champion.

Direct response television is used for its power to drive results not only through infomercials but also in shorter format ads. When Canadian Blood Services launched its "Save a Life" campaign, it exceeded targets by over 50 percent,[38] and took home the Gold award in the Direct Response (DRTV) category at the Canadian Marketing Association (CMA) Awards for the New Donor Drive DRTV campaign.[39]

Kiosks   As discussed in Chapter 11, electronic kiosks can be used to facilitate the way services companies deliver their services to customers, for example, allowing passengers at airports to quickly print pre-booked tickets. However, kiosks can also be used to sell both services and products to end consumers, usually in shopping malls. Some kiosks are temporary, set up in malls primarily to sell gift items in the weeks leading up to Christmas. Others kiosks are permanent. For example, Dell's mall kiosks allow shoppers to talk to a Dell representative face-to-face and find the computer that's just right for them. Consumers can customize their PC, order it, and have it shipped directly to their homes. In Ontario, Virgin Mobile unveiled a network of mall kiosks, which it may use to sell other Virgin products and services in the future.[40] Real estate companies such as Century 21 use kiosks in malls where thousands of potential buyers can connect with property listings. Kiosks from Hallmark allow customers to create their own personalized cards. Disposable cameras, film, and batteries are available at kiosks throughout the Rogers Centre in Toronto.[41]

Business marketers use kiosks as well, particularly at trade shows to collect sales leads and to provide information on their products.

Dell's mall kiosks allow shoppers to find a computer that's just right for them.

Internet and Electronic Retailing

In this section, we discuss the most important innovation in retailing since point-of-sale terminals began scanning UPC (universal product codes) tags in grocery stores more than 20 years ago—electronic, Internet, or simply e-retailing. Prior to 2000, some retailing experts predicted the demise of traditional stores, or **bricks-and-mortar retailers**, as they often are called. These experts argued that everyone would start buying everything over the Internet. Of course, these prophets of doom were wrong, but we have learned several important lessons about what works and what doesn't for e-retailing.

bricks-and-mortar retailer
A traditional, physical store.

At the core of any business strategy is the ability to develop a sustainable competitive advantage.[42] Some aspects of a retailer's strategy are more sustainable than others, whether for e-retailers or bricks-and-mortar players. For instance, when retailers offer pure commodities (building supplies, office supplies) or quasi-commodities (books, CDs), competitors can easily match their offering in terms of both assortment and price.[43] Therefore, a sustainable advantage is difficult for e-retailers of pure commodities to maintain unless the perceived service associated with buying online outweighs the benefits of shopping in a store. For instance, Amazon.ca enhances the shopping experience by providing reviews and making suggestions based on customers' past purchases. Furthermore, many more products are likely to be available at Amazon than in any single store. Whereas some products, such as apparel, can be difficult for customers to purchase over the Internet because of their need to touch, feel, and try on these products, Amazon's offerings do well in the worldwide Internet marketplace. At MuchMusic.com visitors can buy ring tones and other merchandise as described in Internet Marketing 14.1.

With the Internet's low entry costs and constantly improving search engines and shopping bots, smaller niche sources for hard-to-find products, collectibles, and hobbies can expand their trade area—the geographical area that contains the potential customers of a particular retailer or shopping centre—from a few city blocks to the world.

Consumers that shop at multichannel retailers—retailers that sell merchandise in more than one retail channel (such as a Sears Canada store (left), catalogue (middle), and Internet (right)—typically buy more than those who shop in only one retail channel.

Internet Marketing   14.1   MuchMusic.com—Much More in Store

Each year thousands of musicians and music fans anticipate the MuchMusic Video Awards (MMVAs) held in downtown Toronto. Both young and old from Canada and overseas join to celebrate excellence in music videos. In 2006, the event attracted 10,000 people to the concert and awards show. However, its audience was much larger than that. Using a combination of podcasting and television broadcasting, over 3.5 million people actually tuned in.[44] Now MuchMusic is leveraging its strength in multimedia to sell you music through its website in a variety of ways.

While retail has been traditionally confined to bricks-and-mortar buildings, the Internet has made online retailing possible and popular. MuchMusic's website (www.muchmusic.com) has capitalized on this by using the Web to connect with the viewers of its music-focused television channels. In addition to hosting content that supports its lineup of television programming, the site features "MuchShop," an online music retail outlet. Powered by Puretracks, visitors can purchase thousands of songs online for $0.99 each. Shoppers can also purchase full albums at a discounted price. While browsing, you can play samples of any track using the Music Preview tool before committing to their purchase. Furthermore, MuchShop gift cards can be purchased and e-mailed to recipients for online redemption.

MuchMusic's MuchShop also offers content for mobile devices including celebrity cell phone backgrounds and exclusive ringtones from hit artists like Finger Eleven.[45] You can even use the Ringtone Mixer and Image Maker to create your own unique sounds and pictures, and upload them directly to your cell phone. While browsing you can also subscribe to text message updates about when new ringtones become available—a must for anyone who wants to keep up with the latest on the music scene.

MuchMusic also integrates the popularity of text messaging into its programming. In 2005, it introduced the show PunchMuch, a user-controlled, fully automated music request channel, determined by viewer voting through text messaging. The show was so immensely successful that it has become its own channel.

Since the music and mobile products offered through MuchShop appeal to the same demographic that watches MuchMusic, the station knew that its target audience's ability to buy online could be an issue. In an effort to make MuchShop accessible to youth buyers, MuchMusic introduced a branded pre-paid MasterCard. For a one-time fee, cardholders or their parents can load funds onto the card. Accepted as widely as a regular MasterCard, teenagers without their own credits can now make online purchases. By integrating its television and online content with an e-commerce portal, MuchMusic has managed to attract its target consumers and provide them the means to purchase—all from the comfort of their own couch. MuchMusic now brings multichannel marketing to its young customers.

MuchMusic.com allows it customers to buy ringtones and other merchandise online.

The Internet has facilitated market expansions by traditional retailers as well. Not only can a customer in Zurich shop online at Sears.ca or Lee Valley Tools Ltd. (leevalley.com), but a Staples customer can buy a computer online and pick it up at the store. In addition to increasing sales by expanding the current customer base and attracting new customers, an electronic channel enables retailers to collect information about what people looked at or purchased when they visited the website, which the retailer then can use to plan inventories, promotions, and loyalty programs. Furthermore, multichannel retailers can achieve economies of scale by coordinating their buying and logistics activities across channels and consolidating their marketing information and activities. Generally, consumers who shop at **multichannel retailers**—retailers that sell merchandise in more than one retail channel (i.e., store, catalogue, and Internet)—typically buy more than those who shop in only one retail channel.

From customers' points of view, e-stores offer the convenience of a wide selection, available at any time, that they can view from the comfort of their home or office and that can be delivered right to their door. However, e-stores cannot always fulfill all their needs and often have more difficulty providing personalized human contact, prepurchase trial or experience, and low-cost after-sales service (including returns) than their bricks-and-mortar competitors. We summarize the factors that help and hinder the growth and success of e-retailing in Exhibit 14.5.

So what is in store for the future of electronic retailing? There are, and will continue to be, three major categories of e-retailers: Internet niche, large Internet-only, and traditional retailers with Internet offerings. Internet niche retailers offer specific items to interested customers around the world. The second group of large, Internet-only retailers is limited in number, though several quite successful stores exist in this group, such as Amazon.ca. Much of the positive discussion regarding the future of Internet retailing centres on the third group, the large traditional retailers that have opened Internet stores, such as Indigo.com, FutureShop.ca, and CanadianTire.ca. These and many other well-known multichannel retailers have found that customers seem to recognize the potential of having the option to shop in stores, on the Internet, and possibly through a catalogue.

multichannel retailers
Retailers that sell merchandise in more than one retail channel (e.g., store, catalogue, and Internet).

EXHIBIT 14.5	Internet Helpers and Hinderers[46]
Internet Helpers	
Product Category	Standardized and uniquely branded products easier to purchase via Internet.
Access to Information	Consumers can conveniently peruse the entire assortment and obtain product information.
Accessibility	Consumers can access an e-retailer from anywhere Internet service is available.
Convenience	The Internet is open 24 hours a day, seven days a week. Provides tremendous convenience to consumers.
Internet Hinderer	
Lack of Trial	Internet is deficient in offering pre-trial experience and evaluation.
Lack of Interpersonal Trust	Internet retailing is inherently limited in its ability to offer high-trust persuasive communication.
Lack of Instant Gratification	Usually time delay between purchase and obtaining merchandise or service.
Loss of Privacy and Security	Less perceived privacy and security concerns while shopping in an e-retailing environment.
Lack of In-Store Shopping Experience	Perceived as a less entertaining environment.
High Shipping and Handling Costs	Costs of shipping and handling add considerably to the costs of fulfillment in Internet retailing.

Developing a Retailing Strategy and Positioning

So far in this chapter we have discussed the importance of innovation in formats, products, services and prices for the survival and competitive advantage of retailers in the Big Middle. We also looked at how retailers can use the 4Ps to deliver customer value especially in a time when more and more Canadian consumers are becoming very value conscious. We observe that today's consumers are more willing to shop at any retailer or through any retailing channel where they feel they are getting the best value for their money. We also note that the lines between the different types of retailers are increasingly becoming blurred as retailers expand the range of their merchandise and services. For example, Wal-Mart, and to a lesser extent Shoppers Drug Mart, are moving into the grocery business. Thus, it is extremely important for retailers to develop effective retailing strategies and market positioning in order to differentiate themselves in the increasingly competitive landscape and give customers a compelling reason to shop at their stores.

But how can retailers go about creating an effective retailing strategy and positioning? For starters, many of the principles we discussed in Chapter 8 on segmentation, targeting and positioning can be very helpful. As we note in Chapter 8, retailers must first obtain a deep understanding of the consumers in their markets—their attitudes, behaviours, and preferences. Retailers must then use their knowledge of their consumers to develop market segments and then to select those segments they want to serve—target markets. Retailers that try to be all things to all people often end up not being able to serve any particular segment appropriately and soon find themselves in serious trouble. Once the target market is selected, retailers must develop merchandising, pricing, promotion, and place strategies to reach and serve these consumers. Again, these elements must be closely coordinated so that they portray a consistent and clear positioning to consumers of what type of customers the retailer is targeting and how they want to serve them. For example, a retailer such as Harry Rosen, who wants to be perceived as a high-end clothing retailer carries high quality clothing, offers personalized services, and charges premium prices for its merchandise. Harry Rosen's store image and atmospherics (place) also portray an image of affluence and professionalism—an image that is consistent with its customers' perceptions of themselves.

Generally, merchandising strategies pertain to the breadth and depth of product assortments a retailer will offer its target market as well as the range of customer service—from full service to limited service to self-serve. Pricing strategies range from premium pricing to discount pricing to every day low prices and everything in between. Place refers to the retail store image and atmospherics or in the case of online stores, the website's look, feel, and functionality. Place strategy is extremely important since it is the one area in retailing where marketers can establish an emotional connection to its customers and hold their loyalty. Research has shown that the layout of a store and its merchandise, the music, the lighting, the appearance of its sales associates, the location, and other physical elements have a huge impact on consumers shopping behaviour and loyalty. Recognizing the importance of creating effective retailing and positioning strategies, Loblaw has created many different store formats for different target customers. For example, Loblaw's Real Canadian Superstores are for customers who want high quality products, a wide range of product assortments, high levels of service and are willing to pay a premium, while its No-Frills stores are for those looking for narrower product assortments, less service and want to pay much lower prices.

Another important element in creating an effective retail strategy, particularly in today's competitive environment, is what marketers call an integrated multichannel retailing strategy. As we discussed earlier, retailing can be take place at a physical store, through various non-store retailing formats, and through the Internet. In the past, some retailers have used one or two of these retailing channels quite successfully but they often treated each channel as a separate line of business. Today, the competitive environment is forcing retailers to offer their products through multiple channels—physical stores, the Internet, kiosks, catalogues, etc.—rather than a single channel. Even Dell, the once Internet-only computer retailer, is now offering its products through Wal-Mart, a physical store, and through kiosks setup at shopping malls. So why offer multichannel retailing and in particular, why *integrated* multichannel retailing?

Integrated multichannel retailing enables customers to search for or examine goods at one channel, buy them at another channel, and pick them up at yet another channel. To offer this level of service and flexibility to customers, retailers must ensure that all their different channels are seamlessly integrated. This is a huge challenge for most retailers but those who get it right are likely to succeed and do extremely well because integrated multichannel retailing offer several unique benefits to both consumers and retailers. For retailers, integrated multichannel retailing can lead to greater operational efficiencies, higher revenues, and increased market share. As we noted above, consumers who shop at multichannel retailers typically buy more than those who shop in only one retail channel. For consumers, multichannel retailing increases the shopping efficiency and effectiveness of their shopping experiences by offering them greater convenience, flexibility, interactivity, information, and choice, all of which improves their perception of the retailers' value proposition. The unique advantages of four channels—physical store, catalogue, kiosks, and the Web—are highlighted in Exhibit 14.6.

EXHIBIT 14.6	Unique Advantages of Specific Channels
Channel	**Advantage**
Store	• Immediacy—consumer can see item and take home on same trip • No shipping costs for items taken home by shopper • Ability to see, feel, try out, and test item and substitute items • Interaction with store personnel • Satisfies "shopping as a social activity," which other channels cannot
Catalogue	• Portability—catalogue can be read anywhere • Long shelf life • Control over colour is better in catalogue than on website • Access to a global market and to markets without retail stores • 24/7 ordering capability • Transferrable and shareable among customers • Satisfies more sensory needs (visual and smell) than Internet
Kiosk	• Can reach customers without Web access • In-store kiosks can enable retailers to avoid lost sales due to out-of-stock situations • High levels of video/audio quality
Web	• Offers virtually unlimited space to describing an item • Access to a global market and to markets without retail stores • 24/7 ordering capability • No postage or reproduction costs associated with catalogues • Ability to verify shipping status without customer service personnel • Integration of video and audio in sales presentation • Ability to easily compare offerings of merchants, prices, product features • Ability to customize mailings to past and ongoing customers • Enables disabled shoppers to browse and shop in a barrier-free environment • Allows retailers to more effectively stock slow-selling merchandise • Internet sites appeal to market segments that prefer Web-based shopping • Utilizes automatic interface techniques: collaborative filtering, cookies, Web log analysis, and real time • Enables mass customization through visualization and questionnaire to consumers on their specific needs • Enables prices to be easily and quickly changed • Allows for automatic consumption, e.g., flowers sent same day each month

Adapted from: Barry Berman and Shawn Thelen, "A guide to developing and managing a well-integrated multi-channel retail strategy," *International Journal of Retail & Distribution Management, 32* (3), 2004, pp. 147–156.

Learning Objectives Review

1) Explain what will make retailers successful in the future

2) Describe how retailers create value for customers

3) Discuss the forms of non-store retailing

4) Explain how the Internet has changed the way consumers shop

1) Retailers that become market leaders start out by being very innovative, providing a low price, or both. Over time, they come to occupy the Big Middle, the part of the market that provides value for the majority of consumers. If these retailers are able to maintain their innovative or value edge, retain loyal customers, and stay a step ahead of their competition, they'll remain in the Big Middle. Otherwise, they will simply falter and fade away. The next wave of value-oriented retailers may be extreme value retailers and/or innovative entrants coming from specialty and e-retailing.

2) Retailers provide customers with a choice of merchandise in the quantities they want to buy and services that facilitate the sale and use of those products. They offer convenient locations to shop and an atmosphere and presentation that enhance the shopping experience. Promotions, both in the store and outside, provide customers with information. Finally, price provides signals to the customer about the image of the store, its merchandise, and its services.

3) Non-store retailing, or direct marketing, is a form of retailing that involves selling products directly to the final consumer rather than through channel wholesalers and retailers. It uses methods such as catalogues, direct response TV, and kiosks. This type of marketing is increasingly being used by marketers because it is targeted, motivates action, is measurable, and provides information for database marketing. Marketers find direct marketing very cost-effective compared to other methods of promotion and selling and its impact can be easily gauged. Consumers find direct marketing through catalogues, kiosks, direct response television, and other similar methods quite convenient and easy to use. Direct response television such as the Shopping Channel and others demonstrate their product's usage and benefits and encourage consumers to either pick-up the phone and call or go a website and place their order usually immediately or before the end of the show.

4) Customers feel particularly comfortable buying commodities and branded merchandise over the Internet because they can easily judge quality and compare prices. Other products that require consumers to touch or feel them are more difficult. The Internet has expanded the market for many retailers, from small, specialty niche retailers to large global retailers. The group of retailers that appears to be benefiting the most from the Internet channels is multichannel retailers, who can better determine what their customers want and provide them with convenient shopping options.

Key Terms

- big-box food retailer, 400
- bricks-and-mortar retailer, 407
- category killer, 401
- category specialist, 401
- conventional supermarket, 400
- direct mail, 404
- direct response television (DRTV), 405
- discount store, 400
- drugstore, 399
- extreme value retailer, 402
- general merchandise retailer, 400
- multichannel retailers, 409
- off-price retailer, 402
- private-label brands, 396
- retailing, 390
- share of wallet, 398
- specialty store, 400
- wholesalers, 390

Concept Review

1. How has the retail landscape changed in Canada based on the Big Middle concept?

2. How do marketers use the 4Ps to create value in retailing?

3. In this chapter, we discuss the fact that researchers have found that store image and atmospherics exert a huge impact on customers shopping behaviour. What are the key elements of a store's atmospherics and image and why do you think that they affect consumers so strongly?

4. Discuss the types of retailers that operate in Canada and identify some of the issues facing each type.

5. Generally merchandise retailers are classified into several different groups such as discount stores, specialty stores, category killers, and so on. However, it seems that increasingly many of these retailers are looking quite similar. Why is this so and what factors may explain this trend?

6. Identify and discuss four dimensions on which the various forms of retailing operations can be distinguished.

7. What is meant by non-store retailing? How does it benefit both marketers and consumers? Although many have predicted the end of non-store retailing such as telemarketing and mail-order catalogues, these forms of retailing remain strong and are growing for some retailers. What factors do you think may help explain this situation?

8. Explain how the Internet has helped reshape retail marketing strategies. What are some of the unique advantages between physical store retailing, website selling, and kiosks?

9. Discuss the advantages of being a multichannel retailer from the perspectives of both retailers and consumers.

10. Explain why it is important for retailers to develop effective retailing strategy and positioning. How do retailers develop such a strategy? Hint: Look at the various store formats of Loblaw or any national grocery chain.

Marketing Applications

1. How have retail institutions evolved over time according to the Big Middle and Wheel of Retailing concepts? Provide an example of a specific retailer that operates within each of the categories identified in the model.

2. Why don't traditional department stores have the same strong appeal to Canadian consumers that they once enjoyed during their height in the last half of the 20th century? Discuss which types of retailers are now competing with department stores.

3. What do retailers do to increase the value of products and services for consumers? Discuss the extent to which bricks-and-mortar retailers are threatened by Internet-only retailers with regard to these factors.

4. Some argue that retailers can be eliminated from the distribution channel because they only add costs to the final product without creating any value-added services in the process. Do you agree with this perspective? Is it likely that consumers will make most purchases directly from manufacturers in the near future? Provide justification for your answers.

5. Many years ago, the corporations that sold gasoline made the strategic move to include a substantial offering of food items. Today, it is rare to find a gas station that does not sell food items. Into which category of food retailer did these service stations fall? Do you think this was a prudent strategic direction for these corporations? Explain your logic.

6. Identify three categories of products especially suited for sale on the Internet. Identify three categories that are not currently suitable for sale on the Internet. Justify your choices.

7. How does Staples.com or Officedepot.com provide value to their customers beyond the physical products that they sell? Identify some of the ways that the companies have overcome the inhibitors to successful Internet retailing.

8. What options do you have for purchasing food in your town? Under what circumstances would you shop at each option? What about a family with two young children?

9. You can purchase apparel at a discount store, specialty store, category specialist, off-price retailer, department store, or Internet-only store. From which of these types of stores do you shop? Explain why you prefer one type over another.

10. Suppose you are the confectionary buyer for a regional chain of grocery stores. The store policy is to charge a "substantial" listing fee for the placement of new items. Listing fees were originally designed to cover the costs of placing new products on the shelves, such as adjustments to computer systems and realignment of warehouse and store space. Over the years, these fees have become larger, and they are now a significant source of revenue for the chain. A local minority-owned manufacturer of a popular brand of specialty candy would like to sell to your chain, but claims that the listing fee is too high and does not reflect the real cost of adding their candy. Discuss the ethical implications of such a policy. What should the chain do?

Net Savvy

1. Companies like Lee Valley Tools have expanded their offerings beyond their original channels to sell through multiple channels. Visit the company's website (www. leevalley.com) and determine in which channels it operates (Web, stores, and/or catalogue). Discuss the advantages of using a multichannel strategy over a single channel strategy.

2. Using either your own experience or that of a friend, select a familiar Internet website that engages in some form of retailing. Evaluate that website in terms of its helpers and hinderers (Exhibit 14.5), and summarize the extent to which you think the site is successful in sustaining a retailing Web presence.

Chapter Case Study

STAPLES, INC.[47]

Staples operates in the highly competitive, $240-billion office products market, which historically has been served by traditional office products retailers. These traditional retailers purchase a significant portion of their merchandise from wholesalers that purchase merchandise from manufacturers. Traditional office supply retailers often employ commissioned salespeople who use the wholesaler's catalogue to present their business customers with products to select.

But due to their ability to sell at lower prices, mass merchandisers, warehouse clubs, and discount retailers have taken market share away from these traditional retailers, and the industry has grown substantially in the past two decades with the emergence of office supply superstores like Staples, Office Depot, and Office Max. In addition, mail order firms, contract stationery businesses, electronic commerce wholesalers, and manufacturers that sell directly to the consumer all compete for sales. However, though the office products business has changed in recent years, a significant portion of the market is still served by small retailers.

Regardless, the superstores have dramatically changed the landscape of the office supply industry. First, they greatly expanded the use of the retail store format to distribute office supply products, capitalizing in part on the significant increase in the number of home offices. Prior to the mid-1980s, office supply customers primarily placed their orders through commissioned salespeople. Second, an even more recent change in this industry has been the greater use of the Internet for ordering office supply products. These changes have resulted in a very price-competitive market for office supplies, dominated by a small number of providers.

Company Background

Originally opened in 1986 by executive-turned-entrepreneur Tom Stemberg, Staples sales exceeded $16 billion in 2005.[48] Staples has been credited with pioneering the high-volume office products superstore concept. By evolving its original mission of slashing the costs and eliminating the hassles of running an office, to making it easy to buy office products, Staples has become the world's largest office products company.

To distinguish itself in this competitive industry, Staples strives to provide a unique shopping experience to customers in all its market segments. Central to maintaining customer satisfaction is developing strong customer relationship skills and broad knowledge about office products in all associates hired by the company. Therefore, Staples includes formal training as an integral part of the development of its associates. Another truly important aspect of customer service is the availability of merchandise. In the office supply industry, customers have very specific needs, such as finding an ink cartridge for a particular printer, and if the store is out of stock of a needed item, the customer may never come back.

Staples uses various channels of distribution to address the needs of its different segments. Smaller businesses are generally served by a combination of retail stores, catalogue, and the Internet. Retail operations focus on serving the needs of consumers and small businesses, whereas the catalogue and Internet operations focus on customers who need delivery of their office products and other specialized services. The typical Staples retail store has approximately 7000 stockkeeping units (SKUs), but Staples.com offers about 45,000 SKUs.

Staples believes that the Internet channel has helped to increase its sales while reducing its overhead costs. It has developed three standalone websites: Staples.com, a public website; Quill.com, an e-commerce site for medium-sized businesses; and StaplesLink.com, a secure, customized, e-commerce procurement website for large customers with contracts with Staples. In addition, the company has placed Staples.com kiosks in its stores so that customers can make purchases of any product, even if they are not stocked in the store. Customers can pay for these purchases at the register or through Staples.com and have the product delivered to their home or business. This multichannel approach allows Staples to increase its productivity by stocking only fast-moving items in stores but not sacrificing product availability.

Multichannel Integration

Staples' overall goal has been to become the leading office products and service provider by combining its existing experience, extensive distribution infrastructure, and customer service expertise with Web-based information technology. As a result, the integration of different channels of distribution into one seamless customer experience has been of particular interest to the company. Staples, like many other multichannel retailers, has found that many customers use multiple channels to make their Staples purchases and that sales increase when customers use more than one channel (customers that shop two channels spend twice as much as a single-channel shopper; a tri-channel shopper spends about three times as much as a single-channel shopper). Therefore, the greater the number of channels a particular customer shops, the greater the overall expenditure he or she is likely to make.

Staples faces several challenges in integrating its channels of distribution, most of which are related to its Internet channel. First, it must consider the extent to which the Internet may cannibalize its retail store sales. The most attractive aspect of the Internet is its potential to attract new customers and sell more to existing customers. But if overall sales are flat, that is, if online retailing only converts retail store sales to Internet sales, Staples suffers increased overhead costs and poorer overall productivity. Second, Staples must be concerned about the stock position of its retail stores compared with that of alternative channels. Since a retail store cannot carry as much merchandise as the Internet channel, the challenge is keeping an appropriate balance between minimizing stockouts and avoiding the proliferation of too many SKUs in the retail stores.

Questions

1. Assess the extent to which Staples has developed a successful multichannel strategy. What factors have contributed to its success?

2. What are the advantages and disadvantages of using kiosks as a part of its approach?

3. How should Staples assess which SKUs to keep in its stores?

CHAPTER **15**

LEARNING OBJECTIVES

After studying this chapter, you should be able to:

LO **1** Outline the process used to communicate with consumers

LO **2** Explain the six tools of integrated marketing communication campaigns

LO **3** Understand the steps in planning an integrated marketing communication campaign

LO **4** Describe what appeals advertisers use to get customers' attention

LO **5** Identify how firms determine which media to use

LO **6** Describe how firms plan for and measure integrated marketing communications (IMC) success

Integrated Marketing Communications

Love them or hate them, Bell spokes-beavers Frank and Gordon get our attention. In a world where animals in advertising dominate, (Canadians have seen dogs, frogs, pigs, monkeys, birds, and lizards) why have Frank and Gordon been so successful? The beavers made their debut in Quebec late in 2005 as Jules and Bertrand. Research indicated that consumers remembered the ads as being from Bell, helping to make the decision to focus exclusively on the beaver campaign.[1]

The strategy developed one advertising platform to integrate all of Bell's marketing communications. This new platform was used nationally across all business lines. At the heart of the campaign were Frank and Gordon communicating features and benefits of Bell's many products and services, using the tagline, "Making it Simple."

Many Canadians were exposed to the new campaign through television ads during the 2006 Olympic Games. All communication elements featured the beavers, introduced the characters, and reinforced the consumer benefit for each product or service. A Leger Marketing survey conducted after the closing ceremonies showed that almost half of Canadian viewers recognized Bell and the beavers as Olympic sponsors.[2]

While the creative concept has been successful, strategic and tactical changes underlying the campaign are just as important. Bell's switch to using the beavers across all platforms and for all products resulted in ad production costs being cut by almost 50 percent, enabling the company to become more efficient and allowing savings to be re-invested in media buys.[3]

Bell spent an estimated $50 million on mass media in 2006 for more than 20 television ads and countless print, direct, and outdoor ads.[4] According to Bell, the campaign has translated into

yesterday **Turin,**
tomorrow **Vancouver.**

Bravo to our Canadian Olympic Team.
We're so proud and we simply wanted to say thanks.
Thanks for the dedication, and thanks for the
unforgettable moments. Now it's Vancouver's
turn to host the Olympic and Paralympic Winter
Games. We'll be right there beside our athletes
for the next four years, doing everything we can
to help them reach the podium.

Proud supporters of Own the Podium – 2010.

Bell

results. The number of subscribers is up and churn rates (the percentage of customers who leave) are down in three key growth areas—Internet, video, and mobile phone service.[5]

The integrated marketing communication campaign earned Bell a Gold and four other awards at the 2006 Canadian Marketing Awards. Best of all, Frank and Gordon have moved Bell away from price-centric advertising, improved the brand's like-ability factor, and put more focus on new products and services.[6]

Bell launched a new integrated marketing communication campaign featuring spokes-beavers Frank and Gordon using television, print, direct, and outdoor ads.

Throughout the last five chapters, we focused our attention on how firms create value by developing products and services and delivering them to consumers when and where they want to buy them. However, consumers are not likely to come flocking to new products and services unless they are aware of them. Therefore, marketers must consider how to communicate the value of a new product and/or service—or more specifically, the value proposition—to the target market. The Bell Frank and Gordon opening vignette illustrates how a firm can develop a communication strategy to demonstrate the value of its product. Let's begin by examining what IMC is, how it has developed, and how it contributes to value creation.

Integrated marketing communications (IMC) represents the promotion P of the 4Ps. It encompasses a variety of communication disciplines—advertising, personal selling, sales promotion, public relations, direct response marketing, and electronic media—in combination to provide clarity, consistency, and maximum communicative impact.[7] Rather than consisting of separate marketing communication elements with no unified control, IMC programs regard each of the firm's marketing communications elements as part of a whole, each of which offers a different means to connect with the target audience. This integration of elements provides the firm with the best means to reach the target audience with the desired message, and it enhances the value story by offering a clear and consistent message.

There are three components in any IMC strategy: the consumer or target market, the channels or vehicles through which the message is communicated, and the evaluation of the results of the communication. As shown in our chapter roadmap, in the first section, we focus on *consumers*, examining the communication process: how

integrated marketing communications (IMC) Represents the promotion dimension of the four Ps; encompasses a variety of communication disciplines—general advertising, personal selling, sales promotion, public relations, direct marketing, and electronic media—in combination to provide clarity, consistency, and maximum communicative impact.

CHAPTER
ROADMAP

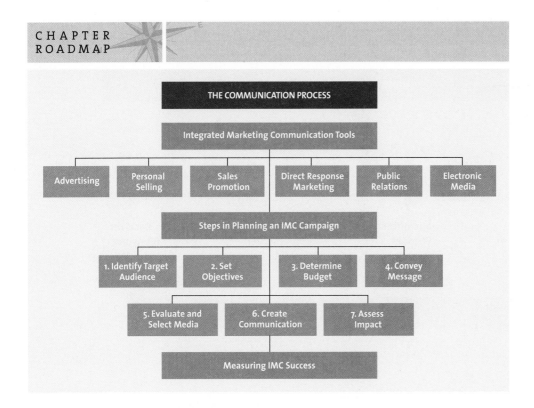

consumers receive communications, whether via media or other methods, as well as how the delivery of that communication affects a message's form and contents. The second section examines the six distinct tools of IMC and how each is used in an overall IMC strategy. We then identify the steps involved in planning successful campaigns, from identifying a target audience to creating an actual ad and assessing its performance. Although we apply these steps specifically to advertising, the same process can be used when planning sales promotions, direct marketing, public relations, and electronic media. The last section considers how the level of complexity in IMC strategies leads marketers to design new ways to measure the *results* of IMC campaigns.

Communicating with Consumers   LO **1**

As the number of communication media has increased, the task of understanding how best to reach target consumers has become far more complex. In this section, we examine a model that describes how communications go from the firm to the consumer and the factors that affect the way the consumer perceives the message. Then we look at how marketing communications influence consumers—from making them aware that a product or service exists to moving them to buy.

The Communication Process

Exhibit 15.1 illustrates the communication process. Let's first define each component and then discuss how they interact.

The Sender The message originates from the **sender**, who must be clearly identified to the intended audience. For instance, an organization such as Home Depot can send a message, using its distinctive logo, that it is having a special "after-holiday sale." Ethical Dilemma 15.1 on page 421 raises the issue of whether it is deceptive to disguise the sender of a message.

sender
The firm from which an IMC message originates; the sender must be clearly identified to the intended audience.

EXHIBIT 15.1 The Communication Process

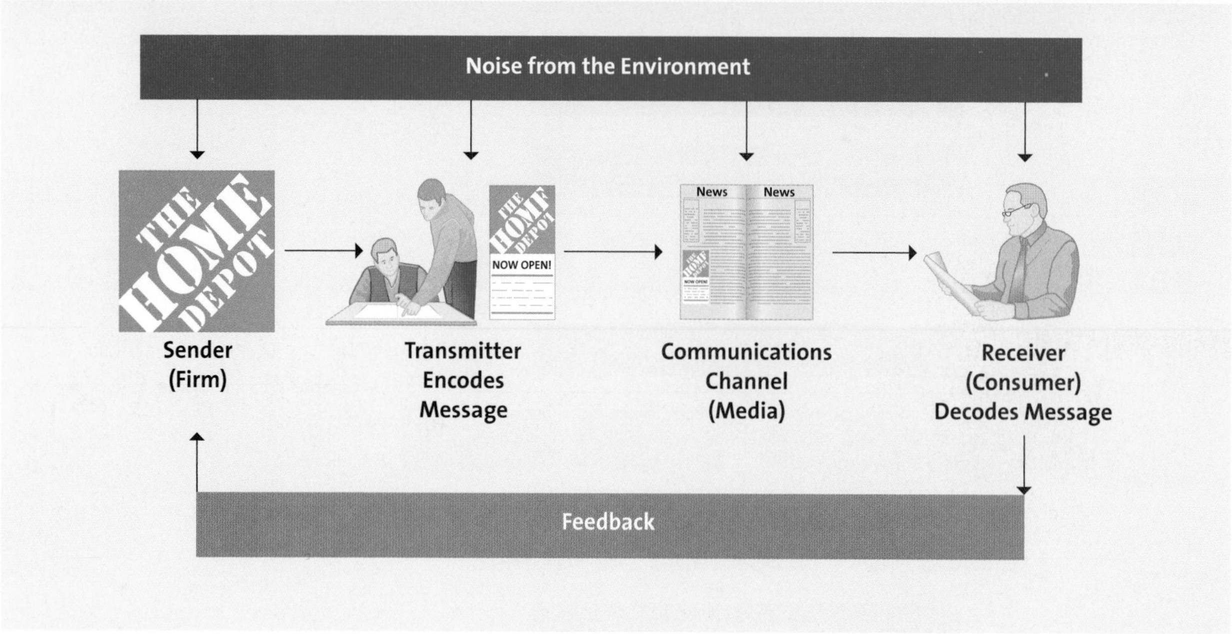
Noise from the Environment
THE HOME DEPOT
Sender (Firm)
NOW OPEN!
Transmitter Encodes Message
News
News
Communications Channel (Media)
Receiver (Consumer) Decodes Message
Feedback

transmitter
An agent or intermediary with which the sender works to develop the marketing communications; for example, a firm's creative department or an advertising agency.

encoding
The process of converting the sender's ideas into a message, which could be verbal, visual, or both.

The Transmitter The sender works with the creative department, whether in-house or from a marketing (or advertising) agency, to develop marketing communications. Home Depot likely works with its advertising agency to develop the message. Such an agent or intermediary is the **transmitter**.

Encoding **Encoding** means converting the sender's ideas into a message, which could be verbal, visual, or both. Home Depot may take out full-page ads in every major newspaper proclaiming: "Amazing Holiday Deals at 25 Percent Off!" A television com-

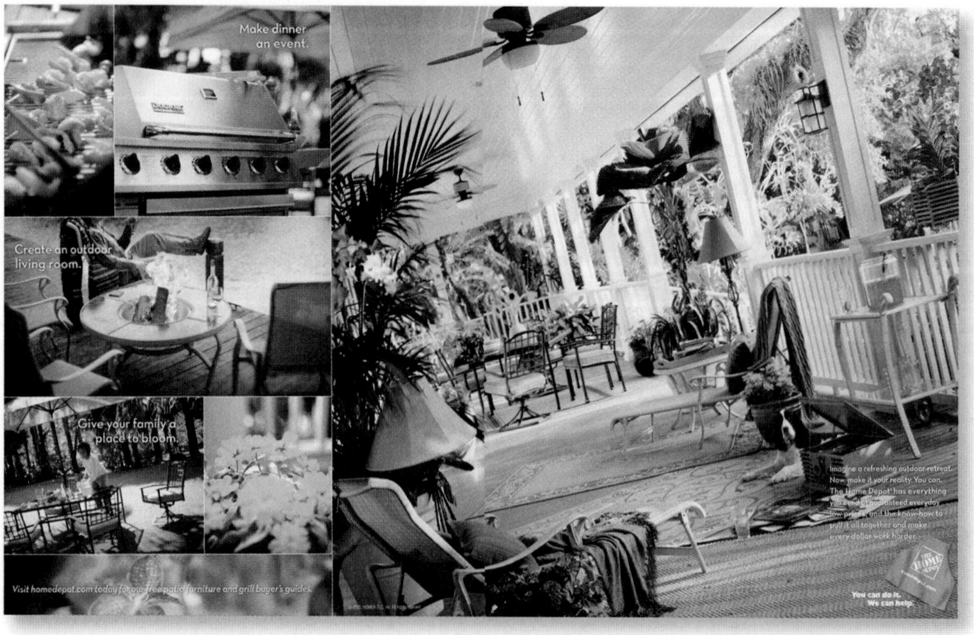
Make dinner an event.
Create an outdoor living room.
Give your family a place to bloom.
You can do it. We can help.

Which component of the communication process exemplifies this Home Depot ad?

Ethical Dilemma 🖐	**15.1**	Is It Deceptive to Disguise the Message Sender?

The quest for innovative ways to reach consumers has led companies to promote some confusion about who the sender of a message really is. Traditionally, the sender of any commercial message had to be identified, and the message was required to indicate that it was a commercial or promotional message.[8] With new media like websites, however, it can become extremely difficult for consumers to know whether a message is commercial. If consumers don't know they are viewing a promotional message, they may be unable to evaluate its claims properly, and deception could ensue. The Competition Bureau regulates **deceptive advertising**, that is, exaggerated claims, false or misleading representations and deceptive marketing practices in promoting products or services

Consider the promotion mix Vancouver-based Lion's Gate Films used for the horror movie *Godsend*, which included a website (www.godsendinstitute.org/) along with traditional movie promotions. However, the website never clearly indicated that it was designed to promote a movie. The film *Godsend* is about cloning, and if you did a Google search for "cloning," the Web page for the Godsend Institute—not a real institute

but rather the setting for the film—would appear in the results list.

The site is very professional and looks very much like a website for a legitimate fertility clinic, including online tours of the facilities and testimonials from parents who had been patients at the centre. Family snapshots supposedly portray the children Godsend has cloned from dying siblings. The effect is dramatic—and completely fake. Nowhere on the site is there a disclaimer stating its true purpose. Tom Ortenberg, president of film releasing for Lion's Gate, stated that the *Godsend* site is "a million dollar idea" built for only about $10,000, in that the site resulted in millions of hits and generated a lot of publicity.[9]

This and other similar websites have sparked controversy primarily because of their realism and lack of clear promotional message. Many believe that a website is deceptive if it does not make clear that the site is actually promoting a product. But is it deceptive or just clever marketing? This challenge remains an open question for now. In the meantime, other movies and television programs, such as *Lost*, have begun using the tactic of creating false websites.

mercial showing people shopping at Home Depot is another way to encode the message that "there are great deals to be had." As the old saying goes, a picture is worth a thousand words. But the most important facet of encoding is not what is sent but rather what is received. Home Depot shoppers must believe that the sale is substantial enough to warrant a trip to a store.

The Communication Channel   The **communication channel** is the medium—print, broadcast, the Internet—that carries the message. Home Depot could transmit through television, radio, and various print advertisements, and it realizes that the media chosen must be appropriate to connect itself (the sender) with its desired recipient. So Home Depot might advertise on HGTV and in *Canadian Homes & Cottages*.

The Receiver   The **receiver** is the person who reads, hears, or sees and processes the information contained in the message and/or advertisement. The sender, of course, hopes that the person receiving it will be the one for whom it was originally intended. For example, Home Depot wants its message received and decoded properly by people who are likely to shop in its stores. **Decoding** refers to the process by which the receiver interprets the sender's message.

Noise   Noise is any interference that stems from competing messages, a lack of clarity in the message, or a flaw in the medium, and it poses a problem for all communication channels. Home Depot may choose to advertise in newspapers that its target market doesn't read, which means the rate at which the message is received by those to whom it has relevance has been slowed considerably. As we have already defined, encoding is what the sender intends to say, and decoding is what the receiver hears. If there is a difference between them, it is probably due to noise.

deceptive advertising
A representation, omission, act, or practice in an advertisement that is likely to mislead consumers acting reasonably under the circumstances.

communication channel
The medium—print, broadcast, the Internet—that carries the message.

receiver
The person who reads, hears, or sees and processes the information contained in the message or advertisement.

decoding
The process by which the receiver interprets the sender's message.

noise
Any interference that stems from competing messages, a lack of clarity in the message, or a flaw in the medium; a problem for all communication channels.

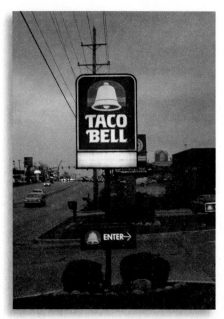

Receivers decode messages differently. What does the Taco Bell sign mean to you?

feedback loop
Allows the receiver to communicate with the sender and thereby informs the sender whether the message was received and decoded properly.

Feedback Loop   The **feedback loop** allows the receiver to communicate with the sender and thereby informs the sender whether the message was received and decoded properly. Feedback can take many forms: a customer's purchase of the item, a complaint or compliment, the redemption of a coupon or rebate, and so forth. If Home Depot observes an increase in store traffic and sales, its managers know that their intended audience received the message and understood that there were great after-holiday bargains to be found in the store.

How Consumers Perceive Communication

The actual communication process is not as simple as the model in Exhibit 15.1 implies. Each receiver may interpret the sender's message differently, and senders often adjust their message according to the medium used and the receivers' level of knowledge about the product or service.

Receivers Decode Messages Differently   Each receiver decodes a message in his or her own way, which is not necessarily the way the sender intended. Different people shown the same message will often take radically different meanings from it. For example, what does the image on the left convey to you?

If you are a user of this brand, it may convey satisfaction. If you recently went on a diet and gave up your favourite Mexican food, it may convey dismay or a sense of loss. If you have chosen to be a nonuser, it may convey some disgust. If you are a recently terminated employee, it may convey anger. The sender has little, if any, control over what meaning any individual receiver will take from the message.[10]

Senders Adjust Messages According to the Medium and Receivers' Traits   Different media communicate in very different ways. So marketers make adjustments to their messages and media depending on whether they want to communicate with

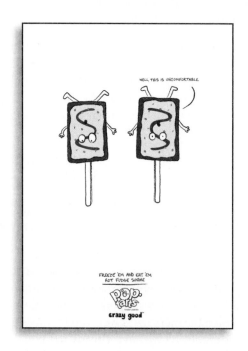

Senders must adjust messages according to the receivers' traits. Kellogg's, for instance, uses different ads to target kids (left) and its retail customers (right).

suppliers, shareholders, customers, or the general public.[11] Kellogg's would not, for instance, send the same message to its shareholders in a targeted e-mail as it would to its consumers on Saturday morning TV.

Now that we've examined various aspects of the communication process, let's look at the specific tools used in IMC programs.

Integrated Marketing Communication Tools

LO

For any communications campaign to succeed, the firm must deliver the right message to the right audience through the right media. Reaching the right audience is becoming more difficult, however, as the media environment grows more complicated and fragmented.

Advances in technology have led to satellite radio, wireless technology, pop-up and banner ads on websites, brand-sponsored websites, PDA messaging, and text messaging, all of which vie for consumers' attention. Not so long ago, advertisers could reach the masses with media buys on three television networks. Today they have to buy on 74 stations to reach the same number of people. Print media have also grown and become more specialized. In Canada there are currently 134 daily newspapers, 1100 plus community newspapers, 800 plus consumer magazines, and 900 trade journals.[12]

This proliferation of media has led many firms to shift their promotional dollars from advertising to direct marketing, website development, product placements, and other forms of promotion in search of the best way to deliver messages to their target audiences. Media fragmentation has also occurred on television. Networks are dedicated to certain types of sports (Outdoor Life Network, Golf Channel), children (Nickelodeon), ethnic minorities (APTN—Aboriginal Peoples Television Network), and religious (CTS, OMNI Television). Each of these channels allows IMC planners to target their desired audience narrowly.

We now examine the individual tools of IMC and the way each contributes to a successful IMC campaign (see Exhibit 15.2). Some tools—advertising, direct response marketing, personal selling, and sales promotion—appear in detail in other chapters; we discuss them only briefly here.

Advertising

Perhaps the most visible of the IMC components, **advertising** is a paid form of communication from an identifiable source, delivered through a communication channel, and designed to persuade the receiver to take some action, now or in the future.[13] In Chapter 16, we discuss the purpose of advertising and its various types, but for now, we note that advertising is extremely effective for creating awareness of a product or service and generating interest. Quarry Integrated Communications, discussed in Entrepreneurial Marketing 15.1 on page 425, helped Research In Motion create awareness for BlackBerry when it was first introduced. And, as mentioned in the opening vignette, many Canadians saw the Frank and Gordon television ads during the 2006 Winter Olympic Games, creating interest in Bell's products and services.

Mass advertising can entice consumers into a conversation with marketers. However, advertising must break through the clutter of other messages to reach its intended audience. And as marketers attempt to find ways to reach their target audiences, advertising has become increasingly pervasive. Not so long ago, the majority of many firms' promotional budgets was spent on advertising. Since the 1990s, however, advertising's share of total promotional dollars has fallen as the budgets for other forms of sales promotion, especially direct marketing and public relations, have increased, resulting in a more balanced approach to the use of marketing communications elements.

advertising
A paid form of communication from an identifiable source, delivered through a communication channel, and designed to persuade the receiver to take some action, now or in the future.

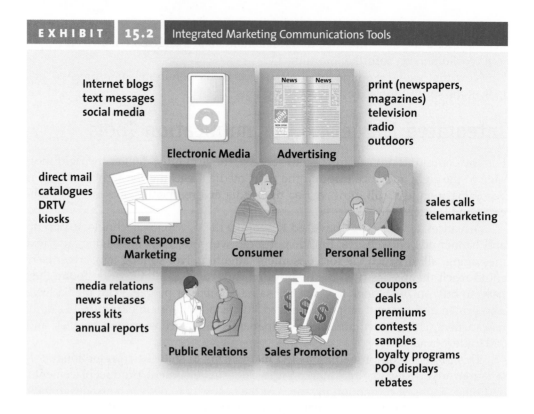

EXHIBIT 15.2   Integrated Marketing Communications Tools

Personal Selling

personal selling
The two-way flow of communication between a buyer and a seller that is designed to influence the buyer's purchase decision.

Personal selling is the two-way flow of communication between a buyer and a seller that is designed to influence the buyer's purchase decision. Personal selling can take place in various settings: face-to-face, video teleconferencing, on the telephone, or over the Internet. Although consumers don't often interact with professional sales people, personal selling represents an important component of many IMC programs, especially in business-to-business (B2B) settings.

The cost of communicating directly with a potential customer is quite high compared with other forms of promotion, but it is simply the best and most efficient way to sell certain products and services. Customers can buy many products and services without the help of a salesperson, but salespeople simplify the buying process by providing information and services that save customers time and effort. In many cases, sales representatives add significant value, which makes the added expense of employing them worthwhile. Chapter 16 devotes more attention to personal selling and sales management.

Sales Promotions

sales promotions
Special incentives or excitement-building programs that encourage the purchase of a product or service, such as coupons, rebates, contests, free samples, and point-of-purchase displays.

Sales promotions are special incentives or excitement-building programs that encourage the purchase of a product or service, such as coupons, rebates, contests, free samples, and point-of-purchase displays. Marketers typically design these incentives for use in conjunction with other advertising or personal selling programs. Many sales promotions, like free samples or point-of-purchase displays, are designed to build short-term sales, though others, like contests and sweepstakes, have become integral components of firms' CRM programs as means to build customer loyalty. We discuss such sales promotions in more detail in Chapter 16.

Direct Response Marketing

direct response marketing
Sales and promotional techniques that deliver marketing communications to individual prospective customers.

The component of IMC that has received the greatest increase in aggregate spending recently is **direct response marketing**, or the sales and promotional techniques that

Entrepreneurial Marketing

15.1 | Ideas that Build Success

Eschewing formal titles, Alan Quarry good-naturedly calls himself the Head Coach and Chief Enthusiasm Officer of Quarry Integrated Communications. Based in Waterloo, Ontario, the 125-plus person company helps its clients build their business through innovative research, advertising, branding, public relations, sales, Web, and digital media.

Alan started his marketing career at Canada Trust, now TD Canada Trust, where he became its youngest ever manager of corporate communications only two and a half years after joining. He left in 1983 to become the third employee at Quarry Integrated Communications, started by his father, Robert Quarry, in the basement of his house 10 years earlier. By 1988, Alan had become the majority shareholder and president. Over the years he contributed to the company's success in a variety of roles including client service director, copywriter, mailroom coordinator, receptionist, media director, integrated communications strategist, U of Q Dean (Quarry has its own in-house university with credit courses for employees), and summer picnic dunk tank target.[14]

While the company's roots go back to an agricultural base, it has successfully expanded to a wide variety of industries and has worked with small and large companies including Bell, Research In Motion, Nortel, Sprint, and FedEx. Working with Bell, Quarry developed in-depth personas to better help them understand customers and structure new service offerings. Forrester Research has recognized Quarry as one of a handful of North American firms with expertise in the development of personas.[15] Quarry's work on early BlackBerry campaigns helped Research In Motion develop brand awareness, gaining a toehold in the all important U.S. market and repositioning it against Palm, HP, and Sony. Building an integrated campaign resulted in a consistent look and feel for all communications whether they were newspaper or magazine ads, billboards, websites, trade show displays, and even packaging. A brand style guide designed for use by business partners, such as Rogers, Bell, and A&T, ensured that their BlackBerry advertising was in sync with RIM's overall integrated marketing communication strategy.

Alan Quarry's approach to integrated marketing communications is manifested in the company's mantra, "Think and Feel Like the Customer, Always Anticipate and Have Fun!" Quarry offices reflect this attitude, helping employees to get their creative juices flowing with meeting rooms named Eureka and Kaboom, gracefully curving walls, and a 1950's style lunch room named Al's Diner after Albert Einstein. The diner is a place where employees and guests meet, work, and access a free supply of healthy food. It comes as no surprise that Quarry has one of the lowest employee turnover rates in the industry. After 34 years in business, and with offices in Waterloo, Toronto, and Raleigh, North Carolina, Quarry builds things to last whether they are campaigns or relationships with employees and clients.

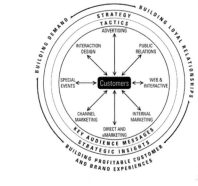

Quarry's Integration Wheel is used to design and integrate positive brand experiences that revolve around customer needs, build demand, and help create loyal, profitable customer relationships.

The unique office design at Quarry Integrated Communications helps employees get their creative juices flowing to create award-winning advertising for products like Research In Motion's BlackBerry.

Direct marketers now use PDAs and cell phones to reach potential customers.

deliver promotional materials individually to potential customers.[16] The direct marketing toolkit contains a variety of marketing communication initiatives, including telephone, mail, direct response television commercials (infomercials), catalogues, the Internet, and e-mail, as well as newer communication technologies such as PDAs, podcasts, and cell phones. Some of these forms of direct marketing are discussed in more detail in Chapter 14. All these initiatives address the customer in very different ways. In our Bell example, many such direct marketing initiatives were crucial to the initial success of its IMC plan, and many others were used only after consumers had identified themselves as wanting to continue their conversation. Unlike mass media, which communicate to a wide audience, direct response marketing allows for personalization of the message, a key advantage.

The increased use of customer databases has enabled marketers to identify and track consumers over time and across purchase situations, which has contributed to the rapid growth of direct response marketing. Marketers have been able to build these databases thanks to consumers' increased use of credit and debit cards, store-specific credit and loyalty cards, and online shopping, all of which require the buyer to give the seller personal information that becomes part of its database. Because firms understand customers' purchases better when they possess such information, they can more easily focus their direct response marketing efforts appropriately. In Adding Value 15.1, we offer some details about how firms can use this information to market to customers one at a time.

Public Relations (PR)

public relations
The organizational function that manages the firm's communications to achieve a variety of objectives, including building and maintaining a positive image, handling or heading off unfavourable stories or events, and maintaining positive relationships with the media.

Public relations is the organizational function that manages the firm's communications to achieve a variety of objectives, including building and maintaining a positive image, handling or heading off unfavourable stories or events, and maintaining positive relationships with the media. Public relations activities support the other promotional efforts by the firm by generating "free" media attention. For example, Bell's spokesbeavers were frequently in the news, featured in numerous newspaper and magazine articles. While it can be very difficult to convince the media to write about a company or its products and services, this media attention can be crucial to a company's success.

Good PR has always been an important success factor. Yet in recent years, the importance of PR has grown as the cost of other forms of marketing communications has increased. At the same time, the influence of PR has become more powerful as consumers have become increasingly skeptical of marketing claims made in other media.[17] In many instances, consumers view media coverage generated through PR as more credible and objective than any other aspects of an IMC program, because the firm does not "buy" the space in print media or time on radio or television. In essence, PR is the free placement of a company's message in the media.

cause-related marketing
Commercial activity in which businesses and charities form a partnership to market an image, a product, or a service for their mutual benefit; a type of promotional campaign.

Yoplait's Save Lids to Save Lives campaign and Champion's Program both illustrate how a well-orchestrated IMC effort using a combination of promotional and PR campaigns can enhance a firm's image while supporting a worthwhile cause.[18] The Save Lids to Save Lives campaign was designed not only to sell yogurt but also to create a positive association between the brand and a social cause, in this case, breast cancer awareness. This form of promotional campaign is called **cause-related marketing,**

Adding Value   **15.1**   One-to-One Marketing

One-to-one marketing is more than a direct marketing tool;[19] it is the total integration of sales, marketing, production, and finance into one system that offers seamless interactions with customers. For instance, if an existing customer comes to a firm with a request or calls with a concern, a good one-to-one marketing system can fill the request or solve the problem immediately because the firm already has an electronic file of that customer that contains his or her purchase information, preferences, and some personal data, like birthdays. Successful one-to-one marketing programs also segment customers so that the best customers receive the attention they deserve. Paying close attention to the most loyal customers is valuable to those customers because they get special treatment; it creates value for the firm because loyal customers are typically the most profitable segment.

Whirlpool Canada research indicated that two-thirds of appliance shoppers entered the retail store without a specific brand in mind.[20] Only 15 percent of shoppers had any brand preferences in the kitchen appliance category.[21] The company identified the need for an integrated customer relationship marketing strategy for its KitchenAid brand. The goal was to build one-to-one relationships with its most favourable customers using the Internet as a key consumer touchpoint. The True

Connoisseur Premier Loyalty Program was launched in November 2005 as an online forum for home enthusiasts. The intent was to provide a place for loyal customers to celebrate their love of all things culinary.[22] The program, which received virtually no public promotion, resulted in conversions of triple the industry standards for existing customers who enrolled.

The following year a mobile "rapid rebate" program was created to create a one-to-one dialogue with consumers. Stickers were placed on KitchenAid appliances in retail locations promoting the rebate and providing the text messaging short code to engage with the program. It resulted in unit sales that were five times higher than projected and 100 percent opt-in permission to communicate with these consumers via the mobile channel in the future.[23]

One-to-one programs create a win–win situation for customers and the firm. Customers get their needs addressed efficiently; firms are able to gather large amounts of data about customers, including their needs and wants, purchase intentions, and levels of satisfaction. This information enables the firm to develop products and services that offer higher value to customers, which in turn gives those customers an incentive to remain loyal to the firm.

which refers to commercial activity in which businesses and charities form a partnership to market an image, product, or service for their mutual benefit.[24] In the Save Lids to Save Lives campaign, Yoplait donates a set monetary amount for each special pink yogurt lid that consumers send in to the Susan G. Komen Breast Cancer Foundation.[25]

Integrally linked to the Save Lids to Save Lives campaign is Yoplait's Champion's Program, another PR campaign. The goal of the nationwide Champion's Program is to identify and recognize "ordinary people doing extraordinary things" in the fight against breast cancer. The 25 individual champions' stories appear in local media, and the program itself often makes the national media. Both initiatives thus are extremely successful in expanding consumers' knowledge about Yoplait's social commitments, as well as Yoplait's brand awareness.[26]

Another very popular PR tool is event sponsorship. **Event sponsorship** occurs when corporations support various activities (financially or otherwise), usually in the cultural or sports and entertainment sectors. For example, Subaru sponsors the Subaru Ironman Canada Triathlon, regarded as one of the best Ironman events in the world. The race helps Subaru promote its vehicles

event sponsorship Popular PR tool; occurs when corporations support various activities (financially or otherwise), usually in the cultural or sports and entertainment sectors.

Yoplait's Save Lids to Save Lives promotional and PR campaign enhances its image while supporting a worthwhile cause.

The annual Subaru Ironman Triathlon in Penticton, British Columbia, lets Subaru link the performance and durability of its vehicles to the grueling race.

electronic media
Tools including e-mail, website content, corporate blogs, online games, text messaging, and social media.

blog (weblog or Web log)
A Web page that contains periodic posts; corporate blogs are new form of marketing communications.

which, like athletes, must possess both the versatility to excel in a variety of environments and the durability to outlast the competition.

Firms often distribute a PR toolkit to communicate with various audiences. Some toolkit elements are designed to inform specific groups directly, whereas others are created to generate media attention and disseminate information. We depict the various elements of a PR toolkit in Exhibit 15.3.

Electronic Media

The Internet has had a dramatic impact on how marketers communicate with their customers. **Electronic media** tools range from simple e-mail and website content to far more interactive features like corporate blogs. Internet Marketing 15.1 examines the viral power of electronic media to quickly spread a message.

Corporate Blogs   Corporate blogging has risen from obscure, random company postings to a valuable Web addition in virtually no time. A **blog (Web log)** contains periodic posts on a common Web page. As a new form of marketing communication, a well-received blog can create positive word of mouth, customer loyalty, valuable feedback, and tangible economic results, whereas a poorly received blog may lead to backlash, decreased customer trust, and tangible but negative economic returns.[27] Corporate blogs that connect with customers also prompt sales increases because the company can respond directly to customers' comments.

Jim Estill started a blog when his company, EMJ Data, was purchased by Synnex Canada, a very large company with operations across the country. As CEO of Synnex, Estill was

Visitors to Synnex Canada's website (www. synnex,ca) can click on CEO blog to get the latest news from chief executive officer, Jim Estill.

Internet Marketing | 15.1 | **A Viral Evolution**

In Canada with Dove products found in one of four homes.[28] The Dove Campaign for Real Beauty set out to widen the definition of beauty in 2004. Two years after the campaign was launched, Unilever's advertising agency for the Dove brand, Toronto-based Ogilvy Mather, wanted to run a low budget campaign with a strong viral component. The Internet was the perfect medium for this kind of initiative. However, Ogilvy knew that any concepts would have to tie back into the Dove masterbrand and the Dove Self-Esteem Fund.

The team came up with the idea for a viral film, not an ad. While brainstorming ideas for the film, Tim Piper, associate creative director at Ogilvy, used his girlfriend, Stephanie Betts, for a rough storyboard titled "Evolution." His proposal was based on the fact that even models don't look like models and so he filmed Betts without make-up, then took her through a transformation from an attractive but plain woman, to glamorous supermodel. The storyboard was so convincing that instead of casting a professional actor, Unilever asked Betts to play the role.

The entire film was pulled together on an extremely low budget, a mere $135,000 investment,[29] with many favours called in from Piper's friends in the industry. No television air time was ever booked for this 75-second film. Instead, it was posted to the Dove website on October 11, 2006. Almost as an afterthought, it was also posted to YouTube. The unique film was exceptionally well received by viewers who quickly spread the word to their friends. Within days, it had received millions of views and continued to spread like wildfire. Viral indeed! Major television networks sensed the film's newsworthiness and jumped on the story which was featured by Ellen DeGeneres, Rosie O'Donnell, *Good Morning America*, *Inside Edition*, *Entertainment Tonight*, CNN, and FoxTV. The film generated

Posted to YouTube, the short film titled "Evolution" was viewed by millions of people within days of being posted, and featured by Ellen DeGeneres and other TV hosts, leading to a barrage of publicity for Unilever and its Dove brand.

well over $150 million in PR and media coverage[30] in the first six months after it was released.

The film continues to win accolades, including being awarded two Grand Prix awards at the Cannes Lions International Advertising Festival in 2007 only seven months after its debut. Ultimately, the film delivered a message people wanted to hear using a simple, but powerful medium. While no one ever expected "Evolution" to be such a phenomenal success, the Internet helped the message spread quickly and easily. Even Ogilvy admits that traditional advertising could never have achieved results like this.

To view this film, visit www.campaignforrealbeauty.ca and click on "Evolution" film.

EXHIBIT 15.3	Elements of a Public Relations Toolkit
PR Element	**Function**
Publications: Brochures, special purpose single-issue publications such as books	Inform various constituencies about the activities of the organization and highlight specific areas of expertise.
Video and audio: Programs, public service announcements	Highlight the organization or support cause-related marketing efforts.
Annual reports	Give required financial performance data and inform investors and others about the unique activities of the organization.
Media relations: Press kits, news releases, speeches, event sponsorships	Generate news coverage of the organization's activities or products/services.
Electronic media: Websites, e-mail campaigns	Websites can contain all the previously mentioned toolbox elements, while e-mail directs PR efforts to specific target groups.

uncomfortable no longer knowing the names of his employees and found that his CEO blog allowed him to put a more personal face forward to employees.

Some universities have started to use student blogs as a recruitment tool to attract undergrads. At the University of Manitoba in Winnipeg, 16 students and alumni have been sharing their experiences at the university through their blogs at www.itsmyfuture.ca. The site attracted more than 60,000 page views by over 6500 visitors in the first four weeks.[31]

Insincere postings or flogs (fake blogs) that are actually disguised advertising campaigns are problematic. By its very nature, a blog is transparent and contains authors' honest observations, which can help customers determine their trust and loyalty levels. Anything less than total honesty will break that bond and damage the relationship. When handled appropriately though, blogs can serve as trusted platforms for damage control. For instance, the vice chairperson of General Motors started a blog to dispel rumours that the company would discontinue its Pontiac and Buick brands.[32]

Visitors to the Tag Body Spray website can view this game in which visitors take on the role of a male character who must get past various virtual roadblocks—the family dog, parents, a younger brother—to gain access to the female "honey" who will find his Tag-enhanced scent appealing.

Online Games One particularly successful way to reach younger consumers is through short online games that allow consumers to interact with the site and possibly other players. In line with its hipster image, young male target market, and claim that it is "uniquely designed to attract the ladies," Tag Body Spray includes on its website a game in which visitors take on the role of a male character who must get past various virtual roadblocks—the family dog, parents, a younger brother—to gain access to the female "honey" who will find his Tag-enhanced scent appealing. Other games appeal to even younger customers, such as Neopet, a site we discuss later under "Stealth Marketing" in Chapter 16.[33]

Text Messaging Using the Internet in novel ways also has led to the growth of text messaging (or short message service [SMS]) as an increasingly important way for marketers to communicate with younger consumers. Recent experiments using text messaging have yielded some impressive results. An average SMS campaign generates a 15-percent response rate, compared with less than half that amount for direct mail. Research also shows that 94 percent of all advertising text messages are read, 23 percent of SMS advertisements are forwarded or shown to other users, and 8 percent of those consumers reply to the text message.[34]

Social Media Social media refers to a broad spectrum of online communities and social networking sites such as Facebook and MySpace. When it comes to social media, there is considerably more transparency and honesty than in most other forms of marketing communication. And, because members share so much personal information, marketers can tailor messages and applications to very specific and desirable target markets. For example, TD Canada Trust launched a Facebook application called Split It, an online calculator that allows roommates to divide household expenses. New Brunswick's Mount Allison University is using Facebook groups and student-made videos on YouTube commissioned and paid for by the university to recruit future students.[35]

The growing demand for social media has spawned new companies and social media divisions within larger Canadian advertising agencies as more mainstream organizations add social media to their suite of IMC tools.

Over time, technology will continue to improve, and other new means of communicating with consumers will be added to the IMC channel mix. For now, let's look at the steps in planning an IMC campaign that achieves the organization's strategic objectives.

Steps in Planning an IMC Campaign

LO **3**

Designing a successful IMC campaign requires much planning; Exhibit 15.4 shows some of the key steps in the planning process, each of which helps ensure that the intended message reaches the right audience and has the desired effect. As mentioned earlier, these steps can be used for all IMC tools. Let's examine each of these steps as they pertain to advertising specifically.

1. Identify Target Audience

The success of an advertising campaign depends on how well the advertiser can identify its target audience. Firms conduct research to identify their target audience, then use the information they gain to set the tone for the advertising program and help them select the media they will use to deliver the message to that audience.

During this research, firms must keep in mind that their target audience may or may not be the same as current users of the product. Think about jewellery. Research shows that in a typical year, some 43 percent of the North American adult population—more than 95 million people—purchase jewellery. Although women have a significantly higher purchase incidence (48 percent) and purchase more often than men (36 percent), men spend significantly more money on their jewellery purchases than do women. Perhaps it is no surprise that the majority of men's jewellery purchases are gifts.[36]

Some advertising messages also may be directed at portions of audiences who are not part of the marketer's target market but who participate in the purchase process. Chrysler, for instance, runs ads for its minivans during Saturday morning children's viewing hours. These ads are designed to build brand awareness on the part of the children, who, Chrysler hopes, will influence their parents' minivan choices.[37]

Who is the target audience for this ad, men or women?

2. Set Objectives

As with any strategic undertaking, firms need to understand the outcome they hope to achieve before they begin. These objectives can be short-term, such as generating inquiries, increasing awareness, and prompting trial. Or they can be long-term in nature, such as increasing sales, market share, and customer loyalty. Selling products and services was the primary and long-term goal of the Bell campaign, but in the short term, Bell needed to establish heightened brand awareness and purchase intentions. Thus, the campaign was designed to get consumers' attention first through television ads during the 2006 Winter Olympic Games. Both short- and long-term goals should be explicitly defined and measured. We discuss how firms measure IMC success later in this chapter.

Advertising campaign objectives are derived from the overall objectives of the marketing program and clarify the specific goals that the ads are designed to accomplish. Generally, these objectives appear in the **advertising plan**, a subsection of the

advertising plan
A section of the firm's overall marketing plan that explicitly outlines the objectives of the advertising campaign, how the campaign might accomplish those objectives, and how the firm can determine whether the campaign was successful.

| EXHIBIT | 15.4 | Steps in Planning an IMC Campaign |

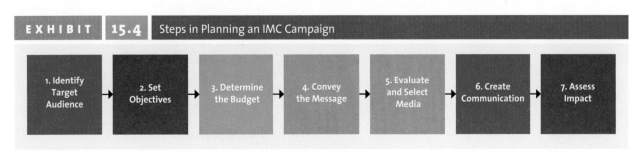

1. Identify Target Audience → 2. Set Objectives → 3. Determine the Budget → 4. Convey the Message → 5. Evaluate and Select Media → 6. Create Communication → 7. Assess Impact

firm's overall marketing plan that explicitly outlines the objectives of the advertising campaign, how the campaign might accomplish those objectives, and how the firm can determine whether the campaign was successful.[38] An advertising plan is crucial because it will later serve as the metric against which advertising success or failure is measured.

All advertising campaigns aim to achieve certain objectives: to inform, persuade, and remind customers. These objectives are examined in more depth in Chapter 16. Communication objectives also need to consider an ad's focus, for example, does the company hope to stimulate demand for a new product or service or to increase awareness for the company general?

To help determine communication objectives, many companies consider the buyer readiness stages shown in Exhibit 15.5A. At each stage of buyer readiness, consumers need information to make judgments which help them progress to the next stage in the process. Companies must ensure that prospective customers are aware of their products and services before they provide them with more details or knowledge in an effort to get them to like their offerings. Then they must build preference for their products and services over competitive offerings to gain a purchase commitment. Lastly, their marketing communications must convince prospective customers to buy.

Not all IMC campaign tools will move consumers to buy as shown in Exhibit 15.5B. For example, advertising may be a useful tool to build awareness and perhaps a bit of knowledge for a new product, but it may take a direct mail offer with a special incentive or a sales representative to convince someone to buy. As such, a mix of tools tailored to each company's unique products and services is required to move them from awareness to purchase.

When setting advertising objectives, the overarching strategy used is one of push versus pull. However, marketers also have to consider other factors such as the nature of the market (consumer versus business), the nature of the product (standardized versus custom or technologically complex), and the stage in the product life cycle. Generally, when advertising to consumers, the objective is a **pull strategy** in which the goal is to get consumers to *pull* the product into the supply chain by demanding it. **Push strategies** also exist and are designed to increase demand by focusing on wholesalers,

pull strategy
Designed to get consumers to pull the product into the supply chain by demanding it.

push strategy
Designed to increase demand by motivating sellers—wholesalers, distributors, or salespeople—to highlight the product, rather than the products of competitors, and thereby push the product onto consumers.

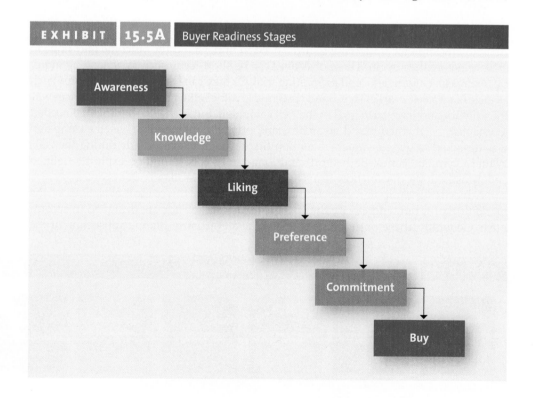

EXHIBIT 15.5A Buyer Readiness Stages

- Awareness
- Knowledge
- Liking
- Preference
- Commitment
- Buy

distributors, or salespeople. These campaigns attempt to motivate the seller to highlight the product, rather than the products of competitors, and thereby push the product onto consumers.

Once the advertising campaign's objectives are defined, the firm sets the advertising budget.

3. Determine the Budget

Firms use a variety of methods to plan their marketing communications budgets. Because all the methods of setting a promotional budget have both advantages and disadvantages, no one method should be used in isolation.[39]

The **objective-and-task method** determines the budget required to undertake specific tasks to accomplish communication objectives. To use this method, marketers first establish a set of communication objectives, then determine which media best reach the target market and how much it will cost to run the number and types of communications necessary to achieve the objectives. This process—set objectives, choose media, and determine costs—must be repeated for each product or service. The sum of all the individual communication plan budgets becomes the firm's total marketing communications budget. In addition to the objective-and-task method, three **rule-of-thumb methods** (competitive parity, percentage-of-sales, and affordable budgeting) can be used to set budgets (see Exhibit 15.6).

These rule-of-thumb methods use prior sales and communication activities to determine the present communication budget. Although they are easy to implement, they obviously have various limitations, as noted in the exhibit. While small companies often

This ad informs consumers about Winners' accessories selection.

objective-and-task method
An IMC budgeting method that determines the cost required to undertake specific tasks to accomplish communication objectives; process entails setting objectives, choosing media, and determining costs.

rule-of-thumb methods
Budgeting methods that bases the IMC budget on either the firm's share of the market in relation to competition, a fixed percentage of forecasted sales, or what is left after other operating costs and forecasted sales have been budgeted.

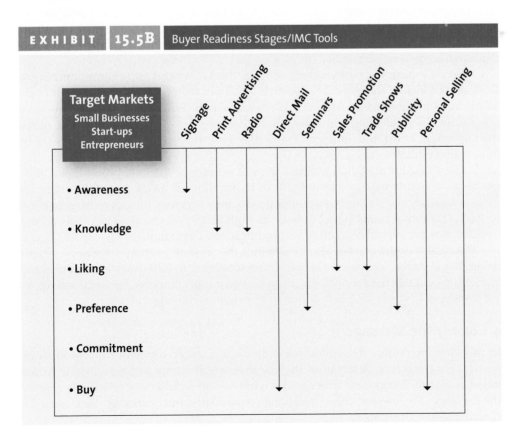

EXHIBIT 15.5B Buyer Readiness Stages/IMC Tools

EXHIBIT 15.6	Rule-of-Thumb Methods	
Method	**Definition**	**Limitations**
Competitive parity	The communication budget is set so that the firm's share of communication expenses equals its share of the market.	• Does not allow firms to exploit the unique opportunities or problems they confront in a market. • If all competitors use this method to set communication budgets, their market shares will stay approximately the same over time.
Percentage-of-sales	The communication budget is a fixed percentage of forecasted sales.	• Assumes the same percentage used in the past, or by competitors, is still appropriate for the firm. • Does not take into account new plans (e.g., to introduce a new line of products in the current year).
Affordable budgeting	Marketers forecast their sales and expenses, excluding communication, during the budgeting period. The difference between the forecast sales and expenses plus desired profit is reserved for the communication budget. That is, the communication budget is the money available after operating costs and profits have been budgeted.	• Assumes communication expenses do not stimulate sales and profit.

use the affordable budgeting method, it generally results in underspending and thus may not accomplish the company's sales objectives. Large companies such as Coca-Cola and Pepsi may use the competitive parity method. However, this method is setting a budget based on market share which may result in Pepsi being outspent. The percentage-of-sales method is popular as well and there are sometimes standard percentages used in some product categories as shown in Exhibit 15.7. Since everyone needs to eat, the grocery industry needs to spend only a small percent—around 1 percent—of its revenues on advertising whereas the toy and game industry must spend around 11 percent. Clearly, budgeting is not a simple process. It may take several rounds of negotiations among the various managers, who are each competing for resources for their own areas of responsibility.

When selecting the various budgeting methods for marketing communications, firms must consider the role that advertising plays in their attempt to meet their overall promotional objectives. Second, advertising expenditures vary over the course of the product life cycle, with considerably higher levels of spending during the introduction stage. Third, the nature of the market and the product influence the size of advertising budgets.

Advertising for the Scion was less than 14 percent of the total promotional budget because Toyota used so many kinds of nontraditional media to get the attention of its young target customers. For other products or services, the advertising portion of the total promotional budget may be as high as 95 percent. It all depends on the objectives of the overall marketing communications campaign.

The nature of the market also determines the amount of money spent on advertising. For instance, less money is spent on advertising in B2B (business-to-business) marketing contexts than in B2C (business-to-consumer) markets. Personal selling, as we discuss in Chapter 16, likely is more important in B2B markets.

4. Convey the Message

In this step, marketers determine what they want to convey about the product or service. First, the firm determines the key message it wants to communicate to the target audience. Second, the firm decides what appeal would most effectively convey the message. We present these decisions sequentially, but in reality, they must be considered simultaneously.

EXHIBIT **15.7** Advertising Spending as a Percent of Sales for Illustrative Product Categories

PRODUCERS:

Category	Value
Petroleum refining	0.7
Computers and office equipment	1.1
Dairy products	1.3
Motor vehicles and care bodies	2.2
Greeting cards	2.4
Investment advice	2.5
Plastic products	2.6
Cable and other pay TV services	3.3
Sporting and athletic goods	3.9
Footwear (except rubber)	4.6
Soft drinks, water	4.8
Business services	5.3
Malt beverages	8.0
Transportation services	9.8
Games and toys	11.1
Perfume and cosmetics	11.2
Soap and detergent	11.3

RETAILERS:

Category	Value
Grocery stores	1.3
Hotels and motels	1.4
Women's clothing stores	3.7
Eating places	3.8
Furniture stores	5.0
Video tape rental	5.8
Catalogue, mail-order houses	8.4
Amusement parks	12.8

Advertising as a percent of sales

The Message The message provides the target audience with reasons to respond in the desired way. A logical starting point for deciding on the advertising message is to tout the key benefits of the product or service. The message should communicate its problem-solving ability clearly and in a compelling fashion. In this context, advertisers must remember that products and services solve problems, whether real or perceived. That is, people are not looking for 1/4-inch drill bits; they are looking for 1/4-inch holes.[40] Because there are many ways to make a 1/4-inch hole, a firm like Black and Decker must convey to consumers that its drill bit is the best way to get that hole.

Another common strategy differentiates a product by establishing its unique benefits. This distinction forms the basis for the **unique selling proposition (USP)**,

Is Black and Decker doing a good job of selling a solution?

unique selling proposition (USP)

A strategy of differentiating a product by communicating its unique attributes; often becomes the common theme or slogan in the entire advertising campaign.

which is often the common theme or slogan in an advertising campaign. Briefly, a good USP communicates the unique attributes of the product and thereby becomes a snapshot of the entire campaign. Some of the most famous USPs include the following:

Ford....Built Tough

Nokia....Connecting People

FedEx....Guaranteed Overnight

The selling proposition communicated by the advertising must be not only *unique* to the brand but also *meaningful* to the consumer; it furthermore must be *sustainable* over time, even with repetition.

LO **4**   **The Appeal**   Advertisers also use different appeals to portray their product or service. We discuss two categories: rational (cognitive) and emotional (affective). Moral appeals are sometimes considered as a third category. Marketers, especially those who work in nonprofit organizations, often use this type of message. Since moral appeals can be rational or emotional, they are not addressed as a separate category.

Rational Appeals   **Rational appeals** help consumers make purchase decisions by offering factual information and strong arguments built around relevant issues that encourage consumers to evaluate the brand favourably on the basis of the key benefits it provides.[41] Rational appeals focus on consumers' sense of reasoning, logic, and learning. Kimberly-Clark, for example, relies heavily on rational appeals to sell Kleenex Anti-Viral tissues. Note the copy used on the company's website:

Only KLEENEX® Anti-Viral Tissue has a moisture-activated middle layer that is scientifically proven to kill cold and flu viruses. When moisture from a runny nose, cough or sneeze comes in contact with KLEENEX® Anti-Viral Tissue's special middle layer, cold and flu viruses are trapped and killed.[42]

This appeal is perfectly suited to this type of product. The source of its competitive advantage is a tangible feature of the product. By stressing the superior benefits of this product over regular facial tissue, the advertising copy directly delivers a rational persuasive message.[43]

Emotional Appeals   An **emotional appeal** aims to satisfy consumers' emotional desires rather than their utilitarian needs. The key to a successful emotional appeal is the use of emotion to create a bond between the consumer and the

This ad for KLEENEX® Anti-Viral Tissue provides a rational appeal that helps consumers make purchase decisions based on factual information and strong favourable arguments.

brand. The emotions most often invoked in advertising include fear, safety, humour, happiness, love, comfort, and nostalgia. Companies must pay attention to cultural influences since humour is not perceived the same way across different cultural groups and sexual appeals are taboo in some cultures.

Kleenex sponsors the TNT Tearjerker Movie that features dramatic films that are renowned for the misty eyes, furtive nose-blowing, and downright weepiness that they inspire in their audiences.

Let's look again at Kimberly-Clark's Kleenex line; it uses a completely different and emotional appeal for its regular facial tissue. Facial tissues can be closely tied to emotional moments that create the need to wipe away tears of joy or sorrow, and Kleenex attempts to reinforce this emotional trigger by sponsoring the TNT Tearjerker Movie.

Unlike the Anti-Viral campaign, this campaign relies on the implied need for Kleenex during dramatic films. Tangible product features, no longer the persuasive mechanism used to deliver the selling message as they are in rational appeals, do not even appear in the emotional appeal. There are many different types of appeals ranging from sex appeal (e.g., Tag Body Spray), need for affiliation, need for guidance (e.g., Betty Crocker), and attention (e.g., cosmetics).[44]

5. Evaluate and Select Media

LO **5**

The content of an advertisement is tied closely to the characteristics of the media that firms select to carry the message, and vice versa. **Media planning** refers to the process of evaluating and selecting the **media mix**—the combination of the media used and the frequency of advertising in each medium—that will deliver a clear, consistent, compelling message to the intended audience.[45] For example, Zellers may determine that a heavy dose of television, radio, print, and billboards is appropriate for the back to school selling season between August and September each year.

Because the **media buy**, the actual purchase of airtime or print pages, is generally the largest expense in the advertising budget, marketers must make their decisions carefully. Television advertising is by far the most expensive. Total ad spending in Canada is $12.6 billion per year. Advertising expenditures per medium have remained roughly constant for some time: television 24 percent, direct mail 12 percent, newspapers 21 percent, radio 10 percent, yellow pages 10 percent, magazines 5 percent, and the Internet 4 percent. Other media, such as out-of-home advertising (e.g., billboards, bus wraps, posters) account for the remainder.[46] To characterize these various types of media, we again use a dichotomy: mass and niche media.

Mass and Niche Media   **Mass media** channels include national newspapers, magazines, radio, and television and are ideal for reaching large numbers of anonymous audience members. **Niche media** channels are more focused and generally used to reach narrower segments, often with unique demographic characteristics or interests. Cable television, direct mail, and specialty magazines such as *Skateboarder* or *Cosmo-Girl* all provide examples of niche media. In some cases, niche media offer advertisers the opportunity to change and even personalize their messages, which is generally not an option with mass media. For example, magazine advertisers can print response cards with the name of the subscriber already on the card or change advertisements to reflect local differences, such as climate or preferences.

media planning
The process of evaluating and selecting the *media mix* that will deliver a clear, consistent, compelling message to the intended audience.

media mix
The combination of the media used and the frequency of advertising in each medium.

media buy
The actual purchase of airtime or print pages.

mass media
Channels that are ideal for reaching large numbers of anonymous audience members; include national newspapers, magazines, radio, and television.

niche media
Channels that are focused and generally used to reach narrow segments, often with unique demographic characteristics or interests.

When Apple teamed up with Irish rock band U2 to create an iPod special edition, it relied heavily on television advertising because of its strong visual and auditory effects.

gross rating points (GRP) Measure used for various media advertising—print, radio, or television; *GRP = reach × frequency.*

Choosing the Right Medium   For each class of media, each alternative has specific characteristics that make it suitable for meeting specific objectives (see Exhibit 15.8). For example, consumers use different media for different purposes, to which advertisers should match their messages. Television is used primarily for escapism and entertainment, so most television advertising relies on a mix of visual and auditory techniques. When Apple teamed up with the Irish rock band U2 to create an iPod special edition, it relied heavily on television advertising to introduce the product, which enabled Apple to create powerful visual images that matched the powerful soundtrack of U2's song "Vertigo" in a memorable ad without providing any detail about the advertised product or even informing viewers what an iPod was.

Communication media also vary in their ability to reach the desired audience. For instance, radio is a good medium for products such as grocery purchases or fast food because many consumers decide what to purchase either on the way to the store or while in the store. Because many people listen to the radio in their cars, it becomes a highly effective means to reach consumers at a crucial point in their decision process. As we discussed in this chapter, each medium also varies in its reach and frequency. Advertisers can determine how effective their media mix has been in reaching their target audience by calculating the total **gross rating points (GRP)** (reach × frequency) of the advertising schedule, which we discuss next.

EXHIBIT 15.8	**Types of Media Available for Advertising**	
MEDIUM	**ADVANTAGES**	**DISADVANTAGES**
Television	• Has wide reach. • Incorporates sound and video.	• Has high cost. • Has cluttered airways. • Has more potential spillover.
Radio	• Is relatively inexpensive. • Can be selectively targeted. • Has wide reach.	• No video limits presentation. • Consumers give less focused attention than TV. • Exposure periods are short.
Magazines	• Is very targeted. • Subscribers pass along to others.	• Is relatively inflexible. • Has long lead times.
Newspapers	• Is flexible. • Is timely. • Can localize.	• Can be expensive in some markets. • Involves potential loss of control over placement. • Advertisements have short life span.
Internet	• Can be linked to detailed content. • Is highly flexible and interactive. • Allows for specific targeting.	• Costs not easily comparable to other media. • Is becoming cluttered. • Blocking software prohibits delivery.
Outdoors	• Is relatively inexpensive. • Offers opportunities for repeat exposure. • Is flexible.	• Is not easily targeted. • Has placement problems in some markets. • Exposure time is very short.
Direct Mail	• Is highly targeted. • Is flexible. • Allows for personalization.	• Is relatively expensive. • Is a cluttered environment. • Is often considered "junk mail."

Determining the Advertising Schedule Another important decision for the media planner is the **advertising schedule**, which specifies the timing and duration of advertising. There are three types of schedules:[47]

- A **continuous** schedule runs steadily throughout the year and therefore is suited to products and services that are consumed continually at relatively steady rates and that require a steady level of persuasive and/or reminder advertising. For example, Procter & Gamble advertises its Tide brand of laundry detergent continuously.

- **Flighting** refers to an advertising schedule implemented in spurts, with periods of heavy advertising followed by periods of no advertising. This pattern generally functions for products whose demand fluctuates, such as tennis racquets, which manufacturers may advertise heavily in the months leading up to and during the summer.

- **Pulsing** combines the continuous and flighting schedules by maintaining a base level of advertising but increasing advertising intensity during certain periods. For example, furniture retailer, Ikea, advertises throughout the year but boosts its advertising expenditures to promote school supplies in August.

Ikea uses a pulsing strategy when they set their advertising schedule. They advertise throughout the year, but have more advertising directed at the back-to-school market in August.

6. Create Communication

After the advertiser has decided on the message, type of ad, and appeal, its attention must shift to the actual creation of the advertisement. During this step, the message and appeal are translated creatively into words, pictures, colours, and/or music. Often, the execution style for the ad will dictate the type of medium used to deliver the message. For example, in one ad campaign, crash tests demonstrating the safety of Toyota cars rely on the visual impact of the crash, softened by children who egg the tester to "Do it again, Bob." This style of execution only works on television. Therefore, it is common for advertisers to make decisions about their message and appeal, the appropriate medium, and the best execution concurrently.

Furthermore, advertisers often employ a combination of media to deliver a message. In such cases, they must maintain consistency across the execution styles so that the different executions deliver a consistent and compelling message to the target audience.

Although creativity plays a major role in the execution stage, advertisers must remain careful not to let their creativity overshadow the message. Whatever the execution style, the advertisement must be able to attract the audience's attention, provide a reason for the audience to spend its time viewing the advertisement, and accomplish what it set out to do. In the end, the execution style must match the medium and objectives. An additional complication in Canada is the necessity to design advertising messages in two official languages. And, as mentioned earlier, Canada's multicultural population means that companies must carefully consider cultural influences so as not to alienate groups with inappropriate messages.

Print advertising can be especially difficult because it is a static medium: no sound, no motion, only one dimension. The advertiser must convey its message using compelling visuals and limited text. One ad in the Stupid.ca campaign was part of a very effective print and Web campaign, so effective that it won two Gold awards at the Cassies, Canadian Advertising Success Stories.

advertising schedule
The specification of the timing and duration of advertising.

continuous advertising schedule
Runs steadily throughout the year and therefore is suited to products and services that are consumed continually at relatively steady rates and that require a steady level of persuasive or reminder advertising.

flighting advertising schedule
An advertising schedule implemented in spurts, with periods of heavy advertising followed by periods of no advertising.

pulsing advertising schedule
Combines the continuous and flighting schedules by maintaining a base level of advertising but increasing advertising intensity during certain periods.

*As the spokesperson
for the Jell-O brand,
Bill Cosby's voice and
image have kept the
brand's image credible,
trustworthy, and
likeable for over
30 years.*

The campaign was based on insights that to kids, parents are lame, teachers are pathetic, and the government is worse. A single, blunt message was needed that kids would relate to. This message, developed in part by an advisory panel of kids, boiled down to a single defining thought: Smoking is just about the stupidest thing you can do. It was delivered in a tone that was honest and funny, not preachy. The results were positive with 91 percent of kids saying that the ads would help prevent their peers from smoking. Better yet, a Statistics Canada study showed that smoking rates declined by 2 percent in 12- to 17-year-olds, as well as a 9-percent increase in the number who never started to smoke at all.[48]

For radio and television, some important execution elements include identifying the appropriate talent (actors or singers) to deliver the message and choosing the correct music and visuals. In 1974, when Jell-O brand was introducing its pudding line, it looked for a spokesperson viewed as credible, trustworthy, and likeable; it found Bill Cosby.[49] For more than 30 years, Cosby has been the voice and image of the Jell-O brand because he possesses all the features Jell-O was looking for, along with a voice and image that are immediately recognizable. Cosby has been featured in more than 70 television, 50 radio, and innumerable print advertisements for the pudding. This continuing relationship has made Cosby the longest-running active spokesperson for any brand.

7. Assess Impact

pretesting
Assessments performed before an ad campaign is implemented to ensure that the various elements are working in an integrated fashion and doing what they are intended to do.

tracking
Includes monitoring key indicators, such as daily or weekly sales volume, while the advertisement is running to shed light on any problems with the message or the medium.

posttesting
The evaluation of an IMC campaign's impact after it has been implemented.

The effectiveness of an advertising campaign must be assessed before, during, and after the campaign has run. **Pretesting** refers to assessments performed before an ad campaign is implemented to ensure that the various tools are working in an integrated fashion and doing what they are intended to do.[50] **Tracking** includes monitoring key indicators, such as daily or weekly sales volume, while the advertisement is running to shed light on any problems with the message or the medium. **Posttesting** is the evaluation of the campaign's impact after it has been implemented. At this last stage, advertisers assess the sales and/or communication impact of the advertisement or campaign.

Measuring sales impact can be especially challenging because of the many influences other than advertising on consumers' choices, purchase behaviour, and attitudes. These influences include the level of competitors' advertising, economic conditions in the target market, sociocultural changes, and even the weather, all of which can influence consumer purchasing behaviour. Advertisers must try to identify these influences and isolate those of the particular advertising campaign.

For frequently purchased consumer goods in the maturity stage of the PLC, such as cola, sales volume offers a good indicator of advertising effectiveness. Because their sales are relatively stable, and if we assume that the other elements of the marketing mix and the environment have not changed, we can attribute changes in sales volume to changes in advertising.

For other types of goods in other stages of the PLC, sales data offer but one of the many indicators that marketers need to examine to determine advertising effectiveness. For instance, in high growth markets, sales growth alone can be misleading because the market as a whole is growing. In such a situation, marketers measure sales relative to those of competitors to determine their relative market share. Firms find creative ways to identify advertising effectiveness; for example, digital cable allows them to present a specific advertisement to certain neighbourhoods and then track sales by local or regional retailers.

Some product categories experience so many influences that it is almost impossible to identify advertising's contribution to any individual consumer's choice to purchase a particular product, especially for addictive products such as cigarettes and alcohol or those with potentially negative health consequences, such as fast food or high-sugar breakfast cereals. The EU is even facing demand for a ban on fast-food ads and other forms of food advertising to children. Although many people firmly believe that advertising for these products contributes significantly to obesity in children, academic research has not been able to show a causal relationship. Other factors, such as parental and peer influence, tend to reflect a higher causality relationship than does advertising.[51]

Results: Measuring IMC Success

LO **6**

Earlier we examined how marketers set strategic goals before implementing any IMC campaign. Once a firm has decided how to set its budget for marketing communications and its campaigns have been developed and implemented, it reaches the point that it must measure the success of the campaigns. Each step in the IMC process can be measured to determine how effective it has been in motivating consumers to move to the next step in the buying process. However, the **lagged effect** influences and complicates marketers' evaluations of a promotion's effectiveness, as well as the best way to allocate marketing communications budgets. Because of the cumulative effect of marketing communications, it may take several exposures before consumers are moved to buy, so firms cannot expect too much too soon. They must invest in the marketing communications campaign with the idea that it may not reach its full potential for some time. In the same way, if firms cut marketing communications expenditures, it may take time before they experience a decrease in sales.

When measuring IMC success, the firm should examine when and how often consumers have been exposed to various marketing communications. Specifically, they use measures of *frequency* and *reach* to gauge consumers' *exposure* to marketing communications. For most products and situations, a single exposure to a communication is hardly enough to generate the desired response. Therefore, marketers measure the **frequency** of exposure—how often the target audience is exposed to a

lagged effect
A delayed response to a marketing communication campaign.

frequency
Measure of how often the audience is exposed to a communication within a specified period of time.

reach
Measure of consumers' exposure to marketing communications; the percentage of the target population exposed to a specific marketing communication, such as an advertisement, at least once.

communication within a specified period of time. The other measure used to determine consumers' exposure to marketing communications is **reach**, which describes the percentage of the target population exposed to a specific marketing communication, such as an advertisement, at least once.[52] Marketing communications managers usually state their media objectives in terms of gross rating points (GRP), which represents reach multiplied by frequency (GRP = reach × frequency).

GRP can be measured for print, radio, or television, but when comparing them, they must refer to the same medium. Suppose that Unilever, the maker of Sunsilk, places five advertisements in *Flare* magazine, which reaches 50 percent of the "fashion forward" target segment. The total GRP generated by these five magazine advertisements is 50 reach × 5 advertisements = 250 GRP. Now suppose Sunsilk includes 15 television ads as part of the same campaign, run during the program *Lost*, which has a rating of 9.2. The total GRP generated by these 15 advertisements is 138 (9.2 × 15 = 138). However, advertisements typically appear during more than one television program, so the total GRP equals the sum of the GRP generated by each program.

Although GRP is an adequate measure for television and radio advertisements, assessing the effectiveness of any Web-based communications efforts in an IMC campaign generally requires Web tracking software to indicate how much time viewers spend on particular Web pages and the number of pages they view. **Click-through tracking** measures how many times users click on banner advertising on websites. Online couponing is a promotional Web technique in which consumers print a coupon directly from a site and then redeem the coupon in a store. Another promotional Web technique is online referring, in which consumers fill out an interest or order form and are referred to an offline dealer or firm that offers the product or service of interest. All these methods can be easily measured and assessed.

As IMC programs become more sophisticated, measurement is not the only concern. There are a host of legal and ethical issues that marketers need to worry about, which we will examine in the next chapter.

click-through tracking
A way to measure how many times users click on banner advertising on websites.

Learning Objectives Review

1) Outline the process used to communicate with consumers

2) Explain the six tools of integrated marketing communication campaigns

3) Understand the steps in planning an integrated marketing communication campaign

4) Describe what appeals advertisers use to get customers' attention

5) Identify how firms determine which media to use

6) Describe how firms plan for and measure integrated marketing communications (IMC) success

1) On the surface, marketing communications look simple: People become aware of a product or service, then grow interested, then desire it, and finally take an action such as purchasing it. But it isn't quite that simple. First, there is the cumulative effect of marketing communications. Ads from the past, for instance, help influence consumers' actions in the future. Second, everyone interprets commercial messages differently, thus making it difficult for a marketer to be assured that a particular, clear signal is getting through. Third, to be effective, marketers must adjust their messages to fit the media and the receiver's knowledge level.

2) The six tools of IMC campaigns are advertising, personal selling, sales promotions, direct response marketing, public relations, and electronic media. In the past, most of a firm's promotional budget was spent on advertising. Although advertising still demands a sizable portion, other media channels have taken up a substantial chunk of the total budget. While the cost of personal selling to reach potential customers directly is quite high, it remains the best and most efficient way to sell certain products and services. Sales promotions are incentives or programs that promote immediate purchase. Many drive sales in the short run, while others exist as part of a company's customer loyalty programs. Direct marketing expenditures are growing because the number of direct marketing media options has increased in recent years. While outbound telephone calls remain a popular form of direct marketing, mail, infomercials, alternative media such as catalogues, the Internet, e-mail, and other new communication technologies such as PDAs and cell phones are all expanding. Public relations also has become increasingly important as other media forms become more expensive and as consumers grow more skeptical of commercial messages. Finally, the Internet has spawned some innovative new ways to promote products and services.

3) Firms (1) identify their target market; (2) set objectives; (3) set the budget; (4) depict their product or service; (5) evaluate and select the media; (6) create the ad; and (7) assess the impact of the ad.

4) Advertising appeals are either rational or emotional. Rational appeals influence purchase decisions with factual information and strong arguments built around relevant key benefits that encourage consumers to evaluate the brand favourably. Emotional appeals indicate how the product satisfies emotional desires rather than utilitarian needs.

5) Firms can use mass media channels like newspapers or television to reach large numbers of anonymous audience members. Niche media, such as cable television, direct mail, and specialty magazines, are generally used to reach narrower segments with unique demographic characteristics or interests. When choosing the media, firms must match their objectives to the media. Also, certain media are better at reaching a particular target audience than others.

6) Planning an IMC budget should encompass a combination of factors. The process could start by setting the overall IMC budget as a percentage of sales. Then, the firm might examine what other firms are spending on similar product categories. When it gets down to planning the budget for individual product categories or items, the firm should set its objectives for the campaign and allocate enough money to meet those objectives.

Marketers rely on a mix of traditional and nontraditional measures to determine IMC success. Because potential customers generally need to be exposed to IMC messages several times before they will buy, firms estimate the degree to which customers are exposed to a message by multiplying frequency (the number of times an audience is exposed to a message) by reach (the percentage of the target population exposed to a specific marketing communication). Measuring Internet IMC effectiveness requires different measures, such as click-through tracking that measures how many times users click on banner advertising on websites.

Key Terms

- advertising, 423
- advertising plan, 431
- advertising schedule, 439
- blog (weblog or Web log), 428
- cause-related marketing, 426
- click-through tracking, 442
- communication channel, 421
- continuous advertising schedule, 439
- deceptive advertising, 421
- decoding, 421
- direct response marketing, 424
- electronic media, 428
- emotional appeal, 436
- encoding, 420
- event sponsorship, 427

- feedback loop, 422
- flighting advertising schedule, 439
- frequency, 441
- gross rating points (GRP), 438
- integrated marketing communications (IMC), 418
- lagged effect, 441
- mass media, 437
- media buy, 437
- media mix, 437
- media planning, 437
- niche media, 437
- noise, 421
- objective-and-task method, 433
- personal selling, 424
- posttesting, 440

- pretesting, 440
- public relations, 426
- pull strategy, 432
- pulsing advertising schedule, 439
- push strategy, 432
- rational appeal, 436
- reach, 442
- receiver, 421
- rule-of-thumb methods, 433
- sales promotions, 424
- sender, 419
- tracking, 440
- transmitter, 420
- unique selling proposition (USP), 435

Concept Review

1. Briefly describe the marketing communication process and identify the possible sources of noise at each stage of the process.

2. What is meant by integrated marketing communication?

3. Describe the integrated marketing communication tools marketers use in campaigns.

4. Explain the differences between advertising and sales promotion.

5. Describe some of the elements in a PR Toolkit. Why would a company include PR in its IMC mix?

6. Identify some of the key electronic media that marketers are using to communicate with their customers. How are these media changing the nature of the communication between the firm and its customers?

7. What are the steps involved in developing an IMC campaign? Briefly explain each step.

8. Describe why a company would use a pull strategy versus a push strategy in its marketing communications.

9. Briefly describe the two main appeals of advertising.

10. Explain the three different ways marketers use to measure the success of their marketing communications? What types of information does each method provide?

Marketing Applications

1. The designer jean company Juicy Couture has embarked on a new IMC strategy. It has chosen to advertise on the NBC *Nightly News* and in *Time* magazine. The message is designed to announce new styles for the season and uses a 17-year-old woman as the model. Evaluate this strategy.

2. It's holiday time, and you've decided to purchase a jewellery item for the person of your choice at Birks. Evaluate how Birks' advertising, personal selling, public relations, and electronic media might influence your purchase decision. How might the relative importance of each of these IMC tools be different if your parents were making the purchase?

3. Choose one of the ads featured in this book and explain whether it uses a rational appeal or an emotional appeal.

4. Bernard's, a local furniture company, target markets college and university students with apartments and households of young people purchasing their first furniture items. If you worked for Bernard's, what type of media would you use for your advertising campaign? Justify your answer.

5. Should Bernard's use continuous, pulsing, or flighting for its advertising schedule? Why?

6. Suppose you saw your instructor for this course being interviewed on TV about the impact of gift certificates on upcoming holiday's sales. Is this interview part of your university's IMC program? If so, do you believe it benefits the university? How?

7. A retail store places an ad in the local newspaper for capri pants. The sales of the featured pants increase significantly for the next two weeks; sales in the rest of the sportswear department go up as well. What do you think are the short- and long-term objectives of the ad? Justify your answer.

8. As an intern for Michelin tires, you have been asked to develop an IMC budget. The objective of the IMC strategy is to raise Michelin's market share by 5 percent in Canada in the next 18 months. Your manager explains, "It's real simple; just increase the budget 5 percent over last year's." Evaluate your manager's strategy.

9. What makes marketing communication deceptive? What are the features of stealth marketing campaigns that make them vulnerable to charges of deception?

10. You were sitting in the school cafeteria yesterday, and a young man from your marketing class, whom you don't know well, asked if he could sit down. He then started telling you about this very cool new Microsoft product that helps you organize your class notes. Although you recognize the merit in the product, you later find out that he works for Microsoft. Do you believe his action constitutes an ethical IMC strategy? How will it affect your attitude toward Microsoft and the potential that you will purchase the product?

Net Savvy

1. Visit www.taxi.ca to view the website of Taxi, a well-known IMC consulting firm. The site contains a lot of information about what IMC is and how it can be used effectively by a wide variety of companies. Of particular interest is the case studies section. Locate the case studies link, read a case, and discuss the following: What were the goals of the IMC campaign? Which IMC components were used in that particular campaign? How do those components contribute to the success of the IMC campaign in achieving its stated goals?

2. The Canadian Marketing Association is the primary source of information about direct marketing activities for both academics and practitioners. The website for the CMA, at www.the-cma.org/, contains a wealth of information about direct marketing practices and self-regulation. How many different target markets does the CMA address on its home page? Click on the "Consumer Information" tab. What services does the CMA provide for consumers? Why do you think it offers those services? Now return to the home page and click on the "Marketing Resources" tab and check out some of the articles, case studies, or white papers and reports.

Chapter Case Study

DOVE WIDENS DEFINITION OF BEAUTY IN INTEGRATED CAMPAIGN

In a world where media depictions of beauty are based on physical attractiveness and airbrushed images, the Dove Campaign for Real Beauty is a breath of fresh air. The campaign, which uses real women not models, was launched by Unilever in Canada in early 2004.

Based on research that came out of a global study of 3200 women, Unilever learned that 76 percent wished there were more realistic portrayals of beauty. Only two percent of women surveyed felt comfortable calling themselves 'beautiful.'

According to Aleksandra Hoszowski, the assistant brand manager on the Dove brand, Unilever's approach to integrated marketing communications is to build a campaign around one true consumer insight. The insight that sprang from the research study was that the current definition of beauty was too narrow and that women wanted it to change. Hoszowski says the Dove mission is to widen the definition of beauty. The Campaign for Real Beauty is based on a belief that beauty comes in different shapes, sizes, ages, and that real beauty can be genuinely stunning.

Work on the campaign began with Unilever sending letters to 58 well-known female photographers around the world asking "What do you think defines a beautiful woman?" Sharon MacLeod, the marketing manager for Dove Canada, says they were overwhelmed with the response and submissions of photos of women and children of all ages, sizes, and ethnic backgrounds. A photo exhibition was launched with 67 of the photos (including some by Annie Leibovitz) all provided at no charge. Donations by attendees went to the Dove Self-Esteem Fund, created to help women and girls celebrate their individual beauty.

As the campaign evolved, the message was delivered via a variety of marketing communication tools: print and TV ads, billboards, free-standing inserts, website, sampling, direct mail, in-store promotion, and public relations.

A good integrated marketing communication strategy must ensure that each tool supports and extends the same integrated and consistent message that is delivered by all the other elements in the campaign. Some people erroneously think that integrated marketing communications means that you always have to do the same thing. But MacLeod says you do the same thing in a different way so that you deliver an integrated message. It's important to have a consistent look, feel and tone. "We're very conscious about Dove's tone of voice," she says. "Dove's brand personality is honest, straight forward, simple. She talks to you like a friend. There's never any puffery."

Examine any of the Dove communications and it's easy to see consistency with predominantly white backgrounds, simple designs, and real women. The overriding message is "Be beautiful, be yourself."

The results of the campaign are impressive with 100 percent of people who attended the photo exhibit making a link back to the Dove brand. There were 50,000 hits to campaignforrealbeauty.ca in its first two months. Unilever had to add staff to its call centre as interest generated in the campaign was the highest in the company's history.

But more importantly, according to MacLeod, is that the campaign got people talking. It engaged them in debate, helping to reframe how people think about beauty. One interactive billboard in downtown Toronto showed a woman in a black dress asked the question "Fat or Fab?" People could call a 1-800 number to submit their vote. In the end, 51 percent said the woman was fat. Voting for the same campaign on the Web resulted in 74 percent saying "Fab."

The "Little Girls" television ad, developed in Canada, was aired on the 2006 Superbowl as a way of starting a dialogue between women and the game's predominantly male audience.

But the campaign didn't stop there. It's a long-term initiative and continues to evolve as Unilever listens to women and hears what they have to say. For example, MacLeod says the global study pointed out how a lack of self-esteem affects young girls and holds them back from being successful in life. As a result, Dove funded a new website (www.realme.ca) developed by the National Eating Disorder Information Centre, designed for young women to explore issues related to self worth and body image.

Dove hosted Real Beauty Workshops for girls aged eight to 12 in major cities across Canada in the fall of 2006. MacLeod says the workshops were designed to help an adult female role model foster self-esteem in girls. In 2007, Dove launched a program with Shoppers Drug Mart allowing customers to collect bonus Optimum points when buying Dove products. It also introduced Pro-Age, a new line of Dove products. IMC initiatives for this new product dovetail with existing communications.

While the campaign has been expensive, the investment has paid off many times over as a result of the publicity it generated. But the real payoff may come from Dove's role in changing how young girls grow up defining real beauty.

The Dove Campaign for Real Beauty was launched by a photo exhibition in the Toronto Eaton's Centre (above). The campaign achieved consistency by using predominantly white backgrounds, simple designs, and real women not models (below).

Case Questions

1. The Dove Campaign for Real Beauty set an objective to widen the definition of beauty versus selling products. How did using an integrated marketing communication campaign help to achieve this objective?

2. In what ways did Dove create value for its target market?

3. The campaign used advertising, however, also received a lot of publicity as time went on. What integrated marketing communication tools will be the most important for this campaign in the future?

LEARNING OBJECTIVES

After studying this chapter, you should be able to:

LO **1** Describe advertising and the objectives of advertising

LO **2** Understand the legal and ethical issues of concern to advertisers

LO **3** Explain how sales promotions supplement a firm's IMC strategy

LO **4** Understand how personal selling adds value

LO **5** Identify the steps in the personal selling process

Advertising, Sales Promotions, and Personal Selling

anadian stock car racing aficionados cheered the news that their favourite brand of sports entertainment—NASCAR racing—would be available in Canada rather than only in the U.S. A multi-year sponsorship deal launched the NASCAR Canadian Tire Series in the spring of 2007. Canadian Tire is the title sponsor of the series, which replaces the CASCAR Super Series.

For Canadian Tire, the country's leading automotive retailer, the sponsorship deal was the perfect promotional opportunity. NASCAR races are the number one motorsport series on television in Canada. There are currently 5.8 million fans in Canada, or about one-quarter of the adult population, with the average Canadian NASCAR fan having followed the sport for approximately 10 years.[1] TSN, which broadcasts the series in Canada, recorded record ratings for its coverage of the 2006 NASCAR series with average Canadian audiences of 332,000 viewers, up 15 percent from the previous year.

The sponsorship deal establishes Canadian Tire as the official automotive retailer of NASCAR in Canada. Canadian Tire shoppers will benefit from exclusive customer promotions, seasonal marketing programs, national advertising, and in-store programs with NASCAR. Contests generate excitement, too. Shoppers who bought a quart of Mobil 1 oil could enter to win a Corvette. Another contest offered the chance to win a trip for two to the NASCAR Nextel Cup Series Dickies 500 Race at the Texas Motor Speedway to shoppers who bought a case of Coke.

The agreement also provides Canadian Tire with the opportunity to increase its in-store product assortment. In the United States, the average NASCAR fan spends $500 a year on memorabilia. Fans will buy just about anything with a NASCAR logo, even blenders and toasters. In contrast, the average Canadian fan spends only $30 a year on NASCAR branded products. Canadian Tire is hoping to change that by developing a new line of NASCAR products for the automotive aftermarket such as windshield washer fluid, batteries, and shock absorbers.

The NASCAR Canadian Tire Series, a multi-year sponsorship agreement, provides many advertising and sales promotion opportunities.

The NASCAR Canadian Tire Series is being touted as a way to build growing popularity of stock car racing and attract new Canadian fans and competitors to the excitement of NASCAR racing. Most fans will likely have a longstanding interest in racing. However, the series has already attracted attention from an unconventional source—federal politicians. Apparently the Conservative Party of Canada realized the advertising potential in the sponsorship deal and recently paid to place its logo on the hood and front side panels of car number 29, driven by Pierre Bourque, in the Canadian Tire NASCAR Series.[2]

In the previous chapter we discussed the tools of integrated marketing communications (IMC) and the steps involved in planning a campaign. While we briefly touched on all of these tools in Chapter 15, we now focus our attention on three elements in particular: advertising, sales promotions, and personal selling, as shown in our chapter roadmap. We begin by introducing the AIDA model, which is the process, or mental stages, marketers try to move consumers through as they are making purchase decisions. As a consumer, you are exposed only to the end product, for example, a finished advertisement, yet many decisions must take place before you actually get to see an ad. We discuss some of these decisions starting with determining the advertising objectives and the focus of advertisements. We consider some of the legal and ethical issues in advertising and those arising from the use of new forms of marketing communications. Then we move on to examine sales promotions and how they add value both in the trade channel and as consumer promotions. The chapter concludes with an examination of how companies use personal selling to influence the buyer's purchase.

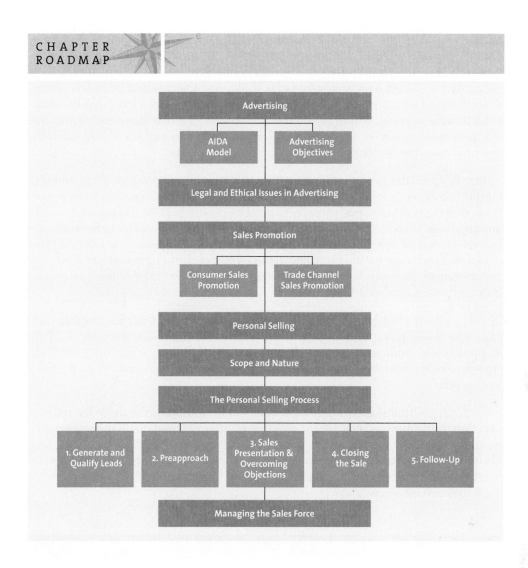

CHAPTER
ROADMAP

Advertising

As we saw in Chapter 15, marketing communication is not a straightforward process. After being exposed to an advertisement, consumers go through several steps before actually buying or taking some other action. There is not always a direct link between a particular marketing communication and a consumer's purchase.

The AIDA Model

To create effective advertising, marketers must understand how marketing communications work. Generally, marketing communications move consumers step-wise through a series of mental stages, for which there are several models. The most common is the **AIDA model** (Exhibit 16.1),[3] which suggests that **A**ttention leads to **I**nterest, which leads to **D**esire, which leads to **A**ction. At each stage, the consumer makes judgments about whether to take the next step in the process. Customers actually have three types of responses, so the AIDA model is also known as the "think, feel, do" model. In making a purchase decision, consumers go through each of the AIDA steps to some degree, but the steps may not always follow the AIDA order. For instance, during an impulse purchase, a consumer may "feel" and "do" before he or she "thinks."

AIDA model
A common model of the series of mental stages through which consumers move as a result of marketing communications: **A**wareness leads to **I**nterests, which lead to **D**esire, which leads to **A**ction.

Attention   Even the best marketing communication can be wasted if the sender doesn't gain the attention of the consumer first. When Ford introduced the redesigned F-150 truck, its first step was to make consumers aware of the new design. So the company placed television ads, radio spots, and Internet and print advertising to reach its desired target audience. This multichannel approach increased the likelihood that the message would be received because even if one of the communication channels were missed or ignored, odds remain good that another would catch the potential customer's attention.

Interest   Once the consumer is aware that the company or product exists, communication must work to increase his or her interest level. It isn't enough to let people know that the product exists; consumers must be persuaded that it is a product worth investigating. Marketers do so by ensuring that the ad's message includes attributes that are of interest to the target audience. To appeal to a customer who likes the great outdoors, Ford's ads for the F-150 show scenes of it performing under extraordinary circumstances. Through these communications, consumers' interest must be piqued enough that they do something about it.

Desire   After the firm has piqued the interest of its target market, the goal of subsequent messages should move the consumer from "I like it" to "I want it." For instance, Ford might devise a communication strategy that offers special financing to make the F-150 appear to be a particularly good deal or highlight special options that make the truck seem unique.

Action   The ultimate goal of any marketing communication is to drive the receiver to action. If the message has caught consumers' attention and made them interested enough to consider the product as a means to satisfy a specific desire of theirs, they likely will act on that interest by making a purchase. Ford dealers may run a special one-week-only sales event for the F-150 to attract prospective buyers and motivate them to purchase a new truck.

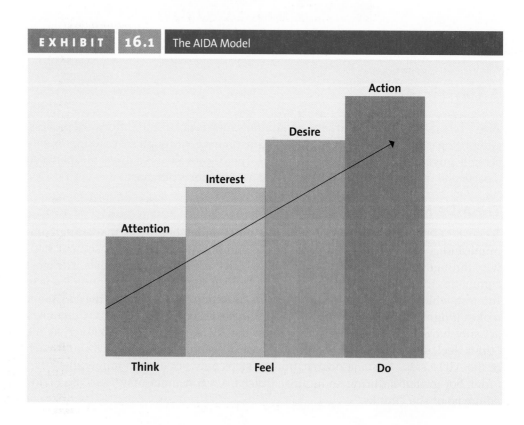

EXHIBIT   16.1   The AIDA Model

The Lagged Effect Sometimes consumers don't act immediately after receiving a marketing communication because of the lagged effect—a delayed response to a marketing communication campaign. It generally takes several exposures to an ad before a consumer fully processes its message.[4] In turn, measuring the effect of a current campaign becomes more difficult because of the possible lagged response to a previous one.[5] Suppose you purchased a Ford F-150 right after hearing a radio ad sponsored by a local dealer. The radio ad may have pushed you to buy, but other communications from Ford, such as television ads and articles in automotive magazines that you saw weeks earlier, probably also influenced your purchase.

Advertising Objectives

As noted in Chapter 15, **advertising** is a paid form of communication, delivered through media from an identifiable source, designed to persuade the receiver to take some action, now or in the future.[6] This definition provides some important distinctions between advertising and other forms of promotion, which we discussed in the previous chapter. First, unlike public relations, advertising is not free; someone has paid, with money, trade, or other means, to get the message shown. Second, advertising must be carried by some medium—television, radio, print, the Web, t-shirts, sidewalks, and so on. Third, legally, the source of the message must be known or knowable. Fourth, advertising represents a persuasive form of communication, designed to get the consumer to take some action. That desired action can range from "Don't drink and drive" to "Buy a new Mercedes."

Some activities that are called advertising really are not, such as word-of-mouth advertising. Even political advertising technically is not advertising because it is not for commercial purposes and thus is not regulated in the same manner as true advertising.

Advertising encompasses an enormous industry and clearly is the most visible form of marketing communications—so much so that many people think of marketing and advertising as synonymous. Global advertising expenditures are projected to exceed $600 billion, with half that amount being spent in the United States alone. It is not just a perception that advertising is everywhere; it *is* everywhere.[7]

Yet how many of the advertisements you were exposed to yesterday do you remember today? Probably not more than three or four. As you learned in Chapter 6, perception is a highly selective process. Consumers simply screen out messages that are not relevant to them. When you notice an advertisement, you may not react to it; even if you react to it, you may not remember it later. Say you remember seeing it—you still may not remember the brand or sponsor of the advertisement, or, worse yet (from the advertiser's point of view), you may remember it as an advertisement for another product.[8]

To get you to remember their ad and the brand, advertisers must first get your attention. As we discussed in Chapter 15, the increasing number of communication channels and changes in consumers' media usage have made the job of advertisers far more difficult.[9] As our opening example demonstrated, advertisers are attempting to use creativity and a mix of promotional elements that offer better opportunities to reach their target markets.

As mentioned in the previous chapter, all advertising campaigns aim to achieve certain objectives: to inform, persuade, and remind customers. Another way of looking at advertising objectives is to examine an ad's focus. Is the ad designed to stimulate demand for a particular product or service, or more broadly for the institution in general? Also, ads can be used to stimulate demand for a product category or an entire industry, or for a specific brand, firm, or item. Let's look at the broad overall objectives of inform, persuade, and remind.

LO

advertising
A paid form of communication from an identifiable source, delivered through a communication channel, and designed to persuade the receiver to take some action, now or in the future.

Informative Advertising

Informative advertising communicates to create and build brand awareness, with the ultimate goal of moving the consumer through the buying cycle to a purchase. Such advertising helps determine some important early stages of a product's life cycle (PLC; see Chapter 10), particularly when consumers have little information about the specific product or type of product. Retailers often use informative advertising to tell their customers about an upcoming sales event or the arrival of new merchandise. Doritos used informative advertising to build brand awareness of a new product discussed in Internet Marketing 16.1.

In the world of financial investments, Dynamic Funds is a smaller mutual fund company. Anxious to increase brand awareness, it launched a campaign featuring pro golfer, Mike Weir, in 2005 with print and billboard ads in major Canadian cities. The next year, radio ads were added to the media mix followed by television ads in 2007. The campaign focused on the relationship between Weir and his caddy, Brennan Little, as an analogy for the trust that Dynamic promotes between financial advisers and their clients. The information advertising campaign resulted in awareness for Dynamic's brand increasing 100 percent since the campaign launched.[10]

Persuasive Advertising

When a product has gained a certain level of brand awareness, firms use **persuasive advertising** to motivate consumers to take action. Persuasive advertising generally occurs in the growth and early maturity stages of the PLC, when competition is most intense, and attempts to accelerate the market's acceptance of the product. In later stages of the PLC, persuasive advertising may be used to reposition an established brand by persuading consumers to change their existing perceptions of the advertised product. Firms, like Cover Girl in the ad below, often use persuasive advertising to convince consumers to take action—switch brands,[11] try a new product, or even continue to buy the advertised product.

Cover Girl's persuasive ads attempt to motivate consumers to take action: try the product, switch brands, or continue to buy the product.

Internet Marketing   **16.1**   **Viral Dare**

Chances are good that you're familiar with Doritos, the best selling flavoured tortilla chip in North America. You've probably seen parts of their IMC campaigns including controversial and entertaining television ads, or their music-centric microsite at DoritosPlay.ca . No doubt you've also heard of the Doritos Juno Fan Choice Award, which picks a contest winner to present a Juno right on stage at the awards. The most popular flavour for the zesty chips is Nacho Cheese, but innovation drives consistent category growth. Based on the success of Jalapeno and Spicy Nacho, and the strong brand messages of bold flavour, Frito Lay developed the spiciest chip ever: Fiery Habanero Doritos.

Rather than launch nationwide in all sizes, they chose instead to keep the distribution selective and place single-serve bags at convenience and drug stores for 100 days as a way to test consumer acceptance and minimize risk. Without channel-wide distribution, national mass media wasn't justified to promote the new flavour, so the Doritos team had to be creative in creating brand and product awareness for the new product. They launched a viral marketing campaign, daring members of the Doritos online mailing list to videotape themselves trying the new fiery chip and then upload the video to a special Doritos microsite. Leveraging a strong consumer e-mail database was important to this promotion.[12]

To make it more enticing for young adult consumers, the team built specific challenges. For example, the Bold challenge asked you to make out with the chip for 30 seconds while in the Fierce Challenge you had to keep the piquant chip in your mouth for the same duration. Each version required consumers to purchase and consume the product in some fashion, helping Doritos achieve their ultimate goal of moving the consumer through the buying cycle to a purchase. All the uploaded videos were featured on the DoritosPlay.ca site and users were highly encouraged to send their videos to friends as well.[13]

While the objectives may have been to support trial and immediate sales, the viral campaign also used informative advertising to build brand awareness of a new product. Consumers suddenly had more touchpoints with the brand: in the convenience store, in their inbox, and later on the website as they went to view their own video and check out other submissions. Capitalizing on their target market's avid use of the Internet, Doritos created an interactive campaign so that consumers would easily remember the new product—a hot idea for any product.

Doritos used informative advertising to build brand awareness for its Fiery Habaneros.

Through focus group research, the Canadian Forces learned that one of its key target markets, young men, were looking for action, not a soft "there's no life like it" type of pitch about career opportunities. As a result, the Department of National Defence launched an action-oriented campaign putting gritty combat life front and centre. The television ads and website showed soldiers patrolling war-torn streets in Afghanistan and used the tagline "Fight fear, fight distress, fight chaos… Fight with the Canadian Forces." The ads proved to be very persuasive as the number of applicants rose 40 percent to 40,000 and 12,862 full-time and reserve members were recruited between April 2006 and March 2007.[14]

Reminder Advertising

Finally, **reminder advertising** is communication used to remind or prompt repurchases, especially for products that have gained market acceptance and are in the maturity stage of their life cycle. For instance, have you ever gone to a restaurant with a group of friends and ordered a Coke when you really wanted iced tea? In this case, the product has achieved **top-of-mind awareness**, or a prominent place in people's memories that triggers a response without them having to put any thought into it. Just the sight of a reminder ad, like a Coca-Cola logo on the menu, may be enough to stimulate the desired response.

reminder advertising
Communication used to remind consumers of a product or to prompt repurchases, especially for products that have gained market acceptance and are in the maturity stage of their life cycle.

top-of-mind awareness
A prominent place in people's memories that triggers a response without them having to put any thought into it.

This umbrella reminds consumers to order a Coke.

Kruger, formerly Scott Paper, faced a challenge. Its licensing agreement with Kimberly-Clark for use of the Cottonelle name was set to expire in June 2007. So it introduced a new brand of toilet paper called Cashmere. Knowing that Kimberly-Clark was expected to reintroduce Cottonelle at some point in the future, Kruger needed not only to build brand awareness, but also to remind consumers about Cashmere in a way that stood out. Given its female target market, the company focused on fashion, an idea relevant to their lives. Television and print ads showed a model wearing a dress that appeared to be made of cashmere but was, in fact, made of toilet paper. The tagline for the ads, "Cashmere. Now in bathroom tissue," helped to remind the target market to take care of herself. Top-of-mind awareness showed significant improvement and market share grew to a historic high of 27.3 percent in May 2007, up from 23.3 percent one year earlier.[15]

Focus of Advertisements

To help determine the focus for advertisements, many companies consider the stages in the AIDA model discussed earlier. Some companies will focus their efforts on attracting attention, for example, in the case of a new product introduction. If consumers are already aware of a product or service, the company will need to build interest and then desire. Lastly, they need to ensure that consumers will be motivated to take action as a result of the company's advertising efforts.

The ad campaign's objectives determine the specific ad's focus. **Product-focused advertisements**, concentrate on informing, persuading, or reminding consumers about a specific product or service. The focus of **institutional advertisements** is to inform, persuade, and remind consumers about issues related to places, politics, an industry, or a particular corporation. In some cases ads are designed to generate demand for the product category or an entire industry, while others are designed to generate demand for a specific brand, firm, or item.

Perhaps the best-known campaign to build demand for a product category is the long-running institutional campaign, "Got Milk?" to encourage milk consumption by appealing to consumers' needs to affiliate with the milk-moustached celebrities shown in the ads.[16] While early campaigns focused on building awareness and knowledge, subsequent campaigns have tried to move consumers further along the buyer readiness continuum. A recent incarnation of the Got Milk? campaign, titled "Bones" highlighted the beneficial properties of milk for building strong bones. This new focus represents a switch to a more informative appeal, combined with a mild emotional fear appeal in its assertion that failing to drink milk can lead to medical problems, perhaps a necessary focus to convince consumers to buy milk.

A special class of demand advertising is the **public service announcement (PSA)**, which focuses on public welfare and generally is sponsored by nonprofit institutions, civic groups, religious organizations, trade associations, or political groups.[17] PSAs represent a form of **social marketing**, which is the application of marketing principles to a social issue to bring about attitudinal and behavioural change among the general public or a specific population segment.[18] Because PSAs are a special class of advertising, under the Canadian Radio-television and Telecommunications Commission (CRTC)

---

product-focused advertisements
Used to inform, persuade, or remind consumers about a specific product or service.

institutional advertisements
Used to inform, persuade, and remind consumers about issues related to places, politics, an industry, or a particular corporation.

public service announcement (PSA)
Advertising that focuses on public welfare and generally is sponsored by nonprofit institutions, civic groups, religious organizations, trade associations, or political groups; a form of *social marketing*.

social marketing
The application of marketing principles to a social issue to bring about attitudinal and behavioural change among the general public or a specific population segment.

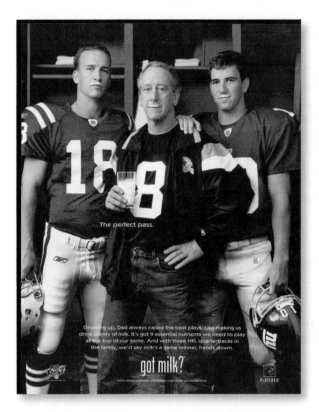

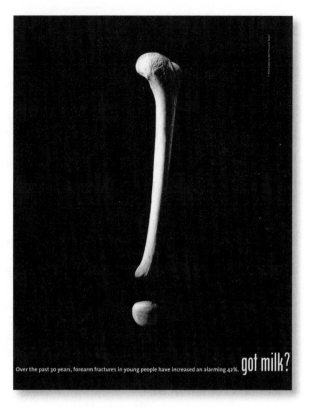

One of the best-known campaigns for generating demand is the "Got Milk?" campaign (left). The latest incarnation of the campaign, titled "Bones" (right) has a more informative appeal, combined with a mild emotional fear appeal.

rules, broadcasters must devote a specific amount of free airtime to them. Some of the most successful PSA campaigns include wildfire prevention (Smokey the Bear), smoking cessation (Stupid.ca), Internet safety (BeWebAware.ca), and breast cancer screening (Breast Cancer Society of Canada).

Because they often are designed by top advertising agencies for nonprofit clients, PSAs usually are quite creative and stylistically appealing. For example, what is your reaction to the Internet safety campaign BeWebAware.ca from the Media Awareness Network? The Ottawa-based nonprofit organization is designed to educate parents about the risks and benefits of letting their kids surf into cyberspace. Supported by Microsoft Canada and Bell Canada, ads highlight eye-opening statistics—such as the fact that 25 percent of kids have been asked to meet someone they've only met online—and include a drive to BeWebAware.ca, a website created to help parents get involved in monitoring their children's online activity. One print ad shows a middle-aged man at a computer, typing away in a kids' chat room. The accompanying copy reads: "To 12 year old Lisa, he was simply 11 year old Jenny."

Regardless of whether the advertising campaign's objective is to inform, persuade, or remind; to focus on a particular product or the institution in general; each campaign's objectives must be specific and measurable. For a brand awareness campaign, for example, the objective might be to increase brand awareness among the target market by 50 percent within six months. Another campaign's goal may be to persuade 10 percent of a competitor's customers to switch to the advertised brand.

Public service advertising, for causes like Internet safety, focus on public welfare and generally are sponsored by nonprofit institutions, civic groups, religious organizations, trade associations, or political groups.

LO **2** # Legal and Ethical Issues in Advertising

Integrated marketing communications brings together many diverse forms of communication under one umbrella. But in Canada, each form of communication media traditionally has been regulated separately. For example, rather than ban cigarette advertising completely the federal 1997 Tobacco Act imposed numerous restrictions including a phased-in ban on tobacco sponsorship of events.[19] However, in 2007, the Supreme Court of Canada struck down the tobacco industry's appeal to remove the advertising ban and opened the door to new advertising. Companies are allowed to advertise in places where only people over the age of 18 are permitted and in magazines whose readerships are more than 85 percent adult.[20] We begin this section by detailing the various agencies that regulate the different forms and media for advertising. Then we discuss some controversies surrounding new forms of potential deception.

In Canada, the regulation of advertising involves a complex mix of formal laws and informal restrictions designed to protect consumers from deceptive practices. Many federal and provincial laws, as well as a wide range of self-regulatory agencies and agreements, affect advertising (Exhibit 16.2). The primary federal agencies that regulate advertising activities are the Competition Bureau, the Canadian Radio-television and Telecommunications Commission (CRTC), the Food and Drug Act, and Advertising Standards Canada. In addition to these agencies, marketers must adhere to other pieces of legislation such as the Consumer Packaging and Labelling Act and the Tobacco Act.

The Competition Bureau enforces the Competition Act, the most comprehensive legislation affecting the marketing activities of companies in Canada. The Competition Act maintains and encourages competition while protecting consumers from misleading and deceptive advertising practices. The CRTC controls the advertising industry and governs broadcast media and licensing. All television and radio advertisements must be approved by the CRTC before they can be broadcast. The Food and Drug Act prohibits the advertising or selling of unsafe or misbranded foods, cosmetics, and drugs. It also requires companies to adhere to regulations regarding health claims. Although used for many years in the United States, diet-related health claims for food products, related to risk reduction of heart disease, cancer, osteoporosis, and high blood pressure, have only recently been allowed in Canada. The Consumer Packaging and Labelling Act requires manufacturers, packers, and distributors to disclose full information about their products. All pre-packaged products must be labelled in both French and English and bear the quantity in metric and imperial for weight, volume, or measures.

Many product categories fall under self-regulatory restrictions or guidelines. For example, the Advertising Standards Canada is a self-regulating body that moni-

EXHIBIT 16.2	Agencies That Regulate Advertising	
Agency	**General Purpose**	**Specific Jurisdiction**
Competition Bureau Canada The Competition Act (1986)	Enforces federal laws that ensure businesses in Canada operate in a fair and equitable manner.	Enforces laws relating to misleading advertising and deceptive marketing practices.
Canadian Radio-television and Telecommunications Commission—CRTC (1968)	Regulates and supervises all aspects of the Canadian broadcasting system, and regulates telecommunications common carriers and service providers that fall under federal jurisdiction.	Establishes standards and requirements for the safety and sanitation of products. Regulates the labelling of food products pertaining to nutrition labelling, nutrient content, and health claims.
Health Canada Food and Drug Act (1954)	Regulates food, drugs, cosmetics, and medical devices.	Establishes standards and requirements for the safety and sanitation of products. Regulates the labelling of food products pertaining to nutrition labelling, nutrient content, and health claims.
Advertising Standards Canada (1957)	ASC is an advertising industry self-regulatory body that monitors voluntary industry codes.	Administers the Canadian Code of Advertising Standards, the Gender Portrayal Guidelines, and the Broadcast Code for Advertising to Children.

tors voluntary industry codes. Advertising to children is regulated primarily through self-regulatory mechanisms designed by Advertising Standards Canada and its Broadcast Code for Advertising to Children. The exception is the province of Quebec, where all advertising to children under the age of 13 is prohibited under the Quebec Consumer Protection Act.

Recently, to make matters even more complicated for advertisers whose products sell in the United States, state Attorneys General's offices have begun to assert their authority to regulate advertising in their states. The EU also has increased its regulation of advertising for EU member nations. Many of these state and European regulations are more restrictive than existing federal or self-regulatory requirements.

Another difference between advertising regulations in Canada and the EU pertains to **puffery**, the legal exaggeration of praise, stopping just short of deception, lavished on a product.[21] In Canada, consumers are viewed as rational and capable of evaluating advertising claims. Does a certain sneaker brand really make you run faster and jump higher? Does Papa John's pizza really have "better ingredients" that make "better pizza"? In the EU, however, puffery is considered deception. For instance, Kraft had no problem advertising its orange-flavored drink Tang surrounded by oranges in North America. But in Germany, the ad was declared deceptive because there are no oranges in Tang. Advertisers must understand these differences to keep from violating EU advertising laws.

Some companies are criticized simply because of their large advertising budgets. Consumers often complain that prices would be lower if companies didn't spend so much money promoting their products. Numerous companies have come under fire for expenditures to advertise Product (RED) collections as discussed in Ethical Dilemma 16.1.

Advertising and direct marketing must adhere to different guidelines than PR. For instance, in the case of *Kasky* v. *Nike*, Nike claimed that a letter to the editor written by its CEO was part of a PR campaign and thus not an advertising message.[22] Unfortunately for Nike, the California courts felt otherwise and found that Nike's letter was an advertisement, which meant that the claims made in the letter had to be substantiated.

Is this billboard ad an example of puffery or deception?

puffery
The legal exaggeration of praise, stopping just short of deception, lavished on a product.

stealth marketing
A strategy to attract consumers using promotional tactics that deliver a sales message in unconventional ways, often without the target audience knowing that the message even has a selling intent.

Stealth Marketing

The *Godsend* website (discussed in the previous chapter in Ethical Dilemma 15.1) is just one example of a growing number of "stealth" promotional campaigns. **Stealth marketing** is a strategy used to attract consumers using promotional tactics that deliver a sales message in unconventional ways, often without the target audience knowing that the message even has a selling intent.[23] Stealth marketing can take many forms and use many different communication channels, and as marketers find more innovative ways to communicate with their target markets, they have crossed into uncharted waters. Consumers thus are starting to lose confidence that they can distinguish a commercial message from a noncommercial one.

Marketers have also begun to employ actual consumers to be, in essence, salespeople for the brand. The average person has 56 word-of-mouth conversations

Do you believe that stealth marketing strategies directed toward children like the one used by Neopet is ethical? Should the government regulate media in which children may not be able to distinguish between entertainment and commercial content?

Ethical Dilemma

16.1 Seeing (RED)

In its short history, Product (RED) is stirring controversy at the same time it is working to fight three of the world's most devastating diseases. The Global Fund to fight AIDS, tuberculosis, and malaria was established in 2002 with the support of world leaders and UN Secretary General Kofi Annan.[24] Four years later, at the 2006 World Economic Forum, Bono and Bobby Shriver announced Product (RED), an economic initiative designed to deliver private sector money to the Global Fund.

Converse, Motorola, Apple, GAP, and other companies created special edition RED products in support of this cause. For example, Apple produced a 4GB iPod nano RED Special Edition while American Express introduced a RED credit card. A portion of the proceeds from RED branded products goes to the Global Fund, for example, 10 percent of a $25 iTunes gift card, 5 to 15 percent depending on the Converse product, or 50 percent of the profits from Gap's sales of RED collections.

It didn't take long for the news to break that more than US$100 million had been spent by companies advertising their RED collections, while only US$18 million had been donated to the Global Fund. Critics claimed the $100 million used for advertising should have simply been donated directly to the cause. Product (RED) promoters argue it is a long-term initiative, designed to build over time and that one year after launch is too soon to measure its success. They claim $25 million was raised (not $18 million) and that the donation is five times the amount given to the Global Fund by the private sector in the past four years.[25] And they point out that money spent to promote RED products, would otherwise have been spent promoting products that made no contribution to the Global Fund at all.[26]

It's too early to determine the long-term impact of the Product (RED) launch or the value of the publicity gener-

Product (RED) was announced by Bono at the 2006 World Economic Forum and later featured on Oprah.

ated by thousands of magazine, newspaper and online articles, hours of TV news coverage, including a profile on *Oprah*.[27] Before the controversy struck, most people didn't even know the Global Fund existed. Still the issue has many observers seeing (RED) and questioning if companies are simply using the cause to their advantage. Is it ethical to profit from a nonprofit cause?

---

every week. Organizations like TheInfluencers.ca are dedicated to helping start, seed, and spread these conversations among Canada's opinion leaders.[28] For example, Dare Foods ran a program to launch its new Simple Pleasures Baked Cookie Bars. Participants received 12 boxes of cookie bars to sample and share with friends and were expected to provide feedback to Dare. The goal for companies is to have such programs become a launching point for **viral marketing**, a marketing phenomenon that encourages people to pass along a marketing message to other potential consumers.[29] There are no current regulations on viral campaigns; the laws that cover deceptive practices have never had to address this new form of marketing.

The use of online games also has been quite effective at getting children's attention and drawing them to firms' websites—as well as at drawing criticism from children's media watchdog groups. These groups believe that the websites do not inform children that the games contain branded messages. One of the most controversial is www.neopet.com, which offers games sponsored by various corporations. By signing up to receive offers from these sponsors, site users get assistance in taking care of their Neopet, a virtual animal they adopt when they register with the site.[30] They can earn points by taking consumer surveys or feeding their Neopet McDonald's products. Young girls, who make up most of the site's visitors, spend an average of 3.5 hours a month on the site.

viral marketing
A marketing phenomenon that encourages people to pass along a marketing message to other potential consumers.

As sites like Neopet become more popular with children, children's media watchers begin to ask: Can children distinguish between entertainment and commercial content?[31] For now, again, there are no formal regulations for children's websites other than those designed to protect children's privacy online. However, regulators are examining the practices used on these sites to determine whether any current regulations are being violated and whether such practices need to be regulated. In the meantime, marketers will continue their quest to find more innovative ways to reach their target audiences using both traditional and nontraditional methods.

Sales Promotion

 LO **3**

Advertising rarely provides the only means to communicate with target customers. As we discussed in Chapter 15, a natural link appears between advertising and sales promotion. **Sales promotions** are special incentives or excitement-building programs that encourage consumers to purchase a particular product or service, typically used in conjunction with other advertising or personal selling programs. In the context of integrated marketing communication campaigns, advertising generally creates awareness, interest, and desire while the value in sales promotions is in closing the deal. Many sales promotions, like free samples or point-of-purchase (POP) displays, attempt to build short-term sales, whereas others, like loyalty programs, contests, and sweepstakes, have become integral components of firms' long-term customer relationship management (CRM) programs, which they use to build customer loyalty. In this section, we examine the various tools firms use for their sales promotions and how those tools complement the advertiser's efforts to achieve its strategic objectives.

sales promotions
Special incentives or excitement-building programs that encourage the purchase of a product or service, such as coupons, rebates, contests, free samples, and point-of-purchase displays.

EXHIBIT 16.3	Kinds of Consumer Sales Promotions		
PROMOTION	**OBJECTIVE**	**ADVANTAGES**	**DISADVANTAGES**
Coupons	Stimulate demand.	• Encourages retailer support. • Allows for direct tracing of sales.	• Has low redemption rates. • Has high cost.
Deals	Encourage trial.	• Reduces consumer risk. • Retaliates against competitive action.	• May reduce perception of value.
Premiums	Build goodwill.	• Increases perception of value.	• Consumers buy for premium not product. • Has to be carefully managed.
Contests	Increase consumer involvement.	• Generates excitement.	• Requires creativity. • Must be monitored.
Sweepstakes	Encourage higher consumption.	• Minimizes brand switching among existing consumers.	• Sales often decline after.
Samples	Encourage trial.	• Offers direct involvement.	• Has high cost to the firm.
Loyalty Programs	Encourage repurchase.	• Creates loyalty.	• Has high cost to the firm.
POP Displays	Increase brand trial.	• Provides high visibility. • Provides in-store support.	• Is difficult to get a good location in the store. • Can be costly to the firm.
Rebates	Stimulate demand.	• Increases value perception.	• Is easily copied by competitors. • May just advance future sales.
Product Placement	Demonstrate product uses.	• Displays products nontraditionally. • Introduces new products.	• Firm often has little control over display. • Product can be overshadowed.

coupon
Provides a stated discount to consumers on the final selling price of a specific item; the retailer handles the discount.

deal
A type of short-term price reduction that can take several forms, such as a "featured price," a price lower than the regular price; a "buy one, get one free" offer; or a certain percentage "more free" offer contained in larger packaging; can involve a special financing arrangement, such as reduced percentage interest rates or extended repayment terms.

premium
An item offered for free or at a bargain price to reward some type of behaviour, such as buying, sampling, or testing.

This sales promotion deal for Payless ShoeSource is a short-term price promotion that encourages consumers to buy a second pair of shoes at one half off.

We present the tools used in sales promotions, along with their advantages and disadvantages, in Exhibit 16.3 on the previous page and discuss them next. As shown in this exhibit, there are many different types of sales promotion tools. Marketers choose which one to use based on their specific marketing objectives. Then, we examine some ways in which integrated marketing communication (IMC) programs make use of sales promotions.

Consumer Sales Promotions

The tools of any sales promotion can be focused on either channel members, such as wholesalers or retailers, or end-user consumers. Just as we delineated for advertising, when sales promotions are targeted at channel members, the marketer is employing a push strategy; when it targets consumers themselves, it is using a pull strategy. Some sales promotion tools can be used with either a push or pull strategy. We now consider each of the tools and how they are used.

Coupons   A **coupon** is a certificate with a stated price reduction for a specific item or percentage of a purchase. More than 300 billion coupons are distributed every year in North America, yet only about 2 percent of them are ever redeemed.[32] However, these redemption rates vary dramatically depending on how consumers obtain the coupon. A segment of the market, the diehard "coupon clippers," devote a great deal of time and effort to searching for, clipping, and redeeming coupons. Many coupon clippers have streamlined this process by using the Internet, which offers entire forums dedicated to coupon sharing and management (e.g., www.couponforum.com). Nonetheless, many consumers dislike the cumbersome coupon process, so redemption rates on coupons average less than 2 percent. In response, coupon distribution has been declining in recent years.[33] Coupons carried in newspapers, magazines, in-store displays, and direct mail have very low redemption rates of only 1 to 2 percent, whereas those downloaded from the Internet experience a 56-percent redemption rate. The reason for this dramatic difference is that consumers seek out online coupons for specific items or stores, whereas many people who have no interest in purchasing the product receive traditional coupons.

Deals   A **deal** refers generally to a type of short-term price reduction that can take several forms, such as a "featured price," a price lower than the regular price; a "buy one, get one free" offer; or a certain percentage "more free" offer contained in larger packaging. Another form of a deal involves a special financing arrangement, such as reduced percentage interest rates or extended repayment terms. Deals encourage trial because they lower the risk for consumers by reducing the cost of the good, but they can also alter perceptions of value.

Premiums   A **premium** offers an item for free or at a bargain price to reward some type of behaviour, such as buying, sampling, or testing. These rewards build goodwill among consumers, who often perceive high value in them. Premiums can be distributed in a variety of ways: They can be included in the product packaging, such as the toys inside cereal boxes; placed visibly on the package, such as a coupon for free milk on a box of Cheerios; handed out in the store; or delivered in the mail, such as the free perfume offers Victoria's Secret mails to customers.

Furthermore, premiums can be very effective if they are consistent with the brand's message and image and highly desirable to the target market. Finding a premium that meets these criteria at a reasonable cost can be serious challenge. At fast food restaurants such as McDonald's and Burger King for instance, the average order cost is around $5, while the average premium distributed costs less than 50 cents.

Contests   A **contest** refers to a brand-sponsored competition that requires some form of skill or effort. In Canada, you cannot give a prize away by chance alone. There must also be a skill component which is why skill-testing questions are used, making the game one of mixed chance and skill. The effort required by these contests often keeps participation lower than that for other forms of promotion. For instance, for more than 40 years, Pillsbury has awarded money and prizes to its bake-off grand prize winner. From all those who submit recipes, 100 finalists are chosen and compete against one another; a panel of experts chooses the ultimate winner. The company also uses cobranding to encourage other brands, such as GE and Jif, to sponsor the runner-up prizes for specific categories.[34]

To be effective, contests must be advertised and enjoy high levels of retailer or dealer support. SportChek recently ran an online contest to drive up its membership database and increase store traffic. Shoppers received unique contest-entry PIN codes on their receipts. They got a discount coupon when they registered at getintogear.ca. In the first week, 3000 people registered for the contest and sent it to friends 1000 times.[35]

Burger King offers premiums like this beetle-shaped ruler in conjunction with movie releases like the "Ant Bully." Premiums are either free or at a bargain price, and encourage buying, sampling, or testing.

Sweepstakes   A form of sales promotion that offers prizes based on a chance drawing of entrants' names, **sweepstakes** do not require the entrant to complete a task other than buy a ticket or fill out a form. Often the key benefit of sweepstakes is that they encourage current consumers to consume more if the sweepstakes form appears inside the packaging or with the product. Unlike contests, sweepstakes winners are determined by a random draw. Reader's Digest Canada runs an annual national sweepstakes for which it invites both subscribers and others to enter.

Samples   **Sampling** offers potential customers the opportunity to try a product or service before they make a buying decision. Distributing samples is one of the most costly sales promotion tools but also one of the most effective. As we describe in Adding Value 16.1, one of the key purposes of Procter & Gamble Canada's "Look Fab Studio" was to help establish P&G as an authority on beauty and to position its beauty brands. Participants received free advice as well as samples.

Loyalty Programs   As part of a sales promotion program, **loyalty programs** are specifically designed to retain customers by offering premiums or other incentives to customers that make multiple purchases over time. Such sales promotions are growing increasingly popular and often tied to long-term CRM systems. In Canada, some of the most popular loyalty programs include Canadian Tire "Money," Air Miles, and the Shoppers Drug Mart Optimum program.

Point-of-Purchase Displays   **Point-of-purchase (POP) displays** are merchandise displays located at the point of purchase, such as at the checkout counter in a grocery store. Marketers spend almost as much on POP materials as they do on consumer

contest
A brand-sponsored competition that requires some form of skill or effort.

sweepstakes
A form of sales promotion that offers prizes based on a chance drawing of entrants' names.

sampling
Offers potential customers the opportunity to try a product or service before they make a buying decision.

loyalty program
Specifically designed to retain customers by offering premiums or other incentives to customers who make multiple purchases over time.

point-of-purchase (POP) display
A merchandise display located at the point of purchase, such as at the checkout counter in a grocery store.

POP displays are merchandise displays located at the point of purchase, such as at the check-out counter in a grocery store.

Adding Value   16.1   Pop-up Beauty

A high traffic area like Yonge and Bloor Street in Toronto is an ideal location to set up a retail store. Procter & Gamble set up its Look Fab Studio in the upscale area—for one month only. The temporary beauty boutique allowed visitors to benefit from free beauty tips, makeovers, and workshops from industry experts such as celebrity makeup artist Paul Venoit.[36] It also offered complimentary hair styling and hair colour services. The goal of the temporary studio was to establish P&G as an authority on beauty and position the Pantene, Cover Girl, Olay, Nice'n Easy, Crest, and Venus brands as everyday beauty aids. The company wanted people to walk into the studio, interact with its brands, and walk out feeling transformed.

Temporary stores are starting to pop up in empty retail spaces, selling everything from tech toys (Motorola) to cat food (Meow Mix), and creating interactive hype.[37] Calvin Klein converted a vacant Toronto store into a club for three nights only to celebrate the launch of its ckIN2U fragrance.[38] The Look Fab Studio campaign generated both publicity and brand trial. Buzz was generated through in-studio interviews with celebrities like singer Holly Cole airing on CTV's *eTalk Daily*. Yorkville fashion fiends told their friends about the unique beauty studio, creating word of mouth. In one month, the studio interacted with over 12,000 consumers and offered over 4000 consultations for complimentary hair styling, hair colour, or make-up services.

The "Look Fab Studio" temporarily offered free beauty tips, makeovers, and workshops from industry experts like celebrity make-up artist Paul Venoit. Pop-up retail stores are set in temporary locations to generate excitement about a brand or product.

magazine advertising, but the key to a successful POP is to make the display "pop out" in a crowded store. In addition, manufacturers must encourage retailers to feature and use the POP displays to maximize their investments. The use of shelf displays along with other promotional tactics led to the successful launch of a new brand of wine as discussed in Entrepreneurial Marketing 16.1.

rebate
A consumer discount in which a portion of the purchase price is returned to the buyer in cash; the manufacturer, not the retailer, issues the refund.

Rebates   **Rebates** refer to a particular type of price reduction. Many products, such as cell phones, now offer significant mail-in rebates that may lower the price of the phone to $0 or even less. Firms offer such generous rebates because the likelihood that consumers will actually apply for the rebate is low, even though consumers indicate that rebate offers are a factor in their purchase decisions. The firms thus garner considerable value from rebates because they attract consumers with a minimal risk that the firm will have to pay off all the rebates offered. Consumers may consider the rebate during their purchase decision process but then never redeem it—an added bonus for the seller.

Recently, heavy rebate users such as Best Buy have begun scaling back their programs.[39] Like any promotional tool, too much of a good thing can be a problem. Best Buy found that consumers were becoming increasingly annoyed by having to mail in the rebate forms and wait to receive their money. Many were requesting that the rebate be given at the time of purchase and wondering why this immediate promotion was not possible. In addition, a growing number of lawsuits claim rebate cheques were never sent to consumers and that rebate offers contain overly detailed clauses that cause consumers to have to submit and resubmit their claims.[40]

| Entrepreneurial Marketing | **16.1** | **Capital Ideas** |

How does a small marketing firm flourish and win not one but two Agency of the Year awards for 2006? With ground-breaking creativity, and a holistic approach to marketing their clients' brands. This is the story of Capital C, a small promotional agency, founded by Tony Chapman in his kitchen in 1992.[41] Since those humble beginnings, "Cap C" has worked with numerous major clients including Microsoft, Investors Group, RBC Financial, Unilever, Bell, Canada Post, McDonald's US, and PepsiCo.

Capital C's strategy involves focusing on the consumer, and executing its clients' promotions across several channels, tailored to each campaign. One brand may require an emphasis on retail marketing and the "in-store theatre," while other promotions may rely more heavily on digital media. Capital C has led the pack because Tony Chapman understands the evolving face of marketing. Less than one-third of all promotional dollars are now spent on advertising, so the company has grown to acquire the database marketing firm Kenna and a stake in the Montreal-based experimental marketing firm P2P. This will help expand Cap C's resource base as it looks to target consumers more precisely.

In 2006, Cap C was named Marketing's 2006 Promotional Agency and Overall Agency of the Year.[42] One of its great success stories was born from the Grimsby, Ontario vintner Andrew Peller Limited. Together, they created the wine brand XOXO and positioned it for a unique, new market. Shying away from traditional wine drinkers, the brand was targeted to women looking to complement a "Girl's Night In." Eye-catching on-shelf displays coupled with simple but recognizable packaging were an instant hit, selling 36,000 bottles in just four weeks. In-store sampling produced a conversion rate of 35 to 50 percent, much higher than the 15 to 20 percent expected from such trials.[43]

While Cap C still tries to shed the veil of being dubbed a "promotional agency," its successes are clear. From championing digital campaigns for brands such as Dove and Thermasilk to dominating the in-store theatre with Frito Lay and Pepsi, Cap C's shift toward becoming a full-service agency continues to progress. Building new brands from scratch exemplifies the depth of its creativity, and will ensure that its list of clients will continue to grow well into the future.

Product Placement When marketers use **product placement**, they include their product in nontraditional situations, such as in a scene in a movie or television program. The first visible movie product placement was Hershey's Reese's Pieces in the film *ET*. The product actually became part of the storyline, offered the candy high levels of visibility, and resulted in a large increase in sales.[44]

product placement Inclusion of a product in nontraditional situations, such as in a scene in a movie or television program.

Although Hershey's did not pay to place Reese's Pieces in *ET*, other firms have been more than willing to shell out for product placements. For example, Exxon paid $300,000 to have its name appear in *Days of Thunder*, Pampers paid $50,000 to be featured in *Three Men and a Baby*, and Cuervo Gold spent $150,000 for placement in *Tequila Sunrise*.[45] The James Bond film *Die Another Day* earned $70 million from companies who paid to have their products featured in the film—a record in the product placement world.[46] Especially because consumers who use digital video recorders report that they skip televised commercials 72.3 percent of the time, product placement is becoming increasingly important. Moreover, research shows that consumers recall product placements relatively well.[47]

How much do you think Coca-Cola had to pay American Idol to get this product placement?

Trade Channel Sales Promotions

Although sales promotions are often associated with coupons, contests, and other consumer tactics, far more money is spent on trade channel sales promotions than on consumer sales promotions. Trade channel promotions help convince retailers and wholesalers to stock a new brand, give it eye level shelf space, and promote it in their flyers and other advertisements. As mentioned earlier, many types of consumer sales promotions can also be used for channel members. Additional trade channel promotions include discounts and allowances, co-operative advertising, and sales force training, each of which is briefly described in the next section.

Discounts & Allowances   Discounts and allowances are effective incentives used to maintain or increase inventory levels in the distribution channel. Manufacturers sometimes offer a case allowance, for example, a discount or dollar amount taken off each case ordered during a specific time period. Alternatively, retailers may receive a set quantity of products free, for example, one case at no charge with an order of 10 cases. A merchandise allowance may be offered in return for extra in-store support or featuring the product in some way by the retailer. For instance, if a store agreed to run an ad with a coupon promoting a specific product, the merchandise allowance may provide a discounted case price for orders received during the promotional period.

Co-operative Advertising   One of the important functions retailers perform is promoting products to consumers. Co-operative (co-op) advertising helps to compensate trade channel members for money they spend promoting products and encourages them to feature products more often. Generally, manufacturers will pay 50 percent of the cost of advertising up to an agreed limit. This limit is usually determined based on the amount of business a retailer does with a manufacturer. To ensure high quality advertisements are placed at the local level, some companies will provide a selection of final ads to choose from, ready to place in a variety of media or adapt as necessary.

Sales Force Training   Because retailers have contact with end consumers and are ultimately responsible for selling the products they carry, manufacturers may offer to train the retailer's sales staff. This training gives a company's sales force more in-depth product knowledge, which enhances their confidence in the product and increases the likelihood of future sales. When Colgate-Palmolive launched its tooth-whitening product, Simply White, it trained cosmeticians at Shoppers Drug Mart since they were most likely the staff members who would field questions about the new product. Other training activities might include providing manuals or brochures, sales meetings, or field visits. Manufacturers sometimes run contests to help motivate trade channel members to sell their products.

Using Sales Promotion Tools

Marketers must be careful in their use of promotions, especially those that focus on lowering prices. Depending on the item, consumers may stock up when items are offered at a lower price, which simply shifts sales from the future to now and thereby leads to short-run benefits at the expense of long-term sales stability. For instance, using sales promotions like coupons to stimulate sales of household cleaning supplies may cause consumers to stockpile the products and decrease demand for those products in the future. But a similar promotion used with a perishable product like Danone yogurt should increase its demand at the expense of competitors like Yoplait.

The tools connected to sales promotions are as varied as the imaginations of the marketers who devise them, and new forms are constantly popping up. For example, **pop-up stores**—like the Look Fab Studio in Toronto featured in Adding Value 16.1 or the Diet Coke Lounges that popped up in Canadian malls—exist only for a limited time and generally focus on a new product or a limited group of products offered by

pop-up stores
Temporary storefronts that exist for only a limited time and generally focus on a new product or a limited group of products offered by a retailer, manufacturer, or service provider; give consumers a chance to interact with the brand and build brand awareness, but are not designed primarily to sell the product.

a retailer, manufacturer, or service provider. These temporary storefronts give consumers a chance to interact with the brand and build brand awareness, but they are not designed primarily to sell the product. Instead, consumers who have visited the pop-up, the company hopes, will follow up with a visit to either another retailer that carries the products or the company's website.[48]

Retailers tend not to mind manufacturers' pop-up stores because most are designed to drive traffic to the retailers through give-aways of coupons and samples. Because pop-ups are short lived, they don't pose any long-term competition to retailers.

Many firms are also realizing the value of **cross-promoting**, when two or more firms join together to reach a specific target market. To achieve a successful cross-promotion, the two products must appeal to the same target market and together create value for consumers. Burger King, for instance recently ran a three-firm cross promotion: Motts Strawberry-Flavored Applesauce, designed to attract health-conscious parents; Star Wars memorabilia, designed to attract collectors and fans of the movie; and BK King of the Courts 3-on-3 College Basketball Tournament, designed to attract university students and fans of U.S. college basketball. Each of these cross-promotions targets a different market and attempts to create value in a slightly different way for Burger King consumers. However, the ultimate, overall goal for Burger King is to generate increased sales and greater brand loyalty.

The goal of any sales promotion is to create value for both the consumers and the firm. By understanding the needs of its customers, as well as how best to entice them to purchase or consume a particular product or service, a firm can develop promotional messages and events that are of interest to and achieve the desired response from those customers. Traditionally, the role of sales promotion has been to generate short-term results, whereas the goal of advertising was to generate long-term results. As this chapter demonstrates, though, both sales promotion and advertising can generate both long- and short-term effects. The effective combination of both types of activities leads to impressive results for the firm and the consumers.

> **cross-promoting** Efforts of two or more firms joining together to reach a specific target market.

Personal Selling and Sales Management

Almost everyone is engaged in some form of selling. On a personal level, you sell your ideas or opinions to your friends, family, employers, and professors. Even if you have no interest in personal selling as a career, a strong grounding in the topic will help you in numerous career choices. Consider, for instance, Harry Porter, a very successful labour attorney. He worked his way through university selling alpaca sweaters to fraternities across the country. Although he loved his part-time job, Harry decided to become an attorney. When asked whether he misses selling, he said, "I use my selling skills every day. I have to sell new clients on the idea that I'm the best attorney for the job. I have to sell my partners on my legal point of view. I even use selling skills when I'm talking to a judge or jury." In this chapter though, we take a straightforward business perspective on selling.

> **personal selling** The two-way flow of communication between a buyer and a seller that is designed to influence the buyer's purchase decision.

> *Many salespeople now can rely on virtual offices, which enable them to communicate via the Internet with colleagues and customers.*

The Scope and Nature of Personal Selling

Personal selling is the two-way flow of communication between a buyer or buyers and a seller that is designed to influence the buyer's purchase decision. Personal selling can take place in various situations: face-to-face, via video teleconferencing, on the telephone, or over the Internet. More than one million people are employed in sales positions in Canada[49], including those involved in business-to-business (B2B) transactions—like manufacturers' representatives selling to retailers or other businesses—and those completing business-to-consumer (B2C)

Professional selling can be a very lucrative career and is very visible to management.

transactions, such as retail salespeople, real estate agents, and insurance agents. Salespeople are referred to in many ways: sales representatives or reps, account executives, agents. And as Harry Porter found, most professions rely on personal selling to some degree.

Salespeople don't always get the best coverage in popular media. In Arthur Miller's play *Death of a Salesman*, the main character, Willie Loman, leads a pathetic existence and suffers from the loneliness inherent in being a travelling salesman.[50] Unfortunately, this powerful Pulitzer Prize–winning piece of literature weighs heavily on our collective conscious and often overshadows the millions of hardworking professional salespeople who have fulfilling and rewarding careers and who add value to their firm and provide value for their customers.

Professional selling can be such a satisfying career for several reasons. First, many people love the lifestyle. Salespeople are typically out on their own. Although they occasionally work with their managers and other colleagues, salespeople are usually responsible for planning their own day. This flexibility translates into an easier balance between work and family than many office-bound jobs can offer. Many salespeople now can rely on virtual offices, which enable them to communicate via the Internet with colleagues and customers. Because salespeople are evaluated primarily on the results they produce, as long as they meet and exceed their goals, they experience little day-to-day supervision.

Second, the variety of the job often attracts people to sales. Every day is different, bringing different clients and customers, often in a variety of places. Their issues and problems and the solutions to those problems all differ and require creativity.

Third, professional selling and sales management can be a very lucrative career. Sales is among the highest-paying careers for college and university graduates, and compensation often includes perks, such as the use of a company car and bonuses for high performance. A top performer can have a total compensation package of over $150,000; even lower-level salespeople can make well over $50,000. Although the monetary compensation can be significant, the satisfaction of being involved in interesting, challenging, and creative work is rewarding in and of itself.

Fourth, because salespeople are the frontline emissaries for their firm, they are very visible to management. Furthermore, it is fairly straightforward for management to identify top performers, which means that those high-performing salespeople who aspire to management positions are in a good position to get promoted.

Personal Selling and Marketing Strategy

Although personal selling is an essential part of many firms' integrated marketing communications strategy, it offers its own unique contribution to the 4Ps. Because of the one-to-one nature of sales, a salesperson is in a unique position to customize a message for a specific buyer—a preplanned sales presentation or demonstration can be altered at any time as the need arises. In a personal selling situation, the salesperson can probe the buyer for his or her potential reservations about a product or service, educate the buyer when appropriate, and ask for the order at the appropriate time. Unlike other types of promotion, the sales presentation can be directed toward those customers with the highest potential. This highly directed approach to promotion is important because experts estimate that the average cost of a single B2B sales call is about $330.[51]

As we discussed in Chapter 13, building strong distribution channel relationships is a critical success factor. Who in the organization is better equipped to manage this relationship than the salesperson, the frontline emissary for the firm? The most successful salespeople are those who build strong relationships with their customers. They don't view themselves as being successful if they make a particular sale or one transaction at a time. Instead, they take a long-term perspective. Thus, building on the strategic relationship concept introduced in Chapter 14, **relationship selling** is a sales philosophy and process that emphasizes a commitment to maintaining the relationship over the long term and investing in opportunities that are mutually beneficial to all parties. Relationship salespeople work with their customers to find mutually beneficial solutions to their wants and needs. An IBM sales team, for instance, may be working with your university to provide you with the computer support and security you need.

Research has shown that a positive customer–salesperson relationship contributes to trust, increased customer loyalty, and the intent to continue the relationship with the salesperson.[52] To help build strong relationships, many firms undertake active customer relationship management (CRM) programs that identify and focus on building loyalty with the firm's most valued customers. Because the sales force interacts directly with customers, its members are in the best position to help a firm accomplish its CRM objectives.

CRM programs have several components. There is a customer database or data warehouse. Whether the salesperson is working for a retail store or manages a selling team for an aerospace contractor, he or she can record transaction information, customer contact information, customer preferences, and market segment information about the customer. Once the data has been analyzed and CRM programs developed, salespeople can help implement the programs. For instance, bankers use a "high-touch approach" in which they frequently call on their best customers or contact them by phone. A salesperson can contact customers when there are new products or changes to existing product lines. He or she can probe customers about what they liked or disliked about their recent transactions with the firm. Or the purpose of the call can be purely social. If done properly, customers will feel special and important when a salesperson calls just to see how things are going.

relationship selling
A sales philosophy and process that emphasizes a commitment to maintaining the relationship over the long term and investing in opportunities that are mutually beneficial to all parties.

The Value Added by Personal Selling

LO 4

Why have salespeople in the supply chain? They are expensive, and as we discuss later in this chapter, they can be a challenge to manage. Some firms, like retailers, have made the decision not to use a sales force and become, for the most part, almost completely self-service. But those that use personal selling as part of their integrated marketing communications program do so because it adds value to their product or service mix—that is, personal selling is worth more than it costs. Personal selling adds value by educating and providing advice, saving the customer time, and making things easier for the customer.[53]

Salespeople Educate and Provide Advice   Imagine how difficult it would be to buy a new suit, a diamond engagement ring, or a plasma TV without the help of a salesperson. Similarly, UPS wouldn't dream of investing in a new fleet of airplanes without the benefit of Boeing's selling team. Sure, it could be done, but customers see the value in and are willing to pay indirectly for the education and advice salespeople provide. Retail salespeople can provide valuable information about how a garment fits, new fashions, or directions for operating products. Boeing's sales team can provide UPS with the technical aspects of the aircraft, as well as the economic justification for the purchase.

Five years ago, many observers thought that travel agents and other service providers would be replaced by more efficient Internet services, and the Internet has certainly changed the way many consumers make travel decisions. Thousands use sites like Expedia.ca and Travelocity.com or visit airlines, rail, hotels, and car rental firms online to make reservations directly. But when booking a complicated trip or cruise or planning to visit an exotic locale, or for those who don't feel comfortable buying online, travel agents add significant value. They can help with itineraries, give helpful tips, and even save the customer money.

Salespeople Save Time and Simplify Buying   Time is money! Customers perceive value in time and labour savings. In many grocery and drugstore chains, salespeople employed by the vendor supplying merchandise straighten stock, set up displays, assess inventory levels, and write orders. In some cases, such as bakeries or soft drink sales, salespeople and truck drivers even bring in the merchandise and stock the shelves. These are all tasks that retail employees would otherwise have to do.

Sometimes, however, turning over too many tasks to suppliers' salespeople can cause problems. If they take over the inventory management function, for instance, they may buy a suboptimal quantity of competitors' products. They might also place competitor products in disadvantageous shelf positions. Salespeople can help facilitate a buying situation, but they shouldn't take it over.

LO 5 The Personal Selling Process

Although selling may appear a rather straightforward process, successful salespeople follow several steps. Depending on the sales situation and the buyer's readiness to purchase, the salesperson may not use every step, and the time required for each step will vary depending on the situation. For instance, if a customer goes into The Bay already prepared to purchase some chino pants, the selling process will be fairly quick. But if IBM is attempting to sell personal computers for the first time to a university, the process may take several months. With this in mind, let's examine each step of the selling process (Exhibit 16.4).

Step 1: Generate and Qualify Leads   The first step in the selling process is to generate a list of potential customers (**leads**) and assess their potential (**qualify**). Salespeople who already have an established relationship with a customer will skip this step, and it is not used extensively in retail settings. In B2B situations, however, it is important to work continually to find new and potentially profitable customers.

Salespeople generate leads in a variety of ways.[54] They can discover potential leads by talking to their current customers and networking at events such as industry conferences or chamber of commerce meetings. The Internet has been a boon for generating leads. For instance, salespeople can gather information collected on the firm's website or Google a few key words and instantly generate enough potential leads to keep them busy for weeks. **Trade shows** also offer an excellent forum for finding leads. These major events are attended by buyers who choose to be exposed to products and services offered by potential suppliers in an industry. For instance, the Canadian Meeting & Incentive Travel Group hosts the IncentiveWorks Show at the Metro Toronto Convention Centre every August. Over 475 exhibit booths representing more than 700 companies from a variety of domestic and international destinations, hotels, resorts, meeting/incentive travel services, business gifts, premium, and reward merchandise exhibit at the show.[55]

Cold calls are a method of prospecting in which salespeople telephone or go to see potential customers without appointments. **Telemarketing** is similar to a cold call, but it always occurs over the telephone. Sometimes professional telemarketing firms, rather than the firm's salespeople, make such calls. However, cold calls and telemarketing have become less popular than they were in the past. First, the success

A great place to generate leads is at a trade show.

leads
A list of potential customers.

qualify
The process of assessing the potential of sales leads.

trade shows
Major events attended by buyers who choose to be exposed to products and services offered by potential suppliers in an industry.

cold calls
A method of prospecting in which salespeople telephone or go to see potential customers without appointments.

telemarketing
A method of prospecting in which salespeople telephone potential customers.

EXHIBIT 16.4	The Personal Selling Process

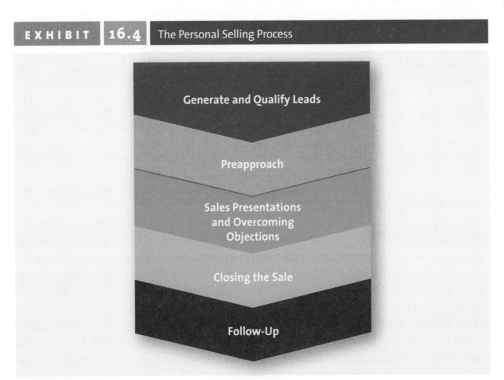

Generate and Qualify Leads

Preapproach

Sales Presentations and Overcoming Objections

Closing the Sale

Follow-Up

Retail salespeople should never "judge a book by its cover" and assume that a person in the store doesn't fit the store's image or cannot afford to purchase there.

rate is fairly low because the potential customer's need has not been established ahead of time. As a result, these methods can be very expensive. Second, both federal and provincial governments have begun to regulate the activities of telemarketers. Federal rules prohibit telemarketing to consumers whose names appear on the national Do-Not-Call list, which is maintained by the Canadian Marketing Association. Even for those consumers whose names are not on the list, the rules prohibit calling before 8:00 a.m. or after 9:00 p.m. (in the consumer's time zone) or after the consumer has told the telemarketer not to call. Federal rules also prohibit unsolicited fax messages and unsolicited telephone calls, as well as e-mail messages to cell phones.

After salespeople generate leads, they must qualify those leads by determining whether it is worthwhile to pursue them and attempt to turn them into customers. In a retail setting, qualifying potential can be a very dangerous and potentially illegal practice. Retail salespeople should never "judge a book by its cover" and assume that a person in the store doesn't fit the store's image or cannot afford to purchase there. Imagine going to an upscale jewellery store to purchase an engagement ring, only to be snubbed because you are dressed in your everyday, casual school clothes. But in B2B settings, where the costs of preparing and making a presentation can be substantial, the seller must assess a lead's potential. Salespeople should consider, for instance, whether the potential customer's needs pertain to a product or a service. They should also assess whether the lead has the financial resources to pay for the product or service.

preapproach
In the personal selling process, occurs prior to meeting the customer for the first time and extends the qualification of leads procedure; in this step, the salesperson conducts additional research and develops plans for meeting with the customer.

Step 2: Preapproach The **preapproach** occurs prior to meeting the customer for the first time and extends the qualification of leads procedure described in Step 1. Although the salesperson has learned about the customer during the qualification stage, in this step, he or she must conduct additional research and develop plans for meeting with the customer. Suppose, for example, a management consulting firm wants to sell a bank a new system for finding chequing account errors. The consulting firm's salesperson should first find out everything possible about the bank: How many cheques does it process? What system is the bank using now? What are the benefits of the consultant's proposed system compared with the competition? The answers to these questions provide the basis for establishing value for the customer.

Having done the additional research, the salesperson establishes goals for meeting with the customer; it is important that he or she know ahead of time exactly what should be accomplished. For instance, the consulting firm's salesperson can't expect to get a commitment from the bank that it will buy on the first visit. But a demonstration of the system and a short presentation about how the system would benefit the customer would be appropriate.

Step 3: Sales Presentation and Overcoming Objections

The Presentation Once all the background information has been obtained and the objectives for the meeting are set, the salesperson is ready for a person-to-person meeting. Let's continue with our bank example. During the first part of the meeting, the salesperson needs to get to know the customer, get his or her attention, and create interest in the presentation to follow. The beginning of the presentation may be the most important part of the entire selling process, because this is where the sales person establishes exactly where the customer is in his or her buying process (Exhibit 16.5). (For a refresher on the B2B buying process, see Chapter 7.) Suppose, for instance, the bank is in the first stage of the buying process, need recognition. It would not be prudent for the salesperson to discuss the pros and cons of different potential suppliers because doing so would assume that the customer already had reached Stage 4, proposal analysis and customer selection. By asking a series of questions, however, the salesperson can assess the bank's need for the product or service and adapt or customize the presentation to match the customer's need and stage in the decision process.[56]

Asking questions is only half the battle; carefully listening to the answers is equally important. Some salespeople, particularly inexperienced ones, believe that to be in control, they must do all the talking. Yet it is impossible to really understand where the customer stands without listening carefully. What if the COO says, "It seems kind of expensive"? If the salesperson isn't listening carefully, he or she won't pick up on the subtle nuances of what the customer is really thinking. In this case, it probably means the COO doesn't see the value in the offering.

When the salesperson has a good feel for where the customer stands, he or she can apply that knowledge to help the customer solve its problem or satisfy its need. The salesperson might begin by explaining the features or characteristics of the system that will reduce chequing account errors. It may not be obvious, based solely on these features, however, that the system adds value beyond the bank's current practices. Using the answers to some of the questions the salesperson posed earlier in the meeting, he or she can clarify the product's advantages over current or past practices, as well as the overall benefits of adopting the new system. The salesperson might explain, for instance, that the bank can expect a 20-percent improvement in chequing account errors and that, based on the size of the bank and number of cheques it processes per year, this improvement would represent $2 million in annual savings.

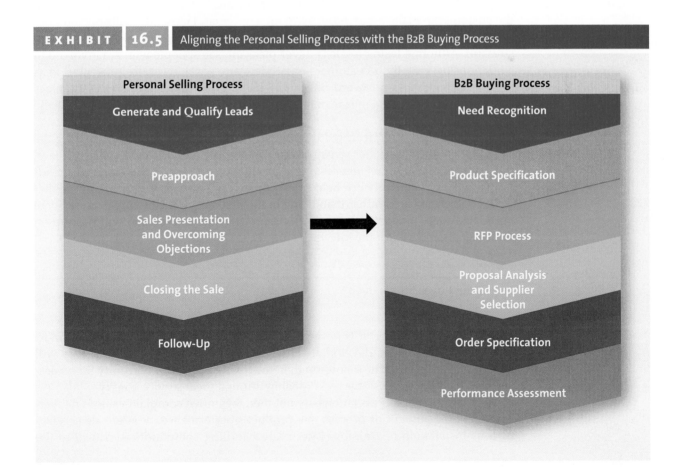

EXHIBIT 16.5   Aligning the Personal Selling Process with the B2B Buying Process

Personal Selling Process

Generate and Qualify Leads

Preapproach

Sales Presentation and Overcoming Objections

Closing the Sale

Follow-Up

B2B Buying Process

Need Recognition

Product Specification

RFP Process

Proposal Analysis and Supplier Selection

Order Specification

Performance Assessment

Because the system costs $150,000 per year and will take only three weeks to integrate into the current system, it will add significant and almost immediate value.

Handling Objections   An integral part of the sales presentation is handling objections that the buyer might have about the product or service. Although objections can arise during each stage of the selling process, they are very likely to occur during the sales presentation. Customers may raise objections pertaining to a variety of issues, but they usually relate in some way to value, such as that the price is too high for the level of quality or service.

Good salespeople know the types of objections buyers are likely to raise. They may know, for instance, that their service is slower than competitors' or that their selection is limited. Although not all objections can be forestalled, effective salespeople can anticipate and handle some. For example, when the bank COO said the cheque service seemed expensive, the salesperson was ready with information about how quickly the investment would be recouped.

Similar to other aspects of the selling process, the best way to handle objections is to relax and listen, then ask questions to clarify any reservations. For example, the salesperson could respond to the COO's objection by asking, "How much do you think the bank is losing through chequing account errors?" Her answer might open up a conversation about the positive trends in a cost/benefit analysis. Such questions are usually more effective than trying to prove the customer's objection is not valid because the latter approach implies the salesperson isn't really listening and could lead to an argument. In an attempt to handle objections and start the process of closing the sale, a salesperson may offer creative deals or incentives that may be unethical.

closing the sale
Obtaining a commitment from the customer to make a purchase.

Step 4: Closing the Sale   Closing the sale means obtaining a commitment from the customer to make a purchase. Without a successful close, the salesperson goes away empty handed, so many salespeople find this part of the sales process very stressful. Although losing a sale is never pleasant, salespeople who are involved in a relationship with their customers must view any particular sales presentation as part of the progression toward ultimately making the sale. An unsuccessful close on one day may just be a means of laying the groundwork for a successful close the next meeting.

Although we have presented the selling process in a series of steps, closing the sale rarely follows the other steps so neatly. However, good salespeople listen carefully to what potential customers say and pay attention to their body language. Reading these signals carefully can help salespeople achieve an early close. Suppose that our hypothetical bank, rather than being in the first step of the buying process, were in the final step of negotiation and selection. An astute salesperson will pick up on these signals and ask for the sale.

Step 5: Follow-Up

> "It ain't over till it's over."
> —Yogi Berra[57]

With relationship selling, it is never really over, even after the sale has been made. The attitudes customers develop after the sale become the basis for how they will purchase in the future. The follow-up therefore offers a prime opportunity for a salesperson to solidify the customer relationship through great service quality.

When customers' expectations are not met, they often complain—about deliveries, the billing amount or process, the product's performance, or after-sale services such as installation or training. Effectively handling complaints is critical to the future of the relationship. As we noted in Chapter 11, the best way to handle complaints is to listen to the customer, provide a fair solution to the problem, and resolve the problem quickly.

The best way to nip a postsale problem in the bud is to check with the customer right after he or she takes possession of the product or immediately after the service has been completed. This speed demonstrates responsiveness and empathy; it also shows the customer that the salesperson and the firm care about customer satisfaction. Finally, a postsale follow-up call, e-mail, or letter takes the salesperson back to the first step in the sales process for initiating a new order and sustaining the relationship.

Managing the Sales Force

Like any business activity involving people, the sales force requires management. **Sales management** involves the planning, direction, and control of personal selling activities, including recruiting, selecting, training, motivating, compensating, and evaluating, as they apply to the sales force.[58]

Managing a sales force is a rewarding yet complicated undertaking. In this section, we examine how sales forces can be structured, some of the most important issues in recruiting and selecting salespeople, sales training issues, ways to compensate salespeople, and finally, how to supervise and evaluate salespeople.

sales management Involves the planning, direction, and control of personal selling activities, including recruiting, selecting, training, motivating, compensating, and evaluating, as they apply to the sales force.

Sales Force Structure

Imagine the daunting task of putting together a sales force from scratch. Will you hire your own salespeople, or should they be manufacturer's representatives? What will be each salesperson's primary duties? Will they work together in teams? We examine these issues here.

Company Sales Force or Manufacturer's Representative A company sales force is comprised of people who are employees of the selling company. **Independent agents**, also known as **manufacturer's representatives,** are salespeople who sell a manufacturer's products on an extended contract basis but are not employees of the manufacturer. They are compensated by commissions and do not take ownership or physical possession of the merchandise.

Manufacturer's representatives are useful for smaller firms or firms expanding into new markets because such companies can achieve instant and extensive sales coverage without having to pay full-time personnel. Good sales representatives have many established contacts and can sell multiple products from noncompeting manufacturers during the same sales call. Also, the use of manufacturers' representatives facilitates flexibility; it is much easier to replace a rep than an employee and much easier to expand or contract coverage in a market with a sales rep than with a company sales force.

Company sales forces are more typically used for established product lines. Because the salespeople are company employees, the manufacturer has more control over what they do. If, for example, the manufacturer's strategy is to provide extensive customer service, the sales manager can specify exactly what actions a company sales force must take. In contrast, because manufacturer's representatives are paid on a commission basis, it is difficult to persuade them to take any action that doesn't directly lead to sales.

Although the life of a professional salesperson is highly varied, salespeople generally play three important roles: order getting, order taking, and sales support.

independent agents (or manufacturer's representative) Salespeople who sell a manufacturer's products on an extended contract basis but are not employees of the manufacturer; also known as *manufacturer's representatives* or *reps.*

Good salespeople, particularly in difficult selling situations like in door-to-door sales, don't easily take no for an answer. They keep coming back until they get a yes.

Recruiting and Selecting Salespeople

When the firm has determined how the sales force will be structured, it must find and hire salespeople. Although superficially this task may sound easy, it must be performed carefully because firms don't want to hire the wrong person—salespeople are very expensive to train.

The most important activity in the recruiting process is to determine exactly what the salesperson will be doing and what personal traits and abilities a person should have to do the job well. For instance, a Coca-Cola sales rep who goes to Safeway to pitch a new product will typically need significant sales experience, coupled with great communication and analytical skills. Coke's order takers, who process routine orders, need to be reliable and able to get along with lots of different types of people in the stores, from managers to customers.

When recruiting salespeople, is it better to look for candidates with innate sales ability, or can a good training program make anyone a successful salesperson? By a margin of 7 to 1 in a survey of sales and marketing executives, respondents believed that training and supervision are more critical determinants of selling success than the salesperson's inherent personal characteristics.[59] Yet some of those same respondents noted that certain personal traits are important for successful sales careers. Those traits, as identified by managers and sales experts [60] are personality, optimism, resilience, self-motivation, and empathy.

Sales Training

All salespeople benefit from training about selling and negotiation techniques, product and service knowledge, technologies used in the selling process, time and territory management, and company policies and procedures.

Firms use varied delivery methods to train their salespeople, depending on the topic of the training, what type of salesperson is being trained, and the cost versus the value of the training. For instance, an on-the-job training program is excellent for communicating selling and negotiation skills because managers can observe the sales trainees in real selling situations and provide instant feedback. They can also engage in role-playing exercises, in which the salesperson acts out a simulated buying situation and the manager critiques the salesperson's performance.

A much less expensive training method is the Internet. Online training programs have revolutionized the way training happens in many firms. Firms can provide new product and service knowledge, spread the word about changes in company policies and procedures, and share selling tips in a user-friendly environment that salespeople can access anytime and anywhere. Distance learning sales training programs through teleconferencing enable a group of salespeople to participate with their instructor or manager in a virtual classroom. While online sales training may never replace the one-on-one interaction of on-the-job training for advanced selling skills, it is quite effective and efficient for many other aspects of the sales training task.

Motivating and Compensating Salespeople

An important goal for any effective sales manager is to get to know his or her salespeople and determine what motivates them to be effective. Some salespeople prize their freedom and like to be left alone, whereas others want attention and are more productive when they receive accolades for a job well done. Still others are motivated primarily by monetary compensation. Great sales managers determine how best to motivate each of their salespeople according to what is most important to each individual. Although sales managers can emphasize different motivating factors, the methods used to compensate salespeople are fairly standardized and can be divided into two categories: financial and nonfinancial.

Financial Rewards Salespeople's compensation usually has several components. Most salespeople receive at least part of their compensation as a salary, a fixed sum of money paid at regular intervals. Another common financial incentive is a commission, money paid as a percentage of the sales volume or profitability. A bonus is a payment made at management's discretion when the salesperson attains certain goals; bonuses usually are given only periodically, such as at the end of the year. A sales contest is a short-term incentive designed to elicit a specific response from the sales force. Prizes might be cash or other types of financial incentives.

Nonfinancial Rewards As we have noted, good salespeople are self-motivated. They want to do a good job and make the sale because it makes them feel good. But this good feeling also can be accentuated by recognition from peers and management. Nonfinancial rewards should have high symbolic value, as plaques, pens, or rings do. Free trips or days off are also effective rewards. More important than what the reward is, however, is the way it is operationalized. For instance, an award should be given at a sales meeting and publicized in the company newsletter. It should also be done in good taste, because if the award is perceived as tacky, no one will take it seriously.[61]

Evaluating Salespeople

Salespeople's evaluation process must be tied to their reward structure. If salespeople do well, they should receive their just rewards. Considering this guiding principle, how should sales managers evaluate their salespeople? The answer is never easy because measures must be tied to performance, and there are many ways to measure performance in a complex job like selling. For example, evaluating performance on the basis of monthly sales alone fails to consider how profitable the sales were, whether any progress was made to build new business that will be realized sometime in the future, or the level of customer service the salesperson provided. Because the sales job is multifaceted with many contributing success factors, sales managers should use multiple measures.[62]

Sales, profits, and the number of orders represent examples of objective evaluation measures. However, such measures do not provide an adequate perspective for a thorough evaluation because there is no means of comparison with other salespeople. For this reason, firms use ratios like profit per customer, orders per call, sales per hour, or expenses compared to sales as their objective measures. Subjective evaluation measures seek to assess salespeople's behaviour: what they do and how well they do it and reflect one person's opinion about another's performance. Thus, subjective evaluations can be biased and should be used cautiously and only in conjunction with multiple objective measures.

Personal selling is an integral component of some firms' integrated marketing communications strategy. Although it doesn't make sense for all firms, it is widely used in B2B markets, as well as in B2C markets in which the price of the merchandise is relatively high and customers need some one-to-one assistance before they can buy. Due to the relatively high expense of maintaining a personal selling force, it is important that salespeople be adequately trained, motivated, and compensated.

Learning Objectives Review

1) Describe advertising and the objectives of advertising

2) Understand the legal and ethical issues of concern to advertisers

3) Explain how sales promotions supplement a firm's IMC strategy

4) Understand how personal selling adds value

5) Identify the steps in the personal selling process

1) Advertising is a paid form of communications delivered by an identifiable source designed to persuade consumers to take action. All advertising campaigns are designed to either inform, persuade, or remind customers. Ads can also be used to stimulate demand for a particular category or industry, or for a specific brand, firm, or item.

2) Advertising is regulated by a plethora of federal and provincial agencies. The most important agencies are the Competition Bureau, which protects consumers against general deceptive advertising; the Canadian Radio-television and Telecommunications Commission, which has jurisdiction over radio, television, wire, satellite, and cable, and covers issues regarding the use of tobacco products and objectionable language; and Health Canada, whose Food and Drug Act regulates food, drugs, cosmetics, and medical devices.

If a message is designed to promote or sell a product or service, it is generally considered to have an economic motivation, but if the message has no promotional or selling intent, it is fully protected by the Charter of Rights and Freedoms. The line becomes blurred, however, when normally noncommercial venues are used to sell something. Another practice that is causing a stir emerges when the sender of a commercial message is not clearly identified. Activities such as bogus websites or certain stealth marketing programs, in which the identity of the sponsor of an activity or event is intentionally kept from prospective customers, can be considered deceptive promotional practices.

3) Sales promotions are special incentives or excitement-building programs that encourage purchase and include coupons, rebates, contests, free samples, and POP displays. They either push sales through the channel, as is the case with contests directed toward retail salespeo-

ple, or pull sales through the channel, as coupons and rebates do. Sales promotions usually occur in conjunction with other elements of a firm's IMC strategy, such as price promotions or loyalty programs. Trade channel sales promotions include discounts and allowances, co-op advertising, and sales force training.

4) Although the cost of an average B2B sales call is expensive (about $330), many firms believe they couldn't do business without their sales force. Customers can buy many products and services without the help of a salesperson, but in many other cases, it is worth the extra cost built into the price of a product to be educated about the product or get valuable advice. Salespeople can also simplify the buying process and therefore save the customer time and hassle.

5) Although we discuss selling in terms of steps, it truly represents a process, and the time spent in each step varies according to the situation. In the first step, the salesperson generates a list of viable customers. During the second step, the preapproach, the salesperson gathers information about the customer and prepares for the presentation. The third step, the sales presentation, consists of a personal meeting between the salesperson and the customer. Through discussion and by asking questions, the salesperson learns where the customer is in its buying process and tailors the discussion around what the firm's product or service can do to meet that customer's needs. During the fourth step, the close, the salesperson asks for the order. Finally, during the follow-up, the salesperson and support staff solidifies the long-term relationship by making sure the customer is satisfied with the purchase and addressing any complaints. The follow-up therefore sets the stage for the next purchase.

Key Terms

- advertising, 453
- AIDA model, 451
- closing the sale, 474
- cold calls, 471
- contest, 463
- coupon, 462
- cross-promoting, 467
- deal, 462
- independent agents, 475
- informative advertising, 454
- institutional advertisements, 456
- leads, 471
- loyalty program, 463
- manufacturer's representative, 475

- personal selling, 467
- persuasive advertising, 454
- point-of-purchase (POP) display, 463
- pop-up stores, 466
- preapproach, 472
- premium, 462
- product placement, 465
- product-focused advertisements, 456
- public service announcement (PSA), 456
- puffery, 459
- qualify, 471

- rebate, 464
- relationship selling, 469
- reminder advertising, 455
- sales management, 475
- sales promotion, 461
- sampling, 463
- social marketing, 456
- stealth marketing, 459
- sweepstakes, 463
- telemarketing, 471
- top-of-mind awareness, 455
- trade shows, 471
- viral marketing, 460

Concept Review

1. What is advertising?

2. What is the AIDA model? How does the AIDA model facilitate the planning and execution of marketing communications?

3. What are the three primary objectives of advertising?

4. List and explain some of the potential legal and ethical issues firms should consider when developing their marketing communications strategy.

5. What is sales promotion? What are the main objectives of sales promotion?

6. List six different kinds of consumer sales promotion tactics and discuss the advantages and disadvantages of each.

7. Describe the different kinds of sales promotion targeted to distribution channel members. Why are these trade channel promotions necessary? Are they ethical?

8. What is personal selling? Describe the steps in the personal selling process. Which stage do you consider to be the most important and why?

9. What is sales management? Why is sales management considered a complicated task?

10. What are the main considerations involved in recruiting, training, and compensating salespeople?

Marketing Applications

1. Choose one of the ads featured in this book and identify its page number. What are the objectives of this ad? Does the ad have more than one objective? Explain your answer.

2. Using the steps in the AIDA model, explain why a potential consumer in Question 1 who views advertising by designer jean company Juicy Couture may not be ready to go out and purchase a new pair of jeans.

3. Suppose Lexus is introducing a new line of light trucks and has already created the advertising campaign. How would you assess the effectiveness of the campaign?

4. Suppose now Lexus is planning a sales promotion campaign to augment its advertising campaign for the new line of light trucks. Which sales promotion tools do you believe would be the most effective? Why?

5. How would the Lexus sales promotion differ if it was geared to a business organization with a fleet of company owned trucks?

6. Choose an ad that you believe unreasonably overstates what the product or service can do. (If you can't think of a real ad, make one up.) Explain whether the ad is actually deceptive or just puffery. How would your answer change if you lived in France?

7. You are invited to your 6-year-old niece's birthday party and bring her the new superhero doll being advertised on television. She's thrilled when she unwraps the gift but is in tears a short time later because her new doll is broken. She explains that on TV, the doll flies and does karate kicks, but when she tried to play with the doll this way, it broke. You decide to call the manufacturer, and a representative

tells you he is sorry your niece is so upset but that the ad clearly states the doll does not fly. The next time you see the televised ad, you notice very small print at the bottom that states the doll does not fly. You decide to write a letter to the Advertising Standards Council about this practice. What information should you include in your letter?

8. "Salespeople just make products cost more." Agree or disagree with this statement and discuss why you've taken that position.

9. Choose an industry or a specific company that you would like to work for as a salesperson. How would you generate and qualify leads?

10. You have taken a summer job in the windows and doors department of a large home improvement store. During sales training, you learn about the products, how to best address customers' needs, why the lifetime value of the customer concept is so important to a store like this, and how to sell the customer the best product to fit their needs regardless of price point. One day your manager informs you that you are to recommend Smith Windows to every window customer. Smith Windows are more expensive and don't really provide superior benefit except in limited circumstances. The manager is insistent that you recommend Smith. Not knowing what else to do, you recommend Smith Windows to customers who would have been better served by lower cost windows. The manager rewards you with a sales award. Later the manager tells you that he received an all-expenses-paid cruise for his family from Smith Windows. What, if anything, should you do with this information?

Toolkit

MAKE AN ADVERTISEMENT

Suppose you have been hired to develop a new ad for a product or service to help target the college and university student market. These ads will appear in student newspapers around the world. Please use the toolkit provided at www.mcgrawhill.ca/olc/grewal to develop the ad.

Net Savvy

1. Go to the website for Concerned Children's Advertisers (www.cca-kids.ca/) an agency that produces and delivers social messaging campaigns on issues of challenge in children's lives. Click on the About Us tab and examine the history and activities of CCA. How does the role they play in responsible advertising complement the formal regulation of other agencies? Now look under the News tab. Choose one of the PSAs and discuss how these ads are used to deliver CCA's message.

2. Go to couponsaver.com (www.couponsurfer.com/) and identify five of the products featured. How effective are coupons for selling these products? Why? What are the benefits to the seller of using couponsaver.com over other integrated marketing communication options? How do you think couponsaver.com makes money?

Chapter Case Study

WEST49.COM—THE CUTTING EDGE OF COOL

Canadians are becoming increasingly involved in online media, ranging from the use of social networking to file sharing with each other. Recent surveys suggest that 42 percent of Canadians have visited at least one social network site, such as Facebook or MySpace.[63] Online video is hot too, with more than a quarter of all Internet users regularly watching videos online.

Canada's largest board sports retailer, West 49, has always had a strong presence on the Web. Its quirky commercials have been a favourite on YouTube, and traditional television advertising had been successful in driving steady traffic to its site. The Web-savvy snowboarding, surfing, and skateboarding consumers who were visiting West49.com posted frequently on message boards and checked out the reams of information about their favourite sports. Consumers returned to the site again and again despite its limited functionality. But West 49 wasn't satisfied with its Web presence.

To stay on the cutting edge of cool, the Canadian skateboarding retail firm revamped the site. Launched in early 2006, different elements were tested in an attempt to inspire stickiness that would translate into sales. The company recognized the need to deliver more engaging content and capitalize on the user-generated trend of the Internet.

Leveraging its existing site, West 49 began by adding video to the site featuring past television commercials. A large video section showcasing cool board tricks was added from its sponsored skateshows. Users were also encouraged to submit their own clips with the chance to be featured on the site. Collaborating with key partners like DC Shoes and Quicksilver, West 49 flooded YouTube with video clips and advertised on skateboarding blogs.

Taking the multimedia experience one step further, West49 set up a user-generated content-inspired feature section where unsigned bands could upload their songs and have them played for free. The audio section highlighted music's cultural connection to board sports. While some monitoring was necessary to filter out inappropriate or copyrighted content, the audio application was extremely effective in attracting traffic. Considering all the new features and applications, overall site membership increased 276 percent.

As West49's Web portal continued to evolve, the company introduced the "All Access Pass."[64] This program integrated the in-store and online experiences to enrich brand loyalty. Exclusive Web benefits included invitees to "chat" events featuring prominent skate, surf, and snowboard icons, as well as online contests and promotions. Membership also tied back to the multimedia experience to include free audio and video downloads each month. Cardholders were privy to member-only deals on merchandise both in-store and online, such as free shipping on all Web orders. Purchases made at West49 stores and BoardZone.com provided cash back in a "piggybank" account—the balance of which could be applied to future purchases.

The increased West49.com activity had a big impact on sales at BoardZone.com. During the 2006 holiday season, the brand destination pushed as much as 40 percent of the e-commerce site's sales. Multimedia downloads skyrocketed during the first 12 to 18 months. Although this tapered off, they are still going strong, growing at nearly 20 percent for videos and around 10 percent for music compared to the same period in 2006.

West49's brand site initiatives successfully relayed traffic to Boardzone.com, its ecommerce site. More importantly, it gave the company a newfound ability to profile users, track website activity, and tie it all back to purchasing patterns.

Source: Adapted from Marketing Sherpa.com. case study, "How Online Video & UCG Lifted Conversions 27 percent for Youth-Oriented Site," www.marketingsherpa.com/article.php?ident=30020, June 20, 2007.

West49 revamped its website to deliver more engaging content and capitalize on the user-generated trend of the Internet.

Questions

1. Identify which West49 tactics would be considered advertising and which would be considered sales promotion. Which of the two elements will be more important in attracting future visitors to the site?

2. Identify and link the various advertising and promotion tactics used by West49 to the buyer readiness model described in this chapter. How effective do you think these tactics are to West49's success?

3. With increased traffic at West49.com, should the company decrease its investment in traditional television and print advertising? Why or why not?

4. Visit West49.com and Boardzone.com. What types of appeals do you see in the messages being communicated on these two sites? How would these appeals change if the company was trying to attract parents buying items for their teenaged children?

LEARNING OBJECTIVES

After studying this chapter, you should be able to:

LO **1** Identify the factors that aid the growth of globalization

LO **2** Explain the factors a firm considers when deciding to enter a global market

LO **3** Describe the ownership and partnership options firms have for entering a new global market

LO **4** Distinguish the similarities and differences between a domestic marketing strategy and a global marketing strategy

LO **5** Explain how ethical issues affect global marketing practices

Global Marketing

I n 1998, Chip Wilson, the creative mind behind Lululemon Athletica, started his yoga-inspired athletic apparel manufacturing and retailing business in Kitsilano, a trendy Vancouver neighbourhood. His original goal was to have one store in Kitsilano, and never grow beyond that. Less than a decade later, Lululemon has been transformed into a global company and a great Canadian success story in the athletic and sportswear indus-try. Lululemon has been growing exponentially since 1998 from just one store to more than 52 company-owned stores across Canada, the U.S., Japan, and Australia, and nine shops at fitness clubs in Hong Kong, Taiwan, Malaysia, Singapore, Mexico, Switzerland, and the UK. It plans to use these nine shops as springboards to setup standalone stores in those countries. Lululemon's global expansion focus has so far resulted in 16 stores in the United States with plans for another 200 company-owned stores, two stores in Japan with plans for another 20 company-owned stores, and two stores in Australia with plans for several more. The com-pany also has its sights set on Europe. In 2007, the company reported annual sales of close to $150 million, more than 1650 employees, a growth rate of 77 percent, and several expansion projects worldwide. About half of its products are manufactured at factories in Vancouver and the other half by third-party, mostly Taiwanese, vendors. Its clothing is distributed from facilities in Vancouver and Washington.

Lululemon finds itself competing head-to-head with established global giants such as Nike, Adidas, Reebok, and other U.S. and European sportswear manufacturers. So far it has been able to successfully steal market share from these global companies that have domi-nated the market for years. And, it's not like its line of sportswear goods and accessories are cheap. If you want to wear a pair of Lululemon pants, prepare to fork out about $100 and over $50 for a top. By any metric, Lululemon's success on the international stage within such

Customers are individuals that work, play, and share Lululemon's vision of creating healthier, happier, and more fun lives!

a short period of time is phenomenal, especially since many excellent Canadian companies have failed in the U.S. and other global markets. So what's the craze all about everywhere that Lululemon sets up shop? Is it its marketing communications campaigns? Its products and fabrics? Its philosophy or what the brand stands for—a healthy, balanced, and fun-filled lifestyle which says, not just to do yoga but be yoga? All of the above and more?[1]

Why was Lululemon so successful in the U.S., Japan, and in so many other Asian countries, where so many others have failed? A huge part of Lululemon's success can be attributed to its understanding of the culture of new markets and the manner in which it enters those markets and connects with customers. First, the company introduced its functional, comfortable, and fashionable tight clothing made of breathable fabric in response to the growing trends of female participation in sports, specifically yoga, and the demand for clothing made from sustainable materials. Second, Lululemon "eyes global markets but seeks local advice,"[2] that is, it works closely with its customers—yogis and athletes in local communities for continuous research and product feedback. These customers help Lululemon set the standard in technical fabrics and functional designs. It has cultivated strong relationships with the local communities where it operates. For example, it encourages interactions with local communities at its regular meetings with local designers and allows local stores to customize their products not only to the Japanese market but to the local communities they serve. Third, Lululemon has developed a strong local organization by partnering with local companies. For example, in Japan, it has partnered with Descente Ltd, a renowned leader in fabric technology for the sports apparel market. It entered Japan through a Japanese joint-venture that clearly understands the Japanese market and serves as a source for further market research.

Lululemon's story demonstrates that success in global markets rests mainly on a deep understanding of the culture of the markets and crafting the 4Ps in such as way as to ensure that the unique needs and wants of customers in the global markets are well served. Of course, other considerations such as the political and economic conditions of the markets will dictate whether a company should enter the market or not. But once the decision is made to go global, cultural considerations should drive the marketing strategy.

The increasing globalization of markets affects all companies—large, small, medium, and entrepreneurial—in Canada, and around the world. Many Canadian companies find themselves becoming part of the global supply chain. Competition is no longer local, provincial, or even national; it is global. Canadian companies not only have to compete with other global companies for raw materials, labour, knowledge, and other inputs, but also for markets for their products. Most people don't think about how globalization impacts their daily lives, but just take a minute and read the labels on the clothing you are wearing right now. Chances are that most of the items, even if they carry Canadian or U.S. brand names, were manufactured in another part of the world such as China, India, Thailand, Mexico, Brazil, and dozens of other developing countries.

In Canada, the market has evolved from a system of local and provincial marketplaces to national markets to geographically regional markets (e.g., Canada and the United States together) to international markets and finally to global markets. **Globalization** refers to the processes by which goods, services, capital, people, information, and ideas flow across national borders. Global markets are the result of several fundamental changes, such as reductions or eliminations of trade barriers by country governments, the decreasing concerns of distance and time with regard to moving products and ideas across countries, the standardization of laws across borders, and globally integrated production processes.[3] For instance, consider the Seven of All Mankind jeans described in Chapter 7, B2B Marketing. It is possible that Seven buys the raw materials (denim and thread) from a supplier in one country, the sewing machines and washers from a supplier in another country, the tiny rocks, knives, and sanders from another supplier in a third country, workers in a fourth county make the jeans, and marketers in several countries around the world are involved in the sale of the jeans, which are bought by consumers in many countries. Thus, globalization creates a lot of interdependencies among firms spread across the globe and among divisions of firms (research and development (R&D), design, engineering, manufacturing, and marketing). For example, Nortel has a research lab in Bangalore, India, several design facilities in the U.S., and a manufacturing facility in Ireland. Nortel also maintains marketing offices in the countries in which it operates.

Globalization has not only created economies of scale because of the global scale in which research, production, and marketing are performed but also made it possible for many market niches that were not profitable at the provincial or national level to become profitable at the global level. For instance, Gennum of Burlington, Ontario, which makes specialized parts for the hearing instrument industry found that the Canadian market is too small for its products, however, on a global scale

globalization
Refers to the processes by which goods, services, capital, people, information, and ideas flow across national borders.

CHAPTER
ROADMAP

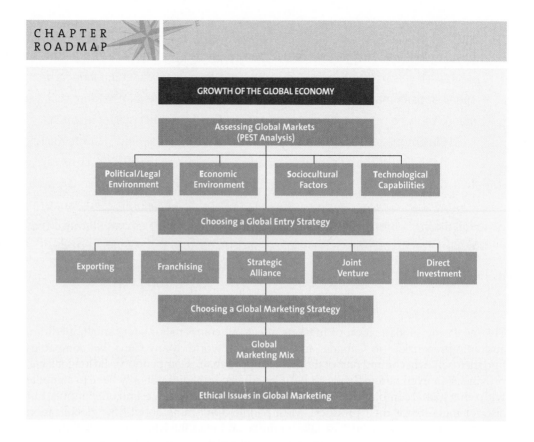

it can profitably serve this market niche. To exploit the global niche, it has global design, R&D, and sales offices in Japan, Taiwan, Korea, and the United Kingdom. Additionally, many Canadian companies are part of the global supply chain supplying inputs and raw materials rather than marketing finished products.

Each of these fundamental changes has paved the way for marketing to flourish in other countries. The elimination of trade barriers and other governmental actions, for instance, allows goods and ideas to move quickly and efficiently around the world, which in turn facilitates the quick delivery of goods to better meet the needs of global consumers. When examining countries as potential markets for global products, companies must realize that these different countries exist at very different stages of globalization. The World Bank ranks countries according to their degrees of globalization on the basis of a composite measure that examines whether the factors necessary to participate in the global marketplace are present. Countries that score well on the scale represent the best markets for globalized products and services; those lowest on the scale represent the most troublesome markets.

Most Canadians tend to take access to global products and services for granted. When we walk into Starbucks, we expect to find our favourite Jamaican Blue Mountain coffee ground and ready for us. But think about the process through which coffee came from a mountainside in Jamaica to your town. Or how a $3 Sri Lankan–made keychain could be produced, transported halfway around the world, and sold for so little money. These are the questions we will be examining in this chapter.

We begin by looking at the growth of the global economy and the forces that led to it. We'll see how firms assess the potential of a given market, make decisions to go global, and—as Lululemon did in the opening vignette—choose markets in which to sell globally. Then we explore how to build the marketing mix for global products and consider some of the ethical and legal issues of globalization. The chapter roadmap illustrates the sequence of this chapter content.

Growth of the Global Economy: Globalization of Marketing and Production

LO **1**

Changes in technology, especially communications technology, have been the driving force for growth in global markets for decades. The telegraph, radio, television, computer, and, now, Internet increasingly connect distant parts of the world. Today, communication is instantaneous. Sounds and images from across the globe are delivered to TV sets, radios, and computers in real time, which enables receivers in all parts of the world to observe how others live, work, and play.

The **globalization of production**, also known as **offshoring**, refers to manufacturers' procurement of goods and services from around the globe to take advantage of national differences in the cost and quality of various factors of production (e.g., labour, energy, land, capital).[4] Although originally focused on relocating manufacturing to lower cost producer countries, the practice of offshoring has now grown to include the products of the knowledge economy: medical services, financial services, technological services, and consulting. The growth of cities such as Bangalore, India, for instance, demonstrates the rapid progression of the globalization of production of both products and services.[5]

Bangalore is now home to divisions of Nortel Networks, GE, Intel, IBM, and a growing number of technology and service firms. Companies in Bangalore provide a broad range of services to customers, including software development, programming, and R&D, as well as customer call centres and help lines. Many consumers have been surprised by disclosures in the media about Indian radiologists who read X-rays taken of U.S. patients and digitally transmitted to India.[6] A similar idea was floated in Canada whereby the X-rays, MRIs, or CT scans of Canadians could be sent to places like India, the U.S., and Switzerland through teleradiology in order to reduce waiting times for results. Proponents suggest that this practice could reduce waiting times for results from about three months to 30 minutes. However, the idea was greeted with opposition from the Canadian Association of Radiologists and many ordinary Canadians.[7]

By globalizing production, companies can lower their total production costs and improve their overall competitive position because they are able to offer higher quality products at lower costs—that is, a better value for the consumer. Yet offshoring leads to a paradox: the problem of invisible beneficiaries and very visible losers.[8] For example, a recent PricewaterhouseCoopers report suggests that Canada stands to lose 75,000 IT jobs due to outsourcing to emerging powerhouses such as India and China.[9] The IT industry employees who have lost their jobs to offshoring are the visible losers, and the consumers who now benefit from the lower cost goods in the marketplace are the invisible winners. Also, the new IT industry employees in India are now able to better afford a better lifestyle.

The growth of global markets also has been facilitated by organizations that are designed to oversee their functioning. Perhaps the most important of these organizations is represented by the **General Agreement on Tariffs and Trade (GATT**—www.gatt.org). The purpose of the GATT was to lower trade barriers, such as high tariffs on imported goods and restrictions on the number and types of imported products that inhibited the free flow of goods across borders. In 1948, 23 countries agreed to 45,000 tariff concessions that affected about one-fifth of world trade.[10] Over the years, successive rounds of trade negotiations have led to further reductions in trade barriers, as well as new rules designed to promote global trade further.

globalization of production (or offshoring)
Also known as *offshoring*; refers to manufacturers' procurement of goods and services from around the globe to take advantage of national differences in the cost and quality of various factors of production (e.g., labour, energy, land, capital).

General Agreement on Tariffs and Trade (GATT)
Organization established to lower trade barriers, such as high tariffs on imported goods and restrictions on the number and types of imported products that inhibited the free flow of goods across borders.

Many goods and services are provided from other countries, an activity known as offshoring. At this call centre in Delhi, India, experts provide information to an Internet service provider in the U.K.

In this photo, World Bank President James Wolfensohn and other officials speak with reporters at the IMF headquarters in Washington.

International Monetary Fund (IMF)
Established with the original General Agreement on Tariffs and Trade (GATT); primary purpose is to promote international monetary cooperation and facilitate the expansion and growth of international trade.

World Trade Organization (WTO)
Replaced the GATT in 1994; differs from the GATT in that the WTO is an established institution based in Geneva, Switzerland, instead of simply an agreement; represents the only international organization that deals with the global rules of trade among nations.

World Bank Group
A development bank that provides loans, policy advice, technical assistance, and knowledge-sharing services to low- and middle-income countries in an attempt to reduce poverty in the developing world.

The original GATT also included the founding of the **International Monetary Fund (IMF**—www.imf.org), but in 1994, the GATT was replaced by the **World Trade Organization** (WTO—www.wto.org). The WTO differs from the GATT in that the WTO is an established institution based in Geneva, Switzerland, instead of simply an agreement. Furthermore, the WTO is the only international organization that deals with the global rules of trade among nations. Its main function is to ensure that trade flows as smoothly, predictably, and freely as possible. The WTO also administers trade agreements, acts as a forum for trade negotiations, settles trade disputes, reviews national trade policies, and assists developing countries in their trade policy issues through technical assistance and training. For instance, in 1995, in order to protect the Canadian magazine industry, the Canadian government imposed an 80-percent tax on split-run magazines—U.S. magazines reprinted in Canada with only a few pages of Canadian content added. The American government appealed the tax before the WTO, which ruled that Canada's tax on split-run magazines is in violation of international trade agreements. The WTO ordered Canada to comply with the decision within 18 months.[11] Currently, the 151 members of the WTO account for 97 percent of global trade.[12]

As we noted, the original GATT established the IMF, whose primary purpose is to promote international monetary cooperation and facilitate the expansion and growth of international trade. Along with the IMF, the **World Bank Group** is dedicated to fighting poverty and improving the living standards of people in the developing world. It is a development bank that provides loans, policy advice, technical assistance, and knowledge-sharing services to low- and middle-income countries in an attempt to reduce poverty.[13] Thus, the key difference between the IMF and the World Bank is that the IMF focuses primarily on maintaining the international monetary system, whereas the World Bank concentrates on poverty reduction through low-interest loans and other programs. For instance, the World Bank Group is the largest external funding source of education and HIV/AIDS programs.

Both these organizations affect the practice of global marketing in different ways, but together, they enable marketers to participate in the global marketplace by making it easier to buy and sell, financing deserving firms, opening markets to trade, and raising the global standard of living, which allows more people to buy goods and services. The financing assistance provided by both the World Bank and the IMF make it possible for firms in the developed world to market their products to developing countries.

However, these organizations have been criticized by a diverse group of nongovernmental organizations, religious groups, and advocates for workers and the poor. The primary criticism of the World Bank is that it is merely a puppet of Western industrialized nations that use World Bank loans to assist their globalization efforts. Others argue that the World Bank loans too much money to third-world countries, which makes it almost impossible for these often debt-ridden nations to repay the loans.[14] Ethical Dilemma 17.1 discusses some of the more general criticisms of globalization.

Globalization obviously has its critics, and those critics very well may have a point. But globalization also has been progressing at a steady and increasing pace. With that development in mind, let's look at how firms determine in which countries to expand their operations.

17.1 Globalization and Its Discontents

One of the most persuasive arguments antiglobalization groups use is that many of the problems related to globalization can be attributed to the seemingly insatiable appetite of countries in North America, Europe, and Asia (e.g., Japan, China, India) and other industrialized nations, for natural resources, oil, gasoline, timber, food, and so forth.[15] These nations consume 80 percent of the world's resources but are home to only 20 percent of the population. Should firms in industrialized nations be able to utilize these natural resources at a disproportionate rate, regardless of whether their shareholders demand profitable growth?

As the industrialized West has put into place laws that protect workers' rights, workers' safety, and the environment, many firms in the industrialized nations have outsourced production to less developed countries that either have no such laws or don't enforce them. Without laws to protect workers and the environment, the factories that produce these goods often exploit both the workers and the environment of these countries. Industrialized nations obtain the goods they crave at low costs, but at what price do these goods come to the country that provides them? Companies such as Coca Cola, Starbucks, and numerous others are often accused of abusing workers' rights and safety in these countries or of supporting governments with a track record of human rights abuse.

In many parts of the world, the changes wrought by globalization have moved so fast that cultures have not had time to adapt. Many countries fear that the price for economic success and participation in the global market may be the loss of their individual identities, cultures, and industry. The challenge thus becomes whether economic needs should be allowed to outweigh cultural preservation. Are governments and firms doing enough to protect indigenous cultures and workers' rights or are they driven primarily by profit motives—cheap labour, raw materials and resources, and low costs?

Assessing Global Markets

LO **2**

Because different countries, with their different stages of globalization, offer marketers a variety of opportunities, firms must assess the viability of various potential market entries. This is done through a situational analysis similar to what is described in Chapter 4 on Analyzing the Marketing Environment. As illustrated in Exhibit 17.1, four sets of factors are often used to assess a country's market: political/legal, economic, sociocultural, and technological factors. The acronym, PEST is used as shorthand to refer to these factors. Analysis of these four factors offer marketers a more complete picture of a country's potential as a market for products and services. Although we describe each factor separately, it is important to note that marketers consider them together in order to obtain a complete picture of a country's marketing potential.

Analyzing the Political and Legal Environment

Governmental actions, as well as the actions of nongovernmental political groups, can significantly influence firms' ability to sell goods and services, because they often result in laws or other regulations that either promote the growth of the global market or close off the country and inhibit growth. Policies aimed at restricting trade and global marketing are called protectionist polices and those that encourage global trade and marketing are referred to as trade liberalization policies. In this section, we discuss various forms of protectionist and liberalization policies. These issues include trade sanctions such as tariffs, quotas, boycotts, exchange controls, and **trade agreements**. (See Exhibit 17.2 on page 491.)

trade agreements
Intergovernmental agreements designed to manage and promote trade activities for specific regions.

Trade Sanctions **Trade sanctions** are penalties or restrictions imposed by one country over another country with respect to importing and exporting of goods or services and investments. In November 2007, Canada imposed sweeping trade sanctions on Burma, also called Myanmar, because of escalating human rights abuses by the Burmese government. Some of the measures announced include a ban on all goods exported from Canada to Burma (except humanitarian goods) and

trade sanctions
Penalties or restrictions imposed by one country over another country for importing and exporting of goods, services, and investments.

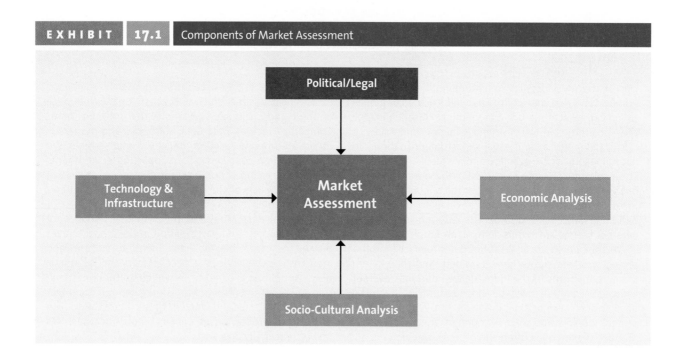

EXHIBIT   17.1   Components of Market Assessment

a ban on all goods imported from Burma into Canada.[16] An embargo is a form of trade sanction that prohibits trading with a certain country or trading in specific goods (e.g., oil embargo) by other signatory countries.

tariff (or duty)
A tax levied on a good imported into a country; also called a *duty.*

Tariffs   A **tariff** (also called a **duty**) is a tax levied on a good imported into a country. In most cases, tariffs are intended to make imported goods more expensive and thus less competitive with domestic products,[17] which in turn protects domestic industries from foreign competition. In other cases, tariffs might be imposed to penalize another country for trade practices that the home country views as unfair. In 2002, for example, the United States imposed a steep duty of 19.31 percent on Canadian softwood lumber exported to the U.S. because the U.S. softwood industry claims that Canada was subsidizing Canadian softwood lumber and Canadian lumber producers were **dumping** low cost softwood lumber on the U.S. market.[18] Dumping is selling a good in a foreign market at a price that is lower than its domestic price or below its cost.[19]

dumping
The practice of selling a good in a foreign market at a price that is lower than its domestic price or below its cost.

quota
Designates the maximum quantity of a product that may be brought into a country during a specified time period.

Quotas   A **quota** designates the maximum quantity of a product that may be brought into a country during a specified time period. Many Canadian quotas on foreign-made textiles were eliminated in 2005, which reduced the cost of imported apparel products sold in the Canada. Some firms have chosen to redistribute the bulk of these savings to consumers—in Wal-Mart's case, 75 percent of them—whereas others, such as Bebe, are planning to distribute only 25 percent and keep the rest as profit.[20]

Tariffs and quotas can impose a potentially devastating blow on a firm's ability to sell products in another country. Tariffs artificially raise prices and therefore lower demand, and quotas reduce the availability of imported merchandise. Conversely, tariffs and quotas benefit domestically made products because they reduce foreign competition. In the case of softwood lumber, tariffs and quotas benefits U.S. lumber producers and reduce competition from Canadian lumber producers. Unfortunately, U.S. consumers end up paying higher prices for U.S. softwood lumber rather than benefitting from cheaper Canadian lumber.

boycott
A group's refusal to deal commercially with some organization to protest against its policies.

Boycott   A **boycott** pertains to a group's refusal to deal commercially with some organization to protest against its policies. Boycotts might be called by governments or nongovernmental organizations, such as trade unions, human rights, or

Many quotas on foreign-made textiles have been eliminated. Some firms have chosen to redistribute the bulk of these savings to consumers—in Wal-Mart's case (left), 75 percent of the savings; whereas other firms, such as Bebe (right), are planning to redistribute only 25 percent of the savings and keep the rest as profit.

environmental groups. The war in Iraq has led to increasing calls for boycotts of U.S. products and services by various countries. According to the results of a recent survey[21] of 8000 consumers in six countries (Canada, China, France, Germany, Russia, and the United Kingdom) more than 20 percent of respondents from Europe and Canada stated that they were consciously avoiding purchasing U.S. products as a form of protest against U.S. foreign policy, especially its actions in Iraq. Corporations viewed as being "more American" fared the worst (e.g., Exxon-Mobile, AOL, Chevron, Texaco, United Airlines, Budweiser, Chrysler, Mattel [Barbie Dolls], Starbucks, and General Motors). Similarly, many U.S. organizations called for U.S. companies and citizens to boycott products from countries that did not support the U.S. going to war with Iraq. There were reports of technology companies refusing to take orders from Canadian companies and a call to avoid Canadian products such as beer, cheese, and hot dogs.[22] The long-term impact of such boycotts on the ability of U.S. firms to market in other countries, as a result of global antiwar sentiment, remains unknown.

exchange control
Refers to the regulation of a country's currency *exchange rate*.

exchange rate
The measure of how much one currency is worth in relation to another.

countertrade
Trade between two countries where goods are traded for other goods and not for hard currency.

Exchange Control Exchange control refers to the regulation of a country's currency **exchange rate**, the measure of how much one currency is worth in relation to another.[23] A designated agency in each country, often the Central Bank, sets the rules for currency exchange. In Canada, the Bank of Canada sets the rules for the currency exchange rates. In recent years, the value of the Canadian dollar against the U.S. dollar has increased significantly from around CAD$0.60 cents for US$1 in 2001 to CAD$1.10 in November 2007. The rise of the Canadian dollar has had a twofold effect on the ability of Canadian firms to conduct global business. For Canadian firms that depend on U.S. imports of finished products, raw materials, or services, the cost of doing business has gone down dramatically. However, U.S. buyers find the costs of Canadian goods and services much more expensive than they were before.

A method of avoiding an unfavourable exchange rate is to engage in countertrade. **Countertrade** is trade between two countries where goods are traded for other

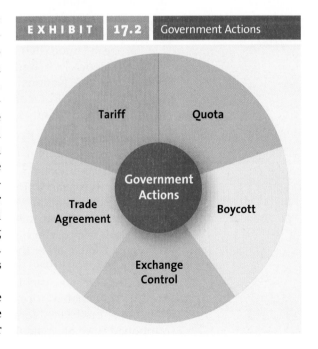

EXHIBIT 17.2 Government Actions

The increase in value of the Canadian dollar against the U.S. dollar has made Canadian exports to the U.S. more expensive, and imports from the U.S. less expensive.

goods and not for hard currency. For instance, the Philippine government has entered into a countertrade agreement with Vietnam. The Philippine International Trading Corp. is importing rice and paying for half of it with fertilizer, coconuts, and coconut by-products.[24] A study of Canadian executives' attitudes to counter trade found that although the majority sees the benefit of countertrade, they are lukewarm to being involved in the practice.[25]

All the restrictions on trade and global marketing discussed so far are deemed protectionist since they, in one way or another, protect a country's domestic industry from foreign competition. A country may also implement protectionist polices for social, economic, or political reasons. The Canadian government, for example, provides subsidies to farmers and technology companies in order for these industries or specific firms to grow and to compete globally. Bombardier and Nortel are two technology companies that benefit substantially from government subsidies. Another example of protectionist policies for political reasons is the action of the Venezuelan government. In 2007 President Hugo Chavez demanded that the state oil company PDVSA be awarded a 60-percent stake in all multinational oil companies. Many Western oil companies were unhappy with this ruling but had to comply or face tough penalties. President Chavez also announced that the government would nationalize companies in the electricity, telecommunications, and petroleum sectors as well as re-write the country's commercial code.[26]

Not all government polices are protectionist. Often, governments will implement policies and agreements to foster global trade and marketing. We now turn our attention to these agreements.

Trade Agreements   Marketers must consider the trade agreements to which a particular country is a signatory or the trading bloc to which it belongs. A trade agreement is an intergovernmental agreement designed to manage and promote trade activities for a specific region, and a **trading bloc** consists of those countries that have signed the particular trade agreement.[27]

trading bloc
Consists of those countries that have signed a particular trade agreement.

Some major trade agreements cover two-thirds of the world's international trade: the European Union (EU), the North American Free Trade Agreement (NAFTA), the Central America Free Trade Agreement (CAFTA), Mercosur, and the Association of Southeast Asian Nations (ASEAN).[28] These trade agreements are summarized in Exhibit 17.3. The EU represents the highest level of integration across individual nations, whereas the other agreements vary in their integration levels.

European Union   The EU is an economic and monetary union that currently contains 25 countries, as illustrated in Exhibit 17.4. Bulgaria and Romania headed a list of additional petitioners for membership, and have since been granted full membership.[29] The European Union represents a significant restructuring of the global marketplace. By dramatically lowering trade barriers between member nations within the union, the complexion of the global marketplace has changed.

Having one currency, the euro, across Europe has simplified the way many multinational firms market their products. For instance, prior to the conversion to the euro on January 1, 1999, firms were unable to predict exchange rates and this made it difficult to set consistent prices across countries in Europe. The introduction of the euro has eliminated price fluctuations due to currency exchange rates. Now products can be preticketed for distribution across Europe. Patent requirements were also simplified since one patent application could cover multiple countries. Similarly the

EXHIBIT 17.3	Trade Agreements
Name	**Countries**
European Union	Austria, Belgium, Denmark, Finland, France, Germany, Greece, Ireland, Italy, Luxembourg, Netherlands, Portugal, Spain, Sweden, United Kingdom of Great Britain, and Northern Ireland. Ten countries joined the EU in 2004: Cyprus, the Czech Republic, Estonia, Hungary, Latvia, Lithuania, Malta, Poland, Slovakia, and Slovenia. Bulgaria and Romania joined in 2007.
NAFTA	United States, Canada, and Mexico.
CAFTA	United States, Costa Rica, the Dominican Republic, El Salvador, Guatemala, Honduras, and Nicaragua.
MERCOSUR	Full Members: Argentina, Brazil, Paraguay, Uruguay, and Venezuela.
ASEAN	Brunei Darussalam, Cambodia, Indonesia, Laos, Malaysia, Myanmar, Philippines, Singapore, Thailand, and Vietnam.

EXHIBIT 17.4	EU Map

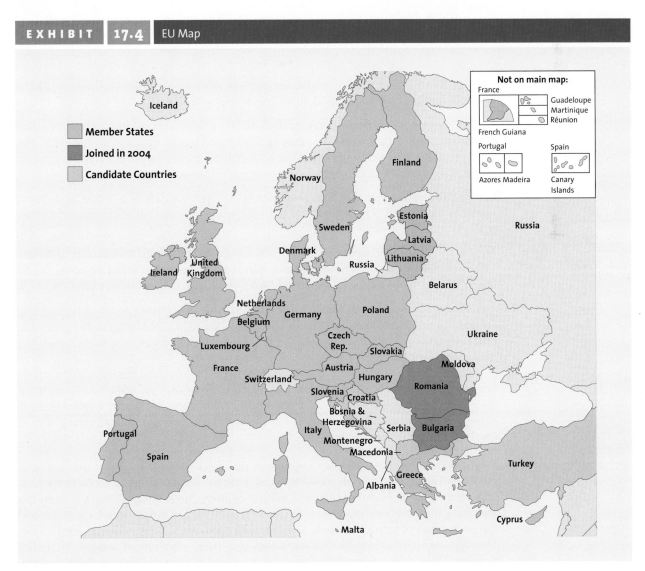

Source: http://en.wikipedia.org/wiki/European_Union, accessed Nov. 2, 2006.

The European Union has resulted in lowering trade barriers and strengthening global relationships among member nations.

rules governing data privacy and transmission, advertising, direct selling, etc., have been streamlined and simplified, allowing seamless trade.

North American Free Trade Agreement (NAFTA)   NAFTA is limited to trade-related issues, such as tariffs and quotas, among the United States, Canada, and Mexico. For example, the softwood lumber and the split-run magazine disputes between Canada and the U.S., two NAFTA partners, were resolved through the WTO.

Central American Free Trade Agreement (CAFTA)   CAFTA is a trade agreement between the United States, Costa Rica, the Dominican Republic, El Salvador, Guatemala, Honduras, and Nicaragua.[30]

Mercosur   Translated from Spanish, Mercosur means the Southern Common Market. This group covers most of South America. In 1995, Mercosur member nations created the Free Trade Area of the Americas (FTAA), primarily in response to NAFTA.

Association of Southeast Asian Nations (ASEAN)   Originally formed to promote security in Southeast Asia during the Vietnam War, ASEAN changed its mission to building economic stability and lowering trade restrictions among the six member nations in the 1980s.

These trading blocs affect how Canadian firms can conduct business in the member countries. Some critics contend that such blocs confer an unfair advantage on their member nations because they offer favourable terms for trade, whereas others believe they stimulate economies by lowering trade barriers and allowing higher levels of foreign investment.

Political Risk Analysis   Before a company decides to engage in global marketing, it must conduct a political risk analysis—assessing the level of political, socioeconomic, and security risks of doing business with a country. Such analysis usually involves weighing the likelihood of certain events such as change in government, violence, and the imposition of restrictive trade policies taking place over a specific period of time. This type of analysis requires sophisticated expertise, which most companies do not possess. Thus, they rely on government agencies (e.g., Export Development Canada, DFAIT) and private companies that specialize in political risk analysis to provide information and guidance. Political risk analysis helps to reduce the risk of a company losing its investment or goods and the possibility of harm to its employees.

Analyzing the Economic Environment

The greater the wealth of a country, generally, the better the opportunity a firm will have in that particular country. A firm conducting an economic analysis of a country's market must look at three major economic factors: the general economic environment, the population size and growth rate, and real income (see Exhibit 17.5).

Evaluating the General Economic Environment Generally, healthy economies provide better opportunities for global marketing expansions, and there are several ways a firm can measure the relative health of a particular country's economy. Each way offers a slightly different view, and some may be more useful for some products and services than for others.

    To determine the market potential for its particular product or service, a firm should use as many measures as it can obtain. One measure is the relative level of imports and exports. Canada, for example, enjoys a trade surplus while the United States suffers a trade deficit. A **trade deficit** means that the country imports more goods than it exports. Firms would prefer to manufacture in a country like Canada that has a **trade surplus**, or a higher level of exports than imports, because it signals a greater opportunity to export products to more markets.

    The most common way to gauge the size and market potential of an economy, and therefore the potential the country has for global marketing, is to use standardized measures of output. One of the most widely used measures is **gross domestic product (GDP)**, which is defined as the market value of the goods and services produced by a country in a year. So what does the size of a country's GDP has to do with global marketing? GDP growth means that production and consumption in the country is expanding, there-

trade deficit
Results when a country imports more goods than it exports.

trade surplus
Results when a country exports more goods than it imports.

gross domestic product (GDP)
Defined as the market value of the goods and services produced by a country in a year; the most widely used standardized measure of output.

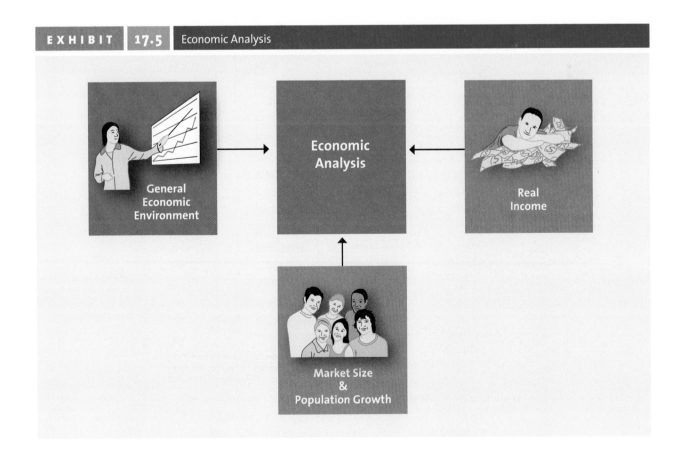

EXHIBIT 17.5 Economic Analysis

General Economic Environment → Economic Analysis ← Real Income

Market Size & Population Growth

purchasing power parity (PPP)
A theory that states that if the exchange rates of two countries are in equilibrium, a product purchased in one will cost the same in the other, expressed in the same currency.

fore, there are greater marketing opportunities for most goods and services. When GDP growth is slowing, it means that the economy is contracting or production and consumption are falling and marketing opportunities for certain goods and services will decline.

Another frequently used measure of an overall economy is the **purchasing power parity (PPP)**, a theory that states that if the exchange rates of two countries are in equilibrium, a product purchased in one will cost the same in the other, if expressed in the same currency.[31] A novel measure that employs PPP to assess the relative economic buying power among nations is *The Economist's* Big Mac Index, which suggests that exchange

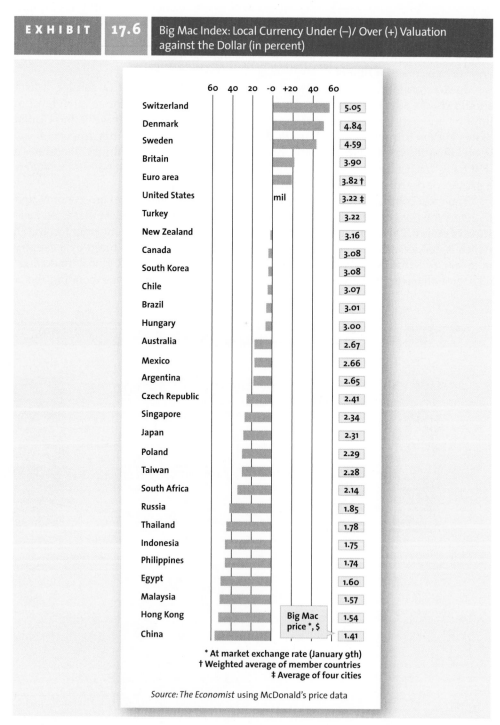

| EXHIBIT | 17.6 | Big Mac Index: Local Currency Under (–)/ Over (+) Valuation against the Dollar (in percent) |

* At market exchange rate (January 9th)
† Weighted average of member countries
‡ Average of four cities

Source: The Economist using McDonald's price data

Source: "Big Mac Index," *The Economist*, February 1, 2007, electronically accessed.

rates should adjust to equalize the cost of a basket of goods and services, wherever it is bought around the world. Using McDonald's Big Mac as the market basket, Exhibit 17.6 on the previous page shows that the cheapest burger is in China, where it costs $1.41, compared with an average Canadian price of $3.08. This implies that the Chinese yuan is 54 percent undervalued, that is, the Chinese yuan is priced "too low" relative to the Canadian dollar. In this case, the undervalued yuan makes China's exports to Canada cheaper than they would otherwise be, thereby providing an unfair trade advantage to China. It also makes Canadian exports to China more expensive.

These various measures help marketers understand the relative wealth of a particular country, though, as scholars have recently argued, they may not give a full picture of the economic health of a country because they are based solely on material output.[32] As a corollary measure to those described previously, the United Nations has developed the **human development index (HDI)**, a composite measure of three indicators of the quality of life in different countries: life expectancy at birth, educational attainment, and whether the average incomes according to PPP estimates are sufficient to meet the basic needs of life in that country. For marketers, these measures determine the lifestyle elements that ultimately drive consumption (recall that Chapter 6, on consumer behaviour, discussed the influence of lifestyle on consumption). The HDI is scaled from 0 to 1; those countries that score lower than .5 are classified as nations with low human development, those that score .5–.8 have medium development, and those above .8 are classified as having high human development. Exhibit 17.7 shows a map of the world with the various HDI scores. Higher HDI means greater consumption levels, especially of discretionary goods and services.

These macroeconomic measures provide a snapshot of a particular country at any one point in time. Because they are standardized measures, it is possible to compare countries across time and identify those that are experiencing economic growth and increased globalization.

Although an understanding of the macroeconomic environment is crucial for managers facing a market entry decision, of equal importance is the understanding of economic measures of individual income and household size.

Evaluating Market Size and Population Growth Rate   Global population has been growing dramatically since the turn of the 20th century (see Exhibit 17.8). From a marketing perspective, however, growth has not been equally dispersed. Less-developed nations, by and large, are experiencing rapid population growth, while many developed countries are experiencing either zero or negative natural popu-

human development index (HDI)
A composite measure of three indicators of the quality of life in different countries: life expectancy at birth, educational attainment, and whether the average incomes are sufficient to meet the basic needs of life in that country.

| **EXHIBIT** | **17.7** | Global Human Development Index Scores |

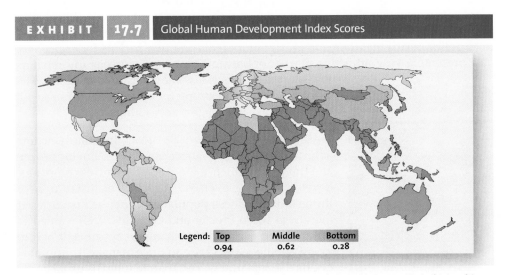

Legend: Top 0.94   Middle 0.62   Bottom 0.28

Source: http://www.nationmaster.com/red/graph/eco_hum_dev_ind-economy-human-development-index&int =-1&b_map=1#.

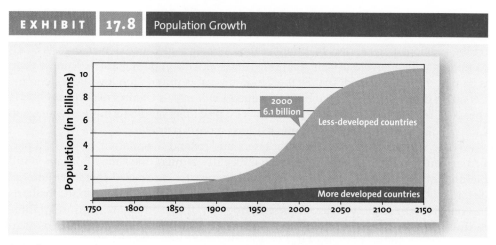

EXHIBIT 17.8 Population Growth

Source: http://www.prb.org/Content/NavigationMenu/PRB/Educators/Human_Population/Population_Growth/Population_Growth.htm

lation growth. Population growth in many developed countries such as Canada is attributed to high levels of immigration. The countries with the highest purchasing power today may become less attractive in the future for many products and services because of stagnated growth.

Another aspect related to population and growth pertains to the distribution of the population within a particular region; namely, is the population located primarily in rural or urban areas? This distinction determines where and how products and services can be delivered. Long supply chains, in which goods pass through many hands, are necessary to reach rural populations and therefore add costs to products. In China, for instance, the previously overwhelmingly rural population is moving toward urban areas to meet the demand of the growing industrial manufacturing centres located outside China's major cities and along its coastal Pearl River Delta. This population shift will facilitate the delivery of goods and services and thereby make China an even more attractive country for global expansion. India's farm goods typically pass through six or seven intermediaries before reaching consumers, and some 40 percent of produce spoils along the way. This situation could lead to huge opportunities for resellers like Wal-Mart with expertise in global supply chain management to serve the Indian market.[33]

Although China has the world's largest population with more than one billion people, its population also is getting older, and the government's single-child policy has effectively capped its previously exponential population growth. Yet the single-child policy means that there are four grandparents and two parents for each child. This presents a very attractive market opportunity for firms such as toy retailers Wal-Mart and Toys R Us, known as Joyo in China. The market is especially strong for educational toys as well as quality toys with high safety ratings.[34]

China's single-child policy means that there are four grandparents and two parents for every child, making the children's market very attractive.

Evaluating Real Income Real income—income adjusted for inflation—affects consumers' buying power, and thus will influence the marketing mixes companies develop for their overseas markets. For instance, two-thirds of the Chinese population earn less than $25 per month, so when Procter and Gamble (P&G) wanted to sell its Head & Shoulders shampoo in China, it had to modify both the package and price to make it affordable to Chinese consumers. P&G had to forgo its usual bottle and package Head & Shoulders in single-use packets, which made the shampoo affordable and practical for the Chinese market.[35] Coke and Pepsi are also making adjustments to their products and prices to be able to compete in India. For example, in the town of Jagadri in Northwest India, composed of 60,000 residents who are mostly farmers, Coke and Pepsi are battling for market share. Each firm has introduced repackaged products to win this market. Coke is producing a 200-ml bottle that sells for 12 cents at small shops, bus stops, and roadside stands in order to offer a more affordable alternative to Pepsi. Why battle for Jagadri? Because each firm knows that 70 percent of the Indian population, some 700 million people, still lives in rural areas and has incomes of less than $42 per month.[36] If they can win in Jagadri, they can win in other rural areas, and the only way to win is to make the product affordable. Speaking of affordable, who would believe that Africa is the fastest growing market for cell phones given the negative stereotypes of poverty in Africa? Today, one in 10 Africans is a cell phone user. The main reason for this explosive growth is a combination of government policy—many African governments privatized their telephone monopolies—and fierce competition among cell phone operators, which led to dramatic decreases in prices for air time and handset.[37]

Coke and Pepsi are battling for market share in India.

Analyzing Sociocultural Factors

While companies wishing to enter global markets can buy commercially available reports about the political, economic, and technological situation in a country fairly easily, they find it more difficult to acquire cultural information. Understanding another country's culture is crucial to the success of any global marketing initiative. **Culture**, or the set of values, guiding beliefs, understandings, and ways of doing things shared by members of a society, exists on two levels: visible artifacts (e.g., behaviour, dress, symbols, physical settings, ceremonies) and underlying values (thought processes, beliefs, and assumptions). Visible artifacts are easy to recognize, but businesses often find it more difficult to understand the underlying values of a culture and appropriately adapt their marketing strategies to them.[38] Even global companies with many years of experience operating in a country region occasionally end up offending their customers, which causes the companies huge embarrassment, lost sales, and even financial losses. Several examples of these 'cultural gaffes' are presented in this section for illustrative purposes.

culture
The set of values, guiding beliefs, understandings, and ways of doing things shared by members of a society; exists on two levels: visible artifacts (e.g., behaviour, dress, symbols, physical settings, ceremonies) and underlying values (thought processes, beliefs, and assumptions).

One important cultural classification scheme that firms can use is Geert Hofstede's cultural dimensions concept, which sheds more light on these underlying values. Hofstede believes cultures differ on five dimensions:[39]

1. **Power distance**: Willingness to accept social inequality as natural.

2. **Uncertainty avoidance**: The extent to which the society relies on orderliness, consistency, structure, and formalized procedures to address situations that arise in daily life.

3. **Individualism**: Perceived obligation to and dependence on groups.

4. **Masculinity**: The extent to which dominant values are male oriented. A lower masculinity ranking indicates that men and women are treated equally in all aspects of society; a higher masculinity ranking suggests that men dominate in positions of power.[40]

5. **Time orientation**: Short- versus long-term orientation. A country that tends to have a long-term orientation values long-term commitments and is willing to accept a longer time horizon for, say, the success of a new product introduction.

To illustrate two of the five dimensions, consider the data and graph in Exhibit 17.9. Power distance is on the vertical axis and individualism is on the horizontal axis. Several Latin American countries cluster high on power distance but low on individualism; Canada, the United States, Australia, and the United Kingdom, in contrast, cluster high on individualism but low on power distance. Using this information, firms should expect that if they design a marketing campaign that stresses equality and individualism, it will be well accepted in the English-speaking countries, all other factors being equal. The same campaign, however, might not be as well received in Latin American countries.

Another means of classifying cultures distinguishes them according to the importance of verbal communication.[41] In Canada, the United States and most European countries, business relationships are governed by what is said and written down, often through formal contracts. In countries such as China and South Korea, however, most relationships rely on nonverbal cues, so that the situation or context means much more than mere words. For instance, business relationships in China often are formalized by just a handshake, and trust and honour are often more important than legal arrangements. Internet Marketing 17.1 describes how socio-cultural factors influence website design and marketing through the Internet.

Business relationships in China often are formalized by just a handshake, and trust and honour are often more important than legal arrangements.

Overall, culture affects every aspect of consumer behaviour: why people buy, who is in charge of buying decisions, and how, when, and where people shop. Essentially, understanding consumer behaviour is all about understanding consumers' culture, particularly in global marketing. For example, in India, McDonald's sells it Maharajah Mac made from lamb instead of beef because the cow is sacred in Hindu culture. In Israel, McDonald's Kosher restaurants use the blue and white colours of Israel's flag instead of its yellow and red Golden Arches.[42] Similarly, Coca-Cola developed a new drink, Vitango, to be sold in Africa, and Procter & Gamble developed its Nutristar for Venezuelan consumers.[43] Both companies claim that their soft drinks have special health benefits for their customers in these markets. In North America, people often use their BlackBer-

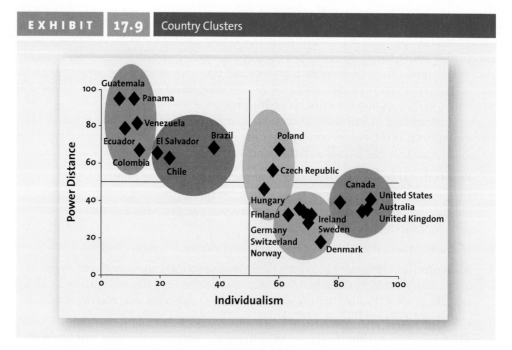

EXHIBIT   17.9   Country Clusters

Source: Based on data available at http://www.geert-hofstede.com. Data from: Geert Hofstede, *Culture's Consequences,* 2nd edition (Thousand Oaks, Sage 2001). Copyright © Geert Hofstede, reproduced with permission.

Internet Marketing

17.1　In the Eyes of the Beholder: Global or Local Web Design?

Once created, a website can be viewed by anyone around the world regardless of country, ethnicity, religion, or culture. For many businesses, this is an appealing idea since they just have to create one website and just try to promote it to as many users around the world as possible. Some companies have gone one step further, offering their Web content in the national language of their target market; for example, McCain offers its content in Spanish, Polish, German, and Dutch. But is this enough? Not according to Internet marketers, researchers, and consultants. Web design involves colours, shapes, sounds, texts, and even personas that usually have different meanings and are interpreted differently in different cultures. Thus, it is strongly recommended that Internet marketers consider the cultural norm, values, and traditions of their target market and develop websites that are more responsive. The argument is that companies who develop culturally appropriate website are more likely to gain the

attention, trust, and loyalty of these customers. In a study of 30 websites in Canada, Germany, Japan, and the United States, Simon Fraser University professor Diane Cyr and her colleagues[44] found statistical evidence that supports the idea that design preference differs across cultures. Specifically, differences were found with respect to Web design elements such as symbols and graphics, colour preferences, site features (links, maps, search functions, and page layout), language, and content. For example, Japanese sites used the colour red twice as often as either the German or American sites. Similarly, the Japanese sites use point form twice as often as either the German or American sites, which use paragraph format. The Japanese and German sites tend to use more culturally specific symbols than American sites. Overall, Canadian and American sites show the highest level of similarity among the sites studied. This supports the call for localization of Web content.

rys almost everywhere—on the roads, subways, lobbies, restaurants, ballparks, and hockey arenas. However, in Japan, typing away on the BlackBerry when in company—say during a sit-down dinner or a child's little league baseball game—could be viewed as bad manners.[45]

The challenge for marketers is that culture is very subtle and a failure to recognize the subtleties could lead to very embarrassing and costly mistakes. The following examples illustrate what happens when marketers have a poor understanding of the culture of their global markets.[46]

- A Canadian importer of Turkish shirts destined for Quebec used a dictionary to help him translate into French the label "Made in Turkey." His final translation: "Fabrique en Dinde." True, "dinde" means "turkey." But it refers to the bird, not to the country, which in French is Turquie.

- An Otis Engineering Corp. display at a Moscow exhibition produced as many snickers among the Russians as it did praise. Company executives were not happy to learn that a translator had rendered in Russian a sign identifying "completion equipment" as "equipment for orgasms."

- Japan's Olfa Corp. sold knives in the United States with the warning "Caution: Blade extremely sharp. Keep out of children."

- In one country the popular Frank Perdue Co. slogan, "It takes a tough man to make a tender chicken," read in local language something akin to "It takes a sexually excited man to make a chicken affectionate."

- One company in Taiwan, trying to sell diet food to expatriates living there, urged consumers to buy its product to add "roughage" to their systems. The instructions claimed that a person should consume enough roughage until "your tool floats." Someone dropped the "s" from "stool."

- How about the Hong Kong dentist who advertised "Teeth extracted by the latest Methodists."

- Or the hotel in notoriously polluted Mexico City that proclaimed: "The manager has personally passed all the water served here."

In Israel, McDonald's Kosher restaurants use the blue and white colours of Israel's flag.

- General Motors Corp.'s promotion in Belgium for its car that had a "body by Fisher" turned out to be, in the Flemish translation, "corpse by Fisher."
- Colgate introduced a toothpaste in France called Cue, which was the name of a local porno magazine.
- Since McDonald's operates over 28,000 restaurants in over 25 countries, you would expect it to be aware of the cultures of its various markets, right? It didn't seem so in India. McDonald's knew that the cow is a sacred religious symbol in India but yet used beef flavouring for its fries. When consumers learnt about this, there were huge protests and a major law suit. McDonald's apologized, changed its practices, and made a large charitable donation to appease Indian consumers.

infrastructure
The basic facilities, services, and installations needed for a community or society to function, such as transportation and communications systems, water and power lines, and public institutions like schools, post offices, and prisons.

Analyzing the Infrastructure and Technological Capabilities

The next component of any market assessment is an infrastructure and technological analysis. **Infrastructure** is defined as the basic facilities, services, and installations needed for a community or society to function, such as transportation and communications systems, water and power lines, and public institutions like schools, post offices, and prisons. Marketers are especially concerned with four key elements of a country's infrastructure: transportation, distribution channels, communications, and commerce. These elements affect the ability of marketers to acquire raw materials and inputs as well as distribution of finished goods—the 4th P of the marketing mix, place.

These four components are essential to the development of an efficient marketing system. First, there must be a system to transport goods throughout the various markets and to consumers in geographically dispersed marketplaces. Second, distribution channels must exist to deliver products in a timely manner and at a reasonable cost. Third, the communications system must be sufficiently developed to allow consumers access to

For a country to be a viable option for a new market entry, firms must assess its transportation, distribution channels, communications, and commercial infrastructure.

information about the products and services available in the marketplace. Fourth, the commercial infrastructure consists of the legal, banking, and regulatory systems that allow markets to function. Marketers, especially, those that are interested in off-shoring research, production, and marketing will be particularly interested in the technical sophistication of the workforce of the country. Generally, a more sophisticated work force means that a higher proportion of product design, development, and marketing activities can be decentralized to the foreign country.

After marketing managers have completed the four parts of the market assessment, they are better able to make informed decisions about whether a particular country possesses the necessary characteristics to be considered a potential market for the firm's products and services. In the next section, we detail the market entry decision process, beginning with a discussion of the various ways firms might enter a new global market.

Choosing a Global Entry Strategy   LO ③

When a firm has concluded its assessment analysis of the most viable markets for its products and services, it must then conduct an internal assessment of its capabilities. As we discussed in Chapter 2, this analysis includes an assessment of the firm's access to capital, the current markets it serves, its manufacturing capacity, its proprietary assets, and the commitment of its management to the proposed strategy. These factors ultimately contribute to the success or failure of a market expansion strategy, whether at home or in a foreign market. After these internal market assessments, it is time for the firm to choose its entry strategy.

A firm can choose from many approaches when it decides to enter a new market. These approaches vary according to the level of risk the firm is willing to take. Many firms actually follow a progression in which they begin with less risky strategies to enter their first foreign markets and move to increasingly risky strategies as they gain confidence in their abilities, as illustrated in Exhibit 17.10. Generally, profit potential increases with higher levels of risks. We examine these different approaches that marketers take when entering global markets, beginning with the least risky.

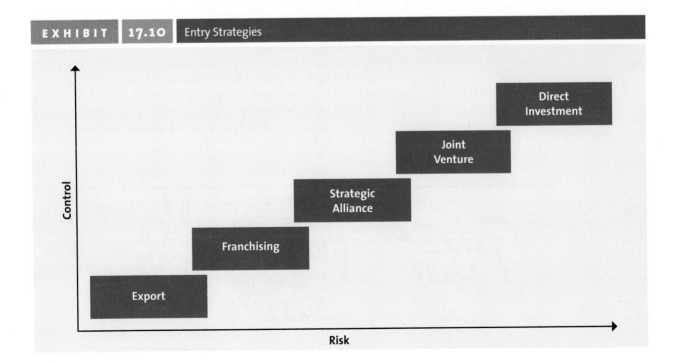

EXHIBIT | **17.10** | Entry Strategies

exporting
Producing goods in one country and selling them in another.

Exporting

Exporting means producing goods in one country (exporting country) and selling them in another (host country). This entry strategy requires the least financial risk but also allows for only a limited return to the exporting firm. Global expansion often begins when a firm receives an order for its product or service from another country, in which case it faces little risk because it can demand payment before it ships the merchandise. By the same token, it is difficult to achieve economies of scale when everything has to be shipped internationally. The Italian bicycle component manufacturer Campagnolo sells relatively small but expensive bicycle parts all over the world. Because its transportation costs are relatively small compared with the cost of the parts, the best way for it to service any market is to export from Italy. Exporting generally provides less employment for citizens of the host country than either joint venture or direct investment.

Exporting may take two forms: indirect or direct. Indirect occurs when the exporting firm sells its goods in the host country through an intermediary, for example, RIM sells its BlackBerry in Japan through NTTDoCoMo Inc., Japan's largest mobile-phone operator.[47] This approach carries the least risk and probably returns the least profit for the exporting company. This approach is likely to be used when the company has limited contacts in the foreign country but wants to market to that country. Direct exporting is when the exporting company sells its products in the host country directly without the intermediaries. This approach carries more risk and offer greater returns to the exporting firm than indirect exporting. For example, Christie Digital, a Kitchener, Ontario-based firm, is a manufacturer of a variety of display technologies and solutions for cinema, large audience environments, control rooms, business presentations, training facilities, 3D and virtual reality, simulation, education, media and government. Christie has installed over 75,000 projection solutions in the U.S., UK, Japan, China, and many other countries around the world.[48] Similarly, Cognos, an Ottawa-based company of business intelligence tools and applications sells its solutions to businesses around the world using its own sales force.

franchising
A contractual agreement between a **franchisor** and a **franchisee** that allows the franchisee to operate a business using a name and format developed and supported by the franchisor.

Franchising

Franchising is a contractual agreement between a firm, the **franchisor**, and another firm or individual, the **franchisee**. A franchising contract allows the franchisee to operate a business—a retail product or service firm or a B2B provider—using the name and business format developed and supported by the franchisor. Many of the best-known retailers in Canada are also successful global franchisers, including McDonald's, Pizza Hut, Starbucks, Dominos Pizza, KFC, and Holiday Inn, all of which have found that global franchising entails lower risks and requires less investment than does opening units owned wholly by the firm. However, when it engages in franchising, the firm has limited control over the market operations in the foreign country, its potential profit is reduced because it must be split with the franchisee, and, once the franchise is established, there is always the threat that the franchisee will break away

These franchise logos are recognized around the world.

The Star Alliance is a strategic alliance with 15 airline members including LOT Polish Airlines.

and operate as a competitor under a different name. In Canada, there are more than 75,000 franchise operations employing more than 1.5 million people and generating over $100 billion in annual sales.

Strategic Alliance   **Strategic alliances** refer to collaborative relationships between independent firms, though the partnering firms do not create an equity partnership; that is, they do not invest in one another. For example, Star Alliance constitutes one of the most complex strategic alliances in the world, with 15 airline members representing 16 countries: Air Canada, Air New Zealand, ANA (Japan), Asiana Airlines (South Korea), Austrian, BMI (United Kingdom), LOT Polish Airlines, Lufthansa (Germany), SAS Scandinavian Airlines (Denmark, Norway, and Sweden), Spanair (Spain), Singapore Airlines, Thai, United (United States), US Airways, and Varig (Brazil).[49]

What began as a series of bilateral agreements among five airlines grew over time into Star Alliance, which now acts as a separate legal entity in which each member is a stakeholder but no member is an equity owner in the others. Star Alliance coordinates the members on projects of mutual interest, such as helping members in their individual brand building efforts by creating value through their membership in the Alliance. This plan offers passengers benefits from individual airlines when they purchase from alliance partners. For instance, an Air Canada frequent flier member could earn Aeroplan miles by flying Spanair. This alliance also allows seamless booking and other transactions across the Alliance membership.

Joint Venture   A **joint venture** is formed when a firm entering a new market pools its resources with those of a local firm to form a new company in which ownership, control, and profits are shared. In addition to sharing the financial burden, the local partner offers the foreign entrant greater understanding of the market and access to resources such as vendors and real estate. Tesco, the UK supermarket, finance, telecom, and insurance superstar, has begun to enter China through a joint venture in which it has purchased a 50-percent share in Ting Hsin—which owns and operates the 25-store hypermarket chain Hymall—for $250 million.[50] China usually requires joint ownership from entering firms, as do many other countries, though these restrictions may loosen as a result of WTO negotiations. Problems with this entry approach can arise when the partners disagree or if the government places restrictions on the firm's ability to move its profits out of the foreign country and back to its home country. Problems can arise with joint ventures if the objectives, responsibilities, and benefits of the venture are not clearly defined from the outset. Conflicts could also arise if larger partners benefit more than smaller partners, which could threaten the venture. Differences in organizational cultures, management styles, and leadership as well

strategic alliance
A collaborative relationship between independent firms, though the partnering firms do not create an equity partnership; that is, they do not invest in one another.

joint venture
Formed when a firm entering a new market pools its resources with those of a local firm to form a new company in which ownership, control, and profits are shared.

Tesco, the UK supermarket chain has a joint venture in China in which it has purchased a 50-percent share in Ting Hsin—which owns and operates the 25-store hypermarket chain Hymall.

disagreements about marketing and investment policies could seriously affect the performance of the venture.

Two variants of joint ventures are contract manufacturing and management contracting. Contract manufacturing is when a foreign firm contracts with a local firm in the host market to manufacture the product. For example, Australian-based manufacturer Moose Enterprises invented Bindeez, one of the hottest toys in 2007, but contracted the production to a Chinese factory in southern China's Guangdong province. Unfortunately, although Bindeez was named toy of the year in Australia in 2007, it was recalled because it had traces of the substance linked to the date-rape drug GHB.[51] This example illustrates the huge risks due to loss of control over the manufacturing process by Moose Enterprises and the tremendous financial loss the company bore.

Management contracting is when the domestic firm provides management consulting and advice to a foreign firm. For example, many Canadian technology companies will supply their technology to firms and governments in developing countries with a specific agreement that only the Canadian supplier can maintain the technology or provide know-how regarding use and repair of the technology. Management contracting is a low-risk method of entering a country's market without setting up operations in the country. It also generates returns immediately upon execution of the agreement. Management contracting tends to be long-term since it extends over the life of the technology.

direct investment
When a firm maintains 100-percent ownership of its plants, operation facilities, and offices in a foreign country, often through the formation of wholly owned subsidiaries.

Direct Investment **Direct investment** requires a firm to maintain 100-percent ownership of its plants, operation facilities, and offices in a foreign country, often through the formation of wholly owned subsidiaries. This entry strategy requires the highest level of investment and exposes the firm to significant risks, including the loss of its operating and/or initial investments. For example, a dramatic economic downturn caused by a natural disaster or war, political instability, or changes in the country's laws can increase a foreign entrant's risk considerably. Many firms believe that in certain markets, these potential risks are outweighed by the high potential returns; with this strategy, none of the potential profits must be shared with other firms. In addition to the high potential returns, direct investment offers the firm complete control over its operations in the foreign country.

ING Group, a financial services firm based in The Netherlands, decided to enter the Canadian market through a wholly owned subsidiary. Attracted by Canada's position as a large financial services market, as well as regulations friendly to ING's desire to provide banking services, insurance, and asset management products (e.g., mortgages, investment accounts), ING began an aggressive entry into Canada in 1997 and has not looked back since. Foregoing traditional bank branches, ING established ING Direct and operates purely online. Although it began with online savings accounts, ING has expanded into investment accounts and online mortgage services and now has over one million customers and more than $10 billion in assets in Canada—as well as an advertising campaign that gently pokes fun at people's lack of awareness about what the company does.[52]

As we noted, each of these entry strategies entails different levels of risk and rewards for the foreign entrant. But even after a firm has determined how much risk it is willing to take, and therefore how it will enter a new global market, it still must establish its marketing strategy, as we discuss in the next section.

Choosing a Global Marketing Strategy

LO **4**

Just like any other marketing strategy, a global marketing strategy includes two components: determining the target market(s) to pursue and developing a marketing mix that will sustain a competitive advantage over time. In this section, we examine marketing strategy as it relates specifically to global markets.

Target Market: Segmentation, Targeting, and Positioning

Global segmentation, targeting, and positioning (STP) is more complicated than local STP for several reasons. First, firms considering a global expansion have much more difficulty understanding the cultural nuances of other countries. Second, subcultures within each country also must be considered. Third, consumers often view products and their role as consumers differently in different countries.[53]

A product or service often must be positioned differently in different markets. For example, Tang, the fruit-flavoured drink produced by Kraft, is positioned as a low-priced drink in the United States, but such a positioning strategy would not work in Brazil, where fresh orange juice already is a low-priced drink. Consequently, Kraft promotes a pineapple-flavoured Tang and positions it as a drink for special occasions. In a similar fashion, McDonald's generally competes on convenience and low price, but in countries like China and India, where consumers already have lower-priced and more convenient alternatives, McDonald's positions itself as an "American" restaurant.[54]

The most efficient route is to develop and maintain a global positioning strategy; one position means only one message to get out. For instance, Tropicana is the best-selling orange juice brand in the United States and owns 6 percent of the global juice market. Tropicana's parent company, PepsiCo, therefore takes a global positioning strategy that stresses around the world that Tropicana is "fresh-squeezed Florida orange juice."[55]

When it identifies its positioning within the market, the firm then must decide how to implement its marketing strategies using the marketing mix. Just as firms adjust their prod-

Tropicana uses a global positioning strategy that stresses around the world that Tropicana is "fresh-squeezed Florida orange juice."

ucts and services to meet the needs of national target market(s), they must alter their marketing mix to serve the needs of global markets.

The Global Marketing Mix

During the early stages of globalization, in the 1950s and 1960s, large U.S. firms were uniquely positioned in the global marketplace because they had the unique skills necessary to develop, promote, and market brand name consumer products. In the 1970s and 1980s, however, Japanese firms dominated the global marketplace because they could exploit their skills in production, materials management, and new product development. Today, retailers such as Wal-Mart, financial services firms such as Citicorp, and software firms such as Microsoft are dominating the newest stage of globalization by exploiting their technological skills.[56] In the following section, we explore the 4Ps (product, place, promotion, price) from a global perspective.

Global Product or Service Strategies   There are three potential global product strategies:

- Sell the same product or service in both the home country market and the host country.
- Sell a product or service similar to that sold in the home country but include minor adaptations.
- Sell totally new products or services.

The strategy a firm chooses depends on the needs of the target market. The level of economic development, along with differences in product and technical standards help determine the need for product adaptation. Cultural differences such as food preferences, language, and religion also play a role in product strategy planning. For example, Frito-Lay discovered that the traditional cheese taste and bright orange colour of Cheetos did not sell well in China, where cheese is not a traditional part of the diet. Therefore, it adapted Chinese Cheetos to offer a choice of either teriyaki or butter flavours.[57] Since that adaptation, Cheetos has been marketed in a variety of flavours and colours, including pink, strawberry-flavoured snacks. The new product retained the Cheetos name though, because the Chinese character *qi duo* is pronounced "CHEE dwaugh" and means "new surprise."[58]

The level of economic development also affects the global product strategy because it relates directly to consumer behaviour. For instance, consumers in developed countries tend to demand more attributes in their products than do consumers in less developed countries. In Canada, Honda does not offer its line of "urban"

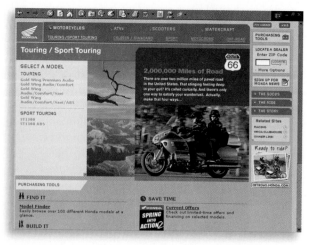

Honda adapts its product line to fit the needs of its customers. Their motorcycles in Mexico (left) are relatively inexpensive and designed for urban use. The much larger sport touring motorcycles sold in the U.S. (right) are designed for highway use.

motorcycles, available in Mexico and China, because the product line resembles a motor scooter more than a motorcycle, which does not tend to appeal to Canadian consumers. Motorcycles sold in Canada have more horsepower and bigger frames and come with an array of options that are not offered in other countries.

Some firms also might standardize their products globally but use different promotional campaigns to sell them. The original Pringles potato chip product remains the same globally, as do the images and themes of the promotional campaign, with limited language adaptations for the local markets, though English is used whenever possible. However, the company does change Pringles' flavours in different countries, including paprika-flavoured chips sold in Italy and Germany.[59] McCain, which markets frozen potato specialties in 100 countries, localizes its product by calling it chips in the UK for instance and developing local advertising for markets and managers by region.[60]

Not just manufacturers must adapt their offering. On the service side, for example, MTV offers a mix of globally standardized and localized content to meet the needs of its diverse and varied markets (see Adding Value 17.1).

Despite the persistent differences across borders, marketers have found a growing convergence in tastes and preferences in many product categories. Starbucks is a good example of a company that has both influenced and exploited this global convergence in tastes. Even in China and Great Britain, traditional strongholds for tea marketers, coffee is quickly gaining as the beverage of choice. Increasingly, because of the Internet and other information and communication technologies, there seems to be not only a convergence of taste among youths but the emergence of global homogenous segments, that is, groups of consumers from around the world who share similar buying characteristics. One study identified the "global teen segment," which they describe as teenagers from around the world—from Japan to Vancouver, London, Beijing, and San Francisco—who pretty much buys the same brand name clothing, electronics, accessories, listens to the same music and eat the same food. Such trends make it easier for marketers to target these consumers with standardized products.[61]

Global Pricing Strategies   Determining the selling price in the global marketplace is an extremely difficult task.[62] Many countries still have rules governing the competitive marketplace, including those that affect pricing. For example, in some countries, firms cannot charge prices lower than the local market prices, and price reductions can be taken only at certain times of the year or according to government-specified

Adding Value | 17.1 MTV Conquers the World

You and millions of others around the globe might watch MTV tonight, but the MTV you see might not be the same as the one a university student in, say, Jakarta views.[63] MTV (Music Television) is now the world's leading youth brand, and can be seen in more than 374.7 million households in 164 countries via 34 channels in 18 languages. When MTV began its globalization efforts, it offered the same programming in every market. Similar to other global brands, MTV soon learned that offering a one size fits all product didn't meet the needs of its target segment, so while maintaining its unique personality and appeal to its target segment, MTV began establishing regional offices, especially in Asia. Today, approximately 80 percent of MTV's programming in Asia is local. This localized content provides an unprecedented venue for local musicians and musical traditions. For example, MTV Indonesia, with 13 million potential view-

ers, stumbled on one of its audiences' favourite shows, MTV Salam Dangdut, almost accidentally.

Salam Dangdut features Indonesia's most popular traditional music, Dangdut, in a show that originally aired simply as a gesture of appreciation for local culture. Ironically, Dangdut has long been unpopular in Indonesia's music industry, viewed as traditional music that was not exciting enough for a contemporary audience. It was only when MTV decided to air the program that local audiences began to appreciate the traditional music again. Young people, who had never been interested in music like Dangdut before, suddenly began seeing it as cool thanks to MTV's generation Y–friendly approach.

The question of what to globalize and what to localize is always difficult to answer. But in this case, MTV seems to have hit a winning note.

percentages. For firms such as Wal-Mart and other discounters, this restriction threatens their core competitive positioning as the lowest-cost provider in the market. Other issues, such as tariffs, quotas, anti-dumping laws, and currency exchange policies, can also affect pricing decisions.[64]

Competitive factors influence global pricing in the same way they do home country pricing, but because a firm's products or services may not have the same positioning in the global marketplace as they do in their home country, market prices must be adjusted to reflect the local pricing structure. Spain's fashion retailer Zara, for instance, is relatively inexpensive in the EU but moderately priced in North America. Similarly, Nintendo's Wii game, boogie, was priced at CAD$65 for the 2007 Christmas season at Best Buy in Ottawa, but it sold for US$45 at Best Buy across the border in New York.

Global Distribution Strategies   Global distribution networks form complex value chains that involve intermediaries, exporters, importers, and different transportation systems. These additional intermediaries typically add cost and ultimately increase the final selling price of a product. As a result of these cost factors, constant pressure exists to shorten distribution channels wherever possible.

The number of firms with which the seller needs to deal to get its merchandise to the consumer determines the complexity of a channel. In most developing countries, manufacturers must go through many different types of distribution channels to get their products to end users, who often lack adequate transportation to shop at central shopping areas or large malls. Therefore, these consumers shop near their homes at small, family-owned retail outlets. To reach these small retail outlets, most of which are located far from major rail stations or roads, marketers have devised a variety of creative solutions. In the Amazon jungle in Brazil, for instance, Avon products are sometimes delivered by canoe. However, even if distribution channels present challenges, some products may be sold the same way in both foreign markets and the home country. Until recently, Dell distributed globally the same way it did in the United States—via the Internet—but in 2007, it began distributing via retailers such as Wal-Mart and Chinese electronics retailer, Gome.

Global Communication Strategies   The major challenge in developing a global communication strategy is identifying the elements that need to be adapted to be effective in the global marketplace. For instance, literacy levels vary dramatically

Distribution can be challenging in some countries if the transportation infrastructure is inadequate. In the Amazon jungle in Brazil, for instance, Avon products are sometimes delivered by canoe.

across the globe. In Argentina, 3.8 percent of the adult population is illiterate, compared with 6 percent in the Philippines and a whopping 61 percent in Liberia.[65] Media availability also varies widely; some countries offer only state-controlled media. Advertising regulations differ too. In an attempt at standardization, the EU recently recommended common guidelines for its member countries regarding advertising to children and is currently reviewing a possible ban on "junk food" advertising.[66]

Differences in language, customs, and culture also complicate marketers' ability to communicate with customers in various countries. Language can be particularly vexing for advertisers. For example, in Australia, a thong is only a sandal, whereas in Canada, it can also be an undergarment. To avoid the potential embarrassment that language confusion can cause, firms spend millions of dollars to develop brand names that have no preexisting meaning in any known language, such as Accenture (a management consulting firm) or Avaya (a subsidiary of Lucent Technologies, formerly Bell Labs).

Within many countries there are multiple variants on a language. For example in China where there are three main languages, firms such as Mercedes Benz adapted the name for each language. Thus, Mercedes-Benz is known by three Chinese names in Asia: pronounced peng zee in Cantonese for Hong Kong; peng chi in Mandarin for Taiwan; and ben chi in Mandarin for mainland China. Other firms such as Nokia only use one name in China, pronounced nuo jee ya in Mandarin.[67] As China continues to develop, having more than one name to represent a product or service will become increasingly inefficient. Unlike these companies, Research In Motion markets its BlackBerry using the same name around the globe.

Even with all these differences, many products and services serve the same needs and wants globally with little or no adaptation in their form or message. Firms whose products have global appeal, like Coca-Cola, can develop global advertising campaigns, an advantage that results in significant savings. According to Coca-Cola's advertising firm, McCann-Erickson, over a 20-year period, it saved Coca-Cola $90 million by reusing advertisements it had already created and changing only a few elements for different local markets.[68]

However, other products require a more localized approach because of cultural and religious differences. In a classic advertisement for Longines watches, a woman's bare arm and hand appear, with a watch on her wrist. The advertisement was considered too risqué for Muslim countries, where women's bare arms are never displayed in public, but the company simply changed the advertisement to show a gloved arm and hand wearing the same watch.

Regulatory actions in the host country can also affect communication strategies. For example, the WTO has become involved in several cases that involve firms' rights to use certain names and affiliations for their products and promotions. Several products in the EU have established worldwide brand recognition on the basis of where they are made. For instance, the EU currently allows only ham made in Parma, Italy, to be called Parma ham and sparkling wine made in the Champagne region of France to be called Champagne. However, the EU has also refused to grant requests from non-EU countries for similar protection, notably Florida orange juice.[69] The WTO is expected to ask the EU to either remove all such protections or grant them to non-EU countries as well. In one case, similar arguments have even led to a global beer brawl, as we describe in Entrepreneurial Marketing 17.1.

Ethical Issues in Global Marketing

LO

Although ethical issues abound domestically, an extra layer of complexity arises for global marketing. Firms that market globally must recognize that they are, in essence, visitors in another country and, as such, must be aware of the ethical concerns of their potential customers, both at home and abroad. In this section, we examine three areas of particular concern: environmental concerns, labour issues, and impact on host country culture.

Entrepreneurial Marketing

17.1 David versus Goliath in the Beer Wars

The Budvar brewery claims that Anheuser-Busch stole the name Budweiser and that its product is, in fact, the one and only true Budweiser.[70] Located in the Czech Republic, a member of the EU, Budvar brewery can trace its roots back 700 years. For years, the two Budweisers coexisted on opposite sides of the Atlantic in relative peace, though the first clash of the Budweisers occurred in 1911 at a trade fair. According to a Budvar spokesperson, the companies then reached an agreement to essentially divide the globe: "We wouldn't sell our beer north of the Panama Canal, and they wouldn't sell their beer in Europe."

After the fall of communism, both Budvar and Anheuser-Busch began to expand. Budvar began placing ads in the United Kingdom, and Anheuser-Busch started exporting to Europe. According to Anheuser-Busch, the company could no longer afford to ignore the lucrative European market.

Budvar argued that consumers expected "Budweiser" to be a premium product produced only by Budvar, and that Anheuser-Busch's "Bud," which was in fact a shortened version of the name of the town in which Budvar was located, simply did not measure up to those standards. In response, Anheuser-Busch argued that Budweiser and Bud are global brand names associated with its product. It has invested hundreds of millions of dollars in the Budweiser and Bud names over the brands' 127-year histories, which has made them among the most valuable brand names in the world. The company believes its trademarks provide the foundation for its beer business, and it plans to protect them aggressively.

European countries have a long tradition of granting protections to local brands and regional products, making it difficult, if not impossible, for foreign manufacturers to enter the market. Thus far, the beer battle has played out on a country-by-country basis and currently sits in

When you think of having a Bud, do you mean Budweiser or Budvar?

an uneasy truce that involves some interesting compromises. Anheuser-Busch has national registrations for "Budweiser" or "Bud" in 20 of the 25 EU countries and sells 31 percent of its foreign beer (by volume) there. In many of these countries, the two Buds exist together on the shelves at the local store.

Budvar is presently looking to expand to the United States. The CEO of Budvar gives a wry chuckle when contemplating the possibility of a U.S. consumer mistakenly taking home a crate of the Czech beer and "accidentally" converting to Budvar.

Meanwhile, the WTO is examining the issue of regional and local product protections. Most indications suggest the WTO will deny both brewers' requests for exclusive use of the Bud and Budweiser names. It looks like the two products will remain side by side for years to come. In the long run, for Budvar, perhaps a little confusion will turn out to be a good thing.

---

environmental concerns
Include, but are not limited to, the excessive use of natural resources and energy, refuse from manufacturing processes, excess trash created by consumer goods packages, and hard-to-dispose-of products like tires, cell phones, and computer monitors.

global labour issues
Includes concerns about working conditions and wages paid to factory workers in developing countries.

Environmental Concerns

Among the various **environmental concerns** that exist, people throughout the world are worried about the amount of waste being generated, especially in developed countries. Waste can include, but is not limited to, the excessive use of natural resources and energy, refuse from manufacturing processes, excess trash created by consumer goods packages, and hard-to-dispose-of products like tires, cell phones, and computer monitors.

Many developed countries produce almost two tonnes of household and industrial waste per person per year![71] Although developing countries do not produce nearly the same level of waste, much of the waste in these areas is not properly disposed of.

Global Labour Issues

Global labour issues, especially concerns about working conditions and wages paid to factory workers in developing countries, have become increasingly prominent.[72] Many large U.S. firms have been questioned by various groups, including nongovernmental organizations and human rights activists, about the degree to which workers the companies employ are paid less than a living wage or forced to work long hours in poor working conditions.[73]

Nike has been repeatedly questioned by a variety of groups about the working conditions in the manufacturing plants around the world that produce its products.[74] For the most part, Nike does not own the plants in which its goods are produced, so it must negotiate with factory owners to improve or ensure adequate working conditions and wages. In response to recent pressure, Nike has made a significant investment in its social responsibility initiatives, such as joining the Fair Labour Association, an organization dedicated to improving working conditions globally and creating a compliance program and code of conduct for its subcontractors. Nike's efforts have been recognized by the United Nations and other international organizations, and its program for contractors serves as a model for other firms. Nike admits it will never be perfect (with 600,000 contract workers in 900 factories in 50 countries, it is almost impossible to avoid some violations), but it is making the effort to bring its subcontractors into compliance with its labour standards. Currently, Coca-Cola is facing a backlash from students across hundreds of university and college campuses in Canada and the U.S. who are calling on their campus presidents to remove Coca-Cola for its poor labour practices in Colombia and other developing countries.[75]

Many developed countries produce almost two tonnes of household and industrial waste per person per year that requires proper disposal.

Impact on Host Country Culture

The final ethical issue involves **cultural imperialism**, or the belief that one's own culture is superior to that of other nations. Cultural imperialism can take the form of an active, formal policy or a more subtle general attitude.[76] Critics of U.S. firms entering foreign markets claim that U.S. products and services overwhelm the local culture, often replacing its foods, music, movies, and traditions with those of the West.

cultural imperialism
The belief that one's own culture is superior to that of other nations; can take the form of an active, formal policy or a more subtle general attitude.

In Iran, for example, the ruling clerics have forbidden the celebration of Valentine's Day.[77] Despite strict Iranian laws regarding the interactions of men and women, especially unmarried men and women, Valentine's Day has become a popular holiday among the youth market. These Iranians were exposed to Valentine's Day through the Internet and satellite television, two information sources the government cannot control. Holiday-themed products arrive through underground distribution channels and are displayed in local shops. Risking legal action, florists, gift shops, and restaurants make special accommodations for the holiday. Many parents sponsor Valentine parties with both men and women in attendance. Apparently, there is no stopping love. Half the Iranian population is younger than 25 years of age, and this youth market has embraced the holiday and continues to celebrate it in traditional Western ways because it represents progress and modernization.

When Western firms enter foreign markets, they must be cognizant of the host country's culture.

For other Iranians though, this type of celebration represents a threat to Iran's culture. Many U.S. firms find themselves squarely in the middle of this cultural conflict.[78] Various countries around the world encompass competing desires: the desire to modernize and participate in the global marketplace versus the desire to hold on to traditional cultural values and ways of life. There is no simple way to resolve these dilemmas. Firms that enter new markets simply must tread lightly to ensure that their business practices, products, and services do not create any unnecessary friction or offence in the host country.

Learning Objectives Review

1) Identify the factors that aid the growth of globalization

2) Explain the factors a firm considers when deciding to enter a global market

3) Describe the ownership and partnership options firms have for entering a new global market

4) Distinguish the similarities and differences between a domestic marketing strategy and a global marketing strategy

5) Explain how ethical issues impact global marketing practices

1) Technology, particularly in communications, has facilitated the growth of global markets. Firms can communicate with their suppliers and customers instantaneously, easily take advantage of production efficiencies in other countries, and bring together parts and finished goods from all over the globe. International organizations such as the World Trade Organization, the International Monetary Fund, and the World Bank Group also have reduced or eliminated tariffs and quotas, worked to help people in less-developed countries, and facilitated trade in many areas.

2) First, firms must determine whether the proposed country has a political and legal environment that favours business. Second, firms must assess the general economic environment. For instance, countries with a trade surplus, strong domestic and national products, growing populations, and income growth generally are relatively more favourable prospects. Third, firms should be cognizant of the cultural and sociological differences between their home and host countries and adapt to those differences to ensure successful business relationships. Fourth, firms should assess a country's technological and infrastructure capabilities. To be successful in a particular country, the firm must have access to adequate transportation, distribution channels, and communications.

3) Firms have several options for entering a new country, each with a different level of risk and involvement. Direct investment is the most risky but potentially the most lucrative. Firms that engage in a joint venture with other

firms already operating in the host country share the risk and obtain knowledge about the market and how to do business there. A strategic alliance is similar to a joint venture, but the relationship is not as formal. A less risky method of entering a new market is franchising, in which, similar to domestic franchise agreements, the franchisor allows the franchisee to operate a business using its name and strategy in return for a fee. The least risky method of entering another country is exporting.

4) The essence of a global marketing strategy is no different than that of a domestic strategy. The firm starts by identifying its target markets, chooses specific markets to pursue, and crafts a strategy to meet the needs of those markets. However, additional issues make global expansion more difficult. For instance, should the product or service be altered to fit the new market better? Does the firm need to change the way it prices its products in different countries? What is the best way to get the product or service to the new customers? How should the firm communicate its product or service offering in other countries?

5) In particular, firms must be cognizant of the impact their businesses have on the environment. When producing merchandise or employing service personnel in another country, they must be certain that the working conditions and wages are fair and adequate, even if the workers are employed by a third party. Finally, marketers must be sensitive to the impact their business has on the culture of the host country.

Key Terms

- boycott, 490
- countertrade, 491
- cultural imperialism, 513
- culture, 499
- direct investment, 506
- dumping, 490
- duty, 490
- environmental concerns, 512
- exchange control, 491
- exchange rate, 491
- exporting, 504
- franchisee, 504
- franchising, 504
- franchisor, 504

- General Agreement on Tariffs and Trade (GATT), 487
- global labour issues, 512
- globalization, 485
- globalization of production, 487
- gross domestic product (GDP), 495
- human development index (HDI), 497
- infrastructure, 502
- International Monetary Fund (IMF), 488
- joint venture, 505
- offshoring, 487
- purchasing power parity (PPP), 496

- quota, 490
- strategic alliance, 505
- tariff, 490
- trade agreements, 489
- trade deficit, 495
- trade sanctions, 489
- trade surplus, 495
- trading bloc, 492
- World Bank Group, 488
- World Trade Organization (WTO), 488

Concept Review

1. What is globalization? What are the factors that facilitate globalization? Explain how globalization has influenced marketing in Canada.

2. List and describe the four components of market assessments firms must conduct in order to evaluate the viability of different global markets.

3. Which of the four components of market assessment do you think are often most difficult to assess? Why?

4. List the five types of strategies companies could use to enter global markets. Compare these strategies in terms of level of risk, expected return, and control.

5. Discuss the advantages and disadvantages of using a global product strategy (offering the same product both at home and in overseas markets).

6. What are the primary considerations marketers should use in deciding whether to customize its 4Ps to specific markets?

7. What is political risk? Why is it important to assess political risks? How is political risk assessed? List two or three organizations in Canada that provide marketers with political risk assessments.

8. Protectionist policies restrict trade and global marketing while trade agreements facilitate global marketing. Explain the reasons why a country may want to impose protectionist policies in some industries and liberalize other industries.

9. Explain how measures such as GDP, PPP (Big Mac Index), and HDI help marketers decide whether to enter a global market. What are the weaknesses of these measures?

10. Explain how useful Hofstede's five dimensions of culture are to our understanding of different cultures around the world. Where and how can marketers learn about the culture of a country to which they are interested in marketing?

Marketing Applications

1. The World Trade Organization, World Bank, and International Monetary Fund all work in different ways to facilitate globalization. What role(s) does each organization play in the global marketplace?

2. Cervélo is a high-end Canadian bicycle manufacturer. Assume the company is considering entering the UK and Chinese markets. When doing its market assessment, what economic factors should Cervélo consider to make its decision? Which market do you expect will be more lucrative for Cervélo? Why?

3. Now consider the political, economic, and legal systems of China versus the United Kingdom. Explain why you think one country might be more hospitable to Cervélo than the other.

4. Volkswagen sells cars in many countries throughout the world, including Mexico and Latin America. How would you expect its market position to differ in those countries compared with that in Canada?

5. Global brands that gain status on a local level have the best of both worlds: local loyalty with all the advantages of global connections. How do huge global companies like McCain Foods, Philips, and McDonald's achieve multi-local status?

6. What is cultural imperialism? Why would a recording company like Def Jam Records need to be aware of and be sensitive to this issue?

7. Provide an example of a potentially ethically troubling practice by a foreign firm doing business in Canada.

8. Many Canadian- and U.S.-based firms are relocating their production facilities and services overseas (outsourcing or offshoring). Why do you believe they are doing so? Do the benefits outweigh the potential losses of Canadian and U.S. jobs? Why or why not?

9. Assume you work for a Canadian-based financial services firm that positions itself as having experts that personally manage the clients' accounts. The clients are unaware that most of the tax preparation work, the bookkeeping, and other record keeping are done by a company in India. The local office simply reviews the file and signs the cover letters. Yet as your manager pointed out, there is still only one person that *manages* each account. After recent news stories about the practice of offshoring sensitive transactions such as tax preparation, clients have been commenting about how grateful they are to have a local firm. What, if anything, should you tell your clients about the firm's practice of offshoring?

10. Lululemon has expanded its global retail operations through company-owned stores. In what instances might it consider using joint ventures as its global market entry strategy into new markets?

Net Savvy

1. For many small businesses, the idea of entering a foreign market is frightening. The Government of Canada, as well as most provincial and territorial governments, now offers assistance designed specifically for small business owners. Two such government departments are DFAIT and Industry Canada. Visit Industry Canada's "expertsource" website at www.exportsource.ca/ and examine the types of services it provides for Canadian businesses wishing to do business in a foreign country. Evaluate the usefulness of the information provided.

2. McCain's is now a global brand, yet in each country, it alters its products and promotions to accommodate local tastes. Go to www.mccain.ca and visit the Canadian site. Now click through to the South American site, the U.S. site, and the site for France. How are these three websites different from the Canadian site? What products are different? What promotional elements are different?

Chapter Case Study

IKEA TAKES ON THE WORLD, ONE COUNTRY AT A TIME

Entrepreneurial ideas can come from anyplace at anytime, and the founding of IKEA is a classic example of a happy accident. Ingvar Kamprad was just 17 years old in 1943 when, using money his father had given him, he began a household goods catalogue. Realizing that his most profitable item was furniture, he began to focus on selling furniture in 1947. Who would have guessed in 1943 that his household goods catalogue would one day become the world's largest furniture retailer, with annual sales of $12 billion to 286 million customers? IKEA now operates in 35 countries and is looking to expand both into more new markets and in the markets it currently serves. Kamprad realized that he had hit on a winning concept—the concept that still drives IKEA today.

It was a simple concept: Offer quality furniture at the lowest possible prices. According to the company's website, "The IKEA Concept is based on offering a wide range of well-designed, functional home furnishing products at prices so low that as many people as possible will be able to afford them. Rather than selling expensive home furnishings that only a few can buy, the IKEA Concept makes it possible to serve the many by providing low-priced products that contribute to helping more people live a better life at home."[79]

Doing business in Russia has been a challenge for IKEA.

The combination of high quality and low price easily translates across global markets. To keep costs down, IKEA must always remain creative. It locates different steps of its production in different parts of the world to take advantage of the savings offered by buying less expensive products overseas. Perhaps the most innovative way IKEA has found to keep costs low is its choice to ship all of its products in flat packages, which keeps both shipping and storage costs to a minimum and also reduces damage during transit. Customers transport their flat purchases home and complete the final assembly themselves.

IKEA stores and the services it provides (or does not provide) differ from those of other furniture retailers.[80] The large, 15,000–35,000 square metre stores are divided into cheerfully decorated model rooms. Customers can lounge on the furniture. The stores are largely self-service, so customers are encouraged to measure the spaces in their homes before they come to the store. Huge price tags appear on the furniture itself, and cards with design tips are displayed in kiosks throughout the store. IKEA also offers elaborate childcare centres and restaurants with Swedish delicacies, like smoked salmon and lingonberry tarts.

Franchising has enabled IKEA to enter new markets but retain control over how those new outlets are organized and managed. Franchisees must demonstrate a firm commitment to the IKEA Concept and possess both extensive retail experience and enough financial resources to absorb the cost of constructing an IKEA store.

As IKEA enters each new market, it must make certain adjustments to its marketing mix. For example, to enter the U.S. market, it altered its European-style mattresses, which did not fit traditional American bed linens. Many Americans found the couches too hard and the dinnerware too small to accommodate their serving sizes. After it had made these necessary adjustments, IKEA took off in the United States.

Entering Russia required different adaptations. While they operate several stores across the country and a warehouse near Moscow, they have had problems getting local producers to deliver on time. Punitive tariffs designed to protect Russia's furniture industry from foreign competition can run as high as 80 percent. Russia's bureaucracy can also be difficult. Many contradictory laws make it almost impossible to follow every one.[81]

This combination of a commitment to its concept, an ability to take full advantage of globalized production, unique stores, carefully chosen franchisees, and the means to adapt the marketing mix to fit local needs have enabled IKEA to become a world-class furniture retailer.

Questions

1. Consumers' tastes for furniture typically vary from region to region within a country, from country to country, and across various demographic dimensions, such as age, income, and education. Yet, though IKEA's product line is fairly narrow, it has been successful in virtually every market it has entered. Who is IKEA's target market? Why does IKEA have such global appeal?

2. IKEA uses franchising to enter new markets. Are there any other entry strategies that would be appropriate for IKEA to use? Why or why not?

3. How is IKEA positioned relative to other furniture retailers?

SLAMKiK

MARKETING PLAN SAMPLE FORMAT

1. **Executive Summary**

2. **Company Description**
   —Overview of Company
   —Mission
   —Goals
   —Core Competency

3. **Situation Analysis**

   —SWOT Analysis
   Assess Strengths and Weaknesses of company and products. Evaluate Opportunities and Threats from the firm's external environment.

   —Market Trend Analysis
   Provide a clear description and a statistical analysis of your industry. How big is the market? What trends are occurring? Why? Are sales going up or down? Why?

   —Environmental Analysis
   What are the *key* environmental factors that influence your market? (e.g., demographic, economic, technology, political/legal, social, culture) Which two or three factors are most relevant to your product or service?

   —Competitive Analysis
   Who are your major competitors? What is their market share? What products and services do they offer that directly compete against yours? How do they promote/distribute/price these products and services? How are they positioned? How are your competitors likely to react to a new competitor?

4. **Marketing Objectives**
   —Short-term Objectives
   —Long-term Objectives

5. **Segmentation and Target Market Analysis**

   What one key market segment will you target? Explain why you have selected it and quantify it, e.g., how many people are in this segment? What percentage will use/buy your product or service? Give your target segment a name and develop an in-depth profile of the characteristics of the people in it, including a brief discussion of their consumer buying behaviour.

6. **Positioning and Marketing Mix**

   Develop an in-depth marketing mix (4Ps) and positioning for your product or service. Be sure to include a clear description of your service/product, how you will price, promote, and distribute. Specific marketing strategies and detailed tactics to capture market share in your target market must be identified. If appropriate, outline some major threats to the success of your strategy.

7. **Financial Analysis**

   Provide a three-year projected financial statement (profit and loss.) What is the break-even point in units? In what year will you make a profit? What are your sales and/or market share projections? Be sure to include details of how you arrive at revenue, costs of goods sold, expenses, and how you allocate your marketing budget.

8. **Marketing Organization**

   Outline an organization chart noting people responsible for implementing the marketing plan.

9. **Evaluate Performance**

   Compare actual performance against planned goals or objectives—ongoing and periodic. Ascertain reasons for performance gaps for both underperformance or overperformance.

MARKETING PLAN FOR SLAMKIK*

Table of Contents

* This sample marketing plan was prepared by a group of students from Wilfrid Laurier University as part of their Marketing course. It is presented here as an illustration and for discussion of marketing plans in general. The authors would like to thank their students—Dan Andrews, Alex Cole, Matthew English, Jaclyn Hougassian, Amit Sen, and Jonathan Snively—for allowing us to use their marketing plan.

EXECUTIVE SUMMARY

SlamKik is a footbag that uses an audio technological component to account for high scores. SlamKik is following the recent trend of using technology to create a fun innovative product to help kids aged 10–19 be active in a society with an ever-growing childhood obesity rate. It will also provide kids with a new physically interactive activity for them to enjoy.

SlamKik will be competing on two different levels in the footbag industry. The first level will be the traditional footbag market where no technology is implemented in the footbags. The second market involves products that implement technology to add special features to the footbag like: audio playback, LED lights, LCD displays, and high score tracking systems. Competitors include Irwin, Wham-O Inc., FunKix, Flying Clipper, and Sipa Sipa.

The initial primary target market of the SlamKik consists of 132,391 males, aged 10–19 in Ontario. These males come from households with an average income level, have lots of disposable income, and are physically active. Our goal is to introduce our products nationally in Canada in three years.

Promotions will mainly consist of distributing sample products to the target market in schools, malls, city street fairs, and some major events such as the Canadian National Exhibition (CNE). Once the product has been established in the market, we will pursue other dynamic Internet marketing channels, including social networking sites such as YouTube, MySpace, and Facebook. An intensive distribution strategy through small local retailers and online sales will be used.

SlamKik will record a net loss for the first two years of operation, and break even in year three when we expand to a national level; recording a net profit of $309,006. This will give us a cumulative net profit of $226,466 over the first three years of operation.

MISSION

The mission of SlamKik is to promote active living among kids through the creation of fun, innovative products.

3. Situation Analysis

• *SWOT Analysis*

→ Strengths and Weaknesses of company and products.

→ Opportunities and Threats from the firm's external environment.

SITUATION ANALYSIS

SWOT Analysis

Strengths	Weaknesses
SlamKik is an innovative product that offers higher levels of technological content and longer battery life	New entrant in a market that is fairly crowded, hence little brand recognition
Opportunities	SlamKik does not have a distribution network and will have to devote considerable marketing efforts and resources to build one
Rising obesity problems and renewed calls for active living	Contracting out manufacturing could reduce SlamKik's ability to ensure high quality toys
Renewal of the ParticipACTION Program that encourages active living	Inexperienced management team and a complete marketing organization would have to be established—takes time and resources
Canada has a growing toy industry	As a start-up, SlamKik has limited financial resources
Greater demand for toys that combine technology and interactivity while encouraging physical activity	**Threats**
The technology for SlamKik is available and has been accepted by kids	Stiff competition, especially price competition, from existing competitors
SlamKik can be played inside so that kids can play with it in the safety of their homes—a growing concern among parents in Canada	Very easy for existing firms to increase the technological content of their toys

• *Market Trend Analysis*

→ Provide a clear description and a statistical analysis of your industry.

→ How big is the market?

→ What trends are occurring? Why?

→ Are sales going up or down? Why?

• *Environmental Analysis*

→ What are the key environmental factors that influence your market? (e.g. demographic, economic, technology, political/legal, social, culture)

→ Which 2 or 3 factors are most relevant to your product or service?

Market Trend Analysis

Canada has a $1.4-billion toy industry, according to the Canadian Toy Association.[1] Retail store sales of toys in Canada for 2006 were $3,026,300,000.[2] Each quarter the sales of toys increased and by the 4th quarter, the industry saw the biggest increase in sales, of more than double the previous quarter, due to the Christmas season. (See Appendix 1 for complete breakdown of quarterly sales trend.) We plan to launch SlamKik at the beginning of November, just in time for the Christmas season in order to increase sales since it is a perfect "stocking stuffer."

This year the trend for new toys is adding electronic and Web-based enhancements to classic toys. These toys are estimated to be the biggest sellers of 2007 in North America.[3] At the 2007 Toy Fair, it was clear that toys in all categories continue to trend toward more electronics, interactivity, technology, and customization.[4] This is one of the driving forces behind the idea for the SlamKik. Another trend in the toy industry is a move towards more physically interactive video games, which include Nintendo Wii, Guitar Hero, and Dance, Dance Revolution. These games attempt to get users involved in physical activity. Among active video game players, light users play for up to five hours a week, while heavy users play for up to 16 or more hours a week.[5] With the strong influence of electronic media in today's society, such as television, movies, computers, and video games, children are spending more time in front of a screen than ever before and less time interacting with each other.[6] Companies have realized that it is important to make games more interactive to get kids to be active while enjoying their favourite video games. In 2006 the sales of outdoor and sports toys decreased by 5 percent, while the sales of youth electronic toys increased by 17 percent worldwide.[7] Our product is a combination of both a sports toy and electronic toy.

Environmental Analysis

The key environmental factors that influence our market are technology and social trends.

Technology   Technology is always changing and it is especially important to stay on top of the latest trends to keep toys current in the market. SlamKik is a basic footbag, but it will incorporate an audio technological component that will count the number of kicks. This technology will be tension activated and will be protected inside the sack by the beads. The audio component will be similar to the Hasbro's Bop It technology[8] and it already exists in other footbag products.

In the U.S., the electronic toy industry is currently $1.6 billion[9] and growing. In 2006, sales in youth electronic toys increased by 22 percent from the previous year.[10] This was the largest increase of all the toy categories and it is expected that this increasing trend will continue in 2007.

Social   In today's society kids and teens are not as active as they used to be. In fact, they are 40 percent less active than they were 30 years ago.[11] This may be due to the increasing number of video games and toys in the market that promote physical inactivity. This is a growing concern for parents, as they want their kids to be active and live a healthy lifestyle. Another concern is that the average Canadian child watches more than 26 hours of television and spends up to 30 hours sitting in school each week.[12] In Canada, the total number of males between age 12 and 19 is 1,716,269 and the number of physically inactive males in that group is 386,366.[13] That is 23 percent of our target market. SlamKik encourages teens to be active and this may appeal to parents who want their children to be healthy and physically active on a regular basis. This fits in with today's culture of promoting healthy choices for healthy active lifestyles. The Canadian Government is also promoting the benefits of physical activity with new million dollar investments into programs to promote healthy eating and activity for Canadians. The Government also renewed funding for ParticipACTION after it was terminated in 2001.[14] ParticipACTION is aimed to ensure that Canadians are the most physically active on earth and encourages Canadians to move more and become active.[15]

Competitive Analysis

In the footbag market, Wham-O Inc. is the leader in sales of Hacky Sacks™, slingshots, hula hoops, and Frisbees. In 2006, Wham-O had $5 million in sales.[16] The top 50 companies in the toy industry hold a combined 75 percent of the market share.[17] This includes major companies such as Mattel and Hasbro.

   SlamKik will be competing with similar products on two levels: traditional and technological. In the traditional market there are many competitors, such as: Irwin, Wham-O Inc., FunKix, Flying Clipper, and Sipa Sipa.[18] We will focus on FunKix because they compete in the technological market and Wham-O Inc. because of its ability to compete in the traditional market.

FunKix   FunKix offers an expansion on the traditional footbag market. Their three products (Digi, Sonic, and Flash) introduce technology into the design of

- *Competitive Analysis*

→ Who are your major competitors?

→ What is their market share?

→ What products and services do they offer that directly compete against yours?

→ How do they promote/distribute/ price these products and services?

→ How are they positioned?

→ How are your competitors likely to react to a new competitor?

the footbag. The Digi product is our direct competition because it has an LCD display that keeps track of your high score. The other two products feature LED lights that light up when you kick it (Flash) and an audio recorder that you can record sayings for play back during kicking (Sonic).[19] All three are offered for £10.00 (CAD$19.60).

FunKix is positioned as an innovative provider, which correlates with higher prices and therefore do not have any traditional footbags in their product line. (See Appendix 2 for perceptual map.)[20] FunKix has tried to capitalize on the Harry Potter craze by making a "golden snitch" style footbag to be won through a promotional contest.[21] One of FunKix's competitive weaknesses is the concern about a short battery life and poor durability of the product. Such concerns will also surround our product but will be overcome using product design and long-life batteries. Although FunKix offers a similar product to our own, their main competitive weakness is their geographical location. Operations are based in the United Kingdom and although they ship internationally they are already priced above our retail price of $17.50, which would mean they are priced out of our market. If they were located in North America our product would be in direct competition with theirs.

Wham-O Inc.   Wham-O is a private toy corporation that is best known for the Slip 'n Slide and the Hula Hoop. Wham-O has created a generic trademark on their footbag product: Hacky Sack. Their Hacky Sack has three varieties: Freestyle ($6.49), Striker, and Impact ($4.99). Wham-O aggressively defends its trademarks citing that, "…Wham-O's intellectual property must be respected."[22] This means that our product must not make any reference to the Hacky Sack trademark otherwise we could wind up with litigation troubles. Promotion is done through point of sale advertising and the use of the generic trademark of Hacky Sack. The product is offered through online sales and also is located in retail stores throughout North America.[23] Wham-O is positioned as a basic, non-innovative provider and is placed on the perceptual map as such (See Appendix 2).[24] Wham-O's product may appeal more to 'footbag purists' as well because of their commitment to the traditional footbag design. Since Wham-O is a large corporation with many product lines supplying steady revenues they are unlikely to let us enter the market easily. They may try to begin a price war between our two products in an attempt to drive us out of the market. We will have to rely on the strength of our innovative product to keep us from entering into a price war. Their competitive weakness is their lack of innovation and commitment to the traditional design. This is how we will differentiate our product from theirs and hopefully capture some of the market share in the industry.

IDENTIFY AND EVALUATE OPPORTUNITIES

Segmentation Analysis and Consumer Buying Behaviour

Our target market is called *Active Hip Boys*. Our primary target market consists of 132,391 individuals who are male and from Ontario. They are between the ages of 10–19 and are physically active on a regular basis. (See Appendix 3 for breakdown of target market.) We chose to target this market because it is substantial and there is a potential to generate profits. There are also growth opportunities in the future to expand the market into other provinces and eventually into the rest of Canada. As sales grow and the product becomes established in the market, we can expand to other provinces targeting the same age group who are looking for the same benefits. The segment is also reachable, since there are many ways to communicate the benefits of our product through advertising on websites, word of mouth, and direct contact with our customers. A potential secondary market would include the inactive kids of the same age group due to the fact that playing with the SlamKik is a social activity. This would make the total target market 817,230 males in size. (See Appendix 4 for secondary market.)

This segment has lots of disposable income because their parents take care of most of their living expenses. They also receive money for birthdays, from allowances, from grandparents, and from part-time jobs, such as a paper route or working in a fast food restaurant. The average household in Ontario spent $4089 on recreation in 2005[25] and sales of toys and games in Canada have increased 19.5 percent since 2002.[26] (See Appendix 5 for Growth of Toy Sales from 2002 to 2006.)

The *Active Hip Boys* segment has an active lifestyle, likes to play with their friends, and is very competitive. These high energy individuals like to watch and participate in sporting events. They go to school during the day and have breaks for lunch where they can play with the SlamKik. They typically have free time on the weekends and more spare time to take part in recreational activities. They are also hip and have all the latest technology, such as iPods and cell phones.

Our target market is looking for something fun, convenient, and easy to use. The SlamKik allows them to stay active and is small and portable, which allows them to throw it in their pocket or backpack.

6. Marketing Mix and Positioning

→ Develop an in-depth marketing mix (4Ps) and positioning for your product or service.

→ Be sure to include a clear description of your service/product, how you will price, promote, and distribute it. Specific marketing strategies and detailed tactics to capture market share in your target market must be identified.

→ If appropriate, outline some major threats to the success of your strategy.

Marketing Mix

Product   Our SlamKik is an innovative new toy incorporating an audio component into a footbag. It is small and compact, making it easy to carry around. It will be available in a variety of colours such as blue, green, red, and black and a variety of patterns such as stripes, checkers, and two-toned. The standard footbag has been around since 1972,[27] with limited innovations being held only to design and size. The SlamKik will bring the footbag up to date with today's technologically advanced society. Our product will be similar in size to original footbags at 6 cm in diameter and 85 g in weight, but will also offer a built in audio device that counts repetitions, records high scores, and offers a fun new spin on the classic footbag. This will be our Rally-Tally technology. The audio component will be activated by a simple firm squeeze. It will keep counting consecutive kicks, until there is a four-second gap because this will indicate that the game has stopped or it has hit the ground. There will be options available to choose counting styles, activated by different types of squeezes. Some examples of options will be sounds to keep count, voices to count the actual number of hits, a summary of hits throughout the game, and finally, an announcement of hits only at the end of the game. Choosing options, as well as turning the device on and off will be done through tension recognition and it will also turn off automatically after five minutes of non-use to preserve battery life. The product will use one battery, which will not be replaceable, but will have a lengthy life, depending on frequency of use. After this time, consumers can buy a SlamKik but the old one will still be a functioning footbag without the audio. The SlamKik will come with an instruction page for use and will be packaged in a bright, colourful cardboard box to attract attention. Each design will have a unique pattern on the box that reflects the pattern on the SlamKik. (See Appendix 6 for a picture of the SlamKik design.)

Price   There are four components to the price of our product. The cost of each SlamKik will include the battery, the Rally-Tally technology, the material (beads and vinyl covering), labour and the packaging for each product. We plan to outsource production at a cost of $1.40 per unit. This will bring the total cost of each SlamKik to $11.40. We plan to sell the SlamKik to retailers for $14 who will mark it up 25 percent to $17.50. We will also sell directly via the Internet and personal selling at a price of $17.50 to match the price set by retailers. We are priced higher than Wham-O's Hacky Sack since we offer more options and technological components. We are also priced higher than our other competitors since we are offering a more innovative, interactive product. We want to keep the prices as low as possible, since the battery is not replaceable and we want consumers to be able to purchase an affordable toy.

Positioning Statement

- Our product is designed for *Active Hip Boys*, who are looking for new, physically interactive games.
- They are up on all the latest technological trends and styles, and are looking for new twists on toys that offer an interactive, cool approach while incorporating social and physically active components.
- The SlamKik is an electronic footbag that tallies your kicks.
- Unlike traditional footbags, SlamKik offers the ability for *Active Hip Boys* to have fun in a competitive environment with our special high score tracking system.

Promotions   In terms of promoting our product, we will use direct contact with our customers to promote the features and benefits of the SlamKik. In the first months of business we will give away free SlamKiks from our booths set up in malls, schools, city street fairs, the CNE, and outside sporting events such as OHL hockey games to let our customers try out the product. There will be contests for kids to win SlamKiks. The trial versions will have a limited battery life (a feature that will be written on the packaging so that the consumer is fully aware this is a trial version), which will expire within roughly 10 hours of play. Hopefully this exposure to the product will encourage consumers to buy a SlamKik when their free trial version expires. These giveaways will create awareness of our brand among our target market and interest in the product's special features. Once we reach major areas of Southern Ontario through direct contact, we expect word-of-mouth advertising to play a large role in building the brand. The Internet is going to be another major way to promote the SlamKik since our target customers are more technologically connected and Internet-savvy than any prior generation. Many toy websites are basic, simple splash-pages with limited information, however, we plan to have a dynamic, interactive portal where users can create accounts, join a loyalty points program for giveaways and access to special online sale discounts, play games and use an interactive design interface to make custom SlamKiks. We'll keep in contact with customers through e-mail to alert them of news and deals. Our database will be updated with names of customers from all the events we put on and attend. This will establish loyalty among our most valued customers who are more likely to buy multiple SlamKiks, all while keeping our marketing hip and down-to-earth with direct customer contact. We could also pursue new, dynamic Internet marketing routes, including social networking sites such as Youtube, where we could introduce a video channel of professionals using the product or Facebook, where we can purchase advertisements that target specific high school-aged markets. Customers can submit videos of themselves and their friends using SlamKik and they can enter a contest on SlamKik.com to win a chance to take part in a private session with professional footbaggers as well as other SlamKik merchandise.

Distribution Strategy   We plan to offer a dynamic, personal approach to our selling. Beginning by introducing our product across Ontario, we eventually plan to expand our operations into other Canadian markets based on our capabilities and opportunities. Our primary focus will remain in Ontario, specifically southern Ontario, where we will maintain the production and promotion of our product. We will introduce our product at a Canadian toy show prior to the Christmas season to gain early buzz among insiders and retailers.

However, we will not focus on trying to get our product shelf space at major toy retailers such as Toys-R-Us or Wal-Mart; we will instead adopt a more direct approach to selling. It's unlikely we would get shelf space at a major retailer, especially with major competitors such as Irwin offering similar electronic footbag products. Therefore, instead of paying high listing fees we will largely distribute the product through small retailers such as West49, local skate shops and hobby shops, and through our own methods.

One direct selling approach, which we will strongly pursue, will be Internet selling, which offers an added bonus of a one-to-one customization approach where for an extra fee a custom design can be applied to the bag. In the future after expanding nationally, we could even promote bulk orders for companies or organizations that wish to buy a large number of logo-branded footbags. Internet selling also decreases our costs and opens up our product to new hard-to-reach markets. In addition to customizing the physical appearance of the bag, online buyers will be able to add in special Internet-only deluxe features, such as lights that flash when the bag is hit, added voice boxes that play music, or different filling types for professional footbaggers who prefer a specific feeling to their footbags (footbags can be filled with sand, plastic pellets, or beans to provide a different feeling depending on personal preference).

Another distribution strategy is direct selling, where a "street team" of young, hip marketers would go into schools or community centres and run demonstrations using our product. This not only promotes brand recognition—a booth set up after the demonstration can be used to sell the product once the audience sees its unique features. Also, schools are likely to allow demonstrations within gym classes, since the product promotes physical fitness in a fun way. Our street team could also set up booths in malls and public places to both demonstrate and sell the product to our target market.

Aside from direct selling, we also plan to sell through small retailers. This avoidance of big-box retailers will earn our product a strong bond with customers. This is specifically important within the social constructs of footbag and skater culture, where reputation and "street cred" are important among consumers who are wary of major corporations and "sellouts." We will be able to approach small toy stores, as well as skateboard shops and young, hip clothing stores that would be able to sell the products at the counter directly to young males who might see it and buy it as an impulse item.

Some threats that may interfere are other companies stealing our idea and creating generic versions of the product for a more competitive price. Another threat may be the costs to make our product. We want to keep the selling price low to fit into our target market's spending patterns, but the audio components may be expensive.

Financials

SlamKik will sell half of our products through retailers and half of the products through the Internet and through direct selling. In year 1, 10 percent of people in the primary target market and 3 percent of people in the secondary target market are projected to buy.

In year 2, 14 percent of people in the primary target market and 4 percent of people in the secondary market will buy. In year 3, 10 percent of people in the primary target market and 3 percent from the secondary market will buy.

In year 1, we plan to launch in southern Ontario and in year 2, we will continue to target our market in Ontario. In year 3, we plan to expand nationally to all of Canada. In year 1, we will have a loss of ($62,330) and in year 2 a loss of ($20,210). In year 3, we will have a profit of $309,006. (See Appendix 7 for the Income Statement and Advertising Budget.)

In the first year we have a high advertising budget of 25 percent of sales because the nature of our product demands a lot of promotion to get the product known in the market. By year 2, we plan to keep a high advertising budget, but drop it to 20 percent of sales. This will give us plenty of money to use for promotional events such as booths and demonstrations in schools to create awareness

7. Financial Analysis

→ Provide a three-year projected financial statement (profit & loss).

→ What is the break-even point in units?

→ In what year will you make a profit?

→ What are your sales and/or market share projections?

→ Be sure to include details of how you arrive at revenue, costs of goods sold, expenses, and how you allocate your marketing budget.

of SlamKik. By year 3, since we are expanding into all of Canada, we will have a lot of travelling expenses to promote SlamKik all across the country.

In years 1 and 2, we will not break even. In year 2, we plan to increase sales and expand into all of Canada near the end of Year 2 in time for the Christmas season. The advertising budget will remain the same as year 1 and R&D costs will be $20,000. By year 3, we will expand our target market into all of Canada; males aged 10–19 and will break even. Our advertising budget will be $403,983 and R&D will be $10,000. (See Appendix 8 for break-even analysis.)

Marketing Organization

SlamKik Organization Chart

8. Marketing Organization

→ Outline an organization chart noting people responsible for implementing the marketing plan.

EVALUATE PERFORMANCE

Our main focus will be on comparing our actual performance against our planned targets in order to identify whether we fall below or surpass our targets. We will also examine the reasons for our performance. Specifically, we will compare our actual sales, expenses, profitability, and market share (broken down by channels and product types) against forecasted sales, expenses, profitability, and market share. These will be measured on an on-going basis in order to ensure we are meeting our quarterly and annual goals. We will measure the effectiveness of our promotion campaigns as well as the level of awareness and acceptance of our brand in the market. We will examine the extent to which our implementation strategy enabled or affected our ability to maximize sales while minimizing expenses. All this information will allow us to identify areas where our strategy needs improvements so that corrective actions can be taken in a timely manner.

9. Evaluate Performance

→ Compare actual performance against planned goals or objectives—ongoing and periodic.
→ Ascertain reasons for performance gaps for both underperformance or overperformance.

Appendices

Appendix 1: Retail Sales for Toys in 2006

- 1st quarter—$484.7 million
- 2nd quarter—$557 million
- 3rd quarter—$569.8 million
- 4th quarter—$1414.8 million (Christmas = good launch time)
- 1st quarter 2007—$583.8 million

Trend shows that toy sales are increasing each quarter and toy sales in Canada have been increasing since 2002.

Appendix 2: Perceptual Map

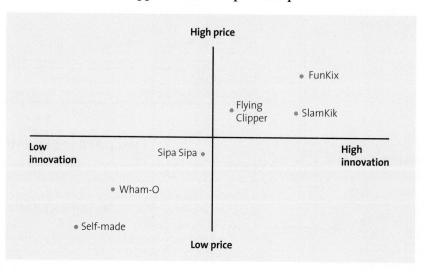

Appendix 3: Target Market Breakdown

Breakdown	Population
Population of Canada	32,623,500[28]
Population of Ontario	12,687,000[29]
Population of Ontario that is male	6,262,100
Population of Ontario males between the ages of 10–19 (13 percent)	817,230
Population of Ontario males 10–19 that is physically active regularly (54 percent)	441,304

We estimated that 30 percent of the 441,304 will be users of our product, so the target market is 132,391.

Appendix 4: Secondary Market

Years 1 and 2
Ontario population of males aged 10–19, inactive regularly = 375,926

Year 3
Canadian population of males aged 10–19, inactive regularly:
Age 10–14 = 1,065,865
Age 15–19 = 1,071,617
Total secondary market = 2,137,482

Appendix 5: Retail Sales for Toys and Games

Year	Sales (in millions)	Percentage Growth from Previous Year
2002	$2,531,500	
2003	$2,595,800	2.5 percent growth from 2002
2004	$2,642,700	2 percent growth from 2003
2005	$2,797,000	5.8 percent growth from 2004
2006	$3,026,300	8.2 percent growth from 2005

There is an increasing growth trend and an overall 19.5 percent increase from 2002 to 2006.

Appendix 6: SlamKik Design

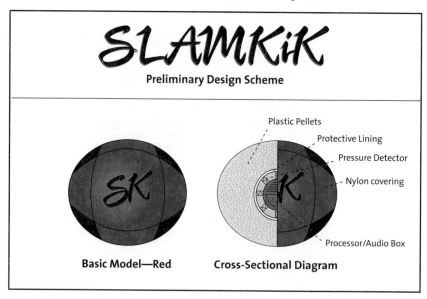

SLAMKiK
Preliminary Design Scheme

Plastic Pellets
Protective Lining
Pressure Detector
Nylon covering
Processor/Audio Box

Basic Model—Red   Cross-Sectional Diagram

Appendix 7: Income Statement and Advertising Budget

SlamKik Division
Income Statement
For the years October 31, 2008, 2009, 2010

	2008	2009	2010
Sales (Note 1)	$386,145	$528,745	$2,693,219
COGS			
Packaging	$24,517	$33,571	$170,998
Transportation	$3,768	$5,036	$25,650
Labour expense	$34,200	$34,200	$102,600
Raw materials	$220,653	$301,653	$1,538,982
Total COGS	$283,138	$374,406	$1,838,230
Gross Profit	$103,007	$154,339	$854,989
Fixed Costs			
Advertising (Note 2)	$96,536	$105,749	$403,983
Office expenses	$28,800	$28,800	$72,000
Office salaries	$20,000	$20,000	$60,000
R&D	$20,000	$20,000	$10,000
Total Fixed Costs	$165,336	$174,549	$545,983
Net Income	($62,330)	($20,210)	$309,006

Note 1: Sales

Total sales for each year will be:

Year	Total Units Sold	Total Sales
1–Retail ($14)	12,258	$171,612
1–Online ($17.50)	12,259	$214,533
2–Retail ($14)	16,785	$234,990
2–Online ($17.50)	16,786	$293,755
3–Retail ($14)	85,499	$1,196,986
3–Online ($17.50)	85,499	$1,496,233

Note 2: Advertising Budget

Total Budget in Year 1 = $386,145 x 25% = **$96,536**	
Demonstrations and Promotions at events (displays, samples, YouTube, contests) = 80 percent	$96,536 x 80% = $77,229
Website (advertisements and design) = 20 percent	$96,536 x 20% = $19,307
Total Budget in Year 2 = $528,745 x 20% = **$105,749**	
Demonstrations and Promotions = 60 percent	$105,749 x 60% = $63,449
Website = 40 percent	$105,749 x 40% = $42,300
Total Budget in Year 3 = $2,693,219 x 15% = **$403,983**	
Demonstrations and Promotions = 65 percent	$403,983 x 65% = $262,589
Website (videos) = 35 percent	$403,983 x 35% = $141,394

Appendix 8: Break-even Analysis

	Year 1	Year 2	Year 3
Selling Price	$15.75*	$15.75*	$15.75*
Variable Cost	$11.40	$11.40	$11.40
Contribution Margin	$4.35	$4.35	$4.35
Fixed Costs	$165,336	$174,549	$545,983
Break-even Units	38,008	40,126	125,513
Sales	$598,631	$631,988	$1,976,834

* average of $14 price to retailers and $17.50 from direct sales

Appendix Bibliography

About.com. "Hacky Sack." About.com. 2007. New York Times Company. 22 Oct 2007 <http://inventors.about.com/library/inventors/blhackysack.htm>.

AllBusiness.com. "The NPD Group Reports U.S. Toy Industry Sales Showed Increases in 2006." AllBusiness. 6 Feb 2007. Business Wire. 15 Nov 2007 <http://www.allbusiness.com/services/business-services/3970448-1.html>.

Belfry, John. "Canadian Children Face Activity and Fitness Crisis." Child and Family Canada. 1996. Canadian Child Care Federation. 15 Nov 2007 <http://www.cfc-efc.ca/docs/cccf/00010_en.htm>.

Canadian Toy Association. "About Us." Canadian Toy Association. 2007. Canadian Toy Association (CTA). 20 Oct 2007 <http://www.cdntoyassn.com/mabout.htm>.

cbc.ca. "Web enhancements, revamped classic toys touted among hot holiday trends." cbc.ca. 1 Nov 2007. CBC. 15 Nov 2007 <http://www.cbc.ca/cp/Home+Family/071101/U110124AU.html>.

Flying Clipper, "Footbags." Flying Clipper. 2005. Flying Clipper. 15 Nov 2007 <http://www.flyingclipper.com/home/fly/smartlist_79>.

Footbag Foundation. "Equipment: Footbags." Footbag Worldwide. 1998. World Wide Footbag Foundation. 13 Nov 2007 <http://www.footbag.org/footbags/ >.

"FunKix."Products." FunKix. 2007. Wicked Vision. 6 Nov 2007 <http://www.funkix com >.

Hasbro. "Bop it–Sounds." Bop it Game. 2007. Hasbro. 23 Oct 2007 <playbopit.com>.

Hoover's Inc. "Wham-O, Inc." Hoover's. 2007. Hoover's Inc.30 Oct 2007 <http://www.hoovers.com/wham-o/--ID__103900--/free-co-factsheet.xhtml>.

Mindbranch. "Toy Manufacture." Mindbranch Market Research. Nov 2007. Mindbranch. 1 Nov 2007 <http://www.mindbranch.com/Toy-Manufacture-R3470-766/>.

NPD. "NPD Press Release." Amount Of Time Kids Spend Playing Video Games Is On The Rise. 16 Oct 2007. The NPD Group. 13 Nov 2007 <http://www.npd.com/press/releases/press_071016a.html>.

Participaction. "Our Mission." Participaction—It's Time For Action. 2007. Participaction. 15 Nov 2007 <http://www.participaction.com/>.

Public Health Agency of Canada. "Canada's New Government Helps to Promote Physical Activity Among Canadians." Public Health Agency of Canada. 26 Sep 2007. Public Health Agency of Canada. 15 Nov 2007 <http://www.phac-aspc.gc.ca/media/nr-rp/2007/2007_10_e.html>.

Research Buy. "Toys Market Research." Market Wikis. 9 Nov 2007. Research Buy. 15 Nov 2007. <http://www.researchbuy.com/marketwikis/Toys_Market_Research>.

Schiller, Gail. "Toy Fair '07 Winds Up With Feature Buzz." AllBusiness. 15 Feb 2007. AllBusiness. 15 Nov 2007 <http://www.allbusiness.com/services/motion-pictures/4771258-1.html>.

Statistics Canada. "Average household expenditures, by province and territory—Ontario." Statistics Canada. 01 Aug 2007. Statistics Canada. 30 Oct 2007 <http://www40.statcan.ca/l01/cst01/famil16d.htm>.

Statistics Canada. "Physical activity, by age group and sex." Statistics Canada. 30 Apr 2007. Statistics Canada. 23 Oct 2007 <http://www40.statcan.ca/l01/cst01/health46.htm>.

Statistics Canada. "Population by sex and age group, by province and territory." Statistics Canada. 26 Oct 2006. Statistics Canada. 23 Oct 2007. http://www40.statcan.ca/l01/cst01/demo31a.htm?sdi= population %20age%20group>.Statistics Canada. "Population estimates and projections." Statistics Canada. 26 Oct 2006. Statistics Canada. 23 Oct 2007. <http://www40.statcan.ca/l01/cst01/demo 10a.htm?sdi =population %20age%20group>.

Statistics Canada. "Retail store sales by selected commodity." Statistics Canada. 15 Oct 2007. Statistics Canada. 30 Oct 2007 <http://www40.statcan.ca/l01/cst01/trad52.htm?sdi=retail>.

Truce. "Toy Action Guides 2007-2008." Truce. 2007. Truce. 15 Nov 2007 <http://www.truceteachers.org/toyactionguide.html>.

Venture Outsource. "Electronic toys and research techniques at CEA Industry Forum." Venture Outsource Trends and Observations. 19 Oct 2007. Venture Outsource. 15 Nov 2007 <http://www.ventureoutsource.com/contract-manufacturing/trends-observations/2007/electronic-toys-and-research-techniques-at-cea-industry-forum>.

Wham-O Inc. "News." Wham-O. 2007. Wham-O Inc. 23 Oct 2007 <http://www.wham-o.com/default.cfm?page=News>.

Wham-O Inc. "Where To Buy—USA." Wham-O. 2007. Wham-O Inc. 15 Nov 2007 <http://www.wham-o.com/default.cfm?page=WhereToBuyUSA>.

Wicked Vision. "FunKix Publicity." Harry Potter. 2007. Wicked Vision. 15 Nov 2007 <http://www.wickedvision.co.uk/harry.html>.

administered vertical marketing system A *supply chain* system in which there is no common ownership and no contractual relationships, but the dominant channel member controls the channel relationship.

advanced shipping notice An electronic document that the supplier sends the retailer in advance of a shipment to tell the retailer exactly what to expect in the shipment.

advertising A paid form of communication from an identifiable source, delivered through a communication channel, and designed to persuade the receiver to take some action, now or in the future.

advertising allowance Tactic of offering a price reduction to channel members if they agree to feature the manufacturer's product in their advertising and promotional efforts.

advertising plan A section of the firm's overall marketing plan that explicitly outlines the objectives of the advertising campaign, how the campaign might accomplish those objectives, and how the firm can determine whether the campaign was successful.

advertising schedule The specification of the timing and duration of advertising.

affective component A component of *attitude* that reflects what a person feels about the issue at hand—his or her like or dislike of something.

AIDA model A common model of the series of mental stages through which consumers move as a result of marketing communications: *Awareness* leads to *Interests*, which lead to *Desire*, which leads to *Action*.

alpha testing An attempt by the firm to determine whether a product will perform according to its design and whether it satisfies the need for which it was intended; occurs in the firm's research and development (R&D) department.

attitude A person's enduring evaluation of his or her feelings about and behavioural tendencies toward an object or idea; consists of three components: *cognitive, affective,* and *behavioural.*

autocratic buying centre A buying centre in which one person makes the decision alone, though there may be multiple participants.

B2B (business-to-business) The process of selling merchandise or services from one business to another.

B2C (business-to-consumers) The process in which businesses sell to consumers.

baby boomers Generational cohort of people born after World War II, between 1946 and 1964.

bait and switch A deceptive practice of luring customers into the store with a very low advertised price on an item (the bait), only to aggressively pressure them into purchasing a higher-priced model (the switch) by disparaging the low-priced item, comparing it unfavourably with the higher-priced item, or professing an inadequate supply of the lower-priced item.

behavioural component A component of *attitude* that comprises the actions a person takes with regard to the issue at hand.

behavioural segmentation Group of consumers based on the benefits they derive from products or services, their usage rate, their user status, and their loyalty.

benefit segmentation The grouping of consumers on the basis of the benefits they derive from products or services.

beta testing Having potential consumers examine a product prototype in a real-use setting to determine its functionality, performance, potential problems, and other issues specific to its use.

big-box food retailer Comes in three types: supercentre, hypermarket, and warehouse club; larger than *conventional supermarket;* carries both food and nonfood items.

blog (weblog or Web log) A Web page that contains periodic posts; corporate blogs are new form of marketing communications.

bonus A payment made at management's discretion when the salesperson attains certain goals; usually given only periodically, such as at the end of the year.

boycott A group's refusal to deal commercially with some organization to protest against its policies.

brand The name, term, design, symbol, or any other features that identify one seller's good or service as distinct from those of other sellers.

brand association The mental links that consumers make between a brand and its key product attributes; can involve a logo, slogan, or famous personality.

brand awareness Measures how many consumers in a market are familiar with the brand and what it stands for; created through repeated exposures of the various brand elements (brand name, logo, symbol, character, packaging, or slogan) in the firm's communications to consumers.

brand dilution Occurs when a brand extension adversely affects consumer perceptions about the attributes the core brand is believed to hold.

brand equity The set of assets and liabilities linked to a brand that add to or subtract from the value provided by the product or service.

brand extension The use of the same brand name for new products being introduced to the same or new markets.

brand licensing A contractual arrangement between firms, whereby one firm allows another to use its brand name, logo, symbols, or characters in exchange for a negotiated fee.

brand loyalty Occurs when a consumer buys the same brand's product or service repeatedly over time rather than buying from multiple suppliers within the same category.

brand personality Refers to a set of human characteristics associated with a brand, which has symbolic or self-expressive meanings for consumers.

brand repositioning (rebranding) A strategy in which marketers change a brand's focus to target new markets or realign the brand's core emphasis with changing market preferences.

break-even analysis Technique used to examine the relationships among cost, price, revenue, and profit over different levels of production and sales to determine the *break-even point.*

break-even point The point at which the number of units sold generates just enough revenue to equal the total costs; at this point, profits are zero.

breakthroughs See *pioneers.*

bricks-and-mortar retailer A traditional, physical store.

business ethics Refers to a branch of ethical study that examines ethical rules and principles within a commercial context, the various moral or ethical problems that might arise in a business setting, and any special duties or obligations that apply to persons engaged in commerce.

business-to-business (B2B) marketing The process of buying and selling goods or services to be used in the production of other goods and services, for consumption by the buying organization, or for resale by wholesalers and retailers.

buyer The buying centre participant who handles the paperwork of the actual purchase.

buying centre The group of people typically responsible for the buying decisions in large organizations.

C2C (consumer-to-consumer) The process in which consumers sell to other consumers.

cash discount Tactic of offering a reduction in the invoice cost if the buyer pays the invoice prior to the end of the discount period.

category depth The number of stock keeping units (SKUs) within a category.

category killer Offers an extensive assortment in a particular category, so overwhelming the category that other retailers have difficulty competing.

category specialist Offers a narrow variety but a deep assortment of merchandise.

cause-related marketing Commercial activity in which businesses and charities form a partnership to market an image, a product, or a service for their mutual benefit; a type of promotional campaign.

channel conflict Results when supply chain members are not in agreement about their goals, roles, or rewards.

checking The process of going through the goods upon receipt to ensure they arrived undamaged and that the merchandise ordered was the merchandise received.

click-through tracking A way to measure how many times users click on banner advertising on websites.

closing the sale Obtaining a commitment from the customer to make a purchase.

cobranding The practice of marketing two or more brands together, on the same package or promotion.

cognitive component A component of *attitude* that reflects what a person believes to be true.

cold calls A method of prospecting in which salespeople telephone or go to see potential customers without appointments.

collaboration, planning, forecasting, and replenishment (CPFR) An inventory management system that uses an electronic data interchange (EDI) through which a retailer sends sales information to a manufacturer.

commercial speech A message with an economic motivation, that is, to promote a product or service, to persuade someone to purchase, and so on.

commission Compensation or financial incentive for salespeople based on a fixed percentage of their sales.

communication channel The medium—print, broadcast, the Internet—that carries the message.

communication gap A type of *service gap*; refers to the difference between the actual service provided to customers and the service that the firm's promotion program promises.

company sales force Comprised of people who are employees of the selling company and are engaged in the selling process.

compensatory decision rule At work when the consumer is evaluating alternatives and trades off one characteristic against another, such that good characteristics compensate for bad ones.

competitive intelligence (CI) Used by firms to collect and synthesize information about their position with respect to their rivals; enables companies to anticipate market developments rather than merely react to them.

competitive parity A firm's strategy of setting prices that are similar to those of major competitors.

competitor orientation A company objective based on the premise that the firm should measure itself primarily against its competition.

competitor-based pricing A strategy that involves pricing below, at, or above competitors' offerings.

competitor-based pricing method An approach that attempts to reflect how the firm wants consumers to interpret its products relative to the competitors' offerings.

complementary products Products whose demand curves are positively related, such that they rise or fall together; a percentage increase in demand for one results in a percentage increase in demand for the other.

complex buying behaviour Consumers are highly involved in the purchase and perceive significant differences among available brands.

concentrated segmentation strategy A marketing strategy of selecting a single, primary target market and focusing all energies on providing a product to fit that market's needs.

concepts Brief written descriptions of a product or service; its technology, working principles, and forms; and what customer needs it would satisfy.

concept testing The process in which a concept statement that describes a product or a service is presented to potential buyers or users to obtain their reactions.

conclusive research Provides the information needed to confirm preliminary insights, which managers can use to pursue appropriate courses of action.

consensus buying centre A buying centre in which all members of the team must reach a collective agreement that they can support a particular purchase.

consultative buying centre A buying centre in which one person makes the decision but he or she solicits input from others before doing so.

consumer decision rules The set of criteria that consumers use consciously or subconsciously to quickly and efficiently select from among several alternatives.

consumerism A social movement aimed at protecting consumers from business practices that infringe upon their rights.

contest A brand-sponsored competition that requires some form of skill or effort.

continuous advertising schedule Runs steadily throughout the year and therefore is suited to products and services that are consumed continually at relatively steady rates and that require a steady level of persuasive or reminder advertising.

contractual vertical marketing system A system in which independent firms at different levels of the supply chain join together through contracts to obtain economies of scale and coordination and to reduce conflict.

contribution per unit Equals the price less the variable cost per unit. Variable used to determine the break-even point in units.

control phase The part of the strategic marketing planning process when managers evaluate the performance of the marketing strategy and take any necessary corrective actions.

convenience goods/services Those for which the consumer is not willing to spend any effort to evaluate prior to purchase.

convenience store Type of retailer that provides a limited number of items at a convenient location in small store with speedy checkout.

conventional supermarket Offers groceries, meat, and produce with limited sales of nonfood items, such as health and beauty aids and general merchandise, in a self-service format.

corporate and product line brands The use of a combination of family brand name and individual brand name to distinguish a firm's products.

corporate brand (family brand) The use of a firm's own corporate name to brand all of its product lines and products.

corporate social responsibility Refers to the voluntary actions taken by a company to address the ethical, social, and environmental impacts of its business operations and the concerns of its stakeholders.

corporate vertical marketing system A system in which the parent company has complete control and can dictate the priorities and objectives of the supply chain; it may own facilities such as manufacturing plants, warehouse facilities, retail outlets, and design studios.

cost of ownership method A value-based method for setting prices that determines the total cost of owning the product over its useful life.

cost-based pricing A pricing strategy that involves first determining the costs of producing or providing a product and then adding a fixed amount above that total to arrive at the selling price.

cost-based pricing method Determines the final price to charge by starting with the cost, without recognizing the role that consumers or competitors' prices play in the marketplace.

countertrade Trade between two countries where goods are traded for other goods and not for hard currency.

country culture Entails easy-to-spot visible nuances that are particular to a country, such as dress, symbols, ceremonies, language, colours, and food preferences, and more subtle aspects, which are trickier to identify.

coupon Provides a stated discount to consumers on the final selling price of a specific item; the retailer handles the discount.

cross-docking distribution centre A distribution centre to which vendors ship merchandise prepackaged and ready for sale. So the merchandise goes to a staging area rather than into storage. When all the merchandise going to a particular store has arrived in the staging area, it is loaded onto a truck, and away it goes. Thus, merchandise goes from the receiving dock to the shipping dock—cross dock.

cross-price elasticity The percentage change in demand for product A that occurs in response to a percentage change in price of product B; see *complementary products*.

cross-promoting Efforts of two or more firms joining together to reach a specific target market.

cross-shopping The pattern of buying both premium and low-priced merchandise or patronizing both expensive, status-oriented retailers and price-oriented retailers.

cultural imperialism The belief that one's own culture is superior to that of other nations; can take the form of an active, formal policy or a more subtle general attitude.

culture The set of values, guiding beliefs, understandings, and ways of doing things shared by members of a society; exists on two levels: visible artifacts (e.g., behaviour, dress, symbols, physical settings, ceremonies) and underlying values (thought processes, beliefs, and assumptions).

cumulative quantity discount Pricing tactic that offers a discount based on the amount purchased over a specified period and usually involves several transactions.

customer excellence Involves a focus on retaining loyal customers and excellent customer service.

customer orientation Pricing orientation that explicitly invokes the concept of customer value and setting prices to match consumer expectations.

customer relationship management (CRM) A business philosophy and set of strategies, programs, and systems that focus on identifying and building loyalty among the firm's most valued customers.

customer service Specifically refers to human or mechanical activities firms undertake to help satisfy their customers' needs and wants.

data Raw numbers or other factual information of limited value.

data mining The use of a variety of statistical analysis tools to uncover previously unknown patterns in the data stored in databases or relationships among variables.

data warehouses Large computer files that store millions and even billions of pieces of individual data.

deal A type of short-term price reduction that can take several forms, such as a "featured price," a price lower than the regular price; a "buy one, get one free" offer; or a certain percentage "more free" offer contained in larger packaging; can involve a special financing arrangement, such as reduced percentage interest rates or extended repayment terms.

deceptive advertising A representation, omission, act, or practice in an advertisement that is likely to mislead consumers acting reasonably under the circumstances.

decider The buying centre participant who ultimately determines any part of or the entire buying decision— whether to buy, what to buy, how to buy, or where to buy.

decision heuristics Mental shortcuts that help consumers narrow down choices; examples include price, brand, and product presentation.

decline stage Stage of the product life cycle when sales decline and the product eventually exits the market.

decoding The process by which the receiver interprets the sender's message.

delivery gap A type of *service gap*; the difference between the firm's service standards and the actual service it provides to customers.

demand curve Shows how many units of a product or service consumers will demand during a specific period at different prices.

democratic buying centre A buying centre in which the majority rules in making decisions.

demographic segmentation The grouping of consumers according to easily measured, objective characteristics such as age, gender, income, and education.

demographics Countable characteristics of human populations and segments, especially those used to identify consumer markets such as age, gender, income, and education.

department store A retailer that carries many different types of merchandise (broad variety) and lots of items within each type (deep assortment); offers some customer services; and is organized into separate departments to display its merchandise.

derived demand The linkage between consumers' demand for a company's output and its purchase of necessary inputs to manufacture or assemble that particular output.

determinant attributes Product or service features that are important to the buyer and on which competing brands or stores are perceived to differ.

differentiated segmentation strategy A strategy through which a firm targets several market segments with a different offering for each.

diffusion of innovation The process by which the use of an innovation, whether a product or a service, spreads throughout a market group over time and over various categories of adopters.

direct investment When a firm maintains 100 percent ownership of its plants, operation facilities, and offices in a foreign country, often through the formation of wholly owned subsidiaries.

direct mail A targeted, printed form of communication sent to a prospective customer's mailbox.

direct marketing Sales and promotional techniques that deliver promotional materials individually to potential customers.

direct response marketing Sales and promotional techniques that deliver marketing communications to individual prospective customers.

direct response television Television commercials or infomercials with a strong call to action.

discount store Offers a broad variety of merchandise, limited service, and low prices.

dispatcher The person who coordinates deliveries to distribution centres.

dissonance-reducing buying behaviour Consumers perceive few differences among brand when buying expensive, infrequent, or risky products.

distribution centre A facility for the receipt, storage, and redistribution of goods to company stores or customers; may be operated by retailers, manufacturers, or distribution specialists.

distribution channel The institutions that transfer ownership of and move goods from the point of production to the point of consumption.

distribution intensity The number of supply chain members to use at each level of the supply chain.

distributive fairness Pertains to a customer's perception of the benefits he or she received compared with the costs (inconvenience or loss) that resulted from a service failure.

diversification strategy A growth strategy whereby a firm introduces a new product or service to a market segment that it does not currently serve.

drugstore A specialty store that concentrates on health and personal grooming merchandise, though pharmaceuticals may represent more than 60 percent of its sales.

dumping The practice of selling a good in a foreign market at a price that is lower than its domestic price or below its cost.

duty See *tariff*.

early adopters The second group of consumers in the diffusion of innovation model, after *innovators*, to use a product or service innovation; generally don't like to take as much risk as innovators.

early majority A group of consumers in the diffusion of innovation model that represents approximately 34 percent of the population; members don't like to take much risk and therefore tend to wait until bugs are worked out.

economic situation Economic changes that affect the way consumers buy merchandise and spend money, both in a marketer's home country and abroad; see *inflation*, *foreign currency fluctuations*, and *interest rates*.

elastic Refers to a market for a product or service that is price sensitive; that is, relatively small changes in price will generate fairly large changes in the quantity demanded.

electronic data interchange (EDI) The computer-to-computer exchange of business documents from a retailer to a vendor and back.

electronic media Tools including e-mail, website content, corporate blogs, online games, text messaging, and social media.

emotional appeal Aims to satisfy consumers' emotional desires rather than their utilitarian needs.

empowerment In context of service delivery, means allowing employees to make decisions about how service is provided to customers.

encoding The process of converting the sender's ideas into a message, which could be verbal, visual, or both.

English auction Goods and services are simply sold to the highest bidder.

environmental concerns Include, but are not limited to, the excessive use of natural resources and energy, refuse from manufacturing processes, excess trash created by consumer goods packages, and hard-to-dispose-of products like tires, cell phones, and computer monitors.

ethical climate The set of values within a marketing firm, or in the marketing division of any firm, that guides decision making and behaviour.

ethnography An observational method that studies people in their daily lives and activities in their homes, work, and communities.

evaluative criteria Consist of a set of salient, or important, attributes about a particular product.

event sponsorship Popular PR tool; occurs when corporations support various activities (financially or otherwise), usually in the cultural or sports and entertainment sectors.

everyday low pricing (EDLP) A strategy companies use to emphasize the continuity of their retail prices at a level somewhere between the regular, nonsale price and the deep-discount sale prices their competitors may offer.

evoked set Comprises the alternative brands or stores that the consumer states he or she would consider when making a purchase decision.

exchange The trade of things of value between the buyer and the seller so that each is better off as a result.

exchange control Refers to the regulation of a country's currency *exchange rate*.

exchange rate The measure of how much one currency is worth in relation to another.

exclusive distribution Strategy of granting exclusive rights to sell to one or very few retail customers so no other customers can sell a particular brand.

exclusive geographic territories Territories granted to one or very few retail customers by a manufacturer using an exclusive distribution strategy; no other customers can sell a particular brand in these territories.

experience curve effect Refers to the drop in unit cost as the accumulated volume sold increases; as sales continue to grow, the costs continue to drop, allowing even further reductions in the price.

experimental research A type of quantitative research that systematically manipulates one or more variables to determine which variable has a causal effect on another variable.

exploratory research Attempts to begin to understand the phenomenon of interest; also provides initial information when the problem lacks any clear definition.

exporting Producing goods in one country and selling them in another.

extended problem solving A purchase decision process during which the consumer devotes considerable time and effort to analyzing alternatives; often occurs when the consumer perceives that the purchase decision entails a lot of risk.

external locus of control Refers to when consumers believe that fate or other external factors control all outcomes.

external reference price A higher price to which the consumer can compare the selling price to evaluate the purchase.

external search for information Occurs when the buyer seeks information outside his or her personal knowledge base to help make the buying decision.

extranet A collaborative network that uses Internet technology to link businesses with their suppliers, customers, or other businesses.

extreme value retailer A general merchandise discount store found in lower-income urban or rural areas.

feedback loop Allows the receiver to communicate with the sender and thereby informs the sender whether the message was received and decoded properly.

financial risk Risk associated with a monetary outlay; includes the initial cost of the purchase, as well as the costs of using the item or service.

first movers Product pioneers that are the first to create a market or product category, making them readily recognizable to consumers and thus establishing a commanding and early market share lead.

fixed costs Those costs that remain essentially at the same level, regardless of any changes in the volume of production.

flighting advertising schedule An advertising schedule implemented in spurts, with periods of heavy advertising followed by periods of no advertising.

floor-ready merchandise Merchandise that is ready to be placed on the selling floor immediately.

focus group interview A research technique in which a small group of persons (usually 8 to 12) comes together for an intensive discussion about a particular topic, with the conversation guided by a trained moderator using an unstructured method of inquiry.

foreign currency fluctuations Changes in the value of a country's currency relative to the currency of another country; can influence consumer spending.

franchisee See *franchising*.

franchising A contractual agreement between a *franchisor* and a *franchisee* that allows the franchisee to operate a business using a name and format developed and supported by the franchisor.

franchisor See *franchising*.

frequency Measure of how often the audience is exposed to a communication within a specified period of time.

functional needs Pertain to the performance of a product or service.

gatekeeper The buying centre participant who controls information or access to decision makers and influencers.

General Agreement on Tariffs and Trade (GATT) Organization established to lower trade barriers, such as high tariffs on imported goods and restrictions on the number and types of imported products that inhibited the free flow of goods across borders.

general merchandise retailer May be a *discount store, specialty store, category specialist, department store, drugstore, off-price retailer,* or *extreme value retailer;* may sell through multiple channels, such as the Internet and catalogues.

generation X Generational cohort of people born between 1965 and 1976.

generation Y Generational cohort of people born between 1977 and 1995; biggest cohort since the original postwar baby boom.

generational cohort A group of people of the same generation—typically have similar purchase behaviours because they have shared experiences and are in the same stage of life.

generic A product sold without a brand name, typically in commodities markets.

geodemographic segmentation The grouping of consumers on the basis of a combination of geographic, demographic, and lifestyle characteristics.

geographic pricng The setting of different prices depending on a geographical division of the delivery areas.

geographic segmentation The grouping of consumers on the basis of where they live.

global labour issues Includes concerns about working conditions and wages paid to factory workers in developing countries.

globalization Refers to the processes by which goods, services, capital, people, information, and ideas flow across national borders.

globalization of production Also known as *offshoring*; refers to manufacturers' procurement of goods and services from around the globe to take advantage of national differences in the cost and quality of various factors of production (e.g., labour, energy, land, capital).

goods Items that can be physically touched.

grey market Employs irregular but not necessarily illegal methods; generally, it legally circumvents authorized channels of distribution to sell goods at prices lower than those intended by the manufacturer.

green marketing Involves a strategic effort by firms to supply customers with environmentally friendly merchandise.

gross domestic product (GDP) Defined as the market value of the goods and services produced by a country in a year; the most widely used standardized measure of output.

gross national income (GNI) Consists of GDP plus the net income earned from investments abroad (minus any payments made to nonresidents who contribute to the domestic economy).

gross rating points (GRP) Measure used for various media advertising—print, radio, or television; *GRP = reach × frequency*.

growth stage Stage of the product life cycle when the product gains acceptance, demand and sales increase, and competitors emerge in the product category.

habitual buying behaviour Consumers make purchase decisions with little or no thought.

habitual decision making A purchase decision process in which consumers engage with little conscious effort.

high/low pricing A *pricing strategy* that relies on the promotion of sales, during which prices are temporarily reduced to encourage purchases.

horizontal price fixing Occurs when competitors that produce and sell competing products collude, or work together, to control prices, effectively taking price out of the decision process for consumers.

human development index (HDI) A composite measure of three indicators of the quality of life in different countries: life expectancy at birth, educational attainment, and whether the average incomes are sufficient to meet the basic needs of life in that country.

hypothesis A statement or proposition predicting a particular relationship among multiple variables that can be tested through research.

ideal point The position at which a particular market segment's ideal product would lie on a *perceptual map*.

ideas Include thoughts, opinions, philosophies, and intellectual concepts.

implementation phase Where marketing managers implement the marketing mix, allocate resources, and develop the marketing organization.

improvement value Represents an estimate of how much more (or less) consumers are willing to pay for a product relative to other comparable products.

impulse buying A buying decision made by customers on the spot when they see the merchandise.

income effect Refers to the change in the quantity of a product demanded by consumers due to a change in their income.

independent (conventional) supply chain A loose coalition of several independently owned and operated supply chain members—a manufacturer, a wholesaler, and a retailer—each attempt to satisfy their own objectives and maximize their own profits, often at the expense of the other members.

independent agents Salespeople who sell a manufacturer's products on an extended contract basis but are not employees of the manufacturer; also known as *manufacturer's representatives* or *reps*.

in-depth interview An exploratory research technique in which trained researchers ask questions, listen to and record the answers, and then pose additional questions to clarify or expand on a particular issue.

individual brands The use of individual brand names for each of a firm's products.

inelastic Refers to a market for a product or service that is price insensitive; that is, relatively small changes in price will not generate large changes in the quantity demanded.

inflation Refers to the persistent increase in the prices of goods and services.

influencer The buying centre participant whose views influence other members of the buying centre in making the final decision.

information Data that has been organized, analyzed, and interpreted, and converted into a useful form for decision makers.

informational appeal Used in a promotion to help consumers make purchase decisions by offering factual information and strong arguments built around relevant issues that encourage them to evaluate the brand favourably on the basis of the key benefits it provides.

informative advertising Communication used to create and build brand awareness, with the ultimate goal of moving the consumer through the buying cycle to a purchase.

infrastructure The basic facilities, services, and installations needed for a community or society to function, such as transportation and communications systems, water and power lines, and public institutions like schools, post offices, and prisons.

initiator The buying centre participant who first suggests buying the particular product or service.

innovation The process by which ideas are transformed into new products and services that will help firms grow.

innovators Those buyers who want to be the first to have the new product or service.

inseparable A characteristic of a service: it is produced and consumed at the same time; that is, service and consumption are inseparable.

institutional advertisements Used to inform, persuade, and remind consumers about issues related to places, politics, an industry, or a particular corporation.

intangible A characteristic of a service; it cannot be touched, tasted, or seen like a pure product can.

integrated marketing communications (IMC) Represents the promotion dimension of the four Ps; encompasses a variety of communication disciplines—general advertising, personal selling, sales promotion, public relations, direct marketing, and electronic media—in combination to provide clarity, consistency, and maximum communicative impact.

intensive distribution A strategy designed to get products into as many outlets as possible.

interest rates These represent the cost of borrowing money.

internal locus of control Refers to when consumers believe they have some control over the outcomes of their actions, in which case they generally engage in more search activities.

internal reference price Price information stored in the consumer's memory that the person uses to assess a current price offering—perhaps the last price he or she paid or what he or she expects to pay.

internal search for information Occurs when the buyer examines his or her own memory and knowledge about the product or service, gathered through past experiences.

International Monetary Fund (IMF) Established with the original General Agreement on Tariffs and Trade (GATT); primary purpose is to promote international monetary cooperation and facilitate the expansion and growth of international trade.

intranet A secure communication system contained within one company, such as between the firm's buyers and distribution centres.

introduction stage Stage of the product life cycle when innovators start buying the product.

joint venture Formed when a firm entering a new market pools its resources with those of a local firm to form a new company in which ownership, control, and profits are shared.

just-in-time (JIT) inventory systems Inventory management systems designed to deliver less merchandise on a more frequent basis than traditional inventory systems; the firm gets the merchandise "just in time" for it to be used in the manufacture of another product; also known as *quick response (QR) systems* in retailing.

knowledge gap A type of *service gap*; reflects the difference between customers' expectations and the firm's perception of those expectations.

laggards Consumers who like to avoid change and rely on traditional products until they are no longer available.

lagged effect A delayed response to a marketing communication campaign.

late majority The last group of buyers to enter a new product market.

lead time The amount of time between the recognition that an order needs to be placed and the arrival of the needed merchandise at the seller's store, ready for sale.

lead users Innovative product users who modify existing products according to their own ideas to suit their specific needs.

leader pricing Consumer pricing tactic that attempts to build store traffic by aggressively pricing and advertising a regularly purchased item, often priced at or just above the store's cost.

leads A list of potential customers.

learning Refers to a change in a person's thought process or behaviour that arises from experience and takes place throughout the consumer decision process.

lifestyles A component of *psychographics*; refers to the way a person lives his or her life to achieve goals.

limited problem solving Occurs during a purchase decision that calls for, at most, a moderate amount of effort and time.

listing allowances Fees paid to retailers simply to get new products into stores or to gain more or better shelf space for their products.

logistics management The integration of two or more activities for the purpose of planning, implementing, and controlling the efficient flow of raw materials, in-process inventory, and finished goods from the point of origin to the point of consumption.

loss leader pricing Loss leader pricing takes the tactic of *leader pricing* one step further by lowering the price below the store's cost.

loyalty program Specifically designed to retain customers by offering premiums or other incentives to customers who make multiple purchases over time.

loyalty segmentation Strategy of investing in loyalty initiatives to retain the firm's most profitable customers.

macroenvironmental factors Aspects of the external environment that affect a company's business, such as competitors, demographics, social/cultural trends, technological advancements, economic conditions, and political/regulatory factors (CDSTEP).

manufacturer brands (national brands) Brands owned and managed by the manufacturer.

manufacturer's representative See *independent agents*.

markdowns Reductions retailers take on the initial selling price of the product or service.

market Refers to the groups of people to whom an organization is interested in marketing its products, services, or ideas.

market development strategy A growth strategy that employs the existing marketing offering to reach new market segments, whether domestic or international.

market growth rate The annual rate of growth of the specific market in which the product competes.

market penetration strategy A growth strategy that employs the existing marketing mix and focuses the firm's efforts on existing customers.

market penetration pricing A pricing strategy of setting the initial price low for the introduction of the new product or service, with the objective of building sales, market share, and profits quickly.

market positioning Involves the process of defining the marketing mix variables so that target customers have a clear, distinctive, desirable understanding of what the product does or represents in comparison with competing products.

market segment A group of consumers who respond similarly to a firm's marketing efforts.

market segmentation The process of dividing the market into groups of customers with different needs, wants, or characteristics—who therefore might appreciate products or services geared especially for them.

marketing A set of business practices designed to plan for and present an organization's products or services in ways that build effective customer relationships.

marketing channel The set of institutions that transfer the ownership of and move goods from the point of production to the point of consumption; consists of all the institutions and marketing activities in the marketing process.

marketing ethics Refers to those ethical problems that are specific to the domain of marketing.

marketing information system (MIS) A set of procedures and methods that apply to the regular, planned collection, analysis, and presentation of information that then may be used in marketing decisions.

marketing mix (four Ps) Product, price, place, and promotion—the controllable set of activities that a firm uses to respond to the wants of its target markets.

marketing plan A written document composed of an analysis of the current marketing situation, opportunities and threats for the firm, marketing objectives and strategy specified in terms of the four Ps, action programs, and projected or pro forma income (and other financial) statements.

marketing research A set of techniques and principles for systematically collecting, recording, analyzing, and interpreting data that can aid decision makers involved in marketing goods, services, or ideas.

mass customization The practice of interacting on a one-to-one basis with many people to create custom-made products or services; providing one-to-one marketing to the masses.

mass media Channels that are ideal for reaching large numbers of anonymous audience members; include national newspapers, magazines, radio, and television.

maturity stage Stage of the product life cycle when industry sales reach their peak, so firms try to rejuvenate their products by adding new features or repositioning them.

maximizing profits strategy A mathematical model that captures all the factors required to explain and predict sales and profits, which should be able to identify the price at which its profits are maximized.

media buy The actual purchase of airtime or print pages.

media mix The combination of the media used and the frequency of advertising in each medium.

media planning The process of evaluating and selecting the *media mix* that will deliver a clear, consistent, compelling message to the intended audience.

micromarketing An extreme form of segmentation that tailors a product or service to suit an individual customer's wants or needs; also called *one-to-one marketing*.

mission statement A broad description of a firm's objectives and the scope of activities it plans to undertake; attempts to answer two main questions: What type of business is it? What does it need to do to accomplish its goals and objectives?

modified rebuy Refers to when the buyer has purchased a similar product in the past but has decided to change some specifications, such as the desired price, quality level, customer service level, options, or so forth.

monopolistic competition Occurs when there are many firms that sell closely related but not homogeneous products; these products may be viewed as substitutes but are not perfect substitutes.

motive A need or want that is strong enough to cause the person to seek satisfaction.

multichannel retailers Retailers that sell merchandise in more than one retail channel (e.g., store, catalogue, and Internet).

need A person feeling physiologically deprived of basic necessities, such as food, clothing, shelter, and safety.

need recognition The beginning of the consumer decision process; occurs when consumers recognize they have an unsatisfied need and want to go from their actual, needy state to a different, desired state.

negative word of mouth Occurs when consumers spread negative information about a product, service, or store to others.

new buy In a B2B setting, a purchase of a good or service for the first time; the buying decision is likely to be quite involved because the buyer or the buying organization does not have any experience with the item.

niche media Channels that are focused and generally used to reach narrow segments, often with unique demographic characteristics or interests.

noise Any interference that stems from competing messages, a lack of clarity in the message, or a flaw in the medium; a problem for all communication channels.

noncompensatory decision rule At work when consumers choose a product or service on the basis of a subset of its characteristics, regardless of the values of its other attributes.

noncumulative quantity discount Pricing tactic that offers a discount based on only the amount purchased in a single order.

North American Industry Classification System (NAICS) codes A classification scheme that categorizes all firms into a hierarchical set of six-digit codes.

objective-and-task method An IMC budgeting method that determines the cost required to undertake specific tasks to accomplish communication objectives; process entails setting objectives, choosing media, and determining costs.

observation An exploratory research method that entails examining purchase and consumption behaviours through personal or video camera scrutiny.

odd prices Prices that end in odd numbers, usually 9, such as $3.99.

off-price retailer A type of retailer that offers an inconsistent assortment of merchandise at relatively low prices.

offshoring See *globalization of production*.

oligopolistic competition Occurs when only a few firms dominate a market.

one-to-one marketing See *micromarketing*.

online couponing A promotional Web technique in which consumers print a coupon directly from a site and then redeem the coupon in a store.

online referring A promotional Web technique in which consumers fill out an interest or order form and are referred to an offline dealer or firm that offers the product or service of interest.

operational excellence Involves a firm's focus on efficient operations and excellent supply chain management.

order getter A salesperson whose primary responsibilities are identifying potential customers and engaging those customers in discussions to attempt to make a sale.

order taker A salesperson whose primary responsibility is to process routine orders or reorders or rebuys for products.

organizational culture Reflects the set of values, traditions, and customs that guides a firm's employees' behaviour.

panel research A type of quantitative research that involves collecting information from a group of consumers (the panel) over time; data collected may be from a survey or a record of purchases.

perceived value The relationship between a product or service's benefits and its cost.

perception The process by which people select, organize, and interpret information to form a meaningful picture of the world.

perceptual map Displays, in two or more dimensions, the position of products or brands in the consumer's mind.

performance risk Involves the perceived danger inherent in a poorly performing product or service.

perishability A characteristic of a service: it cannot be stored for use in the future.

personal needs Relate to ways people satisfy their inner desires.

personal selling The two-way flow of communication between a buyer and a seller that is designed to influence the buyer's purchase decision.

persuasive advertising Communication used to motivate consumers to take action.

physiological needs Those relating to the basic biological necessities of life: food, drink, rest, and shelter.

pioneers New product introductions that establish a completely new market or radically change both the rules of competition and consumer preferences in a market; also called *breakthroughs*.

planning phase Where marketing executives and other top managers (1) define the mission or vision of the business, (2) evaluate the situation by assessing how various players, both in and outside the organization, affect the firm's potential for success, and (3) identify and evaluate different opportunities by engaging in segmentation, targeting, and positioning, and develop the marketing mix, 4Ps.

point-of-purchase (POP) display A merchandise display located at the point of purchase, such as at the checkout counter in a grocery store.

political/regulatory environment Comprises political parties, government organizations, and legislation and laws that promote or inhibit trade and marketing activities.

pop-up stores Temporary storefronts that exist for only a limited time and generally focus on a new product or a limited group of products offered by a retailer, manufacturer, or service provider; give consumers a chance to interact with the brand and build brand awareness, but are not designed primarily to sell the product.

positioning The mental picture that people have about a company and its products or services relative to competitors.

positioning statement Expresses how a company wants to be perceived by consumers.

postpurchase dissonance The psychologically uncomfortable state produced by an inconsistency between beliefs and behaviours that in turn evokes a motivation to reduce the dissonance; buyers' remorse.

posttesting The evaluation of an IMC campaign's impact after it has been implemented.

preapproach In the personal selling process, occurs prior to meeting the customer for the first time and extends the qualification of leads procedure; in this step, the salesperson conducts additional research and develops plans for meeting with the customer.

predatory pricing A firm's practice of setting a very low price for one or more of its products with the intent to drive its competition out of business; illegal under the Competition Act.

premarket test Conducted before a product or service is brought to market to determine how many customers will try and then continue to use it.

premium An item offered for free or at a bargain price to reward some type of behaviour, such as buying, sampling, or testing.

premium pricing A competitor-based pricing method by which the firm deliberately prices a product above the prices set for competing products to capture those consumers who always shop for the best or for whom price does not matter.

prestige products or services Those that consumers purchase for status rather than functionality.

pretesting Assessments performed before an ad campaign is implemented to ensure that the various elements are working in an integrated fashion and doing what they are intended to do.

price The overall sacrifice a consumer is willing to make—money, time, energy—to acquire a specific product or service.

price bundling Consumer pricing tactic of selling more than one product for a single, lower price than what the items would cost sold separately; can be used to sell slow-moving items, to encourage customers to stock up so they won't purchase competing brands, to encourage trial of a new product, or to provide an incentive to purchase a less desirable product or service to obtain a more desirable one in the same bundle.

price discrimination The practice of selling the same product to different resellers (wholesalers, distributors, or retailers) or to the ultimate consumer at different prices; some, but not all, forms of price discrimination are illegal.

price elasticity of demand Measures how changes in a price affect the quantity of the product demanded; specifically, the ratio of the percentage change in quantity demanded to the percentage change in price.

price fixing The practice of colluding with other firms to control prices.

price lining Consumer market pricing tactic of establishing a price floor and a price ceiling for an entire line of similar products and then setting a few other price points in between to represent distinct differences in quality.

price skimming A strategy of selling a new product or service at a high price that *innovators* and *early adopters* are willing to pay in order to obtain it; after the high-price market segment becomes saturated and sales begin to slow down, the firm generally lowers the price to capture (or skim) the next most price sensitive segment.

price war Occurs when two or more firms compete primarily by lowering their prices.

pricing tactics Short-term methods, in contrast to long-term pricing strategies, used to focus on company objectives, customers, costs, competition, or channel members; can be responses to competitive threats (e.g., lowering price temporarily to meet a competitor's price reduction) or broadly accepted methods of calculating a final price for the customer that is short term in nature.

primary data Data collected to address specific research needs.

primary demand advertising Ads designed to generate demand for the product category or an entire industry.

primary package The packaging the consumer uses, such as the toothpaste tube, from which he or she typically seeks convenience in terms of storage, use, and consumption.

private exchange Occurs when a specific firm, either buyer or seller, invites others to join to participate in online information exchanges and transactions; can help streamline procurement or distribution processes.

private-label brands (store brands) Brands developed and marketed by a retailer and available only from that retailer; also called *store brands*.

procedural fairness Refers to the customer's perception of the fairness of the process used to resolve complaints about service.

product Anything that is of value to a consumer and can be offered through a voluntary marketing exchange.

product assortment The complete set of all products offered by a firm; also called the *product mix*.

product category An assortment of items that the customer sees as reasonable substitutes for one another.

product design See *product development*.

product development Also called *product design*; entails a process of balancing various engineering, manufacturing, marketing, and economic considerations to develop a product.

product development strategy A growth strategy that offers a new product or service to a firm's current target market.

product excellence Involves a focus on achieving high-quality products; effective branding and positioning are key.

product life cycle Defines the stages that new products move through as they enter, get established in, and ultimately leave the marketplace and thereby offers marketers a starting point for their strategy planning.

product line A group of products that consumers may use together or perceive as similar in some way.

product line breadth The number of product lines, or variety, offered by the firm.

product line depth The number of categories within a product line.

product lines Groups of associated items, such as those that consumers use together or think of as part of a group of similar products.

product mix See *product assortment*.

product placement Inclusion of a product in nontraditional situations, such as in a scene in a movie or television program.

product-focused advertisements Used to inform, persuade, or remind consumers about a specific product or service.

profit orientation A company objective that can be implemented by focusing on *target profit pricing, maximizing profits*, or *target return pricing*.

projective technique A type of qualitative research in which subjects are provided a scenario and asked to express their thoughts and feelings about it.

prototype The first physical form or service description of a new product, still in rough or tentative form, that has the same properties as a new product but is produced through different manufacturing processes, sometimes even crafted individually.

PSSP hierarchy of needs Argues that when lower-level, more basic needs (physiological and safety) are fulfilled, people turn to satisfying their higher-level human needs (social and personal); see *physiological, safety, social*, and *personal needs*.

psychographics Used in segmentation; delves into how consumers describe themselves; allows people to describe themselves using those characteristics that help them choose how they occupy their time (behaviour) and what underlying psychological reasons determine those choices.

psychological needs Pertain to the personal gratification consumers associate with a product or service.

psychological risk Associated with the way people will feel if the product or service does not convey the right image.

PSYTE clusters The grouping of all neighbourhoods in Canada into 60 different lifestyles clusters.

public relations The organizational function that manages the firm's communications to achieve a variety of objectives, including building and maintaining a positive image, handling or heading off unfavourable stories or events, and maintaining positive relationships with the media.

public service advertising (PSA) Advertising that focuses on public welfare and generally is sponsored by nonprofit institutions, civic groups, religious organizations, trade associations, or political groups; a form of *social marketing*.

puffery The legal exaggeration of praise, stopping just short of deception, lavished on a product.

pull strategy Designed to get consumers to pull the product into the supply chain by demanding it.

pulsing advertising schedule Combines the continuous and flighting schedules by maintaining a base level of advertising but increasing advertising intensity during certain periods.

purchasing power parity (PPP) A theory that states that if the exchange rates of two countries are in equilibrium, a product purchased in one will cost the same in the other, expressed in the same currency.

pure competition Occurs when different companies sell commodity products that consumers perceive as substitutable; price usually is set according to the laws of supply and demand.

push strategy Designed to increase demand by motivating sellers—wholesalers, distributors, or salespeople—to highlight the product, rather than the products of competitors, and thereby push the product onto consumers.

qualify The process of assessing the potential of sales leads.

quantity discount Pricing tactic of offering a reduced price according to the amount purchased; the more the buyer purchases, the higher the discount and, of course, the greater the value.

questionnaire A form that features a set of questions designed to gather information from respondents and thereby accomplish the researchers' objectives; questions can be either unstructured or structured.

quick response An inventory management system used in retailing; merchandise is received just in time for sale when the customer wants it; see *just-in-time (JIT) systems*.

quota Designates the maximum quantity of a product that may be brought into a country during a specified time period.

radio frequency identification (RFID) tags Tiny computer chips that automatically transmit to a special scanner all the information about a container's contents or individual products.

rational appeals Help consumers make purchase decisions by offering factual information and strong arguments built around relevant issues that encourage consumers to evaluate the brand favourably on the basis of the key benefits it provides.

reach Measure of consumers' exposure to marketing communications; the percentage of the target population exposed to a specific marketing communication, such as an advertisement, at least once.

rebate A consumer discount in which a portion of the purchase price is returned to the buyer in cash; the manufacturer, not the retailer, issues the refund.

receiver The person who reads, hears, or sees and processes the information contained in the message or advertisement.

receiving The process of recording the receipt of merchandise as it arrives at a distribution centre or store.

reference group One or more persons whom an individual uses as a basis for comparison regarding beliefs, feelings, and behaviours.

reference price The price against which buyers compare the actual selling price of the product and that facilitates their evaluation process.

relational orientation A method of building a relationship with customers based on the philosophy that buyers and sellers should develop a long-term relationship.

relationship selling A sales philosophy and process that emphasizes a commitment to maintaining the relationship over the long term and investing in opportunities that are mutually beneficial to all parties.

relative market share A measure of the product's strength in a particular market, defined as the sales of the focal product divided by the sales achieved by the largest firm in the industry.

reliability The extent to which the same result is achieved when a study is repeated under identical situations.

reminder advertising Communication used to remind consumers of a product or to prompt repurchases, especially for products that have gained market acceptance and are in the maturity stage of their life cycle.

reps See *independent agents*.

request for proposals (RFP) A process through which buying organizations invite alternative suppliers to bid on supplying their required components.

resellers Marketing intermediaries that resell manufactured products without significantly altering their form.

retailers Sell products directly to consumers.

retailing The set of business activities that add value to products and services sold to consumers for their personal or family use; includes products bought at stores, through catalogues, and over the Internet, as well as services like fast-food restaurants, airlines, and hotels.

retrieval set Includes those brands or stores that the consumer can readily bring forth from memory.

reverse auction The buyer provides specifications to a group of sellers, who then bid down the price until the buyer accepts a specific bid.

reverse engineering Involves taking apart a competitor's product, analyzing it, and creating an improved product that does not infringe on the competitor's patents, if any exist.

ritual consumption Refers to a pattern of behaviours tied to life events that affect what and how people consume.

role playing A good technique for practicing the sales presentation prior to meeting with a customer; the salesperson acts out a simulated buying situation while a colleague or manager acts as the buyer.

rule-of-thumb methods Budgeting methods that bases the IMC budget on either the firm's share of the market in relation to competition, a fixed percentage of forecasted sales, or what is left after other operating costs and forecasted sales have been budgeted.

safety needs Pertain to protection and physical well-being.

salary Compensation in the form of a fixed sum of money paid at regular intervals.

sales contest A short-term incentive designed to elicit a specific response from the sales force.

sales management Involves the planning, direction, and control of personal selling activities, including recruiting, selecting, training, motivating, compensating, and evaluating, as they apply to the sales force.

sales orientation A company objective based on the belief that increasing sales will help the firm more than will increasing profits.

sales promotions Special incentives or excitement-building programs that encourage the purchase of a product or service, such as coupons, rebates, contests, free samples, and point-of-purchase displays.

sales support personnel Employees who enhance and help with a firm's overall selling effort, such as by responding to the customer's technical questions or facilitating repairs.

sample A segment or subset of the population that adequately represents the entire population of interest.

sampling The process of picking a sample; offers potential customers the opportunity to try a product or service before they make a buying decision.

scanner research A type of quantitative research that uses data obtained from scanner readings of UPC codes at checkout counters.

scenario planning A process that integrates macroenvironmental information in an attempt to understand the potential outcomes of different applications of a firm's marketing mix; enables a firm to predict, monitor, and adapt to the ever-changing future.

seasonal discount Pricing tactic of offering an additional reduction as an incentive to retailers to order merchandise in advance of the normal buying season.

secondary data Pieces of information that have already been collected from other sources and usually are readily available.

secondary package The wrapper or exterior carton that contains the primary package and provides the UPC label used by retail scanners; can contain additional product information that may not be available on the primary package.

selective demand Demand for a specific brand.

selective demand advertising Ads designed to generate demand for a specific brand, firm, or item.

selective distribution Lies between the intensive and exclusive distribution strategies; uses a few selected customers in a territory.

self-concept The image a person has of him- or herself; a component of *psychographics*.

self-values Goals for life, not just the goals one wants to accomplish in a day; a component of *psychographics* that refers to overriding desires that drive how a person lives his or her life.

selling teams Combinations of sales specialists whose primary duties are order getting, order taking, or sales support but who work together to service important accounts.

sender The firm from which an IMC message originates; the sender must be clearly identified to the intended audience.

seniors North America's fastest-growing generational cohort; people aged 63 and older.

service Any intangible offering that involves a deed, performance, or effort that cannot be physically possessed.

service Intangible customer benefits that are produced by people or machines and cannot be separated from the producer.

service gap Results when a service fails to meet the expectations that customers have about how it should be delivered.

service quality Customers' perceptions of how well a service meets or exceeds their expectations.

share of wallet The percentage of the customer's purchases made from a particular retailer.

shopping goods/services Those for which consumers will spend time comparing alternatives, such as apparel, fragrances, and appliances.

situation analysis Second step in a marketing plan; uses of a SWOT analysis that assesses both the internal environment with regard to its **S**trengths and **W**eaknesses and the external environment in terms of its **O**pportunities and **T**hreats.

situational factors Factor affecting the consumer decision process; those that are specific to the situation that may override, or at least influence, psychological and social issues.

size discount The most common implementation of a quantity discount at the consumer level; the larger the quantity bought, the less the cost per unit (e.g., per gram).

slotting allowances Fees firms pay to retailers simply to get new products into stores or to gain more or better shelf space for their products.

social marketing The application of marketing principles to a social issue to bring about attitudinal and behavioural change among the general public or a specific population segment.

social needs Relate to one's interactions with others.

specialty goods/services Products or services toward which the customer shows a strong preference and for which he or she will expend considerable effort to search for the best suppliers.

specialty store Concentrates on a limited number of complementary merchandise categories in a relatively small store.

standards gap A type of *service gap*; pertains to the difference between the firm's perceptions of customers' expectations and the service standards it sets.

status quo pricing A competitor-oriented strategy in which a firm changes prices only to meet those of competition.

stealth marketing A strategy to attract consumers using promotional tactics that deliver a sales message in unconventional ways, often without the target audience knowing that the message even has a selling intent.

stock keeping units (SKUs) Individual items within each product category; the smallest unit available for inventory control.

store brands See *private-label brands*.

STP The processes of segmentation, targeting, and positioning that firms use to identify and evaluate opportunities for increasing sales and profits.

straight rebuy Refers to when the buyer or buying organization simply buys additional units of products that had previously been purchased.

strategic alliance A collaborative relationship between independent firms, though the partnering firms do not create an equity partnership; that is, they do not invest in one another.

strategic business unit (SBU) A division of the firm itself that can be managed and operated somewhat independently from other divisions and may have a different mission or objectives.

strategic marketing planning process A set of steps a marketer goes through to develop a strategic marketing plan.

strategic relationship (partnering relationship) A supply chain relationship that the members are committed to maintaining long term, investing in opportunities that are mutually beneficial; requires mutual trust, open communication, common goals, and credible commitments.

structured questions Closed-ended questions for which a discrete set of response alternatives, or specific answers, is provided for respondents to evaluate.

substitute products Products for which changes in demand are negatively related; that is, a percentage increase in the quantity demanded for product A results in a percentage decrease in the quantity demanded for product B.

substitution effect Refers to consumers' ability to substitute other products for the focal brand, thus increasing the price elasticity of demand for the focal brand.

supply chain The group of firms that make and deliver a given set of goods and services.

supply chain conflict (channel conflict) Results when supply chain members are not in agreement about their goals, roles, or rewards.

supply chain management Refers to a set of approaches and techniques firms employ to efficiently and effectively integrate their suppliers, manufacturers, warehouses, stores, and transportation intermediaries into a seamless value chain in which merchandise is produced and distributed in the right quantities, to the right locations, and at the right time.

survey A systematic means of collecting information from people that generally uses a *questionnaire*.

sustainable competitive advantage Something the firm can persistently do better than its competitors.

sweepstakes A form of sales promotion that offers prizes based on a chance drawing of entrants' names.

syndicated data Data available for a fee from commercial research firms such as Information Resources Inc. (IRI), National Purchase Diary Panel, and ACNielsen.

target market The customer segment or group to whom the firm is interested in selling its products and services; potential customers who have both an interest in the product or service and an ability to buy.

target marketing/targeting The process of evaluating the attractiveness of various segments and then deciding which to pursue as a market.

target profit pricing A pricing strategy implemented by firms when they have a particular profit goal as their overriding concern; uses price to stimulate a certain level of sales at a certain profit per unit.

target return pricing A pricing strategy implemented by firms less concerned with the absolute level of profits and more interested in the rate at which their profits are generated relative to their investments; designed to produce a specific return on investment, usually expressed as a percentage of sales.

tariff A tax levied on a good imported into a country; also called a *duty*.

technological advances Technological changes that have greatly contributed to the improvement of the value of both products and services in the past few decades.

telemarketing A method of prospecting in which salespeople telephone potential customers.

test marketing Introduces a new product or service to a limited geographical area (usually a few cities) prior to a national launch.

ticketing and marking Creating price and identification labels and placing them on the merchandise.

top-of-mind awareness A prominent place in people's memories that triggers a response without them having to put any thought into it.

total cost The sum of the *variable* and *fixed costs*.

tracking Includes monitoring key indicators, such as daily or weekly sales volume, while the advertisement is running to shed light on any problems with the message or the medium.

trade agreements Intergovernmental agreements designed to manage and promote trade activities for specific regions.

trade area The geographical area that contains the potential customers of a particular retailer or shopping centre.

trade deficit Results when a country imports more goods than it exports.

trade sanctions Penalties or restrictions imposed by one country over another country for importing and exporting of goods, services, and investments.

trade shows Major events attended by buyers who choose to be exposed to products and services offered by potential suppliers in an industry.

trade surplus Results when a country exports more goods than it imports.

trading bloc Consists of those countries that have signed a particular trade agreement.

traditional distribution centre A warehouse in which merchandise is unloaded from trucks and placed on racks or shelves for storage.

transactional orientation Regards the buyer-seller relationship as a series of individual transactions, so anything that happened before or after the transaction is of little importance.

transmitter An agent or intermediary with which the sender works to develop the marketing communications; for example, a firm's creative department or an advertising agency.

tweens Generational cohort of people born between 1996 and 2000; not quite teenagers, but not young children either: in beTWEEN.

undifferentiated segmentation strategy (mass marketing) A marketing strategy a firm can use if the product or service is perceived to provide the same benefits to everyone, with no need to develop separate strategies for different groups.

uniform delivered pricing The shipper charges one rate, no matter where the buyer is located.

unique selling proposition (USP) A strategy of differentiating a product by communicating its unique attributes; often becomes the common theme or slogan in the entire advertising campaign.

universal product code (UPC) The black-and-white bar code found on most merchandise.

universal set Includes all possible choices for a product category.

unstructured questions Open-ended questions that allow respondents to answer in their own words.

user The person who consumes or uses the product or service purchased by the buying centre.

validity The extent to which a study measures what it is supposed to measure.

value Reflects the relationship of benefits to costs, or what the consumer *gets* for what he or she *gives*.

VALS A psychographic tool developed by SRI Consulting Business Intelligence; classifies consumers into eight segments: innovators, thinkers, believers, achievers, strivers, experiencers, makers, or survivors.

value-based marketing Focuses on providing customers with benefits that far exceed the cost (money, time, effort) of acquiring and using a product or service while providing a reasonable return to the firm.

value-based pricing A pricing strategy that involves first determining the perceived value of the product from the customer's point of view and then pricing accordingly.

value-based pricing method An approach that focuses on the overall value of the product offering as perceived by consumers, who determine value by comparing the benefits they expect the product to deliver with the sacrifice they will need to make to acquire the product.

variability A characteristic of a service: its quality may vary because it is provided by humans.

variable costs Those costs, primarily labour and materials, that vary with production volume.

variety-seeking buying behaviour Consumers have low-involvement but perceive significant differences among brands.

vertical marketing system A supply chain in which the members act as a unified system; there are three types: *administrated, contractual,* and *corporate.*

vertical price fixing Occurs when parties at different levels of the same marketing channel (e.g., manufacturers and retailers) collude to control the prices passed on to consumers.

viral marketing A marketing phenomenon that encourages people to pass along a marketing message to other potential consumers.

voice-of-customer (VOC) program An ongoing marketing research system that collects customer inputs and integrates them into managerial decisions.

want The particular way in which a person chooses to satisfy a need, which is shaped by a person's knowledge, culture, and personality.

Web tracking software Used to assess how much time viewers spend on particular Web pages and the number of pages they view.

wholesalers Those firms engaged in buying, taking title to, often storing, and physically handling goods in large quantities, then reselling the goods (usually in smaller quantities) to retailers or industrial or business users.

World Bank Group A development bank that provides loans, policy advice, technical assistance, and knowledge-sharing services to low- and middle-income countries in an attempt to reduce poverty in the developing world.

World Trade Organization (WTO) Replaced the GATT in 1994; differs from the GATT in that the WTO is an established institution based in Geneva, Switzerland, instead of simply an agreement; represents the only international organization that deals with the global rules of trade among nations.

zone of tolerance The area between customers' expectations regarding their desired service and the minimum level of acceptable service—that is, the difference between what the customer really wants and what he or she will accept before going elsewhere.

zone pricing The shipper sets different prices depending on a geographical division of the delivery areas.

Chapter 1

1. Information for this vignette gathered from Research in Motion's annual reports, 2001–2007, available on its website www.rim.net (accessed November 19, 2007).

2. The Canadian Marketing Association, www.the-cma.org/ (accessed December 17, 2007). More discussion on marketing is provided by Stephen L. Vargo and Robert F. Lusch, "Evolving to a New Dominant Logic for Marketing," *Journal of Marketing* 68 (January 2004), pp. 1–17; and George S. Day, John Deighton, Das Narayandas, Evert Gummesson, Shelby D. Hunt, C.K. Prahalad, Roland T. Rust, and Steven M. Shugan, "Invited Commentaries on 'Evolving to a New Dominant Logic for Marketing,'" *Journal of Marketing* 68 (January 2004), pp. 18–27. Also see W. Stephen Brown, Frederick E. Webster Jr., Jan-Benedict E.M. Steenkamp, William L. Wilkie, Jagdish N. Sheth, Rajendra S. Sisodia, Roger A. Kerin, Deborah J. MacInnis, Leigh McAlister, Jagmohan S. Raju, Ronald J. Bauerly, Don T. Johnson, Mandeep Singh, and Richard Staelin, "Marketing Renaissance: Opportunities and Imperatives for Improving Marketing Thought, Practice, and Infrastructure," *Journal of Marketing*, 69, no. 4 (2005), pp. 1–25.

3. The idea of the four Ps was conceptualized by E. Jerome McCarthy, *Basic Marketing: A Managerial Approach* (Homewood, IL: Richard D. Irwin, 1960). Also see Walter van Watershoot and Christophe Van den Bulte, "The 4P Classification of the Marketing Mix Revisited," *Journal of Marketing* 56 (October 1992), pp. 83–93.

4. Statistics taken from Beverage Marketing Corporation, a New York-based research and consulting firm, www.bottledwaterweb.com (accessed June 12, 2006).

5. Based on David Simchi-Levi, Philip Kaminsky, and Edith Simchi-Levi, *Designing and Managing the Supply Chain: Concepts, Strategies and Case Studies*, 2d ed. (New York: McGraw-Hill Irwin, 2003); and Michael Levy and Barton A. Weitz, *Retailing Management*, 6th ed. (New York: McGraw-Hill Irwin, 2007).

6. Interview with president of The Country Grocer, Ottawa, Ontario; Lisa Morrison, EMBA Consulting Report, University of Ottawa, 2006.

7. 'Seaweed' Clothing Has None, Tests Show, www.nytimes.com/2007/11/14/business/14seaweed.html (accessed December 17, 2007).

8. Websites such as www.whymilk.com/ and www.milkdelivers.org/campaign/index.cfm provide examples of this popular campaign.

9. George S. Day, "Aligning the Organization with the Market," *Marketing Science Institute* 5, no. 3 (2005), pp. 3–20.

10. Dhruv Grewal, Kent B. Monroe, and R. Krishnan, "The Effects of Price Comparison Advertising on Buyers' Perceptions of Acquisition Value and Transaction Value," *Journal of Marketing* 62 (April 1998), pp. 46–60; Kent B. Monroe, *Pricing: Making Profitable Decisions*, 3d ed. (New York: McGraw-Hill, 2004).

11. www.earth-policy.org/Updates/2006/Update51.htm (accessed April 17, 2007); www.finewaters.com/Bottled_Water/Canada/Index.asp (accessed April 17, 2007); www.aqua-store.com/AquaDistribution/_Voss.html (accessed April 17 , 2007); www.vosswater.com/ (accessed April 17, 2007); www.brandchannel.com/features_profile.asp?pr_id=325 (accessed April 17, 2007); www.statcan.ca/Daily/English/070711/d070711b.htm (2007).

12. www.naya.com/en/accueil.html (accessed December 17, 2007).

13. Shelley Emling, "Low-Cost Flying No Longer Just a U.S. Sensation," *Atlanta Journal,* December 26, 2003, p. F1.

14. In 2005, the *Journal of Marketing* ran a special section entirely devoted to relationship marketing. The section included these articles: William Boulding, Richard Staelin, Michael Ehret, and Wesley J. Johnston, "A Customer Relationship Management Roadmap: What Is Known, Potential Pitfalls, and Where to Go," *Journal of Marketing* 69, no. 4 (2005), pp. 155–66; Jacquelyn S. Thomas and Ursula Y. Sullivan, (2005), "Managing Marketing Communications with Multichannel Customers," *Journal of Marketing* 69, no 4 (2005), pp. 239–51; Lynette Ryals, "Making Customer Relationship Management Work: The Measurement and Profitable Management of Customer Relationships," *Journal of Marketing* 69, no. 4 (2005), pp. 252–261; and Martha Rogers (2005), "Customer Strategy: Observations from the Trenches," *Journal of Marketing* 69 no. 4 (2005), pp. 262–3.

15. Rajendra K. Srivastava, Tasadduq A. Shervani, and Liam Fahey, "Marketing, Business Processes, and Shareholder Value: An Embedded View of Marketing Activities and the Discipline of Marketing," *Journal of Marketing* 63, special issue (1999), pp. 168–79; R. Venkatesan and V. Kumar, "A Customer Lifetime Value Framework for Customer Selections and Resource Allocation Strategy," *Journal of Marketing* 68, no. 4 (October 2004), pp. 106–25; V. Kumar, G. Ramani and T. Bohling, "Customer Lifetime Value Approaches and Best Practice Applications," *Journal of Interactive Marketing* 18, no. 3 (Summer 2004), pp. 60–72; and J. Thomas, W. Reinartz, and V. Kumar, "Getting the Most Out of All Your Customers," *Harvard Business Review* (July–August 2004), pp. 116–23.

16. Information based on personal interview with David Blakely, VP, Marketing, ImaSight. Company website www.imasight.com (accessed March 29, 2007).

17. Hennes & Mauritz AB, www.hm.com (accessed October 4, 2005).

18. Zara, www.zara.com (accessed October 4, 2004).

19. Royal Ford, "Automobila: Toyota Makes Emotional Appeal with Zippy New Line," *Boston Globe*, March 13, 2003, p. E1; Zachary Rodgers, "Toyota Bows Web/Mobile Gaming Campaign for Scion," *Clickz*, July 8, 2004, www.clickz.com; April 12, 2006 "Forehead Advertising Goes Mainstream with Toyota," *Adrants* (April 8, 2004). www.adrants.com; and Jason Stein, "Scion National Launch Gets Offbeat Support," *Automotive News* 78, no. 6104 (2004), p. 18.

20. Example based on Loblaws Company Limited Supply Chain Management, www-acad.sheridanc.on.ca/syst35412/patenime/intro.htm (accessed March 29, 2007).

21. www.petro-canada.ca/en/socialresp/77.aspx (accessed June 6, 2007).

22. Calvert, "Corporate Responsibility and Investor Confidence Survey," November 18, 2003, www.harrisinteractive.com. Also see The Trustees of Boston College, "The State of Corporate Citizenship in the United States: 2003," July 2003. Luisa Kroll and Allison Fass, The World's Billionaires, www.forbes.com (accessed March 29, 2007).

23. http://dictionary.reference.com/search?q=Entrepreneurship (accessed May 16, 2005).

24. www.forbes.com/2007/03/07/billionaires-worlds-richest_07billionaires_cz_lk_af_0308billie_land.html (accessed December 17, 2007).

25. Harpo Productions, Inc., www2.oprah.com/about/press/about_press_bio.jhtml (accessed April 11, 2005).

26. This case was written by Jeanne L. Munger in conjunction with the U.S. textbook authors Dhruv Grewal and Michael Levy for class discussion rather than to illustrate either effective or ineffective marketing practices. Jeanne Munger is an Associate Professor at the University of Southern Maine.

27. http://investor.ebay.com/downloads/sund_metrics.pdf; http://investor.ebay.com/downloads/sund_revenue.pdf (accessed August 17, 2006).

Chapter 2

1. Disney, www.wdisneyw.co.uk/palmickey.html (accessed October 14, 2004); Disney, "Mickey Mouse," http://disney.go.com/vault/archives/characterstandard/mickey/mickey.html; Disney, Fact Book and Annual Report, http://disney.go.com/corporate/investors (2003); Debra D'Agostino, "Walt Disney World Resorts and CRM Strategy," eWeek.com, December 1, 2003.

2. Donald Lehman and Russell Winer, Analysis for Marketing Planning, 5th ed. (Burr Ridge, IL: McGraw-Hill/Irwin, 2001); David Aaker, Strategic Market Management, 6th ed. (New York: John Wiley, 2001).

3. www.marketingpower.com/live/mg-dictionary.php?SearchFor=marketing+plan&Searched=1, (accessed August 31, 2006).

4. Andrew Campbell, "Mission Statements," Long Range Planning 30 (1997), pp. 931–33.

5. Alfred Rappaport, Creating Shareholder Value: The New Standard for Business Performance (New York: Wiley, 1988); Robert C. Higgins and Roger A. Kerin, "Managing the Growth-Financial Policy Nexus in Marketing," Journal of Marketing 59, no. 3 (1983), pp. 19–47; and Roger Kerin, Vijay Mahajan, and P. Rajan Varadarajan, Contemporary Perspectives on Strategic Market Planning (Boston: Allyn & Bacon, 1991), Chapter 6.

6. Coca-Cola, www2.coca-cola.com/ourcompany/mission_vision_values.htm (accessed September 2, 2006).;ww2.heartandstroke.ca/Page.asp?PageID=87&CategoryID=10&Src=about.

7. Cynthia Montgomery, "Creating Corporate Advantage," Harvard Business Review 76 (May–June 1998), pp. 71–80; Shelby Hunt and Robert Morgan, "The Comparative Advantage Theory of Competition," Journal of Marketing 59, no. 2 (1995), pp. 1–15; Kathleen Conner and C.K. Prahalad, "A Resource-Based Theory of the Firm: Knowledge versus Opportunism," Organizational Science 7 (September–October 1996), pp. 477–501; David Collins and Cynthia Montgomery, "Competing on Resources: Strategy for the 1990s," Harvard Business Review 73 (July–August 1995), pp. 118–28; William Werther and Jeffrey Kerr, "The Shifting Sands of Competitive Advantage," Business Horizons 38 (May–June 1995) pp. 11–17; "10 Quick Wins to Turn Your Supply Chain into a Competitive Advantage," http://marketindustry.about.com/library/bl/bl_ksao112.htm?terms=competitive+advantage January (2002); "Multi-Channel Integration: The New Market Battleground," Market Forward Inc. www.pwcris.com/ March (2001).

8. www.newswire.ca/en/releases/archive/April2007/23/c8051.html (accessed April 30, 2007).

9. Walt Disney Company, SWOT Analysis, Datamonitor, www.datamonitor.com/companies/company/?pid=8C7AE530-4ECC-4EF5-AC18-370E646FD097 (accessed December 17, 2007).

10. Supra.

11. Supra.

12. Supra.

13. Lisa D'Innocenzo, "Frito Lay Canada: Potato Chips . . . for Dinner?" Strategy Magazine, January 2007, p. 11.

14. www.leevalley.com (accessed April 30, 2007).

15. Interview with owner of the Country Grocer.

16. www.statcan.ca/Daily/English/070420/d070420b.htm (accessed April 30, 2007).

17. www.leevalley.com (accessed April 30, 2007); Conversations on working and well-being: Working by the Golden Rule: Lee Valley Tools www.vifamily.ca/library/social/lee_valley.html (accessed April 30, 2007); Lee Valley Tools Case Study, www.nerac.com/research-victories/lee-valley-tools-case-study (accessed April 30, 2007); A visit to Lee Valley Tools: A Company built on Innovation and Customer Service, www.woodcentral.com/shots/shot643.shtml (accessed April 30, 2007)

18. http://kickinghorsecoffee.com (accessed April 25, 2007).

19. http://contests.rogersconsumerpublishing.com/sears/contest.asp (accessed April 25, 2007).

20. Ned Desmond, "Google's Next Runaway Success: Adwords Select Kicks in a Network Effect for Online Advertising," Business 2.0, November 2002.

21. www.adstandards.com (accessed December 17, 2007).

22. Based on a report by Georgie Binks, CBC New Viewpoint, www.cbc.ca/news/viewpoint/vp_binks/20051212.html (accessed April 30, 2007).

23. www.loblaw.ca/en/abt_corprof.html (accessed April 30, 2007). ® President's Choice, PC Financial, PC are registered trademarks of Loblaws Inc., used with permission.

24. This discussion is adapted from Roger A. Kerin, Eric N. Berkowitz, Steven W. Hartley, and William Rudelius, Marketing, 7th ed. (Burr Ridge, Il: McGraw-Hill/Irwin, 2003), p. 39.

25. Natalie Mizik and Robert Jacobson, "How Brand Attributes Drive Financial Performance," Marketing Science Institute 5, no. 3 (2005), pp. 21–40.

26. Fairmont Hotels and Resort Case Study. www.accenture.com/Global/Services/By_Industry/Travel/Client_Successes/FairmontCrm.htm (accessed April 20, 2007).

27. Roger Kerin, Vijay Mahajan, and P. Rajan Varadarajan, Contemporary Perspectives on Strategic Market Planning (Boston: Allyn & Bacon, 1991), Chapter 6. See also Susan Mudambi, "A Topology of Strategic Choice in Marketing," International Journal of Market & Distribution Management (1994), pp. 22–25.

28. www.fairmont.com (accessed April 30, 2007).

29. Sharon Adams, "Hotels Sweeten the Pot for Travellers," National Post, April 16, 2007, p. IS2.

30. www.fairmont.com (accessed April 30, 2007).

31. Hollie Shaw, "Forever 21 Targets Canadian Teens," National Post, April 15, 2007, p. FP1.

32. The Cisco Mobile Office Solution Power's Fairmont's Hotel E-Business Strategy for Mobile Professionals, www.cisco.com (accessed April 30, 2007); Jens Traenhart, Fairmont's Award-Winning Website Increases Online Bookings and Brand Awareness, www.blastradius.com (accessed April 30, 2007).

33. www.fairmont.com (accessed April 30, 2007).

34. Christina Valhouli, Fairmont Hotel and Resorts, www.forbes.com/travel/2004/02/05/cx_cv_0205feat.html (accessed April 30, 2007).

35. Michael Treacy and Fred Wiersema, *The Disciplines of Market Leaders* (Reading, MA: Addison Wesley, 1995).

36. Based on Jim McElgunn, PROFIT W100: Staying On A Kicking Horse, www.canadianbusiness.com; Tuija Seipell, Kicking Horse Coffee is Brewing Up Growth, www.canadianbusiness.com, and http://kickinghorsecoffee.com/index.php, (accessed April 30, 2007).

37. Gerrard Macintosh and Lawrence Lockshin, "Market Relationships and Store Loyalty: A Multi-Level Perspective," *International Journal of Research in Marketing* 14 (1997), pp. 487–97.

38. R. Venkatesan and V. Kumar, "A Customer Lifetime Value Framework for Customer Selections and Resource Allocation Strategy," *Journal of Marketing* 68, no. 4 (October 2004), pp. 106–25. V. Kumar, G. Ramani, and T. Bohling, "Customer Lifetime Value Approaches and Best Practice Applications," *Journal of Interactive Marketing*, 18, no. 3 (Summer 2004), pp. 60–72. J. Thomas, W. Reinartz, and V. Kumar (2004), "Getting the Most Out of All Your Customers," *Harvard Business Review* (July–August 2004), pp. 116–23.

39. Frederick Reichheld and W. Earl Sasser, Jr., "Zero Defections: Quality Comes to Services," *HBR OnPoint,* September 1, 1990.

40. *Supra.*

41. Jo Marney. "Bringing Consumers Back for More." *Marketing Magazine* 33 (September 10, 2001); Niren Sirohi, Edward McLaughlin, and Dick Wittink, "A Model of Consumer Perceptions and Store Loyalty Intentions for a Supermarket Marketer," *Journal of Marketing* 74, no. 3 (1998), pp. 223–47.

42. Rosemarky McCracken, "Rewards Have Their Own Virtues, *National Post*, April 26, 2007, p. IS1.

43. Mary Jo Bitner, "Self Service Technologies: What Do Customers Expect?" *Marketing Management,* Spring 2001, pp. 10–34; Mary Jo Bitner, Stephen W. Brown, and Matthew L. Meuter, "Technology Infusion in Service Encounters," *Journal of Academy of Marketing Science* 28, no. 1 (2000), pp. 138–49; Matthew L. Meuter, Amy L. Ostrom, Robert I. Roundtree, and Mary Jo Bitner, "Self-Service Technologies: Understanding Customer Satisfaction with Technology-Based Service Encounters," *Journal of Marketing* 64, no. 3 (2000), pp. 50–64; A. Parasuraman and Dhruv Grewal, "The Impact of Technology on the Quality-Value-Loyalty Chain: A Research Agenda," *Journal of the Academy of Marketing Science* 28, no. 1 (2000), pp. 168–74.

44. S.A. Shaw and J. Gibbs, "Procurement Strategies of Small Marketers Faced with Uncertainty: An Analysis of Channel Choice and Behavior," *International Review of Market, Distribution and Consumer Research* 9, no. 1 (1999), pp. 61–75.

45. Virgin Atlantic, www.virgin-atlantic.com/our_story_history.view.do; "Virgin Atlantic Airways Continues to Adhere to its Objective of Supplying Travelers in All Classes with the Best Travel Quality at the Lowest Cost Possible," *Travel Agent* 290, no. 12 (1998), p. 34ff; "Virgin Atlantic's Customer-Service Packages Include a Drive-Through Check-in Service and an Improved Frequent-Flier Program," *Air Transport World* 34, no. 5 (1997).

46. TELUS Consumer Solution: Smart Desktop, www.cipa.com/award_winners/winners_06/Telus.html (accessed April 30, 2007).

47. *BusinessWeek*, "The Top 100 Brands," www.businessweek.com/pdfs/2003/0331_globalbrands.pdf (accessed August 29, 2006). *Report on Business & Interbrand*, "Best Canadian Brands 2006."

48. Lexus, www.lexus.com/about/history/index_1997_1983.html (accessed June 15, 2005).

49. "The Kellogg Way," *Businessline*, Chennai, India, March 20, 2003, p. 1.

50. William Werther and Jeffrey Kerr, "The Shifting Sands of Competitive Advantage," *Business Horizons* 38 (May–June 1995), pp. 11–17.

51. www.newswire.ca/en/releases/archive/April2007/23/c8051.html (accessed April 30, 2007).

52. This case was written by Stacy Biggar in conjunction with Shirley Lichti and Ajax Persaud for a class discussion rather than to illustrate effective or ineffective marketing practices. Stacy Biggar is a research associate with Professor Shirley Lichti.

53. www.globesports.com/servlet/story/RTGAM.20070428.wspt-TorFC-loses-28/GSStory/GlobeSportsSoccer/home.

54. www.usatoday.com/sports/soccer/mls/2007-04-28-kansascity-toronto_N.htm.

55. www.citynews.ca/news/news_10409.aspx.

56. Interview with Paul Beirne.

57. www.citynews.ca/news/news_10409.aspx.

58. Interview with Paul Beirne.

59. http://toronto.fc.mlsnet.com/t280/about/.

60. www.righttoplay.com/site/PageServer.

61. www.thestar.com/Sports/article/208302.

62. Interview with Paul Beirne.

63. www.cbc.ca/sports/soccer/story/2007/05/12/mls-chi-tor.html.

Chapter 3

1. This case was written by Ajax Persaud (University of Ottawa) based on the following publicly available sources of information for the basis of class discussion rather than to illustrate either effective or ineffective marketing practices. David Friend, Menu Foods president says as a pet owner he's angry over poisoned food, www.cbc.ca/cp/world/070323/w032377A.html (accessed May 3, 2007); Colin Perkel, Dog, cat deaths in U.S. prompt $40M recall from Canada's Menu Foods, www.cbc.ca/cp/health/070316/x031617A.html (accessed May 3, 2007); Steven Reinberg, More Pet Food Recalled, www.cbc.ca/cp/HealthScout/070405/6040504AU.html (accessed May 3, 2007); Beth Gorham, U.S. senator complains Canadian pet food firm didn't move fast enough, www.cbc.ca/cp/world/070412/w041256A.html (accessed May 3, 2007); Colin Perkel, Animal death reports did not initially trigger 'alarm bells': pet-food CEO, www.cbc.ca/cp/health/070321/x032135A.html (accessed: May 3, 2007); Allison Jones, Some animal lovers shun once-trusted brands in wake of pet food recall, www.cbc.ca/cp/business/070401/b040104A.html (accessed May 3, 2007); Recalled pet food varieties to be removed from shelves, regardless of date code, www.cbc.ca/cp/health/070326/x032602A.html (accessed May 3, 2007); Zena Olijnyk, Doggone shame, www.canadianbusiness.com/managing/strategy/article.jsp?content=20070409_85396_85396 (accessed May 3, 2007); Menu Foods Struggling to Handle Recall of 89 Brands

of Pet Foods, www.whatsnextblog.com/archives/2007/03/menu_foods_blowing_the_handling_of_recall_of_89_brands_of_pet_foods.asp (accessed May 3, 2007); Menu Foods Income Fund Announces Precautionary Dog and Cat Food Recall, Enhanced Website and Call Center for Precautionary Recall of Dog and Cat Food by Menu Foods Income Fund; Menu Foods Income Fund: Progress in Search for Cause of Pet Illnesses; Menu Foods Initiates Market Withdrawal of All Varieties of Recalled Wet Pet Food to Ensure Consumer Protection; All Menu Foods pet food with ChemNutra wheat gluten voluntarily recalled, http://menu-foods.com/recall/Press_Recall_03162007.htm (accessed May 3, 2007).

2. Theodore Levitt, *Marketing Imagination* (Detroit, MI: The Free Press, 1983).

3. http://en.wikipedia.org/wiki/Business_ethics (accessed August 30, 2006).

4. William L. Wilkie and Elizabeth S. Moore, "Marketing's Contributions to Society," Journal of Marketing 63 (Special Issue, 1999), pp. 198–219.

5. www.gallup.com (accessed September 1, 2006).

6. www.cmomagazine.com/info/release/090104_ethics.html (accessed September 1, 2006).

7. www.bsr.org (accessed September 1, 2006).

8. News Centre, www.ipsos-na.com/news/pressrelease.cfm?id=3054 (accessed April 26, 2007).

9. www.competitionbureau.gc.ca (accessed December 17, 2007).

10. www.competitionbureau.gc.ca/epic/site/cb-bc.nsf/en/02518e.html (accessed December 18, 2007).

11. Corporate Social Responsibility (CSR) In Canada, Ipsos News Centre, www.ipsos-na.com/news/pressrelease.cfm?id=3054 (accessed April 26, 2007).

12. RBC Corporate Responsibility Report, 2006, p. 19, www.rbc.com/responsibility/reports/index.html, (accessed April 26, 2007).

13. Tim Hortons News Archives www.timhortons.com/en/news/news_archive_2006g.html (accessed April 26, 2007).

14. GMability Education: Saturn Kidspace Playgrounds, www.gm.com/company/gmability/edu_k-12/partnerships/saturn_kidspace.html (accessed April 26, 2007).

15. www.newswire.ca/en/media/details.cgi?EventID=155 (accessed May 5, 2007); www.youthaids-aldo.org (accessed April 26, 2007).

16. Malhotra, Naresh K. and Gina L. Miller (1998), "An Integrated Model for Ethical Decisions in Marketing Research," *Journal of Business Ethics,* 17 (February), 263–280; A. Parasuraman, Dhruv Grewal and R. Krishnan (2007), *Marketing Research,* 2nd Edition, Boston, MA: Houghton Mifflin Company, pp. 44–49; J. R. Sparks and S. D. Hunt (1998), "Marketing Researcher Ethical Sensitivity: Conceptualization, Measurement, and Exploratory Investigation," *Journal of Marketing,* April, 92–109; Kimmel, Allan J. and N. Craig Smith (2001), "Deception in Marketing Research: Ethical, Methodological and Disciplinary Implications," *Psychology & Marketing,* 18 (7) 663; Ralph W Giacobbe and Madhav N Segal (2000), "A Comparative Analysis of Ethical Perceptions in Marketing Research: U.S.A. vs. Canada," *Journal of Business Ethics,* 27 (October), 229–246.

17. www.generalmills.com/corporate/index.aspx (accessed August 29, 2006).

18. www.newstarget.com/007572.html (accessed August 29, 2006).

19. www.eatwell.gov.uk/foodlabels/trafficlights (accessed May 2, 2007); British Food Industry Opposes Traffic Light Labelling, *The Guardian (UK),* December 28, 2006 (accessed May 2, 2007); http://findarticles.com/p/articles/mi_qn4158/is_20060310/ai_n16140493 (accessed May 2, 2007); Consumers misled by food labels – report; www.guardian.co.uk/food/Story/0,,2013425,00.html (accessed May 2, 2007); Canada's obesity epidemic worsening, study finds, www.cbc.ca/health/story/2005/04/07/obesity-canada050407.html (accessed May 02, 2007).

20. www.scu.edu/ethics/publications/iie/v7n2/fetzer.html (accessed August 26, 2006).

21. www.scu.edu/ethics/publications/iie/v7n2/fetzer.html.

22. www.caru.org/news/2005/sparkle.pdf (accessed August 30, 2006).

23. www.therecord.com/links/links_070410155331.html (accessed May 2, 2007); www.killercoke.org (accessed May 2, 2007); http://thetyee.ca/News/2007/02/06/CokeOnCampus/ (accessed April 26, 2007).

24. www.drj.com/bookstore/drj502a.htm (accessed August 30, 2006).

25. http://turnitin.com/static/company.html (accessed May 4, 2007); www.cbc.ca/radioshows/AS_IT_HAPPENS/20070410.shtml (accessed April 12, 2007); www.cbc.ca/aih/latestshow.html (accessed April 12, 2007).

26. http://edbrenegar.typepad.com/leading_questions/2005/05/real_life_leade.html (accessed August 30, 2006).

27. Ipsos News Centre, www.ipsos-na.com/news/pressrelease.cfm?id=3054 (accessed April 26, 2007).

28. www.mec.ca/Main/explore.jsp?FOLDER%3C%3Efolder_id=2534374302883315&bmUID=1177625954162 (accessed April 26, 2007).

29. *The Globe and Mail,* April 23, 2007, p. B2.

30. www.ec.gc.ca/epr/inventory/en/DetailView.cfm?intInitiative=72 (accessed May 14, 2007).

31. www.cooperators.ca/en/homepage/homepageEnglish.html (accessed December 17, 2007).

32. http://environment.about.com/od/recycling/a/harry_potter.htm (accessed May 9, 2007).

33. www.cmomagazine.com/info/release/090104_ethics.html (accessed September 1, 2006).

34. Carolyn Hotchkiss, "Business Ethics: One Slide Cases," Babson College, Wellesley, MA, 2004; www.usatoday.com/news/nation/2004-03-23-tshirts_x.htm (accessed August 25, 2006); www.marketingpower.com/live/mg-dictionary.php?SearchFor=direct+marketing&Searched=1 (accessed August 5, 2005).

35. This case was written by Bernadette Franjieh (University of Ottawa) based on publicly available information and a documentary on Carbon Footprints by CBC journalist, Adrianne Arsenault, (under supervision of Ajax Persaud) for the basis of class discussion rather than to illustrate either effective or ineffective marketing practices.

36. www.ec.gc.ca/climate/overview_science-e.html (accessed May 15, 2007).

37. www.carbonfootprint.com/carbon_footprint.html (accessed May 15, 2007).

38. www.cbc.ca/news/reportsfromabroad/arsenault/20070202. html (accessed May 15, 2007).

39. www.cbc.ca/news/background/consumers/carbon-foot-prints.html (accessed May 15, 2007).

40. www.cbc.ca/news/background/consumers/carbon-foot-prints.html (accessed May 15, 2007).

41. www.etravelblackboard.com/index.asp?id=65261&nav=2 (accessed June 6, 2007).

42. www.carbonneutral.com/pages/whatwedo.asp (accessed May 15, 2007).

43. Kerry Gillespie, Province targets plastic, www.thestar.com/news/article/211921 (accessed May 15, 2007).

Chapter 4

1. Loblaw full page ad, *The Record*, May 10, 2007, p. E3.

2. Laura Penny, "Bye-bye, Pooper-scooper. Hello, eco-chic," *The Globe and Mail*, April 21, 2007, p. F3.

3. Tralee Pearce, "Enviro Bags in Demand," *The Globe and Mail*, May 19, 2007, p. L5.

4. *Supra*.

5. Kerry Gillespie, "Campaign to kick the plastic-bag habit," *The Globe and Mail*, May 9, 2007, p. A1.

6. *Supra*.

7. Peter F. Drucker, *The Essential Drucker* (New York: Harper Collins, 2001).

8. Michael Tchong, *Trendscape* (2004), www.trendsetters.com.

9. Valerie Reitman, "Toyota Motor Shows Its Mettle after Fire Destroys Parts Plant," *The Wall Street Journal*, May 8, 1997.

10. AHHA Fashion: Dussault Ink and Gene Simmons Money Bag, www.allhiphop.com/alternatives/?ID=485 (accessed: May 5, 2007); www.dussaultink.com/docs/mar08_07/article.htm (accessed May 5, 2007); www.miw.com.sg/publish/sg/en/looking_good/brand_story/vancouver_raising.html; Interviews on April 4, 2007 with Urban Rush and on March 22, 2007 with 969 City TV, Razer and Much Music available on www.dussaultink.com (accessed May 15, 2007).

11. Matt Fish, "Silicon Belly: The Value of Competitive Intelligence," November 10, 2003, http://lexis-nexis.com (accessed September 6, 2006).

12. *Supra*.

13. Steve Mossop, Companies Not Spending Enough on Business Intelligence Activities, www.ipsos-na.com/news/pressrelease.cfm?id=2874 (accessed May 10, 2007).

14. Steven Gray, "Gillette in a Lather over Schick's Challenge for $1.7 Billion Razor Market," *Seattle Times*, January 14, 2004.

15. Jack Neff, "Gillette, Schick Fight with Free Razors," *Advertising Age* 74, no. 48, p. 8.

16. Andrew Caffey, "Gillette Wins Legal Fight with Schick," *Knight Ridder Tribune Business News*, April 30, 2005.

17. Abelson, Jean, "For Fusion, Gillette Plans a Super Bowl Blitz," *Knight Ridder Tribune Business News*, January 27, 2006, p.1.

18. Air Canada, WestJet Settle Spying Lawsuit, www.cbc.ca/canada/calgary/story/2006/05/29/ca-westjet-settlement-20060529.html (accessed May 15, 2007).

19. "Orthodox," *American Demographics*, May 2004, p. 35.

20. www.statscan.ca (accessed May 15, 2007).

21. Social Welfare Research Institute, "Good Tidings for a New Year: The $41 Trillion Transfer of Wealth Is Still Valid," www.bc.edu/research/swri/meta-elements/ssi/wcvol3.html.

22. www.statscan.ca (accessed May 15, 2007).

23. Kristin Davis, "Oldies but Goodies; Marketers, Take Note: Baby boomers Have Lots of Money to Spend," *U.S. News & World Report*, Washington edition, March 14, 2005, p. 45.

24. Michael Weiss, "Chasing Youth," *American Demographics*, October 2002, pp. 35–41.

25. www.statscan.ca (accessed May 15, 2007); James Tenser, "Ageless Aging of Boom-X," *Advertising Age*, January 2, 2006, 77 (1), pp. 18–19; Tabitha Armstrong, "GenX Family Values," *The Lane Report*, January 1, 2005, p. 41.

26. Lesley Young, Portrait of the New Family, www.marketingmag.ca/magazine/current/feature/article.jsp?content=20040315_61585_61585 (accessed May 11, 2007).

27. www.statscan.ca (accessed May 15, 2007).

28. Pamela Paul, "Getting Inside Gen Y," *American Demographics* 23, no. 9.

29. Noah Rubin Brier, "Move Over Prime-Time!" *American Demographics*, July/August 2004, pp. 14–20; John Hoeffel, "The Next Baby Boom" *American Demographics*, October 1995, pp. 22–31.

30. 2005 YTV Tween Report, Solutions Research Group, A Corus Entertainment Inc. Company; www.corusmedia.com/ytv/research/index.asp (accessed May 15, 2007); J.K. Wall, "Tweens Get Retailers into Parents' Wallets," *Knight Ridder Tribune Business News*, September 12, 2003, p. 1. Research attributed to WonderGroup in Cincinnati.

31. Mindy F. Ji and James U. McNeal, "How Chinese Children's Commercials Differ from Those of the United States," *Journal of Advertising* 30, no. 3 (Fall 2001), pp. 79–91.

32. 2005 YTV Tween Report, Solutions Research Group, A Corus Entertainment Inc. Company; www.corusmedia.com/ytv/research/index.asp (accessed May 15, 2007).

33. The term "Speeders" was coined by Cynthia Cohen, president, Strategic Mindshare.

34. www.statscan.ca (accessed May 15, 2007).

35. www.statscan.ca (accessed May 15, 2007).

36. www.statscan.ca (accessed May 29, 2008).

37. U.S. Bureau of the Census, www.census.gov/population/www/socdemo/educ-attn.html.

38. www.statscan.ca (accessed May 15, 2007).

39. Bethany Clough, "Home-Improvement Store Empower Female Customers with Do-It-Yourself Tools," *Knight Ridder Tribune Business Service*, March 20, 2005, p. 1; Fara Warner, "Yes, Women Spend (And Saw and Sand)," *The New York Times*, February 29, 2004, p. C1.

40. www.statscan.ca (accessed May 15, 2007).

41. www.statscan.ca (accessed May 29, 2008).

42. This section draws heavily from Jacquelyn A. Ottman, *Green Marketing: Opportunity for Innovation* (Chicago: NTC Publishing, 1997), also available online at www.greenmarketing.com.

43. Kerry Gillespie, Province Targets Plastic Bags, www.thestar.com/news/article/211921 (accessed May 15, 2007).

44. Hackers put Winners, HomeSense shoppers at risk, www.ctv.ca/servlet/ArticleNews/story/CTVNews/20070118/fraud_hacker_070118?s_name=&no_ads= (accessed May 15, 2007).

45. www.statscan.ca (accessed May 15, 2007).

46. www.statscan.ca (accessed May 15, 2007).

47. Martin Peers, "Buddy, Can You Spare Some Time?" *The Wall Street Journal*, January 26, 2004, B1, B3.

48. www.theglobeandmail.com/servlet/story/RTGAM.20071205. wcensusmain1005/BNStory/census2006/home (accessed December 18, 2007).

49. www.statscan.ca accessed, May 15, 2007

50. Tapping into the Hot Chinese and South Asian Marketplace, *Ipsos Ideas*, www.ipsos-ideas.com/article.cfm?id=3391 (accessed May 15, 2007).

51. Rebecca Harris, "Skin Deep, Canada's Big Banks Have Taken Great Strides to Reach Newcomers to the Country. But, They Need to Look Beneath the Surface to Truly Connect to Multicultural Consumers," *Marketing Magazine*, January 29, 2007.

52. *Supra.*

53. *Supra.*

54. Michael Solomon, *Consumer Behavior: Buying, Having and Being* (Upper Saddle River, NJ: Prentice Hall, 2006).

55. Rob Gerlsbeck, Research: A Distinct Shopping Society, www. marketingmag.ca/magazine/current/quebec_rpt/article. jsp?content=20070625_69884_69884 (accessed June 25, 2007).

56. John Feto, "Name Games," *American Demographics*, February 15, 2003.

57. www.statscan.ca (accessed May 15, 2007).

58. YourDictionary.com, www.yourdictionary.com (accessed September 5, 2006).

59. www.bankofcanada.ca/en/ (accessed May 15, 2007).

60. Use your Computer to Make Cheap Long-Distance Telephone Calls, VoIP Guru, www.aboutvoip.org/use-your-computer-to-make-cheap-long-distance-telephone-calls. php (accessed May 15, 2007); Converged Communications: The Next Level for IP, http://backbonemag.com/Supplements/ VOIP_Supplement.asp (accessed May 9, 2007).

61. The scenario planning process presented here was adapted from that used first by Royal Dutch/Shell in the early 1970s and follows the steps set forth by consultants at Bain & Co., www.bain.com/bainweb/consulting_expertise/ capabilities_detail.asp?capID=50. See also Michael D. Watkins and Max H. Bazerman, "Predictable Surprises: The Disasters You Should Have Seen Coming," *Harvard Business Review*, March 2003, pp. 5–12.

62. "How Corporations Learn from Scenarios," *Strategy & Leadership* 31, no. 2, p. 5; Liam Fahey and Robert M. Randall, *Learning from the Future Competitive: Foresight Scenarios* (Hoboken, NJ: Wiley, 1998).

63. www.calreinvest.org/PredatoryLending/Top10PredatoryPrac tices7.2.html (accessed August 7, 2005); Class Action Certified in Payday Loan Case, www.cbc.ca/money/story/2006/05/12/ rentcash.html#skip300x250 (accessed May 10, 2007); How Much Will a Payday Loan Cost?, www.fcac-acfc.gc.ca/eng/ publications/PaydayLoans/PaydayLoans-5_e.asp (accessed May 10, 2007); Welcome to the CPLA, www.cpla-acps.ca/ english/home.php (accessed May 10, 2007); B.C. Supreme Court Justice Blasts Payday Loan Predators, www.nupge. ca/news_2006/n17au06b.htm (accessed May 10, 2007).

64. www.weston.ca/en/gwl_ar06e/bus_loblaw_review.html (accessed May 15, 2007).

65. Harry Koza, Comparison shopping, http://magazine.globein vestor.com/servlet//ArticleNews/story/GIGOLD/20050808/ kozao808/GIGOLDMAG/news (accessed May 15, 2007); Hollie Shaw, Wal-Mart Launches Fresh Attack on Loblaw, www.canada.com/nationalpost/financialpost/story. html?id=a8345c2a-acdc-467a-822c-f110a800695d (accessed May 15, 2007).

66. This case was written by the textbook authors Ajax Persaud and Shirley Lichti for use in a class discussion rather than to illustrate either effective or ineffective marketing practices. It is based on an interview with the Simply Audiobooks Chief Marketing Officer, Sanjay Singhal, and Marketing Associate, Jennifer Steele. Press releases on the company's website and an article by Jeffrey Gangemi, Simply Audiobooks Pumps Up the Volume, www.business-week.com were also used in the preparation of the case.

Chapter 5

1. Gary Loveman, "Diamonds in the Data Mine," *Harvard Business Review* 81, no. 5 (May 2003), pp. 109–13; www.har-rahs.com[0] (accessed September 20, 2006).

2. Thomas Hoffman, "Harrah's Bets on Loyalty Program in Caesars Deal," *computerworld.com*. June 27, 2005 (accessed February 22, 2006).

3. A. Parasuraman, Dhruv Grewal, and R. Krishnan, *Marketing Research* (Boston, MA: Houghton Mifflin, 2004), p. 9.

4. Rebecca Harris, Go Big or Stay Small; www.marketing-mag.ca/magazine/current/market_research_rpt/article. jsp?content=20040927_63740_63740 (accessed May 29, 2007); www.marketingpower.com/live/content19312.php (accessed September 20, 2006).

5. Holly Bailey, "Where the Voters Are," *Newsweek* 143, no. 13 (March 29, 2004), p. 67.

6. "Loews Cineplex Boosts Sales by 17 Percent Using Siebel eBusiness Applications," press release, www.siebel.com/ news-events/press_releases/2003/030805_loews.shtm (accessed September 18, 2006).

7. When Companies Lose Customer Data, www.cbc.ca/ news/background/identity-theft/corporate-security.html, (accessed June 1, 2007).

8. Canadian Privacy Legislation, www.media-awareness.ca/ english/issues/privacy/canadian_legislation_privacy.cfm (accessed June 1, 2007).

9. Dick E. Zoutman, B. Douglas Ford, and Assil R. Bassili, A Call for the Regulation of Prescription Data Mining, www. cmaj.ca/cgi/content/full/163/9/1146 (accessed December 18, 2007).

10. www.whirlpool.com/home.jsp (accessed November 12, 2004); Parasuraman, Grewal, and Krishnan, *Marketing Research*; Greg Steinmetz and Carl Quintanilla, "Whirlpool Expected Easy Going in Europe, and It Got a Big Shock," *The Wall Street Journal*, April 10, 1998, pp. A1, A6.

11. Erhard K. Valentin, "Commentary: Marketing Research Pitfalls in Product Development," *Journal of Product & Brand Management* 3, no. 4-6 (1994), pp. 66–69.

12. www.legermarketing.com/eng/qui.asp (accessed December 18, 2007).

13. Edward G. Carmines and Ricahrd A. Zeller, Reliability and Validity Assessment (Quantitative Applications in the Social Sciences), Sage University Press, London (1979).

14. *Supra.*

15. http://en.wikipedia.org/wiki/RFID (accessed June 1, 2007); Privacy Advocates Call for RFID Regulation, http://news.com.com/2100-1029_3-5065388.html (accessed June 1, 2007); Wal-Mart Details RFID Requirement; www.rfidjournal.com/article/articleview/642/1/1/ (accessed June 1, 2007).

16. Emily Nelson, "P&G Wants the Truth: Did You Really Brush Your Teeth?" *The Globe & Mail,* June 1, 2001, p. M2.

17. *Supra.*

18. Lisa D'Innocenzo, Cosying Up to Shoppers to Really Get the Consumer's POV–And a Gain in a Competitive Edge–Talk-Face-To-Face, *Strategy,* November 2006, p. 32.

19. Keith McDevitt, "Driving the Message Home. Why Lexus Chose Newspapers to Convey the Meaning of Luxury for the Launch of the ES 300 and Position the Car as a Personal Oasis of Tranquility and Freedom," *Marketing Magazine* 107, no. 5 (February 4, 2002), p. 14.

20. Allison Fass, "Collective Opinion," Forbes.com November 11, 2005, accessed electronically.

21. Adapted from A. Parasuraman, Dhruv Grewal, and R. Krishnan, *Marketing Research* (Boston: Houghton Mifflin, 2004), p. 64.

22. Stanley E. Griffis, Thomas J. Goldsby, and Martha Cooper, "Web-Based and Mail Surveys: A Comparison of Response, Data and Cost," *Journal of Business Logistics* 24, no. 2 (2003), pp. 237–59; Chris Gautreau, "Getting the Answers," *The Greater Baton Rouge Business Report* 22, no. 29 (September 28, 2004), p. 17; Alf Nucifora, "Weaving Web Surveys That Work," *njbiz* 15, no. 46 (November 11, 2002), p. 28.

23. This example was based on information taken from Coinstar's website (www.coinstar) and a case study about Coinstar, available on the SPSS Inc. company website (www.spss.com) (accessed September 18, 2006).

24. For a more thorough discussion of effective written reports, see Parasuraman, Grewal, and Krishnan, *Marketing Research*, Ch. 16.

25. Jennifer Alsever, "Electronic Stores Discover Women Marketing Survey Spurs New Tactics," *Denver Post,* February 16, 2004, p. C1.

26. This case was written by our co-author, Shirley Lichti, for the basis of class discussion rather than to illustrate either effective or ineffective marketing practices. Shirley Lichti is a marketing professor at Wlifrid Laurier University.

27. Ontario Veterinary Medical Association, "Pets: An Integral Part of the Family," www.ovma.org/pet_owners/ownership_benefits/part_of_family.html (accessed November 25, 2007).

28. Laura Severs, "Pet Power Propels $4.5-billion Industry," www.betheboss.ca/franchise_news_august_2007%5Cpetsmart223.cfm (accessed November 25, 2007).

29. Michelle Halpern, "Heavy Petting," www.marketingmag.ca/magazine/current/feature/article.jsp?content=20050321_67364_67364 (accessed July 12, 2007). "About the Iams Company," www.iamsco.com/en_US/jhtmls/iamsco/about/sw_ia_About_page.jhtml?pti=IA&li=en_US&bc=C (accessed July 12, 2007).

Chapter 6

1. iPod Continues to Dominate, www.afterdawn.com/news/archive/7211.cfm (accessed May 17, 2007); Levi's Releases iPod-compatible Jeans, thestar.com (accessed May 17, 2007); Podcast Named 'Word of the Year', www.afterdawn.com/news/archive/7130.cfm (accessed May 17, 2007); The iPod Creates A Whole New Industry, www.elecdesign.com/Articles/Index.cfm?AD=1&ArticleID=9501 (accessed May 17, 2007); Sony Digital Walkman Upstaged by iPod Nano; www.mp3newswire.net/stories/5002/sony_walkman.html (accessed May 17, 2007); Sony Takes On Apple's iPod; www.cbsnews.com/stories/2006/10/12/business/main2086060.shtml (accessed May 17, 2007); www.Wikipedia.com (accessed May 17, 2007).

2. Dhruv Grewal, Gopalkrishnan R. Iyer, R. Krishnan, and Arun Sharma, "The Internet and the Price-Value-Loyalty Chain," *Journal of Business Research*, 56 (May 2003), p. 391.

3. See Henry Assael, *Consumer Behaviour and Marketing Action* (Boston: Kent Publishing, 1987); John A. Howard and Jadish Sheth, *The Theory of Consumer Behaviour in Marketing Strategy* (Upper Saddle River, N.J.: Prentice Hall, 1989); Philip Kotler, Gary Amstrong, Peggy Cunningham, *Principles of Marketing* (6th Can. Ed. 2005) pp. 279-280.

4. Pamela Sebastian, "'Aspirational Wants' Form the Basis of a Modern Retailing Strategy," *The Wall Street Journal*, October 15, 1998, p. A1; Barry Babin, William Darden, and Mitch Griffin, "Work and/or Fun: Measuring Hedonic and Utilitarian Shopping Value," *Journal of Consumer Research* 20 (March 1994), pp. 644–56.

5. "Prince Charming: Some 30 Years after His First Design, Manolo Blahnik Is Sitting Pretty atop Footwear's Highest Throne," *FN (Footwear News),* December 8, 2003.

6. Harley-Davidson, www.harley-davidson.com/CO/HIS/en/history.asp?locale=en_US&bmLocale=en_US (accessed April 21, 2005); Harley-Davidson, "Harley Owners Group," www.harley-davidson.com/ex/hog/template.asp?locale=en_US&bmLocale=en_US&fnc=miss&loc=join (accessed April 21, 2005); "Technological Breakthrough in the Top 100 Brands: Joanna Doonar Identifies that Technology Brands Are the Interbrand Survey's Three Highest Climbers," *Brand Strategy*, 10 (August 2003); Jeff Morris, "Easy Rider," *Operations & Fulfillment*, November 1, 2002.

7. The term *determinance* was first coined by James Myers and Mark Alpert nearly three decades ago. www.sawtoothsoftware.com/productforms/ssolutions/ss12.shtml (accessed September 4, 2006).

8. www.sawtoothsoftware.com/productforms/ssolutions/ss12.shtml (accessed September 4, 2006).

9. Jim Oliver, "Finding Decision Rules with Genetic Algorithms, www.umsanet.edu.bo/docentes/gchoque/MAT420L07.htm (accessed June 2004).

10. Paul S. Richardson, Alan S. Dick, and Arun K. Jain, "Extrinsic and Intrinsic Cue Effects on Perceptions of Store Brand Quality," *Journal of Marketing* 58 (October 1994), pp. 28–36; Rajneesh Suri and Kent B. Monroe, "The Effects of Time Constraints on Consumers' Judgments of Prices and Products," *Journal of Consumer Research* 30 (June 2003), pp. 92–104.

11. Merrie Brucks, Valerie A. Zeithaml, and Gillian Naylor, "Price and Brand Name as Indicators of Quality Dimensions for Consumer Durables," *Journal of the Academy of Marketing Science* 28, no. 3 (2000), pp. 359–74; Niraj Dawar and Philip Parker, "Marketing Universals: Consumers' Use of Brand Name, Price, Physical Appearance, and Retailer Reputation as Signals of Product Quality," *Journal of Marketing* 58 (April 1994), pp. 81–95; William B. Dodds, Kent B. Monroe, and Dhruv Grewal, "Effects of Price, Brand, and Store Information on Buyers' Product Evaluations," *Journal of Marketing Research* 28 (August 1991), pp. 307–19.

12. Mary Jo Bitner, "Servicescapes: The Impact of Physical Surroundings on Customers and Employees," *Journal of Marketing* 56 (April 1992), pp. 57–71; Dhruv Grewal and Julie Baker, "Do Retail Store Environmental Factors Affect Consumers' Price Acceptability? An Empirical Examination," *International Journal of Research in Marketing* 11 (1994), pp. 107–15; Eric R. Spangenberg, Ayn E. Crowley, and Pamela W. Henderson, "Improving the Store Environment: Do Olfactory Cues Affect Evaluations and Behaviors?" *Journal of Marketing* 60 (April 1996), pp. 67–80; Kirk L. Wakefield and Jeffrey G. Blodgett, "Customer Response to Intangible and Tangible Service Factors," *Psychology and Marketing* 16 (January 1999), pp. 51–68.

13. Youngme Moon and John A. Quelch, "Starbucks: Delivering Customer Service," *Harvard Business Review*, July 31, 2003.

14. www.expedia.com/daily/service/about.asp?rfrr=-1087 (accessed September 4, 2006); www.expedia.ca (accessed May 17, 2007).

15. Jadish Seth, Banwari Mitral and Bruce Newman, *Consumer Behaviour* (Forth Worth: Dryden Press, 1992).

16. www.forbes.com/home/2002/08/21/0821hatesites.html (accessed September 3, 2006); Charles Wolrich, "The Best Corporate Complaint Sites," *Forbes.com*, August 21, 2002; Leslie Jaye Goff, "[Your company name here]sucks. com: When an Angry Consumer Slams Your Organization Online, You Want to Slam Back," www.computerworld. com/printhis/1998/0,4814,31861,00.html; John Simmons, "Stop Moaning about Gripe Sites and Log On," *Fortune*, April 2, 2001, p. 181.; Canadian Tire loses fight for www.crappytire.com, www.cbc.ca/money/story/2001/05/31/crappytire_010531.html (accessed December 18, 2007).

17. See Henry Assael, *Consumer Behaviour and Marketing Action* (Boston: Kent Publishing, 1987); John A. Howard and Jadish Sheth, *The Theory of Consumer Behaviour in Marketing Strategy* (Upper Saddle River, N.J.: Prentice Hall, 1989); Philip Kotler, Gary Amstrong, Peggy Cunningham, *Principles of Marketing* (6th Can. Ed. 2005) pp. 279-280.

18. A.H. Maslow, *Motivation and Personality* (New York: Harper & Row, 1970).

19. William D. Perreault, Jr., and E. Jerome McCarthy, *Basic Marketing: A Global-Managerial Approach*, 15th ed. (Burr Ridge Il.: Irwin/McGraw-Hill, 2005), p. 159.

20. Michael Levy and Barton A. Weitz, *Retailing Management*, 6th ed. (Burr Ridge IL: Irwin/Mc-Graw-Hill, 2007), Chapter 4.

21. 2005 YTV Tween Report, Solutions Research Group, A Corus Entertainment Inc. Company; www.corusmedia.com/ytv/research/index.asp (accessed May 15, 2007).

22. Sandra Yin, "Kids; Hot Spots," *American Demographics*, December 1, 2003; Peter Francese, "Trend Ticker: Trouble in Store," *American Demographics*, December 1, 2003.

23. Survey Reveals Teen Spending Habits, Retail Brand Perceptions; http://money.cnn.com/news/newsfeeds/articles/newstex/VNU-0016-16243010.htm (accessed May 20, 2007).

24. Rebecca Harris, "Skin Deep," *Marketing Magazine*, January 29, 2007.

25. The concept of atmospherics was introduced by Philip Kotler, "Atmosphere as a Marketing Tool," *Journal of Retailing* 49 (Winter 1973), pp. 48–64.

26. Anna S. Mattila and Jochen Wirtz, "Congruency of Scent and Music as a Driver of In-Store Evaluations and Behavior," *Journal of Retailing* 77, no. 2 (Summer 2001), pp. 273–89; Teresa A. Summers and Paulette R. Hebert, "Shedding Some Light on Store Atmospherics; Influence of Illumination on Consumer Behavior," *Journal of Business Research* 54, no. 2 (November 2001), pp. 145–50; for a review of this research, see Joseph A. Bellizzi and Robert E. Hite, "Environmental Color, Consumer Feelings, and Purchase Likelihood," *Psychology and Marketing* 9, no. 5 (September–October 1992), pp. 347–63; J. Duncan Herrington and Louis Capella, "Effects of Music in Service Environments: A Field Study," *Journal of Services Marketing* 10, no. 2 (1996), pp. 26–41; Richard F. Yalch and Eric R. Spangenberg, "The Effects of Music in a Retail Setting on Real and Perceived Shopping Times," *Journal of Business Research* 49, no. 2 (August 2000), pp. 139–48; Michael Hui, Laurette Dube, and Jean-Charles Chebat, "The Impact of Music on Consumer's Reactions to Waiting for Services," *Journal of Retailing* 73, no. 1 (1997), pp. 87–104; and Julie Baker, Dhruv Grewal, and Michael Levy, "An Experimental Approach to Making Retail Store Environmental Decisions," *Journal of Retailing* 68 (Winter 1992), pp. 445–60; Maxine Wilkie, "Scent of a Market," *American Demographics* (August 1995), pp. 40–49; Spangenberg, Crowley, Henderson, "Improving the Store Environment: Do Olfactory Cues Affect Evaluations and Behaviors?"; Paula Fitzgerald Bone and Pam Scholder Ellen, "Scents in the Marketplace: Explaining a Fraction of Olfaction," *Journal of Retailing* 75, no. 2 (Summer 1999), pp. 243–63.

27. Abercrombie and Fitch, http://en.wikipedia.org/wiki/Abercrombie_&_Fitch (accessed May 20, 2007).

28. Julie Baker, Dhruv Grewal, Michael Levy, and Glenn Voss, "Wait Expectations, Store Atmosphere and Store Patronage Intentions," *Journal of Retailing* 79, no. 4 (2003), pp. 259–68.

29. www.zipcar.com/about/ (accessed September 4, 2006); "Growth Is on the Way," *European Rubber Journal*, 184, no. 4 (April 2002), p. 20 (1); Steven Rosenberg, "The Art of Parking: It Works for Candy, so Why Not for Cars? A Boston Architect Proposes a Pez-Like Dispenser to Solve the City's Parking Woes," *The Boston Globe*, March 21, 2004; Brad Grimes, "Leave the Driving to Zipcar; With the Help of the Internet and Wireless Technology, Car Sharing Revs up in Urban Areas," *PC Magazine*, February 17, 2004; www.myrtlebeachonline.com/mld/sunnews/news/local/7668955.htm; www.wjla.com/news/stories/0304/133051.html.; Zipcar Speeds into Vancouver www.zipcar.com/press/releases/press-70 (accessed May 17, 2007).

30. "Canada's Auto Industry Struggling," *Maclean's Magazine*, www.thecanadianencyclopedia.com/index.cfm?PgNm=TCE&Params=M1ARTM0012328 (accessed December 18, 2007).

31. This case was written by Jeanne L. Munger in conjunction with Dhruv Grewal and Michael Levy for the basis of class discussion rather than to illustrate either effective or ineffective marketing practices. Jeanne Munger is an associate professor at the University of Southern Maine.

32. This background information is based on Micheline Maynard, "Get Smart," *Fortune (Europe)*, April 30, 2001, p. 48; Philip Siekman, "The Smart Car is Looking More So," *Fortune*, April 15, 2002, p. 310H.

33. Judy Feldman, "Price Points," *Money*, October 2001, pp. 146–47.

34. Feldman, "Price Points."

35. Jean Halliday, "Mercedes Mimics Mini by Using Offbeat Tactics," *Automotive News*, January 5, 2004, p. 16B.

36. Smart sells out in Canada: No sizzle needed for Smart car, Mercedes says models sold out, Some deliveries will take months' says Toronto Star. www.zapworld.com/zapworld.aspx?id=1140 (accessed May 17, 2007); Advanced Technology

Vehicles Program, www.canadiandriver.com/articles/jk/060112.htm (accessed May 17, 2007); Transport Minister Receives Keys to Smart Car, www.tc.gc.ca/mediaroom/releases/nat/2004/04-h077e.htm (accessed May 17, 2007).

Chapter 7

1. Gary Baker, et al., "An Exchanging Advantage: Supply Chain Innovation in the New Economy," *Arthur Andersen: The White Paper Series*, No. 2 (Autumn 2000), Automotive Industry.

2. Adam Feuerstein, "Private Net Markets Are Taking Off," *Upside Today-The Tech Insider* 24, no. 4, (August 2000), electronically accessed.

3. www.retailcouncil.org/news/media/profile/print/default.asp (accessed May 21, 2007).

4. www.statcan.ca (accessed May 21, 2007).

5. www.charityvillage.com.

6. www.pwgsc.gc.ca accessed (accessed December 18, 2007).

7. http://contractscanada.gc.ca and www.merx.com.

8. www.merx.com (accessed December 18, 2007).

9. www.census.gov/epcd/naics02/SICN02E.HTM#S48; www.census.gov/epcd/www/naics.html;www.census.gov/epcd/naics02/N2SIC51.HTM.

10. Ajay K. Kohli and Bernard J. Jaworski, "Market Orientation: The Construct, Research Propositions, and Managerial Implications," *Journal of Marketing* 54, no. 2 (April 1990), pp. 1–13; John C. Narver and Stanly F. Slater, "The Effect of Market Orientation on Business Profitability," *Journal of Marketing* 54, no. 4 (October 1990), pp. 20–33; Arun Sharma, R. Krishnan, and Dhruv Grewal, "Value Creation in Markets: A Critical Area of Focus for Business-to-Business Markets," *Industrial Marketing Management* 30, no. 4 (2001), pp. 391–402.

11. http://business.telus.com.

12. www.bombardier.com (accessed May 21, 2007).

13. www.probeinternational.org (accessed May 17, 2007).

14. www.shepherd.ca (accessed May 21, 2007).

15. www.shepherd.ca; "Roynat Capital Entrepreneurial Profile," *Financial Post*, May 7, 2007. p. FP12.

16. This illustration, which exemplifies how Toyota works with its suppliers, is based on Jeffrey K. Liker and Thomas Y. Choi, "Building Deep Supplier Relationships," *Harvard Business Review*, December 2004, pp. 104–14.

17. Toyotasupplier.com (accessed September 6, 2006).

18. *Supra*.

19. www.marketingpower.com/live/mg-dictionary-view435.php. These definitions are provided by www.marketingpower.com (the American Marketing Association's website). We have bolded our key terms.

20. www.pulsus.com/clin-pha/08_02/lexc_ed.htm (accessed September 6, 2006).

21. www.goer.state.ny.us/train/onlinelearning/FTMS/500s1.html.

22. Susan Kuchinskas, "Data-Based Dell," *Adweek Magazine's Technology Marketing* 23, no. 6 (September 2003), p. 20.

23. Erika Morphy, "Volkswagen Takes on Covisint in the B2B Auction Arena," *CRM Daily*, July 13, 2001; "The Purchasing Department of Volkswagen," presentation, www.volkswagen-ir.de/download/InvPres_01/20010518VWSanzENG.pdf (accessed May 16, 2005); Martin Hofmann, Emily-Sue Sloane, and Elena Malykhina, "VW Revs its B2B Engine," *Optimize*, March 2004, pp. 22–26; "FAQ," www.vwgroupsupply.com/; "Volkswagen Expands B2B Platform: Volkswagen Has Expanded its Business-to-Business Platform to Allow Suppliers to Easily Manage their Financial Dealings with the Company via the Internet," *Computer World* 9, no. 7 (November 2002).

24. Barton A. Weitz, Stephen B. Castleberry, and John F. Tanner, *Selling Building Partnerships*, 5th ed. (Burr Ridge, IL: McGraw Hill Irwin, 2003), p. 93.

25. Daniel G. Jacobs, "Anatomy of a Supply Chain," *Transportation & Distribution* 44, no. 6 (June 2003), p. 60; F. Andrews, "Dell, It Turns Out, Has a Better Idea than Ford," *The New York Times*, January 26, 2000, p. C12.

26. K.C. Laudon and C.G. Traver, *E-Commerce: Business, Technology, Society*, 2d ed. (Boston, MA: Pearson, 2004).

27. *Supra*.

28. www.covisint.com; accessed May 22, 2007; http://ai.eecs.umich.edu/people/wellman/pubs/phic04.pdf (accessed May 22, 2007); Lee Copeland, Patching the Supply Chain Together; www.computerworld.com (accessed May 22, 2007).

29. Sandy Jap, "An Exploratory Study of the Introduction of Online Reverse Auctions," *Journal of Marketing* 67, no. 3, (July 2003), electronically accessed; R. Tassabehji, W. A. Taylor, R. Beach, A. Wood, "Reverse E-auctions and Supplier-Buyer Relationships: an Exploratory Study," *International Journal of Operations and Production Management*, 26, no. 2, (2006), pp. 1–19; Sandy Jap, Going Going, Gone," *Harvard Business Review*, 78, no. 6, electronically accessed; "Reverse Auctions Gain Momentum as Cost Tool-Chipmakers Grudgingly Join in Online Bids," *Spencer Chin*, March 3, 2003, p. 1.

30. This case was written by Ajax Persaud, the textbook co-author, for the basis of class discussion rather than to illustrate either effective or ineffective marketing practices. Ajax Persaud is a marketing professor at the University of Ottawa.

Chapter 8

1. AC Nielsen latest weeks at August 5, 2006;

2. http://personas.quarry.com/ (accessed May 30, 2007).

3. Melanie Shortman, "Gender Wars," *American Demographics*, April 2002, p. 22.

4. Jagdish Sheth, Banwari Mittal, and Bruce I. Newman, *Customer Behavior: Consumer Behavior and Beyond* (Fort Worth, TX: The Dryden Press, 1999).

5. Tamara Mangleburg, M. Joseph Sirgy, Dhruv Grewal, Danny Axsom, Maria Hatzios, C. B. Claiborne, and Trina Bogle, "The Moderating Effect of Prior Experience in Consumers' Use of User-Image Based versus Utilitarian Cues in Brand Attitude," *Journal of Business & Psychology* 13 (Fall 1998), pp. 101–13; M. Joseph Sirgy et al., "Direct versus Indirect Measures of Self-Image Congruence," *Journal of the Academy of Marketing Science* 25, no. 3 (1997), pp. 229–41.

6. Jagdish Sheth, Banwari Mittal, and Bruce I. Newman, *Customer Behavior: Consumer Behavior and Beyond* (Fort Worth, TX: The Dryden Press, 1999).

7. VALS1, the original lifestyle survey, assessed general values and lifestyles. The VALS survey focuses more on values and lifestyles related to consumer behaviour and thus has more commercial applications. Another lifestyle segmentation system is Yankelovich's Monitor Mindbase, yankelovich.com.

8. Michael D. Lam, "Psychographic Demonstration: Segmentation Studies Prepare to Prove Their Worth," *Pharmaceutical Executive*, January 2004.

9. Stowe Shoemaker and Robert Lewis, "Customer Loyalty: The Future of Hospitality Marketing," *Hospitality Management* 18 (1999), p. 349.

10. V. Kumar and Denish Shah, "Building and Sustaining Profitable Customer Loyalty for the 21st Century," *Journal of Retailing* 80, no. 4 (2004), p. 317–330.

11. Rebecca Harris, "Canadians Love Loyalty," *Marketing Daily*, May 31, 2007.

12. Aricanada.com (accessed June 1, 2007).

13. Michael J. Weiss, *The Clustered World* (Boston: Little, Brown, 2000).

14. PSYTE Advantage, www.tetrad.com/pricing/can/psyteadvantage.html (accessed June 1, 2007).

15. www.tetrad.com/demographics/canada/environics/prizmce.html (accessed June 1, 2007).

16. Pete Jacques, "Aspirational Segmentation," *LIMRA's MarketFacts Quarterly* 22 (Spring 2003), p. 2[0].

17. www.aa.com/content/AAdvantage/programDetails/eliteStatus/main.jhtml (accessed March 3, 2005).

18. www.microsoft.com/info/cookies.htm (accessed September 30, 2005).

19. Dhruv Grewal, "Marketing Is All about Creating Value: 8 Key Rules," in *Inside the Mind of Textbook Marketing* (Boston, MA: Aspatore Inc., 2003), 79–96.

20. LaSenza.com (accessed December 18, 2007).

21. G.R. Iyer, A.D. Miyazaki, D. Grewal, and M. Giordano, "Linking Web-Based Segmentation to Pricing Tactics," *Journal of Product & Brand Management* 11, no. 5, (2002), pp. 288–302; B. Jaworski and K. Jocz, "Rediscovering the Consumer," *Marketing Management*, September/October 2002, pp. 22–27; L. Rosencrance, "Customers Balk at Variable DVD Pricing," *Computer World*, September 11, 2000, p. 4; M. Stephanek, "None of Your Business: Customer Data Were Once Gold to E-Commerce. Now, Companies are Paying a Price for Privacy Jitters," *BusinessWeek*, June 26, 2000, p. 78; D. Wessel, "How Technology Tailors Price Tags," *The Wall Street Journal*, June 23, 2001, p. A1

22. James L. Heskett, W. Earl Sasser Jr., and Leonard A. Schlesinger, *The Service Profit Chain: How Leading Companies Link Profit and Growth to Loyalty, Satisfaction, and Value* (New York: Simon & Schuster Adult Publishing Group, 1997); Christopher D. Ittner and David F. Larcker, "Are Nonfinancial Measures Leading Indicators of Financial Performance? An Analysis of Customer Satisfaction," *Journal of Accounting Research* 35 (Supplement 1998), pp. 1–35; Thomas O. Jones and E. Earl Sasser Jr., "Why Satisfied Customers Defect," *Harvard Business Review*, November/December 1995, pp. 88–99; A. Parasuraman and Dhruv Grewal, "The Impact of Technology on the Quality-Value-Loyalty Chain: A Research Agenda," *Journal of the Academy of Marketing Science* 28, no. 1 (2000), pp. 168–74; Frederick F. Reichheld, "Loyalty-Based Management," *Harvard Business Review* 2 (March/April 1993), pp. 64–73; Frederick F. Reichheld, "Loyalty and the Renaissance of Marketing," *Marketing Management* 2, no. 4 (1994), pp. 10–21; Frederick F. Reichheld and Phil Schefter, "E-Loyalty," *Harvard Business Review*, July/August 2000, pp. 105–13; Anthony J. Rucci, Richard T. Quinn, and Steven P. Kirn, "The Employee-Customer-Profit Chain at Sears," *Harvard Business Review*, January/February 1998,

pp. 83–97; Roland T. Rust, Valarie Zeithaml, and Katherine N. Lemon, *Driving Customer Equity* (New York: The Free Press, 2000); Russell S. Winer, "A Framework for Customer Relationship Management," *California Management Review* 43, no. 4 (2001), pp. 89–105; Valarie Zeithaml, Roland T. Rust, and Katherine N. Lemon, "The Customer Pyramid: Creating and Serving Profitable Customers," *California Management Review* 43, no. 4 (2001), pp. 118–42.

23. Datamonitor: Hallmark Cards, Inc., "Greeting Cards Facts and Figures," *Souvenirs, Gifts & Novelties*," May 2005.

24. LaSenza.com (accessed December 18, 2007).

25. Amy Merrick, "Christopher & Banks Shuns Trends in Fashion, Targets Mothers in 40s," *The Wall Street Journal*, May 9, 2003, wsj.com.

26. www.canada.com/vancouversun/news/arts/story.html?id=1d14b6e4-926e-4702-9107-a6f30ba8c828&k=28195&p=1;www.balmshell.com/about.aspx; www.workopolis.com/servlet/Content/qprinter/20070209/RSWAG09; www.dermstore.com/product_BalmShell+Holiday+Gift+Set_8313.htm; www.dermstore.com/product_BalmShell+Holiday+Gift+Set_8313.htm; www.enterprisetoronto.com/index.cfm?linkid=99&linktype=mainlink&content_id=623&fromurl=box (accessed June 1, 2007).

27. B. Joseph Pine, *Mass Customization: The New Frontier in Business Competition* (Cambridge, MA: Harvard Business School Publishing, 1999); James H. Gilmore and B. Joseph Pine, eds., *Markets of One: Creating Customer-Unique Value through Mass Customization* (Cambridge, MA: Harvard Business School Publishing, 2000).

28. www.cspinet.org/liquidcandy/index.html (accessed September 12, 2006).

29. Jean Halliday, "Maloney Wants Volvo Viewed as Both Safe and Luxurious," *Advertising Age* 75, no. 12 (2004), p. 22.

30. www.jacob.ca; www.lasenza.com; www.abercrombie.ca (accessed June 1, 2007).

31. Avis: We Try Harder, www.buildingbrands.com/didyouknow/16_avis_we_try_harder.php (accessed December 18, 2007).

32. McDonald's legal cases http://en.wikipedia.org/wiki/McDonald's_legal_cases (accessed December 18, 2007).

33. Crane et al., *Marketing*, 6th Canadian Ed. (Whitby, ON: McGraw-Hill Ryerson, 2006), p. 243.

34. McDonald's Global Sales Advance 4.8%: Burger Giant Now Top Seller of Chicken, *Bloomberg News*, accessed June 1, 2007.

35. Gogi Anand, Janine Chin, Cam Christie, Jonathan Lee, Jessica Liu, Rebecca Muise, and Tobi Schlager, "Can Junk Food be Healthy? A Consumer Behaviour Response to Repositioning Junk Food as a Healthy Alternative," unpublished paper for WLU Consumer Behaviour Project (Wilfrid Laurier University, Waterloo, ON, 2007).

36. Stephen Brown, Robert V. Kozinets, and John F. Sherry Jr., "Teaching Old Brands New Tricks: Retro Branding and the Revival of Brand Meaning," *Journal of Marketing* 67, no. 2 (July 2003), p. 19.

37. Chuck Salter, "Whirlpool Finds Its Cool," *Fast Company* 95 (June 2005), p. 73.

38. Christine Bittar, "Cosmetic Changes beyond Skin Deep," *Brandweek*, May 17, 2000, pp. 20, 22.

39. Lisa Granatstein, "Back to Cool," *Mediaweek*, June 21, 2004, pp. 25–26.

40. Michelle Halpern, "Wonderland goes Hollywood," www.marketingmag.ca/magazine/marketingdaily/article.jsp?content=20040430_102845_3948 (accessed June 7, 2007).

41. Brian Wansink, "Making Old Brands New," *American Demographics*, December 1997, pp. 53–58.77. Wansink,

42. "Making Old Brands New."

43. This case was written by Shirley Lichti, the textbook co-author, for the basis of class discussion rather than to illustrate either effective or ineffective marketing practices. Shirley Lichti is a marketing professor at Wilfrid Laurier University.

44. Matt Semansky, "M&M Goes Downtown with Uptown," www.marketingmag.ca/daily/20071017/topstory.html (accessed October 16, 2007).

Chapter 9

1. www.unileverusa.com/ourbrands/personalcare/dove.asp (accessed June 6, 2007).

2. Karen Mazurkesich, "Dove Story," www.strategymag.com/articles/magazine/20070101/dove.html?word=dove&word=story (accessed June 6, 2007).

3. American Marketing Association, *Dictionary of Marketing Terms* (Chicago, IL: American Marketing Association, 2004), available at www.marketingpower.com/live/mg-dictionary-view329.php?.

4. "All Colgate Toothpastes," www.colgate.com (accessed September 16, 2006).

5. William P. Putsis Jr. and Barry L. Bayus, "An Empirical Analysis of Firms' Product Line Decisions," *Journal of Marketing Research* 38, no. 1 (February 2001), pp. 110–18.

6. Bruce G.S. Hardie and Leonard M. Lodish, "Perspectives: The Logic of Product-Line Extensions," *Harvard Business Review*, November–December 1994, p. 54.

7. John A. Quelch and David Kenny, "Extend Profits, Not Product Lines," *Harvard Business Review*, September–October 1994, pp. 153–60.

8. Rekha Balu, "Heinz to Trim Its Work Force as Much as 9%," *The Wall Street Journal*, February 18, 1999 (ProQuest Document ID 39039688).

9. Jim Mateja, "Chicago Tribune New Cars Column," *Knight Ridder Tribune Business News*, July 13, 2003 (ProQuest Document ID: 357908581).

10. "J&J to Buy Skin-Care Business," *The Wall Street Journal*, December 18, 1998, p. 1.

11. http://scjohnson.com/products/ (accessed September 20, 2006).

12. Ibid; Louis Lee, "Jean Therapy, $23 a Pop," *BusinessWeek*, June 28, 2004, pp. 91, 93.

13. Ernest Beck, "Unilever to Cut 25,000 Jobs, Close Factories—Consumer-Goods Company to Focus on Core Brands in Restructuring Asian," *The Wall Street Journal*, February 23, 2000, p. 2.

14. www.rbc.com/aboutus/index.html (accessed June 6, 2007).

15. www.rbcroyalbank.com/RBC:RmcqJo71A8UAAWzg3w8/products/deposits/view-all-bank-accounts.html (accessed June 6, 2007).

16. Kevin Lane Keller, *Strategic Brand Management: Building, Measuring, and Managing Brand Equity*, 2d ed. (Upper Saddle River, NJ: Prentice Hall, 2003).

17. This discussion on the advantages of strong brands is adapted from Keller, *Strategic Brand Management*, pp. 104–12; Elizabeth S. Moore, William L. Wilkie, and Richard J. Lutz, "Passing the Torch: Intergenerational Influences as a Source of Brand Equity," *Journal of Marketing* 66, no. 2 (April 2002), p. 17.

18. Angela Y. Lee and Aparna A. Labroo, "The Effect of Conceptual and Perceptual Fluency on Brand Evaluation," *Journal of Marketing Research* 41, no. 2 (May 2004), pp. 151–65.

19. www.interbrand.com/best_brands_2004.asp (accessed September 14, 2006). The net present value of the earnings over the next 12 months is used to calculate the value.

20. David A. Aaker, *Managing Brand Equity*, New York: Free Press, 1991.

21. www.interbrand.com/best_brands_2006.asp (accessed December 22, 2007).

22. Polo Ralph Lauren Corporate Report 2004, available at http://media.corporate-ir.net/media_files/NYS/RL/reports/04ar/PRL2004AR.pdf (accessed September 16, 2006).

23. David A. Aaker, "Measuring Brand Equity Across Products and Markets," *California Management Review* 38 (Spring 1996), pp. 102–20.

24. http://en.wikipedia.org/wiki/List_of_generic_and_genericized_trademarks (accessed December 22, 2007).

25. Keller, *Strategic Brand Management*.

26. Jennifer L. Aaker, "Dimensions of Brand Personality," *Journal of Marketing Research* 34, no. 3 (August 1997), pp. 347–56.

27. Kevin Lane Keller, "Conceptualizing, Measuring, and Managing Customer-Based Brand Equity," *Journal of Marketing* 57, no. 1 (January 1993), pp. 1–22.

28. Dave Larson, "Building a Brand's Personality from the Customer Up," *Direct Marketing*, October 2002, pp. 17–21.

29. www.marketingpower.com/live/mg-dictionary.php?SearchFor=brand+loyalty&Searched=1 (accessed September 17, 2006).

30. James H. McAlexander, John W. Schouten, and Harold F. Koenig, "Building Brand Community," *Journal of Marketing* 66, no. 1 (January 2002), pp. 38–54.

31. Christine Bittar, "Big Brands: Stronger than Dirt," *BrandWeek*, June 23, 2003, pp. S52–53.

32. www.petitiononline.com/No2010Bd/petition.html (accessed June 8, 2007).

33. http://policyalternatives.ca/index.cfm?act=news&call=610&do=article&pA=BB736455 (accessed June 8, 2007).

34. www.vancouver2010.com/en/LookVancouver2010/ProtectingBrand (accessed June 8, 2007).

35. *Supra.*

36. www.canada.com/vancouversun/news/story.html?id=a9509d93-a94c-4d2e-bb22-9903cf2c760e (accessed June 8, 2007).

37. "President's Choice Continues Brisk Pace," *Frozen Food Age*, March 1998, pp. 17–18.

38. Laura Liebeck, "Private Label Goes Premium," *Discount Store News*, November 4, 1996, p. F38; "New Private-Label Alternatives Bring Changes to Supercenters, Clubs," *DSN Retailing Today*, February 5, 2001, p. 66.

39. www.marketinghalloflegends.ca/visionaries_david_nichol.php (accessed June 7, 2007).

40. Michael Levy and Barton A. Weitz, *Retailing Management*, 6th ed. (New York: McGraw-Hill/Irwin, 2007).

41. www.pg.com.

42. Harvey Schacter, "What's in a name? Plenty," *The Globe and Mai,l* May 5, 2004, p. C4.

43. Eve Lazarus, "New beer goes with flies and a croak," www.marketingmag.ca/magazine/marketingdaily/article.jsp?content=20060914_102950_5424 (accessed June 7, 2007).

44. For recent research on brand extensions, see Subramanian Balachander and Sanjoy Ghose, "Reciprocal Spillover Effects: A Strategic Benefit of Brand Extensions," *Journal of Marketing* 67, no. 1 (January 2003), pp. 4–13; Kalpesh Kaushik Desai and Kevin Lane Keller, "The Effects of Ingredient Branding Strategies on Host Brand Extendibility," *Journal of Marketing* 66, no. 1 (January 2002), pp. 73–93; Tom Meyvis and Chris Janiszewski, "When Are Broader Brands Stronger Brands? An Accessibility Perspective on the Success of Brand Extensions," *Journal of Consumer Research* 31, no. 2 (September 2004), pp. 346–57.

45. David Aaker, "Brand Extensions: The Good, the Bad, and the Ugly," *Sloan Management Review*, 31 (Summer 1990), pp. 47–56.

46. www.braun.com.

47. www.dell.com.

48. www.fritolay.com/consumer.html.

49. Vanitha Swaminathan, Richard J. Fox, and Srinivas K. Reddy, "The Impact of Brand Extension Introduction on Choice," *Journal of Marketing* 65, no. 3 (October 2001), pp. 1–15.

50. Jennifer Aaker, Susan Fournier, and S. Adam Brasel, "When Good Brands Do Bad," *Journal of Consumer Research* 31, no. 1 (June 2004), pp. 1–16.

51. Barbara Loken and Deborah Roedder John, "Diluting Brand Beliefs: When Do Brand Extensions Have a Negative Impact?" *Journal of Marketing* 57, no. 3 (July 1993), pp. 71–84.

52. Aaker, "Brand Extensions," pp. 47–56.

53. David A. Aaker and Kevin Lane Keller, "Consumer Evaluations of Brand Extensions," *Journal of Marketing* 54, no. 1 (January 1990), pp. 27–41.

54. Susan M. Broniarczyk and Joseph W. Alba, "The Importance of the Brand in Brand Extension," *Journal of Marketing Research* 31, no. 2 (May 1994), pp. 214–28.

55. www.ritzcarlton.com/corporate/about_us/history.asp (accessed September 16, 2006).

56. Kate Fitzgerald, "A New Addition to Cobranding's Menu," *Credit Card Management*, 16 (November 2003), pp. 40–44.

57. This section is based on Akshay R. Rao and Robert W. Ruekert, "Brand Alliances as Signals of Product Quality," *Sloan Management Review*, 36 (Fall 1994), pp. 87–97.

58. Hoover's Company Information, *Hoover's Online*, 2004; Melissa Master, "Overreaching," *Across the Board*, March/April 2001, pp. 20–26; David Taylor, *Brand Stretch: Why 1 in 2 Extensions Fail and How to Beat the Odds* (New York: John Wiley & Sons, 2004); Melanie Wells, "Red Baron," *Forbes*, July 3, 2000, p. 150.

59. www.hoovers.com/virgin-group/—ID__41676—/free-co-factsheet.xhtml (accessed August 30, 2005).

60. "FedEx Expands Alliance with Kinko's," *Journal of Commerce*, August 11, 2000, p. WP.

61. "FedEx and Kinko's to Deliver Increased Threat," *DSN Retailing Today*, May 17, 2004, p. 17.

62. T. Kippenberger, "Co-Branding as a Competitive Weapon," *Strategic Direction* 18 (October), pp. 31–33.

63. Tom Blacket and Bob Boad, eds., *Branding: The Science of Alliance* (London: Macmillan Press, 1999).

64. David A. Aaker, *Brand Portfolio Strategy* (New York: The Free Press, 2004).

65. Keller, *Strategic Brand Management*.

66. Doug Desjardins, "LIMA Foresees Huge 2nd Half for Entertainment Properties," *DSN Retailing Today*, June 21, 2004, pp. 6, 37.

67. "NASCAR Launches New Stock Car Racing Series in Canada and National Title Sponsorship Agreement with Canadian Tire." Canada Newswire, www.newswire.ca/en/releases/archive/September2006/12/c5003.html (accessed June 7, 2007).

68. Keller, *Strategic Brand Management*.

69. www.lacoste.com/usa/.

70. Dwight Oestricher, "Marvel: Powerhouse Potential? Other Heroes Spawned by Spider-Man Creator Could Pay Off," *The Wall Street Journal*, May 8, 2002, p. B9 ff.

71. Anna Wilde Mathews, "Lord of the Things—Separate Companies Hold Rights to the Products from 'Rings' Books, Films," *The Wall Street Journal*, December 17, 2001, p. B1ff.

72. William Makely, "Being the Beauty, Being the Brand," *Global Cosmetic Industry*, January 2004, pp. 28–30.

73. "Packages: Tracing an Evolution," *Packaging Digest*, December 2003, pp. 37–42.

74. www.packagingdigest.com/articles/200605/6.php (accessed June 8, 2007).

75. Annette Bourdeau, "A green future: Three eco-friendly trends you should be keeping an eye on," www.strategymag.com/articles/magazine/20070501/what.html?word=biodegradable&word=palm&word=fibre-based&word=packaging (accessed June 7, 2007).

76. Annette Bourdeau, "P&G rallies allies (and foes)," www.strategymag.com/articles/magazine/20071001/upfront-tide.html (accessed December 22, 2007).

77. "Danone Expands Goodies Low-Fat Line of Desserts," *Marketing*, February 12, 2004, p. 4; www.landwriter.co.uk/landwriter/premium/TemplateParser.asp?aId=3778&page=FreeTemplate ((accessed August 30, 2005).

78. www.smartspot.com/about/criteria/ (accessed June 8, 2007).

79. Laura Penny, "When Health Meets Hedonism," *The Globe and Mail*, June 2, 2007, p. F7.

80. This case was written by Jeanne L. Munger and Julie Rusch in conjunction with the U.S. textbook authors Dhruv Grewal and Michael Levy for the basis of class discussion rather than to illustrate either effective or ineffective marketing practices. Jeanne Munger is an associate professor at the University of Southern Maine.

81. www.bandaid.com/brand_story.shtml; www.bandaid.com/new_products.shtml; Christine Bittar, "J&J Stuck on Expanding BAND-AID® Franchise," *Brandweek*, March 3, 2003, p. 4; Richard Gutwillig, "Billion-Dollar Bandages," *Supermarket Business*, August 15, 2000, p. 58; "United States Top 10 First Aid Tape/Bandages/Gauze Brands Ranked by Dollar Sales and Unit Volume for 2003," *Chain Drug Review*, June 21, 2004, p. 238; Andrea M. Grossman, "Personal and Beauty Care: News Bites," *Drug Store News*, January 11, 1999,

p. 61; "O-T-C Health Care: United States Over-the-Counter Heath Care Product Sales in Dollars and Percent Change for 2003," *Chain Drug Review*, May 24, 2004, p. 32.

82. Christine Bittar, "J&J Stuck on Expanding Band-Aid Franchise," *Brandweek* 44, no. 9 (March 3, 2003), p. 4.

Chapter 10

1. Adapted from Natalia Williams, "For the Love of Jam," *Strategy Magazine*, www.strategymag.com/articles/magazine/20050701/mediaed.html?word=e.d.&word=smith (accessed June 11, 2007); www.edsmith.com/web/edsmith.nsf/eng/WhatsNew (accessed June 11, 2007).

2. www.dove.com.

3. Koen Pauwels, Jorge Silva-Risso, Shuba Srinivasan, and Dominique M. Hanssens, "New Products, Sales Promotions, and Firm Value: The Case of the Automobile Industry," *Journal of Marketing* 68, no. 4 (October 2004), p. 142.

4. A number of articles on variety seeking are available. For example, see Andrea Morales, Barbara E. Kahn, Cynthia Huffman, Leigh McAlister, and Susan M. Bronizrszyk, "Perceptions of Assortment Variety: The Effects of Congruency between Consumer's Internal and Retailer's External Organization," *Journal of Retailing* 81 (2) (2005), pp. 159–69.

5. Kalpesh Kaushik Desai and Kevin Lane Keller, "The Effects of Ingredient Branding Strategies on Host Brand Extendibility," *Journal of Marketing* 66, no. 1 (January 2002), pp. 73–93.

6. Rajesh K. Chandy, Jaideep C. Prabhu, and Kersi D. Antia, "What Will the Future Bring? Dominance, Technology Expectations, and Radical Innovation," *Journal of Marketing* 67, no. 3 (July 2003), pp. 1–18; Harald J. van Heerde, Carl F. Mela, and Puneet Manchanda, "The Dynamic Effect of Innovation on Market Structure," *Journal of Marketing Research* 41, no. 2 (May 2004), pp. 166–83.

7. Clayton M. Christensen and Michael E. Raynor, *The Innovator's Solution*. Boston, MA: Harvard Business School Press, 2003.

8. Philip Kotler, *Marketing Management*, 11th ed. (Upper Saddle River, NJ: Prentice-Hall, 2003), pp. 330–31. Kotler's work was based on the following research: William T. Robinson and Claes Fornell, "Sources of Market Pioneer Advantages in Consumer Goods Industries," *Journal of Marketing Research* 22, no. 3 (August 1985), pp. 305–17; Glen L. Urban, T. Carter, S. Gaskin, and Z. Mucha, "Market Share Rewards to Pioneering Brands: An Empirical Analysis and Strategic Implications," *Management Science* 32 (June 1986), pp. 645–59; and G.S. Carpenter and Kent Nakamoto, "Consumer Preference Formation and Pioneering Advantage," *Journal of Marketing Research* 26, no. 3 (August 1989), pp. 285–98.

9. Raji Srinivasan, Gary L. Lilien, and Arvind Rangaswamy, "First in, First out? The Effects of Network Externalities on Pioneer Survival," *Journal of Marketing* 68, no. 1 (January 2004), p. 41.

10. Cyndee Miller, "Little Relief Seen for New Product Failure Rate," *Marketing News*, June 21, 1993, pp. 1, 10; *BusinessWeek*, "Flops," August 16, 1993, p. 76ff.; Lori Dahm, "Secrets of Success: The Strategies Driving New Product Development at Kraft," *Stagnito's New Products Magazine* 2 (January 2002), p. 18ff.

11. www.marketingpower.com (accessed September 18, 2006).

12. www.appleinsider.com/articles/04/11/29/ipod_adoption_rate_faster_than_sony_walkman.html (accessed December 23, 2007).

13. www.quickmba.com (accessed September 16, 2006).

14. Subin Im and John P. Workman Jr., "Market Orientation, Creativity, and New Product Performance in High-Technology Firms," *Journal of Marketing* 68, no. 2 (April 2004), p. 114.

15. Standard & Poor's, Industry Surveys: Healthcare: Pharmaceuticals, June 24, 2004.

16. Geoffrey York and Simon Avery, "China's got RedBerry," www.theglobeandmail.com/servlet/story/RTGAM.20060411.wredberry11/BNStory/Business/home (accessed June 11, 2007).

17. Glen L. Urban and John R. Hauser, "'Listening In' to Find and Explore New Combinations of Customer Needs," *Journal of Marketing* 68, no. 2 (April 2004), p. 72; Steve Hoeffler, "Measuring Preferences for Really New Products," *Journal of Marketing Research* 40, no. 4 (November 2003), pp. 406–20.

18. Glen L. Urban and John R. Hauser, *Design and Marketing of New Products*, 2nd ed. (Upper Saddle River, NJ: Prentice Hall, 1993), pp. 120–21.

19. Lisa D'Innocenzo, "Frito Lay Canada: Potato chips...for dinner?" www.strategymag.com/articles/magazine/20070101/biz.html (accessed June 12, 2007).

20. *Supra.*

21. www.betterproductdesign.net/tools/user/leaduser.htm (accessed November 12, 2004); Eric von Hippel, "Successful Industrial Products from Consumers' Ideas," *Journal of Marketing* 42, no. 1 (January 1978), pp. 39–49; Eric von Hippel, "Lead Users: A Source of Novel Product Concepts," *Management Science* 32 (1986), pp. 791–805; Eric von Hippel, *The Sources of Innovation* (New York: Oxford University Press, 1988); Glen L. Urban and Eric von Hippel, "Lead User Analysis for the Development of Industrial Products," *Management Science* 34 (May 1988), pp. 569–82.

22. Karl T. Ulrich and Steven D. Eppinger, *Product Design and Development*, 2nd ed. (Boston, MA: Irwin-McGraw-Hill, 2000).

23. www.marketingpower.com (accessed September 18, 2006).

24. Ulrich and Eppinger, *Product Design and Development*, p. 166.

25. Ely Dahan and V. Srinivasan, "The Predictive Power of Internet-Based Product Concept Testing Using Visual Depiction and Animation," *Journal of Product Innovation Management* 17 (2000), pp. 99–109.

26. www.marketingpower.com (accessed September 18, 2006).

27. Ulrich and Eppinger, *Product Design and Development*.

28. Tonya Vinas, "P&G Seeks Alternatives to Animal Tests," *Industry Week* 253, no. 7 (July 2004), p. 60; "EU to Ban Animal Tested Cosmetics," www.cnn.com (accessed March 31, 2006); www.leapingbunny.org; Gary Anthes, "P&G Uses Data Mining to Cut Animal Testing," www.computerworld.com (accessed December 6, 1999).

29. Noriko Suzuki, "The Truth about the Body Shop," www.tsujiru.net/compass/compass_1996/reg/suzuki_noriko.htm (accessed June 12, 2007).

30. www2.acnielsen.com/products/crs_bases2.shtml (accessed September 20, 2006).

31. www.blackberrypearl.com (accessed June 12, 2007).

32. http://crunchgear.com/2007/01/29/blackberry-pearl-tel-enav-gps-hearts (accessed June 12, 2007).

33. http://72.14.205.104/search?q=cache:9IEQogzGu8J: www.internetnews.com/infra/article.php/630791+price+ of+blackberry+pearl&hl=en&ct=clnk&cd=5&gl=ca (accessed June 12, 2007).

34. Philip Kotler, *Marketing Management*, 11th ed. (Upper Saddle River, NJ: Prentice-Hall, 2003).

35. Patricia Sellers, "P&G: Teaching an Old Dog New Tricks," *Fortune*, May 31, 2004, pp. 166–80.

36. Norma Ramage, "Testing, testing 1-2-3," www.marketingmag.ca/magazine/current/in_context/article.jsp?content=20050718_69775_69775 (accessed June 12, 2007).

37. www.infores.com/public/us/analytics/productportfolio/bscannewprodtest.htm, (accessed April 2, 2006).

38. J. Daniel Sherman and William E. Souder, "Managing New Technology Development," http://books.google.com/books?id=6p3hdSUXOlsC&pg=PA104&lpg=PA104&dq=kellogg+%22toast+ems%22&source=web&ots=xP30aQrfMe&sig=YAxE8134Djzngytp3DcC_H8g_FA (accessed June 12, 2007).

39. Lisa D'Innocenzo, "Frito Lay Canada: Potato Chips...for dinner?" www.strategymag.com/articles/magazine/20070101/biz.html (accessed January 12, 2008).

40. Product Development Management Association, *The PDMA Handbook of New Product Development*, 2nd ed., Kenneth K. Kahn, ed. (New York: John Wiley & Sons, 2004).

41. BestNewProducts.ca maintains a list of best new products launched each year. The products listed were winners in the 4th Annual Best New Products Awards, a competition judged by 10,000 Canadian consumers coast to coast, www.BestNewProducts.ca.

42. Ashwin W. Joshi and Sanjay Sharma, "Customer Knowledge Development: Antecedents and Impact on New Product Success," *Journal of Marketing* 68, no. 4 (October 2004), p. 47.

43. "BlackBerry Pearl 8130 smartphone," www.businessonthego1.com/english/wp_blackberry_bb8130.asp (accessed January 12, 2008).

44. Yuhong Wu, Sridhar Balasubramanian, and Vijay Mahajan, "When Is a Preannounced New Product Likely to Be Delayed?" *Journal of Marketing* 68, no. 2 (April 2004), p. 101.

45. www.pdma.org/ (accessed September 15, 2006).

46. Theodore Levitt, *Marketing Imagination* (New York: The Free Press, 1986).

47. Donald R. Lehmann and Russell S. Winer, *Analysis for Marketing Planning*, 6th ed. (Boston: McGraw-Hill/Irwin, 2004).

48. Urban and Hauser, *Design and Marketing*.

49. Thomas K. Arnold, "VHS Is on Its Way to Becoming a Modern-Day Dinosaur," *Video Store Magazine*, October 6–October 12, 2002, p. 20; Erik Gruenwedel, "MPAA: Rising DVD Penetration at VHS Expense," *Video Store Magazine*, March 28–April 3, 2004, p. 44.

50. Geoffrey Colvin, "Admit It: You, too, Are Paris Hilton," *Fortune*, December 29, 2003, p. 57.

51. Miriam Jordan and Jonathan Karp, "Machines for the Masses; Whirlpool Aims Cheap Washer at Brazil, India and China; Making Due with Slower Spin," *The Wall Street Journal*, December 9, 2003, p. A19.

52. Om Malik, "The New Land of Opportunity," *Business 2.0*, July 2004, pp. 72–79.

53. Claire Briney, "Wiping Up the Market," *Global Cosmetic Industry* 172, no. 4 (April 2004), pp. 40–43.

54. Kara Swisher, "Home Economics: The Hypoallergenic Car; Wave of Cleaning Products Caters to Finicky Drivers; Premoistened Auto Wipes," *The Wall Street Journal* (eastern edition), May 6, 2004, p. D.1.

55. www.toiletwand.com (accessed September 20, 2006).

56. www40.statcan.ca/l01/cst01/arts28.htm (accessed June 12, 2007).

57. "Vinyl lovers spur new boom for old medium," www.cbc.ca/consumer/story/2007/01/03/vinyl-boom.html (accessed June 12, 2007).

58. "Vinyl lovers spur new boom for old medium," www.cbc.ca/consumer/story/2007/01/03/vinyl-boom.html (accessed June 12, 2007).

59. Kevin J. Clancy and Peter C. Krieg, "Product Life Cycle: A Dangerous Idea," *Brandweek*, March 1, 2004, p. 26; Nariman K. Dhalla and Sonia Yuseph, "Forget the Product Life-Cycle Concept," *Harvard Business Review* (January–February 1976), p. 102ff.

60. Peter Golder and Gerard Tellis, "Cascades, Diffusion, and Turning Points in the Product Life Cycle," *MSI* Report No. 03-120, 2003.

61. Jay Bolling, "DTC: A Strategy for Every Stage," *Pharmaceutical Executive*, November 2003, pp. 110–17.

62. This case was written by Susan White Newell and Jeanne L. Munger in conjunction with the U.S. textbook authors Dhruv Grewal and Michael Levy for the basis of class discussion rather than to illustrate either effective or ineffective marketing practices. Jeanne Munger is an associate professor at the University of Southern Maine.

63. "Apple unveils video iPod," AppleInsider October 12, 2005; www.appleinsider.com/article.php?id=1315 (accessed September 20, 2006); "Video iPod Shocks Affiliates, Spawns New TV Industry," www.adrants.com/2005/10video-ipod-shocks-affiliates-spawns-new.php (accessed October 17, 2006); Kenhi Hall, "Sony's iPod Assault Is No Threat to Apple," *Business Week*, March 13, 2006. p. 53; David Pogue, "Almost iPod, but in the End a Samsung," *The New York Times*, March 9, 2006, www.nytimes.com (accessed September 20, 2006); David Becker, "It's All about the iPod," *CNET Networks*, www.news.com, April 18, 2005. Scott VanCamp, "They March to His Rhythm," *Brandweek* 45, no. 36 (October 11, 2004), Special Section, pp. M36–40; Beth Snyder Bulik, "The iPod Economy," *Advertising Age* 75, no. 42 (October 18, 2004), pp. 1–2.

Chapter 11

1. Eve Lazarus, "Trash Talk," www.marketingmag.ca/magazine/current/in_context/article.jsp?content=20070226_68767_68767 (accessed June 13, 2007).

2. Matt Semansky, "1-800-Got-Junk? Makes a Beer Run," www.marketingmag.ca/daily/20070320/national2.html (accessed June 13, 2007).

3. Eve Lazarus, "Trash Talk," www.marketingmag.ca/magazine/current/in_context/article.jsp?content=20070226_68767_68767 (accessed June 13, 2007).

4. Leonard L. Berry and A. Parasuraman, *Marketing Services: Competing through Quality* (New York: The Free Press, 1991), p. 5.

5. Valarie A. Zeithaml, A. Parasuraman, and Leonard L. Berry, *Delivering Quality Service: Balancing Customer Perceptions and Expectations* (New York: The Free Press, 1990).

6. Alison Overhold, "Listening to Starbucks," *Fast Company* 84 (July 2004), pp. 50–57.

7. Konrad Yakabuski, "The Greatest Canadian Company on Earth," *Report on Business Magazine* (September 2007), p. 57.

8. "Developing a Deeper Understanding of Post-Purchase Perceived Risk and Repeat Purchase Behavioral Intentions in a Service Setting," (with M. Levy, Jerry Gotlieb and Gopal Iyer), 2006, Unpublished Working Paper, Babson College; Mary Jo Bitner, Stephen W. Brown, and Matthew L. Mueter "Technology Infusion in Service Encounters," *Journal of the Academy of Marketing Science,* 28 (1) (2000), pp. 138–49; Jerry Gotlieb, Dhruv Grewal, Michael Levy, and Joan Lindsey-Mullikin, "An Examination of Moderators of the Effects of Customers' Evaluation of Employee Courtesy on Attitude toward the Service Firm," *Journal of Applied Social Psychology* 34 (April 2004), pp. 825–47.

9. Tim Shufelt, "Immersive drives a long, long, long path to Google's door," www.theglobeandmail.com/servlet/story/LAC.20070531.RIMMERSIVE31/TPStory/Business (accessed June 14, 2007).

10. Choice Hotels, "Special Guest Policies," 2004, www7.choicehotels.com/ires/en-US/html/GuestPolicies?sid=hPTj.2R60elpGw.7 (accessed September 10, 2006).

11. www.clubmed.com (accessed June 17, 2007).

12. Greg Michetti, "Webify Your Workout," www.backbonemag.com/Magazine/Hot_Tech_12310602.asp (accessed June 17, 2007).

13. Jeff Bennett, "Technology Trends: More Shoppers Find Self-Checkout Easy; Major Retailers Turn to Automation for Customers," *Detroit Free Press Business*, March 1, 2003, www.freep.com/money/business/scan1_20030301.htm (accessed November 10, 2004); www.ncr.com/products/pdf/hardware/fastlane_capabilities.pdf (accessed November 11, 2004); Matt Pillar, "Self-Checkout: Self-Serving or Customer Centric?" *Integrated Solutions for Retailers*, July 2004, http://ismretail.com/articles/2004_07/040710.htm (accessed November 10, 2004).

14. Rebecca Harris, "Confident Customers," www.marketingmag.ca/magazine/current/in_context/article.jsp?content=20060410_76174_76174 (accessed June 17, 2007).

15. Andrew Willis, "Sports fan munchies fatten Cineplex's bottom line," www.theglobeandmail.com/servlet/story/LAC.20070104.RCINEPLEX04/TPStory/Entertainment (accessed June 17, 2007).

16. The discussion of the Gap Model and its implications draws heavily from Michael Levy and Barton A. Weitz, *Retailing Management,* 6th ed. (Burr Ridge, IL: Irwin/McGraw-Hill, 2007) and also is based on Deon Nel and Leyland Pitt, "Service Quality in a Retail Environment: Closing the Gaps," *Journal of General Management* 18 (Spring 1993), pp. 37–57; Zeithaml, Parasuraman, and Berry, *Delivering Quality Customer Service*; Valerie Zeithaml, Leonard Berry, and A. Parasuraman, "Communication and Control Processes in the Delivery of Service Quality," *Journal of Marketing* 52, no. 2 (April 1988), pp. 35–48.

17. Kenneth Clow, David Kurtz, John Ozment, and Beng Soo Ong, "The Antecedents of Consumer Expectations of Services: An Empirical Study across Four Industries," *The Journal of Services Marketing* 11 (May–June 1997), pp. 230–48; Ann Marie Thompson and Peter Kaminski, "Psychographic and Lifestyle Antecedents of Service Quality Expectations," *Journal of Services Marketing* 7 (1993), pp. 53–61.

18. Zeithaml, Berry, and Parasuraman, *Delivering Quality Customer Service.*

19. Rebecca Harris, "Marketing 2.0," www.marketingmag.ca/magazine/current/feature/article.jsp?content=20070430_69539_69539 (accessed June 17, 2007).

20. *Supra.*

21. *Supra.*

22. Leonard Berry and A. Parasuraman, "Listening to the Customer—The Concept of a Service-Quality Information System," *Sloan Management Review* 38, no. 3 (1997), pp. 65–77; A. Parasuraman and Dhruv Grewal, "Serving Customers and Consumers Effectively in the 21st Century," working paper (1998), University of Miami, Coral Gables, FL.

23. Teena Lyons, "Complain to Me—If You Can," *Knight Ridder Tribune News,* December 4, 2005, p. 1.

24. Rick Spence, "Canadian Beauty," www.canadianbusiness.com/entrepreneur/columnists/rick_spence/article.jsp?content=20070405_144036_5628 (accessed June 16, 2007).

25. Bernadette Morra, "Barry slowly breaking barriers," www.thestar.com/article/189388 (accessed June 16, 2007).

26. www.benbarry.com/fashioningreality.htm (accessed June 16, 2007).

27. www.nwa.com/plan/index.html (accessed September 20, 2006).

28. 2006 Annual Report, http://c1dsp.westjet.com/guest/about/investor_reportsTemplate.jsp (accessed June 17, 2007).

29. Joe Castaldo, "Just be nice: providing good customer service," www.canadianbusiness.com/managing/strategy/article.jsp?content=20061009_81513_81513 (accessed June 17, 2007).

30. 2006 Annual Report, http://c1dsp.westjet.com/guest/about/investor_reportsTemplate.jsp (accessed June 17, 2007).

31. Jim Poisant, *Creating and Sustaining a Superior Customer Service Organization: A Book about Taking Care of the People Who Take Care of the Customers* (Westport, CT: Quorum Books, 2002); "People-Focused HR Policies Seen as Vital to Customer Service Improvement," *Store,* January 2001, p. 60; Michael Brady and J. Joseph Cronin, "Customer Orientation: Effects on Customer Service Perceptions and Outcome Behaviors," *Journal of Service Research,* February 2001, pp. 241–51; Michael Hartline, James Maxham III, and Daryl McKee, "Corridors of Influence in the Dissemination of Customer-Oriented Strategy to Customer Contact Service Employees," *Journal of Marketing* 64, no. 2 (April 2000), pp. 25–41.

32. Conrad Lashley, *Empowerment: HR Strategies for Service Excellence* (Boston: Butterworth/Heinemann, 2001).

33. "Future Success Powered by Employees," *DSN Retailing Today* 44 (January 2006), pp. 22–24.

34. 2006 Annual Report, www.kegincomefund.com/financial-info/financialreports.htm (accessed June 17, 2007).

35. Alicia Grandey and Analea Brauburger, "The Emotion Regulation behind the Customer Service Smile," in *Emotions in the Workplace: Understanding the Structure and Role of Emotions in Organizational Behavior,* eds. R. Lord, R. Klimoski, and R. Kanfer (San Francisco: Jossey-Bass, 2002); Mara

Adelman and Aaron Ahuvia, "Social Support in the Service Sector: The Antecedents, Processes, and Consequences of Social Support in an Introductory Service," *Journal of Business Research* 32 (March 1995), pp. 273–82.

36. Colin Armistead and Julia Kiely, "Creating Strategies for Managing Evolving Customer Service," *Managing Service Quality* 13, no. 2 (2003), pp. 64–171; www.robertspector.com/NordWay_extract.html (accessed September 20, 2006).

37. Barton Goldenburg, "Customer Self-Service: Are you Ready?" *CRM Magazine,* May, 2004, www.destinationcrm.com/articles/default.asp?ArticleID=4011 (accessed September 20, 2006).

38. Rhett H. Walker, Margaret Craig-Lees, Robert Hecker, and Heather Francis, "Technology-Enabled Service Delivery: An Investigation of Reasons Affecting Customer Adoption and Rejection," *International Journal of Service Industry Management* 13, no. 1 (2002), pp. 91–107; Mary Jo Bitner, Steven W. Brown, and Matthew L. Meuter, "Technology Infusion in Service Encounters," *Journal of the Academy of Marketing Science* 28, no. 1 (2000), pp. 138–49; Stephen W. Brown, "Service Recovery through IT," *Marketing Management* 6 (Fall 1997), pp. 25–27; P.A. Dabholkar, "Technology-Based Service Delivery: A Classification Scheme for Developing Marketing Strategies," in *Advances in Services Marketing and Management*, Vol. 3, eds. T.A. Swartz, Deborah E. Bowen, and Stephen W. Brown (Greenwich, CT: JAI Press, 1994), pp. 241–71.

39. "Everyone's Internet = Poor Service & False Advertising," www.complaints.com, June 11, 2000 (accessed September 20, 2006).

40. Subimal Chatterjee, Susan A. Slotnick, and Matthew J. Sobel, "Delivery Guarantees and the Interdependence of Marketing and Operations," *Production and Operations Management* 11, no. 3 (Fall 2002), pp. 393–411; Piyush Kumar, Manohar Kalawani, and Makbool Dada, "The Impact of Waiting Time Guarantees on Customers' Waiting Experiences," *Marketing Science* 16, no. 4 (1999), pp. 676–785.

41. K. Douglas Hoffman, Scott W. Kelley, and H.M. Rotalsky, "Tracking Service Failures and Employee Recovery Efforts," *Journal of Services Marketing* 9, no. 2 (1995), pp. 49–61; Scott W. Kelley and Mark A. Davis, "Antecedents to Customer Expectations for Service Recovery," *Journal of the Academy of Marketing Science* 22 (Winter 1994), pp. 52–61; Terrence J. Levesque and Gordon H.G. McDougall, "Service Problems and Recovery Strategies: An Experiment," *Canadian Journal of Administrative Sciences* 17, no. 1 (2000), pp. 20–37; James G. Maxham III and Richard G. Netemeyer, "A Longitudinal Study of Complaining Customers' Evaluations of Multiple Service Failures and Recovery Efforts," *Journal of Marketing* 66, no. 3 (October 2002), pp. 57–71; Amy K. Smith, Ruth N. Bolton, and Janet Wagner, "A Model of Customer Satisfaction with Service Encounters Involving Failure and Recovery," *Journal of Marketing Research* 36, no. 3 (August 1999), pp. 356–72; Scott R. Swanson and Scott W. Kelley, "Attributions and Outcomes of the Service Recovery Process," *Journal of Marketing Theory and Practice* 9 (Fall 2001), pp. 50–65; Stephen S. Tax and Stephen W. Brown, "Recovering and Learning from Service Failure," *Sloan Management Review* 40, no. 1 (1998), pp. 75–88; Stephen S. Tax, Stephen W. Brown, and Murali Chandrashekaran, "Consumer Evaluations of Service Complaint Experiences: Implications for Relationship Marketing," *Journal of Marketing* 62, no. 2 (April 1998), pp. 60–76; Scott Widmier and Donald W. Jackson Jr., "Examining the Effects of Service Failure, Customer Compensation, and Fault on Customer Satisfaction with Salespeople," *Journal of Marketing Theory and Practice* 10 (Winter 2002), pp. 63–74; Valarie A. Zeithaml and Mary Jo Bitner, *Services Marketing: Integrating Customer Focus across the Firm* (New York: McGraw-Hill, 2003).

42. James Maxham III, "Service Recovery's Influence on Consumer Satisfaction, Positive Word-of-Mouth, and Purchase Intentions," *Journal of Business Research* (October 2001), pp. 11–24; Michael McCollough, Leonard Berry, and Manjit Yadav, "An Empirical Investigation of Customer Satisfaction after Service Failure and Recovery," *Journal of Service Research* (November 2000), pp. 121–37.

43. "Correcting Store Blunders Seen as Key Customer Service Opportunity," *Stores,* January 2001, pp. 60–64; Stephen W. Brown, "Practicing Best-in-Class Service Recovery: Forward-Thinking Firms Leverage Service Recovery to Increase Loyalty and Profits," *Marketing Management,* Summer 2000, pp. 8–10; Tax, Brown, and Chandrashekaran, "Customer Evaluations"; Amy Smith and Ruth Bolton, "An Experimental Investigation of Customer Reactions to Service Failures and Recovery Encounters: Paradox or Peril?" *Journal of Service Research* 1 (August 1998), pp. 23–36; Cynthia Webster and D. S. Sundaram, "Service Consumption Criticality in Failure Recovery," *Journal of Business Research* 41 (February 1998), pp. 153–59.

44. Ko de Ruyter and Martin Wetsel, "The Impact of Perceived Listening Behavior in Voice-to-Voice Service Encounters," *Journal of Service Research* (February 2000), pp. 276–84.

45. Hooman Estelami, "Competitive and Procedural Determinants of Delight and Disappointment in Consumer Complaint Outcomes," *Journal of Service Research* (February 2000), pp. 285–300.

46. Michael Tsiros, Anne Roggeveen, and Dhruv Grewal (2006), "Compensation as a Service Recovery Strategy: When Does It Work?" Unpublished Working Paper, Babson College. Amy K. Smith, Ruth N. Bolton, and Janet Wagner, "A Model of Customer Satisfaction with Service Encounters Involving Failure and Recovery," *Journal of Marketing Research* 36 (August 1999), pp. 356–72. Scott R. Swanson and Scott W. Kelley, "Attributions and Outcomes of the Service Recovery Process," *Journal of Marketing: Theory and Practice* 9 (Fall 2001), pp. 50–65.

47. www.commerce.usask.ca/faculty/boyd/comm401/CanadianTireA.doc (accessed June 14, 2007).

48. www2.canadiantire.ca/CTenglish/h_ourstory.html (accessed June 14, 2007).

49. *Supra.*

50. www.myctfs.com/Products/HighIntSavings/ (accessed June 15, 2007).

51. Sarah Dobson, "Great Reputations," www.marketingmag.ca/magazine/current/feature/article.jsp?content=20060508_67052_67052 (accessed June 14, 2007).

52. David Brown, "Canadian Tire begins campaign for new bank services," www.marketingmag.ca/magazine/marketingdaily/article.jsp?content=20061024_110355_5184 (accessed June 14, 2007).

Chapter 12

1. Doug Burn, "On the Rise," www.bizlink.com/foodfiles/PDFs/jan2007/food_on_the_rise.pdf (accessed June 18, 2007).

2. "Commitment to the Community," www.acebakery.com/about/charities.cfm (accessed June 18, 2007).

3. Kent B. Monroe, *Pricing: Making Profitable Decisions*, 3rd ed. (New York: McGraw-Hill, 2003); Dhruv Grewal, Kent B. Monroe,

and R. Krishnan, "The Effects of Price Comparison Advertising on Buyers' Perceptions of Acquisition Value and Transaction Value," *Journal of Marketing* 62 (April 1998), pp. 46–60.

4. "American Shoppers Economize, Show Greater Interest in Nutrition and Awareness of Food Safety Issues, According to Trends in the United States: Consumer Attitudes and the Supermarket 2003," www.fmi.org/media/mediatext.cfm?id=534 (accessed December 10, 2005): A key finding was that, low price third most important feature in selecting a supermarket and viewed important by 83%; see also "The New Value Equation," *Supermarket News* 50 (June 10, 2002), p. 12.

5. Anthony Miyazaki, Dhruv Grewal, and Ronnie Goodstein, "The Effects of Multiple Extrinsic Cues on Quality Perceptions: A Matter of Consistency," *Journal of Consumer Research* 32 (June 2005), pp. 146–53; William B. Dodds, Kent B. Monroe, and Dhruv Grewal, "The Effects of Price, Brand, and Store Information on Buyers' Product Evaluations," *Journal of Marketing Research* 28 (August 1991), pp. 307–19.

6. Robert J. Dolan, "Note on Marketing Strategy," *Harvard Business School* (November 2000), pp. 1–17; Dhruv Grewal and Larry D. Compeau, "Pricing and Public Policy: An Overview and a Research Agenda," *Journal of Public Policy & Marketing* 18 (Spring 1999), pp. 3–11.

7. www.paradigm.com/en/paradigm/company/ (accessed June 19, 2007).

8. www.gnb.ca/0398/share/Success/general/sabian/index-e.asp, (accessed June 18, 2007).

9. www.arbiter.co.uk/sabian/news/sabian_xs20_171005.htm, (accessed June 18, 2007).

10. *Supra*.

11. Suntanu Dalal, "If you can't join 'em, beat 'em," www.canadianbusiness.com/article.jsp?content=4581 (accessed June 18, 2007).

12. Monroe, *Pricing: Making Profitable Decisions*.

13. www.corporate.canada.travel/en/ca/research_statistics/trends_outlook/tib/tib.html.

14. www.marketingpower.com/mg-dictionary-view669.php? (accessed September 19, 2006).

15. Ruth N. Bolton and Venkatesh Shankar, "An Empirically Derived Taxonomy of Retailer Pricing and Promotion Strategies," *Journal of Retailing* 79, no. 4 (2003), pp. 213–24; Rajiv Lal and Ram Rao, "Supermarket Competition: The Case of Every Day Low Pricing," *Marketing Science* 16, no. 1 (1997), pp. 60–80.

16. A. R. Rao, M. E. Bergen, and S. Davis, "How to Fight a Price War," *Harvard Business Review* 78 (March–April 2000), pp. 107–16.

17. Rao, Bergen, and Davis, "How to Fight a Price War."

18. Tara Perkins and Tavia Grant, "White-label Cash Kings," www.globeinvestor.com/servlet/WireFeedRedirect?cf=GlobeInvestor/config&vg=BigAdVariableGenerator&date=20070423&archive=rtgam&slug=wrabm_Bsection23 (accessed June 18, 2007).

19. *Supra*.

20. Tavia Grant and Tara Perkins, "Red flags on white-label ABMS," www.theglobeandmail.com/servlet/story/RTGAM.20070424.wxrabm24/BNStory/Business (accessed June 18, 2007).

21. Tara Perkins and Tavia Grant, "White-label Cash Kings."

22. www.ndp.ca/endatmfees, (accessed June 18, 2007).

23. Merriam-Webster's Dictionary of Law, 1996.

24. "Fujitsu Institutes New Warranty Policy For Plasmavision® Monitors," May 15, 2002, www.plasmavision.com/buying_online.htm[o] (accessed January 25, 2005).

25. Joseph P. Bailey, "Electronic Commerce: Prices and Consumer Issues for Three Products: Books, Compact Discs, and Software," *Organization for Economic Cooperation and Development, OECD, GD* 98 (1998), p. 4; J. Yannis Bakos, "Reducing Buyer Search Costs: Implications for Electronic Marketplaces," *Management Science* 43, no. 12 (1997), pp. 1676–92; Erik Brynjolfsson and Michael D. Smith, "Frictionless Commerce? A Comparison of Internet and Conventional Retailers," *Management Science* 46, no. 4 (2000), pp. 563–85; Rajiv Lal and Miklos Sarvary, "When and How Is the Internet Likely to Decrease Price Competition?" *Marketing Science* 18, no. 4 (1999), pp. 485–503; Xing Pan, Brian T. Ratchford, and Venkatesh Shankar, "Can Price Dispersion in Online Markets be Explained by Differences in E-Tailer Service Quality?" *Journal of the Academy of Marketing Science* 30, no. 4 (2002), pp. 433–45; Michael D. Smith, "The Impact of Shopbots on Electronic Markets," *Journal of the Academy of Marketing Sciences* 30, no. 4 (2002), pp. 446–54; Michael D. Smith and Erik Brynjolfsson, "Consumer Decision-Making at an Internet Shopbot: Brand Still Matters," *The Journal of Industrial Economics* 49 (December 2001), pp. 541–58; Fang-Fang Tang and Xiaolin Xing, "Will the Growth of Multi-Channel Retailing Diminish the Pricing Efficiency of the Web?" *Journal of Retailing* 77, no. 3 (2001), pp. 319–33; Florian Zettlemeyer, "Expanding to the Internet: Pricing and Communications Strategies When Firms Compete on Multiple Channels," *Journal of Marketing Research* 37 (August 2000), pp. 292–308; Dhruv Grewal, Gopalkrishnan R. Iyer, R. Krishnan, and Arun Sharma, "The Internet and the Price-Value-Loyalty Chain," *Journal of Business Research* 56 (May 2003), pp. 391–98; Gopalkrishnan R. Iyer, Anthony D. Miyazaki, Dhruv Grewal, and Maria Giordano, "Linking Web-Based Segmentation to Pricing Tactics," *Journal of Product & Brand Management* 11, no. 4/5 (2002), pp. 288–302.

26. Amy Verner, "Carried Away with Eco-bags," www.theglobeandmail.com/servlet/story/LAC.20070623.BAG23/TPStory/?query=%22holt+renfrew%22 (accessed June 23, 2007).

27. Thomas T. Nagle and Reed K. Holden, *The Strategy and Tactics of Pricing*, 3rd ed. (Upper Saddle River, NJ: Pearson, 2002).

28. Dhruv Grewal and Jeanne Munger, "Carpet Pro Solutions," case study (2005), unpublished case study, Babson College.

29. www.amazon.ca/ (accessed June 19, 2007).

30. Lisa E. Bolton, Luk Warlop, and Joseph W. Alba, "Consumer Perceptions of Price (Un)Fairness," *Journal of Consumer Research* 29 (March 2003), pp. 474–91; Margaret C. Campbell, "Perceptions of Price Unfairness: Antecedents and Consequences," *Journal of Marketing Research* 36 (May 1999), pp. 187–99; Peter R. Darke and Darren W. Dahl, "Fairness and Discounts: The Subjective Value of a Bargain," *Journal of Consumer Psychology* 13, no. 3 (2003), pp. 328–38; Sarah Maxwell, "What Makes a Price Increase Seem 'Fair'?" *Pricing Strategy & Practice* 3, no. 4 (1995), pp. 21–27.

31. A. Biswas, E.J. Wilson, and J.W. Licata, "Reference Pricing Studies in Marketing: A Synthesis of Research Results," *Journal of Business Research* 27, no. 3 (1993), pp. 239–56; A. Biswas, "The Moderating Role of Brand Familiarity in Reference Price Perceptions," *Journal of Business Research* 25 (1992), pp. 251–62; A. Biswas and E. Blair, "Contextual Effects

of Reference Prices in Retail Advertisements," *Journal of Marketing* 55 (1991), pp. 1–12; Larry D. Compeau and Dhruv Grewal, "Comparative Price Advertising: An Integrative Review," *Journal of Public Policy & Marketing* 17 (Fall 1998), pp. 257–73; Rajesh Chandrashekaran and Dhruv Grewal, "Assimilation of Advertised Reference Prices: The Moderating Role of Involvement," *Journal of Retailing* 79, no. 1 (2003), pp. 53–62; David M. Hardesty and William O. Bearden, "Consumer Evaluations of Different Promotion Types and Price Presentations: The Moderating Role of Promotional Benefit Level," *Journal of Retailing* 79, no. 1 (2003), pp. 17–25.

32. "About Giant Tiger—History," www.gianttiger.com/en/about_gt/history/index.php (accessed June 20, 2007).

33. "Facts and Questions," www.gianttiger.com/en/faq.php accessed June 20, 2007.

34. *Supra*.

35. "Community/Murals," www.gianttiger.com/en/community/murals/ (accessed June 20, 2007).

36. "The North West Company: Alberta," www.northwest.ca/BackOffice/DesktopDefault.aspx?tabindex=0&tabid=100 80 (accessed June 20, 2007).

37. Dhruv Grewal, Kent B. Monroe, and R. Krishnan, "The Effects of Price Comparison Advertising on Buyers' Perceptions of Acquisition Value and Transaction Value," *Journal of Marketing* 62 (April 1998), pp. 46–60.

38. Noreen M. Klein and Janet E. Oglethorpe, "Reference Points in Consumer Decision Making," in *Advances in Consumer Research*, Vol. 14, eds. Melanie Wallendorf and Paul Anderson (Provo, UT: Association for Consumer Research, 1987), pp. 183–87.

39. J.E. Urbany, W.O. Bearden, and D.C. Weilbaker, "The Effect of Plausible and Exaggerated Reference Prices on Consumer Perceptions and Price Search," *Journal of Consumer Research* 15 (1988), pp. 95–110.

40. Michael Levy and Barton A. Weitz, *Retailing Management*, 6th ed. (Burr Ridge, IL: Irwin/McGraw-Hill, 2007).

41. Robert Schindler, "The 99 Price Ending as a Signal of a Low-Price Appeal," *Journal of Retailing* 82, no. 1 (2006).

42. Merrie Brucks, Valerie A. Zeithaml, and Gillian Naylor, "Price and Brand Name as Indicators of Quality Dimensions for Consumer Durables," *Journal of the Academy of Marketing Science* 28, no. 3 (2000), pp. 359–74; William B. Dodds, Kent B. Monroe, and Dhruv Grewal, "Effects of Price, Brand, and Store Information on Buyers' Product Evaluations," *Journal of Marketing Research* 28 (August 1991), pp. 307–19.

43. Brucks, Zeithaml, and Naylor, "Price and Brand Name as Indicators"; Niraj Dawar and Philip Parker, "Marketing Universals: Consumers' Use of Brand Name, Price, Physical Appearance, and Retailer Reputation as Signals of Product Quality," *Journal of Marketing* 58 (April 1994), pp. 81–95; Dodds, Monroe, and Grewal, "Effects of Price, Brand, and Store Information"; Paul S. Richardson, Alan S. Dick, and Arun K. Jain, "Extrinsic and Intrinsic Cue Effects on Perceptions of Store Brand Quality," *Journal of Marketing* 58 (October 1994), pp. 28–36; Anthony Miyazaki, Dhruv Grewal, and Ronnie Goodstein, "The Effect of Multiple Extrinsic Cues on Quality Perceptions: A Matter of Consistency," *Journal of Consumer Research* 32 (June 2005), pp. 146–153.

44. This section draws from Levy and Weitz, *Retailing Management*.

45. Sha Yang and Priya Raghubir, "Can Bottles Speak Volumes? The Effect of Package Shape on How Much to Buy," *Journal of Retailing* 81, no. 4 (2005), pp. 269–281.

46. "Competition Bureau Investigation Leads to $1-Million Settlement with Suzy Shier Inc.," www.competitionbureau.gc.ca/internet/index.cfm?itemID=305&lg=e (accessed June 24, 2007).

47. Compeau and Grewal, "Comparative Price Advertising"; Larry D. Compeau, Dhruv Grewal, and Diana S. Grewal, "Adjudicating Claims of Deceptive Advertised Reference Prices: The Use of Empirical Evidence," *Journal of Public Policy & Marketing* 14 (Fall 1994), pp. 52–62; Dhruv Grewal and Larry D. Compeau, "Comparative Price Advertising: Informative or Deceptive?" *Journal of Public Policy & Marketing* 11 (Spring 1992), pp. 52–62; Larry Compeau, Joan Lindsey-Mullikin, Dhruv Grewal, and Ross Petty, "An Analysis of Consumers' Interpretations of the Semantic Phrases Found in Comparative Price Advertisements," *Journal of Consumer Affairs* 38 (Summer 2004), pp. 178–87.

48. Joanna Grossman, "The End of Ladies Night in New Jersey," *Find Law's Legal Commentary*, 2004, writ.news.findlaw.com/grossman/20040615.html (accessed November 29, 2005); Joyce Howard Price, "Ladies Night Ruled Discriminatory," *The Washington Times*, 2004, washingtontimes.com/national/20040602-111843-2685r.htm (accessed November 29, 2005).

49. This case was written by Larry D. Compeau in conjunction with the U.S. textbook authors Dhruv Grewal and Michael Levy for the basis of class discussion rather than to illustrate either effective or ineffective marketing practices.

Chapter 13

1. www.zara.ca (accessed May 4, 2007); Pankaj Ghemawat and Jose Luis Nueno, "Zara: Fast Fashion," Harvard Business School Case Number 9-703-497 (April 1, 2003); www.inditex.com/english/home.htm (accessed July 20, 2006); Guillermo D'Andrea and David Arnold, "Zara," Harvard Business School Case Number 9-503-050 (March 12, 2003); www.gapinc.com/financmedia/financmedia.htm (accessed March 13, 2005); www.hm.com/us/start/start/index.jsp# (accessed June 4, 2005); www.benetton.com/press/ (accessed September 3, 2006); Stephen Tierney, "New Look's Supply Chain Obsession," *Frontline Solutions* 12, no. 6 (October 2003), pp. 24–25.; David Bovet and Joseph Martha, "E-Business and Logistics Unlocking the Rusty Supply Chain," *Logistics Quarterly* 6, no. 4 (Winter 2000), pp. 1–3; Jane M. Folpe, "Zara Has a Made-to-Order Plan for Success," *Fortune* 142, no. 5 (September 2000), pp. 80–82; Carlta Vitzthum, "Just-in-Time Fashion: Spanish Retailer Zara Makes Low-Cost Lines in Weeks by Running Its Own Show," *The Wall Street Journal* (Eastern Edition), May 18, 2001, p. B1.

2. Rebecca Harris, "Buy a coffee, remember a veteran," www.marketingmag.ca/magazine/current/the_briefing/article.jsp?content=20041101_64784_64784 (accessed January 2, 2008).

3. Shirley Lichti, "When it comes to packaging, it pays to be different," www.marketingmagic.ca/articles/Packaging.htm (accessed January 2, 2008).

4. www.marketingpower.com/live/mg-dictionary.

5. Based on David Simchi-Levi, Philip Kaminsky, and Edith Simchi-Levi, *Designing and Managing the Supply Chain: Concepts, Strategies and Case Studies*, 2d ed. (New York: McGraw-Hill Irwin, 2003); Michael Levy and Barton A. Weitz, *Retailing Management*, 5th ed. (New York: McGraw-Hill Irwin, 2004).

6. www.marketingpower.com/live/mg-dictionary. Definition from the Council of Logistics Management.

7. Shirley Won, "Arctic Glacier Seeks to Ice Competition," *The Globe & Mail*, May 29, 2007.

8. *Supra.*

9. "Industry History," www.arcticglacierinc.com/history.htm (accessed June 27, 2007).

10. *Supra.*

11. Shirley Won, "Arctic Glacier Seeks to Ice Competition."

12. Jon Pareles, "The Once and Future Prince," www.nytimes.com/2007/07/22/arts/music/22pare.html?ei=5124&en=b52b49b65411b345&ex=1342670400&adxnnl=1&partner=per&adxnnlx=1185567590-yTMSuMcGbwfz6rtKV0Jjhw (accessed January 3, 2008).

13. Thomas W. Gruen, Daniel S. Corsten, and Sundar Bharadwaj, "Retail out of Stocks: A Worldwide Examination of Extent, Causes, and Consumer Responses," unpublished working paper, May 7, 2002; Nirmalya Kumar, "The Power of Trust in Manufacturer-Retailer Relationships," *Harvard Business Review*, November–December 1996, pp. 92–106; Mark E. Parry and Yoshinobu Sato, "Procter & Gamble: The Wal-Mart Partnership," University of Virginia case #M-0452 (1996).

14. www.marketingpower.com/live/mg-dictionary.

15. Canadian Franchise Directory, www.franchisedirectory.ca/ (accessed June 28, 2007).

16. Ghemawat and Nueno, "ZARA: Fast Fashion."

17. Navi Radjou, Henry H. Harteveldt, and Colin Teubner, "Airlines: Fix Your MRO Supply Chains to Save Big," *Forrester*, February 4, 2004 (including footnotes 2–5).

18. www.marketingpower.com/live/mg-dictionary.

19. Sharyn Leaver, Joshua Walker, and Tamara Mendelsohn, "Hasbro Drives Supply Chain Efficiency with BPM," *Forester Research*, July 22, 2003.

20. Erin Anderson and Anne Coughlan, "Structure, Governance, and Relationship Management," in *Handbook of Marketing*, eds. B. Weitz and R. Wensley (London: Sage, 2002).

21. Erin Anderson and Barton Weitz, "The Use of Pledges to Build and Sustain Commitment in Distribution Channels," *Journal of Marketing Research* 29 (February 1992), pp. 18–34.

22. This section draws from Levy and Weitz, *Retailing Management*, Chapter 10.

23. Larry Kellam, "P&G Rethinks Supply Chain," *Optimize*, October 2003, p. 35.

24. This case was written by Jeanne L. Munger in conjunction with the U.S. textbook authors Dhruv Grewal and Michael Levy for the basis of class discussion rather than to illustrate either effective or ineffective marketing practices. Jeanne Munger is an associate professor at the University of Southern Maine.

25. Mellissa S. Monroe, "Wal-Mart Is Rewriting Rules, Dominating World's Supply Chain," *Knight Ridder Tribune Business News*, November 10, 2003, p. 1.

26. Richard J. Schonberger, "The Right Stuff, Revisited," *MSI* 21, no. 9 (September 2003), p. 26.

27. Staff, "Logisticstoday's 10 Best Supply Chains," *Logisticstoday*, December 2003, p. 20.

Chapter 14

1. www.roots.com/index.php?/canada/content/view/26/70/lang,en/ (accessed June 24, 2007).

2. *Supra.*

3. Birte Pampel, "Behind the Brand: The Triumphs and the Tragedies," www.brandchannel.com/features_profile.asp?pr_id=194 (accessed June 24, 2007).

4. www.roots.com/index.php?/canada/content/view/27/71/lang,en/ (accessed June 24, 2007).

5. Birte Pampel, "Behind the Brand: The Triumphs and the Tragedies," www.brandchannel.com/features_profile.asp?pr_id=194 (accessed June 24, 2007).

6. Geoffrey York, "Roots Plants the Flag in China," www.reportonbusiness.com/servlet/story/RTGAM.20070921.wrroots21/BNStory/robNews/home - 93k (accessed January 4, 2008).

7. Kara Aaserud, Camilla Cornell, Jim McElgunn, Kim Shiffman and Richard Wright, "The golden rules of growth: Michael Budman," www.canadianbusiness.com/entrepreneur/managing/article.jsp?content=20070419_095717_4492 (accessed June 24, 2007).

8. www.stores.org/pdf/GlobalRetail04.pdf.

9. www.retailcouncil.org/news/media/profile/print/default.asp (accessed January 4, 2008).

10. For descriptions of the Wheel of Retailing theory, see Stanley Hollander, "The Wheel of Retailing: What Makes Skilled Managers Succumb to the 'Prosper, Mature, and Decay' Pattern?" *Marketing Management*, Summer 1996, pp. 63–65; Stephen Brown, "Postmodernism, the Wheel of Retailing, and Will to Power," *The International Review of Retail, Distribution, and Consumer Research*, July 1995, pp. 387–412; Arieh Goldman, "Institutional Change in Retailing: An Updated Wheel of Retailing," in *Foundations of Marketing Channels*, eds. A. Woodside, J. Sims, D. Lewison, and I. Wilkenson (Austin, TX: Lone Star, 1978), pp. 193–201. For a description of the Accordion Theory, see Stanley C. Hollander, "Notes on the Retail Accordion," *Journal of Retailing* 42 (Summer 1966), pp. 20–40, 54. For a description of the Dialectic Process theory, see Thomas J. Maronick and Bruce J. Walker, "The Dialectic Evolution of Retailing," in *Proceedings: Southern Marketing Association*, ed. Barnett Greenberg (Atlanta: Georgia State University, 1974), p. 147. For descriptions of Natural Selection theory, see A.C.R. Dreesmann, "Patterns of Evolution in Retailing," *Journal of Retailing* (Spring 1968), pp. 81–96; Murray Forester, "Darwinian Theory of Retailing," *Chain Store Age*, August 1995, p. 8. A summary of these theories can be found in Michael Levy and Barton A. Weitz, *Retailing Management*, 6th ed. (Burr Ridge, IL: Irwin/McGraw-Hill, 2007).

11. Michael Levy, Dhruv Grewal, Robert A. Peterson, and Bob Connolly, "The Concept of the Big Middle," *Journal of Retailing* 81, no. 2 (2005), pp. 83–88.

12. Michael Treacy and Fred Wiersema, *The Disciplines of Market Leaders* (Reading, MA: Addison Wesley, 1995).

13. Marina Strauss, "Struggling Saan Seeks Financing," www.reportonbusiness.com/servlet/story/LAC.20071213.RSAAN13/TPStory/?query= - 79k – (accessed January 4, 2008).

14. Reuters, "Would You Like Fries with your Tiramisu?" www.theglobeandmail.com/servlet/story/LAC.20070628.RTICK28SEC/TPStory/Business (accessed June 28, 2007).

15. Paul Brent, "McLatte Anyone?" *Marketing Magazine,* December 10, 2007, p. 10.

16. Aaron Bernstein, "A Major Swipe at Sweatshops," *BusinessWeek,* May 23, 2005, p. 98; "The Gap (clothing retailer)," www.wikipedia.org (accessed September 24, 2006); "Landmark Workers' Rights Lawsuit Settled," February 16, 2003, www.cleanclothes.org (accessed September 20, 2006); Don Tapscott, "Time of Transparency," *Intelligent Enterprise* 7, no. 10 (June 12, 2004), pp. 12–24; "Workers Sue Wal-Mart over Sweatshop Conditions," September 13, 2005, www.nosweat.org.uk//article.php?sid=1390 (accessed October 21, 2005); "Disney in China: Making Children's Books at the Nord Race Factories," National Labor Committee, August 2005, www.nlcnet.org (accessed September 26, 2006).

17. www.sa-intl.org (accessed September 26, 2006).

18. Wes Lafortune, "Concept Retailing Trend Costly But Growing," www.businessedge.ca/article.cfm/newsID/11401.cfm (accessed June 24, 2007).

19. Julie Baker, A. Parasuraman, Dhruv Grewal, and Glenn Voss, "The Influence of Multiple Store Environment Cues on Perceived Merchandise Value and Patronage Intentions," *Journal of Marketing,* 66 (April 2001), pp. 120–41; Eric R. Spangenberg, Ayn E. Crowley, and Pamela W. Henderson, "Improving the Store Environment: Do Olfactory Cues Affect Evaluations and Behaviors?" *Journal of Marketing* 60 (April 1996), pp. 67–80; Michael K. Hui and John E.G. Bateson, "Perceived Control and the Effects of Crowding and Consumer Choice on the Service Experience," *Journal of Consumer Research* 18 (September 1991), pp. 174–84.

20. "About Us," www.pleasemum.com/about_us.php (accessed June 25, 2007).

21. "Vancouver 2010 Brand and Image," www.vancouver2010.com/en/LookVancouver2010 (accessed June 25, 2007).

22. Leonard Berry, Kathleen Seiders, and Dhruv Grewal, "Understanding Service Convenience," *Journal of Marketing* 66 (July 2002), pp. 1–17.

23. "About The Frootique—Frequently Asked Questions," www.petesfrootique.com/faqs.asp (accessed June 25, 2007).

24. "Nutrition Center," www.petesfrootique.com/LorieMcNeil.asp (accessed June 23, 2007).

25. "Meet Pete," www.petesfrootique.com/meet_pete.asp (accessed June 23, 2007).

26. "Our History," www.petesfrootique.com/our_history.asp (accessed June 23, 2007).

27. "Shoppers Drug Mart Opens its 1,000th Drug Store in Canada," www.shoppersdrugmart.ca/english/corporate_information/investor_relations/press_releases/articles/april_26_2007.html (accessed June 25, 2007).

28. "An Industry That's Regaining Its Fighting Trim," *Chain Drug Review,* June 7, 2004, p. 20.

29. The Canadian Marketing Association, www.the-cma.org (accessed June 24, 2007).

30. Ruth Stevens, "Crash Course in Direct Marketing," www.marketingprofs.com/premium/seminar_detail.asp?adref=semsrch&semid=104 (accessed June 25, 2007).

31. Canadian Media Directors' Council, "Media Digest," 2007.

32. Marketing Research Group Fact Sheet: Canadian Consumer Attitudes to Direct Mail (Part II), www.canadapost.ca/business/prodserv/mdm/market-e.asp (accessed June 26, 2007).

33. Heart & Stroke Foundation of Canada, "About Us," ww2.heartandstroke.ca/Page.asp?PageID=88&CategoryID=10&Src=about (accessed June 26, 2007).

34. Heart & Stroke Foundation of Canada, "Annual Report 2006," ww2.heartandstroke.ca/Images/HSFC_AR_2006_eng.pdf (accessed June 26, 2007).

35. Marketing and Selling Solutions: Catalogues, www.canadapost.ca/tools/pdf/getpdf.asp?pdf=/offerings/catalogue_mail/pdf/cat-e.pdf&lang=e(accessed June 26, 2007).

36. Marketing Research Group Fact Sheet: Canadian Consumer Attitudes to Direct Mail (Part II), www.canadapost.ca/business/prodserv/mdm/market-e.asp (accessed June 26, 2007).

37. Direct Response Television, www.direct-response-television.com/ (accessed June 26, 2007).

38. Canadian Blood Services & Northern Lights to Present at Interactive Marketing Conference," www.nldrtv.com/news/CBS_CaseStudy_PressRelease.htm (accessed June 26, 2007).

39. "Northern Lights and Canadian Blood Services Capture Gold at CMA Awards," www.nldrtv.com/news/CMA_PressRelease.htm (accessed June 26, 2007).

40. Paul-Mark Rendon, "Virgin Builds on Buzz," www.marketingmag.ca/magazine/current/feature/article.jsp?content=20051212_73030_73030 (accessed June 26, 2007).

41. "About Rogers Centre," www.rogerscentre.com/inaround/visitors/policies/index.html (accessed June 26, 2007).

42. This section draws from Dhruv Grewal, Gopalkrishnan R. Iyer, and Michael Levy, "Internet Retailing: Enablers, Limiters, and Market Consequences," *Journal of Business Research* 57 (2004), pp. 703–13.

43. John M. de Figueiredo, "Finding Sustainable Profitability in Electronic Commerce," *Sloan Management Review* 41 (Spring 2000), pp. 41–52.

44. Kohl, Jesse. "MuchMusic Puts Awards on Mobile—Live," www.mediaincanada.com/articles/mic/20070615/mmvas.html?word=music (accessed June 26, 2007).

45. "MuchShop," http://shopmobile.muchmusic.com/ (accessed June 26, 2007).

46. Grewal, Iyer, and Levy, "Internet Retailing."

47. This case was written by Jeanne L. Munger (University of Southern Maine) in conjunction with the U.S. textbook authors Dhruv Grewal and Michael Levy for the basis of class discussion rather than to illustrate either effective or ineffective marketing practices. The authors thank Max Ward, vice president of Technology at Staples, who provided valuable input for the development of this case. They also acknowledge that parts of the case are based on information provided by W. Caleb McCann (in collaboration with J.P. Jeannet, Dhruv Grewal, and Martha Lanning), "Staples," in *Fulfillment in E-Business,* ed. Petra Schuber, Ralf Wolfle, and Walter Dettling (Germany: Hanser, 2001) pp. 239–52 (in German).

48. www.bizjournals.com/boston/stories/2004/03/01/daily53.html (accessed September 20, 2006).

Chapter 15

1. Keith McArthur, "Annoying But Successful. Whither the Beavers?" www.theglobeandmail.com/servlet/ArticleNews/freeheadlines/LAC/20070423/RBEAVERS23/business/ROB (accessed June 30, 2007).

2. Dave Scholz and Jean Marc-Leger, "Year of the Beavers," www.marketingmag.ca/magazine/current/top_mind/article.jsp?content=20060410_76142_76142 (accessed June 30, 2007).

3. David Brown, "The year of Frank and Gordon," www.marketingmag.ca/magazine/current/feature/article.jsp?content=20061120_67344_67344 (accessed June 30, 2007).

4. Paul-Mark Rendon, "Working Overtime," www.marketingmag.ca/magazine/current/feature/article.jsp?content=20070312_68988_68988 (accessed June 30, 2007).

5. Keith McArthur, "Annoying but Successful. Whither the Beavers?" www.theglobeandmail.com/servlet/ArticleNews/freeheadlines/LAC/20070423/RBEAVERS23/business/ROB (accessed June 30, 2007).

6. Paul-Mark Rendon, "Working Overtime," www.marketingmag.ca/magazine/current/feature/article.jsp?content=20070312_68988_68988 (accessed June 30, 2007).

7. T. Duncan and C. Caywood, "The Concept, Process, and Evolution of Integrated Marketing Communication," in Integrated Communication: Synergy of Persuasive Voices, eds. E. Thorson and J. Moore (Mahwah, NJ: Lawrence Erlbaum Associates, 1996); http://jimc.medill.northwestern.edu/2000/pettegrew.htm.

8. Roger Parloff, "Talk Ain't Cheap: First Amendment Ruling against Nike," Marketing Magazine, September 9, 2002; Roberto Ceniceros, "Suit over Nike Public Statements Upheld," Business Insurance, May 12, 2002; Eugene Volokh, "Nike and the Free Speech Knot," The Wall Street Journal, June 30, 2003, p. A16; Anonymous, "Supreme Court Won't Hear Nike Speech Case," The Quill 91, no. 6 (2003), p. 6; Russell Mokhiber, "Nike's Come from Behind Win," Multinational Monitor 24, no. 10 (2003), p. 7.

9. www.cnn.com/2004/TECH/internet/04/26/godsend.controversy.reut/ (accessed September 5, 2005).

10. Deborah J. MacInnis and Bernard J. Jaworski, "Information Processing from Advertisements: Toward an Integrative Framework," Journal of Marketing 53, no. 4 (October 1989), pp. 1–23.

11. Deborah J. MacInnis, Christine Moorman, and Bernard J. Jaworski, "Enhancing and Measuring Consumers' Motivation, Opportunity," Journal of Marketing 55, no. 4 (October 1991), pp. 32–554. Joan Meyers-Levy, "Elaborating on Elaboration: The Distinction between Relational and Item-Specific Elaboration," Journal of Consumer Research 18 (December 1991), pp. 358–67.

12. Canadian Media Directors' Council, "Media Digest," 2007.

13. www.oxygen.com/basics/founders.aspx (accessed September 5, 2006); www.oxygen.com/press (accessed September 6, 2006); Nadine Heintz, "Thinking Inside the Box," Inc. 26, no. 7 (July, 2004), pp. 90–95; Jon Lafayette, "Oxygen Turns to Its Stars," TelevisionWeek, 24, no. 9, (February 28, 2005), pp. 3–4.

14. "Our Partners," www.quarry.com/who_we_are/partnership/alan_quarry.cfm (accessed June 29, 2007).

15. "Quarry to participate in Forrester Marketing Forum 2007," www.quarry.com/who_we_are/news_and_events/pr/show_release.cfm?id=32 (accessed June 30, 2007).

16. www.onlinewbc.gov/docs/starting/glossary.html#d (accessed October 11, 2004).

17. Carl Obermiller and Eric R. Spangenberg, "On the Origin and Distinctness of Skepticism toward Advertising," Marketing Letters 11, no. 4 (2000), p. 311.

18. www.yoplait.com/breastcancer_lids.aspx (accessed September 22, 2006).

19. Don Peppers, Martha Rogers, and Bob Dorf, "Is Your Company Ready for One-to-One Marketing?" Harvard Business Review 77, no. 1 (1999), pp. 151–61; www.managingchange.com/guestcon/highimp.htm (accessed September 26, 2006).

20. Building Loyalty 2006, "KitchenAid Brand Cooking up Relationships in the Kitchen," www.marketingmag.ca/workingknowledge/images/BuildingLoyaltyHandbook_Eng.pdf (accessed July 2, 2007).

21. "Seven Rules for Increasing Customer Value," www.realmarket.com/required/peppers1.pdf (accessed July 2, 2007).

22. Building Loyalty 2006, "KitchenAid Brand Cooking up Relationships in the Kitchen," www.marketingmag.ca/workingknowledge/images/BuildingLoyaltyHandbook_Eng.pdf (accessed July 2, 2007).

23. Building Loyalty 2007, "Loyalty and Relationship Marketing Can Work in the Mobile Channel," http://qml.quiettouch.com/files/publishing/marketing/roadshows/BuildingLoyalty_English.pdf (accessed July 2, 2007).

24. Jackie Huba, "A Just Cause Creating Emotional Connections with Customers," 2003, www.inc.com/articles/2003/05/25537.html.

25. www.yoplait.com/breastcancer_lids.aspx (accessed October 25, 2004).

26. www.coneinc.com/Pages/buzz3.html (accessed October 22, 2004).

27. "iUpload Takes Datamations First Blogging Win," February 28, 2006, www.itmanagement.eartweb.com, (accessed April 19, 2006); Nicole Ziegler Dizon, "Corporations Enter into World of Blogs," San Francisco Gate, June 6, 2006, www.sfgate.com (accessed September 26, 2006); Mark Berger, "Annie's Homegrown: 'Bernie's Blog' Case Study," www.backbonemedia.com (accessed September 26, 2006); "Corporate Blogging Survey" www.backbonemedia.com (accessed September 26, 2006).

28. Karen Mazurkewich, "Dove Story," www.strategymag.com/articles/magazine/20070101/dove.html?word=dove&word=story (accessed June 29, 2007).

29. David Brown and Chris Powell, "The Beauty of Evolution," www.marketingmag.ca/magazine/current/feature/article.jsp?content=20070212_68561_68561 (accessed June 29, 2007).

30. Matt Semansky and David Brown, "It's an Evolution at the Marketing Awards," www.marketingmag.ca/daily/20070330/topstory.html (accessed June 29, 2007).

31. Carey Toane, "U of M Using Student Blogs as Recruitment Tool," www.mediaincanada.com/articles/mic/20071129/recruitment.html (accessed January 5, 2008).

32. "iUpload Takes Datamations First Blogging Win," February 28, 2006, www.itmanagement.eartweb.com, (accessed April 19, 2006); Dizon, "Corporations Enter into World of Blogs"; Mark Berger, "Annie's Homegrown: 'Bernie's Blog' Case Study," www.backbonemedia.com (accessed September 24, 2006); "Corporate Blogging Survey" www.backbonemedia.com (accessed September 24, 2006).

33. www.consideryourselfwarned.com (accessed September 20, 2006); www.childrennow.org/newsroom/news-04/cam-ra-05-03-04.cfm (accessed October 11, 2004).

34. Michael Singer, "Microsoft, SINA Send SMS Message to China," 2004, http://internetnews.com/ent-news/article.php/1585181 (accessed September 25, 2006).

35. Elizabeth Church, "Newsfeed Update: Universities Sign onto Facebook," *The Globe and Mail*, December 26, 2007, p. A14.

36. http://retailindustry.about.com/library/bl/q2/bl_um041701.htm (accessed September 26, 2006).

37. www.inastrol.com/Articles/990601.htm (accessed September 26, 2006).

38. http://advertising.utexas.edu/research/terms/index.asp#O (accessed September 26, 2006).

39. This section draws from Michael Levy and Barton A. Weitz, *Retailing Management*, 6th ed. (Burr Ridge, IL: McGraw-Hill/Irwin, 2007).

40. Theodore Leavitt, *The Marketing Imagination* (New York: The Free Press, 1986).

41. George E. Belch and Michael A. Belch, *Advertising and Promotion: An Integrated Marketing Communications Perspective*, 7th ed. (New York: McGraw-Hill/Irwin, 2007).

42. www.kleenex.com/us/av/index.asp (accessed September 26, 2006).

43. Bret A.S. Martin, Bodo Lang, and Stephanie Wong, "Conclusion, Explicitness in Advertising: The Moderating Role of Need for Cognition and Argument Quality on Persuasion," *Journal of Advertising* 32, no. 4 (2004), pp. 57–65.

44. Michael Petracca and Madeleine Sorapure, eds., *Common Culture: Reading and Writing about American Popular Culture* (Upper Saddle River, NJ: Prentice Hall, 1998).

45. wps.prenhall.com/ca_ph_ebert_busess_3/0,6518,224378-,00.html.

46. The Television Bureau of Canada.

47. William F. Arens, *Contemporary Advertising*, 8th ed. (New York: McGraw Hill, 2003).

48. Cassies Canadian Advertising Success Stories 2006, http://cassies.ca/winners/2006Winners/winners_04.html (accessed July 4, 2007).

49. www.kraftfoods.com/jello/main.aspx?s=&m=jlo_news_jun04.

50. Dean M. Krugman, Leonard N. Reid, S. Watson Dunn, and Arnold M. Barban, *Advertising: Its Role in Modern Marketing* (New York: The Dryden Press, 1994), pp. 221–26.

51. Stanford L. Grossbart and Lawrence A. Crosby, "Understanding Bases of Parental Concern and Reaction to Children's Food Advertising," *Journal of Marketing* 48, no. 3 (1984), pp. 79–93; Brian M. Young, "Does Food Advertising Influence Children's Food Choices? A Critical Review of Some of the Recent Literature," *International Journal of Advertising* 22, no. 4 (2003), p. 441.

52. www.riger.com/know_base/media/understanding.html (accessed November 15, 2004).

Chapter 16

1. Robert MacLeod, "NASCAR roars its way into Canada," www.theglobeandmail.com/servlet/story/RTGAM.20060913.wxauto13/BNStory/Sports/home (accessed July 3, 2007).

2. "Conservative Party Supports Canadian Tire NASCAR Series," www.dianefinley.ca/EN/5922/56716 (accessed July 2, 2007).

3. E.K. Strong, *The Psychology of Selling* (New York: McGraw Hill, 1925).

4. John Philip Jones, "What Makes Advertising Work?" *The Economic Times*, July 24, 2002.

5. www.legamedia.net/lx/result/match/0591dfc9787c111b1b24dde6d61e43c5/index.php.

6. Jef I. Richards and Catherine M. Curran, "Oracles on 'Advertising': Searching for a Definition," *Journal of Advertising* 31, no. 2 (Summer 2002), pp. 63–77.

7. www.brandweek.com/bw/news/financial/article_display.jsp?vnu_content_id=1001615315 (accessed September 26, 2006); "Global Ad Spending Expected To Grow 6%," *Brandweek*, December 6, 2005.

8. Raymond R. Burke and Thomas K. Srull, "Competitive Interference and Consumer Memory for Advertising," *Journal of Consumer Research* 15 (June 1988), pp. 55–68; Kevin Lane Keller, "Memory Factors in Advertising: The Effect of Advertising Retrieval Cues on Brand Evaluation," *Journal of Consumer Research* 14 (December 1987), pp. 316–33; Kevin Lane Keller, "Memory and Evaluation Effects in Competitive Advertising Environments," *Journal of Consumer Research* 17 (March 1991), pp. 463–77; Robert J. Kent and Chris T. Allen, "Competitive Interference Effects in Consumer Memory for Advertising: The Role of Brand Familiarity," *Journal of Marketing* 58, no. 3 (July 1994), pp. 97–106.

9. Anthony Bianco, "The Vanishing Mass Market," *BusinessWeek*, July 12, 2004, pp. 61–68.

10. Robert Thompson, "Making the Green," *Marketing Magazine*, August 27, 2007, p. 11.

11. Matthew Shum, "Does Advertising Overcome Brand Loyalty? Evidence from the Breakfast Cereal Market," *Journal of Economics and Management Strategy* 13, no. 2 (2004), pp. 77–85.

12. Doritos Canada email message, Subject: "We dare you to try new Doritos brand Fiery Habanero!" sent on May 8, 2007.

13. "The Screening Room," www.DoritosPlay.ca (accessed July 6, 2007).

14. Rob Gerlsbeck, "The Military Draws Recruits by Putting Combat Life Front and Centre," *Marketing Magazine*, November 26, 2007, p. 22.

15. "Cashmere," *Strategy Magazine*, November 2007, p. 48.

16. www.gotmilk.com/fun/decade/year_1993.html (accessed September 26, 2006).

17. http://advertising.utexas.edu/research/terms/index.asp#P (accessed November 15, 2004).

18. www.grantstream.com/glossary.htm (accessed September 26, 2006).

19. "The Battle to Ban Advertising," www.idrc.ca/en/ev-28820-201-1-DO_TOPIC.html (accessed July 2, 2007).

20. Grant Robertson, "Tobacco Ban Stays, But Expect Ad Blitz Anyway," www.theglobeandmail.com/servlet/ArticleNews/freeheadlines/LAC/20070629/TOBACCO29/national/National (accessed July 2, 2007).

21. http://advertising.utexas.edu/research/terms/index.asp#O (accessed September 26, 2006).

22. Richard Kielbowicz and Linda Lawson, "Unmasking Hidden Commercials in Broadcasting: Origins of the Sponsorship Identification Regulations 1927–1963," 2004, www.law.indiana.edu/fclj/pubs/v56/no2/Kielbowicz%20Finals%20round%20IV.pdf (accessed September 4, 2005). More case/settlement details in IM.

23. www.onpoint-marketing.com/stealth-marketing.htm (accessed September 20, 2006).

24. "The Global Fund," www.joinred.com/globalfund/ (accessed July 4, 2007).

25. "Letter to the Editor," www.joinred.com/archive/adage/ (accessed July 4, 2007).

26. "Point/Counter Point," www.joinred.com/archive/adage/pcp.asp (accessed July 4, 2007).

27. Ricardo Alleyne, www.marketingmag.ca/magazine/current/letters_to_editor/article.jsp?content=20070528_69658_69658 (accessed July 4, 2007).

28. The Influencers, "What We Do," www.theinfluencers.ca/whatwedo.php (accessed July 2, 2007).

29. www.marketingterms.com/dictionary/viral_marketing/ (accessed September 26, 2006).

30. K. Onah Ha, "It's a Neopet World: Popular Site for Kids Stirs Controversy," *San Jose Mercury News*, September 14, 2004.

31. Christopher Reynolds, "Game Over," *American Demographics* 26, no. 1 (2004), pp. 35–39.

32. This section draws from Tom Duncan, *Principles of Advertising and IMC*, 2nd ed. (Burr Ridge, IL: Irwin/McGraw-Hill, 2005).

33. "Merger and Acquisition Activity Impacts Coupon Promotion Volume, Study Finds," *The Food Institute Report*, March 5, 2001, p. 4.

34. www.pillsbury.com/bakeoff/index.asp (accessed May 25, 2007).

35. Annette Bourdeau, "Sport Chek, Contiki and Subaru Rally for Data," www.strategymag.com/articles/magazine/20070601/sportchek.html (accessed July 5, 2007).

36. "Pop-up branding," www.strategymag.com/articles/magazine/20070601/escapism.html (accessed July 3, 2007).

37. Amy Verner, "Get It While It's Free," www.theglobeandmail.com/servlet/story/RTGAM.20070413.store14/BNStory/lifeStyle/home (accessed July 3, 2007).

38. Jeromy Lloyd, "Calvin Klein Nightclub Pops Up for Three Days," www.marketingmag.ca/daily/20070704/national2.html (accessed July 4, 2007).

39. www.msnbc.msn.com/id/7357071/ (accessed September 26, 2006).

40. www.engadget.com/entry/1234000103038638/ (accessed September 26, 2006).

41. Capital C Blog, "Being Capital C," http://capitalc.typepad.com/my_weblog/being_capital_c/index.html (accessed June 26, 2007).

42. Annette Bourdeau, "Capital C: From Mass to My," www.strategymag.com/articles/magazine/20070601/bizc.html (accessed June 25, 2007).

43. Capital C Blog, "Agency of the Year" by Paul-Mark Rendon. http://capitalc.typepad.com/my_weblog/agency_of_the_year/index.html (accessed June 25, 2007).

44. www.itvx.com/SpecialReport.asp (accessed September 26, 2006).

45. www.snopes.com/business/market/mandms.asp (accessed September 26, 2006).

46. "Product Placement to Triple in Films, TV, Report Says," www.cbc.ca/arts/story/2006/08/20/productplacement-report.html (accessed July 3, 2007).

47. www.itvx.com/SpecialReport.asp (accessed September 26, 2006).

48. Betsy Spethmann, "For a Limited Time Only," *Promo: Ideas, Connections and Brand*, 2004, http://promomagazine.com/mag/marketing_limited_time/.

49. Statistics Canada, *Canada Year Book*, (Ottawa, 2005).

50. This section draws from Mark W. Johnston and Greg W. Marshall, *Relationship Selling and Sales Management* (Burr Ridge, IL: Irwin/McGraw-Hill, 2004).

51. Reed Research Group, "Evaluating the Cost of Sales Calls," *Corporate Advertising Research Reports (CARR)*, www.cahnerscarr.com (accessed October 26, 2004).

52. Michael Beverland, "Contextual Influences and the Adoption and Practice of Relationship Selling in a Business-to-Business Setting: An Exploratory Study," *Journal of Personal Selling and Sales Management*, Summer 2001, p. 207.

53. Bill Stinnett, *Think Like Your Customer*, 1st ed. (Burr Ridge, IL: McGraw-Hill, 2004).

54. Johnston and Marshall, Relationship Selling and Sales Management.

55. IncentiveWorks, Canada's Meetings & Promotions Show, www.meetingscanada.com/cmits_pi/exhibitinfo_cmits.jsp (accessed June 24, 2007).

56. Barton A. Weitz, Harish Sujan, and Mita Sujan, "Knowledge, Motivation, and Adaptive Behavior: A Framework for Improving Selling Effectiveness," *Journal of Marketing*, October 1986, pp. 174–91.

57. www.quotedb.com/quotes/1303 (accessed September 20, 2006).

58. www.marketingpower.com/live/mg-dictionary.

59. Rene Y. Darmon, "Where Do the Best Sales Force Profit Producers Come From?" *Journal of Personal Selling and Sales Management* 13, no. 3 (1993), pp. 17–29.

60. Julie Chang, "Born to Sell?" *Sales and Marketing Management*, July 2003, p. 36.

61. Johnston and Marshall, *Relationship Selling* p. 368; Bill Kelley, "Recognition Reaps Rewards," *Sales and Marketing Management*, June 1986, p. 104 [reprinted from Thomas R. Wotruba, John S. Macfie, and Jerome A. Collem, "Effective Sales Force Recognition Programs," in *Industrial Marketing Management* 20, pp. 9–15].

62. For a discussion of common measures used to evaluate salespeople, see Johnston and Marshall, *Churchill/Ford/Walker's Sales Force Management*, p. 482.

63. Patti Summerfield, "Canadian Families Increasingly 'Living on the Internet,'" www.mediaincanada.com/articles/mic/20070626/srg.html?word=music (accessed June 29, 2007).

64. West49 website, www.west49.com/ (accessed June 30, 2007).

Chapter 17

1. www.lululemon.com (accessed May 23, 2007); http://en.wikipedia.org/wiki/Lululemon (accessed May 23, 2007); www.mindspring.com/~wilma-munsey/uhcw/BBCNews (accessed May 23, 2007); http://sev.prnewswire.com/retail/20061003/LAM02203102006-1.html (accessed May 23, 2007); www.hoovers.com/lululemon/--ID__156721--/free-co-factsheet.xhtml (accessed May 23, 2007); Laura Bogomolny, "Toned and Ready," *Canadian Business*, April 24-May 7, 2006, pp. 59-63; Martha Strauss, "As It Stretches, Lululemon Tries Not to Bend, *The Globe and Mail*, October 2, 2006.

2. Martha Strauss, "As It Stretches, Lululemon Tries Not to Bend," *The Globe and Mail,* October 2, 2006.

3. Pierre-Richard Agenor, *Does Globalization Hurt the Poor?* (Washington, DC: World Bank, 2002); "Globalization: Threat or Opportunity," International Monetary Fund, www.imf. org/external/np/exr/ib/2000/041200.htm#II (accessed on September 18, 2006).

4. Charles W.L. Hill, *Global Business Today,* 3rd edition (New York: Irwin McGraw-Hill, 2004).

5. David Rosenbaum, "Next Stop, New Delhi; The Strategic Debate Over Off-Shoring is Over," *CIO* 19, no. 8, (February 1, 2006) p. 1.

6. Rachel Kronrad, "Outsourcing Backlash Brewing," CBS News, 2004, www.cbsnews.com/stories/2004/01/19/national/ main594119.shtml (accessed August 28, 2005).

7. "Outsourcing Your CT Scan," *Ottawa Citizen,* October 22, 2006, www.epiphan.com/solutions/index.php?stid=15&P HPSESSID=tto9nft8gv7bp2kt5b3gm1thh7 (accessed May 23, 2007).

8. www.pbs.org/wgbh/commandingheights/hi/people/pe_ name.html.

9. www.thestandard.com.

10. www.econ.iastate.edu/classes/econ355/choi/wtoroots. htm.

11. www.canadians.org/media/trade/1997/30-June-97.html.

12. www.wto.org/english/thewto_e/whatis_e/tif_e/org6_e.htm.

13. web.worldbank.org/WBSITE/EXTERNAL/EXTABOUTUS/ 0,,pagePK:50004410~piPK:36602~theSitePK:29708,00.html.

14. For a full description of criticisms of the IMF, see www.imf. org/external/np/exr/ccrit/eng/cri.htm; for a list of criticisms of the World Bank, see www.artsci.wustl.edu/~nairobi/wbissues.html (accessed August 28, 2005).

15. Social Science Research Council, www.ssrc.org/sept11/ essays/teaching_resource/tr_globalization.htm (accessed September 2, 2005); www.acdi-cida.gc.ca/CIDAWEB/webcountry.nsf/VLUDocEn/Cameroon-Factsataglance#def.

16. "Canada Imposes New Sanctions on Myanmar," *The Globe and Mail Update* and *Reuters,* November 14, 2007, www. theglobeandmail.com/servlet/story/RTGAM.20071114. wburmasanction1114/BNStory/National/home (accessed December 18, 2007).

17. David L. Scott, *Wall Street Words: An A to Z Guide to Investment Terms for Today's Investor* (Boston: Houghton Mifflin, 2003).

18. www.international.gc.ca/eicb/softwood/menu-en.asp (accessed May 26, 2007).

19. http://economics.about.com/library/glossary/bldef-dumping.htm (accessed September 11, 2006); Scott, *Wall Street Words.*

20. www.bloomberg.com/apps/news?pid=10000103&sid=ajt pC2UYVKwk&refer=us.

21. "Half of Europeans Distrust American Companies," 2004 www.gmi-mr.com/gmipoll/press_room_wppk_pr_ 12272004.phtml (accessed September 11, 2006).

22. www.cbc.ca/canadavotes2004/politicalcanada/iraq.html (accessed May 26,, 2007).

23. http://en.wikipedia.org/wiki/Exchange_rate.

24. "Philippines Implement Countertrade Program for Vietnamese Rice," *Asia Pulse Pte Limited,* April 27, 2005.

25. Nicolino Strizzi and G. S. Kindra, "A Survey of Canadian Countertrade Practices with Asia-Pacific Countries," *Revue Canadienne des Sciences de l'Administration,* 1997.

26. 2007 Investment Climate Statement–Venezuela, www. state.gov/e/eeb/ifd/2007/80762.htm (accessed December 18, 2007).

27. http://ucatlas.ucsc.edu/trade/subtheme_trade_blocs.php (accessed March 5, 2005).

28. www.unescap.org/tid/mtg/postcancun_rterta.pps#1.

29. www.answers.com/main/ntquery?method=4&dsid=2222 &dekey=European+Union&gwp=8&curtab=2222_1.

30. www.fas.usda.gov/itp/CAFTA/cafta.html (accessed September 10, 2006).

31. http://en.wikipedia.org/wiki/Purchasing_power_parity (accessed September 19, 2005); O'Sullivan-Sheffrin, *Macroeconomics: Principles and Tools activeBook,* 3rd edition: (Upper Saddle River: Prentice Hall, 2002).

32. http://hdr.undp.org/reports/global/2001/en/. Nobel Prize–winning economist Amartya Sen has proposed that developing countries should also be measured according to the capabilities and opportunities that people within that particular country possess.

33. Emily Kaiser, Wal-Mart Takes Its China Lessons to India, www.boston.com/business/articles/2006/03/27 (accessed May 26, 2007).

34. www.tdctrade.com/econforum/tdc/tdc050101.htm.

35. "Who's Getting It Right? American Brands in the Middle Kingdom," *Time* 164, no. 17 (October 25, 2004), p. A14; "Cracking China," www.chiefexecutive.net 199 (June 2004); Normandy Madden and Jack Neff, "P&G Adapts Attitude towards Local Markets," *Advertising Age* (Midwest region edition) 75, no. 8 (February 23, 2004), p. 28; www.pg.com. eg/history4.cfm.

36. "Rural India, Have a Coke," www.businessweek.com/magazine/content/02_21/b3784134.htm.

37. Cellphones Catapult Rural Africa to 21st Century, www. nytimes.com/2005/08/25/international/africa/25africa. html (accessed December 18, 2007).

38. Training Management Corporation (TMC), Doing Business Internationally: The Cross Cultural Challenges, Seminar and Coursebook (Princeton, NJ: Trade Management Corporation, 1992).

39. Geert Hofstede, "Management Scientists Are Human," *Management Science* 40 (January 1994), pp. 4–13; Geert Hofstede and Michael H. Bond, "The Confucius Connection from Cultural Roots to Economic Growth," *Organizational Dynamics* 16 (Spring 1988), pp. 4–21; Masaaki Kotabe and Kristiaan Helsen, *Global Marketing Management* (Hoboken, NJ: John Wiley & Sons, 2004).

40. www.geert-hofstede.com/ (accessed September 10, 2006).

41. Donghoon Kim, Yigang Pan, and Heung Soo Park, "High versus Low Context Culture: A Comparison of Chinese, Korean and American Cultures," *Psychology and Marketing* 15, no. 6 (1998), pp. 507–21.

42. www.brandchannel.com/features_effect.asp?pf_id=261.

43. Betsy Mckay, Procter & Gamble, "Coca-Cola Formulate Vitamin Drinks for Developing Countries," *The Wall Street Journal* cited at www.chelationtherapyonline.com/articles/p9.htm (accessed May 26, 2007).

44. Diane Cyr and Trevor-Smith Haizley, "Localization of Web Design: An Empirical Comparison of German, Japanese, and United States Web Site Characteristics," *Journal of the American Society for Information Science and Technology*, 55 (13), 1199-1208, 2004; Diane Cyr, Carole Bonnani, John Bowes, Joe Ilsever, "Beyond Trust: Web Site Design Preferences Across Cultures," *Journal of Global Information Management*, 13, 4, Oct–Dec 2005.

45. Amy Chozick, "Japan Finally Opens," *The Globe and Mail*, September 26, 2006.

46. Laurel Delaney, Global Marketing Gaffes, March 19, 2002, www.marketingpofs.com (accessed December 18, 2007).

47. Amy Chozick, "Japan Finally Opens."

48. www.christiedigital.com/ (accessed December 18, 2007).

49. Angela Andal-Ancion and George Yip, "Smarter Ways to Do Business with the Competition," *European Business Forum* (Spring 2005), pp. 32–37.

50. "Joint Venture with Ting Hsin Brings Tesco to China," *MMR[o]* 11, no. 11 (July 26, 2004), p. 13.

51. Aqua Dots Recall, Bindeez Recall: Contains 'Date Rape' Drug, www.cjreport.com/news/777/aqua-dots-recall-bindeez-recall-contains-date-rape-drug.html (accessed December 18, 2007).

52. www.ingcanada.com; www.cyber-ark.com/networkvault-news/pr_20031110.asp.

53. Bruce D. Keillor, Michael D'Amico, and Veronica Horton, "Global Consumer Tendencies," *Psychology and Marketing* 18, no. 1 (2001), pp. 1–20.

54. www.consumerpsychologist.com/food_marketing.htm.

55. http://ro.unctad.org/infocomm/anglais/orange/market.htm; www.tropicana.com/index.asp?ID=27.

56. Charles W.L. Hill, *Global Business Today*, 3rd edition (New York: Irwin McGraw-Hill, 2004).

57. Supra.

58. Glenn Collins, "Going Global Involves More Than Many US Companies Think," *The New York Times*, January 2, 1997, p. C10.

59. www.pringles.it/.

60. Local Success on a Global Scale, www.brandchannel.com/features_effect.asp?pf_id=261 (accessed December 18, 2007).

61. Hayes, H.M., P.V. Jenster, and N.-E. Aaby (1996), *Business Marketing: A Global Perspective*, Boston: Irwin/McGraw-Hill.

62. Mary Anne Raymond, John F. Tanner Jr., and Jonghoon Kim, "Cost Complexity of Pricing Decisions for Exporters in Developing and Emerging Markets," *Journal of International Marketing* 9, no. 3 (2001), pp. 19–40.

63. Kelly Santana, "MTV Goes to Asia: Entertainment Giant Woos and Wows Audiences with Combination of Foreign and Local Talent," *Yale Global Online*, 2003, http://yaleglobal.yale.edu/display.article?id=2211.

64. Terry Clark, Masaaki Kotabe, and Dan Rajaratnam, "Exchange Rate Pass-Through and International Pricing Strategy: A Conceptual Framework and Research Propositions," *Journal of International Business Studies* 30, no. 2 (1999), pp. 249–68.

65. www.literacyonline.org/explorer/compare.iphtml?ID1=78&ID2=79&ID3=27&ID4=12&ID5=127.

66. www.aeforum.org/latest.nsf.

67. www.brandchannel.com/features_effect.asp?pf_id=274.

68. Charles W.L. Hill, *Global Business Today*, 3d edition (New York: Irwin McGraw-Hill, 2004).

69. George Hager, "Bush Plays Free-Trade Game," *USA Today*, May 2, 2002.

70. Paul Meller, "The W.T.O. Said to Weigh In on Product Names," *The New York Times*, November 18, 2004, p. 1; Mark Jarvis, "Which Bud's for You?" *BrandChannel*, January 5, 2004 www.brandchannel.com/start1.asp?fa_id=191 (accessed September 5, 2005); Paul Byrne, "Austrian Court Rules in Favor of Anheuser Busch," *PR Newswire*, December 31, 2004.

71. BBC News "Disposable Planet," http://news.bbc.co.uk/hi/english/static/in_depth/world/2002/disposable_planet/waste/statsbank.stm (accessed September 5, 2005).

72. Alladi Venkatesh, "Postmodernism Perspective for Macromarketing: An Inquiry into the Global Information and Sign Economy," *Journal of Macromarketing* 19, no. 12 (1999), p. 153 –169.

73. Michael R. Czinkota and Ilkka A. Ronkainen, "An International Marketing Manifesto," *Journal of International Marketing* 11, no. 1 (2003), pp. 13–27.

74. www.nike.com/nikebiz/nikebiz.jhtml?page=25&cat=businessmodel.

75. Haider Rizvi, Coca-Cola Faces Mounting Pressure over Abusive Practices at Plants Worldwide; http://corporationscreatefascism.blogspot.com/2005/12/coca-cola-faces-mounting-pressure-over.html (accessed May 26, 2007).

76. http://users.aber.ac.uk/pjm04/linguisticimperialism.html#culturalimperialism.

77. Farnaz Fassihi, "As Authorities Frown, Valentine's Day Finds Place in Iran's Heart; Young and in Love Embrace Forbidden Holiday; A Rush on Red Roses," *The Wall Street Journal*, February 12, 2004, p. A.1.

78. Thomas Friedman, *The Lexus and The Olive Tree: Understanding Globalization* (New York: Anchor, 2000).

79. www.ikea.com.

80. Youngme Moon, "IKEA Invades America," *Harvard Business School Publications*, #9-504-094 (2004).

81. James Schofield, "Ikea Wows the Russians," February 22, 2002, http://news.bbc.co.uk/1/hi/business/1836004.stm.

Appendix

1. Canadian Toy Association. "About Us." Canadian Toy Association. 2007. Canadian Toy Association (CTA). 20 Oct 2007, www.cdntoyassn.com/mabout.htm.

2. Statistics Canada. "Retail store sales by selected commodity." Statistics Canada. 15 Oct 2007. Statistics Canada. 25 Oct 2007, www40.statcan.ca/l01/cst01/trad52.htm?sdi=toys.

3. cbc.ca. "Web enhancements, revamped classic toys touted among hot holiday trends." cbc.ca. 1 Nov 2007. CBC. 15 Nov 2007, www.cbc.ca/cp/Home+Family/071101/U110124AU.html.

4. Schiller, Gail. "Toy Fair '07 Winds Up With Feature Buzz." AllBusiness. 15 Feb 2007. AllBusiness. 15 Nov 2007, www.allbusiness.com/services/motion-pictures/4771258-1.html.

5. NPD. "NPD Press Release." Amount Of Time Kids Spend Playing Video Games Is On The Rise. 16 Oct 2007. The NPD Group. 13 Nov 2007, www.npd.com/press/releases/press_071016a.html.

6. Truce. "Toy Action Guides 2007-2008." Truce. 2007. Truce. 15 Nov 2007, www.truceteachers.org/toyactionguide.html.

7. Research Buy. "Toys Market Research." Market Wikis. 9 Nov 2007. Research Buy. 15 Nov 2007, www.researchbuy.com/marketwikis/Toys_Market_Research.

8. Hasbro. "Bop it—Sounds." Bop it Game. 2007. Hasbro. 23 Oct 2007, www.playbopit.com.

9. Venture Outsource. "Electronic toys and research techniques at CEA Industry Forum." Venture Outsource Trends and Observations. 19 Oct 2007. Venture Outsource. 15 Nov 2007, www.ventureoutsource.com/contract-manufacturing/trends-observations/2007/electronic-toys-and-research-techniques-at-cea-industry-forum.

10. AllBusiness.com. "The NPD Group Reports U.S. Toy Industry Sales Showed Increases in 2006." AllBusiness. 6 Feb 2007. Business Wire. 15 Nov 2007, www.allbusiness.com/services/business-services/3970448-1.html.

11. Belfry, John. "Canadian Children Face Activity and Fitness Crisis." Child and Family Canada. 1996. Canadian Child Care Federation. 15 Nov 2007, www.cfc-efc.ca/docs/cccf/00010_en.htm.

12. Belfry, John. "Canadian Children Face Activity and Fitness Crisis." Child and Family Canada. 1996. Canadian Child Care Federation. 15 Nov 2007, www.cfc-efc.ca/docs/cccf/00010_en.htm.

13. Statistics Canada. "Physical activity, by age group and sex." Statistics Canada. 30 Apr 2007. Statistics Canada. 23 Oct 2007, www40.statcan.ca/l01/cst01/health46.htm.

14. Public Health Agency of Canada. "Canada's New Government Helps to Promote Physical Activity Among Canadians." Public Health Agency of Canada. 26 Sep 2007. Public Health Agency of Canada. 15 Nov 2007, www.phac-aspc.gc.ca/media/nr-rp/2007/2007_10_e.html.

15. ParticipAction. "Our Mission." ParticipAction—It's Time For Action. 2007. ParticipAction. 15 Nov 2007, www.participaction.com/.

16. Hoover's Inc. "Wham-O, Inc." Hoover's. 2007. Hoover's Inc. 30 Oct 2007, www.hoovers.com/wham-o/--ID__103900--/free-co-factsheet.xhtml.

17. Mindbranch. "Toy Manufacture." Mindbranch Market Research. Nov 2007. Mindbranch. 1 Nov 2007, www.mindbranch.com/Toy-Manufacture-R3470-766/.

18. Footbag Foundation. "Equipment: Footbags." Footbag Worldwide. 1998. World Wide Footbag Foundation. 13 Nov 2007, www.footbag.org/footbags/.

19. "FunKix." "Products." FunKix. 2007. Wicked Vision. 6 Nov 2007, www.funkix com.

20. Flying Clipper, "Footbags." Flying Clipper. 2005. Flying Clipper. 15 Nov 2007, www.flyingclipper.com/home/fly/smartlist_79.

21. Wicked Vision. "FunKix Publicity." Harry Potter. 2007. Wicked Vision. 15 Nov 2007 www.wickedvision.co.uk/harry.html.

22. Wham-O Inc. "News." Wham-O. 2007. Wham-O Inc. 23 Oct 2007, www.wham-o.com/default.cfm?page=News.

23. Wham-O Inc. "Where To Buy—USA." Wham-O. 2007. Wham-O Inc. 15 Nov 2007, www.wham-o.com/default.cfm?page=WhereToBuyUSA.

24. Flying Clipper, "Footbags." Flying Clipper. 2005. Flying Clipper. 15 Nov 2007, www.flyingclipper.com/home/fly/smartlist_79.

25. Statistics Canada. "Average household expenditures, by province and territory—Ontario." Statistics Canada. 01 Aug 2007. Statistics Canada. 30 Oct 2007, www40.statcan.ca/l01/cst01/famil16d.htm.

26. Statistics Canada. "Retail store sales by selected commodity." Statistics Canada. 15 Oct 2007. Statistics Canada. 30 Oct 2007, www40.statcan.ca/l01/cst01/trad52.htm?sdi=retail.

27. About.com. "Hacky Sack." About.com. 2007. New York Times Company. 22 Oct 2007, http://inventors.about.com/library/inventors/blhackysack.htm.

28. Statistics Canada. "Population estimates and projections." Statistics Canada. 26 Oct 2006. Statistics Canada. 23 Oct 2007, www40.statcan.ca/l01/cst01/demo 10a.htm?sdi=population percent20age percent20group.

29. Statistics Canada. "Population by sex and age group, by province and territory." Statistics Canada. 26 Oct 2006. Statistics Canada. 23 Oct 2007, www40.statcan.ca/l01/cst01/demo31a.htm?sdi= population percent20age percent20group.

Chapter 1

Photos/ads: p. 4, Courtesy Research In Motion; p. 5, AP Photo/Keystone, Walter Bieri; p. 7, © Reuters/CORBIS; p. 8, Courtesy of Clearly Canadian; p. 9, Photo by Thos Robinson/Getty Images; p. 10, Courtesy The Country Grocer; p. 10, Courtesy Parasuco Jeans Ltd.; p. 11, www. peta.org; p. 13, H. Armstrong Roberts/Retrofile/ Getty Images; p. 13, Courtesy National Fluid Milk Processor Promotion Board; Agency: Lowe Worldwide, Inc.; p. 15, © VOSS USA Inc.; p. 17, CP PHOTO/Steve White; p. 18, Courtesy easyJet; p. 19, Dr. Jan Bellows, All Pets Dental, Weston, Florida; p. 20, Courtesy of Nestle S.A.; p. 20, Courtesy of Honda North America, Inc.; p. 20, Courtesy H&M, Hennes & Mauritz L.P.; p. 20, McGraw-Hill Companies, Inc./Gary He, photographer; p. 21, Courtesy Scion, Toyota Motor Sales, U.S.A., Inc.; p. 23, Courtesy Research In Motion; p. 23, Photo by Thomas Cooper/Getty Images; p. 27, These Materials have been reproduced with the permission of eBay, Inc. COPYRIGHT © 2006 EBAY INC. ALL RIGHTS RESERVED.

Chapter 2

Photos/ads: p. 29, Photo by Pascal Le Segrtain/ Getty Images; p. 36, ©Michael Hruby; p. 37, Courtesy of Frito-Lay Inc.; p.38, Courtesy SIRIUS Satellite Radio; p. 40, Courtesy of Lee Valley Tools Ltd.; p. 42, President's Choice, PC Financial, PC are registered trademarks of Loblaws Inc., used with permission; p. 43, Courtesy Loblaw Inc.; p.45,© Kristi J. Black/CORBIS; p.47, Courtesy Kicking Horse Coffee; p. 49, Roger Tully/Stone/ Getty Images; p. 50, Courtesy Crispin Porter & Bogusky/Miami; p. 51, Courtesy Team One Advertising; p. 51, CP PHOTO/Richard Lam; p. 55, CP PHOTO/Toronto Sun/Dave Thomas.

Chapter 3

Photos/ads: p. 58, AP PHOTO/Reed Saxon, file; p. 63, THE CANADIAN PRESS/Tom Hanson; p. 63, © Dennis MacDonald/Photo Edit; p. 66, General Motors of Canada Ltd.; p. 66, Aldo Groupe Inc.; p. 70, © Michael Hruby, p. 71, ©Rob Melnychuk/ CORBIS; p. 72, Courtesy Brown-Forman Wines; p. 73, © 2007 Waterloo Region Record, Ontario, Canada; p. 77, ©McGraw-Hill Ryerson.

Exhibits/boxes: Exhibit 3.1, Gallup Poll, "Attitudes about the Ethical Standards of Various Professions." Used by permission; Exhibit 3.6, Adapted by permission of the author from Kate McKone-Sweet, Danna Greenberg, and Lydia Moland, "Approaches to Ethical Decision Making," Babson College Case Development Center, 2003; Exhibit 3.8, Tom Morris, *The Art of Achievement: Mastering the 7Cs of Success in Business and in Life*, Fine Communications, 2003. Used by permission.

Chapter 4

Photos/ads: p. 83, © McGraw-Hill Ryerson; p. 86, AP Photo/Al Behrman; p. 87, Dussault Apparel Inc.; p. 88, Courtesy The Gillette Company; p. 88, Courtesy Energizer Holdings, Inc.; p. 90, Jack Hollingsworth/Getty Images; p. 91, Photo by Brian Bahr/Getty Images; p. 92, ©Chuck Savage/CORBIS; p. 93, BananaStock/ JupiterImages; p. 94, Courtesy of Hammacher Schlemmer, www.hammacher.com; p. 94, CP PHOTO/Don Denton; p. 95, ©Brent Jones; p. 96, Courtesy Ford Motor Company; p. 97, Photo by CBS Photo Archive/Getty Images; p.97, AP Photo/Ric Feld; p. 98, Comstock/PictureQuest; p. 100, Kaz Chiba/Getty Images; p. 104, © Ashley Cooper/CORBIS; p. 105, CP PHOTO/Ryan Remiorz; p.107, © Scott Houston/CORBIS; p.107, CP PHOTO/Halifax Chronicle Herald—Ingrid Bulmer; p. 111, Printed with permission of Sanjay Singhall/Simply Audiobooks.

Exhibits: Exhibit 4.3, "Gen Y and the future of mall retailing," *American Demographics*, December 2002 24. (11) p. J1. Used by permission of Crain Communications.

Chapter 5

Photos/ads: p. 116, AP Photo/Jose F. Moreno; p. 117, ©Bill Aron/PhotoEdit, Inc.; p. 118, ©James Leynse/Corbis; p. 119, The McGraw-Hill Companies, Inc./John Flournoy, Photographer; p. 120, Courtesy Whirlpool Corporation; p. 121, ©Spencer Grant/PhotoEdit, Inc.; p. 122, ©Royalty-Free/Corbis; p. 125, Courtesy of Leger Marketing; p. 129, ©Photodisc; p. 130, The McGraw-Hill Companies, Inc./ John Flournoy, Photographer; p. 131, Photo courtesy Staples, Inc.; p. 132, ©2006 The LEGO Group; p. 133, The McGraw-Hill Companies, Inc./John Flournoy, Photographer; p. 134, Courtesy Coinstar, Inc.; p. 144, Coutesy of Iams.

Exhibits: Exhibit 5.7, A. Parasuraman, Dhruv Grewal, and R. Krishnan, *Marketing Research*, Second Edition. Copyright © 2007 by Houghton Mifflin Company. Adapted with permission.

Chapter 6

Photos/ads: p. 148 (left), CP Photo/Don Denton; p. 148 (right), Comstock Images/Alamy; p. 150, AP Photo/Jennifer Graylock; p.151, AP Photo/ Ann Johansson; p.153, ©M. Hruby; p.153, Andrew Wakeford/Getty Images; p.153, ©M. Hruby; p. 154, Getty Images; p. 156, Courtesy of General Motors of Canada Ltd.; p.157, Courtesy Expedia, Inc.; p. 160, kbb.com used with permission of Kelley Blue Book Co., Inc.; p.163, The McGraw-Hill Companies, Inc./Andrew Resek, photographer; p.164, Copyright ©Ron Kimball/Ron Kimball Stock—All rights reserved; p. 165, © Alessandro Garofalo/Reuters/Corbis; p.166, Thinkstock/ JupiterImages; p. 168, ©Richards Cummins/ Corbis; p.168, Courtesy Albertson's, Inc.; p.169, Courtesy Zipcar; p.173, Courtesy smart GmbH; p.174, Courtesy smart GmbH; p. 175, Chris Wattie/Reuters/Corbis.

Chapter 7

Photos/ads: p.178, Photo by Paul McConnell/ Getty Images; p. 179, Courtesy of Corporate Couriers Logistics Ltd.; p. 180, Reprinted with permission from MERX; p.181, Janis Christie/ Getty Images; p.181, Nick Koudis/Getty Images; p.185, Copyright ©Ron Kimball/Ron Kimball Stock—All rights reserved; p.186, ©Toyota Motor Engineering & Manufacturing North America; p.187, ©Worth Canoy/Icon SMI/Corbis; p. 190, ©Custom Medical Stock Photo; p.192, AP Photo/Fabian Bimmer; p.195, AP Photo/Harry Cabluck.

Chapter 8

Photos/ads: p. 204, SUNSILK is a trademark owned or used under license by Unilever Canada, Toronto, Ontario M4W 3R2; p. 207 *both*, Courtesy The Gillette Company; p. 208, ©Benetton Group SPA; Photo by: Oliviero Toscani; p. 209, © Catherine Wessel/Corbis; p. 210, Ryan McVay/Getty Images; p. 210, Ryan McVay/Getty Images; p. 212, Stockbyte/ Punchstock Images; p. 212, Getty Images; p. 212, Ryan McVay/Getty Images; p. 214, Ed Taylor/ Taxi/Getty Images; p. 216, La Senza Girl Spring 2008 website homepage; p. 217, ©Jerry Arcieri/ Corbis; p. 217, The McGraw-Hill Companies, Inc./ Andrew Resek, photographer; p. 218, Courtesy Carhartt, Inc.; p. 219, © Digital Vision/Punch Stock, © Bananastock, © Bananastock/Punch Stock, Royalty-Free/CORBIS, Image State Royalty-Free/Alamy, © Digital Vision; p. 220, Courtesy of Kettleman Bagel Co.; p. 220, CP PHOTO/Peter McCabe; p. 221, Courtesy of BALMSHELL; p. 222, Courtesy Lands' End; p. 225, Courtesy Volvo Cars of North America, LLC; p. 229, Photo provided by MABE Canada Inc.; p. 230, ®Registered trademark/™Trademark of Whirlpool, U.S.A., Whirlpool Canada LP licensee in Canada. Trademarks and photograph used with permission of Whirlpool Corporation; pp. 234 and 235, Courtesy of M&M Meat Shops.

Exhibits/boxes: Exhibit 8.3, Source: SRI Consulting Business Intelligence, www. sric-bi.com/VALS/; Exhibit 8.5: Pitney Bowes MapInfo PSYTE¨ Cluster Segmentation System; Adding Value 8.1, Reprinted by permission of LIMRA, a financial services research and consulting organization.

Chapter 9

Photos/ads: p. 238, DOVE is a trademark owned or used under license by Unilever Canada, Toronto, Ontario M4W 3R2; p. 239 *all*, Courtesy Colgate-Palmolive Company; p. 241, PORSCHE, CAYENNE, the Porsche Crest are registered trademarks and the distinctive shapes of Porsche automobiles are trademarks of Dr. Ing. h.c.F. Porsche AG. Used with permission of Porsche Cars North America, Inc. All rights reserved. Do not copy without the permission of Porsche Cars North America, Inc.; p. 244, The Canadian Press/Richard Lam; p. 245, ©American Honda Motor Co., Inc.; p. 246, ©M. Hruby.; p. 247, AP PHOTO/Mary Altaffer; p. 248, DOVE is a trademark owned or used under license by Unilever Canada, Toronto, Ontario M4W 3R2; p. 250, VANOC 2010; p. 251, ©M. Hruby; p. 252, Courtesy General Electric Company; p. 252, ©2006 Kellogg North America Company; p. 253, ©M. Hruby; p. 255, Photo by Stephane L'hostis/Getty Images; p. 256 *both*, Lacoste S.A; p. 257, THE COCA-COLA COMPANY; p. 258, ©M.

company index

subject index